HANNES SCHMID
REAL STORIES

Edited by
Museum of Fine Arts Bern, Matthias Frehner
and Ildegarda E. Scheidegger

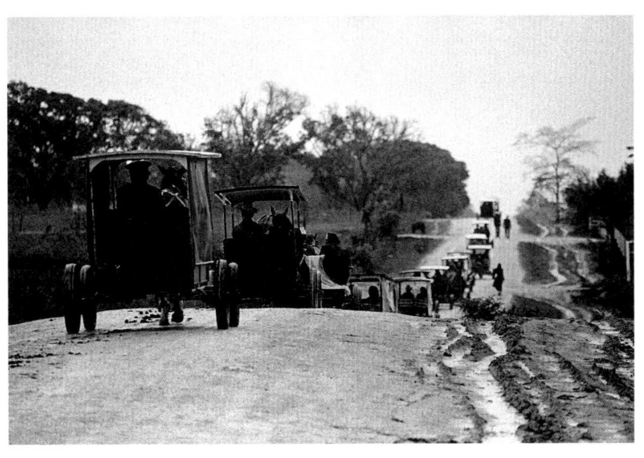

Preface

His images are moving, captivating, and leave no one cold. The same applies to Hannes Schmid as a person. His energy is infectious, his spontaneity disarming. From the very first time we met it was already clear that we would one day collaborate on a project. So I am all the more delighted that I didn't have to wait long for this opportunity. With *Real Stories* we can hold in our hands a unique selection of the photographic accomplishments of Hannes Schmid — a look back over several decades of work by one of Switzerland's most important contemporary artists.

Hannes Schmid is interested in what lies behind the façade, and it is this curiosity that forms a theme running through his work. He offers us an intimate glimpse into private worlds, stories of people in the midst of life, and educates us about powerful moments in time. Glancing at his pictures we see pop and rock stars, among others, and how normal human beings become heroes on the stage — and the other way around. Or millions of pilgrims in India, and how individually, each in a state of profound emotion, they cross the sacred Ganges at the Maha Kumbh Mela, the oldest festival of Hinduism. And, last but not least, we are introduced to the actors of the Kim-Eng troupe, a ritualistic Chinese street opera from Singapore, and how they staged their last performance for the gods alone, in front of 200 empty red seats. This cultural project was organized under the patronage of UNESCO Switzerland in 2004.

Hannes Schmid's delight in experimentation is something he also carries over to entirely different worlds, for example, to international fashion labels, glossy magazines and the roaring engines of the circus that is Formula One. Spirituality meets high-tech, and at the heart of it all there is always humankind. This mix of tradition and innovation never fails to fuel my fascination for Hannes Schmid. A fusion, incidentally, that is not entirely without similarities to my world. As a company with a longstanding tradition, we also have to focus on long-term values, innovation and particularly on people in the thick of life. Their needs for protection and security are always snapshots of a particular time in their lives.

With *Real Stories,* Zurich is supporting a visually stunning contemporary record of one of the most multi-faceted photographers of our times. In his images, Hannes Schmid always captures a special moment: a moment that transports the essence of an emotion. With this in mind, I wish the observers of this inspiring visual spectacle fun and emotion-filled moments.

Joachim Masur, CEO Zurich Switzerland

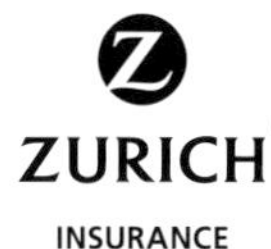

Foreword

Rarely does such an exciting and felicitous opportunity arise to present a leading artist of our time, with an oeuvre spanning more than forty years. Hannes Schmid embodies the paradox of operating at the very cutting edge of artistic developments over a long period, without ever becoming an integral part of the art world. He remained an outsider precisely because, until recently, he created images without declaring them to be art. From the 1970s until 2008, Schmid pursued a highly successful career as a commissioned photographer, which allowed him at times to work on his own projects without any commercial pressure. In his fashion and journalistic photography, he developed a keen sense of staging his models in unexpected locations. His lavish photo campaigns featuring the iconic cowboy figure of the Marlboro Man show how this self-taught photographer acquired a stupendous knowledge of his chosen medium.

Hannes Schmid, as everyone who knows him personally can attest, leads an impatient, restless, even driven existence. Unwilling to wait for happenstance, he helps that exceptional moment of a lifetime to occur, entirely in keeping with his maxim that if you're not at the right place at the right time, you have to create the specific situation you need. Accordingly, Schmid's commissioned photography is almost always staged. It begins with classic precursors such as William Klein and Richard Avedon, whereby Schmid places the main emphasis on atmospherically embedding the figure within the surroundings. Schmid often intensifies this by using exotic and mountainous locations, such as the jungles of Borneo, the treacherous north wall of the Eiger or the glaciers of the Himalayas at 5545 meters above sea level. The thrill of real danger, for the photographer and his models alike, is one of the hallmarks of Schmid's fashion shots. His success in capturing such extraordinary scenes is testament to his phenomenal ability to inspire enthusiasm for his ideas. And so, he thinks nothing of persuading models to balance precariously on the backs of unpredictable elephants in Sumatra rather than having them pose, as Avedon did, between two trained circus elephants. Nobody so far has ever emulated him in this regard.

Hannes Schmid is the 007 of photography. His empathy and his existential interest in his fellow human beings have resulted in some unlikely constellations. He is capable of integrating fully into social groups, building a relationship of trust over a period of weeks or months, and living among them according to their rhythm of life. This is what gives Schmid's photographs, be they of indigenous tribespeople in the West Papuan rainforests or international rock stars backstage, such a compelling authenticity and a sense of actually being there with them, camouflaged. When we look at Schmid's photographs, we always see something that we have never seen quite that way before. Schmid creates new images, expands our visual reservoir, and lets us see familiar things in new ways.

In an act of appropriation, Schmid has translated his own photographs of the Marlboro Man into monumental photorealist paintings. This transition from photography to painting was prompted by a chance encounter with Richard Prince's Cowboy series, which was based on Hannes Schmid's advertising shots. Schmid has since adopted the strategies of contemporary art with consummate technical and artisanal mastery, transposing his own photographs into other media and, in doing so, redefining their meaning and purpose. Discovering Richard Prince's adaptation of his Marlboro Man cowboy figures and reappropriating them in his own photorealist painting marks the point at which Schmid begins to position himself in the art world as a contemporary artist. He had his first gallery exhibition in New York in 2008. Zurich publisher Patrick Frey came across Schmid's rockstar series and made them the subject of a first publication. Soon, Schmid's name was spreading like wildfire in the art world. Further exhibitions followed: the rockstar photos were shown at the Museum Folkwang in Essen, and at the Brooklyn Museum and the Rubin Museum in New York. In 2010, Peter Pfrunder presented Schmid's Cowboy series at the Fotostiftung Schweiz in Winterthur under the title *Never Look Back*.

I first saw Hannes Schmid's photographs and some of his photorealist paintings at the Chelsea Gallery in New York in 2008. "He's Swiss?" I asked, and was told that he was indeed, and that he lived near Zurich. As soon as I got back to Switzerland, I arranged to meet him and, within just half an hour, I was determined to show his work at an exhibition in Bern. I have indelible memories of my subsequent talks with photographic specialist Markus Schürpf, who was just as unfamiliar with Schmid's work as I was, and whose initial skepticism quickly gave way to genuine enthusiasm. Further meetings with the artist followed and these, too, remain unforgettable, for they opened up a whole cosmos of immensely fascinating visual worlds from every nook and cranny of our planet. I realized that Schmid, from the very beginning of his career as a photographer, had always been an open-minded, cosmopolitan individual and artist who always acts out of emotional perception and empathy. That makes his work enormously important in terms of the globalization discourse in the world of art.

Hannes Schmid was enthused by the idea of the exhibition and once again demonstrated his talent not only for teaching himself the ropes, this time in mounting an exhibition, but also for achieving the highest standards in doing so. He provided full access to his incredibly wide-ranging archives, with the result that most of the photographs on display have been printed in large format for the first time specifically for the exhibition. The retrospective exhibition in Bern includes monumental formats, classic prints, films and paintings. A satellite exhibition is also being held at the same time at Zurich Airport, for which Schmid has digitally processed some of his works. The exhibition has also been extended to the internet. Thanks to the technical help and the financial support of Markus Huber, head of BNC — Business Network Communications AG, the Kunstmuseum Bern could be equipped with wifi. Therefore, our visitors may download for free the app with further information about the concept, the themes and the artworks of the exhibition. Yet even though these various forms of presentation involve hundreds of works, they still represent only the tip of the proverbial iceberg. This exhibition and the accompanying publication mark the beginning of an expedition into uncharted territory requiring an extension of photographic history.

I wish to thank Hannes Schmid most sincerely for making his work available in such breadth for this retrospective exhibition. Without his enthusiasm for the project, nothing would be as it is. The exhibition and the catalogue have been a team effort and are the fruits of an enriching exchange between the artist, the exhibition curator Christiane Kuhlmann, and the art historian Ildegarda Scheidegger, in charge of the catalogue. I owe them both a debt of gratitude for their months of unstinting commitment. I wish to express my appreciation and gratitude to the authors Elisabeth Bronfen, Gail Buckland, Rainer Egloff and Kornelia Imesch Oechslin for their authoritative and scholarly contributions. I also offer my sincere thanks to the translators, editors and proof-readers for their outstanding work under so much pressure, as well as to the team of assistants from Hannes Schmid's studio, Elisa Bütler, Giglio Pasqua, Susanne Zoller and Jürg Wey, who undertook the graphic design and layout of the accompanying publication. Thanks also go to Stefan Laeng, whose liaison with sponsors was indispensable. The publication is issued under the "Sélection d'Artistes" label of the Binding Foundation, which presents the life's work of leading contemporary Swiss artists. We are indebted to the Binding Foundation for their support. In order to mount this exhibition, the works had to be produced from the negatives and from digitally stored image data, respectively. For this, the artist received the generous support of a number of patrons and sponsors. Particular thanks in this regard go to Guido Persterer, gallerist, friend and mentor of Hannes Schmid, who provided contacts with various sponsors. I wish to thank our partner ZURICH Schweiz for so generously and enthusiastically embracing the project, and for jumping aboard when it was already in motion. We are also very grateful to the second sponsor PwC for their support, as well as to Raiffeisen as the third sponsor to support the project, who, in addition, have helped to promote visits to many Swiss museums as part of their Member Plus Programme. Sincere thanks also go to Highlight Communications for their involvement.

A photographic exhibition of such scope and complexity, with the added dimension of electronic visual media, undoubtedly sets a new milestone for the Kunstmuseum Bern. As such, it demanded an immense effort on the part of our entire in-house team as well as all those involved externally. This effort was coordinated by exhibition manager René Wochner to produce a homogeneous overall result. I thank him most sincerely for that. His specialist team was highly motivated and professional. Thanks also go to Nathalie Bäschlin, Thomas Bieri, Mike Carol, Andres Meschter, Martin Schnidrig, Roman Studer, Dorothea Spitza and Wilfried von Gunten. Our communications department delivered sterling work under the leadership of Ruth Gilgen Hamisultane, for which I thank her, along with Brigit Bucher, Aya Christen, Marie Louise Suter and Christian Schnellmann. Thanks are also due to the museum's educational team for their creative outreach programmes, especially to Anina Büschlen, Magdalena Schindler and Beat Schüpbach.

And, last but not least, there is someone else I wish to thank: Hillary Schmid, wife of the artist, as well as the artist's children: They enabled Hannes Schmid to work tirelessly and relentlessly for more than a year, sometimes putting in twenty-hour days, to bring this truly unique project to fruition.

Matthias Frehner Director of Kunstmuseum Bern

Introduction

Ildegarda E. Scheidegger

It began by moving away from Switzerland to South Africa. Swiss photographer Hannes Schmid embarked on his adventure in 1970. Having trained initially as an electrical engineer, he enrolled at the Ruth Prowse School of Art in Capetown. Yet he soon found that institutionalized coursework, which would lead to formal qualification as proof of his creative ability, was unsuited to his restless nature. Instead, his curiosity drove him to explore aspects of life and cultures at first hand. The camera became a friend and fellow traveler, at times endowing him with a certain sense of empowerment.

This book is intended to give the reader an insight into the character and work of the largely self-taught artist Hannes Schmid. The global encounters, both serendipitous and sought, that inform his work, indirectly made Schmid into an artist who now ranks as a photographer of international stature. Schmid has honed his gaze traveling the world, meeting and portraying people from all walks of life, with a wide diversity of sensibilities, vocations, social viewpoints, and religious mores.

In 1974, while staying at an orangutan rehabilitation center on Sumatra, Schmid stumbled upon a photographic report by anthropologist Michael Rockefeller. A scion of the powerful American oil dynasty, Rockefeller was conducting an expedition to what was then known as Dutch New Guinea, now West Papua, to study the art and culture of the Asmat, Dani, and Lani tribes on behalf of Harvard University. He disappeared without trace under circumstances that have never been clarified. Deeply moved by this true story, Schmid decided to find out more about this island, where ritual cannibalism is still practiced. Secretly, he hoped he might even find Rockefeller. For a year, he wandered through the valleys and highlands of Irian Jaya, meeting the indigenous Korowai, Dani, and Lani. The photographs he took in this remote corner of the world might be expected to reflect a harsh life of raw physical survival. Instead, they show groups of people whose gaze is more curious than distrustful. Schmid's empathetic and respectful approach to his subject matter is clearly evident here for the first time.

The next project, which would change the direction of his work, more or less fell into his lap. A chance encounter with a music manager on the Maldives in the Indian Ocean prompted him to return to Switzerland with the rock band Status Quo, who were then at the pinnacle of their career. Easy-going and approachable, Schmid valued shared experiences more highly than the conventional methods of voyeuristic photojournalism. His attitude won him the trust and friendship of 257 rock bands, which he went on to photograph in the course of almost a decade from 1977 to 1984. Living and touring with the big names of rock and pop shaped the way Schmid related to people and characters; he also saw photography more as a vocation than a profession. The path to the picture was more important to him than the picture itself. Most of the photographs he took in this way remained unpublished for years. It was not until 2009 that a selection of them appeared in the publication *Hannes Schmid Rockstars*. When we leaf through the book, the title appears almost provocative, or at least ironic, for the photographs seem almost like snapshots in a respectable family album, with neither glamour, nor diva-like airs and graces.

Nina Hagen, however, was an exception, even for Schmid. She was unpredictably creative. Constantly staging her appearance, she became Schmid's bridge to the world of fashion photography. The groundbreaking *Punk is Sweet* spread for German *Vogue*, shot in London in 1985, shows an iconic Nina Hagen in her self-styled boundary-crossing role between fashion, punk, and rock.

Equipped with such an array of knowledge and experience, Schmid began a new and important phase in the world of fashion photography. His innovative, unorthodox approach, in particular the unusually natural staging of his models and outfits, brought him commissions from leading magazines such as *Vogue*, *Harper's Bazaar*, *Elle*, and many others. Together with his team, he would propose traveling to selected locations all over the world: from rock faces in Switzerland to Himalayan mountainsides, from the Bolivian salt flats to the Cape Verde Islands—always in the spirit of his own guiding principle that if you move forward, you will always discover something new. At the same time, he never let himself be distracted from his own projects, fueled by a curiosity about other cultures and social systems that went far beyond any merely touristic interest. In Bolivia, for example, Schmid photographed the wives of the miners in Potosi and was instrumental in setting up a social project to ensure a pension for miners' widows. In Belize he happened to come into contact with Mennonites, who offered him their hospitality. His portrayal of these people, whose lives are based on upholding a simple, modest way of life rooted in conservative Christian values, is remarkable for the monochrome images that convey a profound faith in their right to this existence. With his distinctly complex and sensitive approach, Schmid invariably succeeds in getting to the heart of the situation and conveying the lives of his protagonists. Whether in photographs of Hindu rituals and ceremonies (*Maha Kumbh Mela - The Flow of Life* and *Thaipusam*) or in portraits of disabled young people and their families (*Models*), he always takes his time—months or even years. His feature film *Bonneville Final Run*, documenting a Formula 1 speed record in the salt flats of the Utah desert, beautifully transports a long cherished personal vision.

Rainer Egloff touches particularly on the empathy that marks Schmid's approach, especially in his images of rock stars. It is directly comparable to the anthropological practice of "participant observation" and goes hand in hand with a nonjudgmental approach to different cultures and peoples. Most notably, however, Schmid never loses sight of his own aesthetic vision, according to his proviso that work of the highest quality is the route to survival. In his project *For Gods Only,* Schmid spent years observing a Chinese theater troupe perform operas in front of empty seats on a street in Singapore until, five years later, they finally gave their last performance due to a lack of new blood. The artistic handling of this cultural and aesthetic performance is in itself remarkable. Schmid had all 138 of his photographs inscribed in red ink by Chinese master calligrapher Simon Huang, using traditional characters in direct relation to the visual content of the images. In her essay, Gail Buckland explores the distinguishing features of Schmid's photographs and the qualities that make them so unforgettable. According to Buckland, Schmid's creative implementation of his vision in stills and films is directly related to his emotional, intellectual, and aesthetic commitment to everything he experiences. The photographer's strength lies in a personal involvement that enables him to embed his protagonists in situations to which the viewer can relate. It is precisely because of such factors that Hannes Schmid has been hailed since the 1980s as a major discovery and in the following 20 years as one of the foremost exponents of international fashion photography. In her article on the fashion photographs and the related Formula 1 images, Kornelia Imesch Oechslin addresses the so-called time codes—the cultural and social mechanisms that make viewers receptive to a specific aesthetic. She traces the development of an expanded concept of art, which has led to the pairing of art and branding, as demonstrated by Schmid's iconic advertising images of the Cowboy. Elisabeth Bronfen looks at the same figure of the Cowboy, analyzing how it has become mythically anchored in the collective consciousness of North America. She develops her analysis of this icon from a historical standpoint, while at the same time setting Schmid clearly apart from any retrospectively determined reception and specifically emphasizing his visionary outlook, as demonstrated by the painterly reappropriation of his Cowboy in response to the art of Richard Prince.

Encountering his own appropriated images at the Venice Biennale in 2003 was an eye-opener, which completely upended Schmid's enduring interest in the action rather than the image. Schmid did all he could to reappropriate his images, enlisting the medium of painting to establish their status as originals. These images inspired the idea behind this exhibition and the accompanying publication. Kunstmuseum Bern hosts the first representative retrospective of the oeuvre of Hannes Schmid, in a themed presentation mounted by freelance curator Christiane Kuhlmann. The book seeks to bring together the disparate oeuvre of Hannes Schmid in a way that does justice to its cohesion and diversity.

A retrospective view of any artist's work is bound to shed light only on selected aspects of the entire oeuvre. It is impossible to draw a red thread through every station of the artist's life. This is particularly true of Hannes Schmid, whose restless curiosity has led him through countless facets of human existence. His ability to be part of everything around him and yet always the keen observer is truly remarkable. He fearlessly stands eye to eye with the world that appears before the lens of his camera. We hope that, in this book, his images will speak for themselves and tell the real stories.

Never Standing Still – Hannes Schmid Answers 10 Questions

Matthias Frehner

*Being at the right place at the right time—or you have to create precisely
what you need for a specific result.*
Hannes Schmid, 2012

Hannes Schmid is a self-taught photographer. Yet he is a consummate master of the
medium, who has carved out a meteoric career as an advertising photographer, campaign
photographer, fashion photographer, and photojournalist. Some of the most iconic images
of recent photographic history, most notably the Marlboro Man, were created by him.
Just a few years ago, Schmid operated alone, interested only in projects in which he was
totally immersed. One of his key strategies was to integrate himself into a place, a scene,
or a social group so fully that he would not be perceived as an outsider. This chameleon-
like approach allowed him to capture unique insights into the inner world of 70s and 80s
rock stars. Schmid himself is the very antithesis of a paparazzo. He photographs people
as though he were camouflaged—from Mennonites in Belize, to tough guys and bad girls
at a Harley bikers' rally in Daytona Beach, to the indigenous peoples of the West Papuan
jungle. His photographs have an intensity and truth redolent of Nan Goldin. Wherever
Schmid was able to blend into a group, it was a case of being at the right place at the
right time. Wherever that did not happen, he adopted a different tack and became a
director, staging his own vision of reality in order to photograph it uncompromisingly.
In doing so, he has often gone to remarkable lengths, as witnessed by his iconic images
of models on elephants, of Himalayan glaciers, or of lasso-toting cowboys silhouetted
against the magnificent sunsets of New Mexico. The quest for visual authenticity coupled
with the invention of visionary reality in staged images are central aspects of Schmid's
photographic creed. In an oeuvre so vast, it is astonishing that such diametrically opposed
strategies have resulted in a body of photographic work that bears such a uniquely
distinctive signature. His extraordinary sensibility for atmospheric lighting is the key
to the artistic homogeneity of his work and at the same time the basis for his leap
from photography to painting. The photorealist style that Schmid has adopted as a
painter—again, self-taught, to a high degree of technical perfection—is a medium
that allows him to come even closer to his vision of reality by engaging artifice. In the
following interview, Hannes Schmid talks about how he sees himself as an artist
and photographer.

Matthias Frehner: When I saw your 2008 exhibition *Men and Machismo* in a New York gallery, I was particularly impressed by the cowboys. What is the importance of this figure to your oeuvre as a whole?

Hannes Schmid: The work with the western cowboy is one of my most important artistic projects. You could say he is the central figure, and the point from which I rethought my work. The New York exhibition showed oil paintings of cowboys. In other words, I reconstructed photography in another visual medium. Reappropriating that figure or, quite literally, taking it in hand, led me in a new direction. I see this form of revival as an artistic act in the spirit of Appropriation Art. It was triggered by my encounter with the works of Richard Prince, but ultimately it goes much further than that, because my own picture archive has been the starting point for other art projects too. For instance, I also redefined portrait photographs of rock stars by enlarging them to XXL format so that the visual structure appears to be ripped open. What's more, the works are divided into individual segments and assembled poster-style. *Divas+Heroes* is the title of this series, which was also shown in the New York exhibition. Referencing my archives is one of my creative and conceptual principles, which I learned from doing the cowboy pictures.

Matthias Frehner: The cowboy photographs, which are the basis for many of your more recent works, are probably instantly associated by people of our generation with the advertising campaign for a certain cigarette brand. How should we imagine your work in situ?

Hannes Schmid: Well, it started with photography. It is still my starting point, even though I have since moved on to large-scale installations and video works, far away from the classic photo. But I still use analog technology, because that demands a different way of seeing. In the exhibition, the cowboy works are included in the *Visions* section. That says a lot, because for me it was always about staging my own vision of a scene and implementing that as an image.

My work on set can be compared to the work of a Hollywood director, who is also a circus trainer. There were these real guys, the cowboys, who actually did this work for a living in real life, and, of course, an entire herd of horses. You can only photograph when you are in the right place at the right time—or you have to create precisely what you need for a specific result. That begins with the clothing and is far from ending with the camera position. I was always prepared for everything, which is why the cowboy photographs are not spontaneous, as they might appear to be in the dynamic horseback scenes, but part of a wider script that I devised beforehand.

Matthias Frehner: This campaign has existed since the 1950s. You have been working with the figure of the Marlboro Man since the mid-90s. Apart from you, were there other photographers working for Philip Morris at the time?

Hannes Schmid: Actually, they held onto that identifying figure for a very long time, because it describes a myth and a dream of western freedom. There were certainly many photographers before me, and there were some who were working on other aspects of the advertisement at the same time. I was not the only one, but my work consisted in creating a new image for this cowboy figure. It was important to me to show a certain color scheme and to direct attention to certain details—things I have reprised in my oil paintings. Ultimately, that is the fascination of photography, which necessarily shows just part of what is actually happening in front of the camera.

Matthias Frehner: What about copyrights and such?

Hannes Schmid: For my freelance work, which includes the photographic series and the individual shots as well as my oil paintings, I only use images that have never been used for a campaign. Of course, they were created within that context, but they are my creations nonetheless. Within the art world, this is a question that can't really be answered. After all, you have to wonder whether a figure such as the cowboy, who started out as a western hero in literature and film, can ever be "copyrighted" at all. The works of Richard Prince show just how difficult it is to recognize and distinguish what is actually reproduction: take an individual billboard that was once displayed in a specific place and is now presented with no indication of a specific brand or user—what about that? Of course, we know in which context the figure was once used, and that's something that people of our generation will recognize in my work as well. But for a lot of young people that simply doesn't work anymore, because the figure of the cowboy is no longer part of everyday life and doesn't appear in any street scene. But on the whole, this just goes to show how much we are influenced by images and photography. Within the framework of art, it is possible to read various levels of meaning into the figure of the cowboy and relate those meanings to one another. After all, art has to be seen as autonomous and free of purpose.

Matthias Frehner: Does the reprise of your photographic images in oil paintings represent your own personal path to freedom and adventure?

Hannes Schmid: If you like … it was the start of something new, and whenever that happens it's exciting. For me, the cowboy was the start of a visual adventure. Painting is a process that is organized in an entirely different way from photography—detached from the scene itself and therefore liberated from the actual conditions such as light, weather, or the mood of the individuals involved. Painting also taught me that you simply can't stop the wheel from turning. These days I'm interested in the new media potential of film and video and installation. How can you present photography in a public space? How can you capture an image of a moment and make that accessible? Those are the issues that I am currently interested in as an artist and that is why I would like to show part of the exhibition at Zurich Airport.

Matthias Frehner: Another part of the *Visions* section of the exhibition includes your staged fashion photography. How does that fit in?

Hannes Schmid: I've worked for labels from A for Armani to V for Vogue, right through to double Z for ZZ Top. It's fashion photography, in particular, that has given me the opportunity to tell stories about people, longings, and nature, and the clash of cultures. Real stories, for me, are the ones that have a touch of melancholy or show people in relation to their environment. I've always worked in real situations, such as the Himalayas or Mongolia, and I've always used analog photography. In other words, whatever I wanted to show and describe has always taken place right in front of my camera lens—and that directness is evident in my pictures. One crucial factor for me, though, is light—the ur-substance of photography. For me, it has a certain tenderness: light envelops what is shown, rather than merely revealing or unmasking. The main focus of my photography was not the dress or the suit itself. Instead, I wanted to capture a certain mood, describe feelings, appeal to emotions. My stories work by appealing to people rather than shocking them.

Matthias Frehner: What were your influences?

Hannes Schmid: When I started with photography, I was exploring uncharted territory. Television and digital media were still a long way off. Of course, I was aware of newspaper images and books, but on my travels I was very much left to my own devices. It was only from the mid-80s onwards, when my photo series were being published internationally, that the magazine culture was gaining a stronger foothold. By that time, however, I had already covered a lot of ground, had followed my own path, and continued to do so. I was inspired by films and by the everyday stories I witness all around me, and I interpreted them visually in my own way.

Matthias Frehner: In your freelance work, you often reference Asian culture. You even got involved in a Cambodian charity project. What is it that connects you to Asia? What's the fascination there?

Hannes Schmid: I've always traveled a lot in Africa and South America, and have lived in New York. The Cambodia project was a new milestone. I've always been drawn to new paths, to discovering new things, even though I am deeply rooted in my own homeland of Toggenburg. When you speak of Asia in general, you have to bear in mind how vast that continent is and how many diverse cultures that word harbors. In recent years, it has become increasingly obvious how much all these civilizations have influenced our own. I'm interested in understanding that exchange and in seeing what happens, and I want my work to express, above all, the energy that generates. We can no longer regard Europe as a singular society dissociated from the rest of humanity, but have to see it as part of a globalized world. Making that transition visible is an aspect of my work that I want to show at the airport as an extension of the exhibition in Berne. The collaboration between the Kunstmuseum and the airport is new and, for me, conceptually important.

Matthias Frehner: The *Real Stories* exhibition at Kunstmuseum Bern is being shown alongside a major exhibition of Swiss Symbolists whose works focus to a large extent on landscape and nature. Do your pictures have some kind of symbolic content too?

Hannes Schmid: Photography can be interpreted in very different ways; it speaks to people directly, frontally. I've often noticed that, and sometimes photographs are even described in terms of wishful thinking—as images that make people wish to be in certain places or situations. Perhaps those are ideal images, but they also appeal to the importance of preserving and looking after them. In that respect, yes, they do have a symbolic content, though it is not in the foreground. I am personally very curious to see what effect these images will have in a museum setting and what associations they will bring about.

Matthias Frehner: The exhibition is not so much a retrospective as an overview of your work so far. What plans and themes are you pursuing now?

Hannes Schmid: First and foremost, I am looking forward to seeing all these works together in one place, and of course, that gives me the impetus to continue. I am a person who can never really stand still, so I would like to use my many years of experience as a springboard to address new topics, using new media and branching out into spatial installations.

Real Stories – A Survey

Christiane Kuhlmann

Real Stories: what more appropriate title than this for an exhibition of photography. And no one is more suited to representing it than a photographer who takes it upon himself to capture more than meets the eye; a photographer who does not record what presents itself to the camera lens but actively plans and stages what he wants to see and show; a photographer who explores the places where his wishes and dreams are at home. Hannes Schmid is a photographer who lives his stories and his portraits; he is part of them. In translating and transforming them, he has become one of Switzerland's great contemporary visual storytellers and living proof of the difference between the idea of "taking" a picture in the sense of Henri Cartier-Bresson's decisive moment, and of "making" a picture by staging a visual event.

Photography is Schmid's point of departure and the camera the tool that he uses to "write" his stories. John Berger puts it succinctly in *Another Way of Telling*: "Cameras are boxes for transporting appearances." A comparable approach to photography is found in Schmid's work. In his photographs, we see segments from the world of fashion, advertising, and the stars of entertainment, but we also see an unusual take on daily life, reinforced by optical scraps of conversation that testify to his intensely personal study of people, animals, and nature.

The exhibition at Kunstmuseum Bern is distinctive in that it is both a retrospective survey and a premiere, a rediscovery, the first-ever presentation of Hannes Schmid's oeuvre from 1974 to the present day. Some of the works are familiar, others are on view for the first time, having been unearthed through renewed exploration of the artist's archives. Pictures that were never intended to be mounted on a wall are juxtaposed with series that have already been on view elsewhere, such as the installation *The Flow of Life* presented at New York's Rubin Museum, the *Cowboys* at Fotostiftung Schweiz in Winterthur, and the *Rockstars* at Museum Folkwang in Essen.

Schmid's archives resemble a warehouse; they are not an immutable, fixed inventory but a source of study that reveals ever new perspectives. This testifies to the artist's fundamental insight that photography, with its medial structure, is open-ended by definition.

The stories that take place in front of and behind the camera are closely interwoven with the course of Schmid's life, which has shaped his artistic identity. But the exhibition proposes a different approach: it does not follow a biographical trail, but rather seeks to reveal the artistic principles underlying this prolific oeuvre. The legibility of Schmid's work is based on several modes of perception: emphatic, narrative, and dialogic. The exhibition opens with three series that were not commissioned but rather initiated by the artist himself: *For Gods Only, The Flow of Life*, and *Daytona.*

Rituals shows religious and social ceremonies, some that take place in concealment, others that signify moments of transition from the secular to the spiritual, and still others that call for specific physical and mental states. Perception in Schmid's work is closely related to the desire to keep a record. The photographer is not detached; he participates in everything that is happening around him. The meaning of rituals in this case is twofold: on one hand, it refers to content and subject matter; on the other, photography itself is linked to ritual. The works are motivated by wanting to preserve something that would otherwise fade into oblivion. Intrinsic to photography is the principle of its own mortality since, as Roland Barthes observes, it can only show us what has already passed: transitory transience in every picture, which is consistently updated and quickened with renewed life through the act of viewing. Viewers are confronted with analog photography's characteristic gesture of pointing and the direct path laid out between what the picture shows and their own perception.

Visions juxtaposes two equivalent concerns, cowboys and fashion, their presentation guided by the principles of essay and narrative in the medium of photography. These appellative pictures and photo spreads have been commissioned in a variety of contexts. Their common ground lies in a combination of form and content that evokes personal memories and expands the potential of the imagination. The narrative charge in Schmid's meticulously staged photography merges with personal images, experiences, television reports, and films. In historical terms, Schmid's oeuvre can be assigned to the field of contemporary art photography, whose semantic impact lies in the cultural knowledge of generalized and specific imagery. Typically, Schmid's creations for the fashion and advertising industries bridge the gap between the rendition of exotic events and a personal visual universe. The inclusion of his photorealistic cowboy oil paintings in this section is telling. The photographer has reappropriated his own visual material in another genre, but even more importantly, he has chosen to do so in a rhythm diametrically opposed to that of photography, thus reinforcing the ambiguity of the distinction between original and copy. The principle of appropriating and reiterating popular visual subject matter has informed contemporary art since the 1960s. Inescapable in photography, it is both a curse and a blessing. Schmid's iteration of the cowboy in a decelerated, unique semiotic system once again makes of the figure the construct it has in fact always been from its very first appearance. In addition, Schmid uses pictorial archives as a point of departure for a theoretical engagement with his medium, joining the roster of such photographers as Hans-Peter Feldmann, Peter Piller, and Joachim Schmid.

Dialogs investigates the communicative principle of photography. Especially relevant in portraiture, it raises fundamental questions that apply both in front of and behind the camera: Who are you and who do you want to be? Schmid addresses these questions in many different conversations, the most immediate and provocative being the portraits made of rock stars in the 1980s and early 1990s.
This section reveals Schmid's intuitive approach to his work. His mastery of the dialogical principle of photography, of question and answer, calling for curiosity as well as an emotional commitment, is particularly manifest when he pursues projects in foreign cultures: in West Papua, in Bolivia, or among the Mennonites in the United States.

Movements deals, in closing, with rhythm and velocity, phenomena that are basically a conundrum in a medium that immobilizes its subject matter and whose product is a silent object. Capturing the experience of rhythm and sound, velocity and physical effort, on a two-dimensional plane is a challenging artistic venture.
Schmid's series speak a language that evokes the "pathos formula" conceived by Aby Warburg well over a century ago to describe the body rendered with utmost vitality and passion. Expanded to signify the energy stored in the picture atlas accumulated by Warburg, the pathos formula positively explodes in Schmid's concert photographs of such musicians as AC/DC, Queen, Blondie, or Mick Jagger. This section also highlights the cultic potential of photography in portraying heroes, celebrities, and stars.

The exhibition shows Hannes Schmid as a contemporary artist, who has created a highly distinctive, unmistakably ambiguous oeuvre that straddles the fine and applied arts. As art photography, his work not only relies on specific strategies, but actually generates the circumstances required for the photographic process. The artistic act originates in a plan, long before the camera comes into play. It is a strategy rooted, according to Charlotte Cotton, in the conceptual art of the 1960s and 70s. Schmid himself speaks of visions, well aware that his works are not merely vessels of information, but rather atmospheric and conceptual vehicles of expression.

Participant Photography

Rainer Egloff

Angus Young is sweating. He has taken off the top of his school uniform. Wearing only shorts, he is standing on the stage, bent over his guitar, playing and sweating. Hannes Schmid's close-up has isolated AC/DC's lead guitar in the spotlight, foregrounding his scraped knees. His face, rolled up into pouting lips, can barely be distinguished; his body is squished into the corner of the picture, cropped. But this sweating troll against a black ground is not only obviously Angus; he is Angus incarnate—devil and angel, half joke, half serious.

Schmid's *Blackstage* series highlights the stage presence of the stars of pop and rock music, capturing instantaneous moments with a precision that epitomizes the iconic quality of each single figure on stage. He isolates his subjects from their surroundings—from the situation on stage and from the other members of the band. These sculptural studies make an impact even without the music. The exaggerated visualization distils the role-play of the stars, essentially objectivizing it—although objectivity is not the ambition of this photography. Nor is reportage. Schmid thinks in terms of his own images and stories, and seeks to visualize his inner visions by capturing them with the camera. He scrutinizes his subjects, analyzes how they act and operate, until he has acquired a familiarity that enables him to illuminate them from his own perspective. He condenses appearances, leaves things out, shifts perception, estranges.

Schmid stages pop and rock stars as quasi-divine creatures of light, his studies underscoring their charismatic impact, skilled showmanship and virtuoso techniques. There is no need to see Angus's face in detail and even less so that of Freddie Mercury, who is shown to us in head-on rear view. Queen's singer is just as physical as AC/DC's guitarist, though different in style. No terrycloth socks for him. He too is naked to the waist but his torso rises up out of full-length black, faux leather skin-tight pants, held up by red suspenders. This body is in even better physical condition; we see no sweat and the neck-length hair is well groomed. Freddie's sexuality is more in-your-face but more ambiguous too. And he exploits the freedom to use his arms. Angus, when he plays, is strapped to his guitar with both hands while singer Freddie turns his mike into an active prop. In Schmid's photograph, he is holding it in front of his mouth with one hand, while lifting his other arm with consummate elegance to slide the cable up his thigh and to the front again between his spread-eagled legs. The cable is actually the focus of the photograph, the central axis, the lasso of an electric cowboy, the feather boa of a male rock queen perfectly versed in microphonic choreography.

Hannes Schmid freely admits that he was not particularly taken with the music of the groups he accompanied on tour between 1977 and 1984. While shooting pictures of them on-, back- and offstage, he was much more interested in the star cult as a social phenomenon and also in the concert as its preferred site and most intense embodiment. Significantly, the modern rituals of largely youthful subculture were not the exclusive domain of the musicians; they were also intimately associated with the nature of specific locations: the dark concert hall and the brightly lit stage on which the shamans of pop performed their song and dance. Crucially, however, they rely on wildly enthusiastic masses of fans, shaking their heads, succumbing to open-mouthed ecstasy, screaming, waving their arms, and frantically reaching for their gods, clamoring for the intoxication of a single touch. All of this is embodied in Schmid's rear view of Freddie Mercury. He shows the master of ceremonies facing his fans on a matt-reflecting stage—and in the lower right of the photograph, there is even room for the head of a security guard. Schmid consummately distills the quality of this event in a photograph that has been reduced to absolute essentials: the star and his fans constitute a system that functions only through mutual participation. That interdependence is visually symbolized by the cable of Freddie's microphone. Not only does it represent the cord that connects the rock star to amplifier, power, and light; it also reveals him to be a vulnerable puppet strung up on the expectations of the music industry and a community of fans.

What happens before and after the concert is also part of the ritual: arriving in a tour bus or by taxi from the airport, contact with fans, waiting backstage, then the excitement building before going on stage, the stage fright, the tension and a brief moment to collect oneself, and after the concert, exhaustion and emptiness, relaxation on days off, private life between tours, promotional campaigns and studio visits. We see astonishingly middle-class living rooms and bedrooms; we see family photographs and excursions to the beach; we see stars without makeup; we see people.

Schmid's oeuvre might be considered a form of anthropological photography; he clearly makes use of anthropological methods and practices, though he lays no claim to being an anthropologist. Actually, he talks about "participant observation" to describe his personal involvement and his role as communicator between people and various cultural and social systems. This touches on the classical controversy regarding the method of participant observation in the social sciences. The concept was introduced at the beginning of the 20th century specifically to counteract the armchair anthropologist whose desk was the locus of his social research. In contrast, scholars like Franz Boas or Bronislaw Malinowski considered direct, long-term participation in the life of the tribe indispensable to understanding and communicating a "foreign" culture. They advanced the theory that cultural elements can only be comprehended by adopting, at least partially, the natives' perspective of the world and by studying its underlying practices and functions. Participant observation fostered an insight into the functional rationalism of religious practices or into social interaction, which had hitherto been classified as superstition or primitive irrationalism. The growing significance of participant observation in comparative anthropology gave enormous impetus to cultural relativism and, with it, the premise that mental faculties are basically and universally equivalent. This, in turn, led to an analytical interest in the specific ways in which human beings cope with existence as expressed in language, customs, economy, and ritual.

Photography played a crucial role in participatory, observing anthropology: on one hand, the medium was used to keep a record of dwellings, costumes, or pieces of jewelry that were too difficult to describe or too complex to draw; on the other, it played an aestheticizing, artistic role. As early as the late 1930s, photography featured crucially as a means of analysis in research projects, initiating the field of visual anthropology. In 1942, the anthropologists Gregory Bateson and Margaret Mead published an ethnopsychological study on the Balinese mentality, in which they used photography as their primary research tool. However, the method of participant observation is freighted with a fundamental paradox: the more one becomes immersed in a culture, the less one can maintain the detachment required to communicate the characteristics of that culture to others. This phenomenon has been dubbed "going native." Conversely, anyone who is not entirely at home within a culture can only function as an observing outsider. Schmid resolves the issue by being at home in several cultures, by changing both perspective and forms of transformation. As a photographer, he may become a member of a specific group and an aesthetic community, but he never abandons Hannes Schmid, always remaining true to his own aesthetic vision. His devotion to the ideal of aesthetic autonomy is actually what motivates him to become a member of the scene that he is interested in. The quasi-anthropological photographs that result are neither snapshots nor are they elaborately staged. Instead, they are situational arrangements of reality captured at the decisive moment, in the right place, with the right objects and the right people.

Hannes Schmid's early life set the stage for his affinity with anthropology and his delight in things foreign, giving him a faculty for empathizing with others and adapting to the most

varied cultural groups and lifestyles as well as building confidence and patiently waiting for
the right moment.

He was born in Zurich in 1946 as the fourth and youngest child of a baker's family. Since
his father's income was not enough to cover the family's expenses, his mother used
to travel to local fairs where she first sold pottery from Heimberg in Emmental and later
costume jewelry. Being 13 years younger than his next oldest sibling, Hannes grew up
between bakery and county fairs and soon became accustomed to a constant stream of
different people. He learned to cope and coped well, becoming a persuasive vendor in his
own right, selling day-old goods from the bakery, picking snowdrops and heather to make
little bouquets, taking the hawker's place at the fair grounds at lunchtime, and peddling
ox gall or vegetable slicers. During the summer holidays, he went to his family's native
Toggenburg to work as a goatherd on the slopes of the Kurfirsten Mountains. Equally
at home in the settings of urban trade and rural farming, Schmid was quick to acquire
substantial social and cultural competence alongside a delight in difference and novelty.
"I was a curious child," he confirms, a child who longed to know what it was like on the
other side of mountains.

He also faced challenging circumstances: his childhood and schooling were rudely
interrupted when he contracted glandular tuberculosis at the age of seven, as a result
of which he spent three years in sanatoriums in Davos and Wald. With only one hour of
lessons per day, he fell behind so that the only opportunity open to him after reaching
school-leaving age was to take an apprenticeship. Half-heartedly he decided to train as
an electrician and later specialized in lighting technology. This solid, practical education
paid off. Driven by wanderlust, he joined three friends from Toggenburg and emigrated to
South Africa in 1970, where skilled craftsmen were in great demand thanks to rampant
industrial growth. Hired to work on the construction of a radar station in Cape Town with
monthly wages of SFr.7000, Schmid had plenty of money and even more time on his
hands: there was no work on the job because the required copper tubing had been stolen
upon arrival at the harbor and had never reached the construction site. He bought himself
a camera and started exploring his surroundings. It was the time of apartheid and, not
knowing any better, he frequently ended up in the black ghetto of Cape Town. Fascinated
by the notorious "District 6," he started conversing with the inhabitants, who were not only
friendly but also wanted to have their pictures taken. Why wasn't this white photographer
despised, shunned, a victim of aggression? Schmid feels that it is because of his
reticence and his ability to show respect for others and wait patiently to gain confidence.

Before taking a single picture, he would visit people five or six times. They made his acquaintance first as a human being and only later as a photographer.

From the very beginning, his studies as a photographer were direct and causally linked to crossing cultural boundaries and engaging in participant observation. Later these self-taught steps in photography were complemented by formal, university studies in art and photography, but it did not take long for Schmid to realize that only he himself would be able to flesh out his ideas on photography. Lucrative jobs as an electrician enabled him to continue honing his photographic skills without commercial pressure. He traveled, did a great deal of reading, followed his curiosity, and became involved in a variety of projects, among them the protection of orangutans. In addition, Schmid pursued his life of photographic discovery free from the constraints of art or scientific documentation. He had charted his own photographic continent. A prolonged stay in 1975 with the Dani and Lani tribes in Indonesia was to prove crucial to his future development. These tribal societies still practiced ritual cannibalism and Schmid had decided to follow the trail of anthropologist Michael Rockefeller, who had vanished years before in the same region. He gave the lie to the cliché of absolute otherness by living with these people, getting to know them, and finally capturing them on film. Equipped with only 60 rolls of film and no means of developing his photographs on site, he was compelled to restrict himself; his limited supplies were compounded by being unable to look at or evaluate the pictures he was taking. Relying on his inner vision and technical expertise, he waited for the right moment to press the release—two or three times a day. He says it was then that he realized the necessity of becoming part of what he wanted to photograph; he simply had to be there and wait until people no longer took note of him.

Even in those days he already had the urge to go beyond documentary photography by actively orchestrating his images. Having such restricted means at his disposal, he did the next best thing: "I had to wait for things to fall into place by themselves." Even so, he was already interested in reduction. Instead of the spotlights and smoke machines that he later exploited for his *Blackstage* series, he simply made do with the smoke from the open fire and the right daylight moment to stage pictures of proudly smiling Dani men with their penis sheaths, necklaces, and headbands. To create entire series of such photographs, Schmid had to pay meticulous attention to daily rhythms, to the light, and to the people, in order to seize an opportune moment or to anticipate when a specific vision that he had in mind might materialize for his camera lens. Although the research he conducted was specifically visual, Schmid acquired a substantial body of anthropological knowledge regarding tribal structures and culture: the way of life and the economy, animistic beliefs and religious rituals.

On coming back to Switzerland in 1977, Schmid was invited to a Status Quo concert—his first rock concert—at the Hallenstadion in Zurich. He couldn't help thinking in terms of comparative anthropology; to him, the audience was a tribe in uniform with ribbons around their arms: "They were all shaking their fists, nodding their heads, shaking their long hair, then this band came on stage, they were the leaders, and they shook their hair, shook their heads, and then this fearful roar came out of these boxes. It was completely tribal to me, it wasn't music, it was a social event and that was what fascinated me." Schmid was introduced to the band and the manager after the concert and when the latter learned that Schmid had just come back from photographing people in the jungle, he promptly invited him to take pictures of Status Quo. Seven years of rock and pop photography followed, during which he accompanied and photographed over 250 acts.

The *Rockstars* footage selected from Schmid's archive is promotional material originally made for the music industry and primarily intended for print magazines, like Jürg Marquard's *Pop*. However, these pictures are fascinating because of something that is diametrically opposed to the marketing strategies of stardom or the voyeuristic gratification of fans. They do not dish out home stories, backstage revelations, or embarrassing disclosures but instead offer a subtle insight into star-related cultural systems, into stardom, its way of life, codes, and customs and, in particular, the rituals of celebration and faith. Schmid's photographs are clearly invaluable contributions to an anthropology of pop culture. Unpretentious, nonacademic, and nonjudgmental, they render an impression of rock and pop music that ages gracefully and still has us in thrall. Today they can claim a space that has been overlooked and, in fact, unforgivably neglected by academic anthropology. Social anthropology and sociology ignored rock and pop stars and their fan communities in the 1970s and 1980s. Those fields of study were just emerging at the time especially in Great Britain and the United States, and were still largely under the normative sway of traditions in art, literature, and music. The subject matter of anthropology in those days was devoted primarily to non-European and preliterate tribal cultures, and researchers were just beginning to take a tentative look at Western culture. Folk studies in Europe focused on traditions of the past, while pop and rock were disparagingly written off as industrially commercialized mass entertainment with no cultural value. Schmid ignores polarization and hierarchical thinking of this kind, nor does he take a fan's point of view. His forte lies in skillfully combining social and spatial intimacy with respectful aesthetic detachment.

His detachment distinguishes him from the majority of rock photographers, and his staging does not merely serve to highlight the stars: it is the subject matter of the picture itself and thus generates ambivalence. Take, for instance, the portrait of Bob Geldof in the *Divas+Heroes* series. The obvious flirtation with kitsch in the red of the retouched background, of glasses, lips, and carnation, is underscored by the light reflected on Geldof's glasses. For his portrait of Polo Hofer, Schmid uses the same devices, though less blatant and therefore to different effect. Once again, he successfully seeks the alienation inherent in the rhetoric of the photographic studio to generate a sustained tension between charismatic identification and ambivalent detachment.

That tension actually brings differences and relations to the fore that expose and epitomize the essence of the music, whether embodied by a solo performer, a band, or a genre. Facets of stardom and the people behind it are also revealed, as in the portrait of Debbie Harry, who appears invincibly strong on stage but tired and vulnerable in her coat and scarf.
Sexuality and gender identity are richly resonant in these photographs. A singer, naked to the waist, flaunts his macho body, his undulating, blow-dried tresses, and his androgynous jewelry: necklaces and bracelets, rings on fingers and ears. The orchestration of gender shows an impressive subtlety in the juxtaposition of Rob Halford (1981) and Nina Hagen (1978) with motorcycle caps. Shades of Marlon Brando from *The Wild One*—stereotypical emblem of masculinity—have been reconfigured as ambivalent contributions to the discourse on gender. In the portrait of Judas Priest singer Halford, who did not out himself until the end of the 1990s, the homosexual connotations of sunglasses, studs, and whip are incontestable. In contrast, Nina Hagen not only sports a buxom bosom under her striped tank top but also a delicately painted moustache. In addition, she's wearing a regular skirt and an undefinable cape of some kind. Her message is one of feminine strength without ascribing to a fixed sexual orientation. The pictures of fans also offer a fruitful insight into the gender issue. The demography of the fans changes depending on the band and genre. Teens and Bay City Rollers were typical girly bands while Kiss attracted a mixed audience and Motorhead tended to target young males.
Fans are the disciples of the cult; they are the members of the respective "tribe." They want to share the radiance and power of their idols, and they do so by emulating the clothing, hairdos, and jewelry of their gods. Schmid's photographs of Kiss fans in makeup, rapt

disciples who mirror their band in adoration, speak volumes. Contemporary social research describes fandom as reiterated, interactive, ritualized practices based on the premise of the physical co-presence of a group of people with a common focal point, a shared state of mind, and clearly delimited group borders. Could these characteristics be pinpointed any more precisely than in Schmid's fan photographs?

Schmid's rock and pop photography coincided with a period of transition in those genres. Disco, Abba, and Boney M. had passed their zenith and Punk, New Wave, and Neue Deutsche Welle were taking their place. New aesthetic forms acquired ascendancy that eclipsed those of classical hard rock. Schmid's photographs also testify to the transformation of individual bands like Genesis that morphed from classical art rock to the more successful pop. After the departure of colorful Peter Gabriel, the new singer chosen by the band—former drummer Phil Collins—had to embody a different image. Schmid documents the search for a trenchcoat gangster look. Punk and New Wave changed the look of their singers even more: Schmid shows Ian Dury as a carnivalesque, theatrical court jester. Affected by polio, he had made his handicap the subject of some his songs, taking an entirely different approach from the Adonis type cultivated by singers from Mick Jagger to David Lee Roth, whose acrobatics on stage dramatically displayed their sinewy muscular prowess. The burgeoning role of front women is also conspicuous, with the likes of Nina Hagen, Kim Wilde, and Debbie Harry casting a justified spell on Schmid. In this period of transition, Schmid did not take sides. Personal affinities barely make an appearance: Schmid allows them all to garner an enthusiastic response.
This was also a time of far-reaching changes in technology and media. The key role played by the microphone cable on stage gradually yielded to a new freedom of movement thanks to the wireless microphone, which led to a new visual dynamic. Upcoming bands like Depeche Mode demonstrated the inexorable advance of electronic music, which had already been cultivated by Kraftwerk since the early 1970s. In addition, music videos proliferated, competing with concerts as a primary means of promotion. This epoch also saw a highlight in magazine publishing, with *Bravo*'s life-sized star poster, pieced together from partial cut-outs in each issue, decorating practically every teenager's room. Visual pop culture also flourished on LP covers with a flamboyance unequaled in the age of the CD. The design of the covers took a visual approach that was analog, haptic, and explicitly physical. In the digitally modified, large-format series of *Divas+Heroes*, individually printed and pasted together in 2008, Schmid pays tribute not only to the "star cut" invented by *Bravo* but also to pop visual culture per se.

As of the mid-1980s, Hannes Schmid's non-hierarchical approach to culture and increasingly focused concentration on staging led him to move away from music and devote himself more to fashion and advertising. Even so, his interest in social groups and their aesthetics never flagged, its visibility underscored by his technique of participant observation. The affinity with anthropology and its procedures logically plays a crucial role in this oeuvre—whether patent as in Schmid's Mennonite series and the photographs of the motorcycle meet in Daytona, or more subtly as in the Pro Infirmis campaign where certain attitudes, gestures, and styles of clothing recall the earlier staging of rock and pop stars.

Sources referenced:

Bateson, Gregory and Margaret Mead, *Balinese Character: A Photographic Analysis*, New York, 1942.

Hannes Schmid - A Journey into Perspectives, Zurich, 2011.

Hannes Schmid - Rockstars, Zurich, 2009.

Interview between the writer and Hannes Schmid, 21 August 2012.

Fashion and Formula One Photographs as Time Codes

Kornelia Imesch Oechslin

Time Codes

What are Giorgio Armani's creations doing in New York's Guggenheim (2000) or Miuccia Prada's in the Metropolitan (2012)? And why does Benetton choose the Centre Pompidou in Paris for a fashion extravaganza to celebrate its 40th anniversary? Just what is it that attracts fashion and other advertising imagery to the museum and the gallery?

Fashion as art and art as fashion—fashion as a time code and as one of those cultural and social high-end media of the kind that have emerged especially since the 1960s and 1980s, turning fashion designers and models into stars and artists, and, conversely, artists into stars and models. This phenomenon was spawned by the meltdown of boundaries between genres that characterizes postmodernism's expanded notion of art. Design plays a constitutive role in this process. Within the framework of a post-Fordist economy of attention and creativity, fashion and art are united as trademarks, as brands, offering a lifestyle and literally designing life. Both fashion and art thus take the limelight as brands that exploit the aura and theatrical strategies of the white cube, as in the forms of display cultivated by such luxury brands as Prada, Armani, and Chanel, and their artistic reinvention in the installations and photographs of Silvie Fleury or Andreas Gursky.

In the wake of these developments, the distinction between fine and commercial art has become obsolete: this is where Hannes Schmid's fashion photography comes in. Selected pictures are on view in the Kunstmuseum Bern alongside his Formula One photographs. Commissioned by the fashion and automobile industries since the 1980s, they illustrate the new advertising strategies Schmid helped to devise, and testify to the time codes of aestheticized consumption and marketing. The emergence of such time codes made a tentative appearance as far back as the 19th century and gradually acquired momentum in the second half of the 20th century, but it was not until recent decades that the phenomenon burst into full bloom with movements in both art and fashion exploiting the medium of photography—its theatrical, inter-textual, narrative, and conceptual potential—to highlight postmodernist paradoxes, such as the authenticity of the fake or the uniqueness of the copy. Fashion photography fosters the interests of romanticizing and ennobling consumption and luxury; it celebrates appropriative, hybrid affinities with the ethno style of Benetton, punk and global art, with glamour, cult, and the sublime.

"Their fiction seemed to be terrifyingly beautiful."
Richard Prince

Much like Joseph Beuys, who claimed that "expanded art" was his best work of art, Leo Burnett of the eponymous Chicago advertising agency created imagery that was tantamount to a new, expanded form of marketing. He has made a lasting impact on today's culture in our late capitalist, aestheticized age of marketing. In the early 1950s, Burnett successfully linked the American myth of the cowboy, functionalized by Hollywood, with Marlboro cigarettes, transforming them into a masculine brand and the embodiment of a lifestyle. The climate of the 1950s in the United States clearly explains why the image chosen to reinvent a cigarette initially launched for women in the 19th century was not incorporated by an Afro-American Wrangler, who did after all account for a third of the broncos in the decades around the turn of the 19th century. Instead, the cigarette was embodied by a white cowboy as the heroic, nature-bound, and intellectualized counterpart to the urban population. The lonely, male hero, exuding authenticity and authentically engrossed in a dialogue with animals and nature, smokes the filter cigarette that Marlboro had just introduced in the now omnipresent red and white pack simultaneously developed by Frank Gianninoto. Ever since that hero took the stage in 1956, photographers, enthralled by the image, have reimagined it in a mixture of reportage, documentary, and patently fabricated, conceptual photography. The trend culminated in the dramatic, strikingly reductionist, and sublimely chromatic, iconic images of the Marlboro Man created by Schmid between 1993 and 2002 and rarely seen smoking, in keeping with the times. Some of these photographs even garnered him the honor of "cannibalistic" appropriation by Richard Prince, who effected their first appearance in the white cube, albeit under his own name.

The postmodernist strategy of divested authorship implied by Prince through the veritable "death of the author" ultimately turned into an act of reappropriation: Schmid reclaimed his own photographic imagery in the photorealistic paintings he made of the Marlboro Man after 2007. And he did so by means of a technique that stands for originality, authenticity, and authorship. In the act of creating a "photograph in painting," the Swiss photographer reversed the postmodernist appropriation of his icon and "resurrected" his authorship. This is an unmistakable and indeed perfectly logical consequence of his eminently painterly Marlboro photographs. The cowboy, a fiction that "never existed as an original" (Hannes Schmid), had become a reality in the here and now.

This author, Hannes Schmid, considers himself an interloper, who came to photography in the course of extended travels since the 1970s through Africa and Asia, where he acted as a "participant observer" (Bronislaw Malinowski). His involvement is also reflected in the staging and conceptual nature of the work that followed in the 1980s for such fashion magazines as *Vogue, Elle*, and *Marie-Claire*. These photographs incorporate the above-mentioned mutual insemination of art, fashion, advertising, body cult, sports, and lifestyle. Yet they are also informed with an insight into marketing, akin to what Leo Burnett anticipated when he launched his Marlboro Man. In the timeline of Hannes Schmid's photographic oeuvre, they follow the *Rockstars* series, whose intimate snapshot style resembles "family pictures," not unlike the photographs Warhol took of the members of his Factory.

"Every good photograph has a history. My strength lies in uncovering it."
Hannes Schmid

Fashion photography, an undeniably significant social phenomenon and field of endeavor, does, of course, tell stories that connote specific lifestyles and attitudes; it stands for a way of life and its ideologies; it creates images. For Schmid, the history that belongs to every good photograph is not only embodied in the narrative potential of his works but also in the staged reality captured in long exposures, as has been widely featured in fashion photography since the 1980s and 90s. In those decades, art, design, and fashion began rubbing shoulders to the point of interchangeability, with new advertising strategies giving precedence to brand recognition over the advertised object. Schmid adopted such strategies early on, for instance, linking the authentic, pristine, singular universe of the mountains with fashion or rather with a fashion label in his 1984 shoots on the north face of the Eiger for the German edition of *Vogue*. We will come back to that later.
In Schmid's fashion series, the history of a photograph can also be read as an ongoing process involving the appropriation of historical photography as well as his own early, noncommercial photography. In the series shot in the 1990s on location in the Indonesian jungles of Sumatra and Borneo, woman, nature, and animal life merge with the photographer's own environmental and political commitment. Significantly, they are inconceivable without the anthropological record he made of the Dani and Lani tribes in West Papua, where he lived as a freelance photographer in the 1970s and followed the trail of Michael Rockefeller, who had disappeared there. The attitude that inspired his early photography resonates in works of art like the video *Maha Kumbh Mela* and the photo installation *Thaipusam*, with their urgency of detail and close-up effects. The last mentioned series also testifies to Schmid's subtle rhetorical choice of black-and-white or color photography to render the spirit of a given context. A similarly intense gaze, attention to detail, and recognition of the singularity of otherness mark several other fashion series

that cultivate an anthropological or "Benetton style." Strong coloring and a sophisticated close-up technique link the staging of his Marlboro Man with contemporary African art. The symbiosis of art and fashion, the lack of distinction between fashion and art photography, between reportage, documentary, or staged work in these pictures is also characteristic of Schmid's fashion series in black-and-white. The latter show variations in depth, a subtle pathos, and an internalized sublime that recall the documentary style of Walker Evans, on one hand, and his own photographs of the Mennonites, on the other.

What does the Marlboro Man have to do with the Mountain Girl?

None of these works from Hannes Schmid's varied artistic oeuvre shows such a great affinity with his Marlboro Man—albeit an antithetical affinity—as the photographs in which the myth of the Prairie is juxtaposed with the myth of the Alps. The cowboy is to the United States what William Tell and the mountains are to Switzerland. The latter belong to our country's commercially and touristically high-yield founding tale from the days of enlightenment, romanticism, and early industrialization. Such devices as the above-mentioned use of the north face of the Eiger for *Vogue* or Mount Everest, which suggest the auratic and the sublime, define Schmid's innovative contribution to magazine fashion photography. In those years, Schmid worked both with a wide-angle panorama effect and with the authentication strategies of the immediacy evoked by close-up photography and starkly contrasting colors, often deployed in his depictions of the Marlboro Man as well. The two themes, the American Marlboro Man and the Swiss Mountain Girl, converge in a photograph of 2001 taken on the Cape Verde Islands. A reclining beauty, her face averted, is gazing into distant sandy hills while clinging to the arm of her Marlboro Man, of whom we see only his naked muscular torso. The Marlboro Man as the incarnation of masculinity is in danger of becoming obsolete in the 21st century, which belongs to women (Matthias Horx). Moreover, the occasionally homoerotic implications of Schmid's interpretation lap over into his Formula One series, being intimately associated with fashion imagery and, in fact, the shared branding of fashion and cars. Man and machine are either linked to the mountainous Alps in fashion photography staged in a snow-covered landscape or to a lifestyle rendered in a deconstructivist, futuristic architectural ambience that takes its cue from the automobile or fashion industry, specifically Pierre Cardin's bubble house on the French Côte d'Azur. A case in point: the Formula One car is staged as a work of art, depicted up ended or immersed in a pool. In only a few shots does Schmid picture the race—courted alike by the cigarette, automobile, and fashion industries—for what it is, namely an elite sport, as in the full-figure photograph of Formula One racing driver

Takuma Sato. In contrast, Sato's colleague Jenson Button is placed in the feminized world of the bubble house not as a high-speed hero but rather as a model of the fashion industry, whose irresistible appeal impacts not only the art world but the auto industry as well.

The Reality and Facticity of the Fictional
The postmodern artificiality or simulation of brands and events that marks Schmid's mixture of reportage, documentation, and staging is reined in by the reality and facticity of the fictional, achieved through the production of photographs that evoke the above-mentioned modernist notion of the author in the digital age. Schmid's settings are not fictional; they are not computer simulations; they are not simply staged in the studio. He, his crew, and his models really do climb the north face of the Eiger or Mount Everest; they really do explore the freedom and adventure connoted by the expanses and loneliness of the American prairie or the Cape Verde Islands; racing driver Alan van der Merwe's attempt to break the land speed record in a BAR-Honda F1 team car really is re-enacted on Utah's icy Bonneville salt flats. Hannes Schmid's insistence on the reality and authenticity of a staged, narrational, empathetic photographic practice, in which simulated and fictional experience return to reality, may also yield unanticipated results, such as being compelled to flee from that same reality, specifically from a raging female elephant trying to protect her baby in Kenya's Masai Mara in a setting borrowed from Karen Blixen's book *Out of Africa* and consequently receiving the *Life Magazine* award of Best Fashion Picture of the Year.

Sources referenced:

Ackeret, Matthias, "Hannes Schmid, Fotograf und Konzeptkünstler" in: *persönlich, Zeitschrift für Werbung und Medien*, Rapperswil, Switzerland, November 2008, pp. 10–50.

Brüderlin, Markus and Annelie Lütgens, eds., *Art & Fashion. Zwischen Haut und Kleid* (exh. cat.), Kunstmuseum Wolfsburg, Bielefeld/Leipzig et al., 2011.

Die Erfindung der Schweiz 1848–1998. Bildentwürfe einer Nation (exh. cat.), Swiss National Museum, Zurich, 26 June – 4 October 1998.

Heusser, Hans-Jörg and Kornelia Imesch, eds., *Art & branding. Principles – interaction – perspectives* (outlines 3), Zurich, 2006.

Hollein, Max and Christoph Grunenberg. eds., *Shopping. 100 Jahre Kunst und Konsum* (exh. cat.), Schirn Kunsthalle Frankfurt and Tate Liverpool, 2002/2003.

Pagnucco Salvemini, Lorella, *Toscani: Benetton (1984 – 2000)*, Paris, 2002.

Poschardt, Ulf, Marion de Beaupré and Stéphane Baumet, *Archaeology of Elegance. 1980 – 2000. 20 Years of Fashion Photography*, New York, 2003.

Schmitt, Bernd and Alex Simonson, *Marketing Aesthetics. The Strategic Management of Brands, Identity and Image*, New York, 1997.

Perspective: For Gods Only

Gail Buckland

One might compare the art of photography to the act of pointing.
It must be true that some of us point to more interesting facts,
events, circumstances, and configurations than others....
John Szarkowski, The Work of Atget, 1981

Perhaps there is no more potent word than *perspective* when discussing photography. One of the most critical—even radical—decisions we make is where we place ourselves, and what we choose to look at. Our field of vision is one of the most vital ways we define ourselves as individuals—and as artists.

Photographers first locate themselves in time and space; then they determine their *perspective.* The most common meaning of *perspective* refers to the technique of depicting volumes and spatial relationships on a flat surface. But the word also connotes a way of seeing the world, an individual's relationship with all things beheld.

The dynamic relationship of the word *perspective* with the medium of photography is further celebrated by its etymology: it derives from the Latin *perspectivus*, referring to an optical glass, and to *perspicere* which means "to look at closely." Hannes Schmid has spent a lifetime placing himself in extraordinary environments. He not only "shows up" in remarkable places; he is intellectually and emotionally present to all he witnesses. Through photography he brings the subjects of his encounters into *perspective.*

Schmid is physically fit. This remark is not incidental. To know this photographer is to feel his physical energy. He is forever putting his taut, lithe body (which comes with a camera as an accoutrement) in the most singular situations. The analogy John Szarkowski, former Director of Photography at MoMA in New York, makes between pointing and photographing cannot be more apt. There is a wow factor to everything Schmid points to; he is in awe of the things he has witnessed during forty years of adventures all across the globe. "Look, look," is his mantra. "See this. It is amazing, it is magical, it is heroic, it is wonderful, it is extraordinary, it is important," his pictures seem to say. What makes him a remarkable photographer is not only that he sees well, but that he is not afraid to reconfigure his photographs. Sometimes a straight print illuminates the subject most exactly. Sometimes, however, he reimagines that original exposure and translates it into something beyond straight photography. He sees a potential to enlarge and transform the image. We witness this in the scale and pixilation of *Divas+Heroes*; the conceptualization and execution of the multi-media series on the mythic cowboy; the washed-out, claustrophobic and tightly cropped *Maha Kumbh Mela* photographs and film; and most poignantly in *For Gods Only* with bold calligraphy applied directly on the photographic print.

There are many roads to great photography. Robert Frank, also born in Zurich, Switzerland, left his homeland as a young man, as did Schmid. Frank, however, settled in the United States and concentrated on ordinary people engaged in daily life. The drama in Frank's photography is found in the mental attitudes and body language of the people he photographed. Schmid, too, might photograph people in their daily routines, but while Frank, in his early work, explored the habits of Americans in the continental United States, Schmid's photography knows no boundaries. Schmid takes us to places we would rarely go ourselves and shows us customs that are foreign to most Westerners' experience. If he photographs everyday activities, they are of the Lani and Dani tribes in West Papua or Mennonites refusing to embrace modern amenities in rural America. The most familiar settings in his photographs are ironically the homes of rock musicians. The contrast between these wild, music men and the banality of their homes results in some of the most humorous and surprising of his photographs. Floral wallpaper just seems out-of-place in the home of a heavy metal musician.

With his energy, physical stamina, perseverance, excitement, sense of adventure, talent, professionalism, and *joie de vivre*, Schmid takes us on a great journey—in time, place, and perspective.

A photograph is never neutral. William Henry Fox Talbot, the inventor of positive/negative photography (as opposed to the one-off daguerreotype) never believed his invention *captured* reality. He understood that the photographic process has an uncanny relationship with external reality. It is not the real thing that photographers present to the world but their *perspective* on what they have experienced—emotionally, intellectually, aesthetically. The last part is often the most difficult because no matter what the subject, the end product is a picture with artistic demands and criteria.

All photographs, good and bad, offer the opportunity for contemplation. They are two-dimensional witnesses, silent but never neutral. Photographs transform their subjects; they are not the reality. No photograph can be violent even if its subject is violence. A photograph can, however, be beautiful. Pictorial beauty traditionally has attributes of balance, grace, unity of purpose—even as these attributes are under attack and constantly changing. Every artist gives some kind of form to the chaos of the world and photography is, of course, inherently capable of creating deeply aesthetic experiences.

The proverbial photographic sunset snap gets us nowhere towards understanding. Beauty without depth is boring. That is why *equivalent*, a term introduced by the great American photographer, editor, and gallery director, Alfred Stieglitz, is crucial to explaining how a machine-made image can be art. A photograph has the potential to reflect (and let the viewer reflect on) a place or event or person, but it is more than that, for it can also convey an emotional/spiritual experience—an *equivalent*. A photograph itself can never depict reality, but it can have a powerful relationship with that reality.

Throughout the history of photography, there has been a raging battle: It started in 1839 with the announcement of the invention of photography. People asked, "How can a machine make art?" When Kodak introduced the first true amateur snapshot camera, the Kodak No.1, in 1888, anyone could take a picture because all they had to do was press the button, advance the film, and let Kodak do the rest. Professional photographers and art photographers felt threatened. The former because of their livelihood; the latter because a quick snapshot could have some of the same attributes as a photograph that a dedicated, creative photographer spent days, weeks, even years conceptualizing and executing.

Two incredibly simple points settled the debate: 1) humans make art, not cameras or paintbrushes; 2) you decide for yourself if you have had a deep, meaningful, transformative, aesthetic experience. Today photography and film are not only recognized art forms; they initiate and drive much of the intellectual discourse in the art world.

Photography was born of man, not machine. And handiwork was present from the beginning. Fox Talbot made an "x" on his plain writing paper before brushing on the chemicals, so that when the paper dried, he knew which side had the light sensitive chemicals. But seeing that handwritten "x" on a Talbot print, an "x" made for the most practical of purposes, connects us directly to the man. The early daguerreotypists hired miniature portraitists (the daguerreotype had put many of them out of business) to hand-color their portraits, to give a rosy blush to the cheeks, a sparkle to the gold necklace. With the growing popularity of cartes-de-visite and family albums in the 1860s and 70s, it was the rage among amateurs to add their handiwork to these tiny sepia prints. Drawing on photographs, coloring them, making collages by cutting them up, and pasting them in family albums and elsewhere gave photographs something they seemingly lacked—uniqueness.

Talbot's marvelous invention—and the realization that a negative can produce any number of identical copies—did, however, produce a backlash. People value what is unique and what actually shows effort. This attitude prevailed during the Pictorialist period in art photography, dating from around the 1890s to the First World War. It started, in part, as a reaction to the Kodak camera, but acquired ascendancy because photographers had to find a dramatic means of distinguishing their aesthetically driven photographs from common snapshots. Photographers made their pictures look like etchings, watercolors, and drawings. Sometimes they worked on the negative; almost always they worked on the final print, adding colors, brushstrokes, scratches, layers of emulsion—all the

while removing photographic detail to convey an impression, reverie, a deep emotion.
Sometimes handwork was for practical purposes, as with Talbot; sometimes it was for
purely aesthetic reasons, as with the great Pictorialists; sometimes a blending of the two.
In 1878, the Chinese photographer Liang Shitai (commonly known as See Tay) inscribed
(or had someone else inscribe) beautiful Chinese characters directly on his albumen
photograph of the powerful politician Li Hongzhang. In the Introduction to *Brush & Shutter:
Early Photography in China*, Wu Hung, professor of Chinese Art History, explains that the
writing identifies "the time and place the picture was taken" and "the inscription's literary
style and ink-and-brush (*maobi*) manner disclose the impact of traditional paintings,
for which inscriptions often identify the work as a gift and include a dedication to the
recipient." Photographs taken in China in the 19th century sometimes had the seal of
the sitter stamped on the face of the print, a way of authenticating that the photograph
was indeed the correct likeness of the individual. From an aesthetic point of view, these
stamps balance and enhance the image. Professor Hung observes that these seals are
"flanking the figure and confronting the viewer," emphasizing that the "bold imprints are
integrated into the composition and should be recognized as the prince's [Yixuan, 1840
– 91, the Seventh Prince of the Qing imperial house] self-presentation." Schmid also
uses calligraphy on his prints to energize, inform, and balance his pictures.

*The function of the artist in society is to put layer upon layer, stone upon stone,
in the organization of emotions: to record feelings with his particular means.
The artist unconsciously disentangles the most essential strands of existence
from all the contorted and chaotic complicities of actuality,
and weaves them into an emotional fabric of compelling validity.*
László Moholy-Nagy (1947) 2005

Hannes Schmid's *For Gods Only* builds on many traditions in the history of photography.
Initially, foreigners documented the traditions and practices of other cultures. A Westerner
took the first photographs in China in 1842. (The earliest extant daguerreotype, however,
dates from 1844 and the earliest known daguerreotype by a Chinese photographer dates
from nine years later.) Soon after photography was introduced into China, European
merchants, army officers, or customs officials presumably brought the new invention to
Singapore. We do know for certain that the great Scottish photographer John Thomson
moved to Singapore in 1863. He then traveled between 1868 and 1872 across China
and notably, for this essay, included photographs of actors in his survey. The Chinese

photographic studio Hing-Qua John & Co. also photographed actors in the 1860s. About this profession Thomson wrote: "Although the Chinese had a great fondness for theatricals, the profession of actor was considered among the most debased and disreputable. A severe course of training went into the apprenticeship of an actor which usually began when a boy was either indentured or sold to a troupe."

In 1998 during a visit to Singapore, Schmid unexpectedly stumbled upon a secluded theatrical stage, not easily seen by people casually walking by. It was the Kim Eng Teochew Opera Troupe, founded by Chua Hung Kee. They performed ritualistic opera in front of hundreds of empty red chairs. What Schmid witnessed was not a dress rehearsal; it was an opera performed *for gods only.*

In a recent correspondence, I asked Schmid the obvious question: can people stand in the back or on the sides and discreetly watch this opera? His answer was, "To watch is considered wrong or even dangerous. It is only okay for young children and the mentally handicapped to do so if they do not disturb the actors and stay at a distance."

How was it possible for Schmid to photograph this clandestine form of ritual street theatre when even watching it was prohibited? He did it through perseverance. Schmid befriended the members of the ensemble and finally, after years of developing trust and friendships, was allowed to start photographing the company. He shows the actors and musicians rehearsing, spiritually preparing themselves to perform, slowly and meticulously putting on their makeup, offering sacrifices to propitiate the spirits of the ancestors, and, finally, presenting the play. From 2002 until February 11, 2007 when the Kim Eng Theatre disbanded, Schmid did not just document the opera company; he created a body of work that serves as an *equivalent* of this deeply spiritual, esoteric, transitory art form.

As strange as this form of opera, with its component of ritual sacrifice to the gods and ancestors, may seem to the Western mind, a beginning explanation may be found in Confucianism. As the scholar Xinzhong Yao explains in his *Introduction to Confucianism*: "Confucianism appreciates that sacrifice may bring about good fortune, such as material gain, physical longevity and spiritual protection, but it constantly emphasizes that personal gain is not the primary purpose. The important thing is to have a sincere attitude, a reverential heart and a virtuous motive, and to offer 'sacrifices without seeking for anything to be gained.' Those who are engaged in ritual should experience a spiritual and moral reunion with the spirits. 'Sacrifice as if present,' is taken to mean 'sacrifice to the gods as if the gods were present.' (Lunyu, 3:12). This requires more than merely ceremonial performance. Confucians stress the importance of ceremonies in refining human piety and emphasize the moral effect of ritual on the people. Ritual is not merely about playing music and offering jade and silk. (Lunyu,17:11) It is meant to achieve moral perfection." Chinese street theater is both a form of drama and musical theater, at times mixed with martial art elements. In Singapore, it probably dates back to the opening of the Thian Hock Keng temple in 1840. It is performed in the various dialects spoken by immigrant groups, most notably Cantonese, Hainanese, Hokkien, and Teochew, who emigrated to southeast Asia for economic and political reasons. Writing about its significance, Professor Jung Sai Shing of the National University of Singapore observes: "As reflected in the Lat Pau, the earliest Chinese newspaper of Singapore, ritual performance served as a major theatrical form of Chinese opera in 19th century Singapore. In fact, the street opera in Singapore was a continuation of a long established tradition of the Chinese drama culture. From an academic point of view, it is believed that the street opera culture of Singapore had preserved the performance practices and religious culture that might have been lost in Mainland China during the Cultural Revolution."

Through prescribed ritual, the Chinese actors communicate with the spirits and the gods and try to please them. Schmid was fascinated by the dance, theater, and music integral to an art form that has been handed down through generations of oral tradition within a clan via secret rites. It is a traditional form of street opera combined with offerings to propitiate the ancestors and the spirits.

Until the 1970s, Chinese street theater flourished. Street operas were very public events, taking place at temples, cemeteries, housing estates—anywhere in a city that had large numbers of Chinese. Hundreds of people watched as the stories of gods and heroes, supernatural challenges and human failings, magical events and mundane happenings unfolded. A linguistic policy mandating Mandarin as the official language of Singapore meant young people could not understand the dialects used in the performances. Nor could they relate to this stylistic, antiquated form of entertainment. Only the elderly were happy to sit for three hours watching equally elderly actors enact ancient stories. Traditional Chinese street opera cannot compete with cell phones, the internet, TV, and cinema in the minds and hearts of the young. But "Natural Law" in Confucianism contains the concept of constant change, by which all things are given life and all events run their course. For the most part, this noble art has come to an end in Singapore, making Schmid's photographs of the Kim Eng Troupe even more important and significant. His work has won the patronage of UNESCO, in recognition of its contribution to the preservation of world culture. A new edition of Schmid's 2008

short, subtle, eloquent, and magical multipart video received the prestigious Delphic Art
Movie Award (DAMA) in 2011.

*I want to alter the photographic surface—that is, move from the transparent,
window-on-the world form that has been photography's primary reason for
being since its invention, to making it a physical object, an object to be looked
at for its own presence and not for a surrogate experience.*
Thomas Barrow, 1984

Schmid understands, as did many of his predecessors, that black-and-white photography
has an inherent aesthetic that allows the viewer to focus on core elements of the subject.
Black-and-white helps reduce the photograph to its essence. His decision to use black-
and-white in *For Gods Only* is made even more commendable because Chinese street
opera is one of the most colorful forms of theater. The vibrant hues of the costumes, sets,
and make-up assault the senses. Had Schmid photographed in color, the viewer would be
drawn to the surface elements—the silks, the brocades, the shiny swords, the jeweled
headdresses. He has slowed things down by using black-and-white. This is a meditative
form of theater, paced to allow for spiritual transformation. Schmid wants us to slow
down as well, in order to experience this transformation. Rather than be overwhelmed
by the sensations that color photography can generate, Schmid has given the viewer the
opportunity to see not only the subject, but *into* the subject.
Art photography has its roots in monochromatic prints, but Schmid is building on more
than one tradition in the 138 prints of his visual narrative. He is also paying tribute to
the centuries-old practice of Chinese painting done with brush and black ink on white
surfaces. Traditionally painting must have what the Chinese call *qiyun*, spirit or breath of
life. Schmid found a means of imbuing his photographs with *qiyun*.
For Gods Only combines Schmid's black-and-white photographs with master calligrapher
Simon Huang's red ideographs. It is a brilliant partnering of two inherently different art
forms. The photograph holds the moment; the brushstroke sets it free. Like yin-yang, the
Baryt photographic print and the acrylic paint are complementary forces, balancing each
other like hot and cold, water and fire, earth and air. In Daoist metaphysics, yin-yang is an
indivisible whole. Schmid and Huang make the whole manifest.
Schmid is a wonderful portraitist; his studies of the actors are deeply probing. The black-
and-white prints are rich with a full range of tone, sensually going from the deepest blacks
to the whitest highlights. Schmid uses the entire gray scale to maximum effect. Areas of

black create mystery and help isolate the actor within the frame. The brilliant whites are used most effectively in dramatizing the painted faces, porcelain-like on stage but simply craggy with age behind the scenes. And the 6 x 6 cm square format of the negative works well, both visually and emotionally. The tight geometric form evokes order, structure, and precision—all inherent in traditional Chinese opera.

Red is potent. It is energy as well as good luck. Master Huang sits in front of Schmid's large-format black-and-white photographs, brush in hand, preparing himself not to violate but to liberate the pristine print. Starting from top left to bottom right, a spirit born of experience, passion, understanding, and communion guides his hand. Like a Chinese red seal stamp that is placed just exactly right to balance and complete a painting or drawing, Huang's characters complement Schmid's pictures in a remarkable way. Art historian Ildegarda Scheidegger helps us understand: "…the redness [of the Chinese characters] renders the world of the Gods vividly present… Indeed, the characters chosen have an expressive weight that goes well beyond their immediate significance. What is more, the Chinese calligraphy used in this work is performative and requires bodily action for its realization, a balance of cognition and intuition and thus one of Schmid's recurrent topics." Huang makes the calligraphy both semantically and graphically meaningful. The ideograph must work pictorially with the content of the photograph; it must also illuminate the subject and serve as a caption. A wonderful example is the photograph titled *Yi* meaning "to apply makeup for the role." The affinity between the actor applying his makeup and Huang's brushstrokes is perceptible. There is a tangible fluidity and hand movement with both. One feels the connection immediately. Applying painted eyebrows in Chinese opera is a form of body calligraphy.

The photograph titled *Dao* shows an elderly actor of the company looking intensely at the viewer, a lifetime of experience carved into the deep crevices of his face. The Chinese character which means "leader of the ritual procession" dominates the picture. The "leader" himself is receding—almost withdrawing out of the picture—as he did in real life. But Huang's forceful lines move forward, confronting the viewer and demanding recognition. Both the meaning of the calligraphy and the elegant brushwork pay tribute to the "leader." The picture is no longer still or a thing of the past; it moves and breathes life—and has something of the eternal.

One does not need to understand the meaning of the character painted on the photograph to absorb the rightness of the mark. In the photograph titled *Ban*, the meaning of the word "treatment of a particular play" hardly matters. The joy of seeing brushstrokes copy the old man's long beard is enough.

One of the most haunting photographs in this series shows a woman looking into a mirror, the red painted lines framing her face and echoing the rectangular shape of the mirror. The title of the picture is *Cun*, meaning "to ponder upon one's completed mask." Oscar Wilde once said "Man is least himself when he talks in his own person. Give him a mask and he will tell you the truth." One cannot help wonder what the actress is seeing as she looks so intently at herself in the mirror.

The acrylic brushstrokes direct the viewer's gaze to specific details in the picture. They often serve as a frame within the frame. Even more radically, Huang consistently extends his brush mark beyond the edge of the photograph, taking the power of the red mark into the meditative white space that surrounds the image. Every character applied by Huang is positioned to balance, to enhance, to dramatize, to isolate, to emphasize something vital in the picture. Graphically, the red marks speak of the fluidity of the human condition. It was a brilliant insight on the part of Schmid to invite Huang to collaborate in this series. *Qiyun* is present. Every print is unique. Art and spirit are one.

Still photography is just that—no motion. Just as photographs of violence are never violent, a photograph can show action, but it cannot be active. Huang's brushstrokes throb with vital energy and animate the image in a multitude of ways. There is the paint itself, semi-transparent so that the photographic image comes through the brushstroke, adding a physical layer on top of the smooth light-sensitive paper. There is the flow of the paint, like blood coursing through veins—a life force dancing on the surface of the print. And, as noted, no Chinese character stays strictly within the square frame. Each is rebellious, each breaks out, goes from dark to light. The calligraphy is deeply spiritual, enhancing the spirituality inherent in Schmid's subject.

There are photographers, like William Klein, who mark their black-and-white contact prints and enlargements with red or blue paint; there are photographers, like Duane Michaels and Jim Goldberg, who write on the face of their photographs. Rarely has a photographer used paint on photographic paper to such emotional, aesthetic, and meaningful purpose as Hannes Schmid has done in *For Gods Only*. He has given us his perspective on a sacred and transitory art form. The performances may have stopped but something precious and profound has been preserved.

Sources referenced:

Cody, Jeffrey W. and Frances Terpak, eds., *Brush & Shutter: Early Photography in China,* Los Angeles, California, 2011.

Moholy-Nagy, Lazlo, *The New Vision: Fundamentals of Bauhaus Design, Painting, Sculpture, and Architecture,* New York, 2005.

Scheidegger, Ildegarda, "Hannes Schmid: For Gods Only" in: *Friends: Zilla Leutenegger & Hannes Schmid,* St. Moritz, 2010.

Schuman, Aaron, "Thomas Barrow's Cancellations" in: *Aperture 208,* Fall 2012.

Sherman, Lee E., *A History of Far Eastern Art,* New York, 1994.

Spence, Jonathan D. and Annping Chin, *The Chinese Century: A Photographic History of the Last Hundred Years,* New York, 1996.

Strauss, David Levi, *Between the Eyes: Essays on Photography and Politics,* New York, 2003.

Szarkowski, John and Maria Morris Hambourg, *The Work of Atget: Volume I: Old France,* New York, 1981.

Thomson, John, *Illustrations of China and Its People,* 1873–1874, London, 1874.

White, Stephen, *John Thomson: A Window to the Orient,* London, 1985.

Worswick, Clark and Jonathan Spence, *Imperial China: Photographs 1850-1912,* New York, 1978.

Yao, Xinzhong, *An Introduction to Confucianism,* Cambridge, England, 2000.

Reappropriations of the Cowboy

Elisabeth Bronfen

An Iconic Figure

We know him as a lone ranger, riding over mountain ridges, through prairies and dunes, crossing raging rivers. His horse is an extension of his body, allowing him to search, wander, and if need be take flight from danger. Looking for his trail, he traverses the wide plains or plunges into a crevice in the rocky hills, becoming part of the Western landscape. We also know him to bond with other like-minded men, herding cattle, each with a lasso in hand, or sitting around a fireside at night, resting from their day's hard labor. Standing for rugged individualism, for the solitary freedom of unconstrained mobility, the cowboy has become a myth in the cultural imaginary of America. As Roland Barthes notes in his seminal text "Myth Today," the mythic sign evolves by separating the signifier (be it a word or an image) from what it signifies, namely the actual person or object to which it refers, and instead attaching to it a different idea or set of ideas. Myth thus proves to be a second-order sign system, in which the original meaning loses its value by becoming pure form: "It empties itself, it becomes impoverished, history evaporates, only the letter remains." The iconic image of an agile man on his horse, wearing a Stetson and cowboy boots, does not refer to the multitude of inconspicuous cowhands who worked on ranches tending cattle in the past as they still do today. Instead, it signifies on the level of a form that puts the original meaning at a distance, even while holding it at one's disposal. Barthes adds to his definition that "the form must constantly be able to be rooted again in the meaning and to get there what nature it needs for its nutriment; above all, it must be able to hide there. It is this constant game of hide-and-seek between the meaning and the form which defines myth."

There is, however, something specific about why the cowboy, like no other cultural icon, represents the transformation of American history into myth. As the lone wanderer who blazes trails in the wilderness, familiarizing himself with the undiscovered frontier and its strange inhabitants so that settlers may follow, he embodies the Manifest Destiny first declared by Democrats in the 1840s to support their effort at bringing civilization to the Western territories. The stories that emerged around the figure of the cowboy are thus mythic in that they contain, as their secondary meaning, a political agenda, an agenda that screens out the genocide of the indigenous population and the exploitation of the region's natural resources by transforming the settling of the West into a narrative of cultural progress. However, from the start, the cowboy was also a nostalgic figure, recalling a frontier that was already in the process of being superseded by its own legend. Ironically, the fascination of the West was always predicated on its provisional, transient nature and the promise that the modern civilized world would replace it. In the same vein, the nomadic cowboy is excluded from the inevitable march of progress he helps bring about. Although he works in the name of the community of settlers and rangers, there is no place for him in their settled world. The only home for his nomadic way of life is the wide prairie.

The cowboy perfects the masculine will to win the West as well as the moral fortitude necessary to combat hostile forces—be it the harsh law of nature, the Indians seeking to repossess their land, or the violence of outlaw rogues. With his resilient self-reliance he stands for the American dream par excellence, repeatedly taking flight from the encumbering conventions of the ordinary civil world and finding in the open landscape the perfect site for his radical will to freedom. And yet, because the *raison d'être* of this mythic figure is to bring about the very civilization whose social conventions must exclude him (because they restrict his desire for mobility), he is caught up in the process of making himself obsolete: a scapegoat sacrificed to an idea of law, order, and civilization along with the frontier he has helped turn into a garden. At play is, thus, the following aporia: The cowboy has become such a powerful mythic figure precisely because, as a hero of adventure stories in which he distances himself from the ordinary world, he has, in a second step, also become depleted of any real context, his actual history evaporated with only the character remaining. In addition, the cowboy is more than merely one popular folklore figure among many, serving as the mythic form able to transmit and negotiate the ideology of the American project of expansionism. He was a stereotype from the beginning, standing in for the dreams of ordinary people, living the radical but unattainable freedom to which they aspire.

Emptied of his historical singularity, he embodies the legend that is to be told about him after his demise. In this iconic figure, meaning and form perfectly match in that both— the story of masculine adventure he embodies and the body gestures that represent this dream—are removed from any reference outside the mythic sign. Regarding the resilient cultural afterlife of the cowboy, this process of evaporation and appropriation involves intricate genre memory as well. If myth recasts historical reality to support a particular narrative of the nation—in the case of the cowboy the Manifest Destiny of the United States to expand its political hegemony all the way to the Pacific Ocean—the forms in which this refiguration occurs themselves partake of a complex cycle of reformulations. It is useful, therefore, to recall that the actual settling of America, which began in the

16th century, first produced a plethora of stories and paintings of valiant explorers, oscillating between the settlements they helped found and the wilderness of the as yet undiscovered new world. By the 19th century, a specifically American literature took shape in James Fenimore Cooper's *Leatherstocking Tales*, whose hero serves as the father of all subsequent cowboy legends—much as a specifically American visual style has its roots in the early landscape paintings and photography of the West.

Once the frontier had successfully been rendered obsolete, this layering of visual and narrative reappropriations of Westward expansion took a new turn. By the 1880s, Buffalo Bill's infamous Wild West Shows came to offer their version of how the West was won, only to migrate to the new medium of cinema when Hollywood became the key producer of imaginary re-conceptualizations of America's mythic past. The Western, one of the first Hollywood film genres, has been reconceived throughout the 20th century according to the needs of each new generation of directors, cinematographers, and screenwriters. The constant game of hide-and-seek between meaning and form not only writes itself into the way each subsequent period has recourse to previous cinematic transformations of the history of the West into a mythic narrative; it also underpins the global dissemination the American cowboy has found on the silver screen. With each new wave of recycling, only the contours of this mythic figure remain, and yet it is repeatedly replenished with the materiality of the medium (be it photography, painting, graphic art, or computer design) that taps over and again into its vital force. From the onset of genre movies, Hollywood turned the cowboy into the star of the Western film and male stars, such as John Wayne, Gary Cooper, and James Stewart, came to stand in for this iconic figure. In classic Hollywood, the cinematic image thus took the mythic distancing (and oblique recollection) of real historical men to yet another level: Cowboys, having become the icons of an American way of life, are transformed into stars of an American way of aesthetically refiguring national ideology.

Hannes Schmid's Reappropriation Loops

In 1954 Leo Burnett first developed the concept of the Marlboro Man for Philip Morris, using the mythic cowboy to sell not a political project but rather cigarettes. Hannes Schmid's photographs for this advertising campaign idiosyncratically interpret the particular notion of masculinity attached to the solitary, free-spirited wanderer, recalling the poses and scenes immortalized by Hollywood's silver screen. Given the fact that Schmid would later find himself compelled to reappropriate his own photographs as images painted in oil on canvas, it is fruitful to invoke another correspondence, namely to the paintings of Charles M. Russell (1864-1926). Contemporaneous with the emergence of the cowboy in Hollywood, Russell depicted the West on canvas. Highlighted in these paintings are scenes of bodily intensity. We see a group of men synchronize their lasso throwing to rope in a stray animal. Or our attention is drawn to the agility of a rider, put to the test by a bucking horse. In other paintings we find cowboys sitting proudly erect on their horses to scan the horizon or traversing the prairie, their individual bodies starkly contrasting with the immensity of the wilderness. Foregrounded also are moments of nocturnal repose, with the camp fire drawing a circle of light that holds the men together in a world falling into darkness. These paintings freeze the movement so characteristic for the cowboy, intensifying it in the stillness of the painted image, even while they pit the intimacy of shared adventure against the anonymity of the wide-open frontier.

If, in his photographs, Hannes Schmid picks up on poses that Russell's Western paintings installed in the first decades of the 20th century, he gives them a particular visual spin. The focus is on the detail of a gesture—pouring coffee from a thermos bottle, filling a cup with water at the edge of a river, carrying a saddle, and, of course, lighting up a cigarette or leaning against a pole while enjoying a quiet smoke. Often the individuality of his cowboys is indiscernible—the Stetson covers the actual face, or, in one picture of a cowboy resting, we see only his hat from behind. Sometimes the image is cropped to focus on the hands or the boots, foregrounding the accoutrements of cowboy life rather than any particular man. Sometimes the picture is taken from such a distance that only the outline of a pose is recognizable. Then again, the cowboys herding horses or sitting on fences evaporate into the all-encompassing yellow, orange, or blue light cast on the scene. Indeed, most often they appear as dark silhouettes against an intensely colored sky, drawing attention not to their unique traits but to the iconic gestures they share. Even as Schmid refigures the poses of Russell's Western painting—the perfect pitching of a lasso, the skillful horseman who can stay on a bucking horse, men walking or riding in formation—he embellishes the mythic quality of the cowboy by explicitly staging his body as pure visual form. Whether the image captures him in motion or in repose, he is primarily the embodiment of an intense emotion, whose resilient transmission depends on its depletion of any specific context: its reduction to pure energy contained in a culturally codified form. What these photographs capture is the spirit of cowboy life, not its reality. Schmid is less interested in the nostalgic narrative of the cowboy; he is not concerned with the cowboy who pits his forces against the indigenous Native American population. Instead, he focuses on moments of fragility that celebrate a state of exception from the ordinary, repeatedly drawing on one specific aspect of the myth: group rituals among men, coming together in moments of action, their movements perfectly coordinated even as they pause to survey the land. When only one rider can be seen, we are called upon to imagine the other men around him watching. These images touch us because the adventure they encapsulate is an excitement which is at risk in more senses than one. There is the implicit danger of the work itself, but more importantly there is the certainty that the thrill cannot be sustained indefinitely. The intimacy amongst men which these photographs transform into mythic signs commemorates time detached from the ordinary. Rather than being endangered by the immensity of the landscape surrounding them, its openness offers up the stage that protects their union. On it they come together as a band of brothers not so much striving to bring civilization to the wilderness as partaking in a shared flight from the settled community.

The nostalgia flooding these photographs is joyful, a tribute to the fact that on the level of the mythic sign at least, the freedom of the cowboy can be resurrected. Having emptied itself of historicity and context, it can turn into a permanent aesthetic form. The elegance of the body movements becomes monumental because the freedom Schmid's cowboys incorporate is explicitly larger than life, each individual man subsumed into the group scenario of which he is but a part. If these photographs touch us because we know that the scenes they depict are precarious, sustainable only in a special place and time outside the ordinary, the artificiality of the color and the reduction of the individual to a figure underscore the process of derealization on the formal level as well. The mythic cowboys they resurrect are explicitly elevated to an aesthetic form. By celebrating the cowboy as an image formula, Schmid puts the process of iconic mythification itself on display. Even as he offers a poignant comment on the cultural reception of historical reality, he resurrects the affective power contained in and by the visual formalization of its images.

The Genre Memory of Aesthetic Forms

Given that over the past decades Schmid has been compelled to literally undertake a recollection of previous imagings, there is a further twist to his play with the genre memory revolving around the iconic Marlboro cowboy. It is fruitful to recall that the original advertisements deployed photographs in both magazines and billboard posters. The strategy of the campaign, in turn, tapped into a particularly resilient aspect of the American Dream so as to sell filter cigarettes, meant to mitigate fears about the health risk of smoking. Working against the image of being a feminine product, the Marlboro

Man was designed to recast the typical smoker of filter cigarettes along the lines of an ideal American masculinity. In the 1960s, the advertisements also showed urban men of leisure on sporting, boating, or fishing trips, yet the cowboy soon emerged as the most efficient mythic figure to sell this brand. His image perfectly fused two meanings: a particular tobacco flavor and the fantasy of rugged masculine adventure. By using the cowboy as a second-order sign and attaching to him a meaning traditionally not associated with him, the advertisements successfully suggest that smoking is the stuff that men's dreams are made of. When one lights up a Marlboro—thus the rhetorical wager of the campaign—one can imagine stepping into the shoes of the most prominent embodiment of American self-reliance. Smoking allows for an imaginary appropriation of the cowboy experience. The cinematic touch to the secondhand emotions the advertisements sought to evoke is particularly evident in one image from 1963, in which we see a cowboy lighting up in front of a nocturnal cityscape. Given the interchangeability of scenery, the urban night here functions as the last frontier: a man's world that arises as an imaginary backdrop out of the flavor of a particular cigarette.

Over decades, the campaigns primarily involved scenes appropriated from Westerns, with Marlboro Country as mythic a geography as John Ford's Monument Valley. This reveals a crucial point about Hollywood's celebrity system. Though they are embodied by actual actors, film stars are themselves commodities, their specific visual aura exploited to advertise a particular film studio. When advertisement strategists, in turn, recycle film images to sell their products, the second-order signification becomes ever more layered. The image of a particular product (a cigarette) is implicitly coupled with the image of another commodity (the Western star). The affective power of both resides in the fact that they stand in for, and thus call forth, an immaterial item, namely the emotion connected to a particular way of life. Given that the cowboy, as a mythic figure, himself served as an advertisement for the American project of expansion, he is rhetorically connected to the Marlboro cigarette brand and the Western star whom the Marlboro man emulates not in any reality but on the level of a culturally shared imaginary. As the second-order signs multiply (a photograph recycling a film image recycling a painted image recycling a political ideology) any first-order meaning (the historical West) becomes ever more depleted. The figure remaining in the photo image instead refers primarily to the multiple layers of visualization preceding it, each of which had already emptied itself of any reference to a world beyond the sign. And yet, as each subsequent, multi-layered image taps into previous formalizations, it also releases if not the meaning then the emotion contained in and by the preceding image formulas. The affective effect is nourished by the intensity that is evoked along with the pure visual form.

In the work of Hannes Schmid, this looping came to find its own idiosyncratic twist when, in response to Richard Prince's appropriation art, he decided to reclaim his work in various media. He has since reappropriated his original photographs by painting them in oil on canvas, by photographing these paintings and enlarging them into billboard posters, and by enlarging his photographs to the size of big canvases. The paint blurs the distinction between original and recycling, between realism and aestheticism. By repainting photographs and rephotographing paintings, Schmid confronts us with various image layers in such a way as to raise both the photographic and the painted image to the level of a self-reflexive game with refigurations in which even the claim to an original point of reference beyond the image recedes. The endless loop of reappropriation recalls both the earlier medium of the Western painting but also the format of the billboard poster that preceded the conceptual art of the 1980s. The "preposterous" twist these reappropriations perform by conceiving, as Mieke Bal proposes with this term, previous images through the lens of their subsequent recycling, is essential. Schmid returns to the original photographs, implicitly recalling even while screening out the advertisement campaign that brought them into circulation, but he does so by adding yet another layer of aesthetic mediation: oil paint on canvas. As his work shifts from one medium to the next, it draws ever more attention to the way the cowboy figure empties itself to become a vibrant mythic figure, by foregrounding the medium through which we perceive this transmission—the sharply contoured, vibrantly colorful paint on canvas.

If Andy Warhol's Pop Art reclaimed iconic advertisement images such as the Campbell soup can, Schmid reappropriates his *own* advertisement images in response to their deployment (and depletion) by another conceptual artist. His photo-realistic paintings produce a hyper-reality whose visual form seduces us into recalling the array of previous meanings in which it is rooted: a nostalgia not only for the mythic cowboy and the cigarette culturally associated with him until the late 1990s but also for a particular art and cinema genre. By reappropriating both his original photographs and the recycling to which they were subjected, Schmid comments on the layering of previous images involved in the cowboy's cultural survival as a mythic figure. Facing his work, we may find ourselves compelled to ask where the original may be located but, even more pointedly, what an original is. Like the scenarios his photographs depict, the visual form is itself precarious not only because it can be refigured and recycled, but also because its privileged thematic form—the cowboy, his accoutrements, his poses and gestures—was, from the start, the visual embodiment of a dream, of an immaterial idea, of a national project. Hannes Schmid does not engage art for art's sake; his art is about the power of the art medium, the vitality it precariously encapsulates. In the course of a complex loop of reappropriations, his cowboy images have transformed into mythic time capsules which hide historical meaning only to open up to its resilient force.

Sources referenced:

Bal, Mieke, *Quoting Caravaggio. Contemporary Art, Preposterous History,* Chicago, 1999.

Barthes, Roland, "Myth Today" in: *A Barthes reader,* edited, with an introduction by Susan Sontag, New York, 1982.

Bellour, Raymond, *Le Western*, Paris, 1993.

Bronfen, Elisabeth, *Home in Hollywood. The Imaginary Geography of Cinema*, New York, 2004.

Wood, Michael, *America in the Movies*, New York, 1975.

Photographs 1974 – 2005

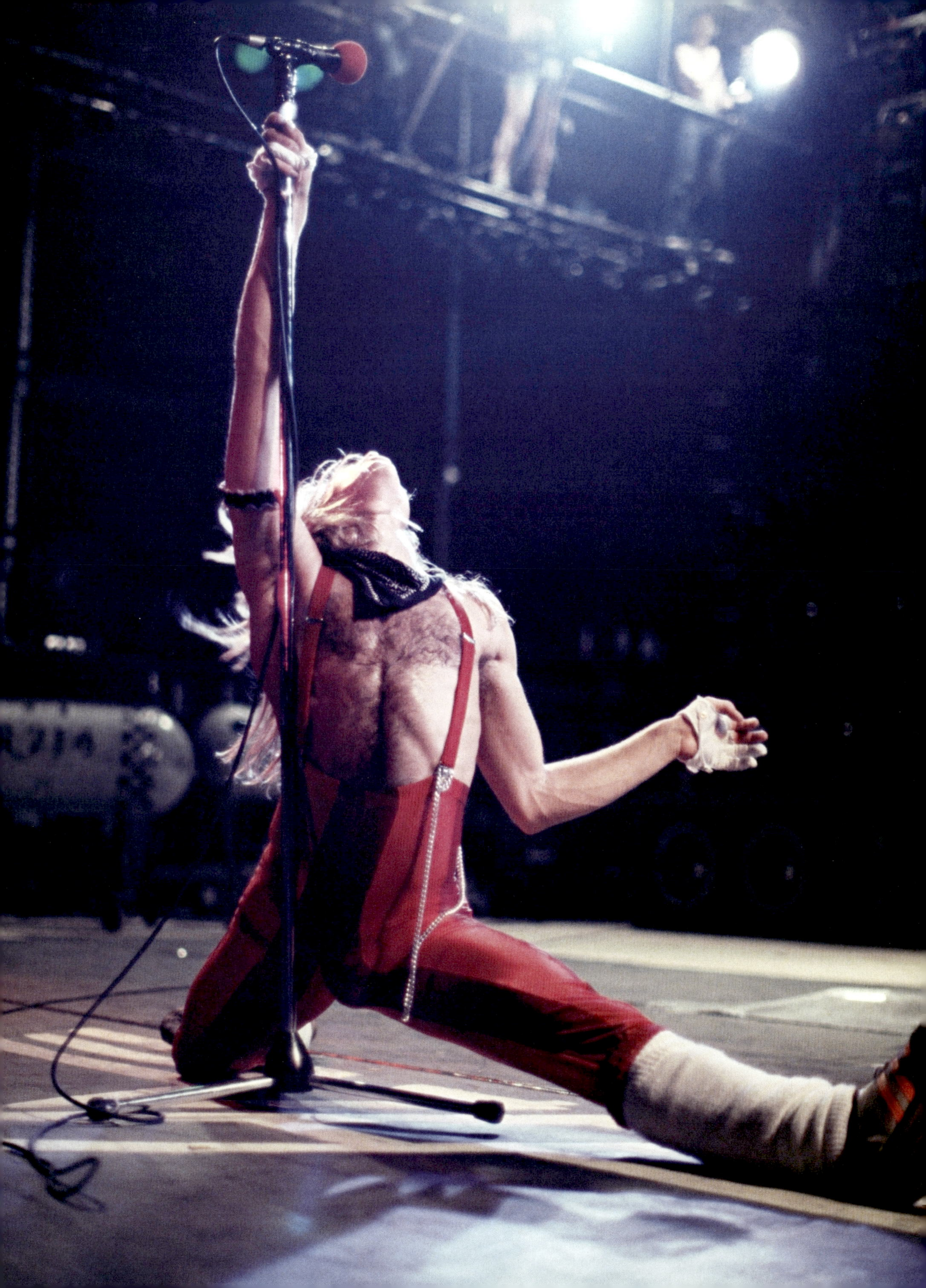

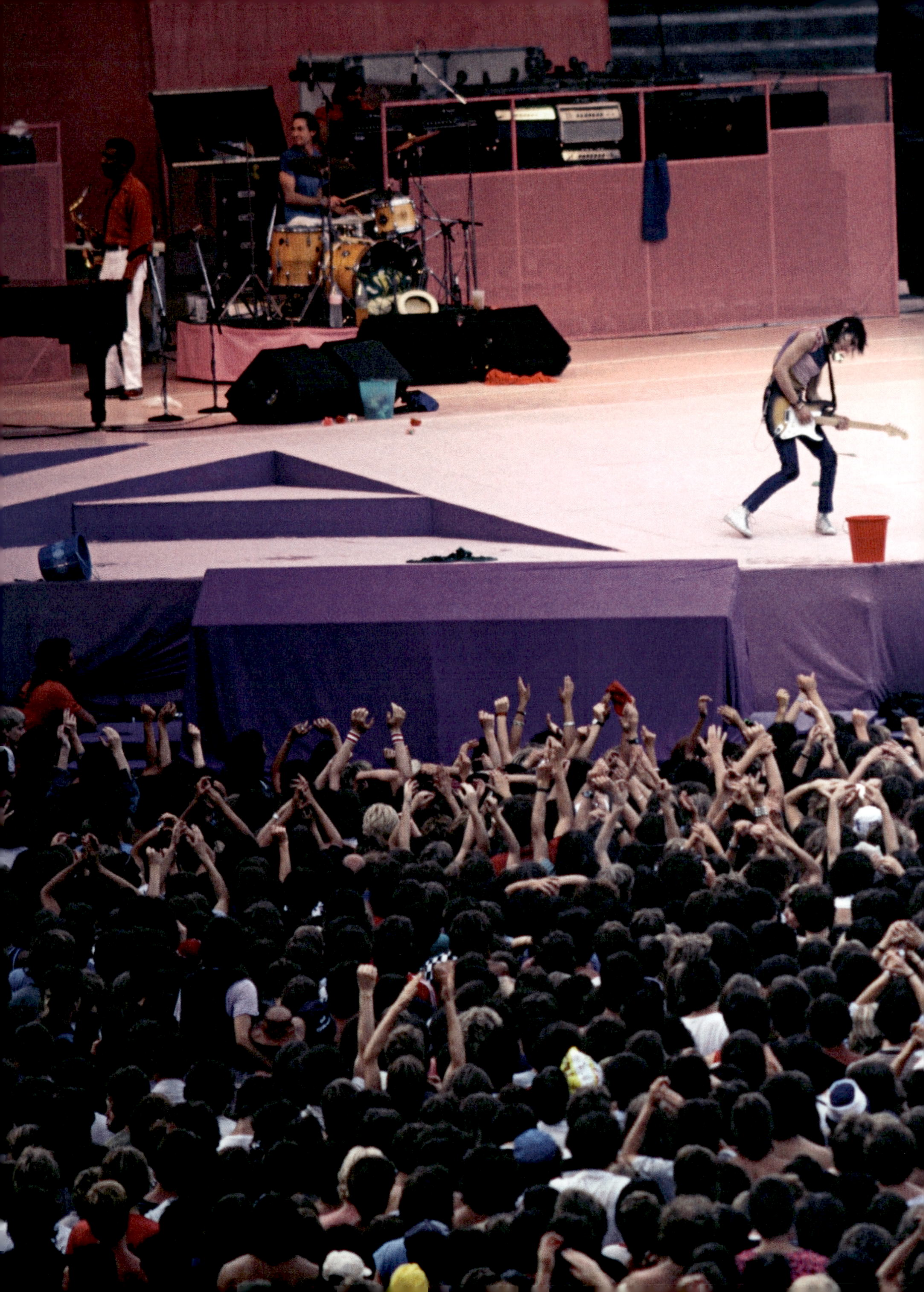

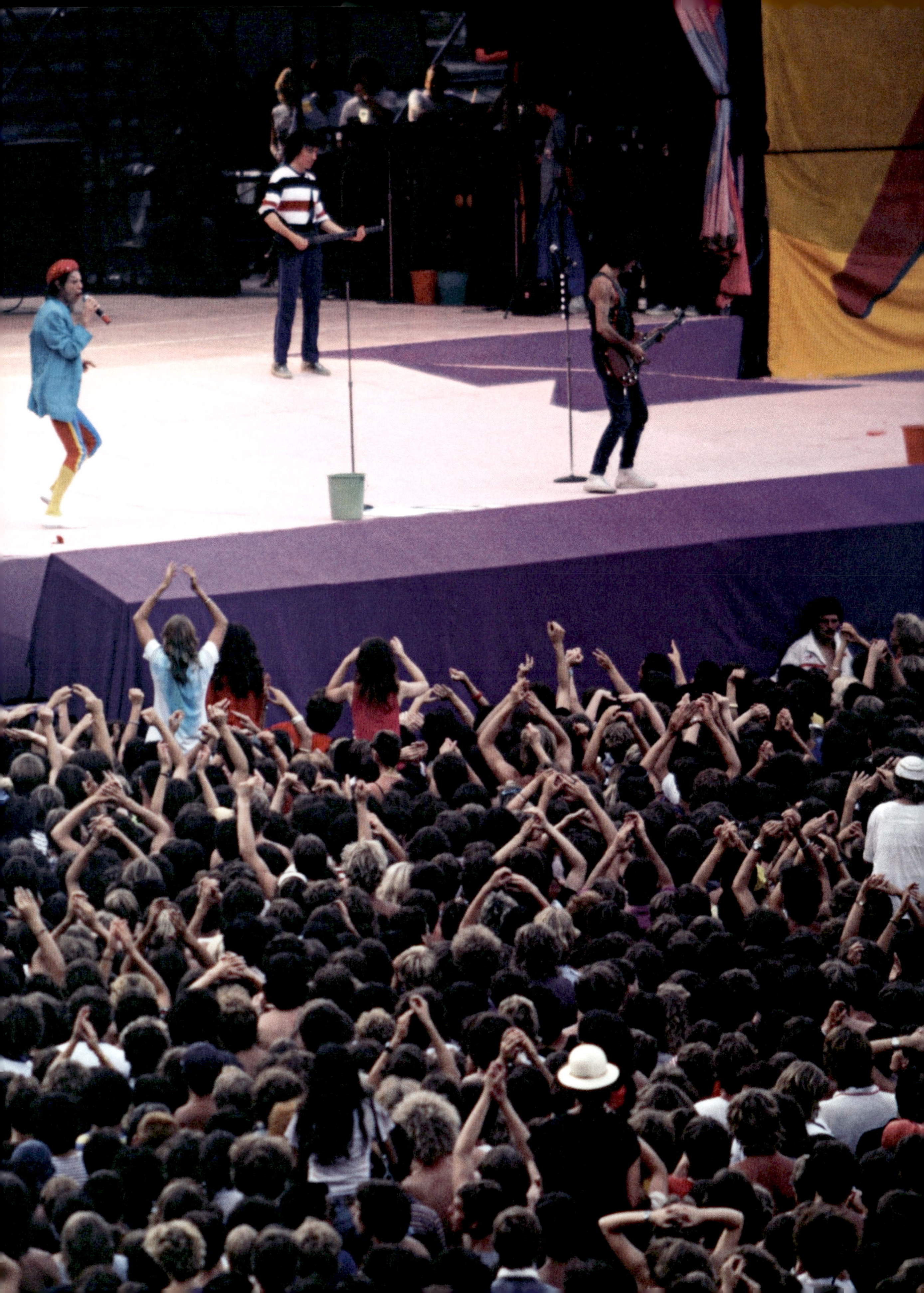

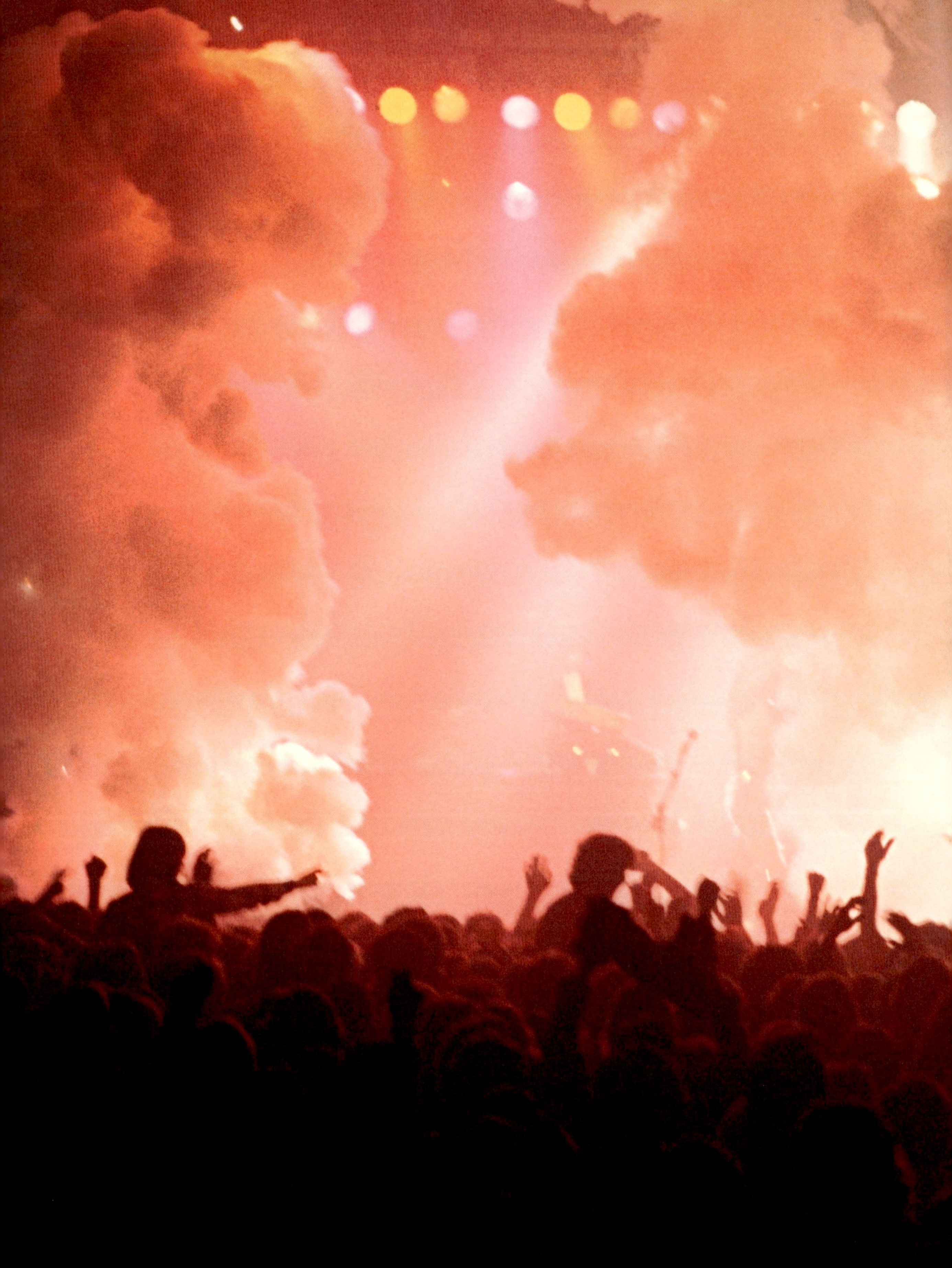

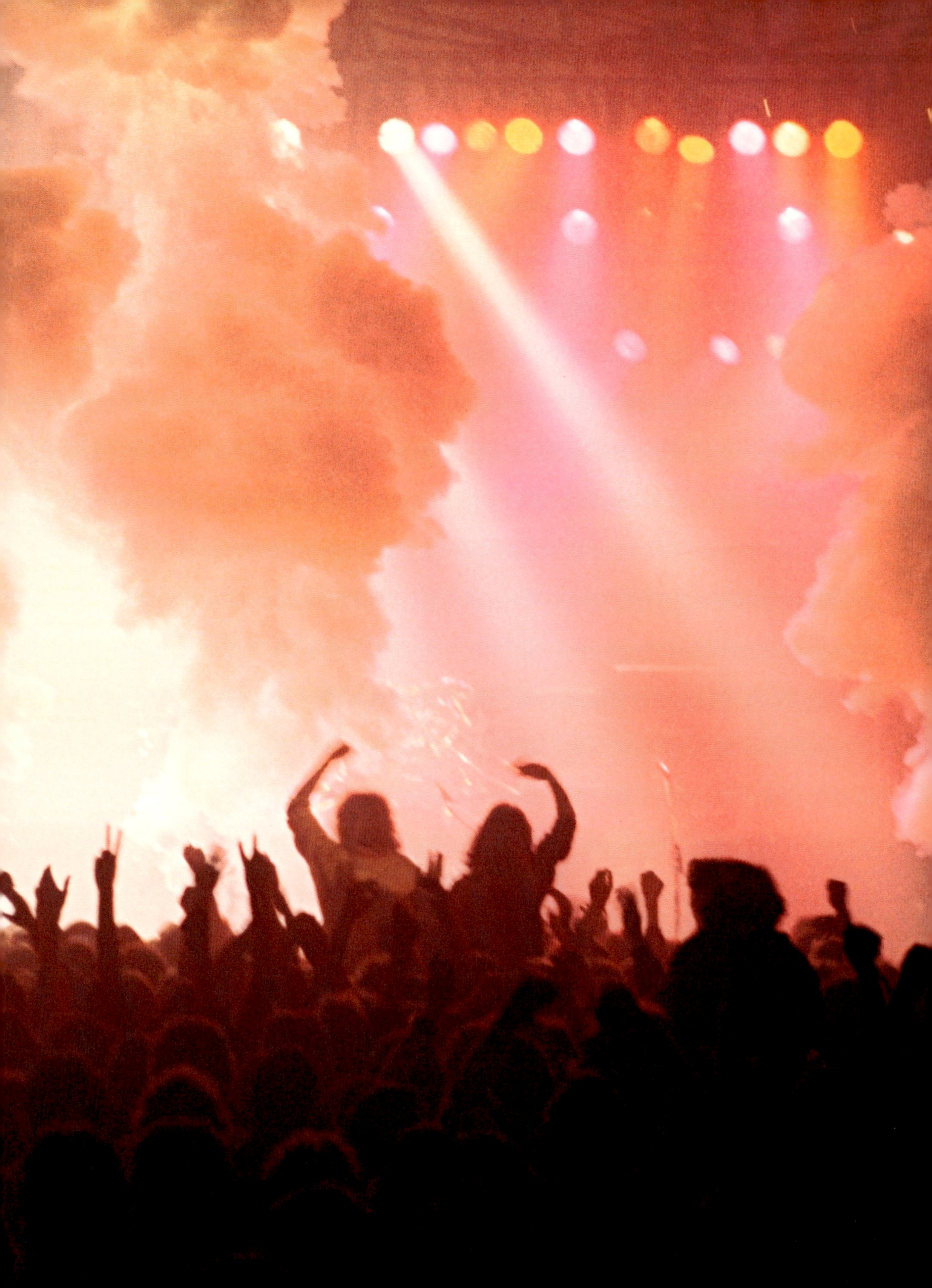

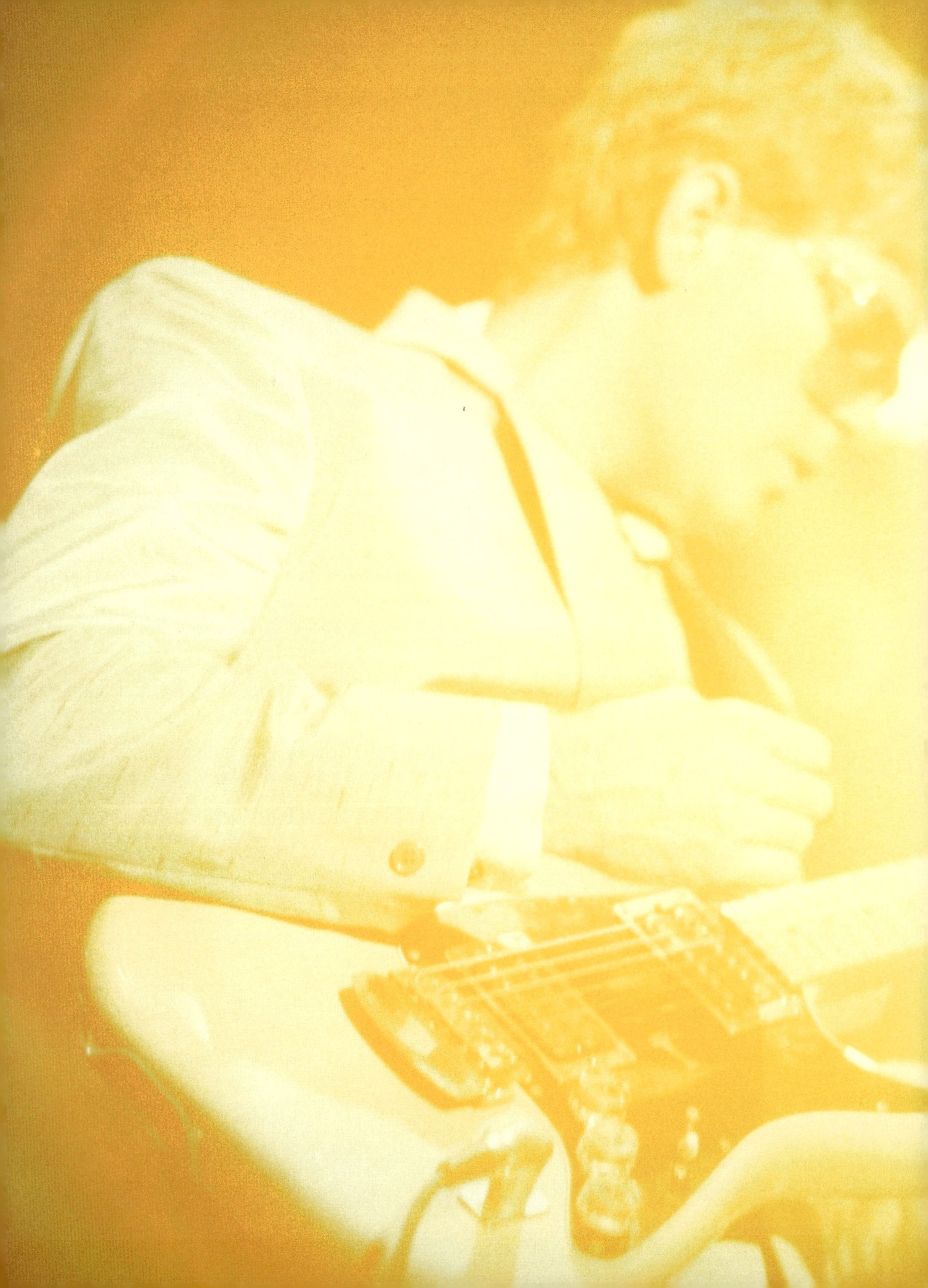

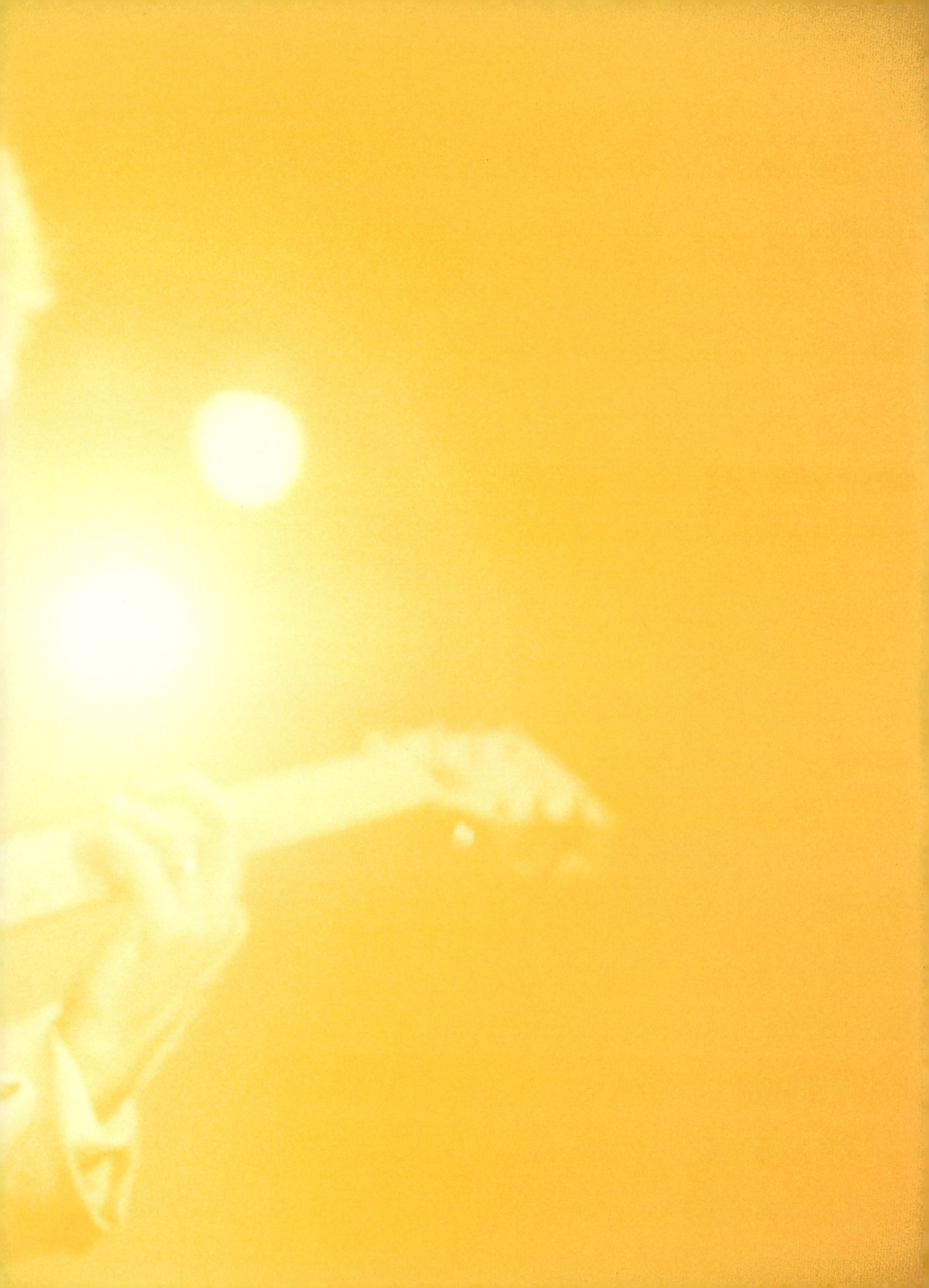

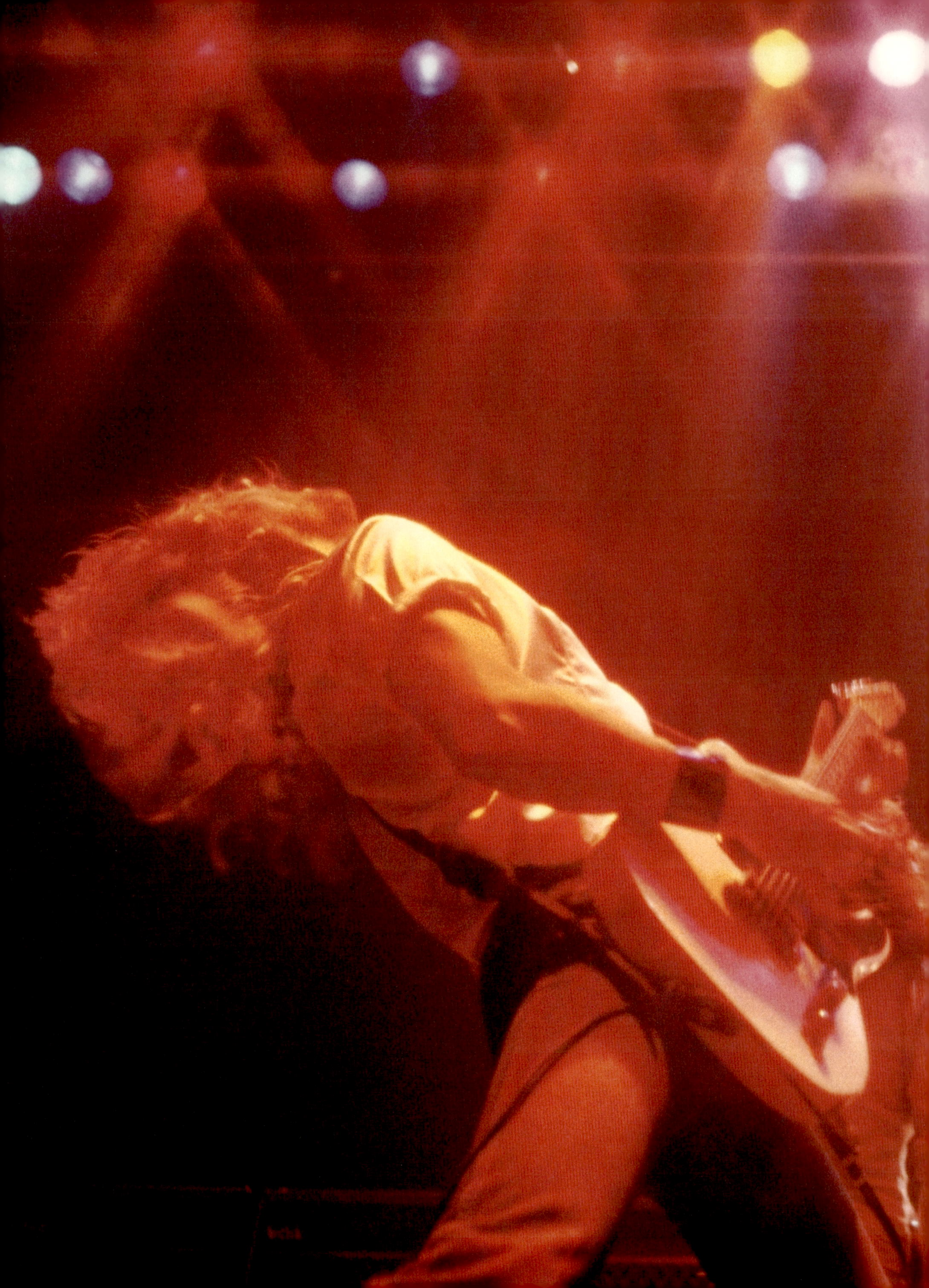

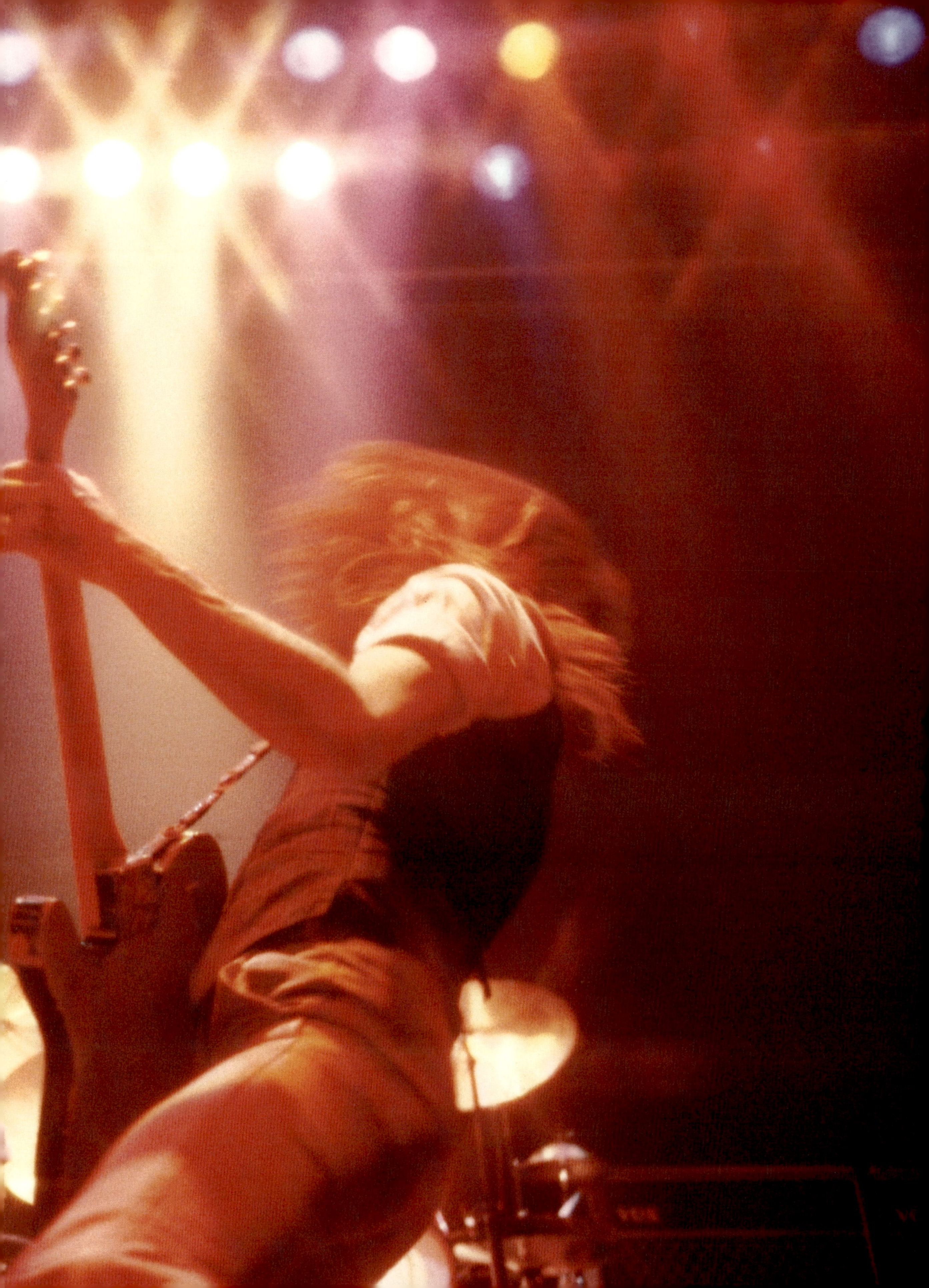

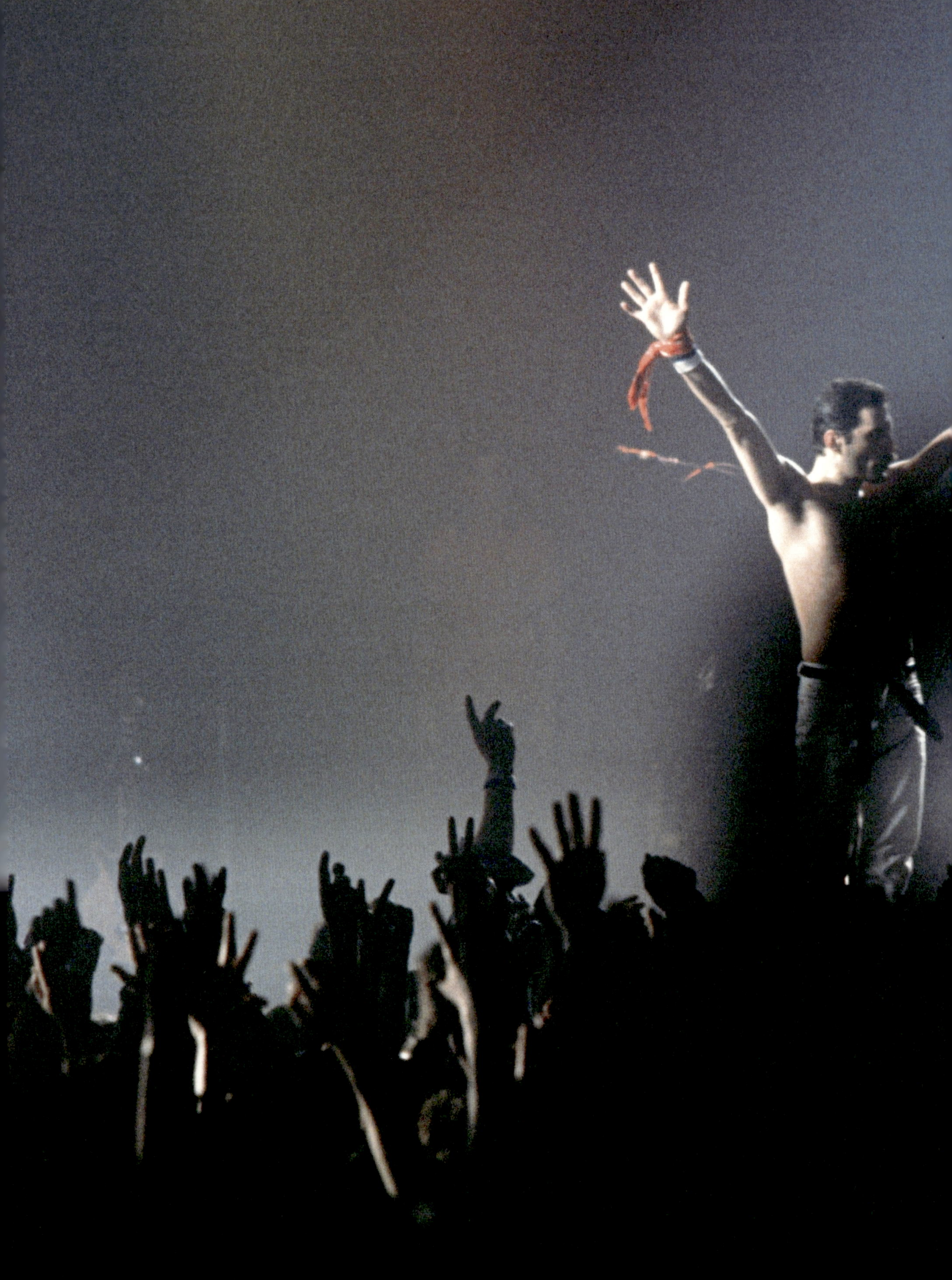

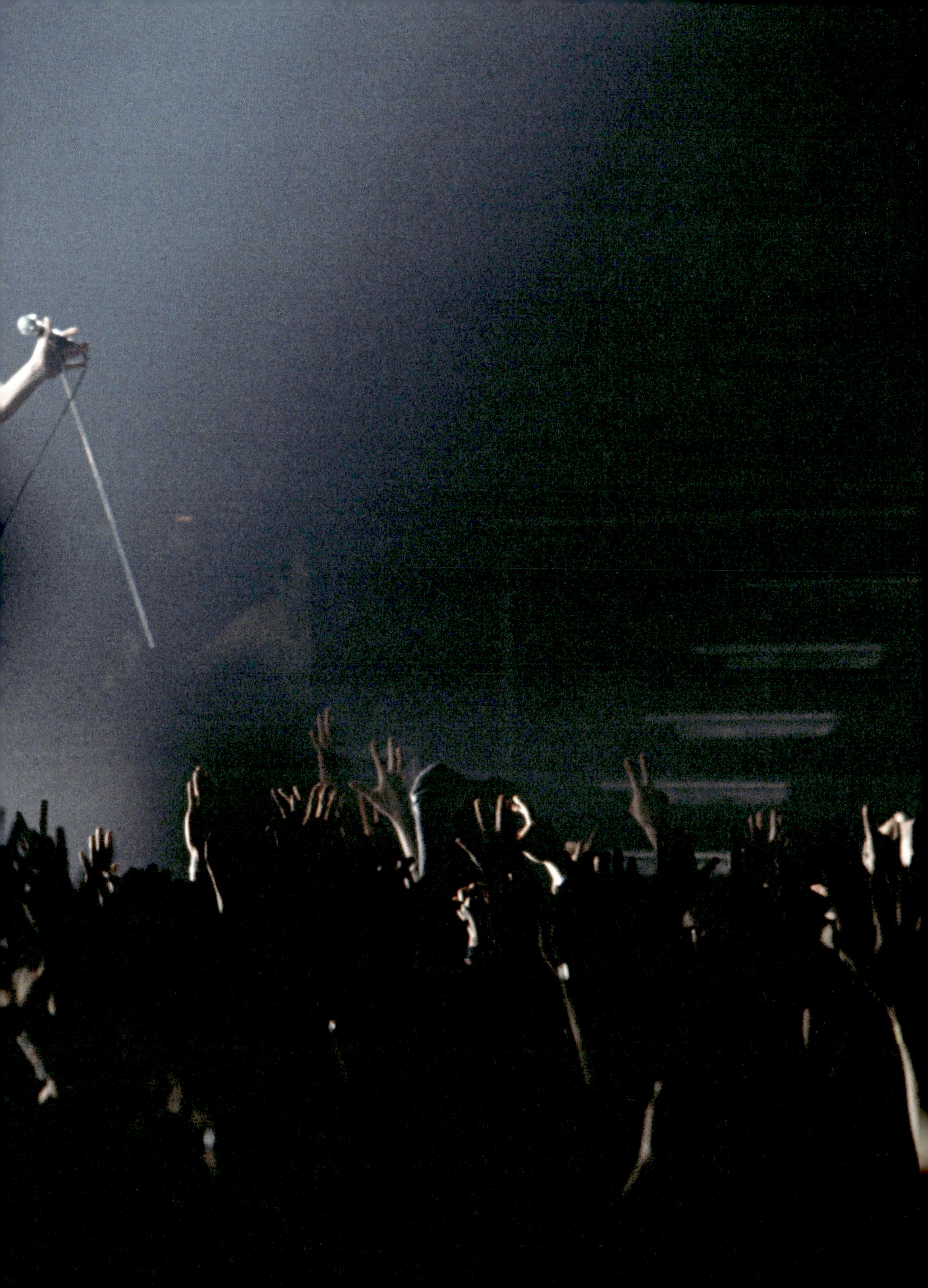

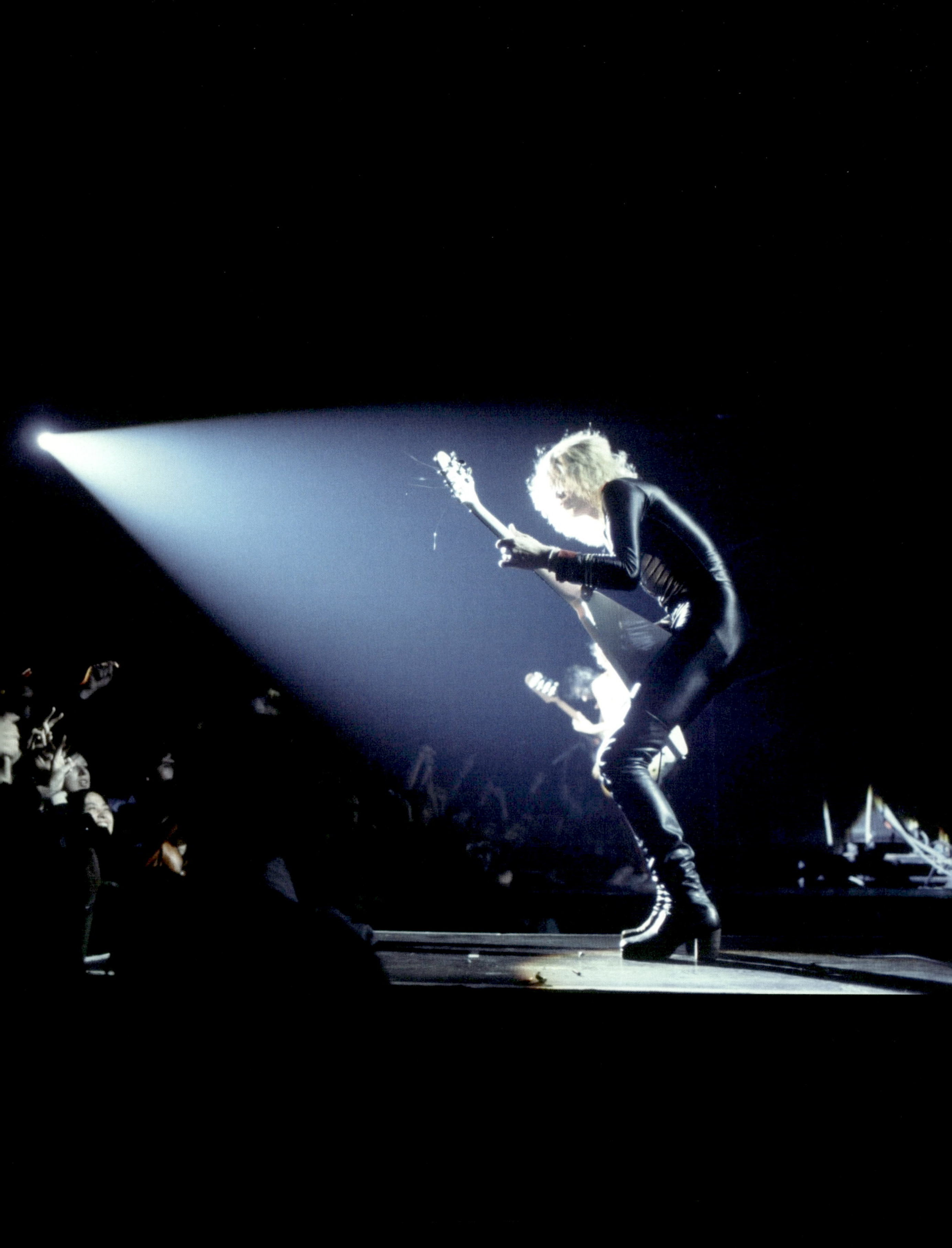

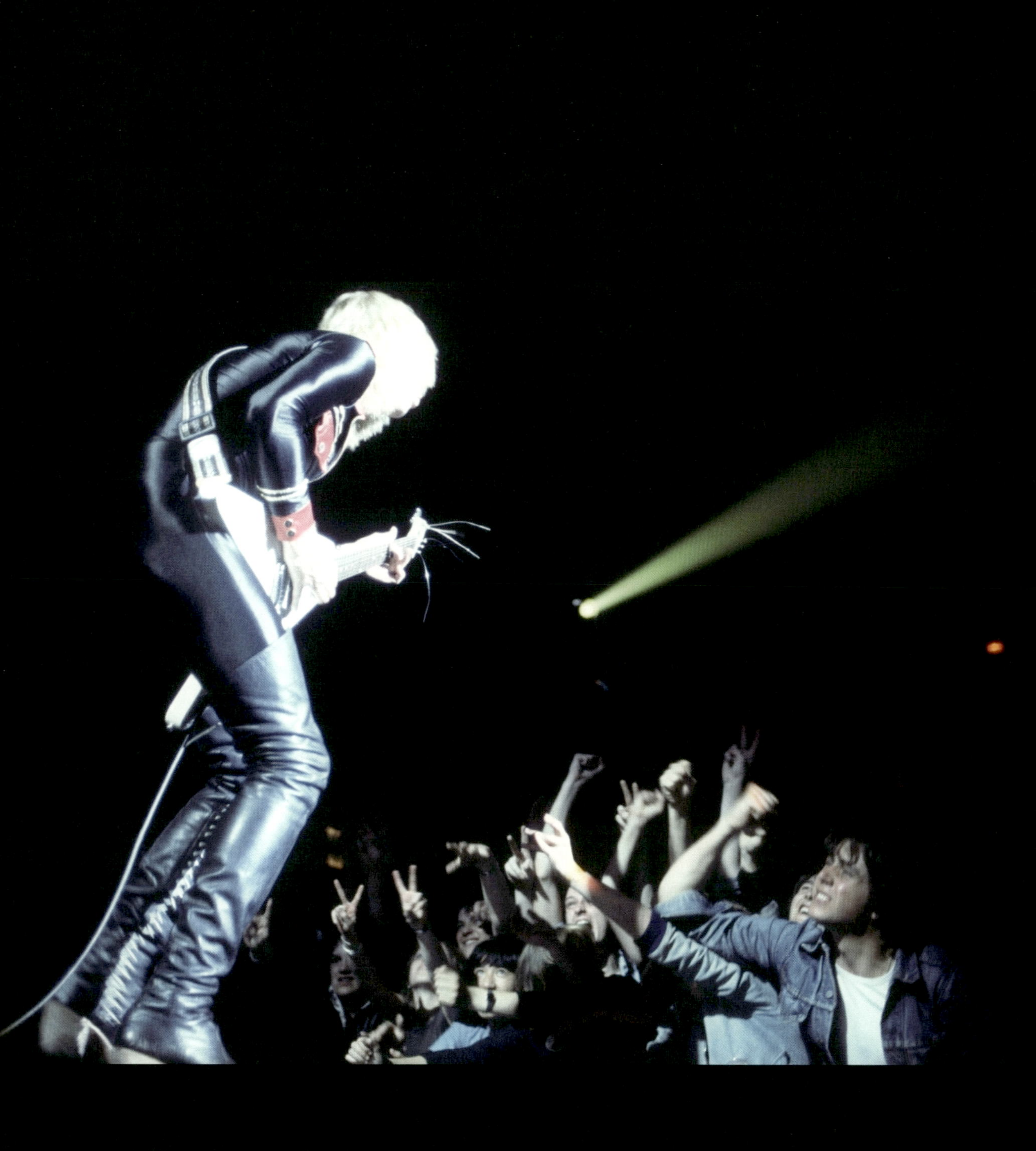

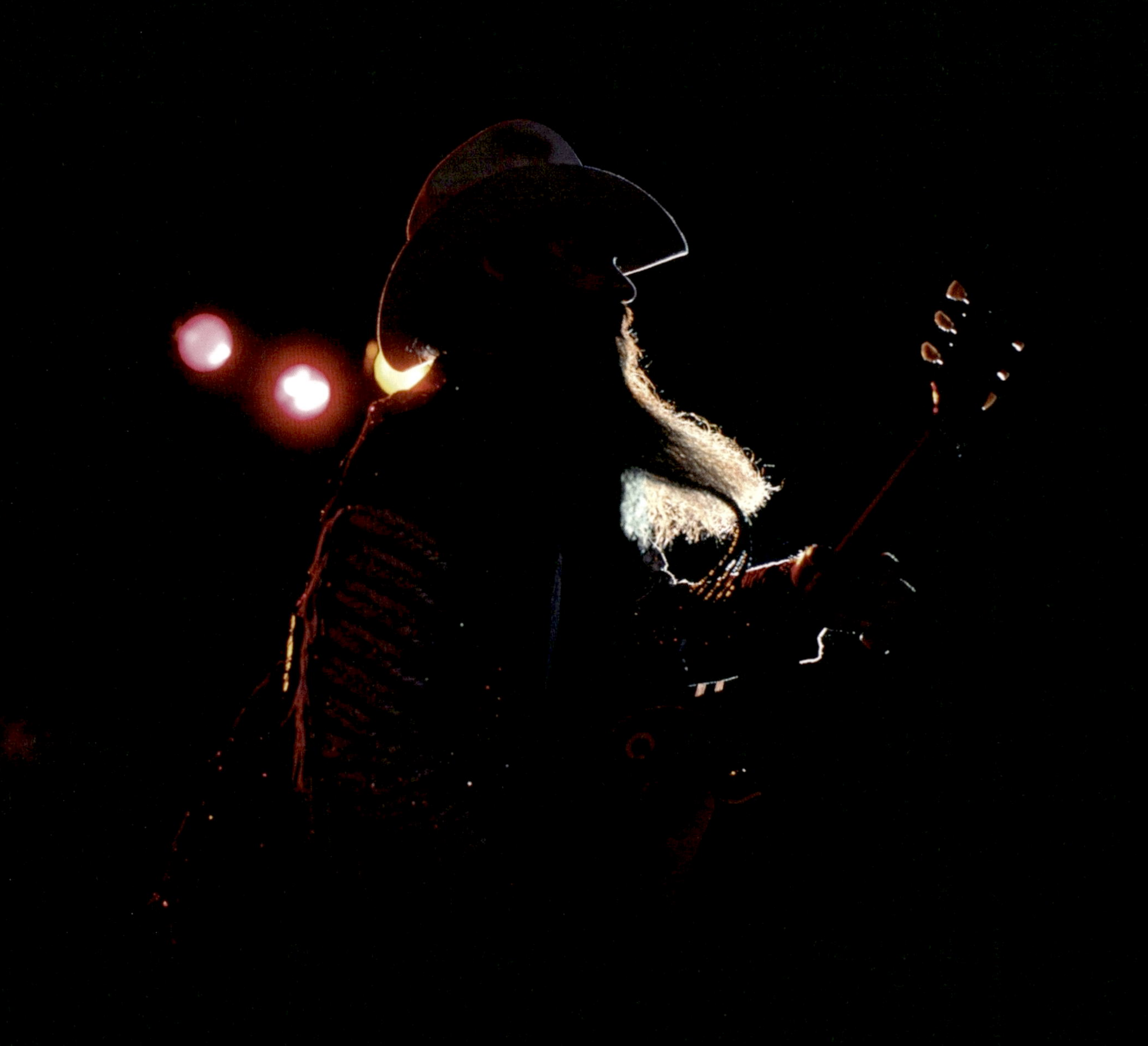

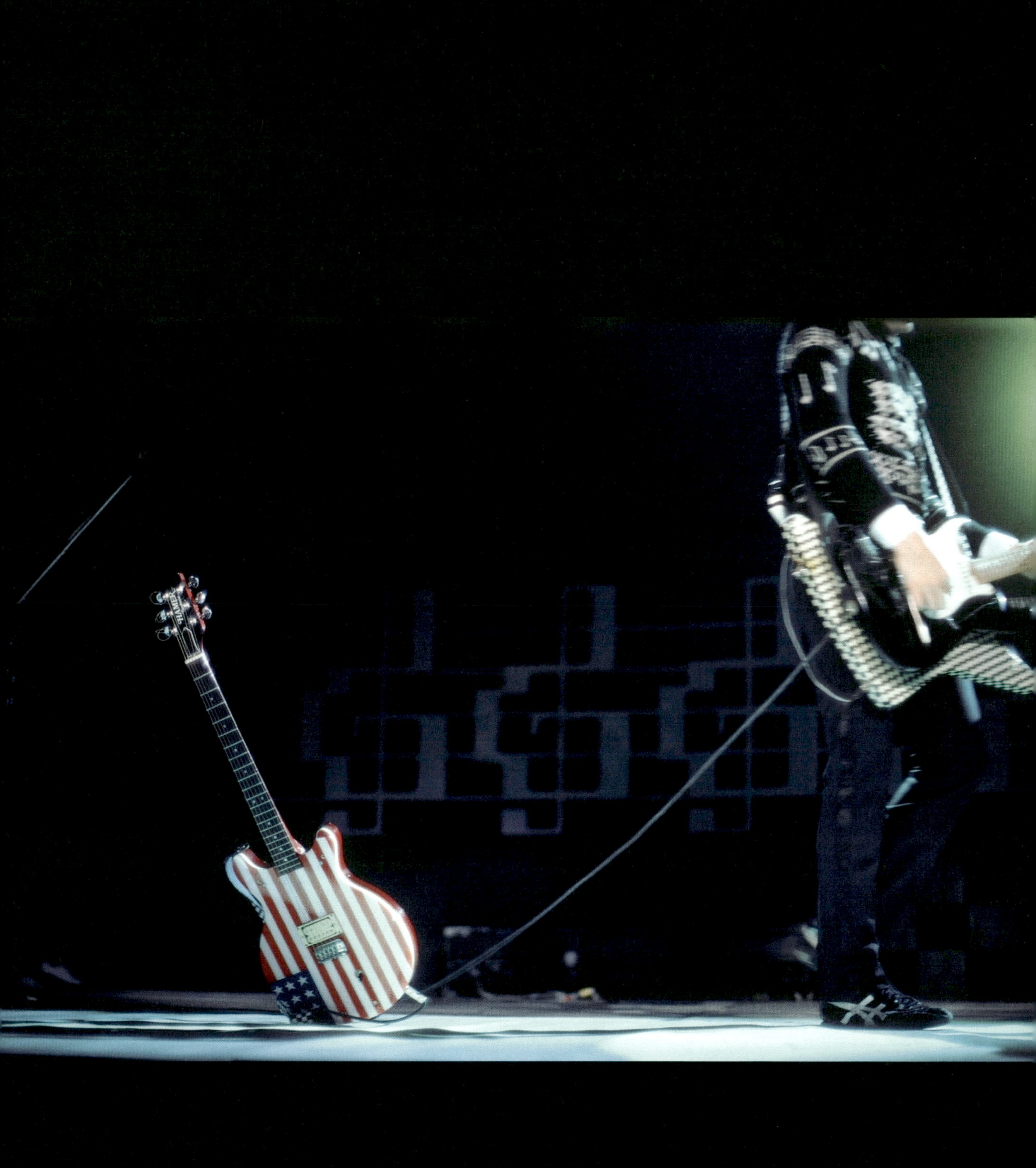

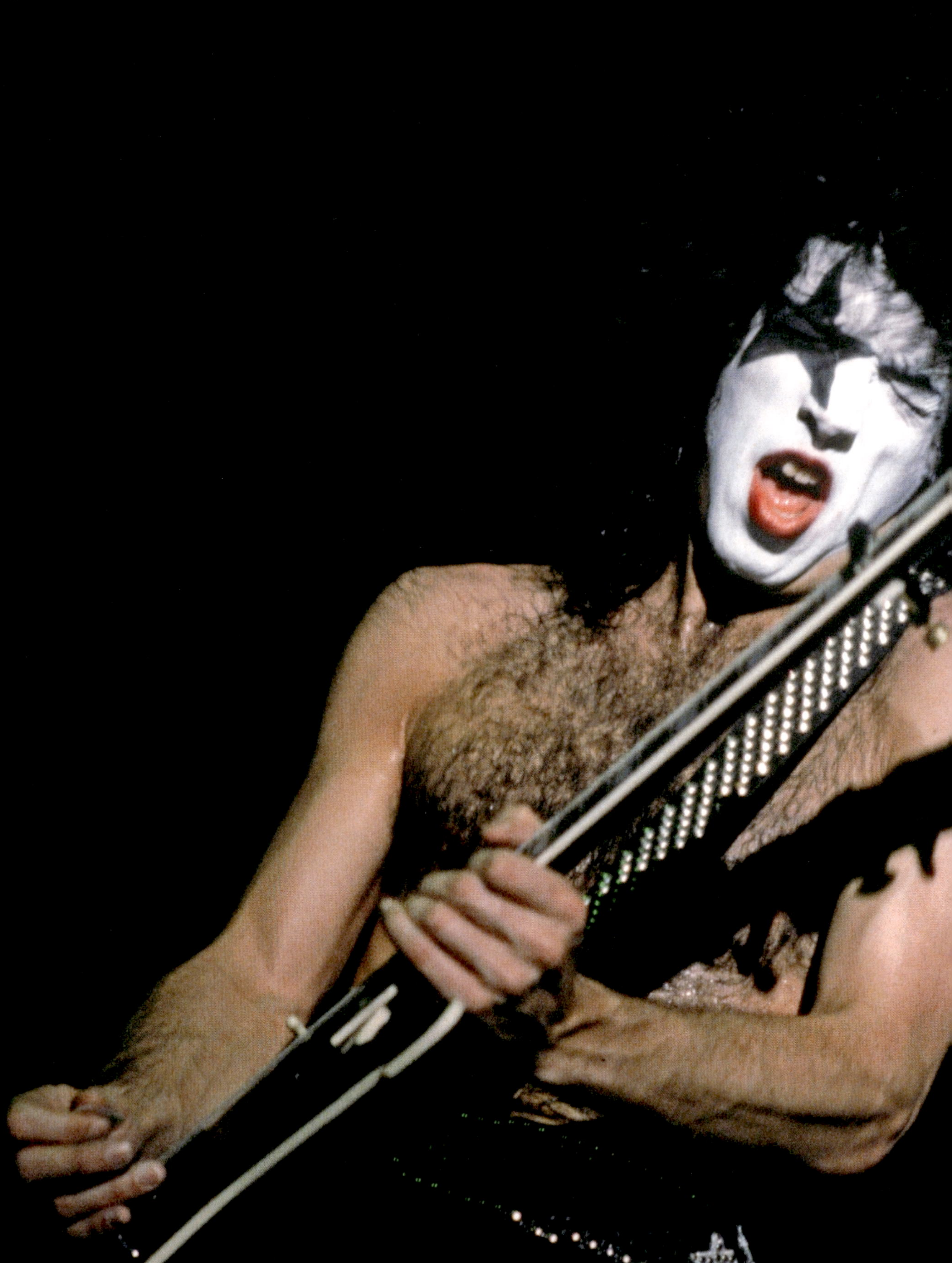

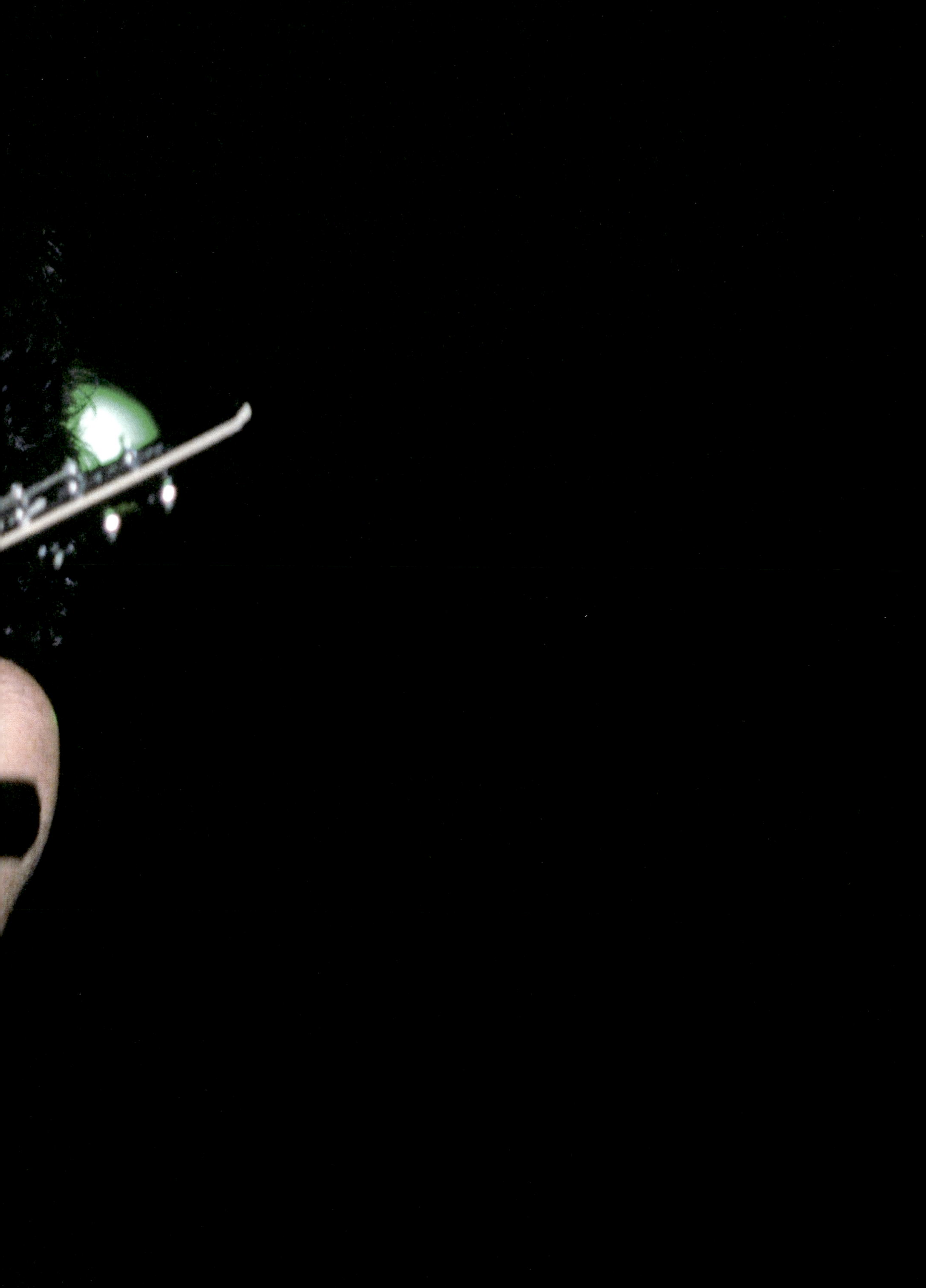

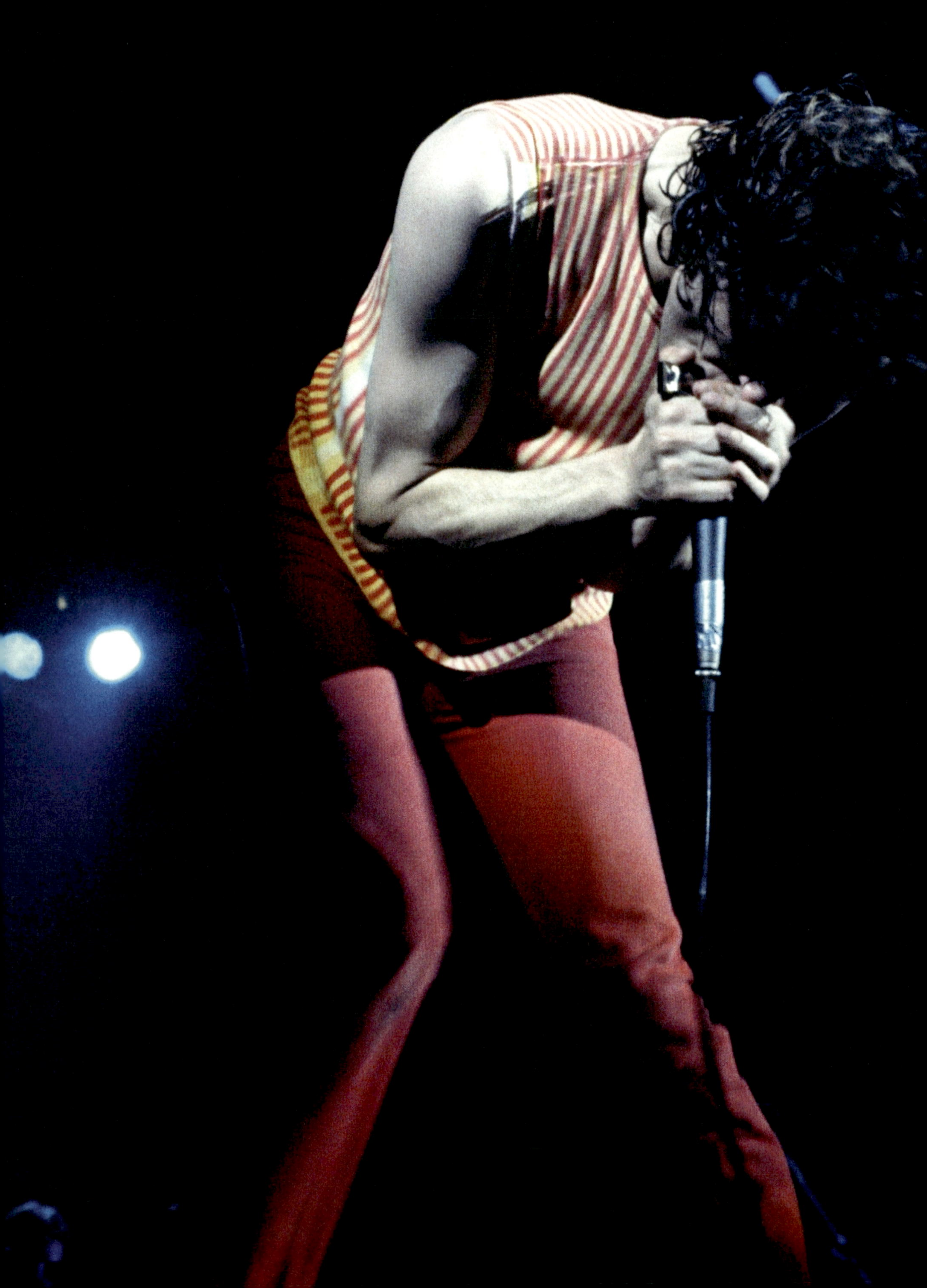

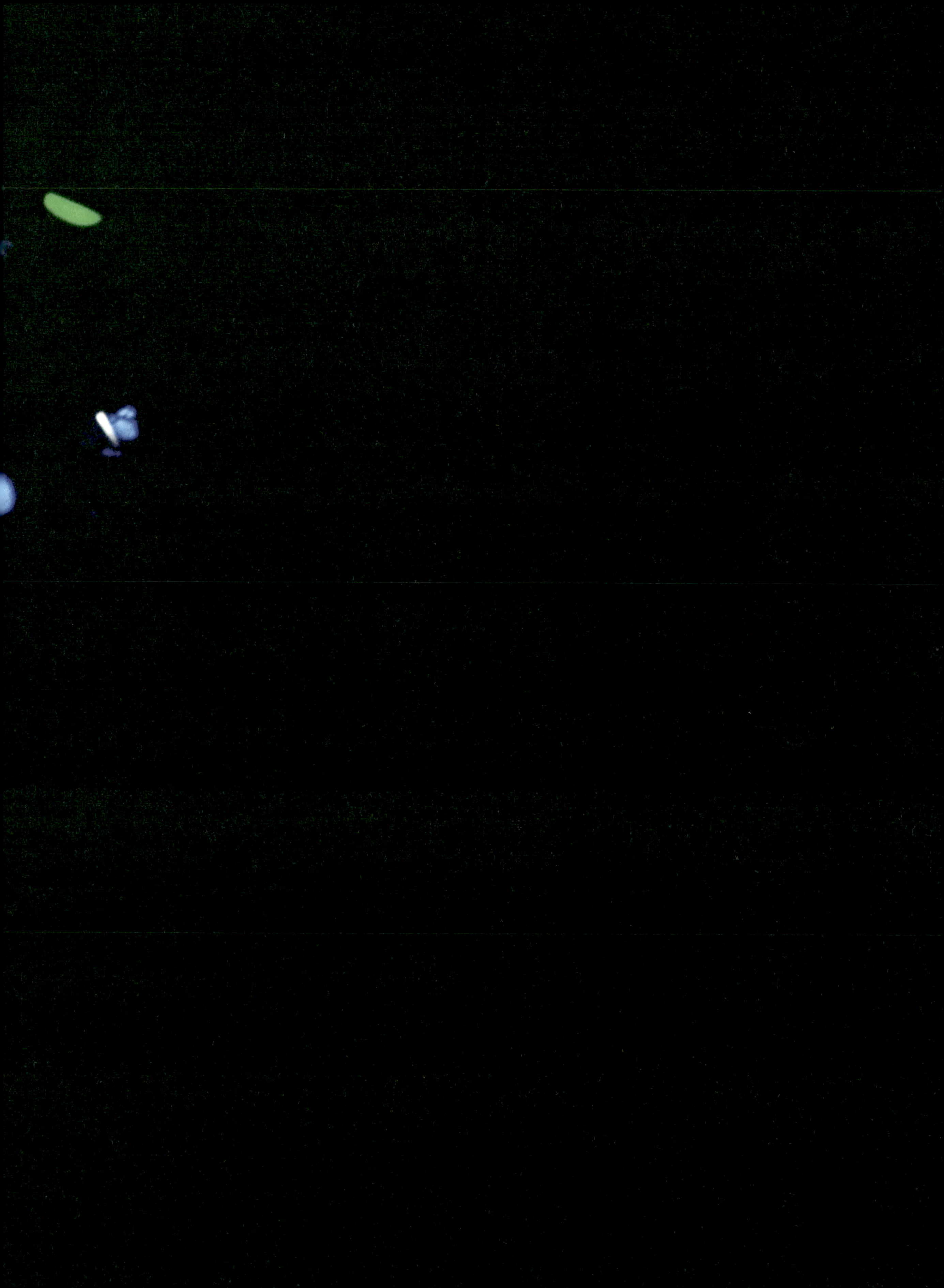

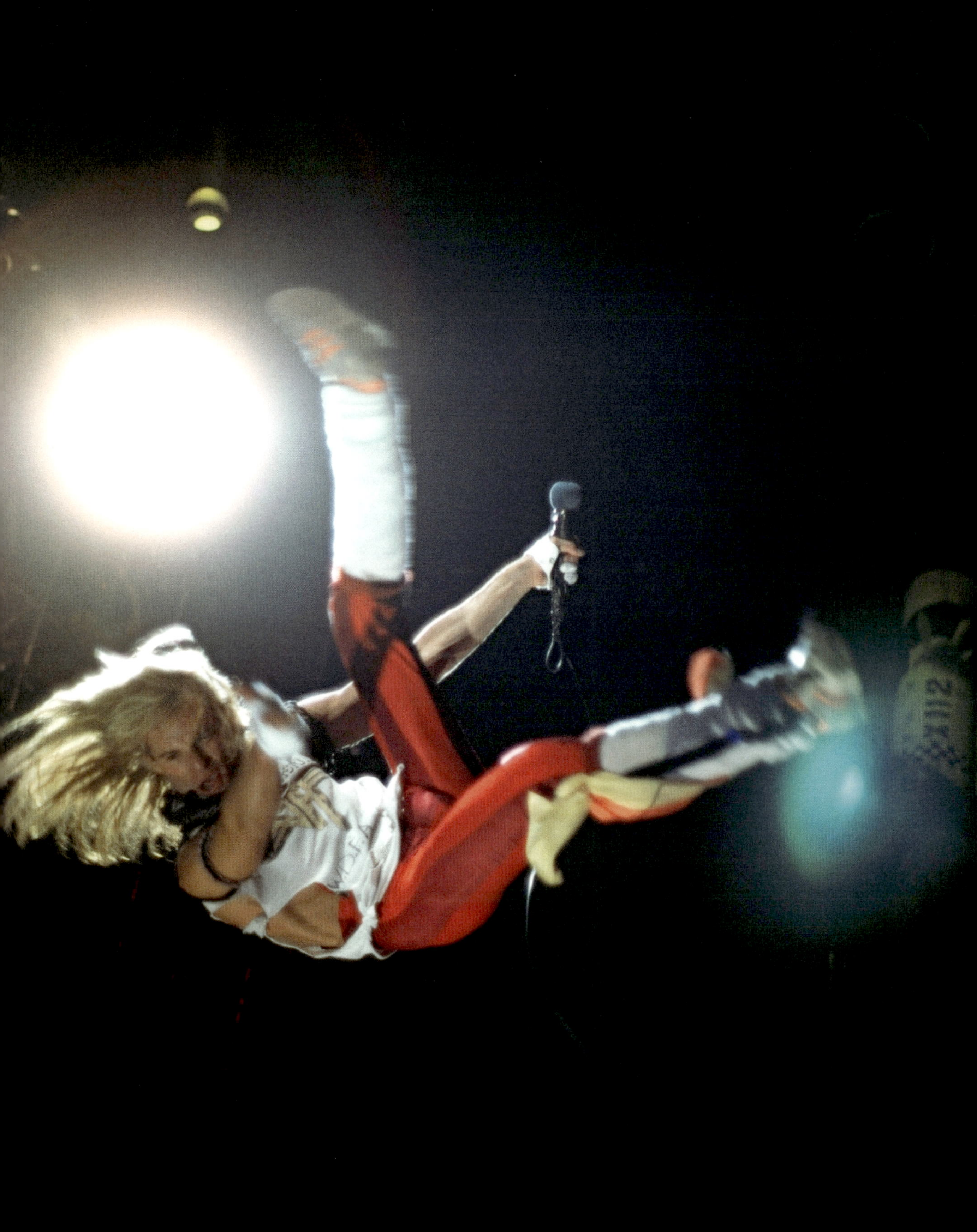

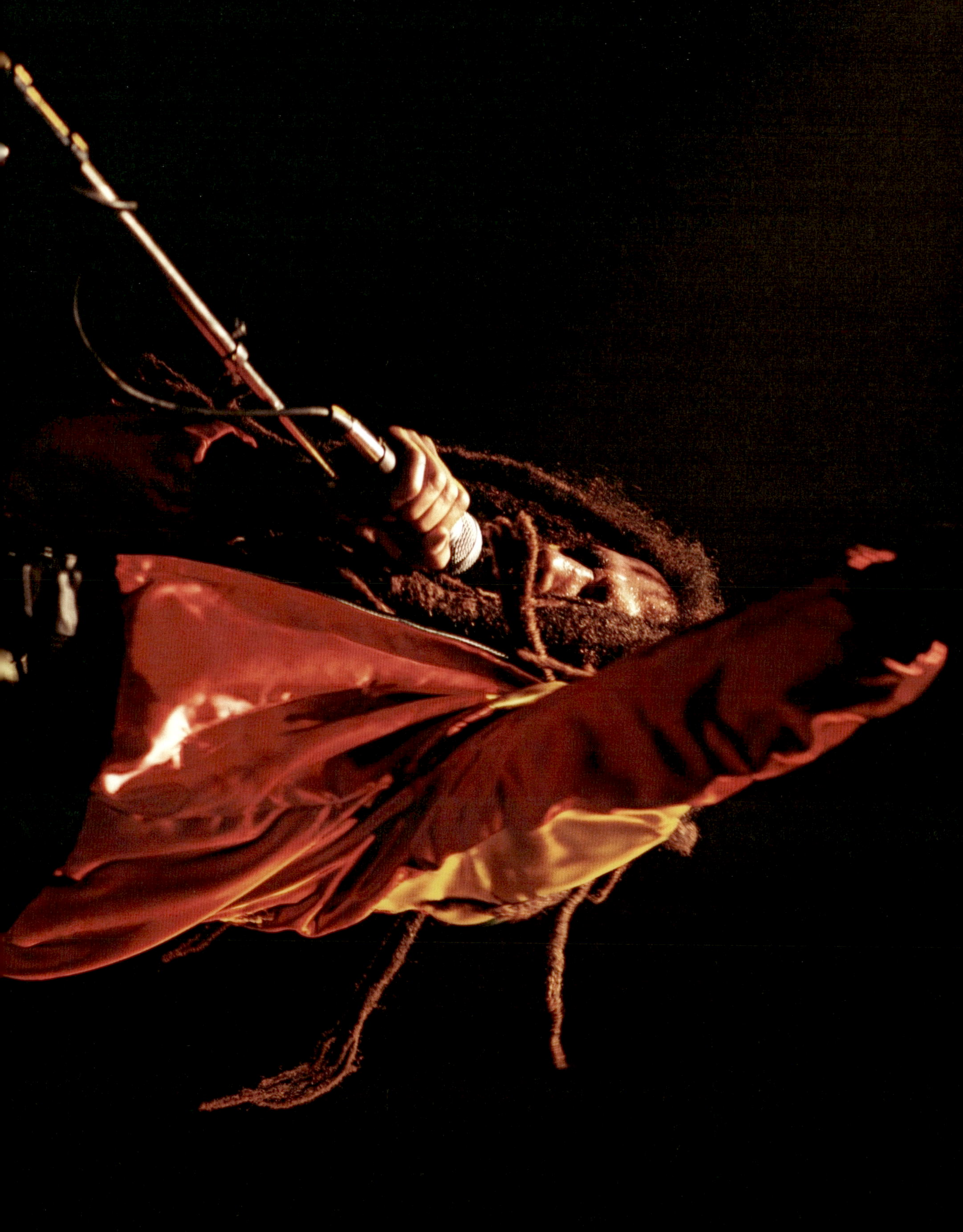

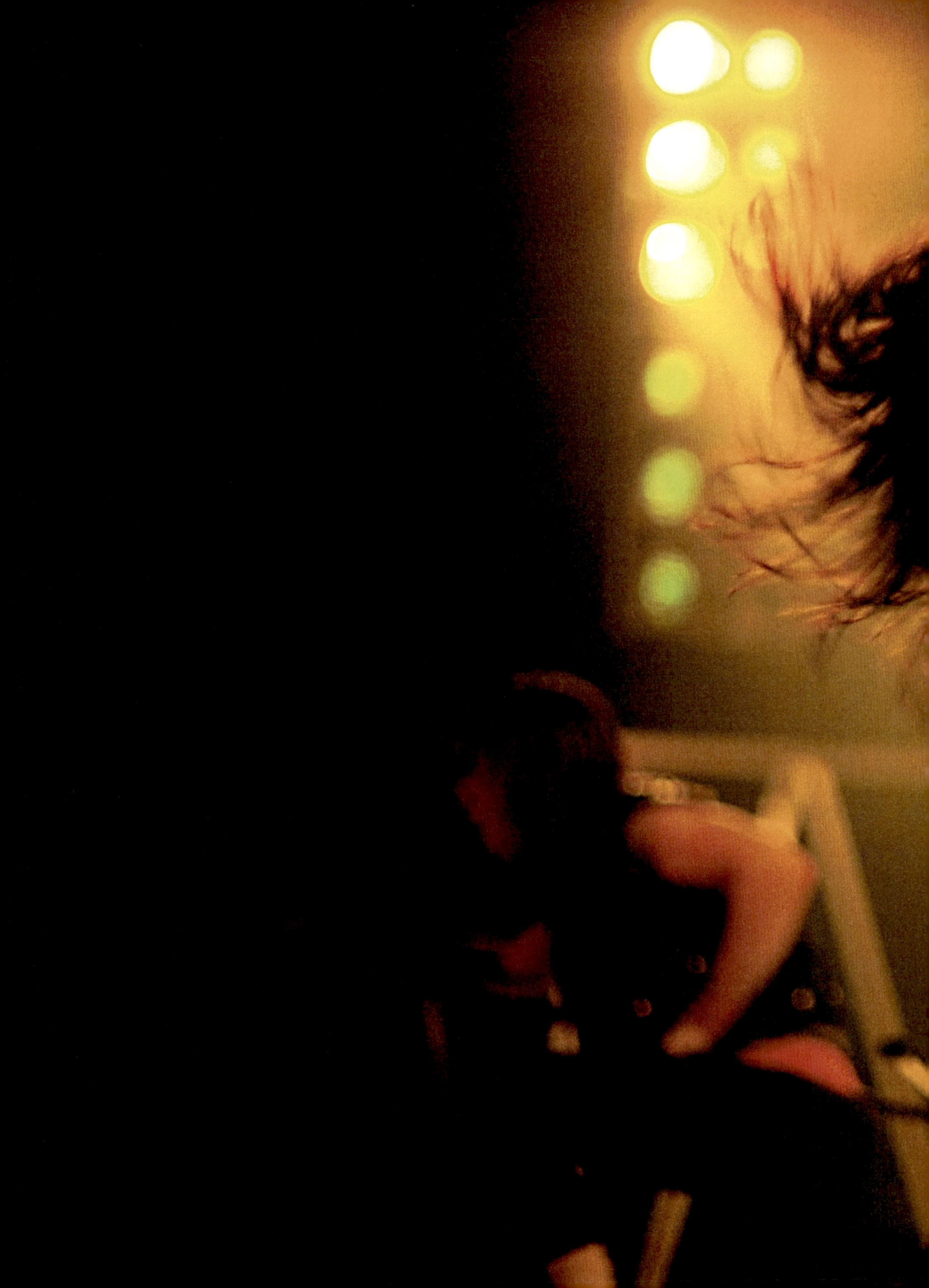

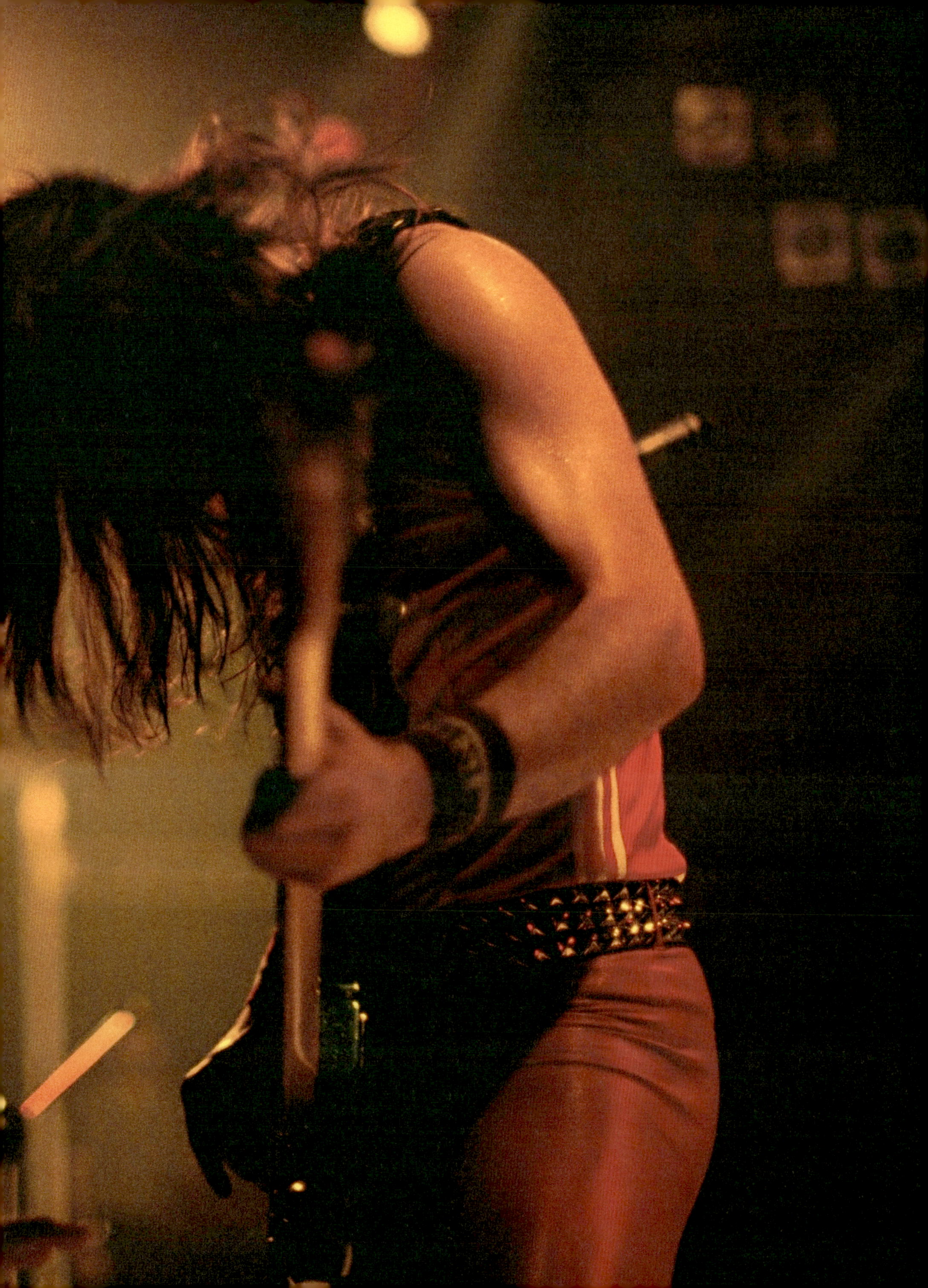

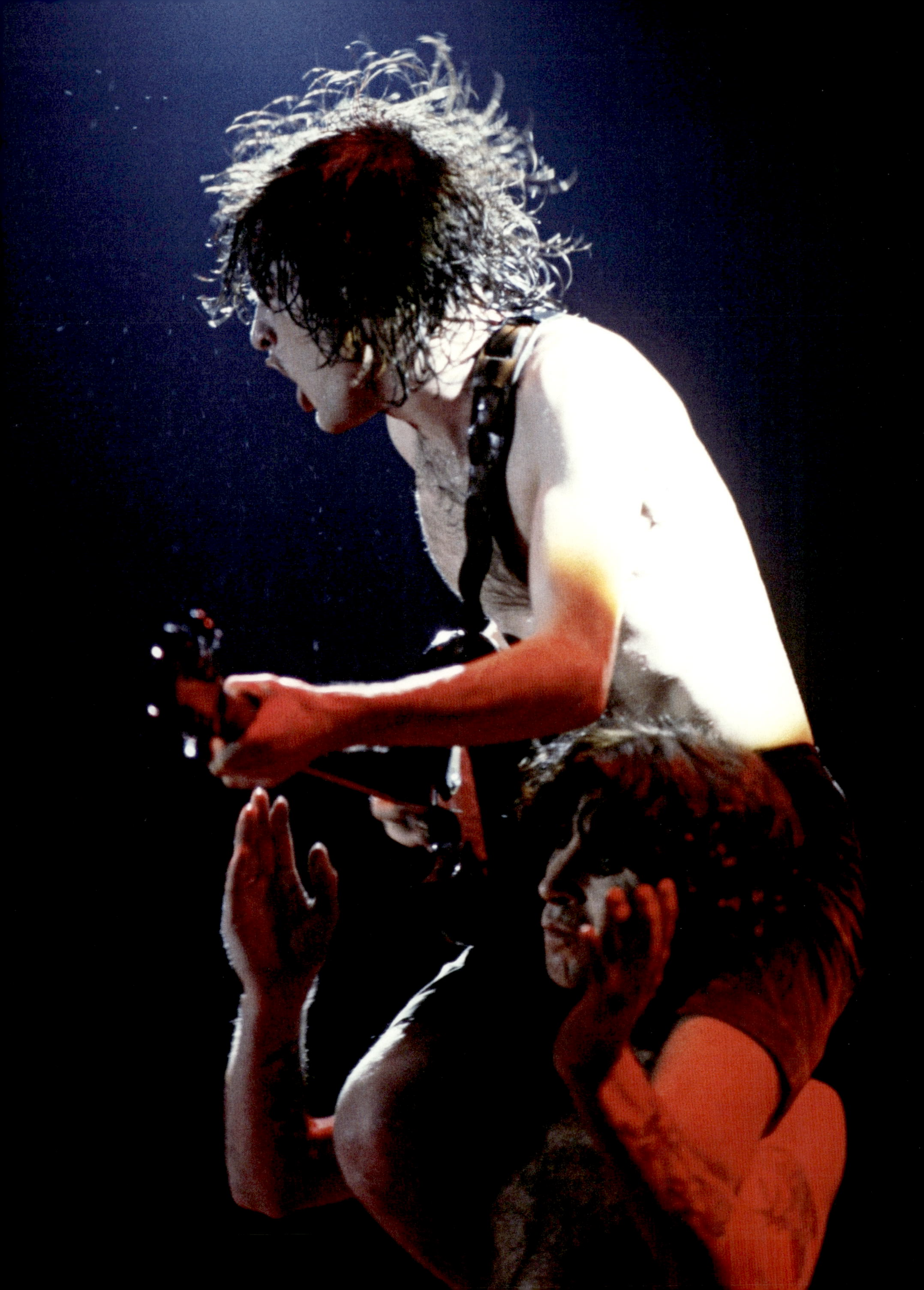

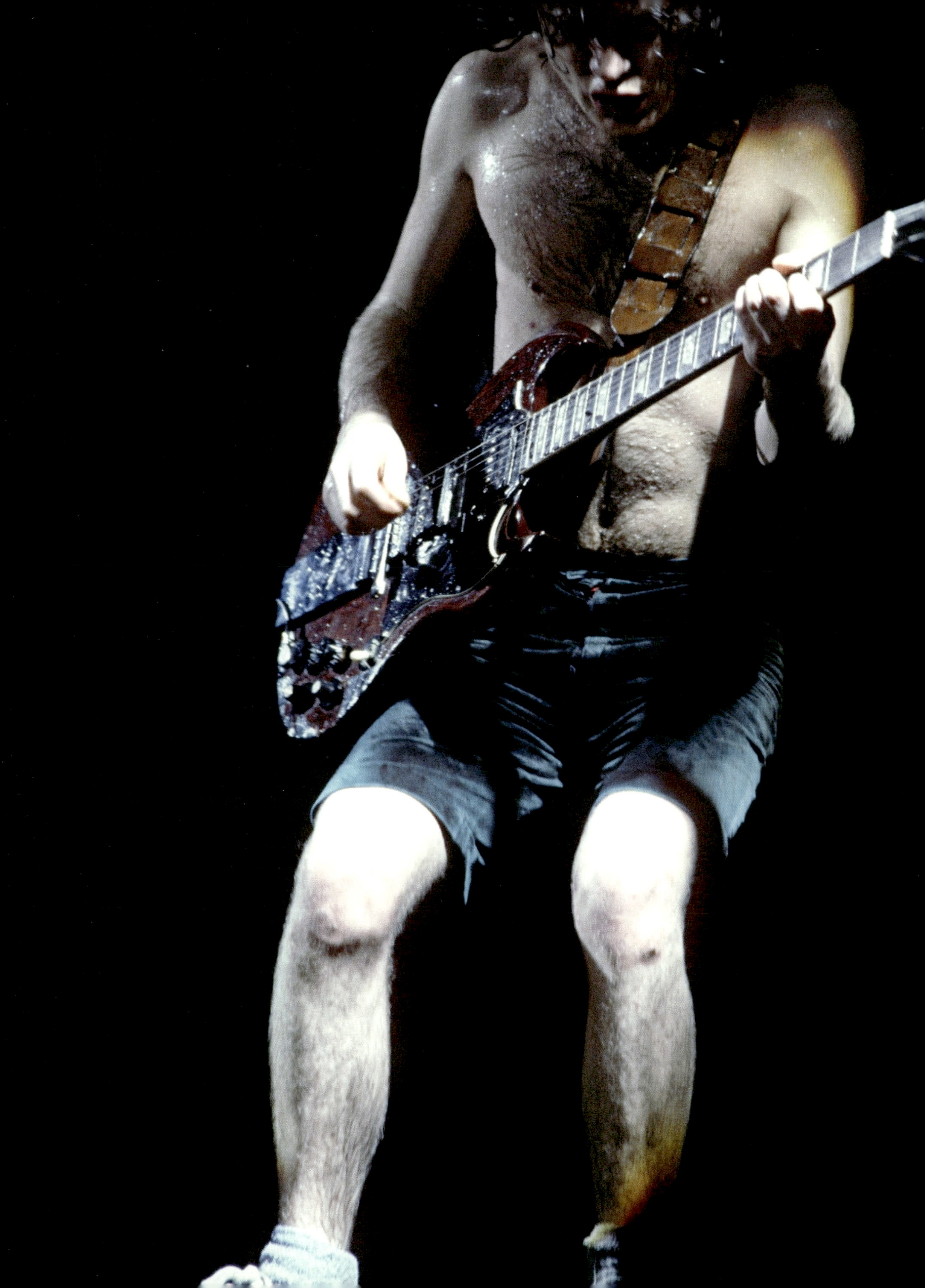

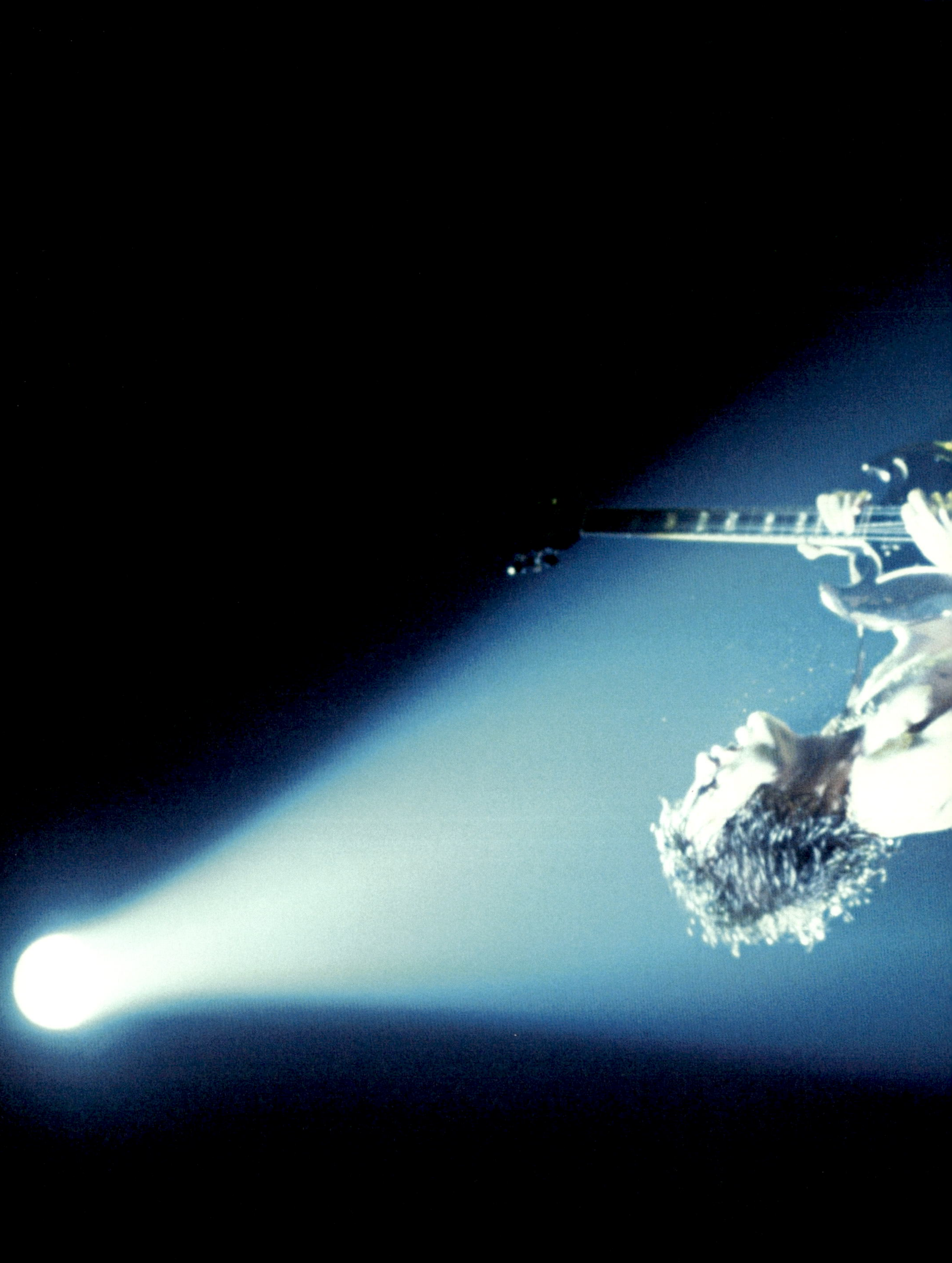

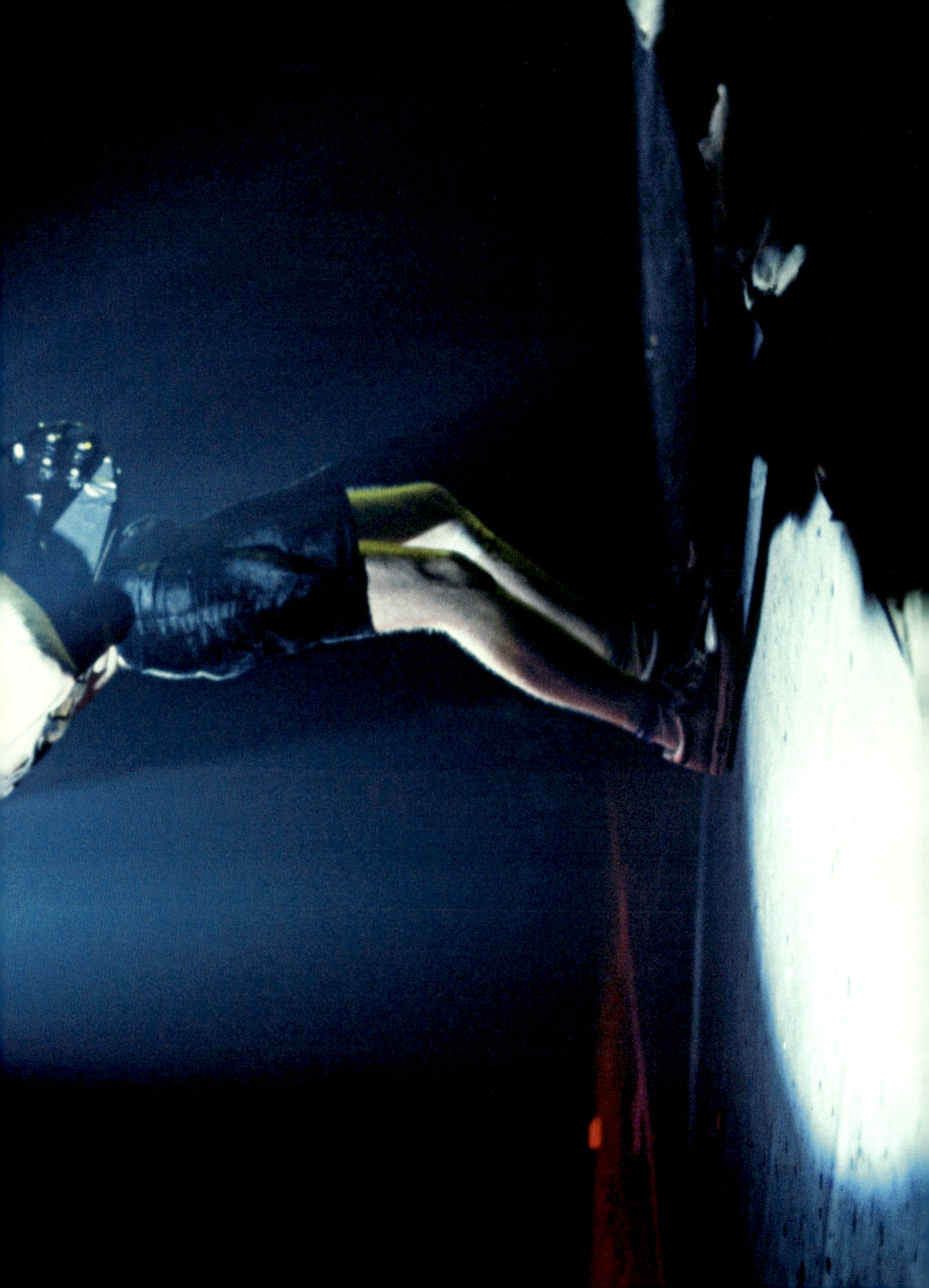

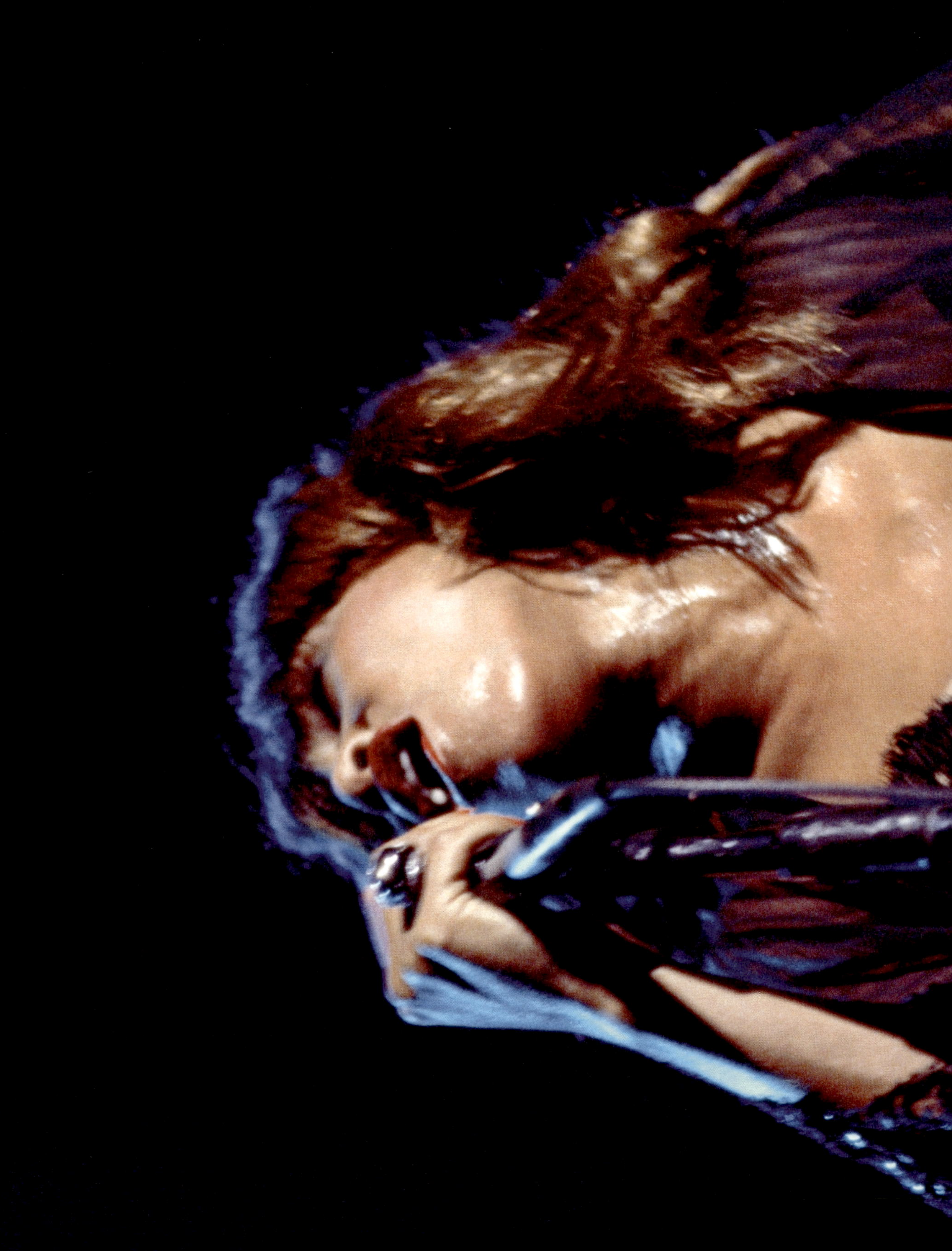

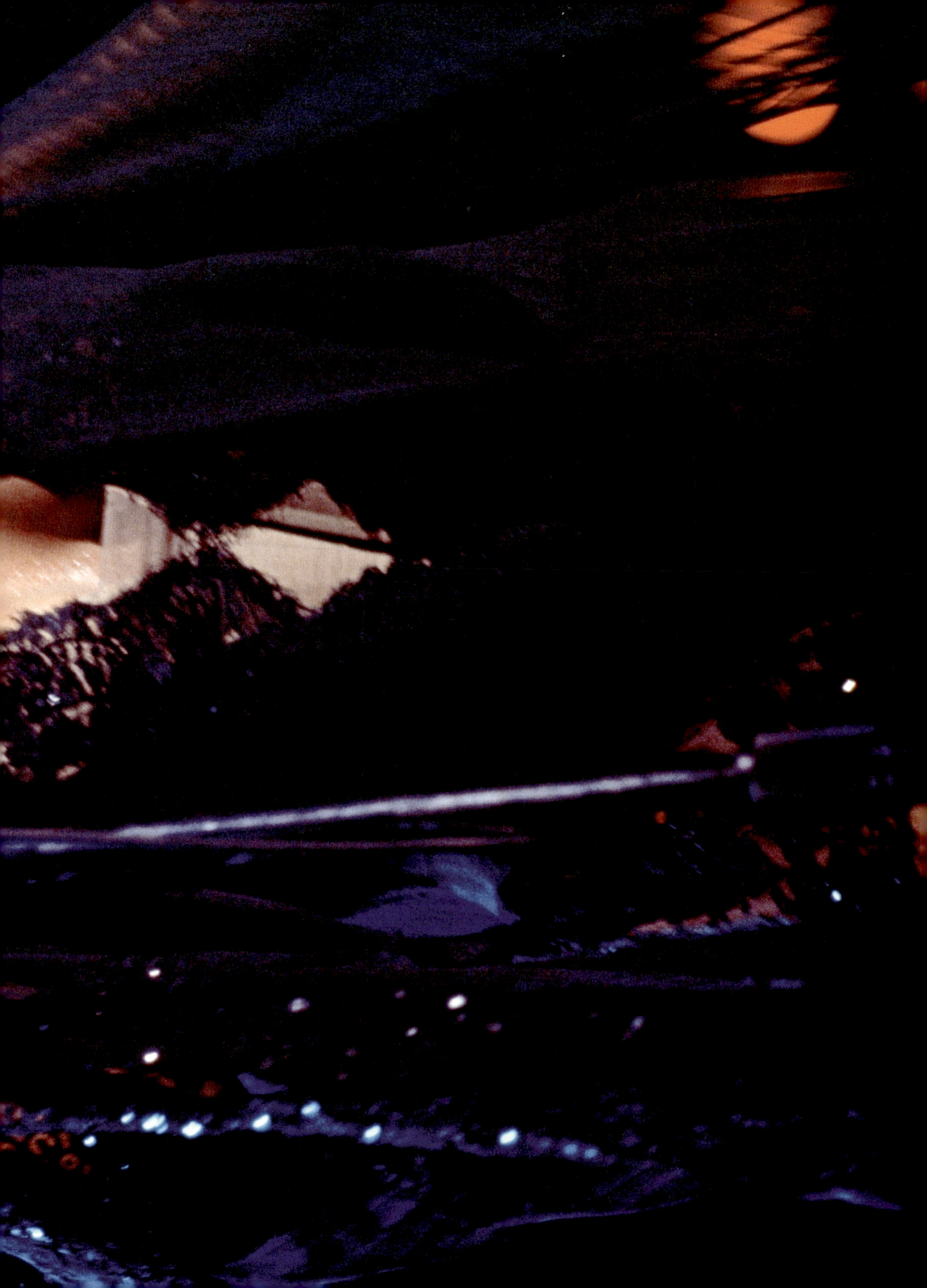

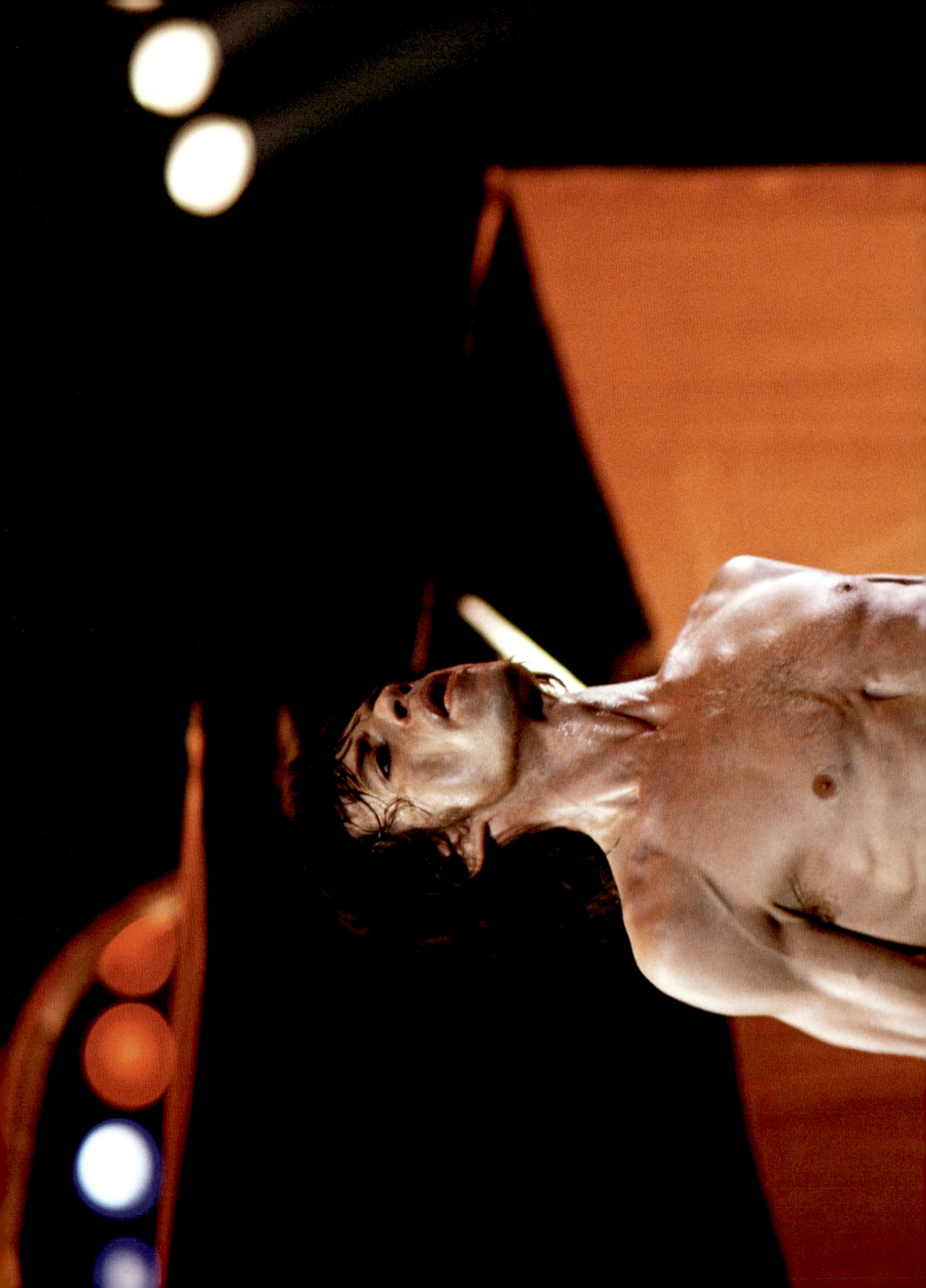

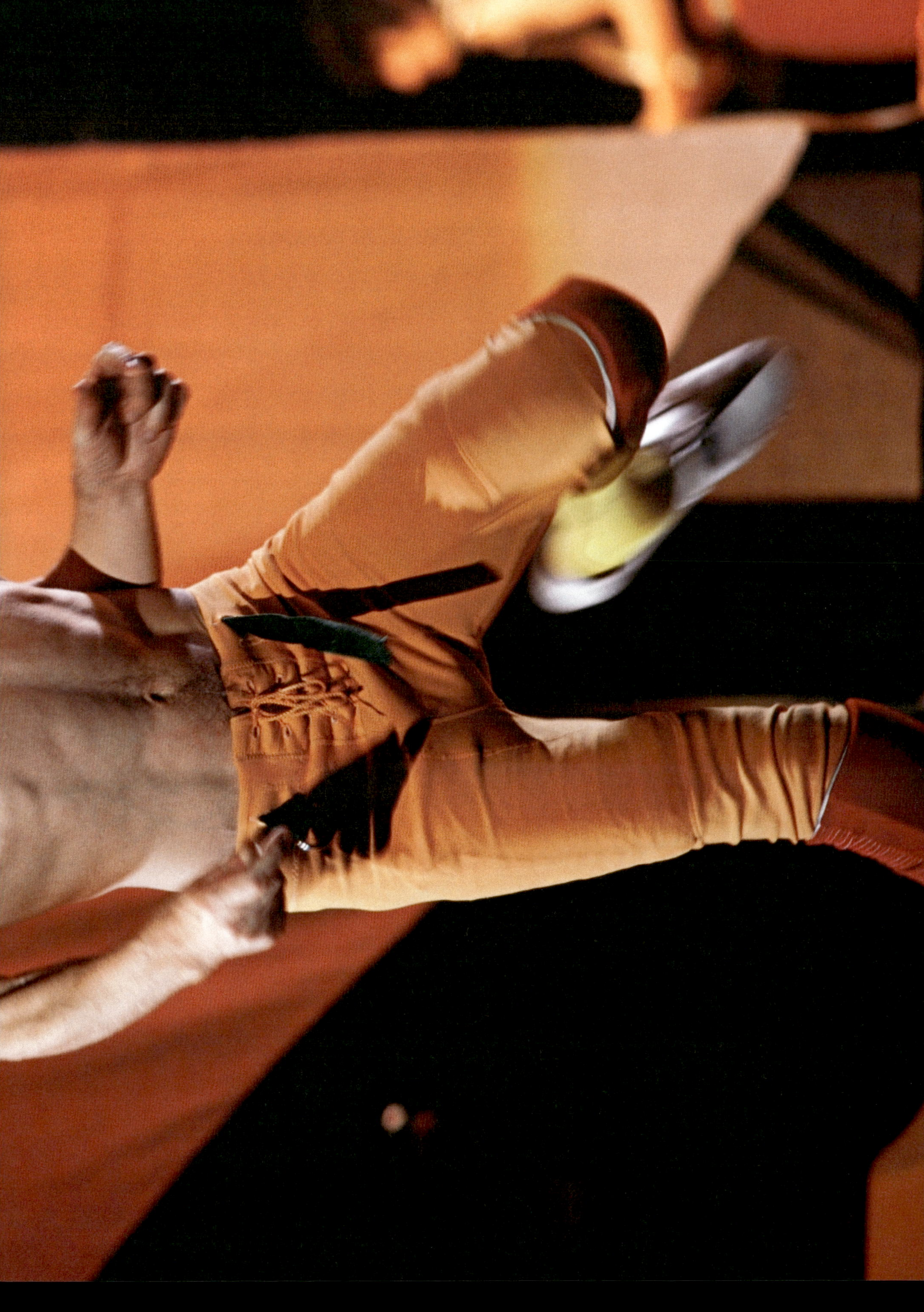

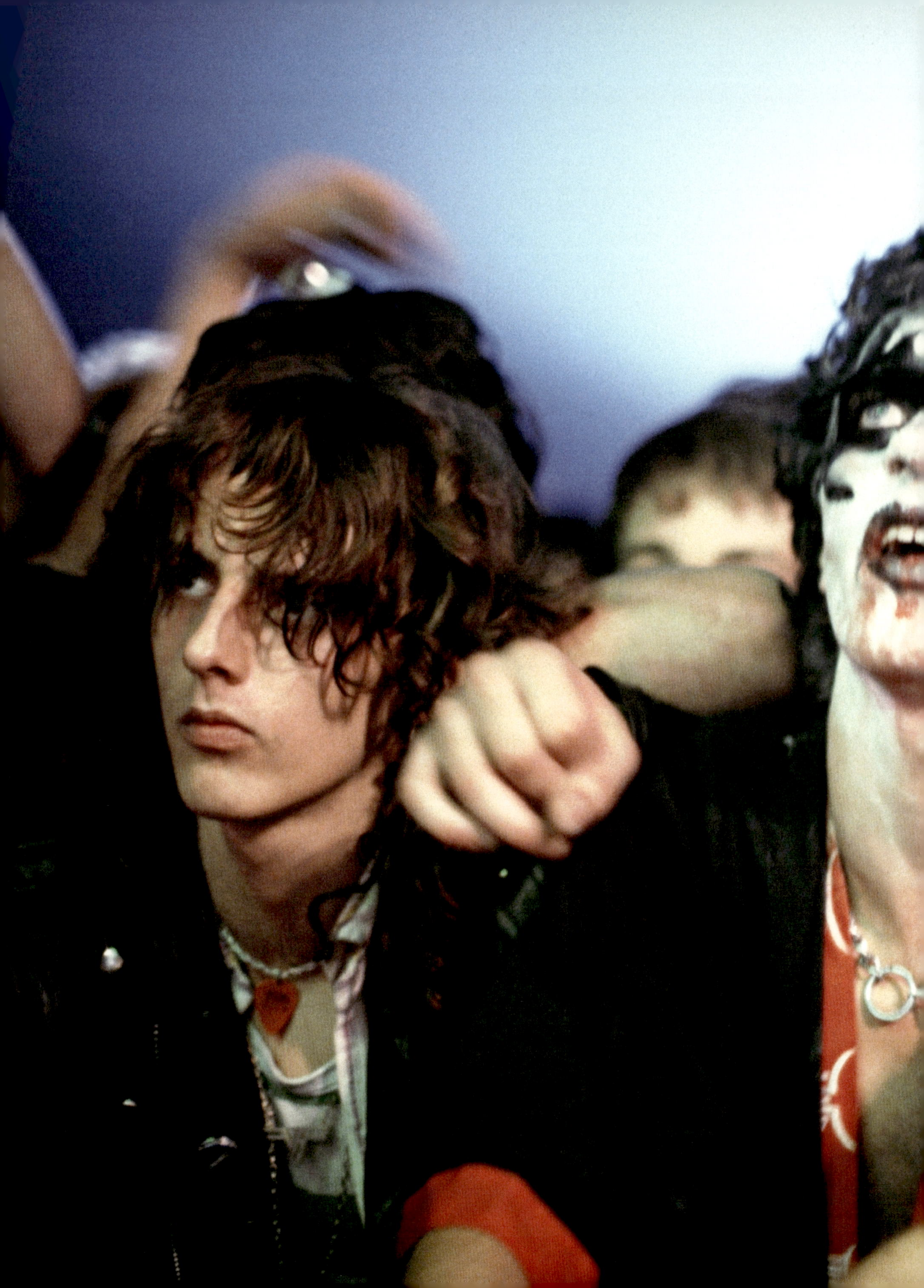

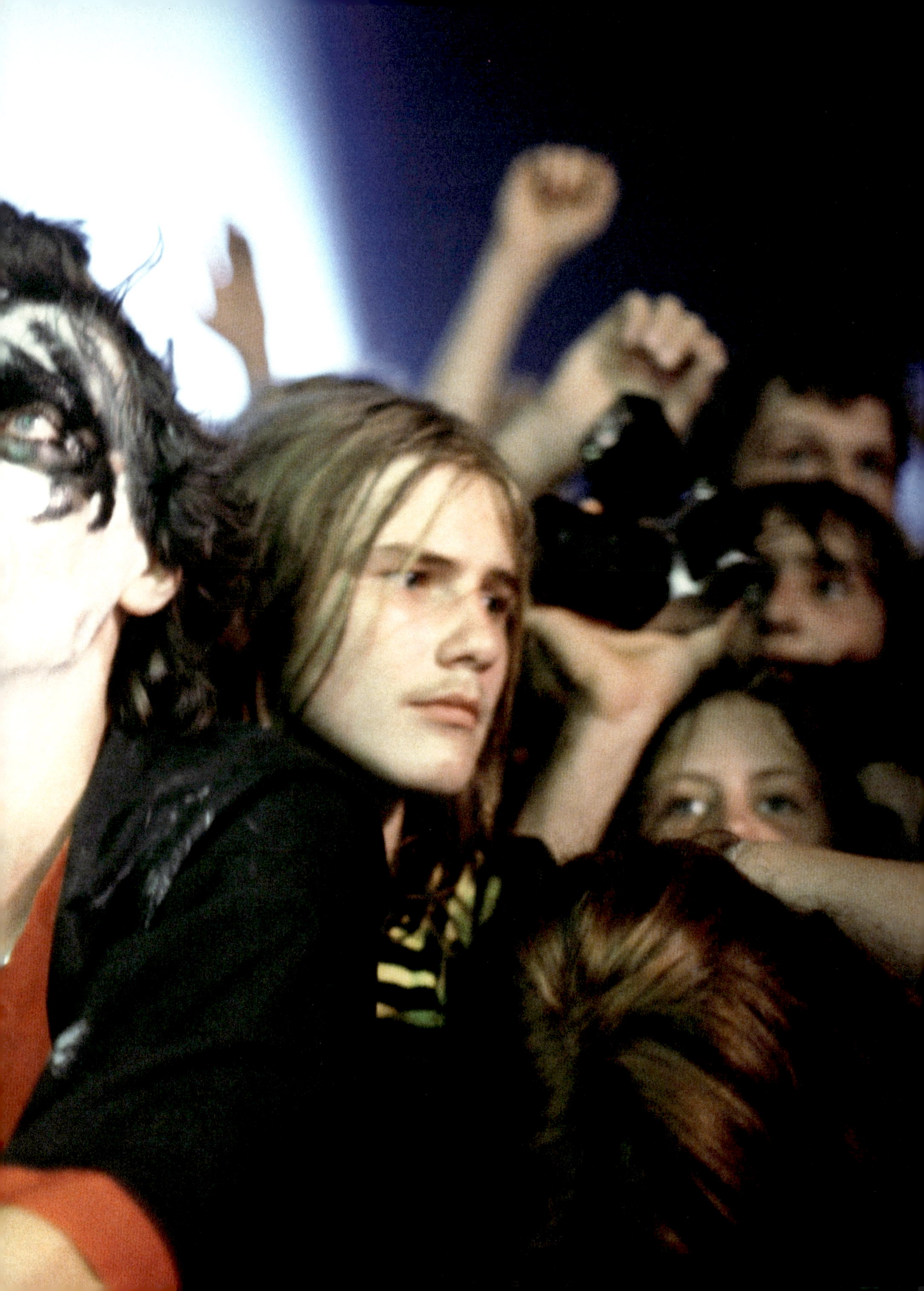

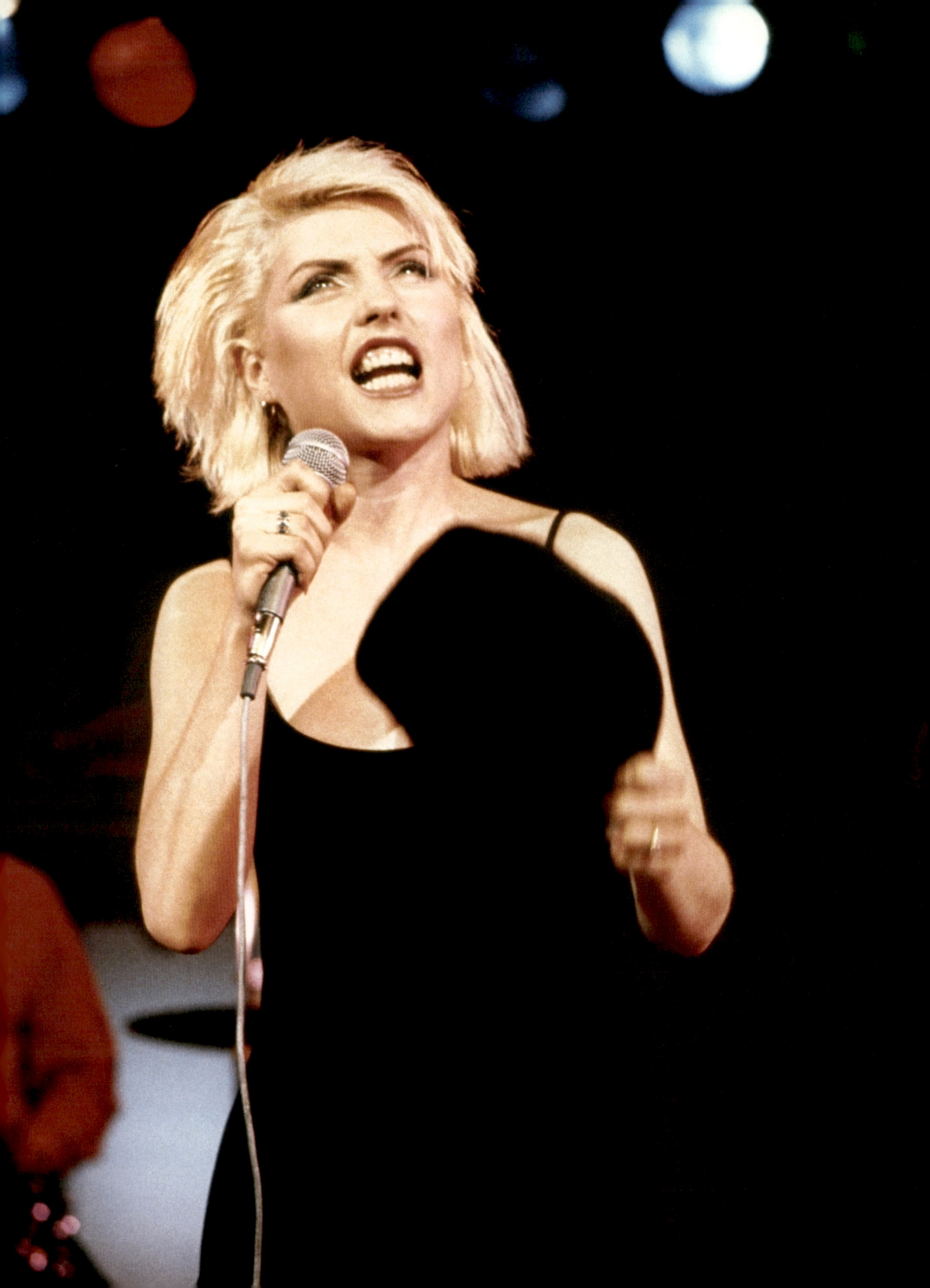

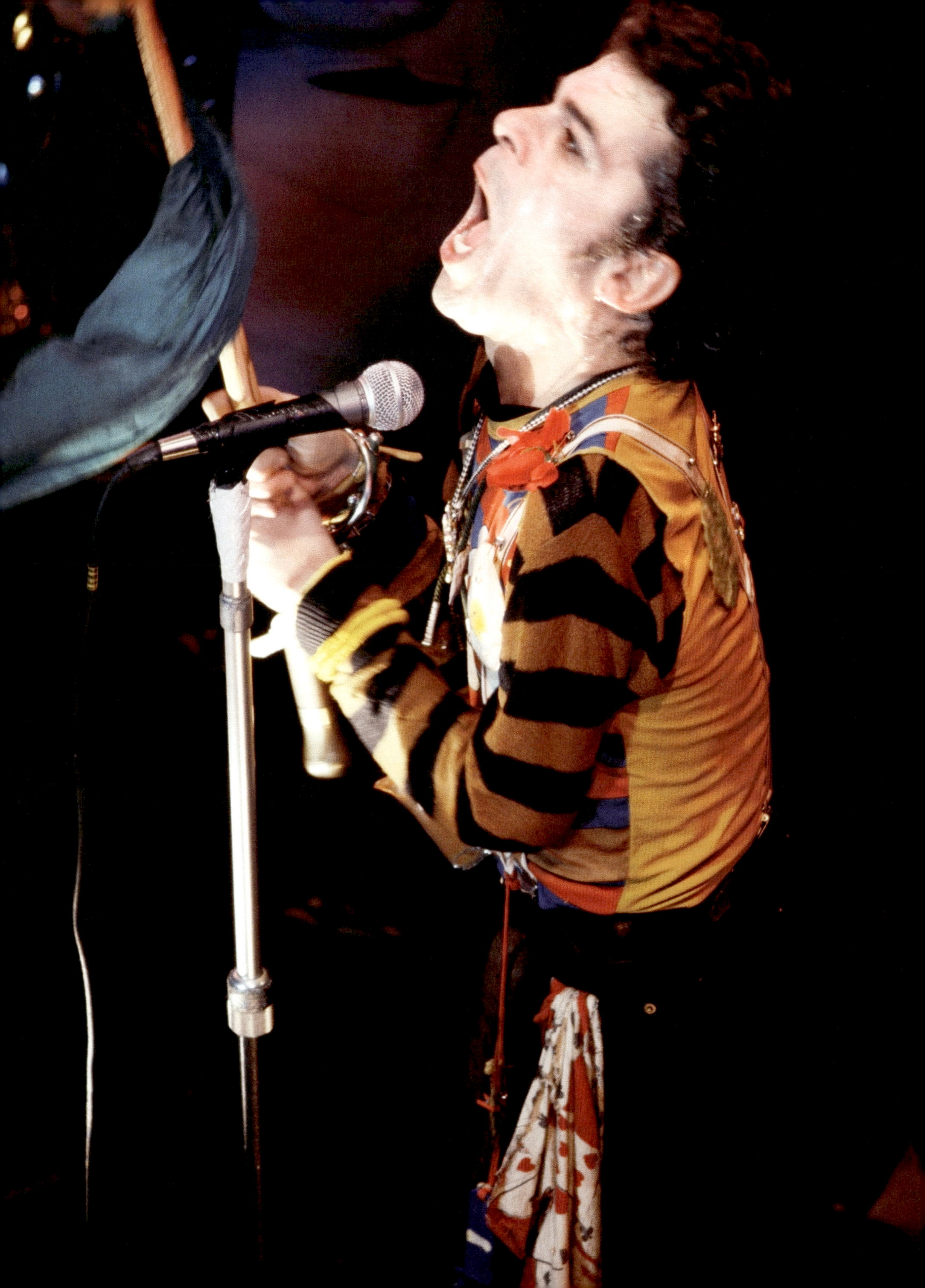

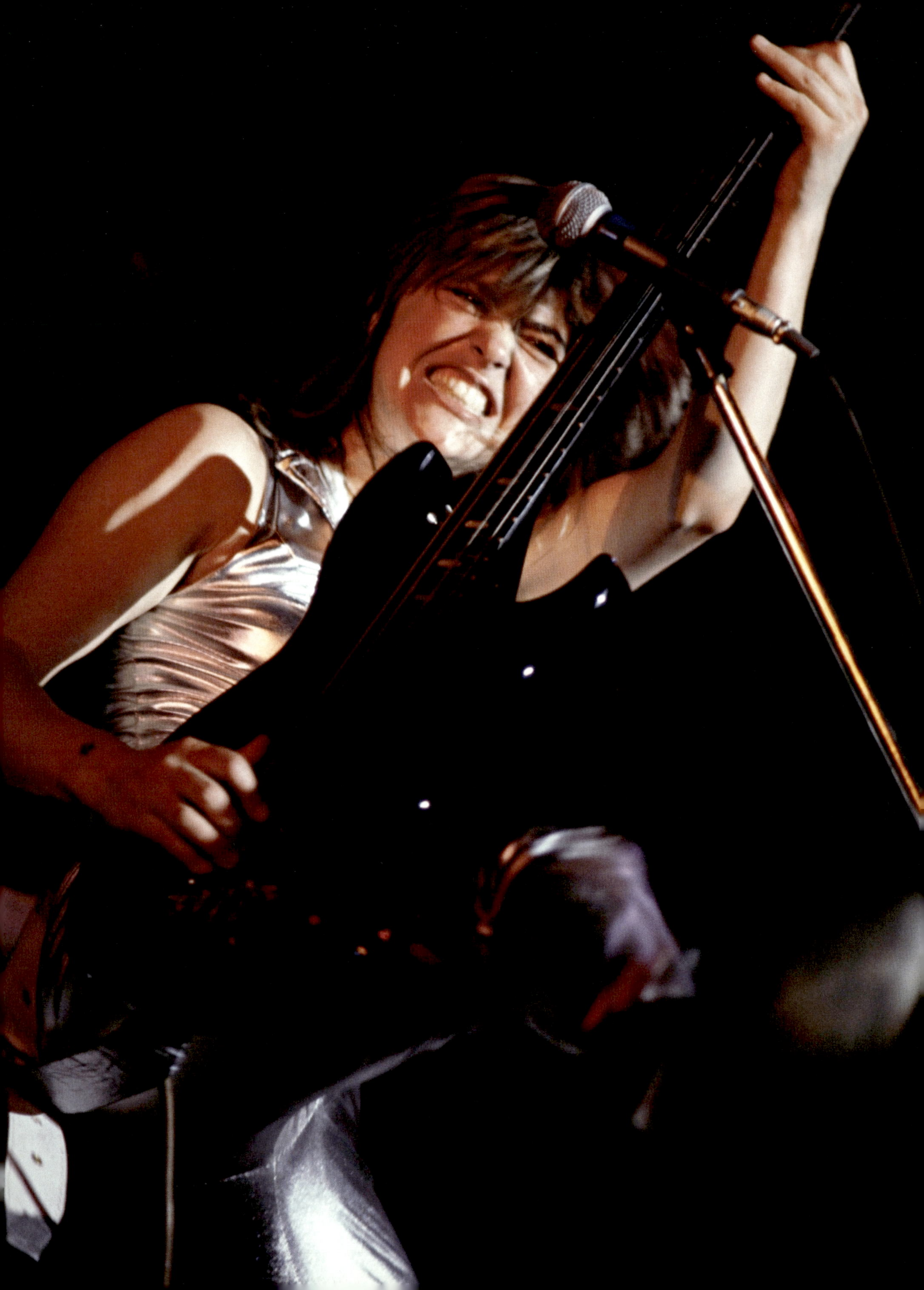

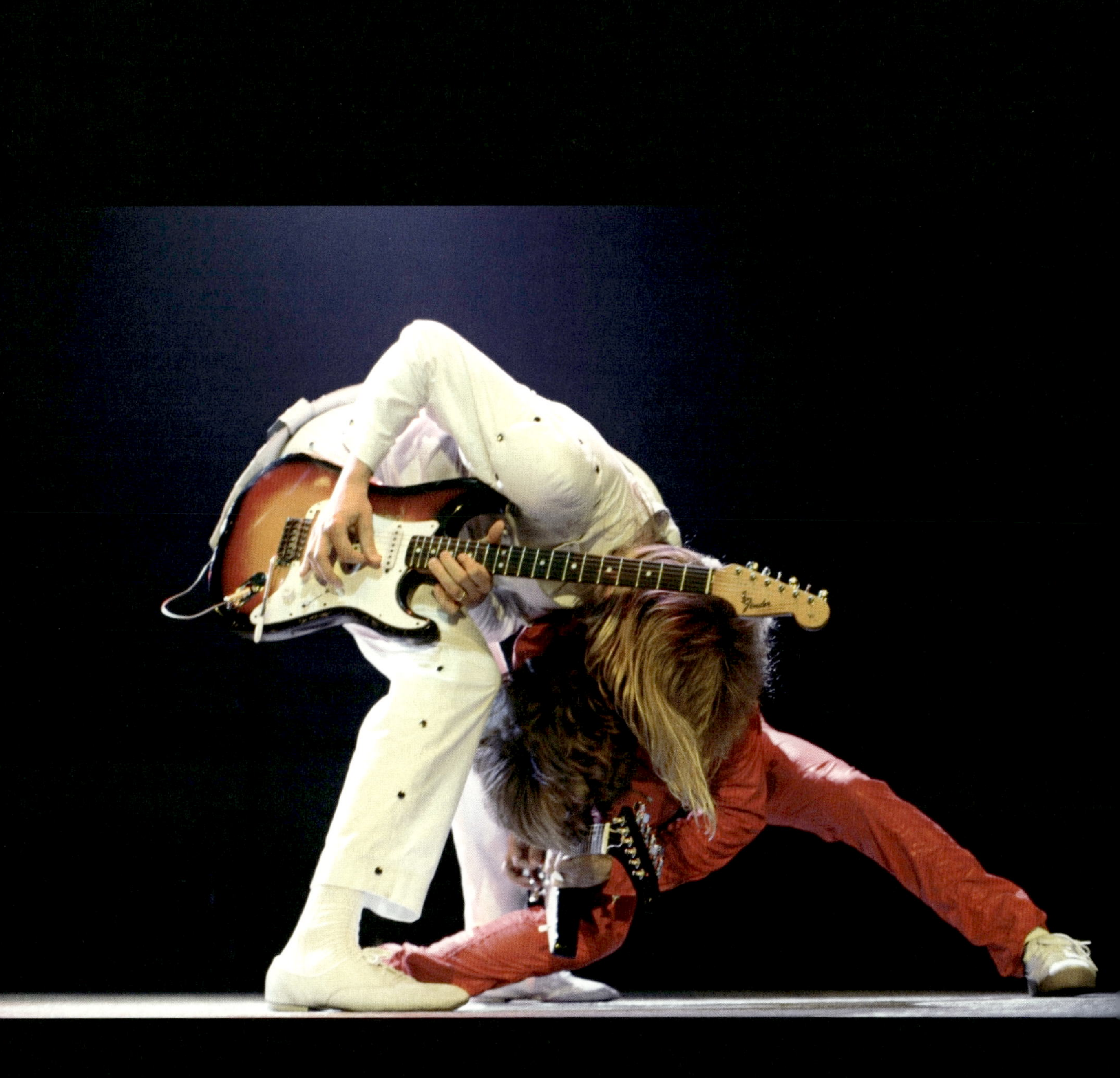

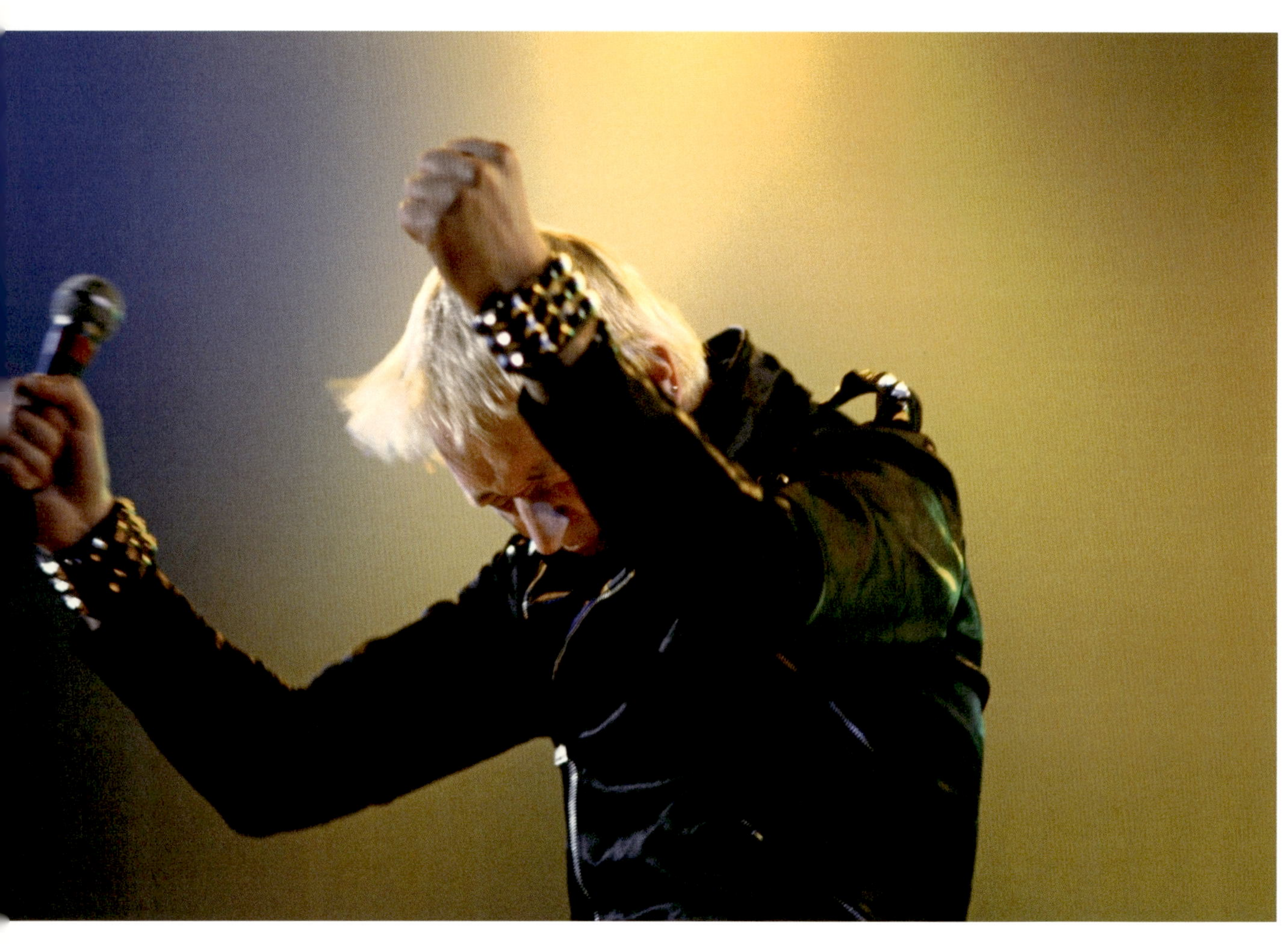

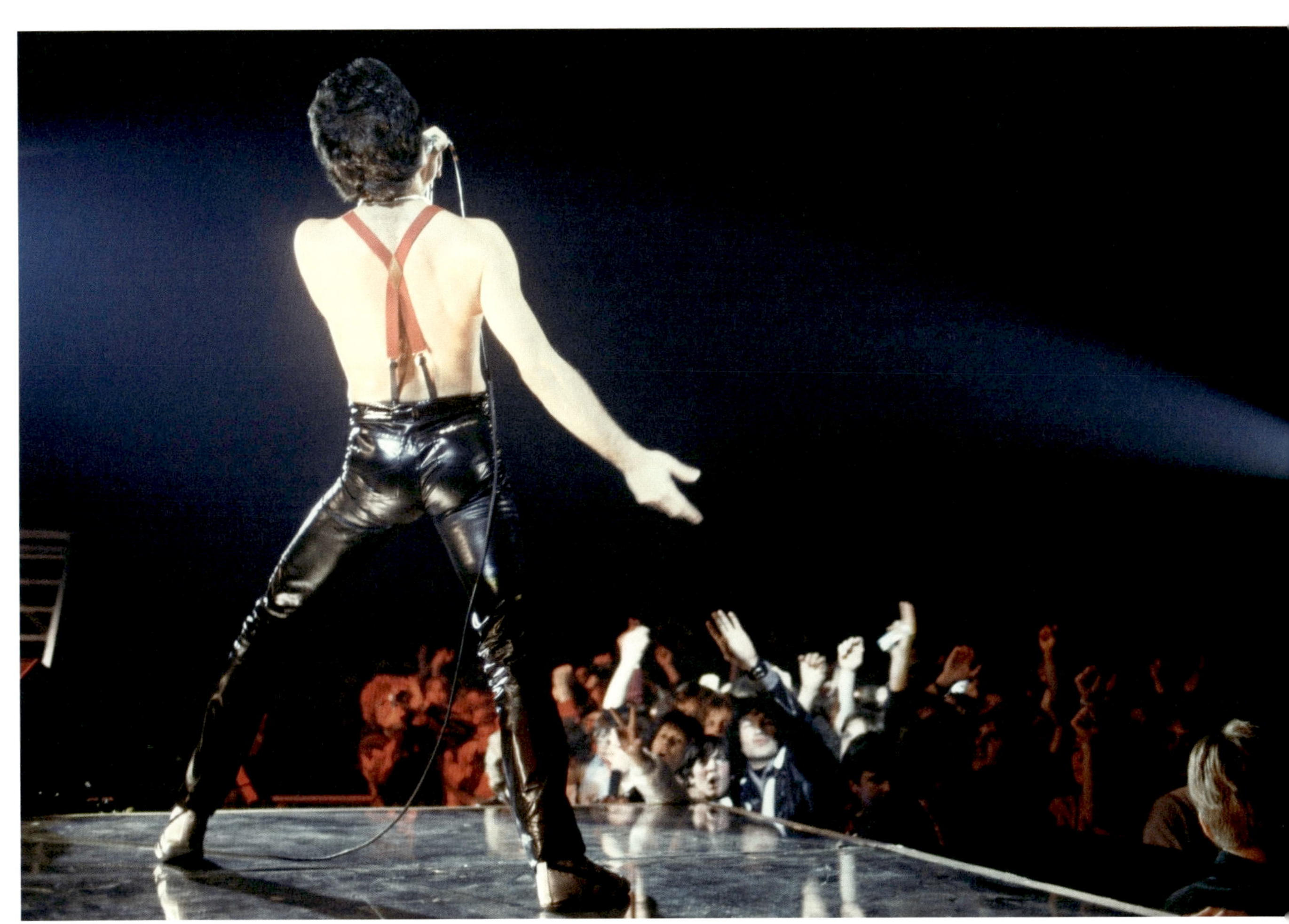

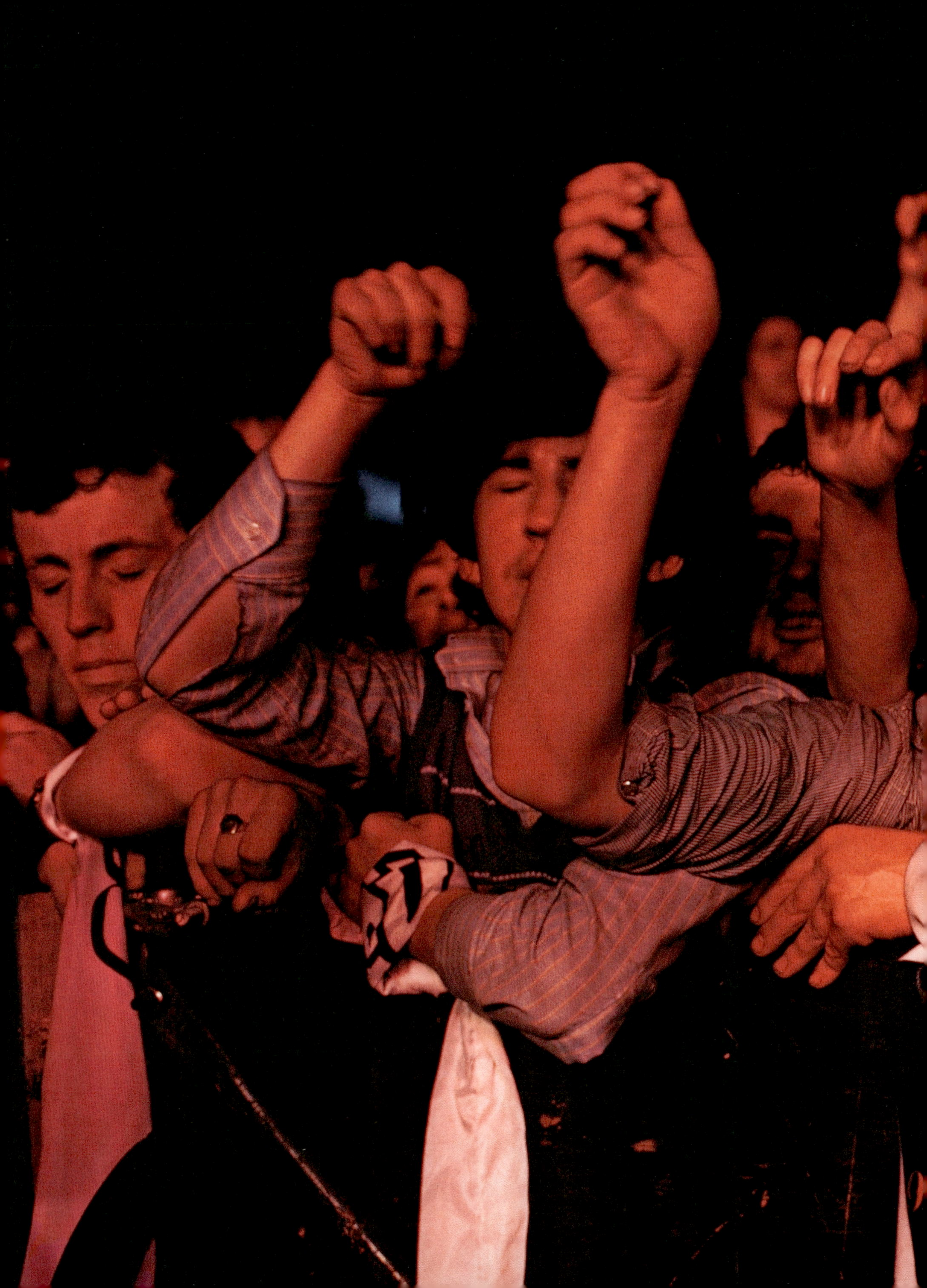

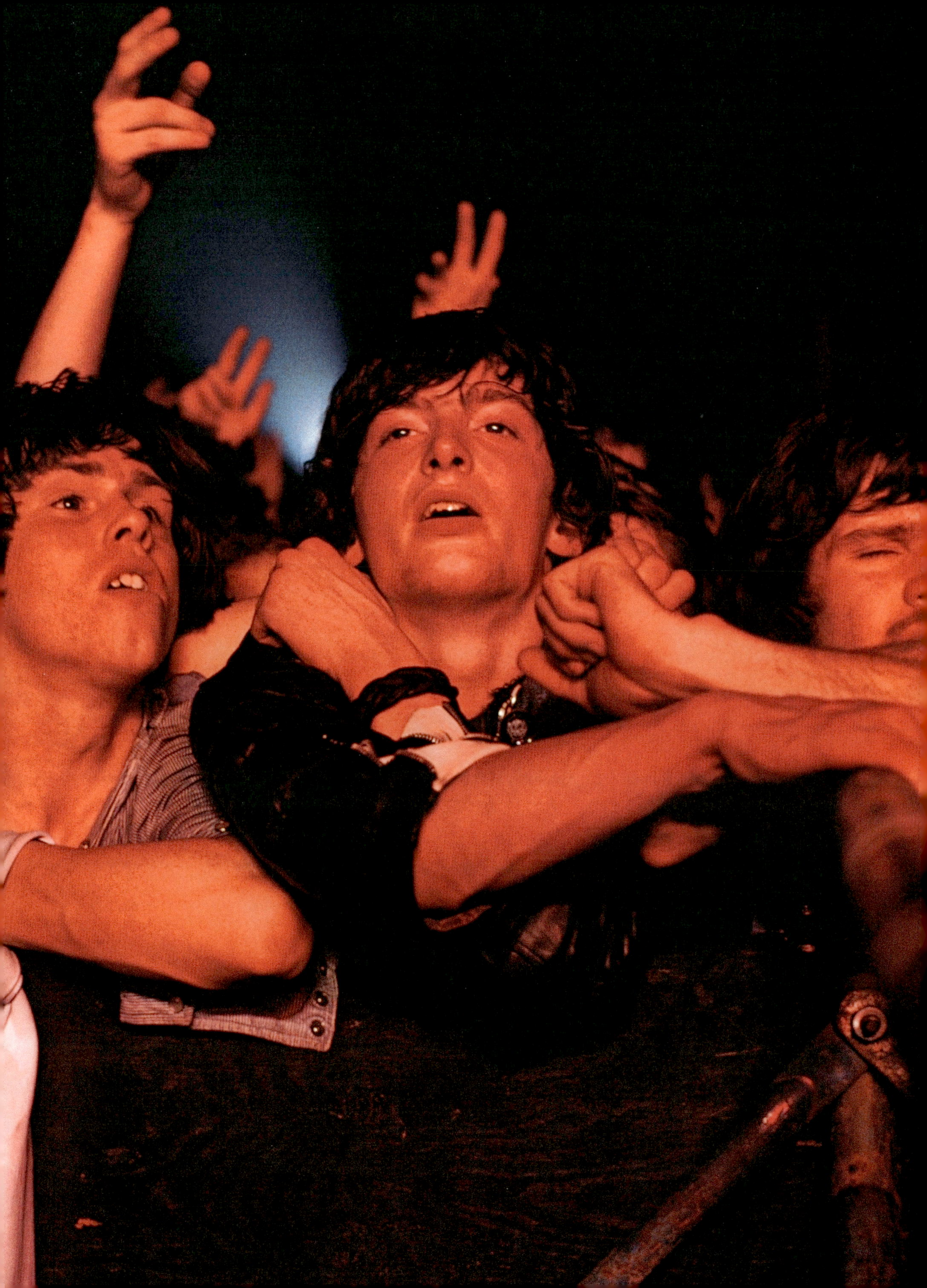

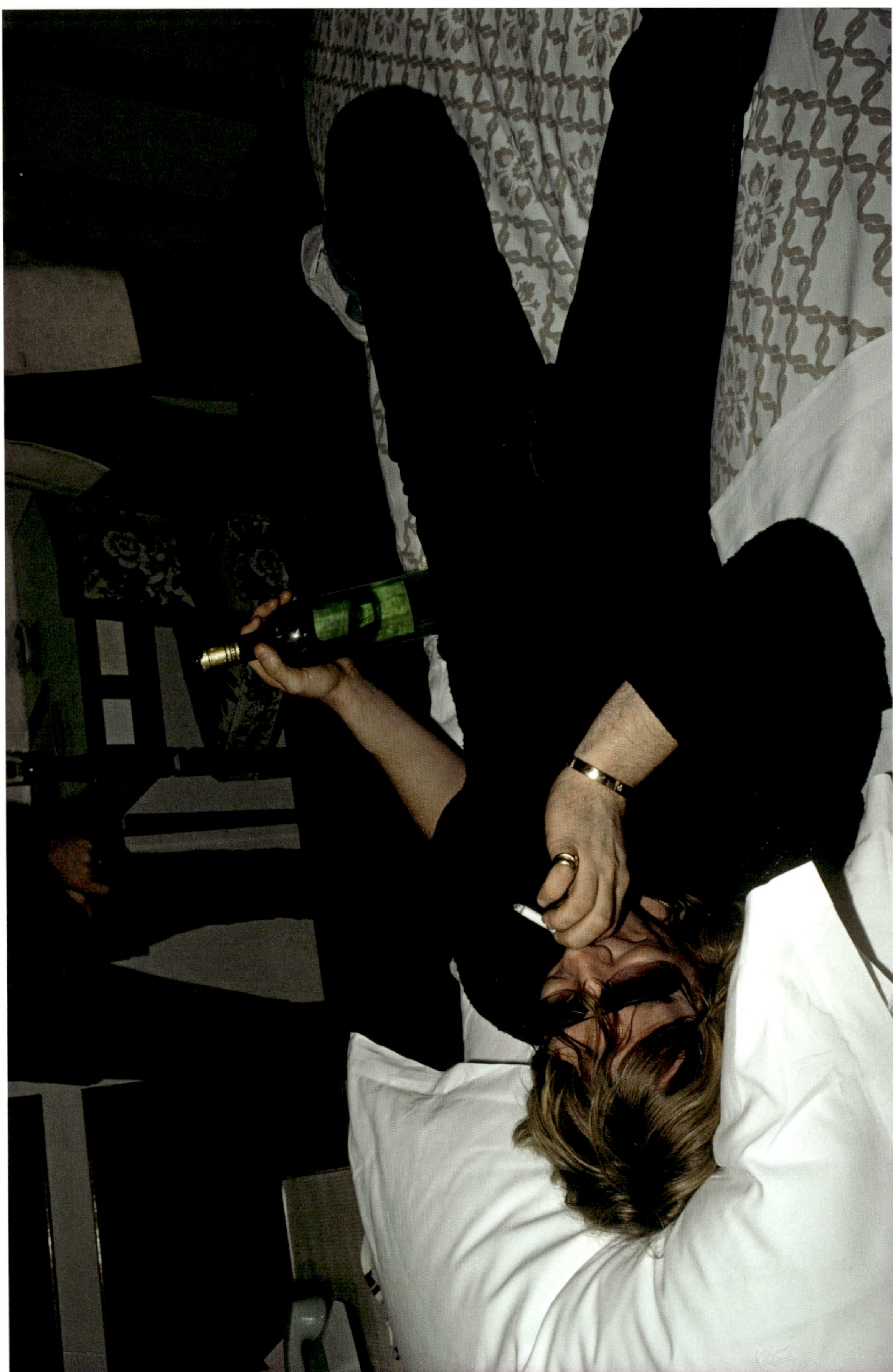

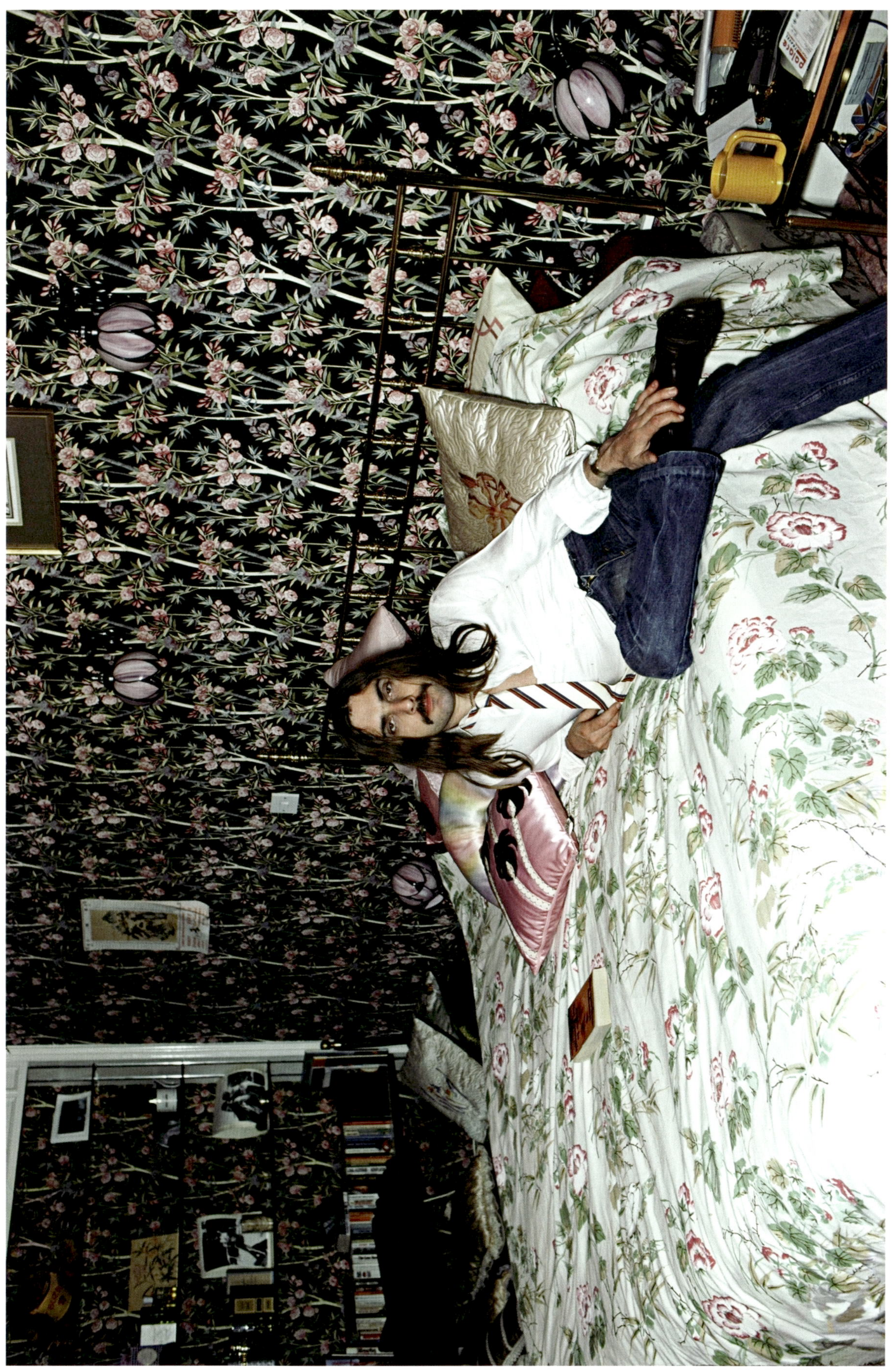

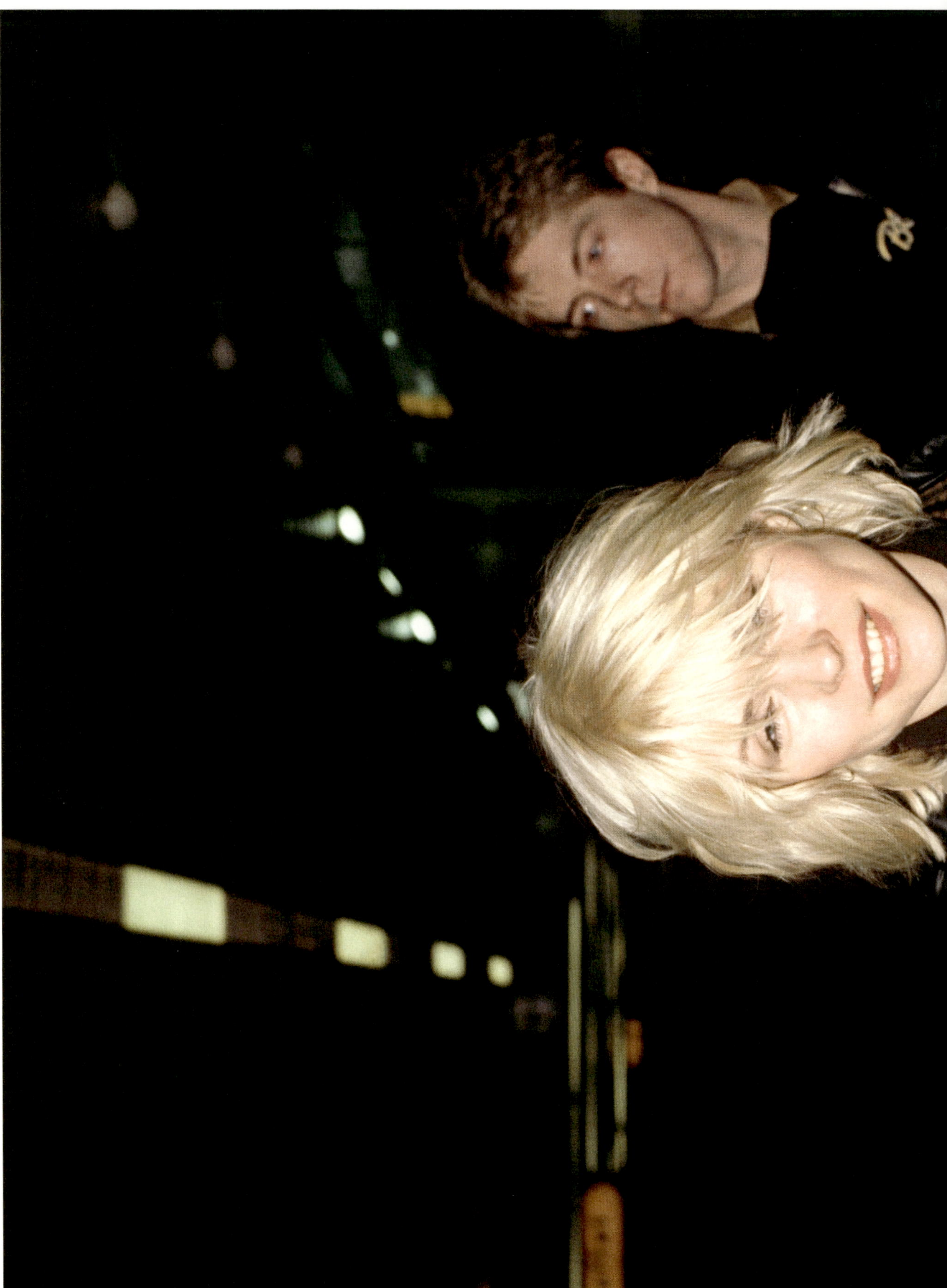

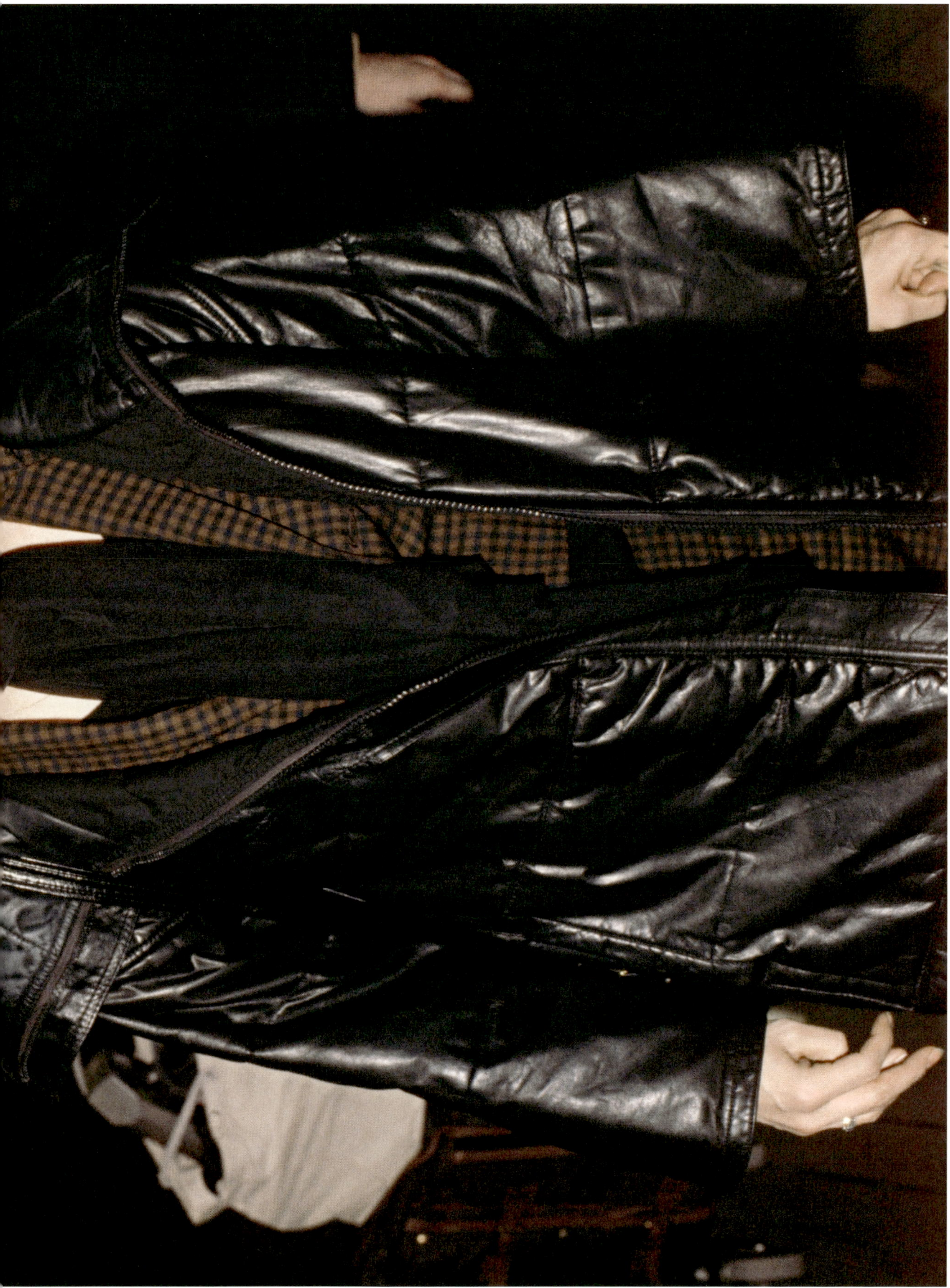

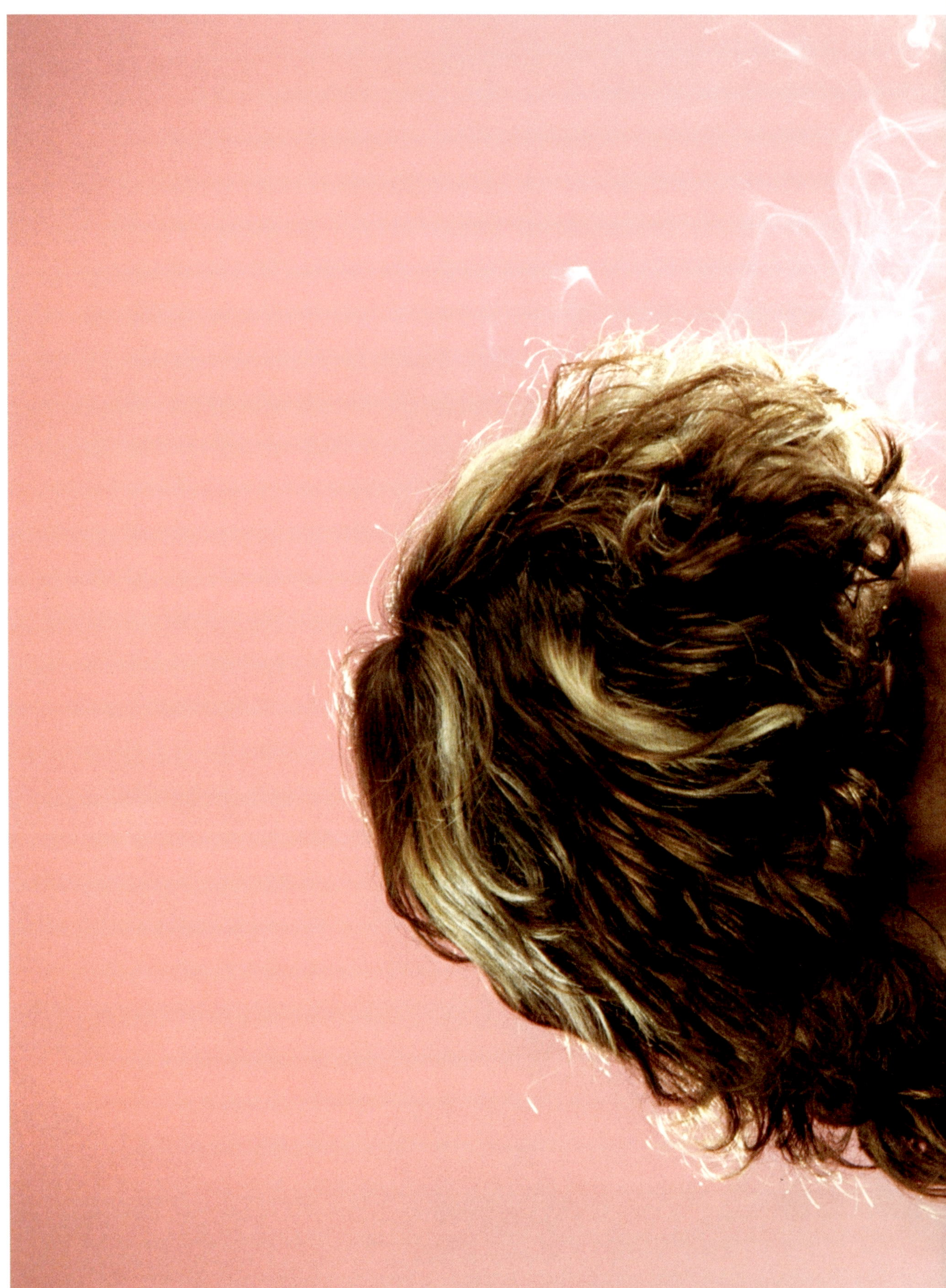

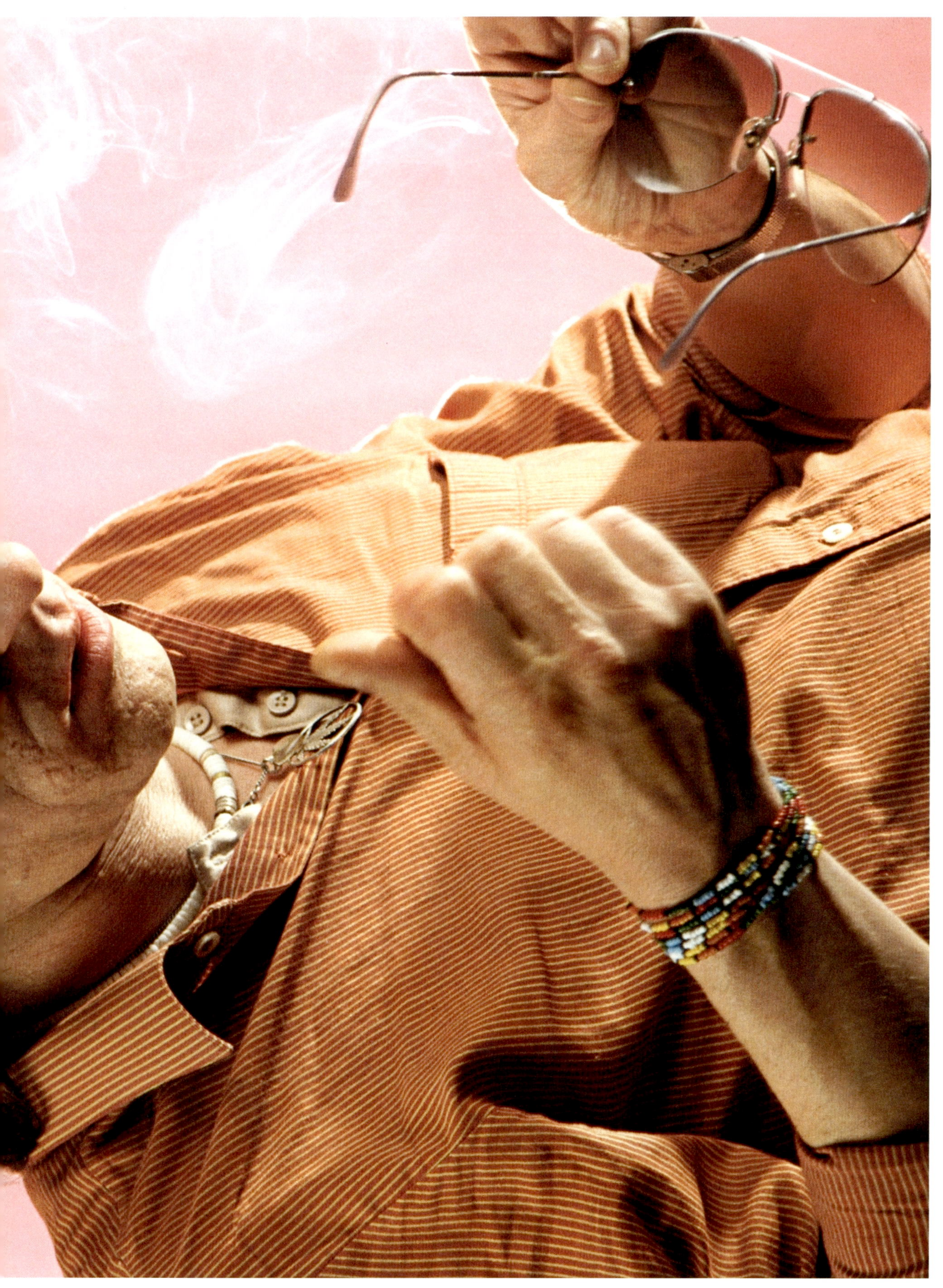

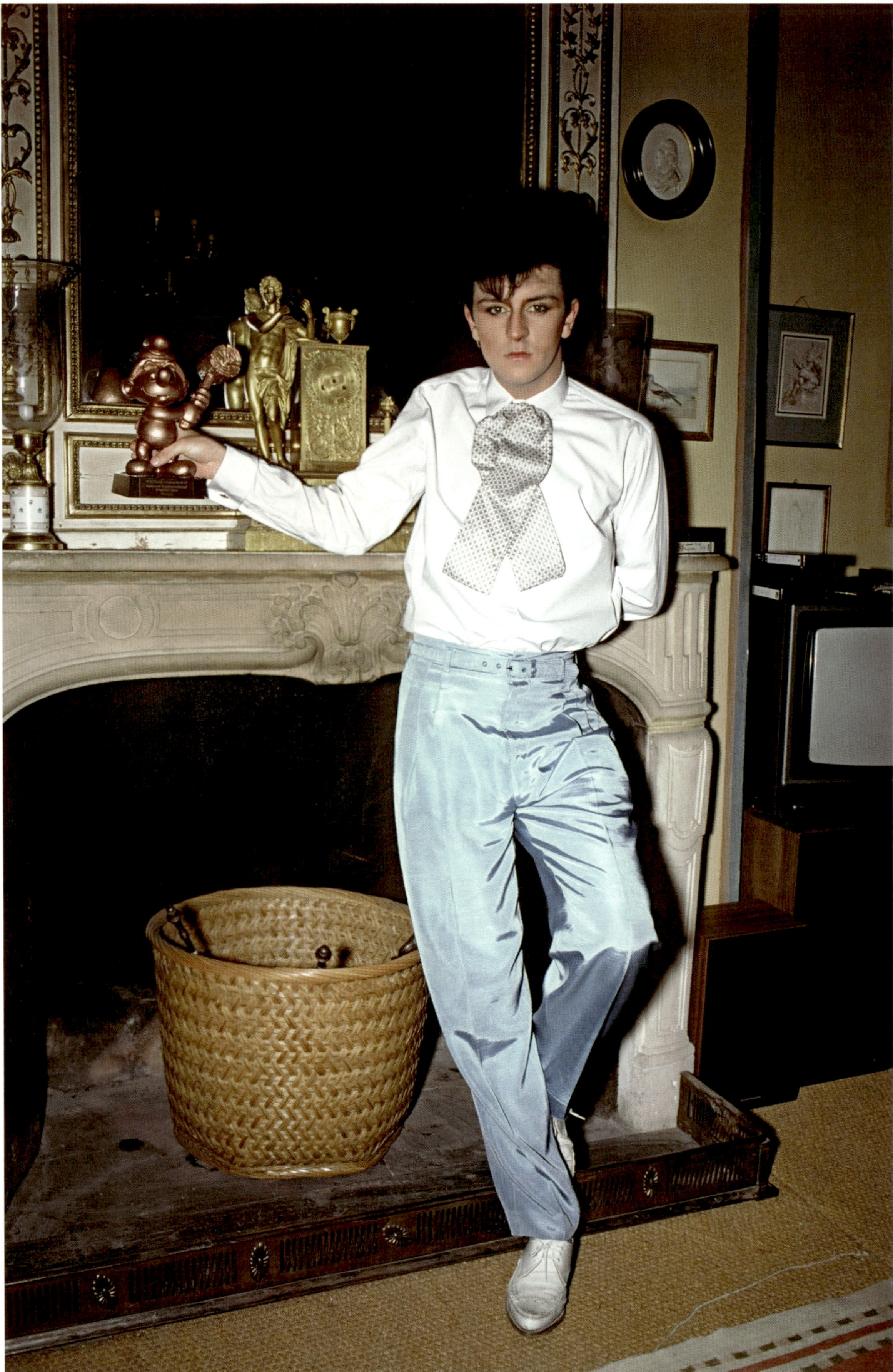

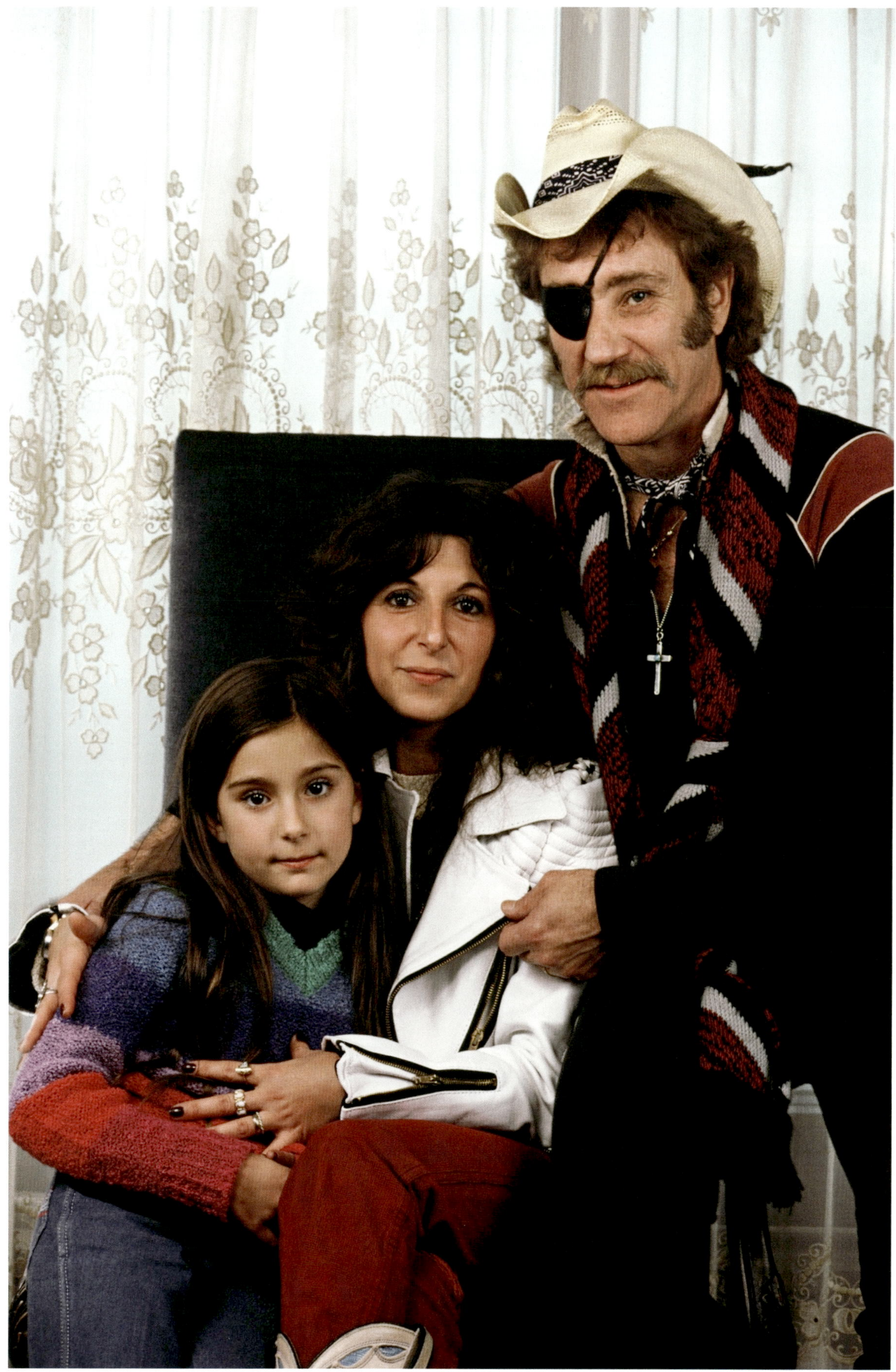

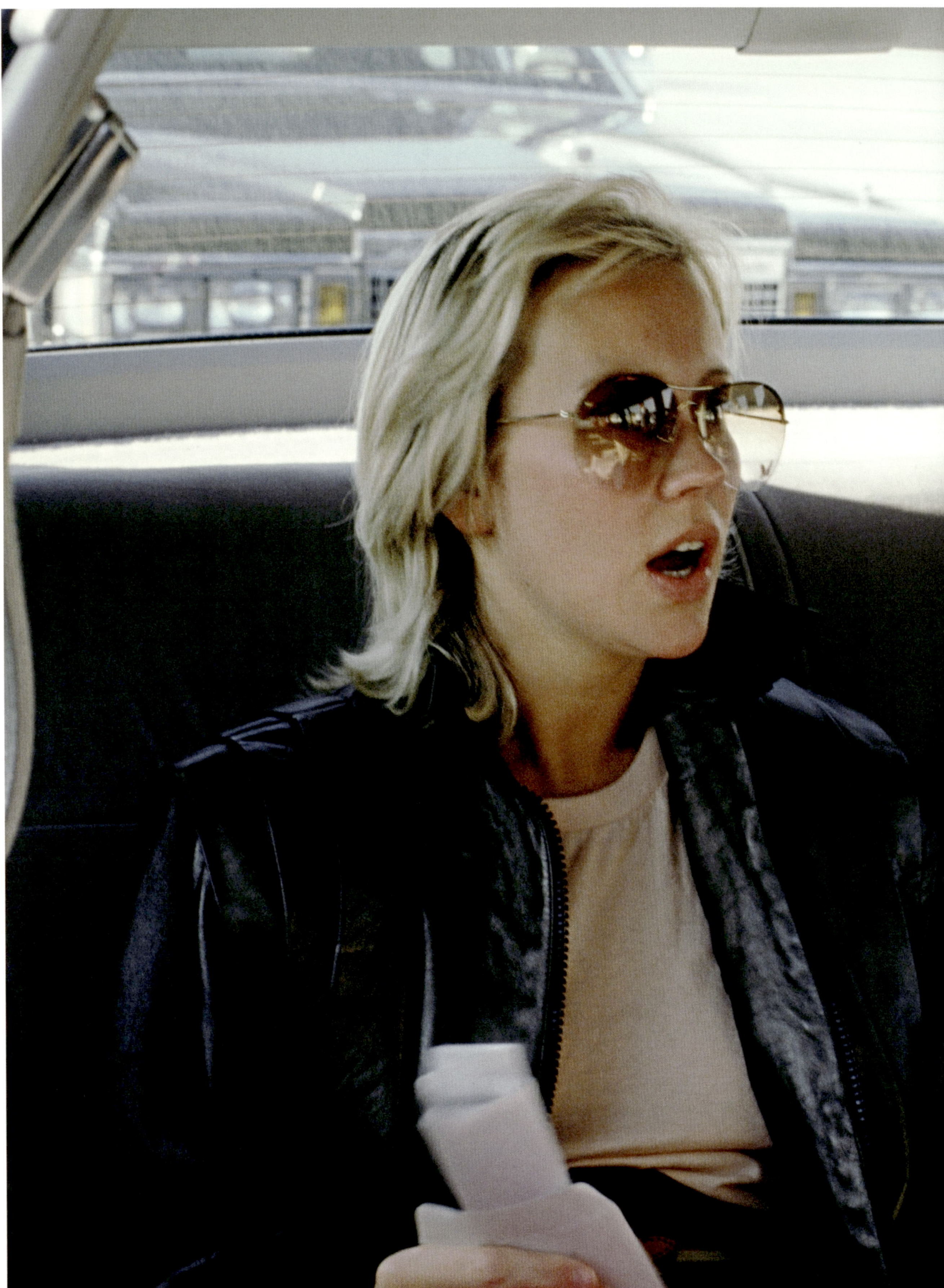

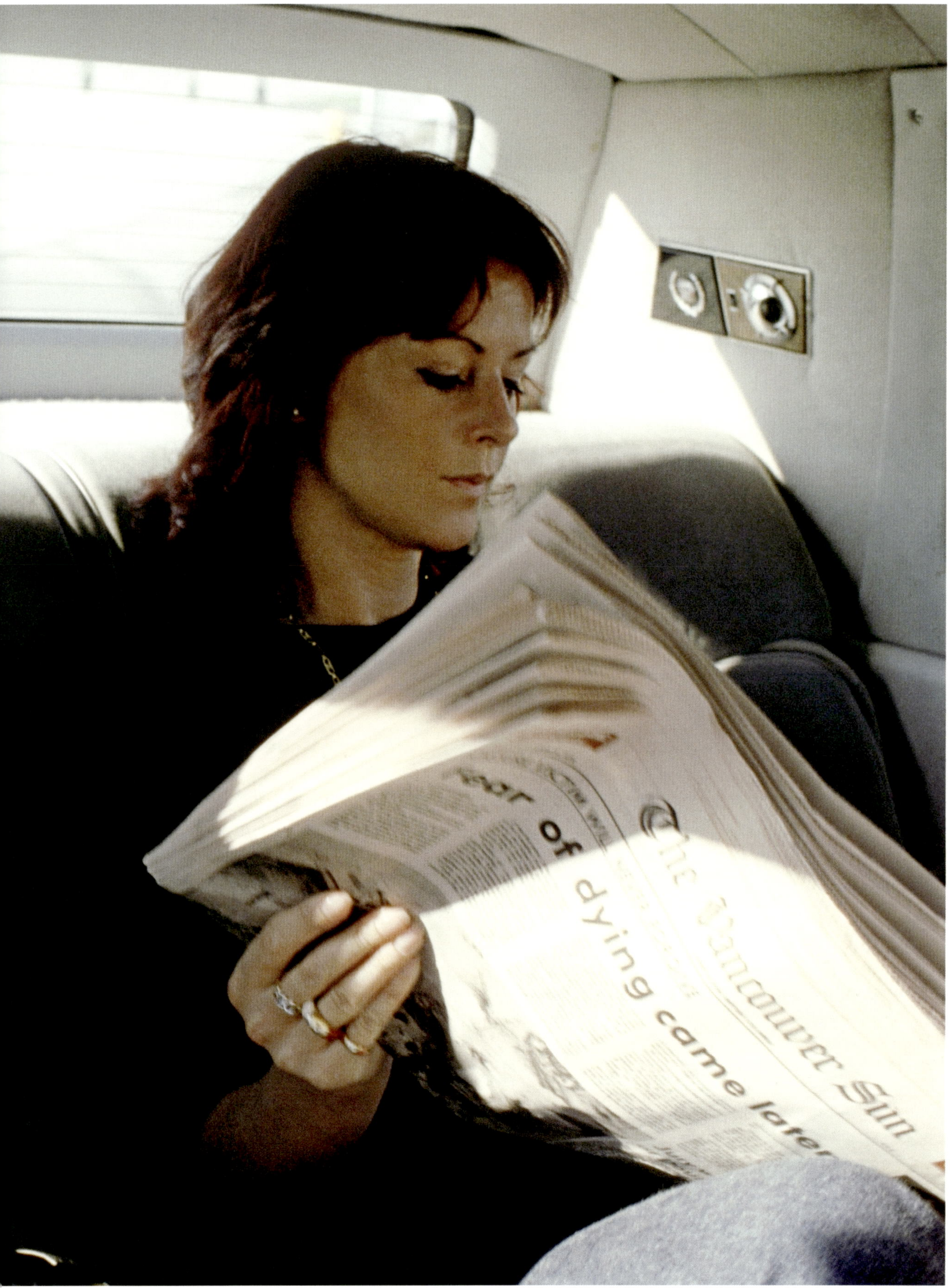
The Vancouver Sun
of dying came later

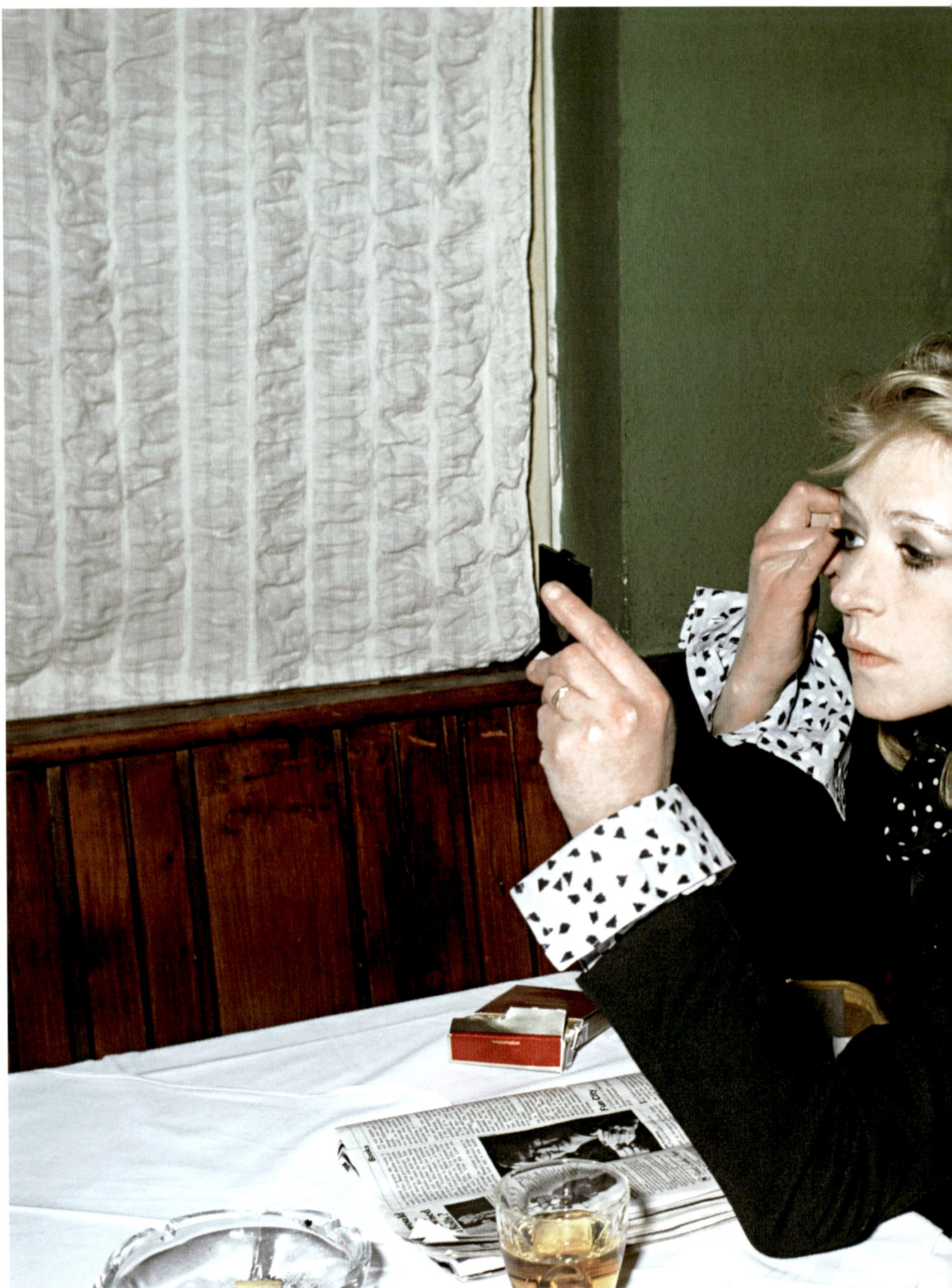

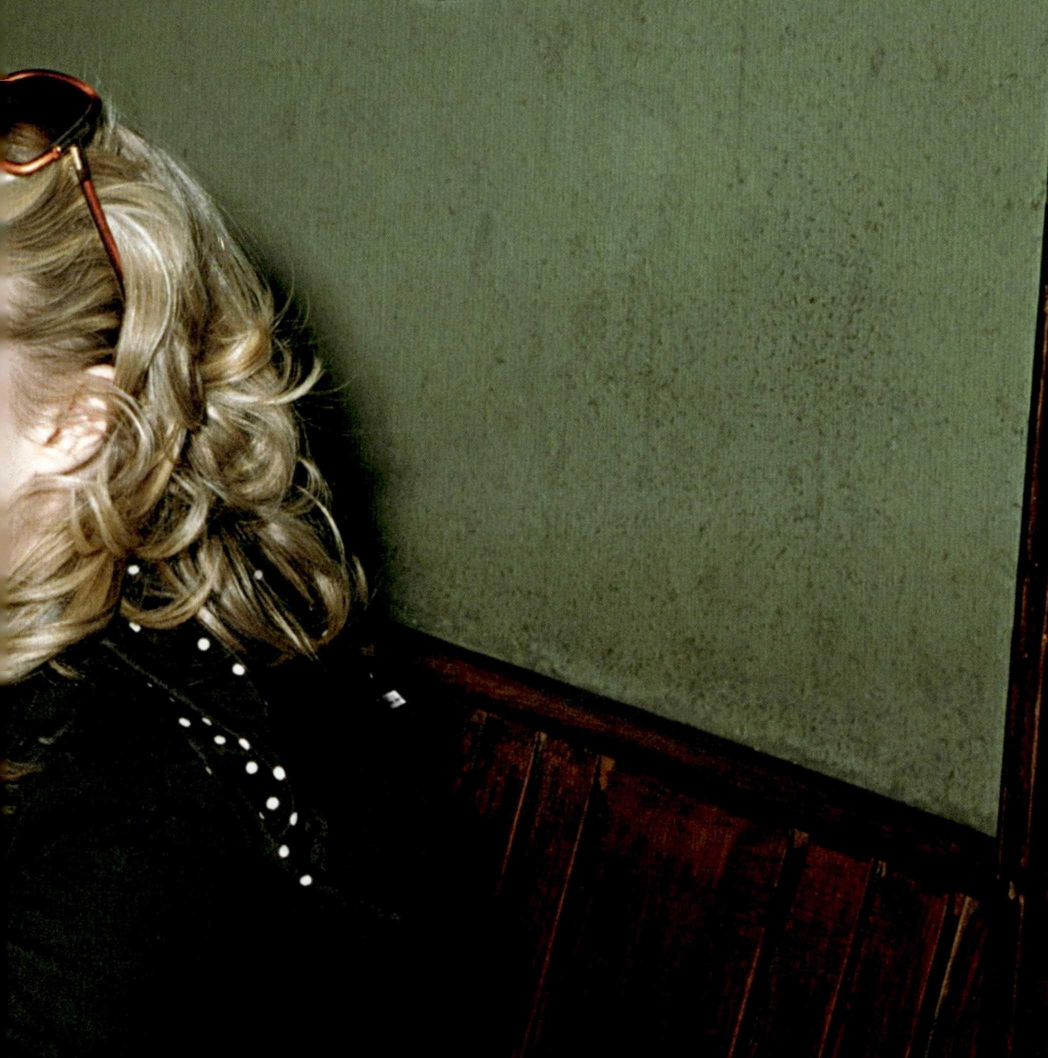
QUEENS ROAD
BATTERSEA

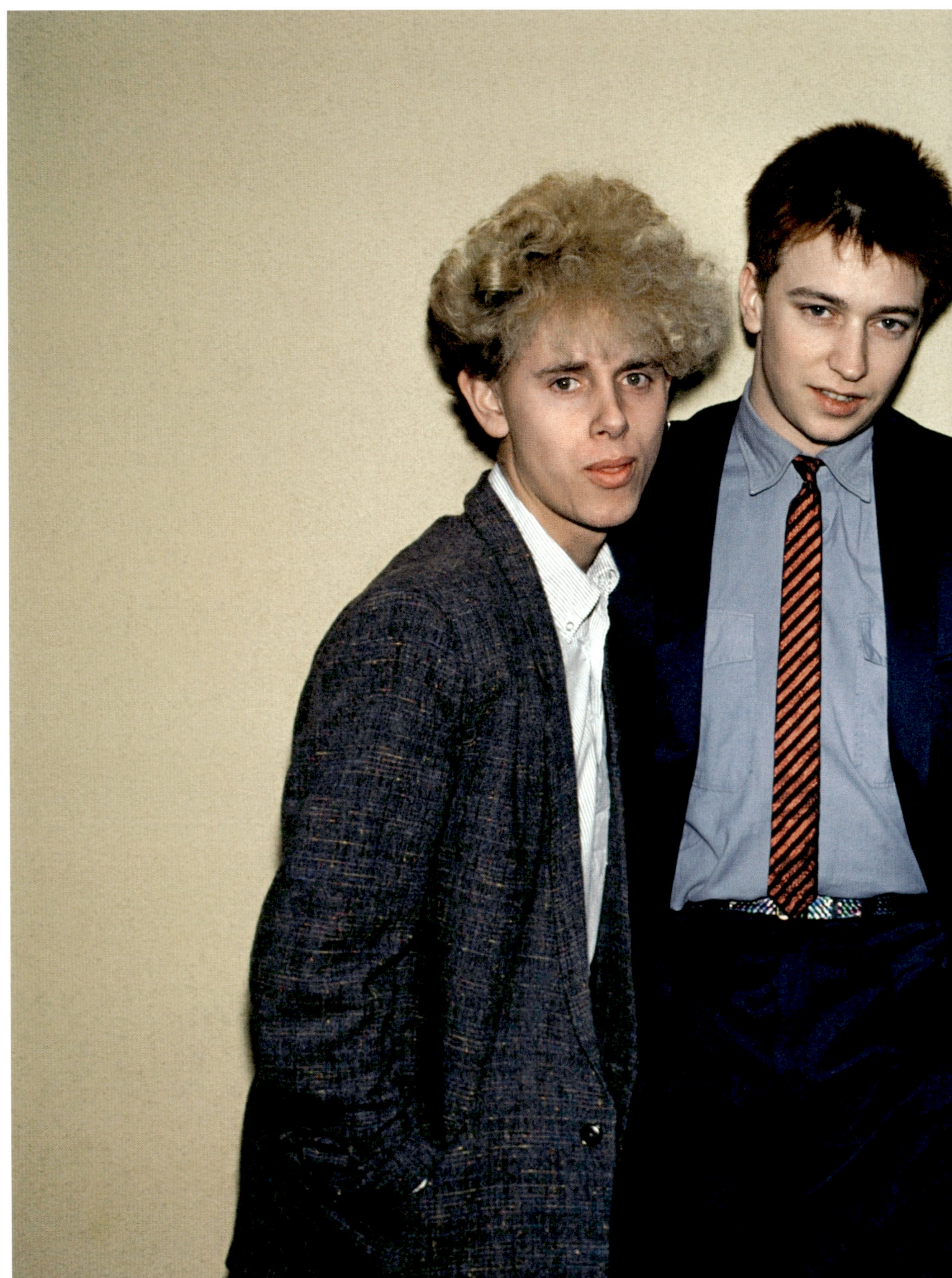

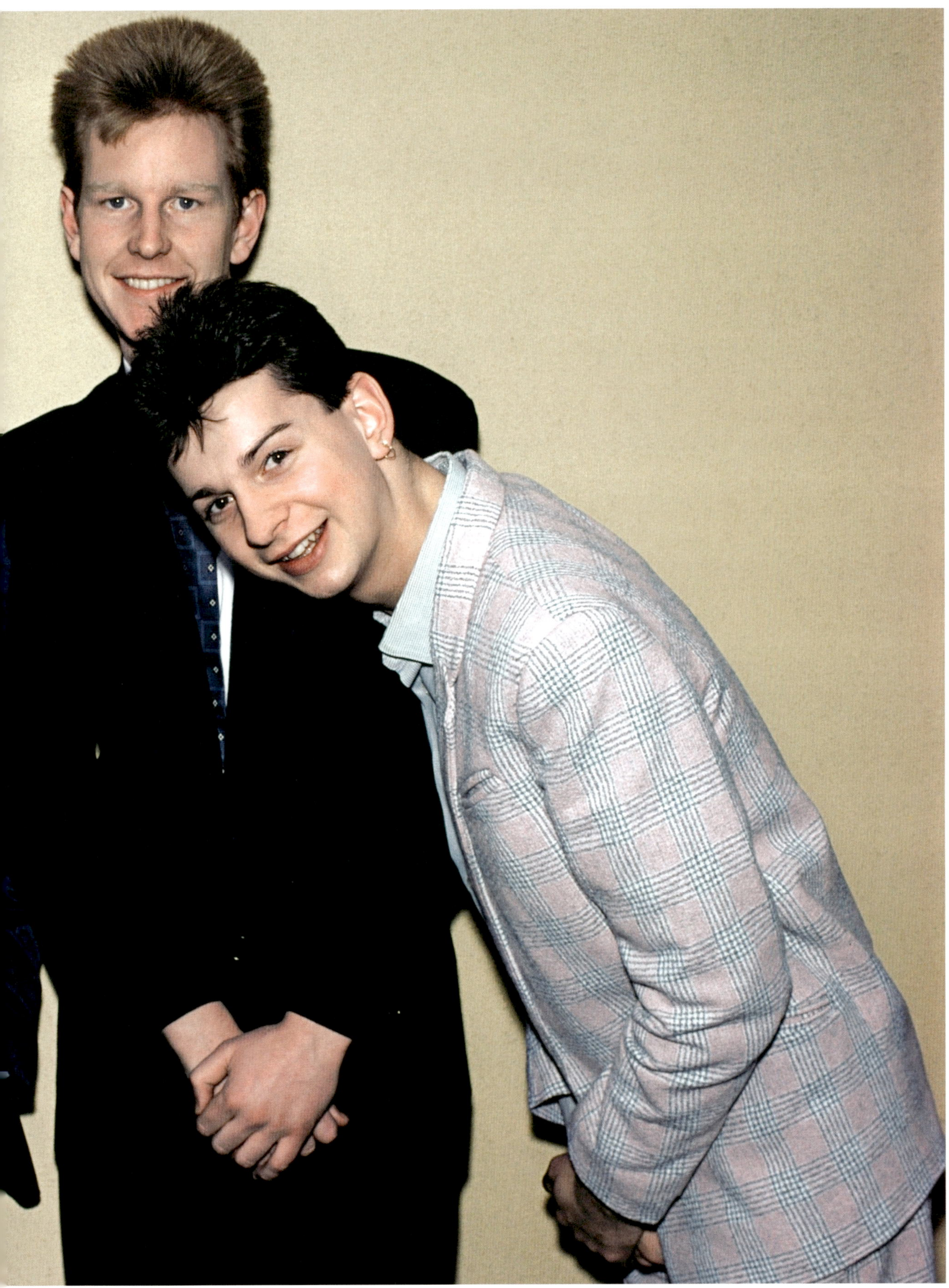

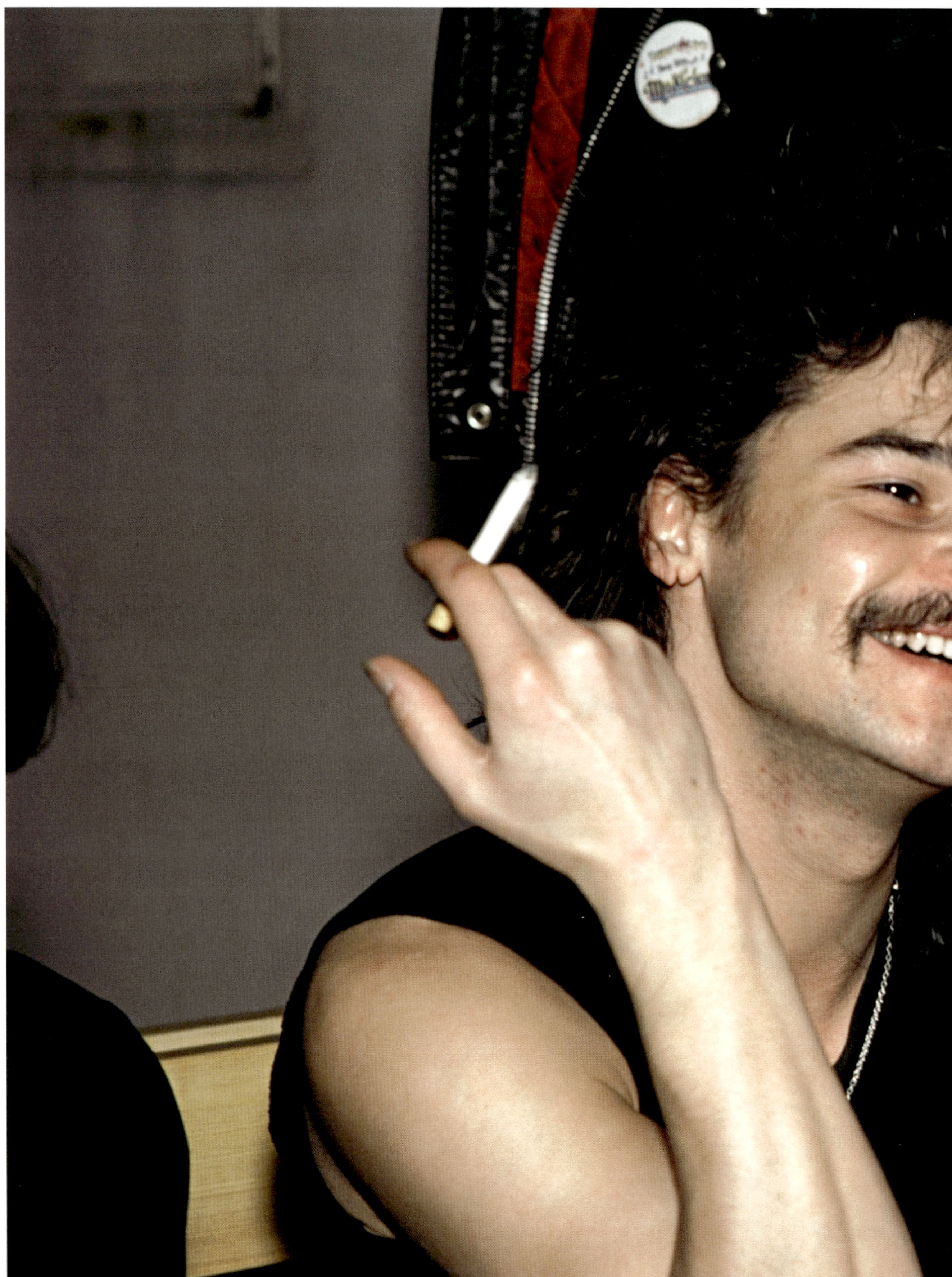

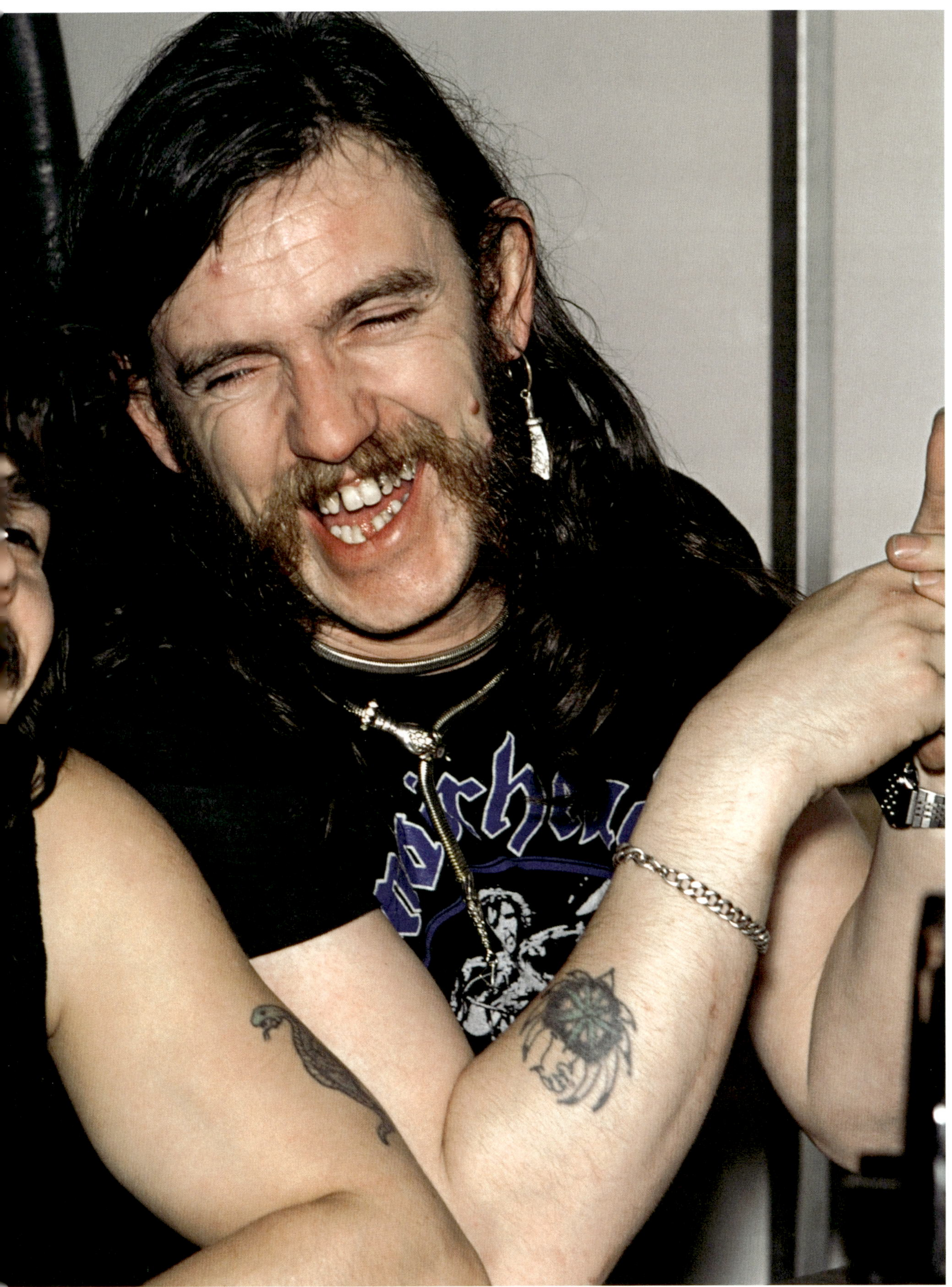

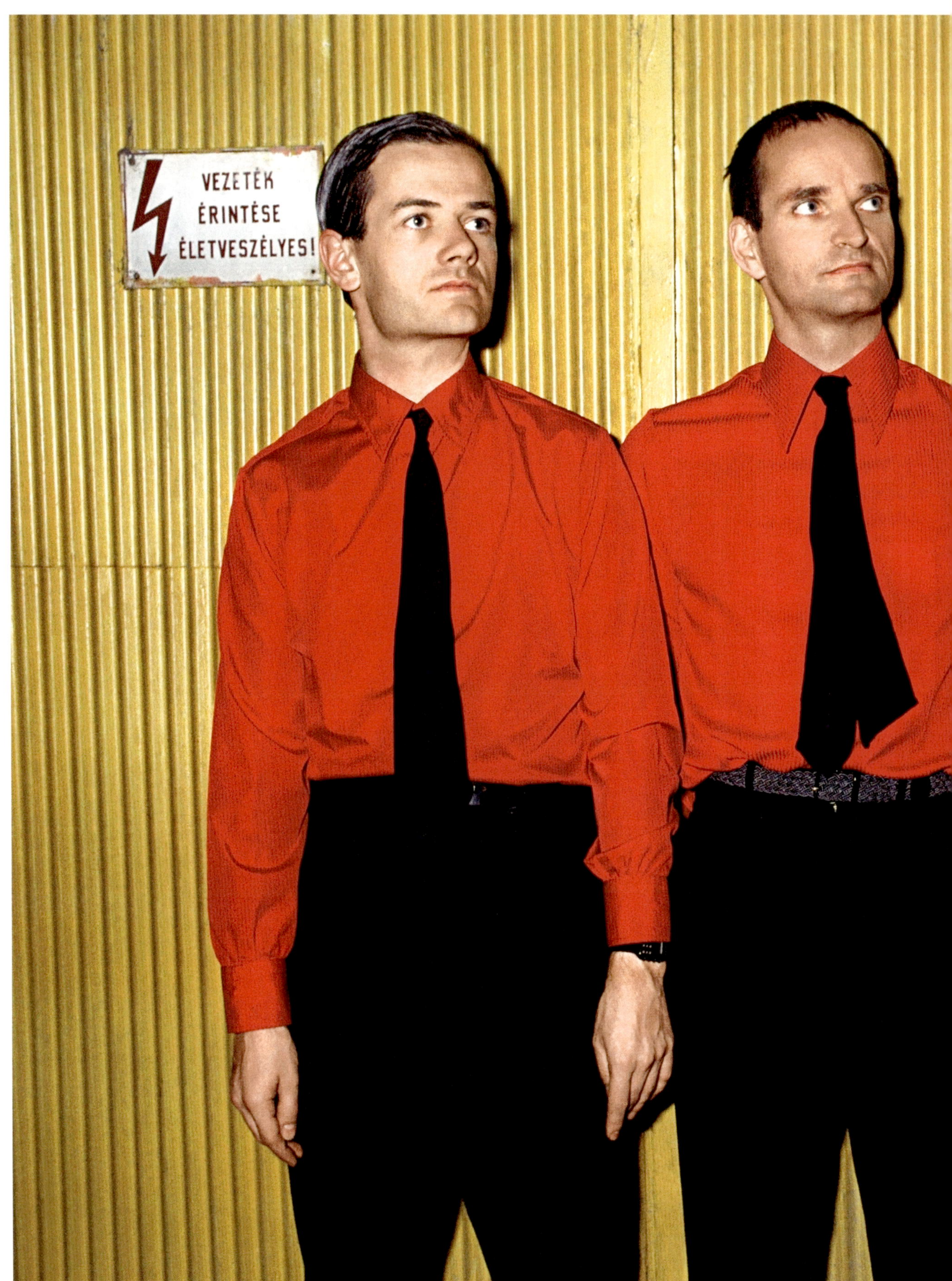

VEZETÉK
ÉRINTÉSE
ÉLETVESZÉLYES!

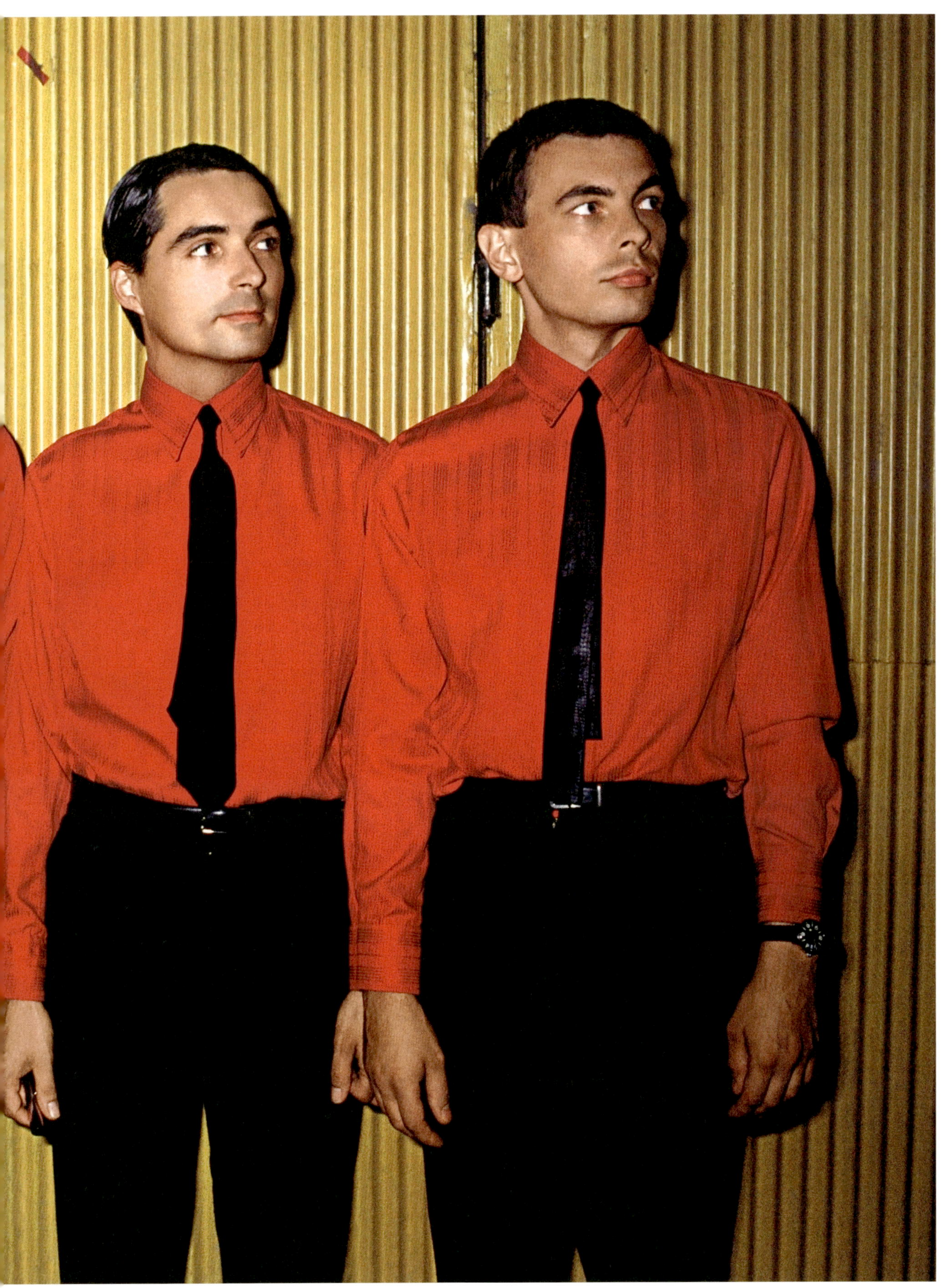

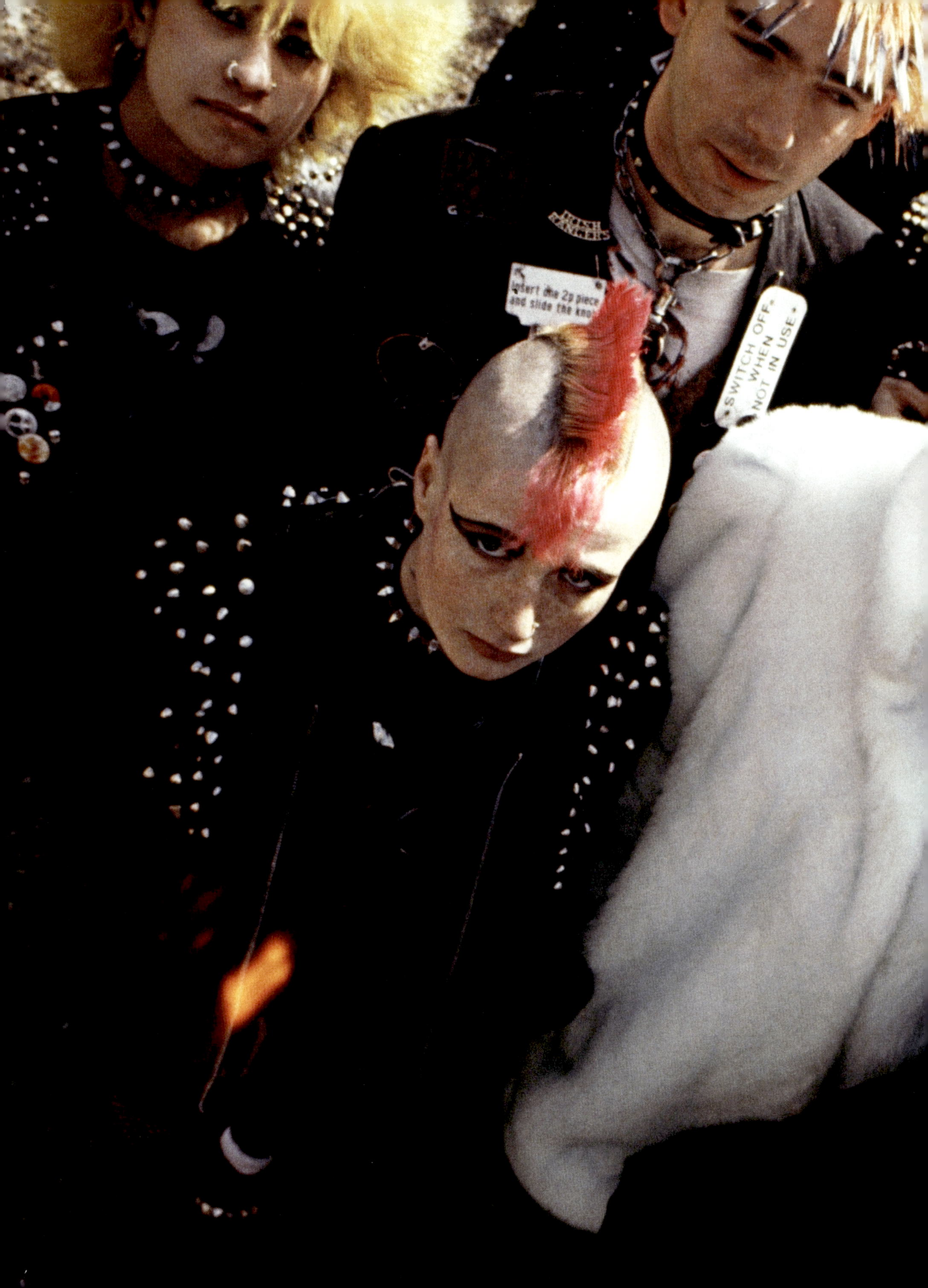

Insert the 2p piece
and slide the knob
* SWITCH OFF *
WHEN IN USE *
* NOT IN USE *

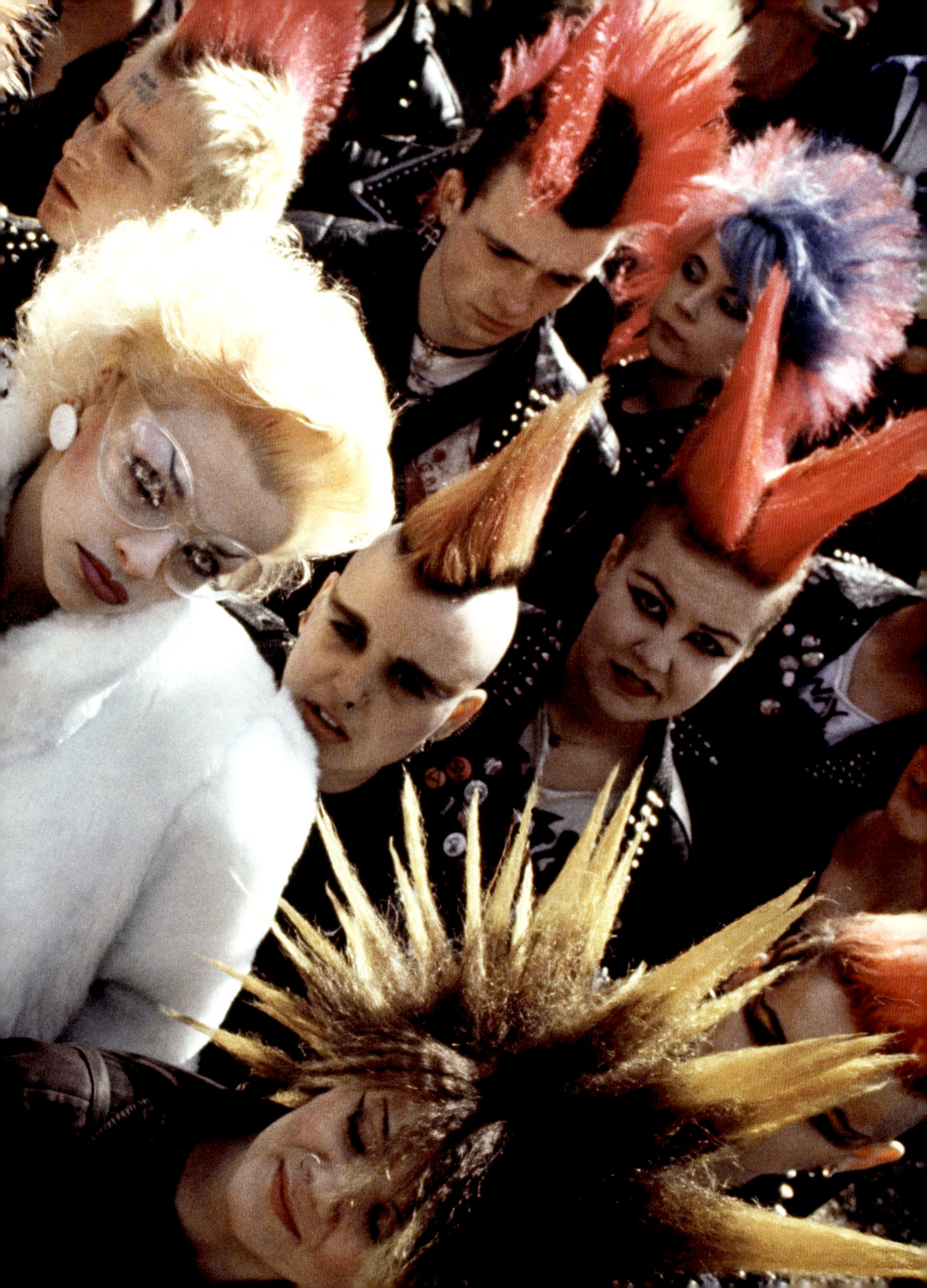

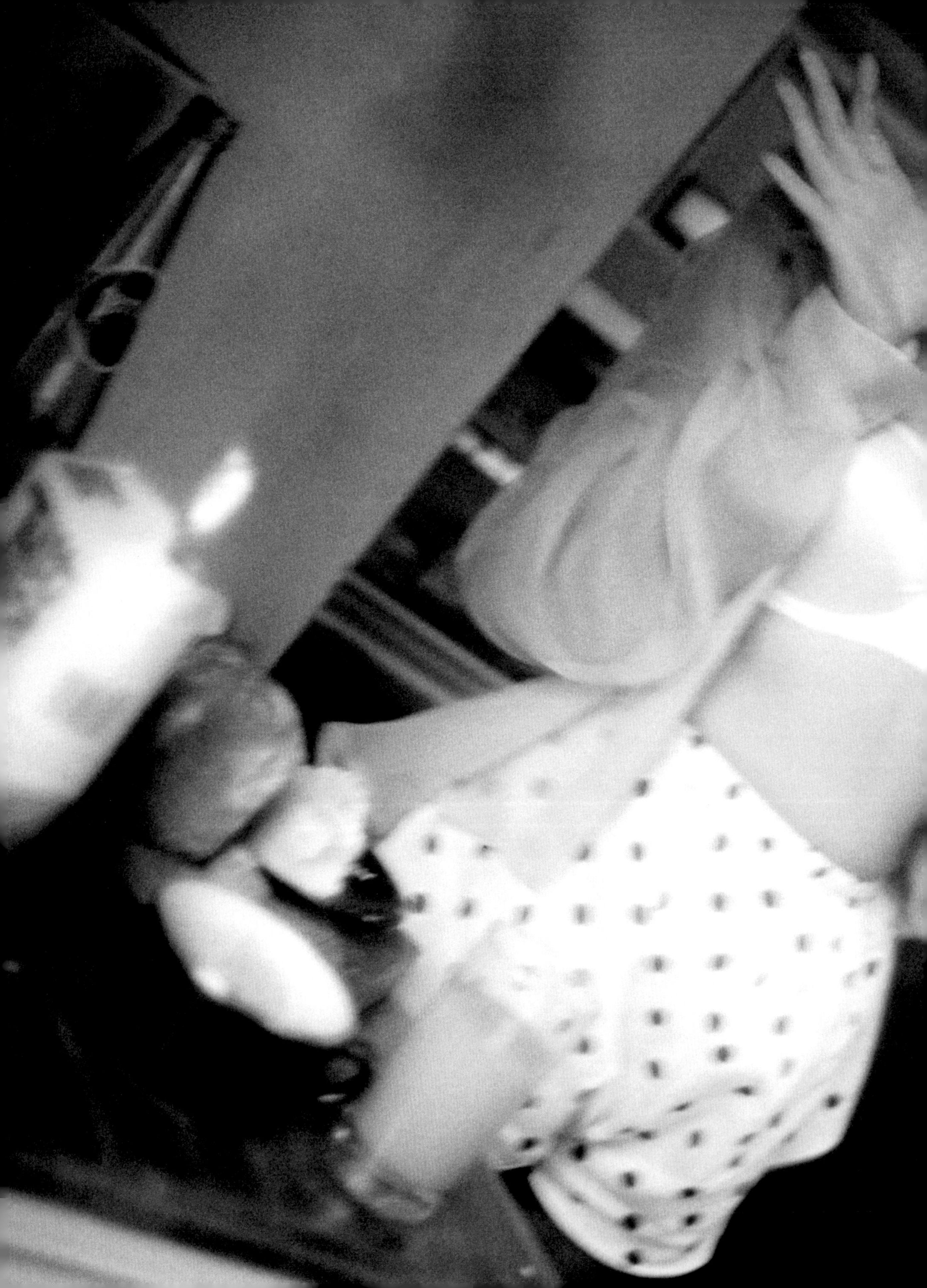

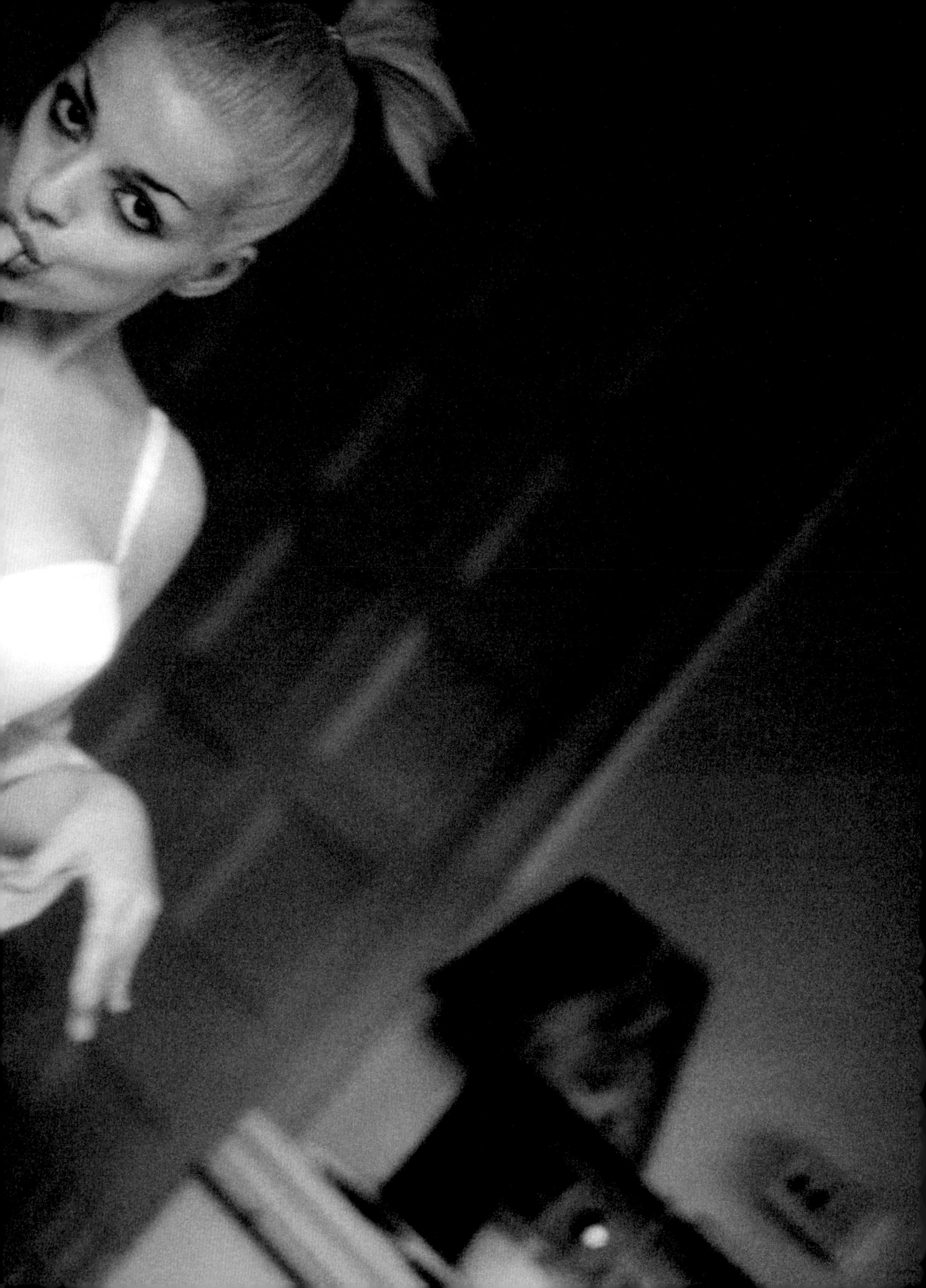

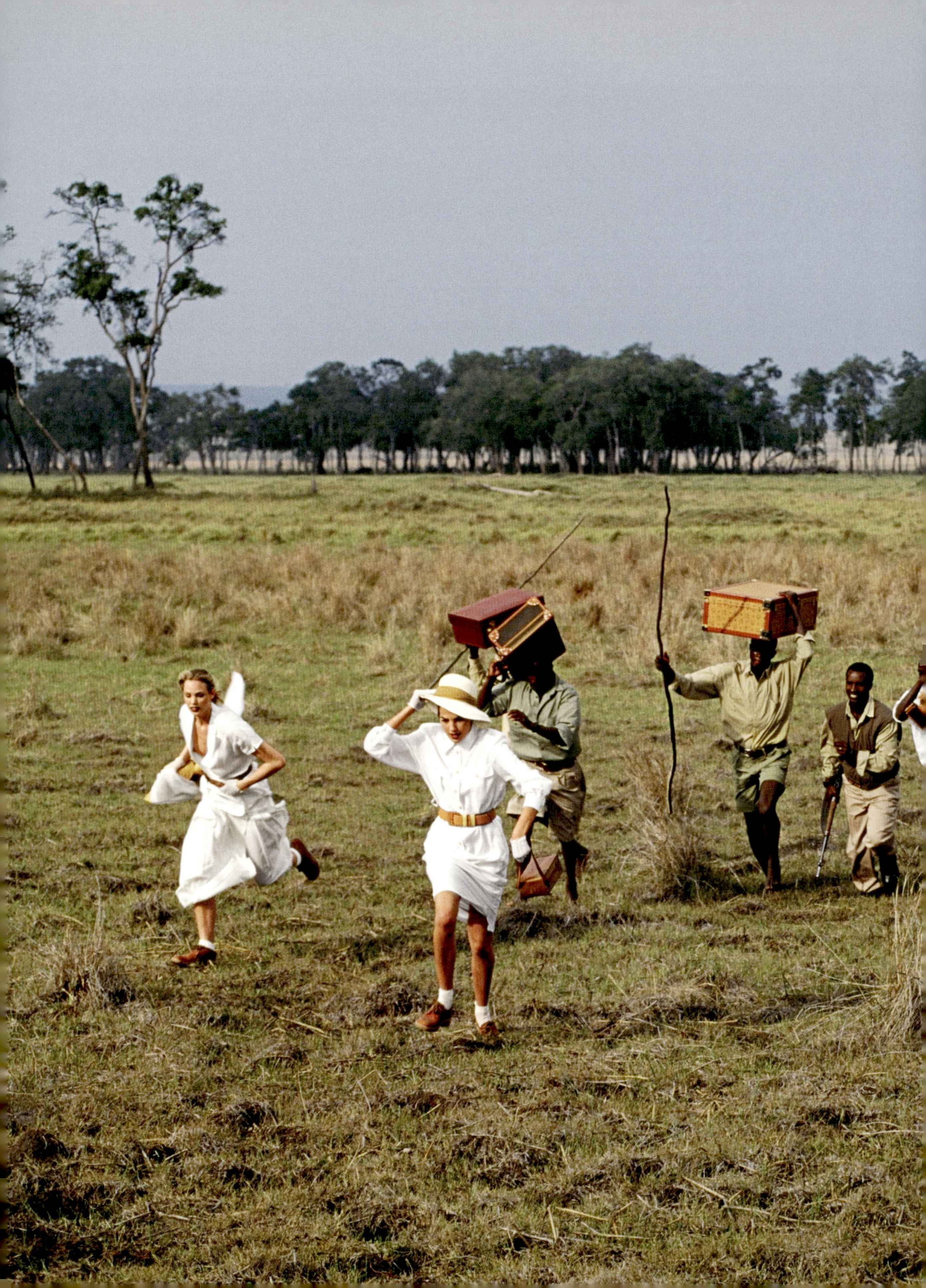

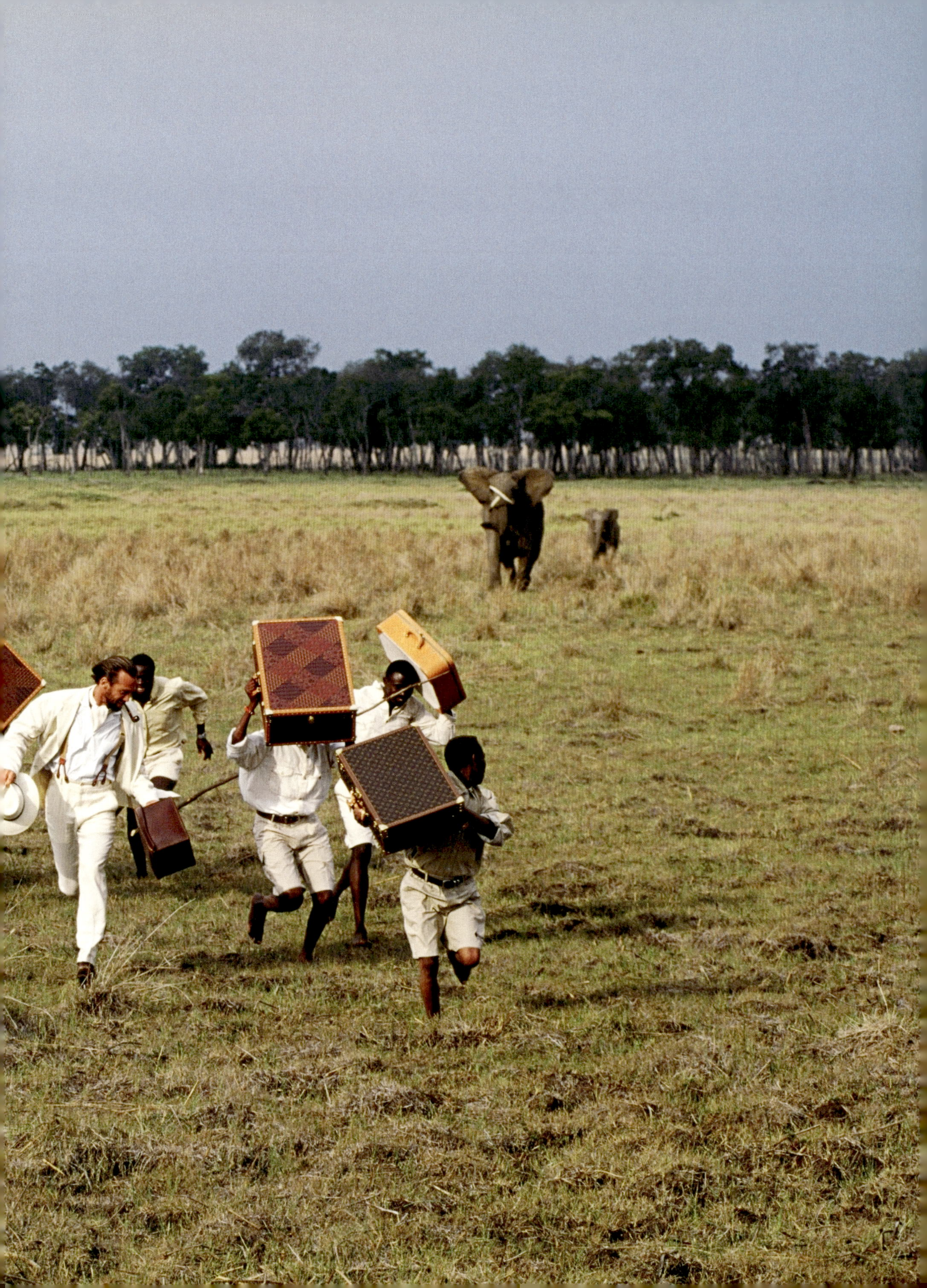

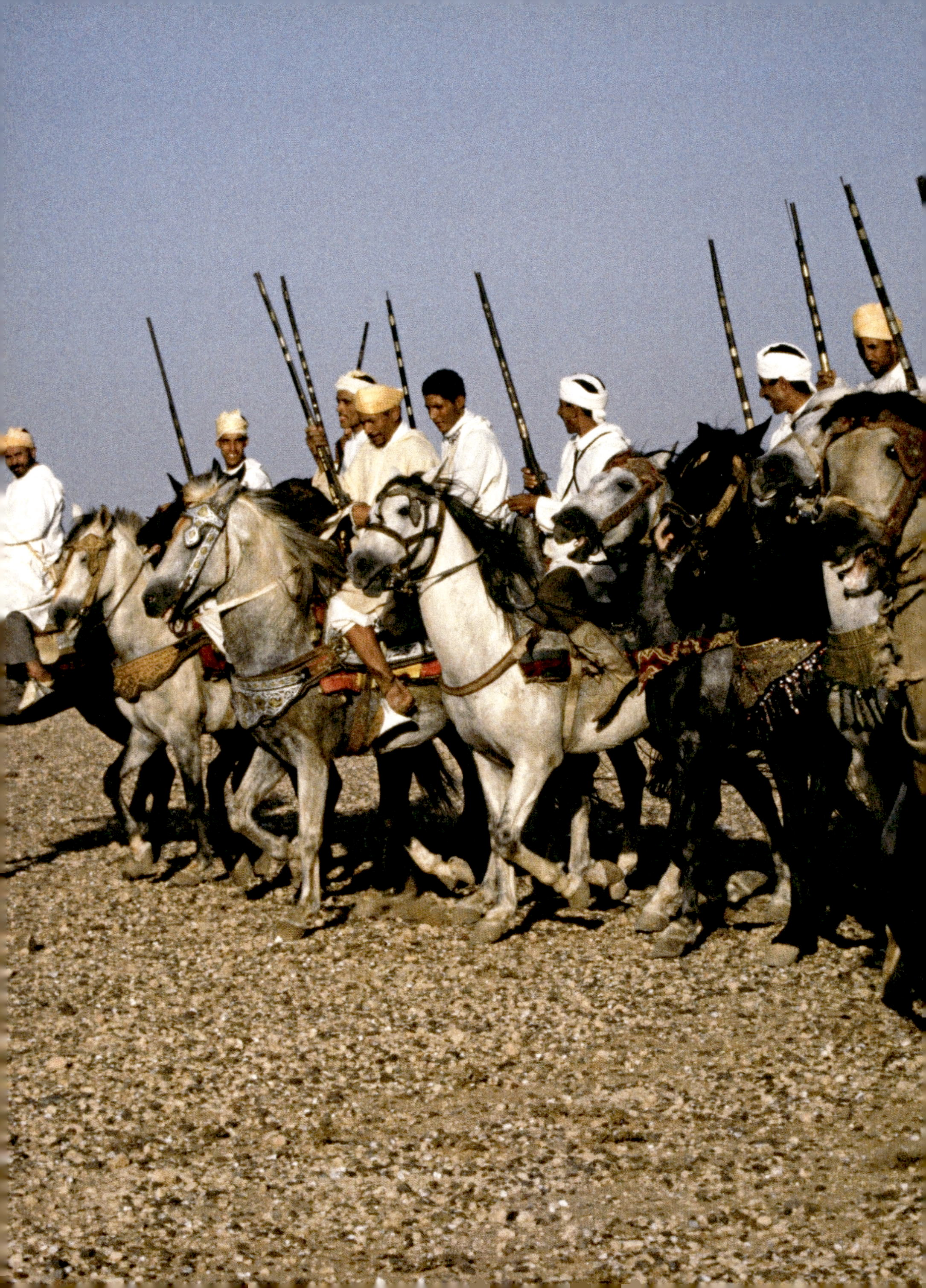

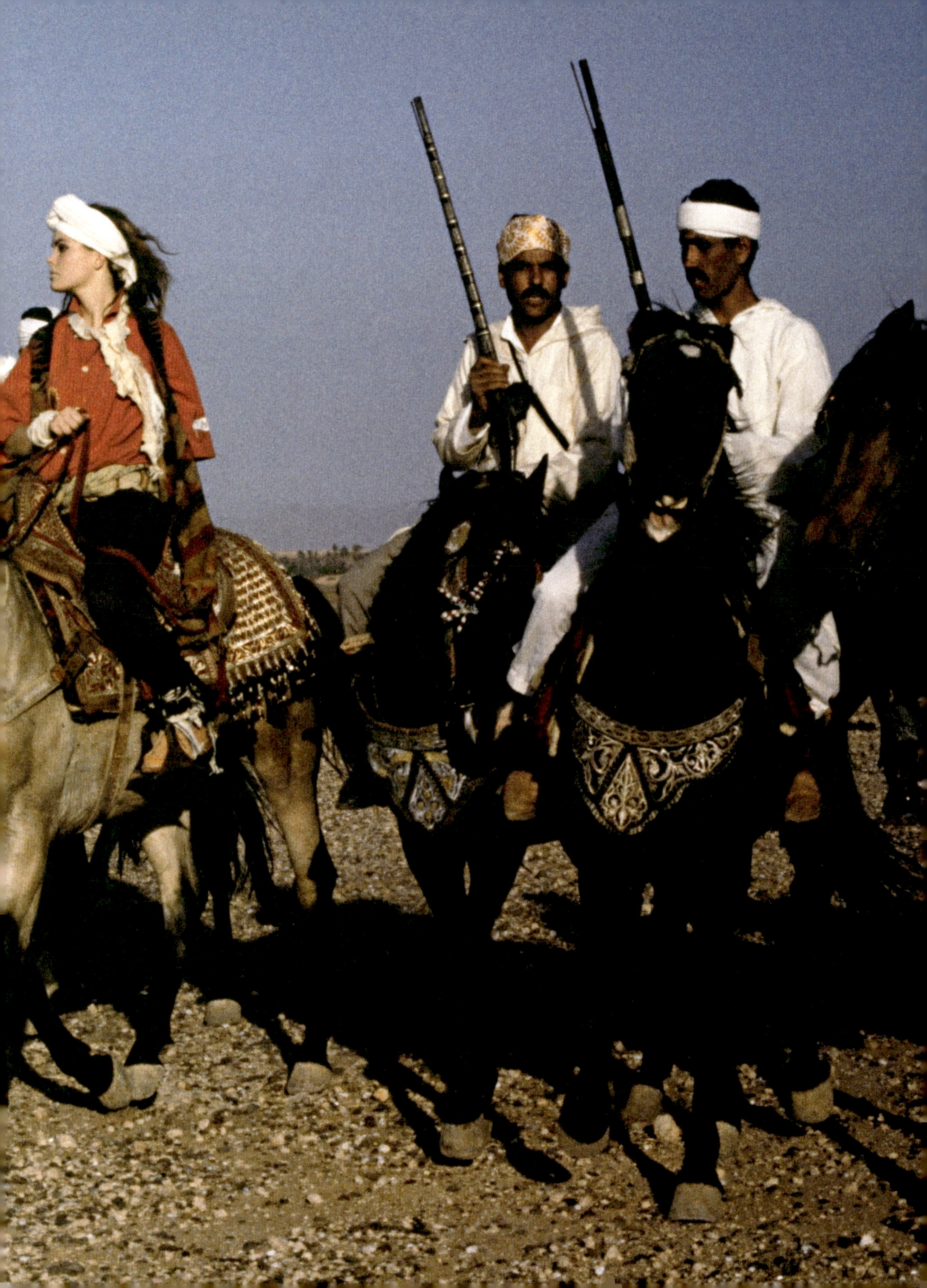

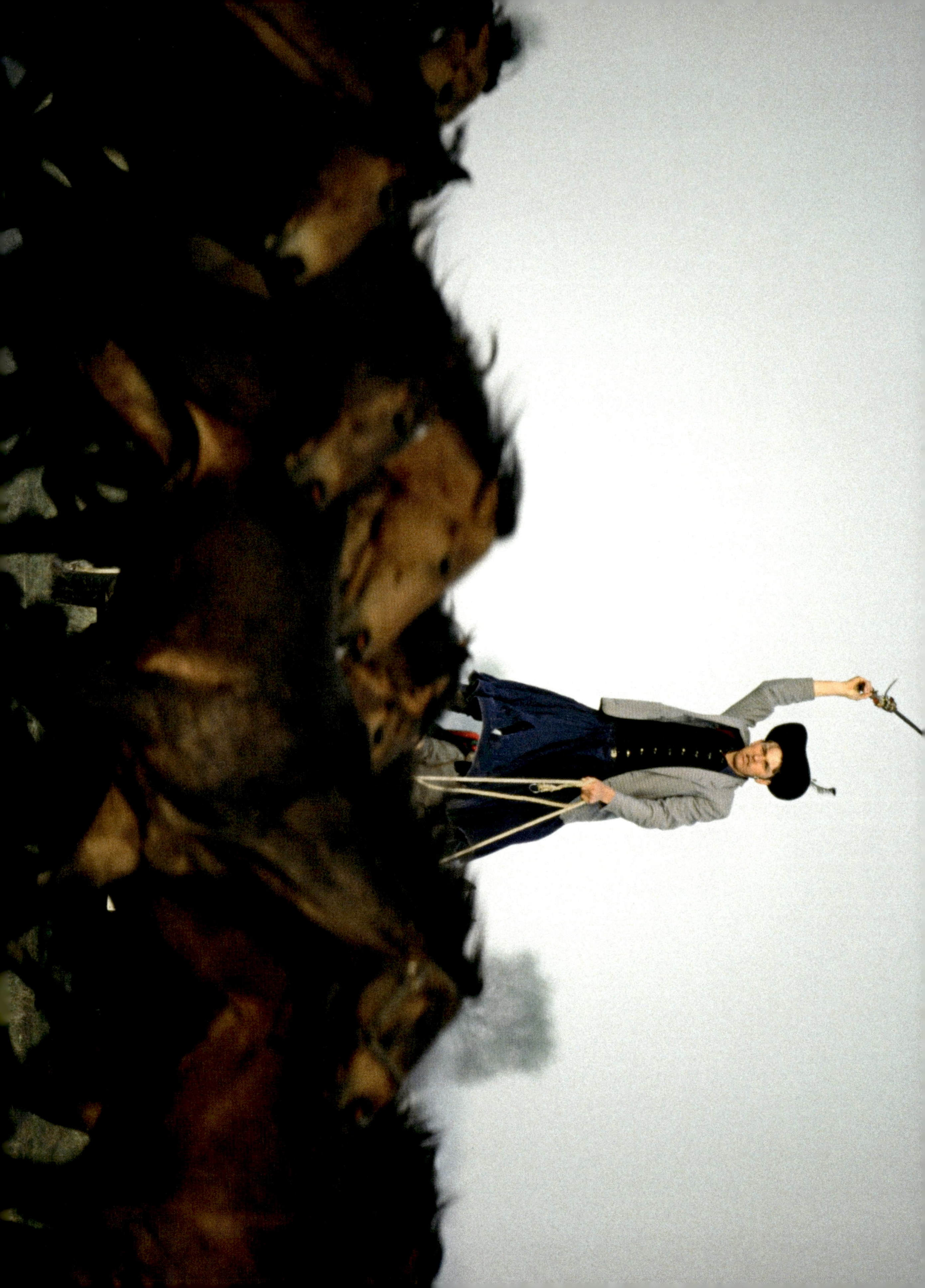

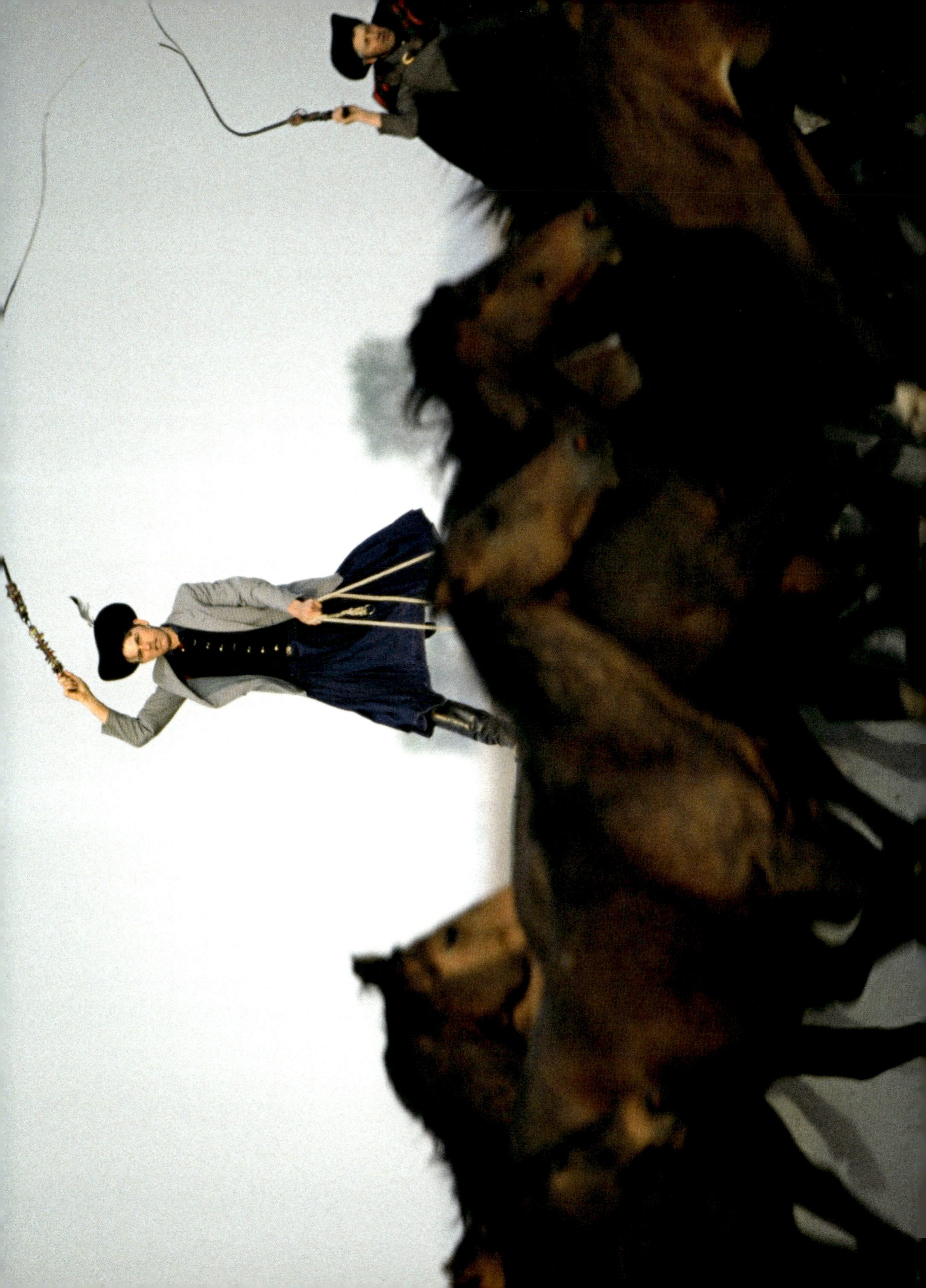

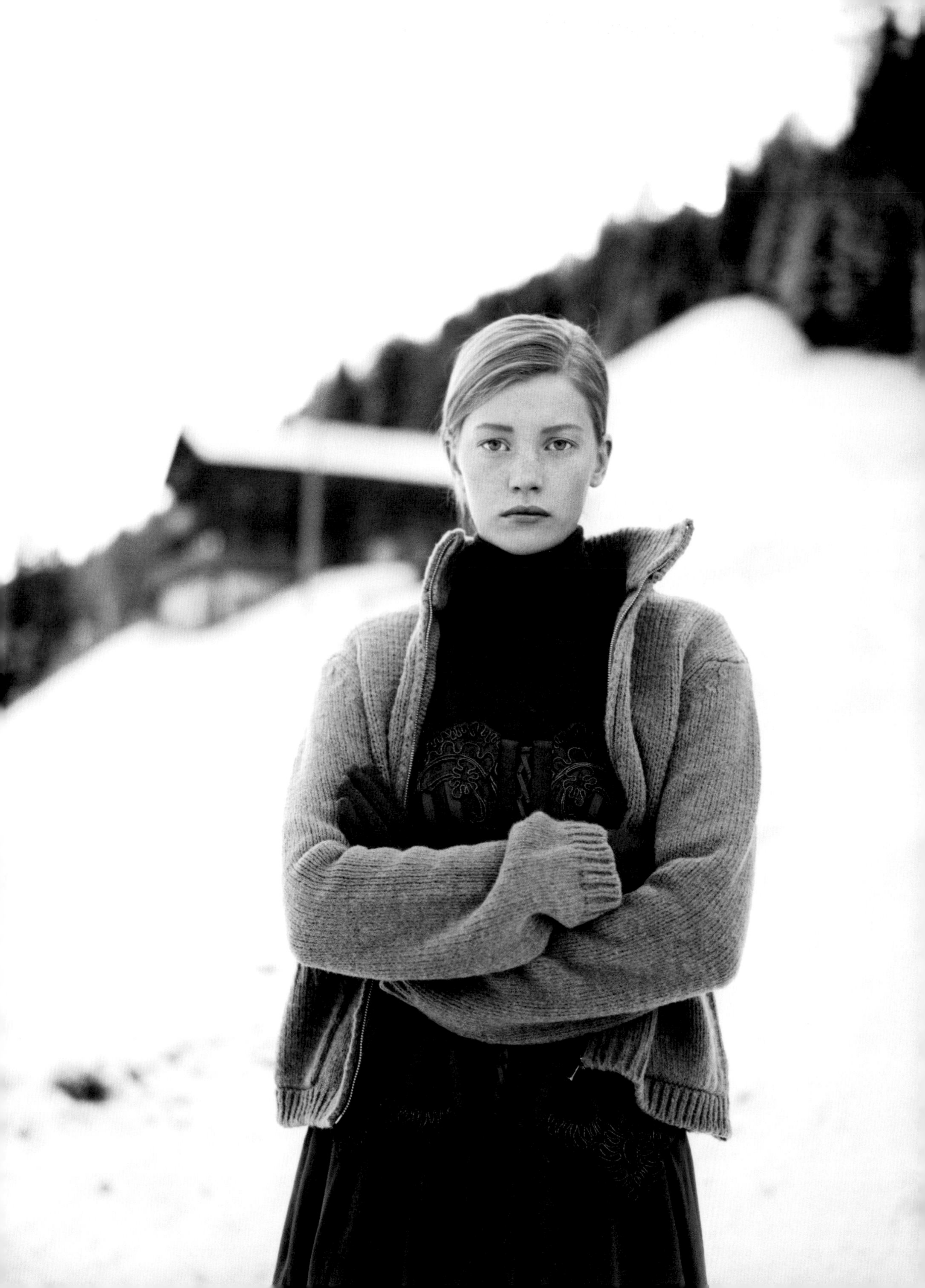

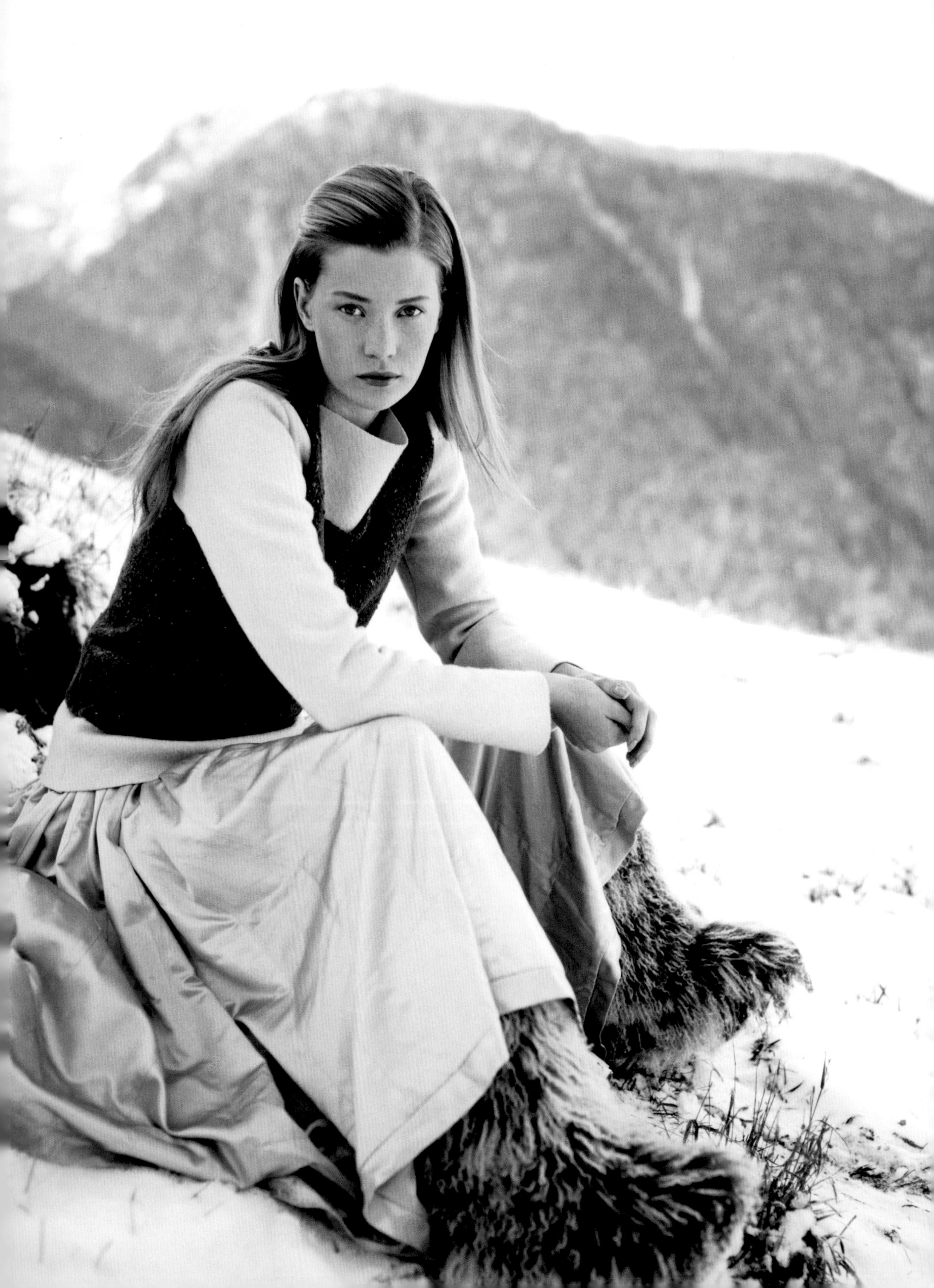

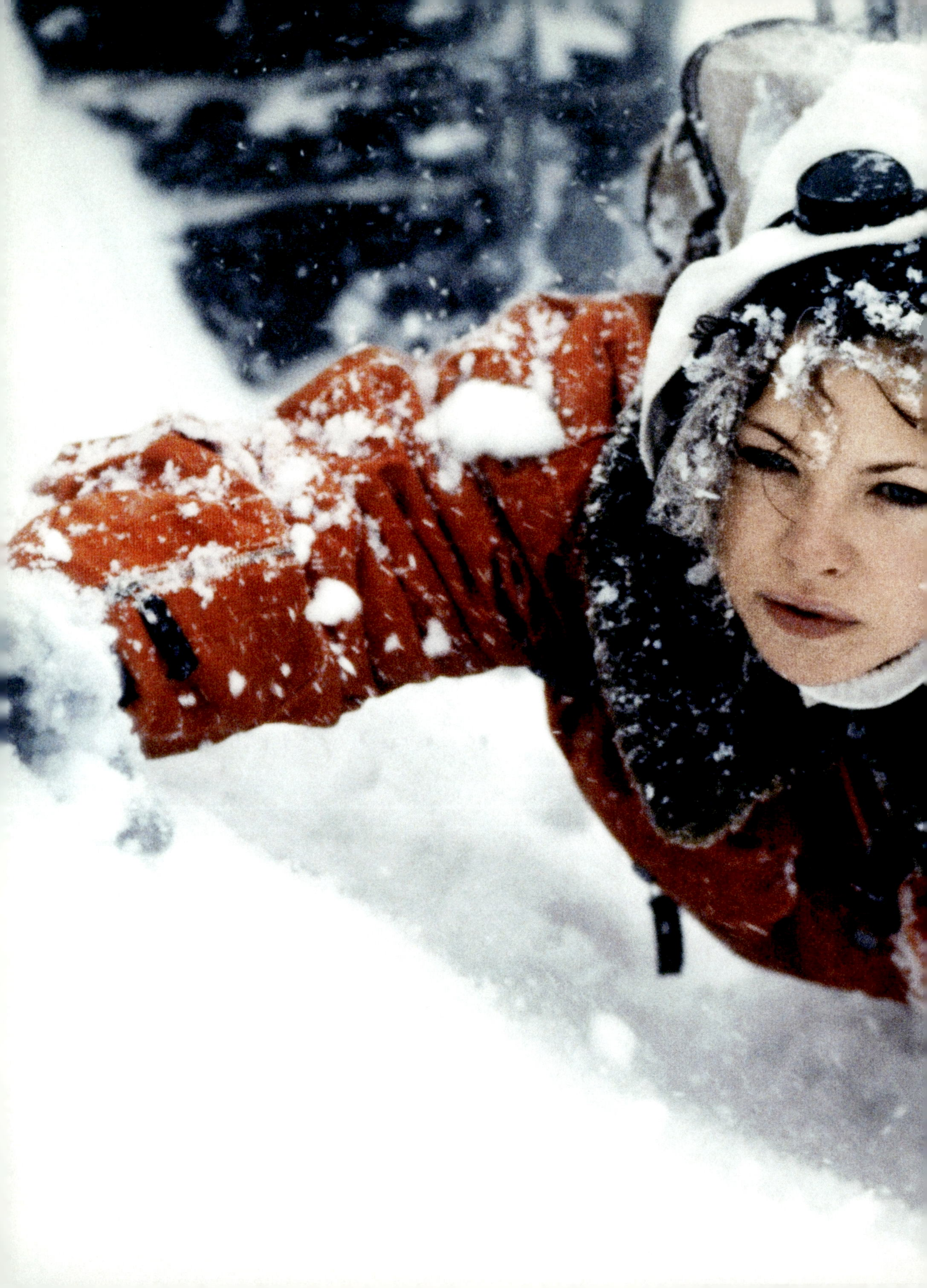

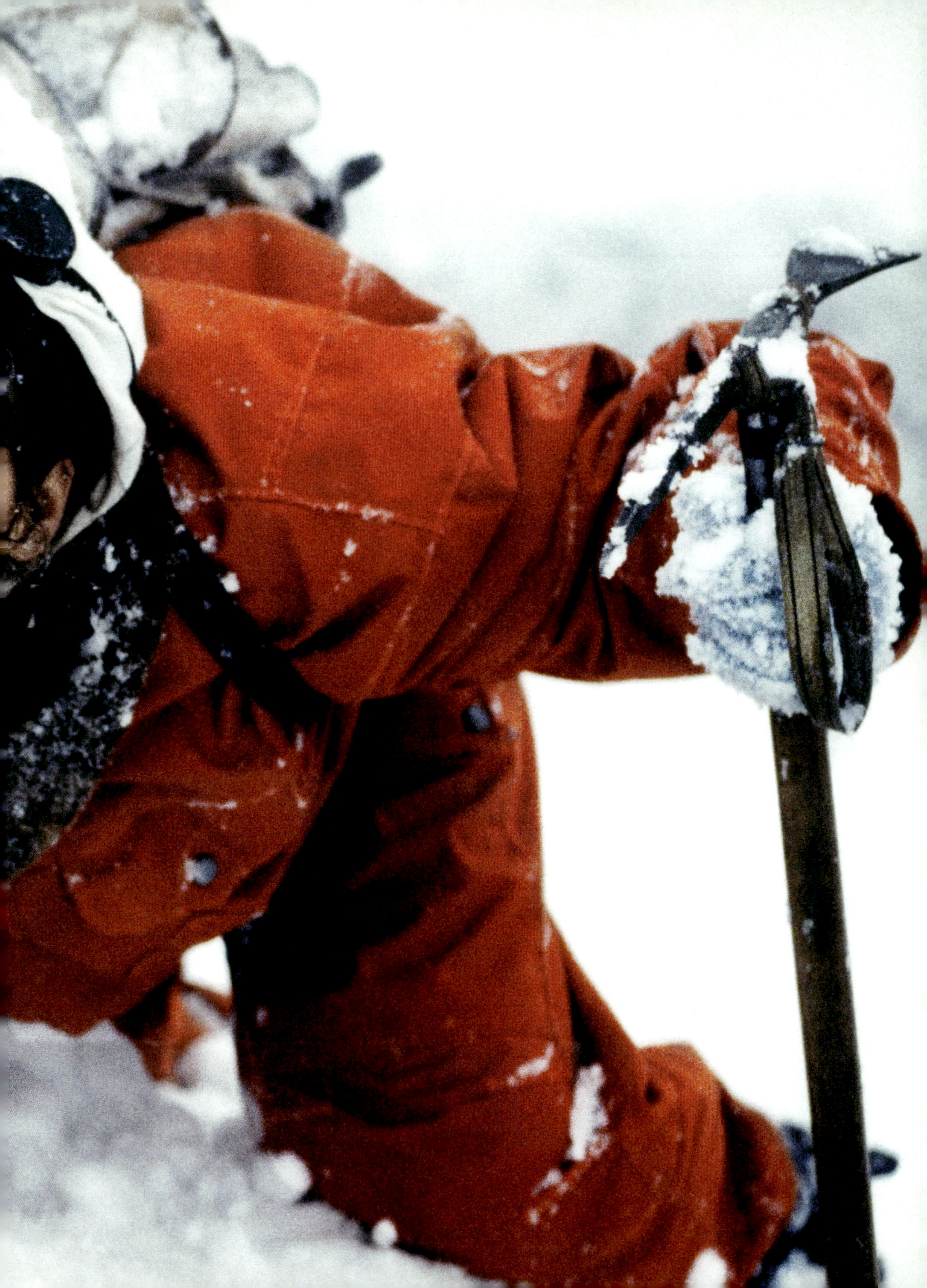

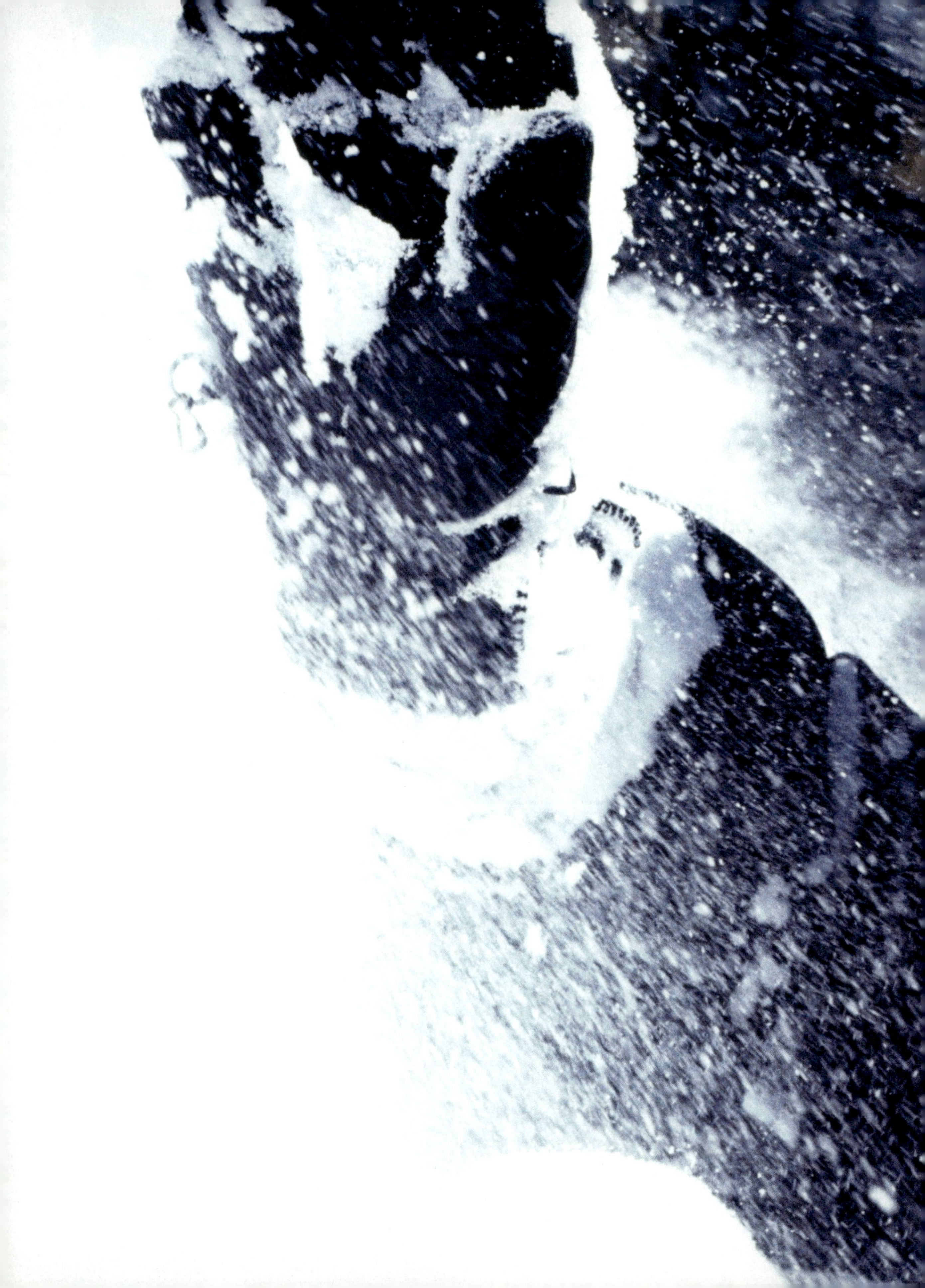

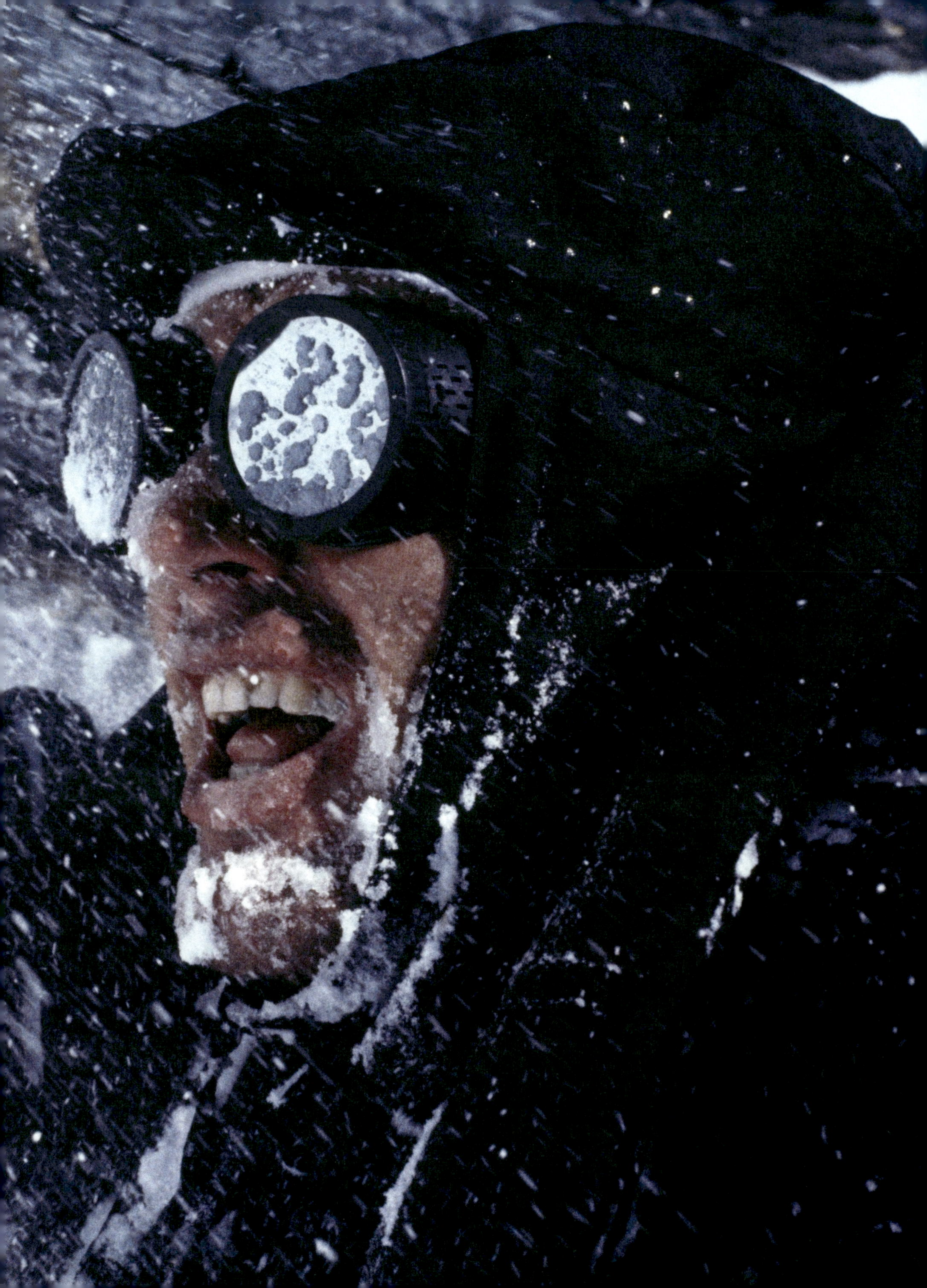

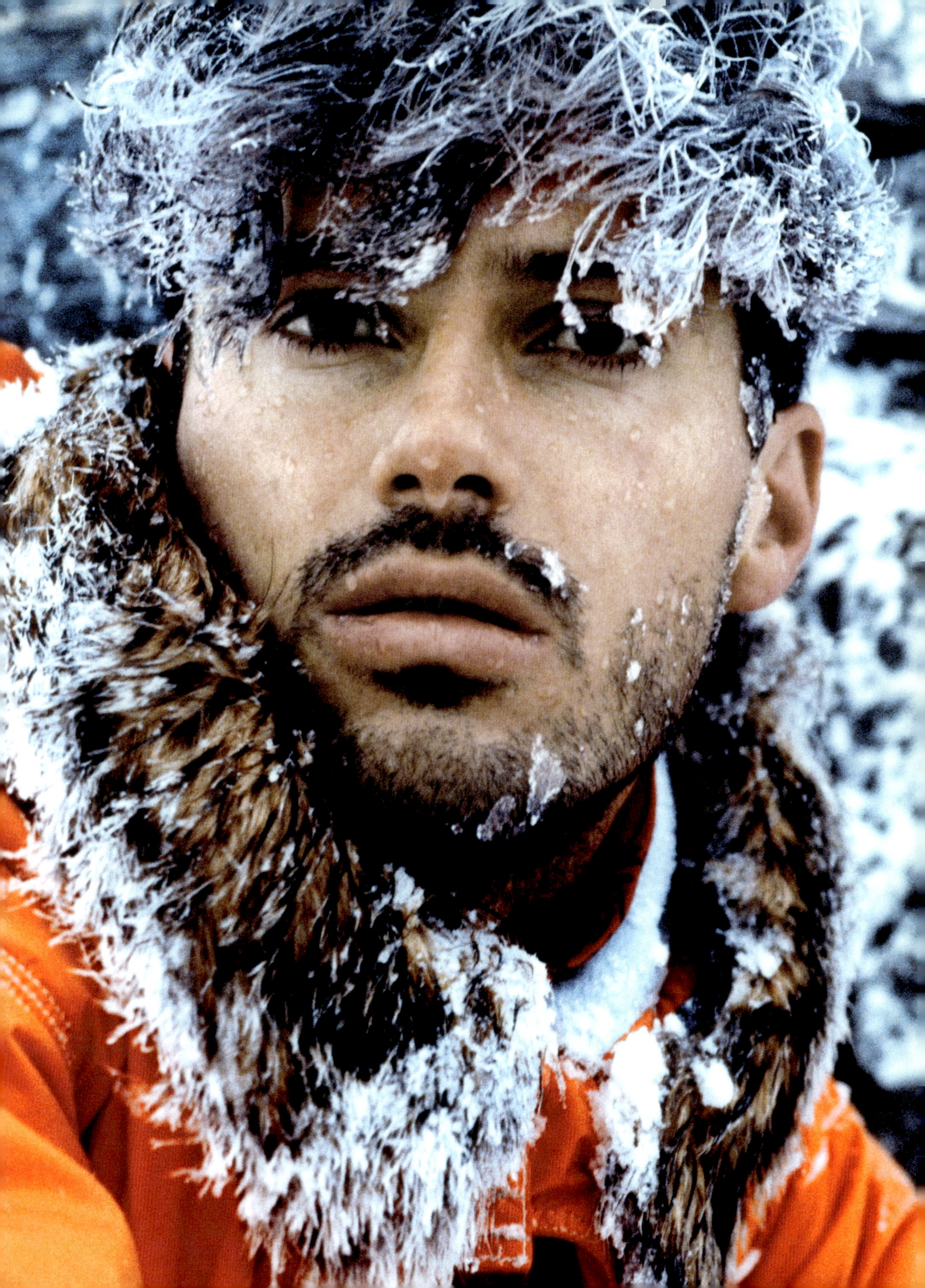

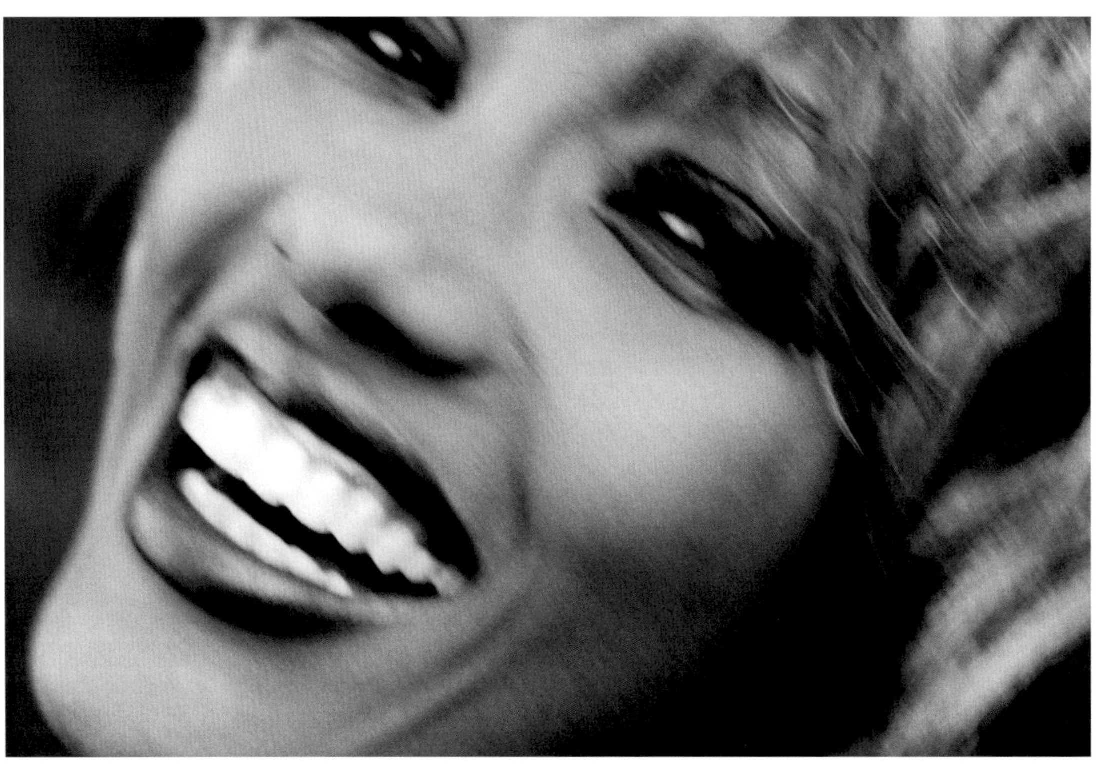

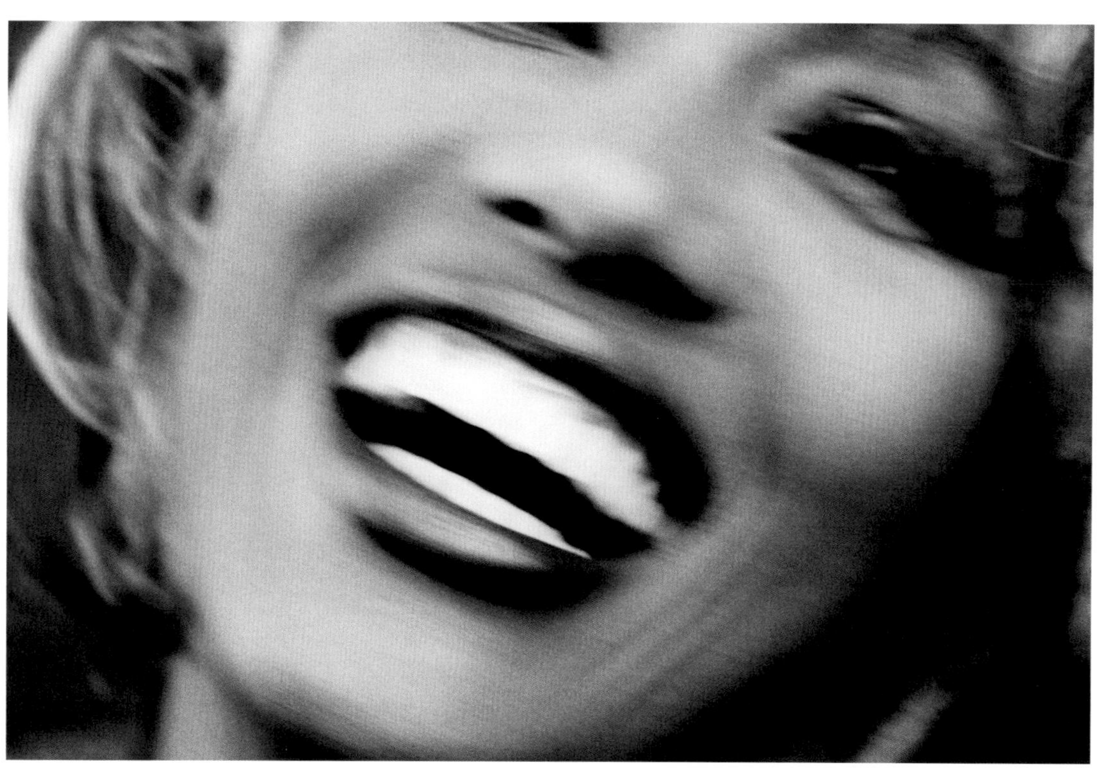

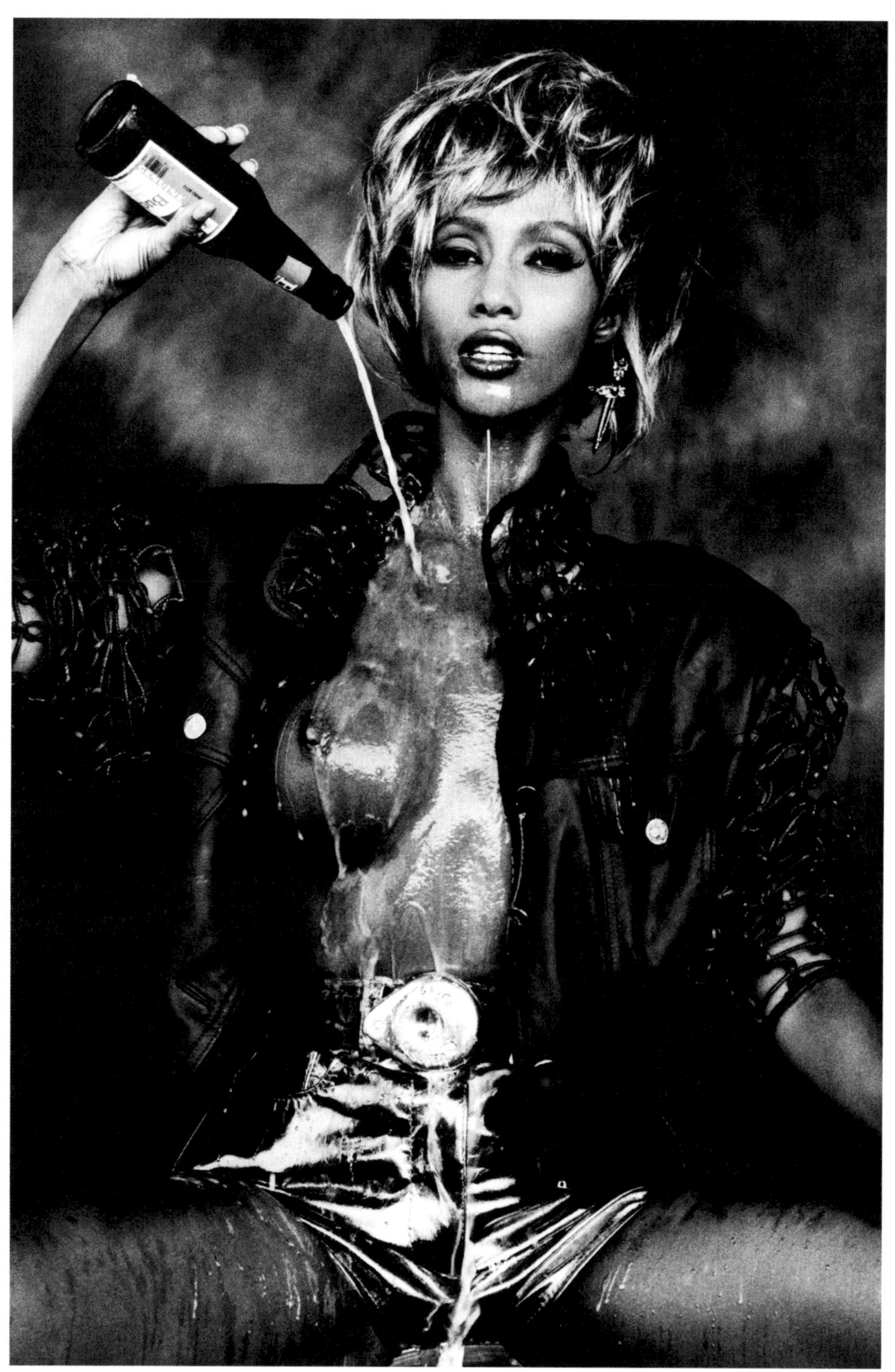

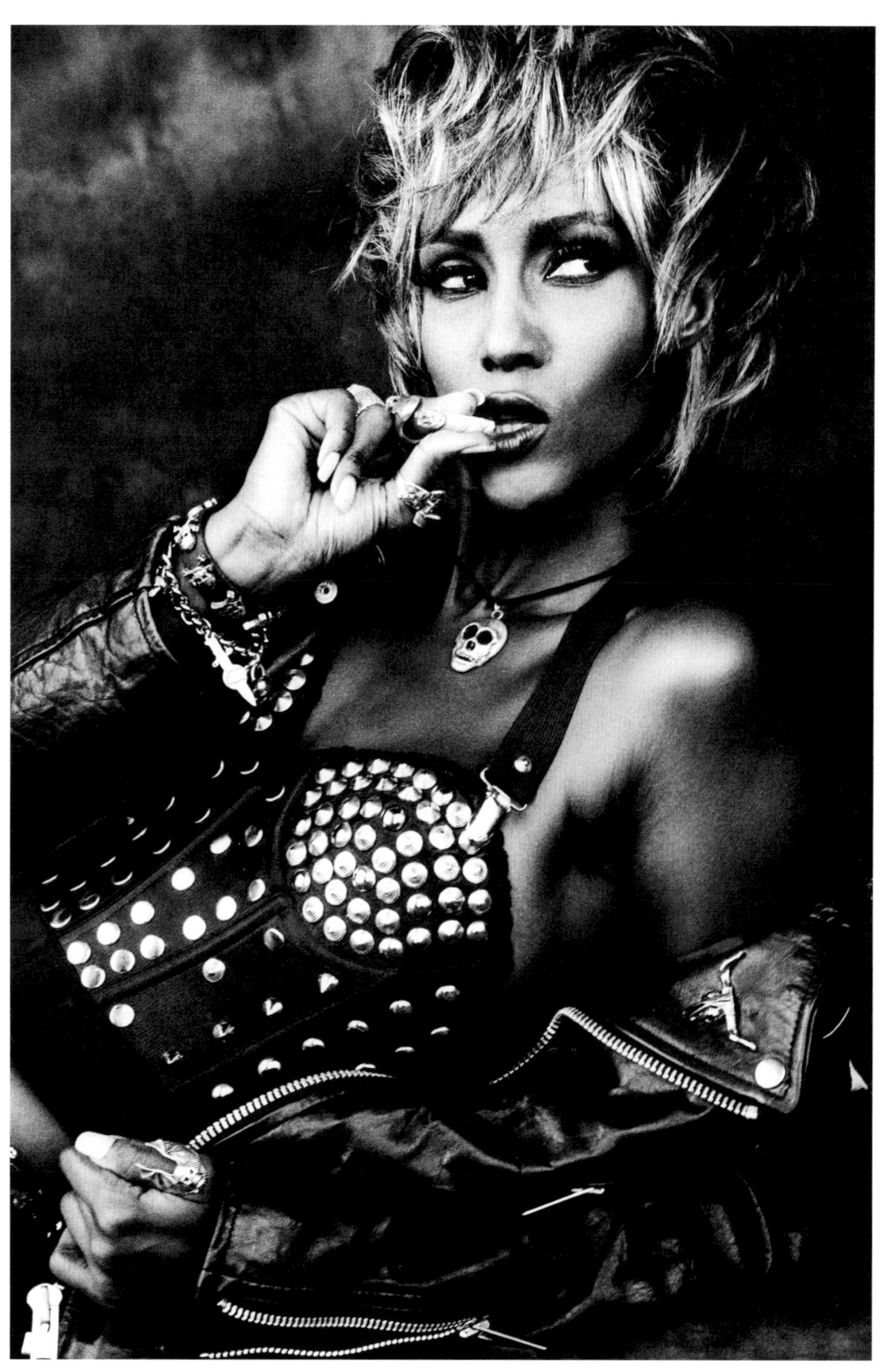

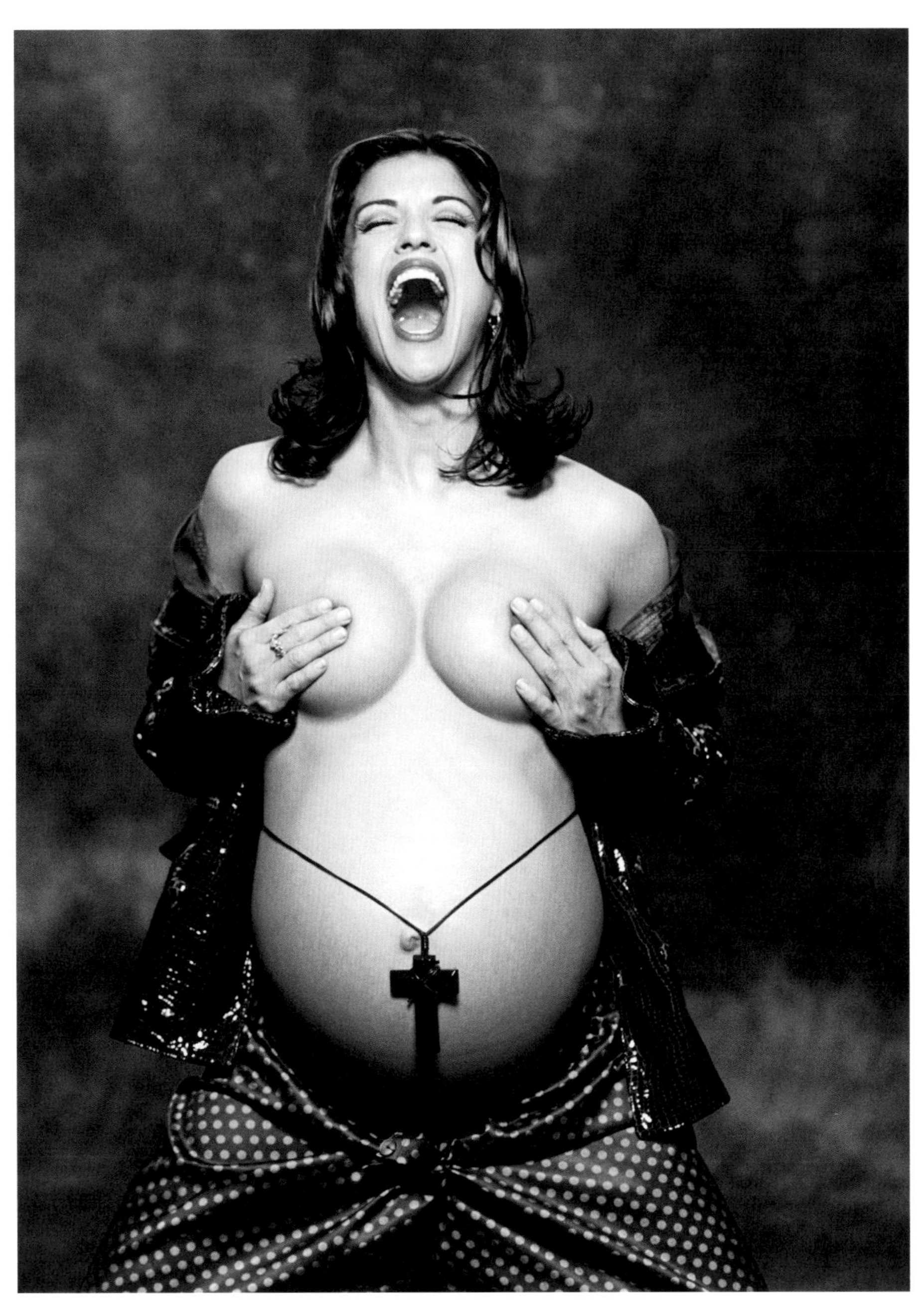

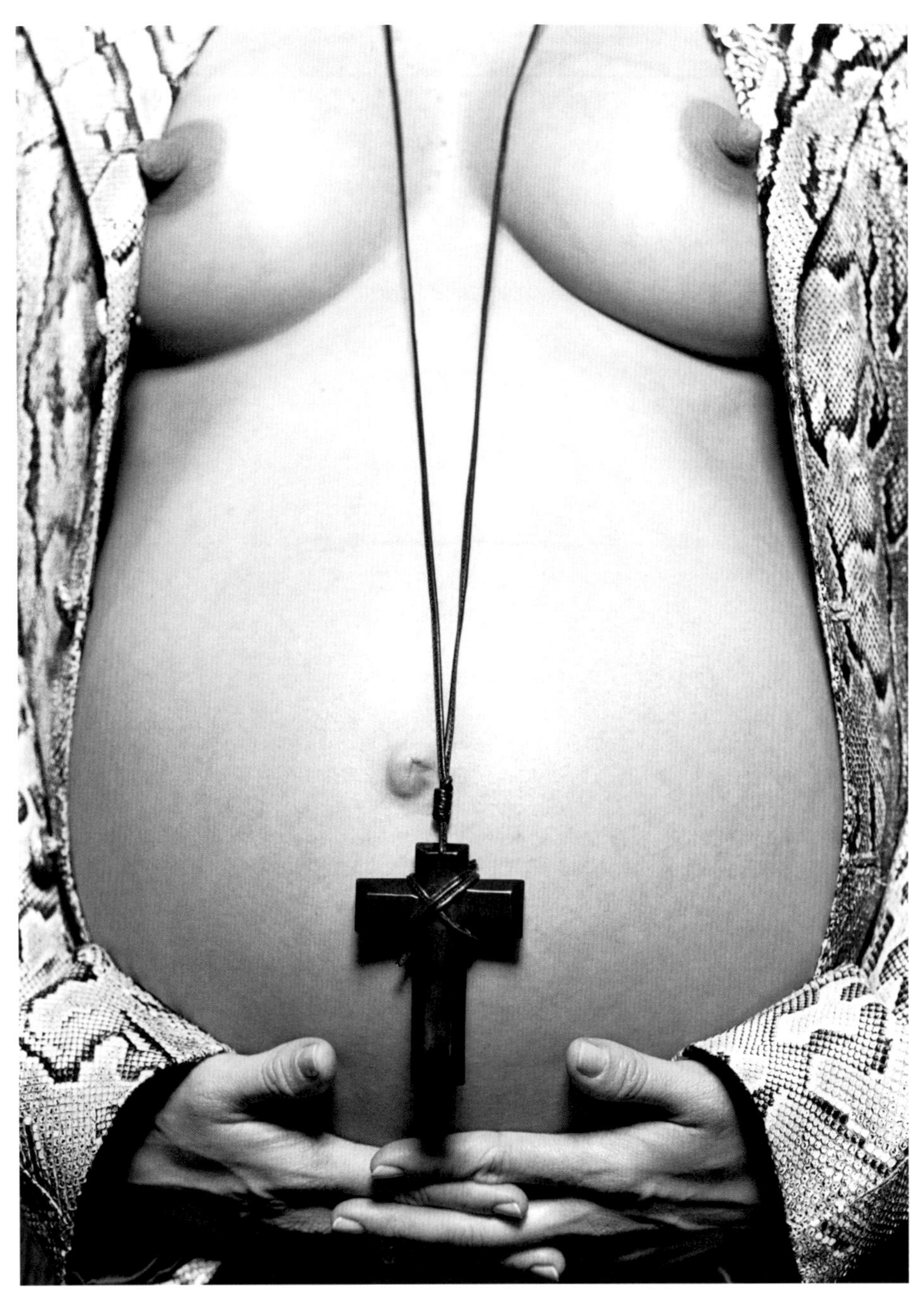

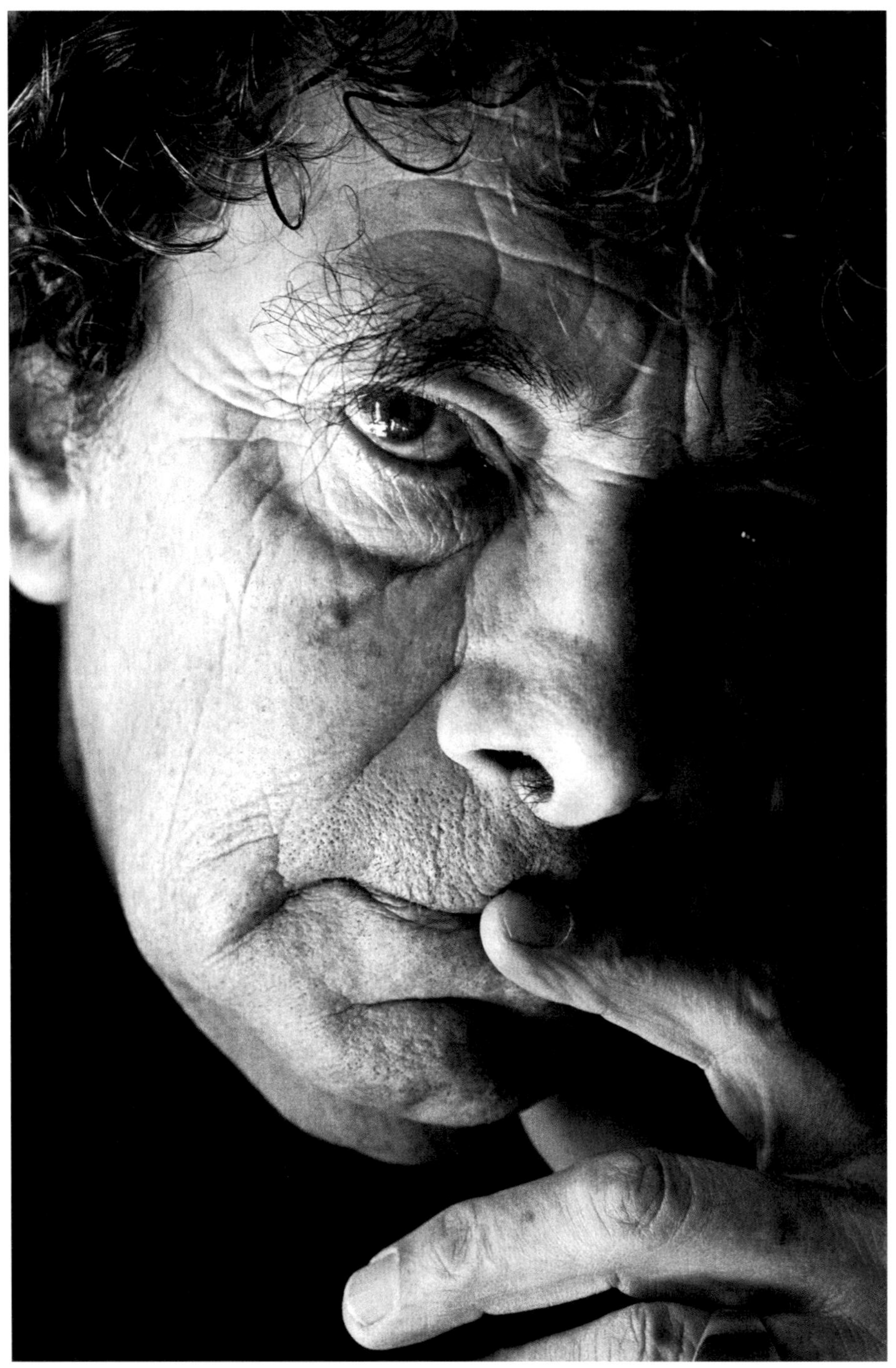

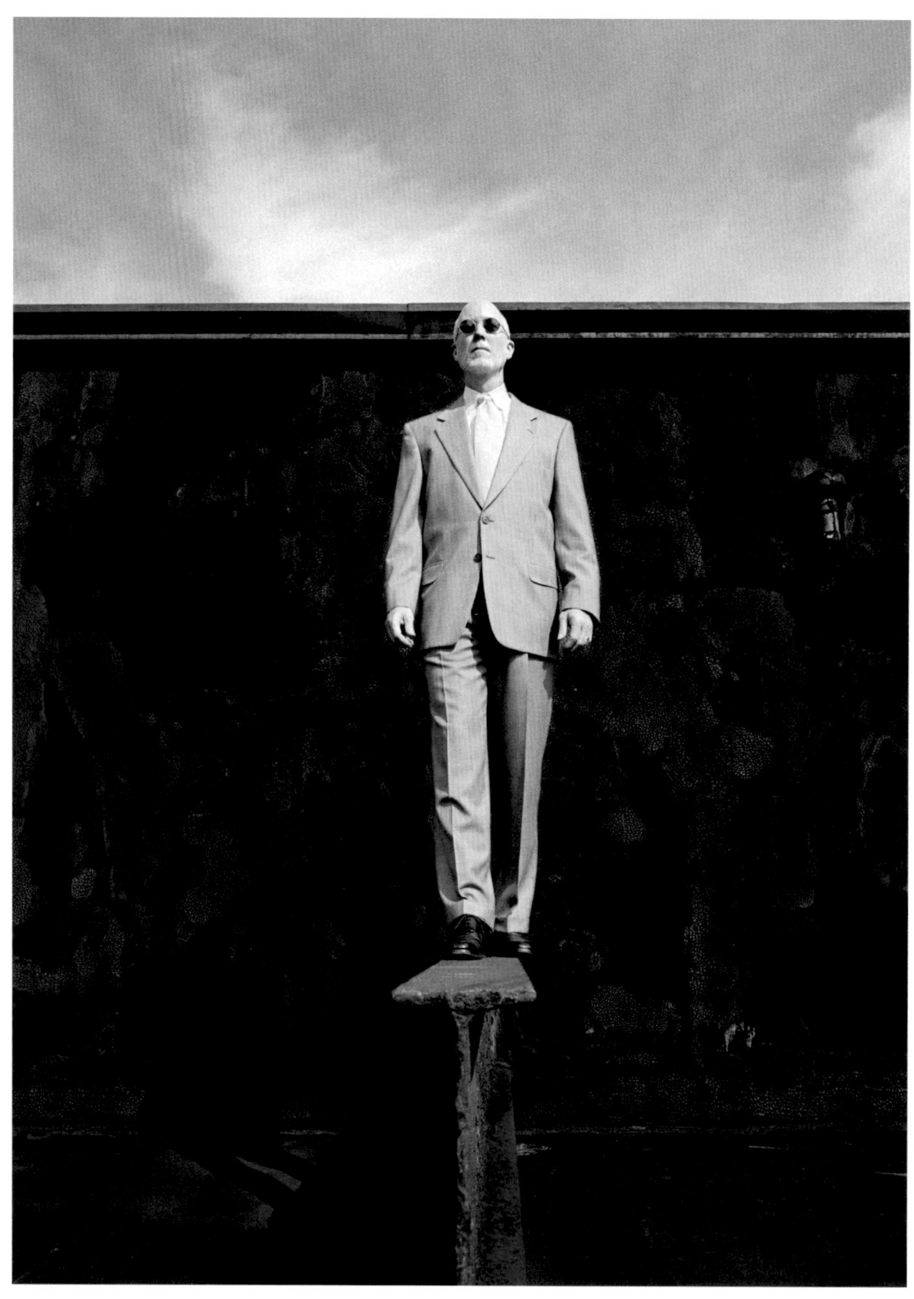

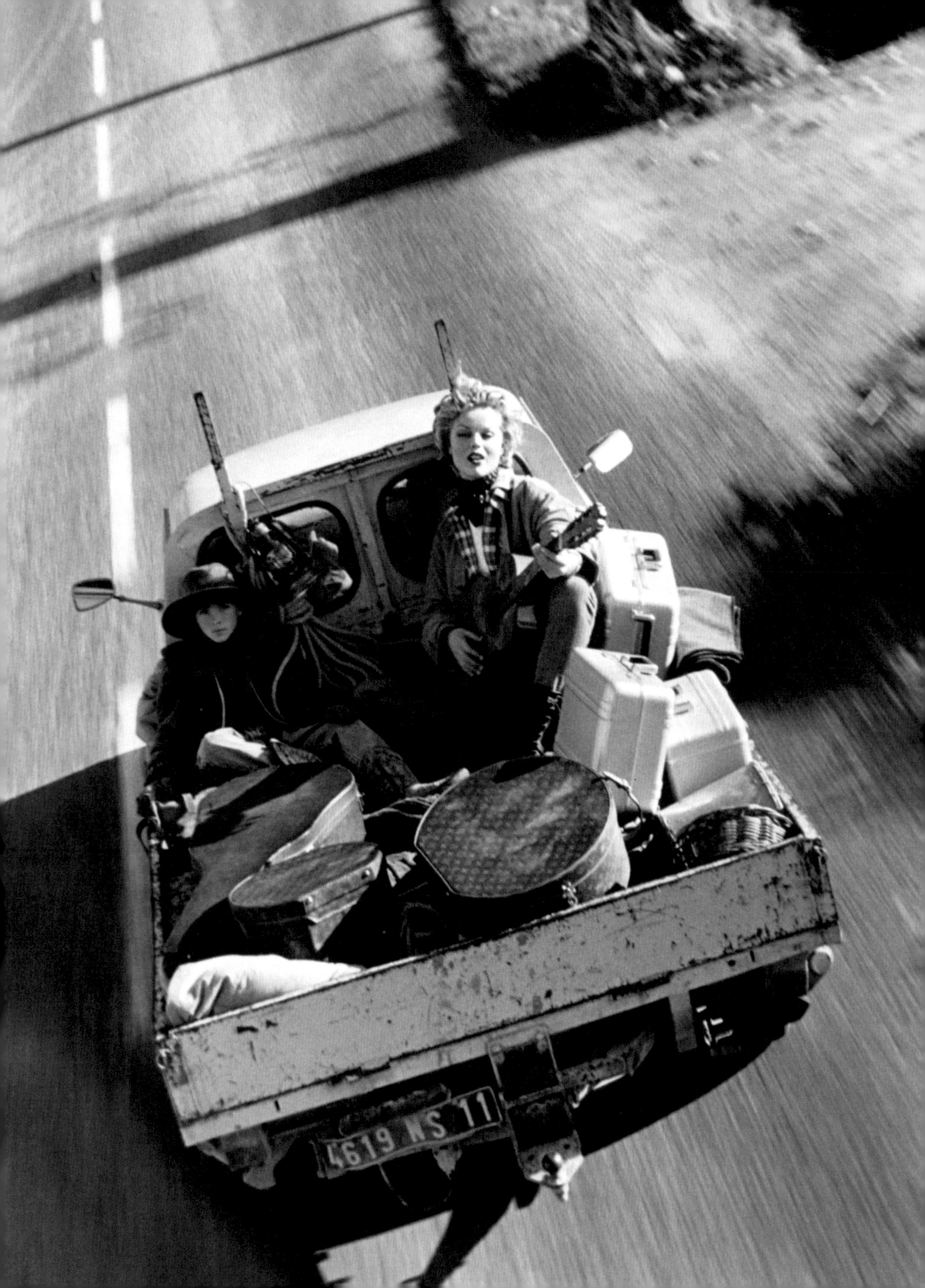

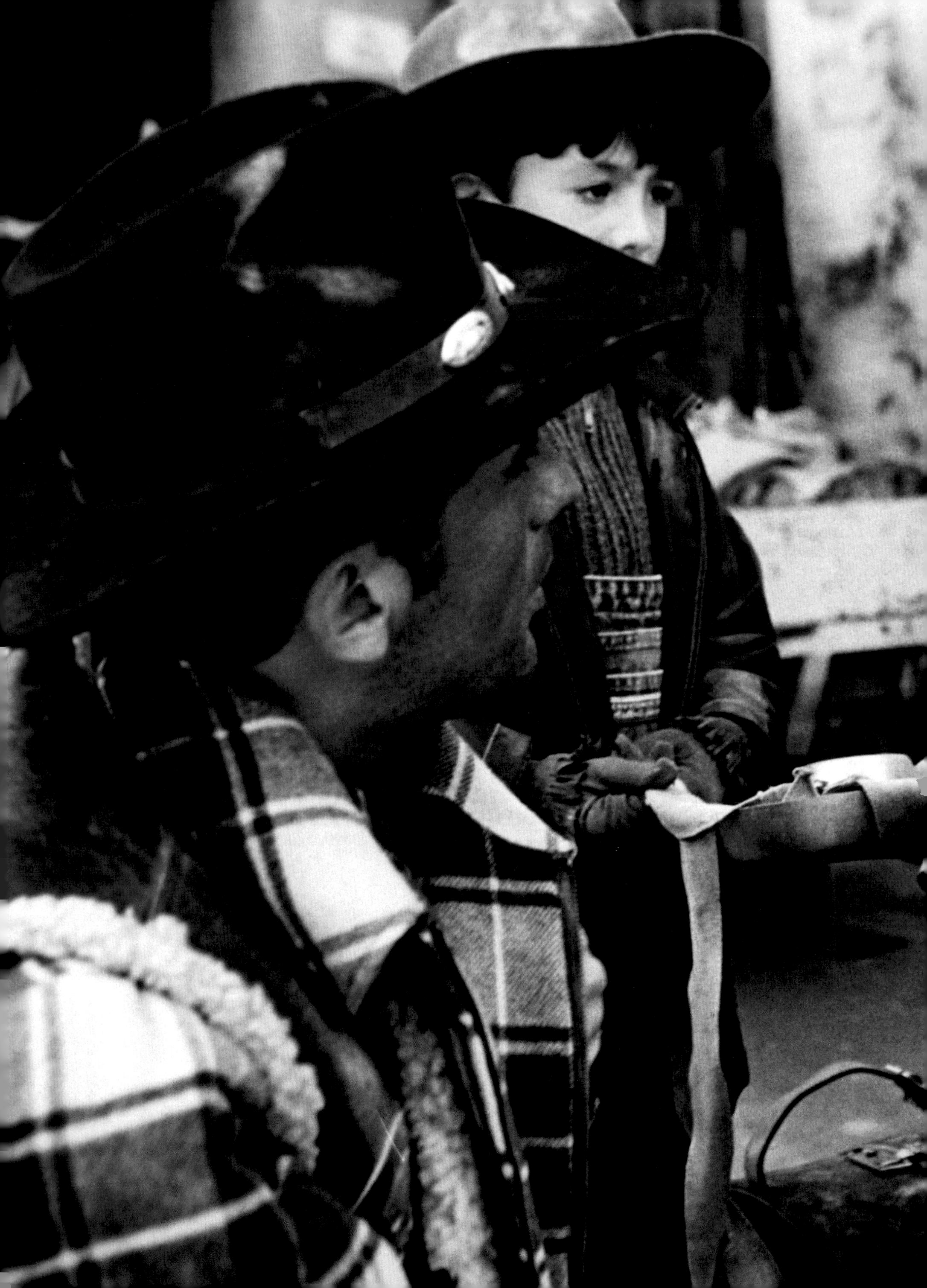

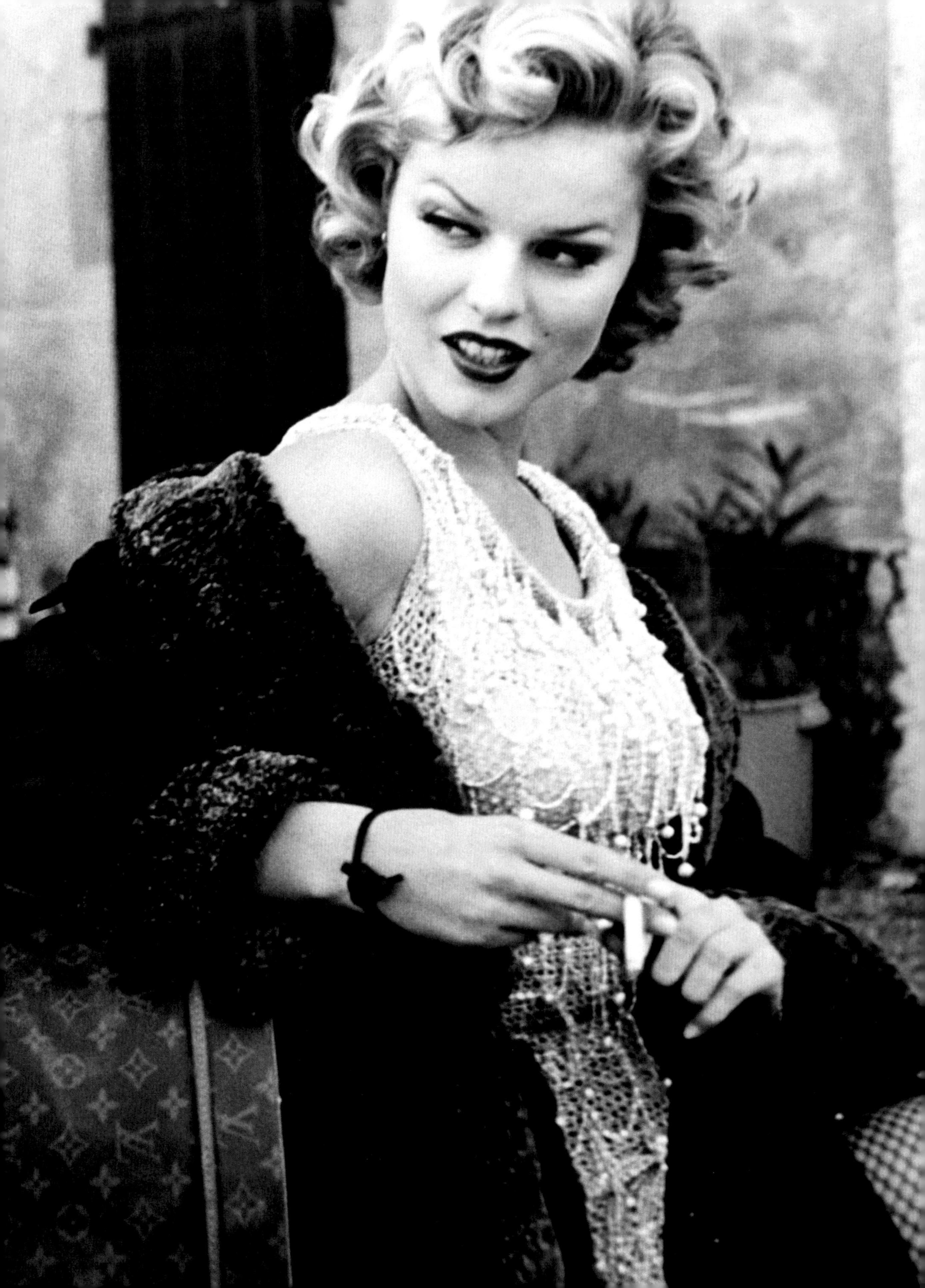

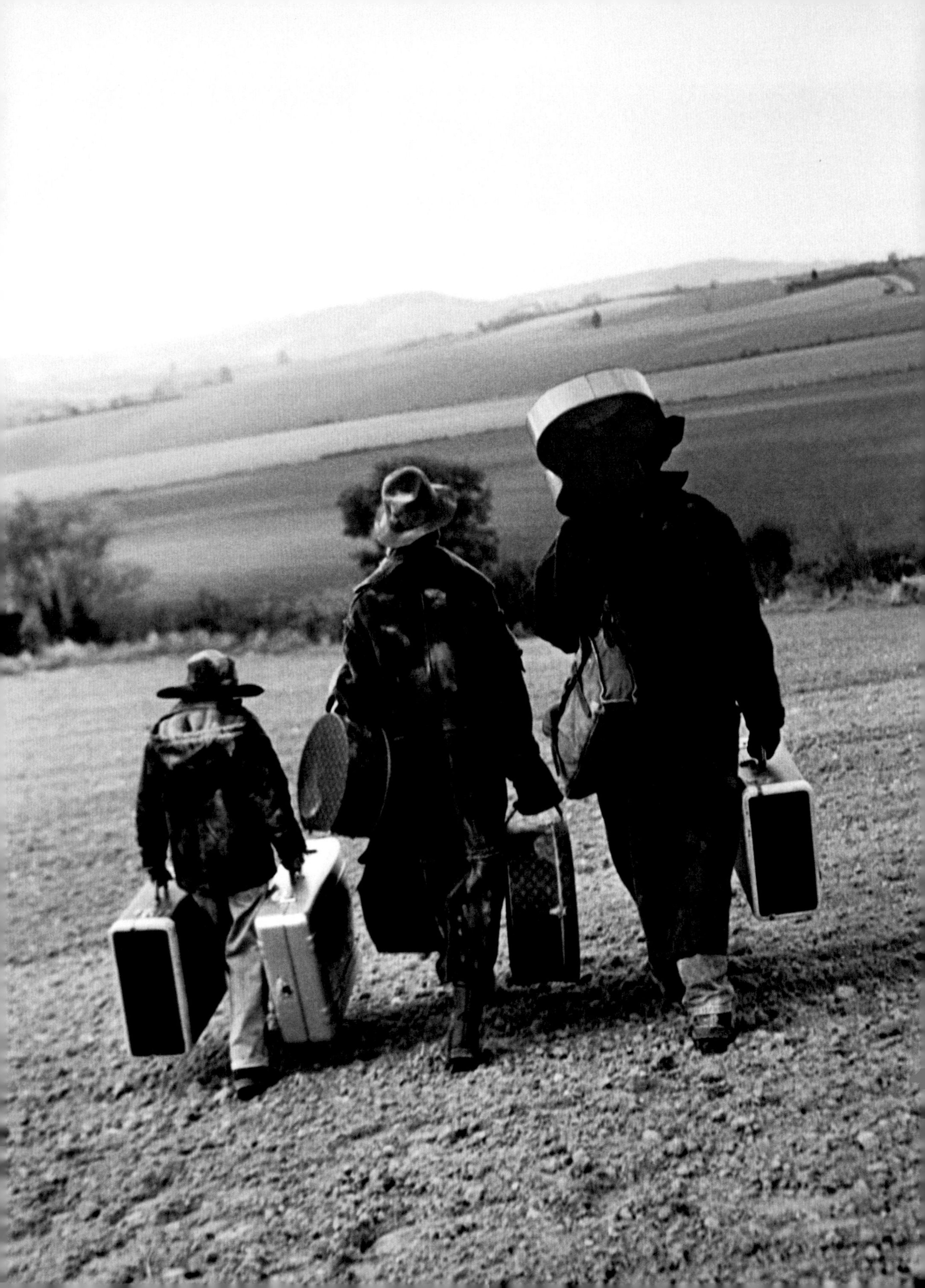

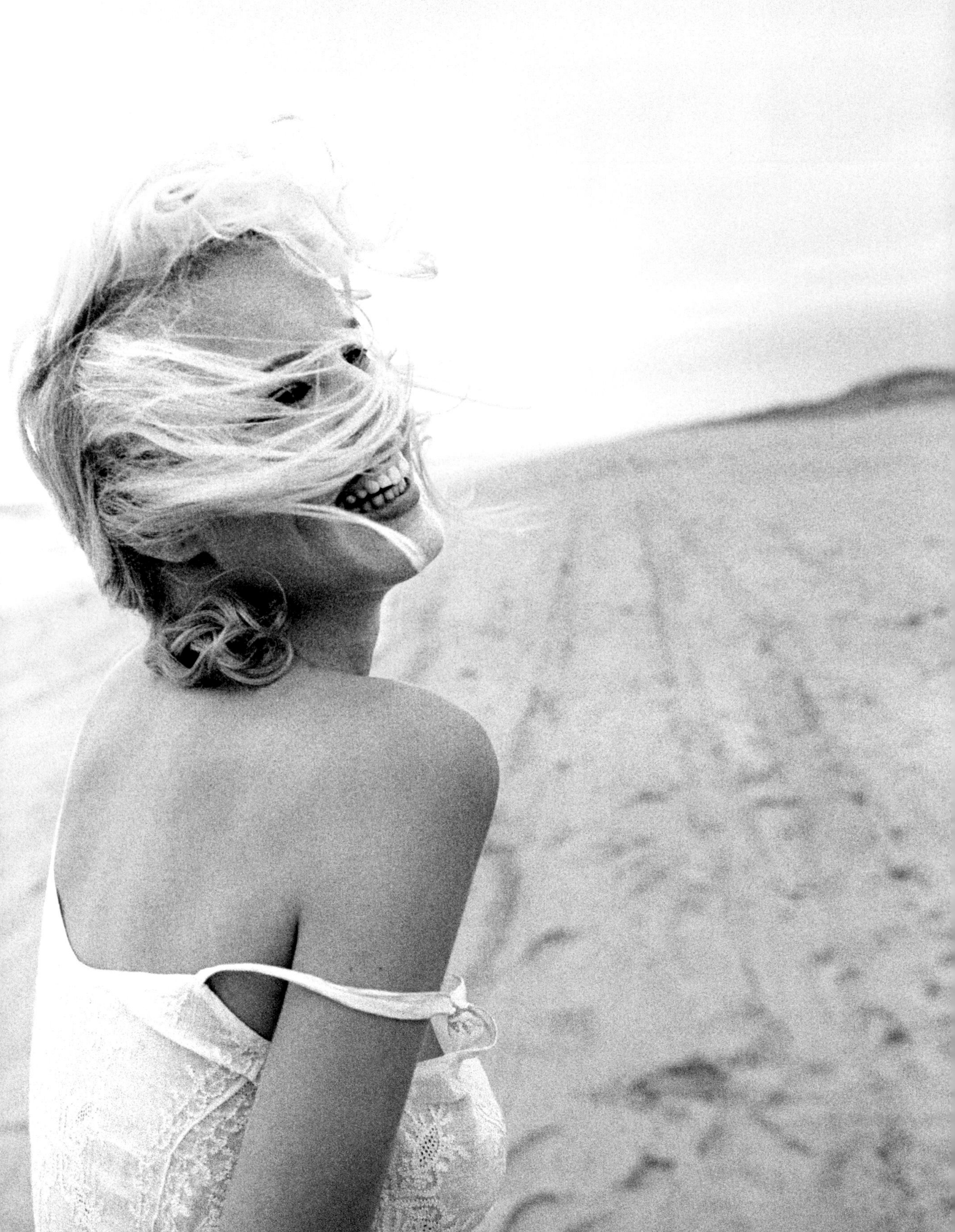

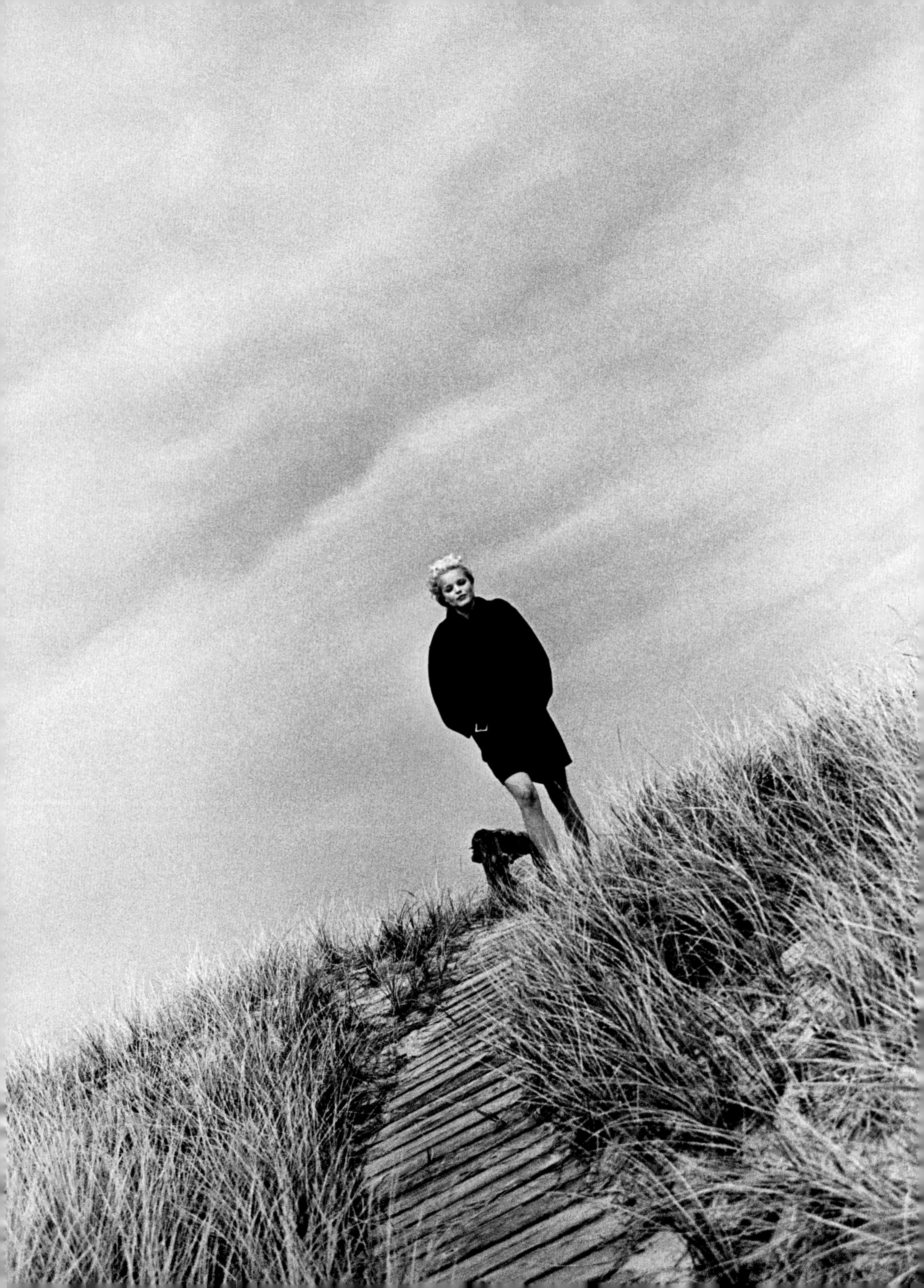

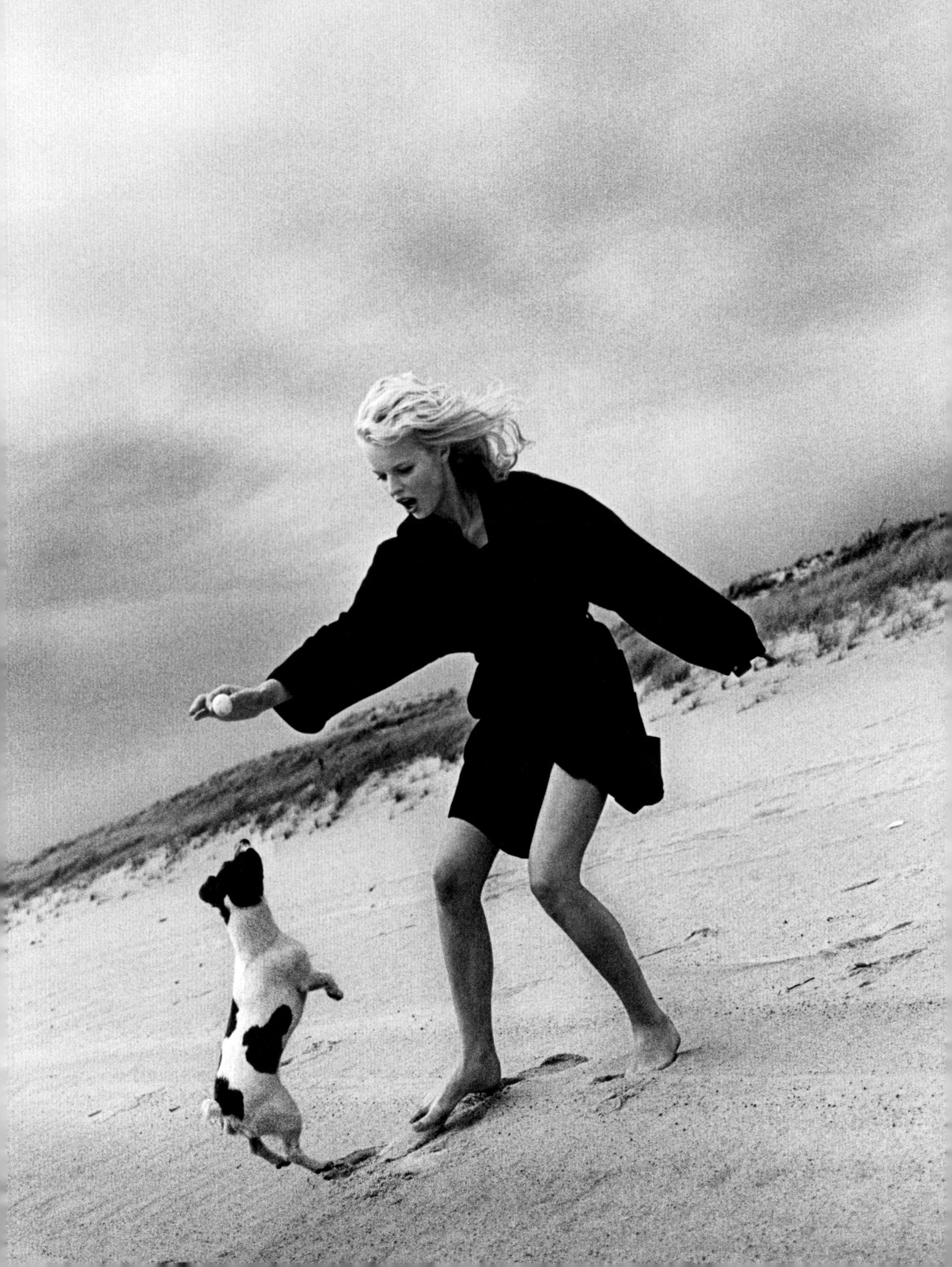

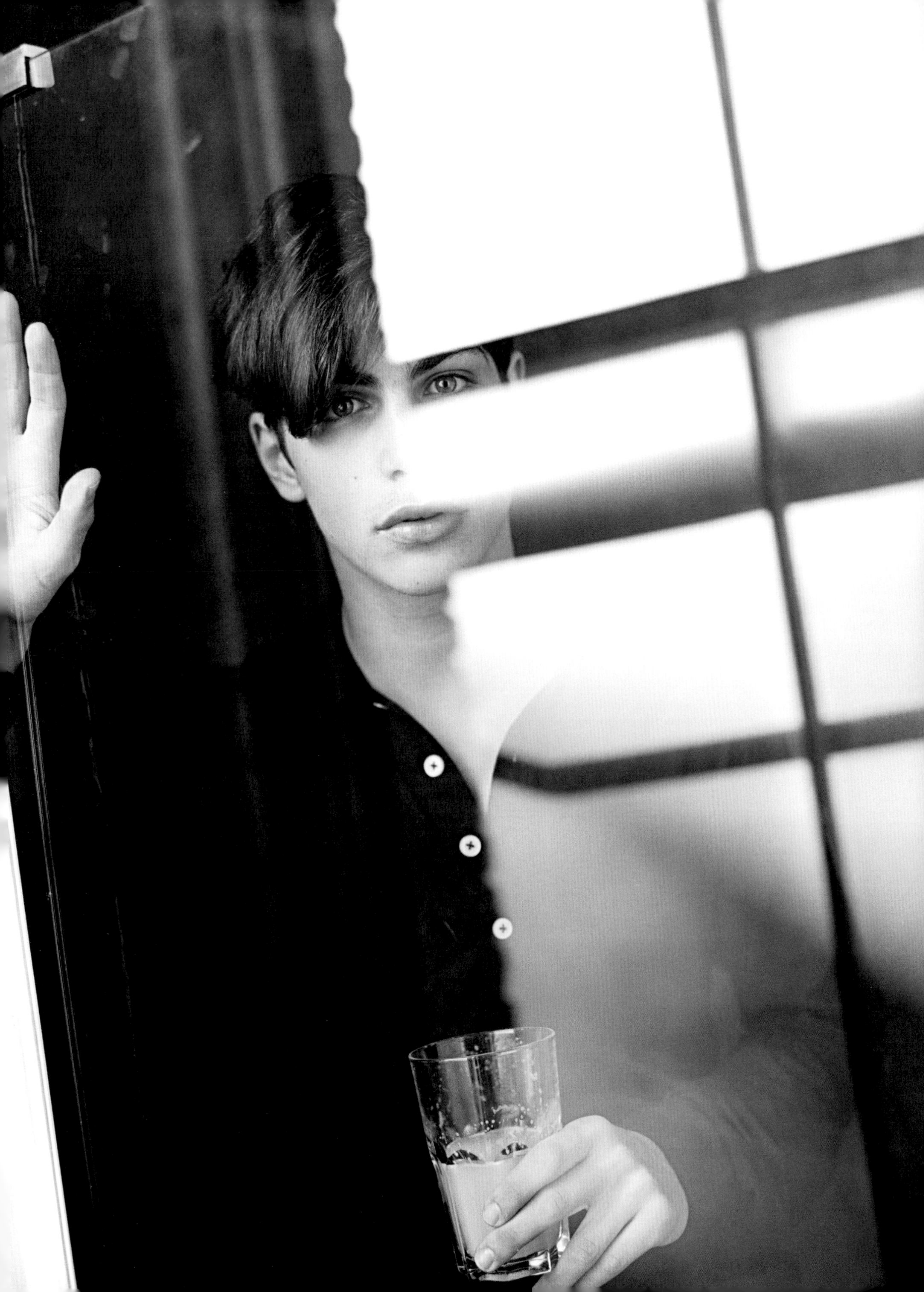

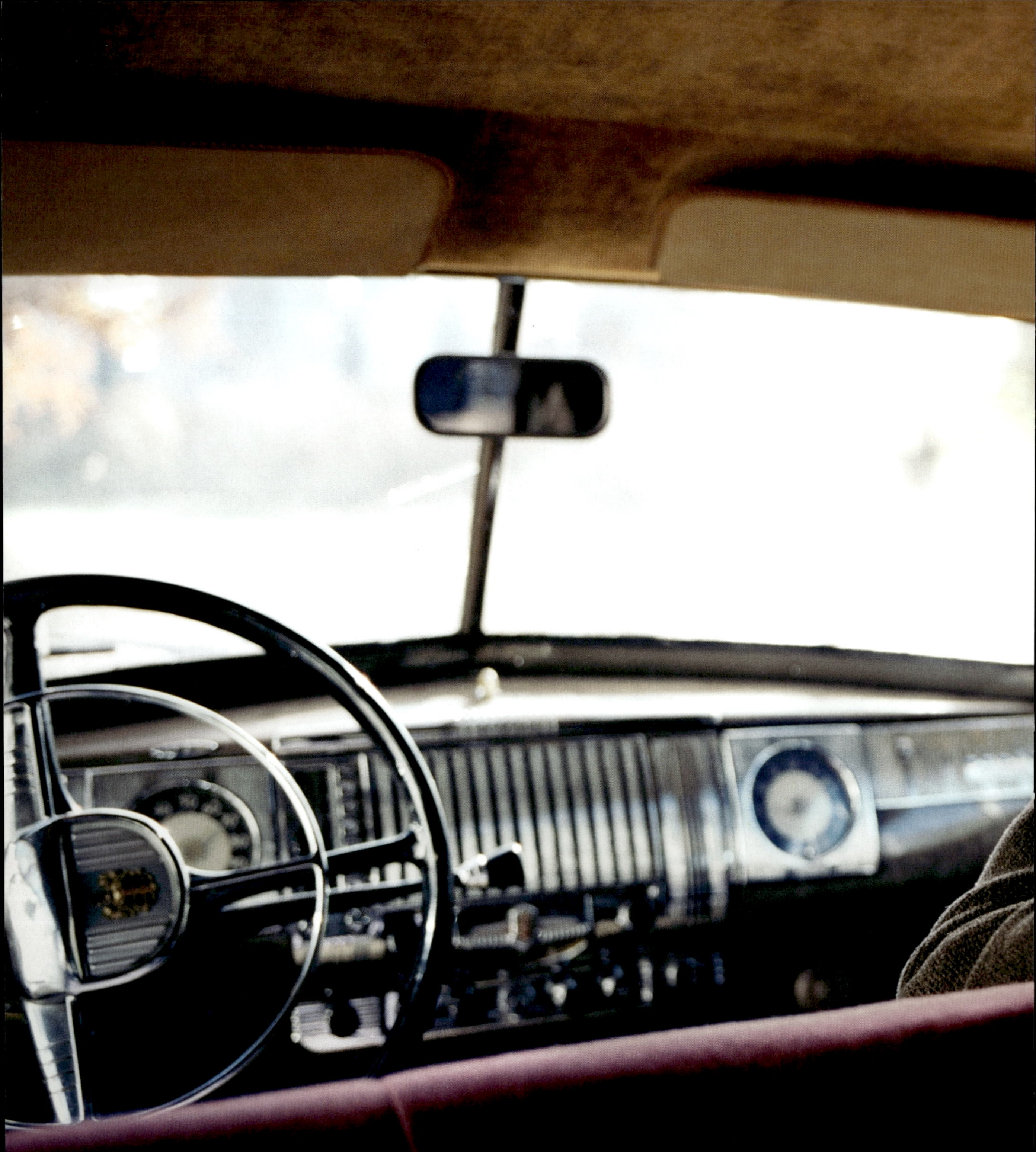

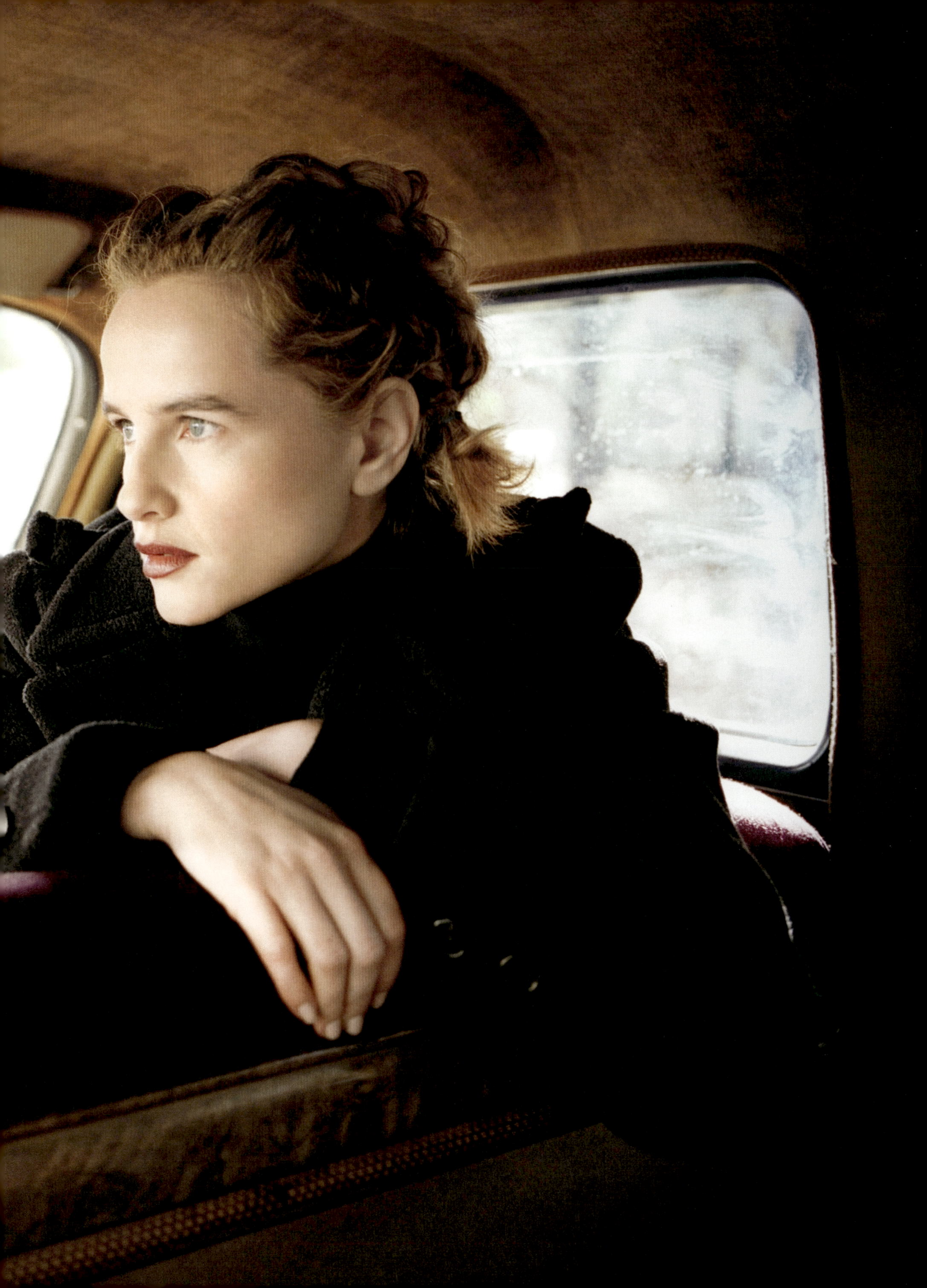

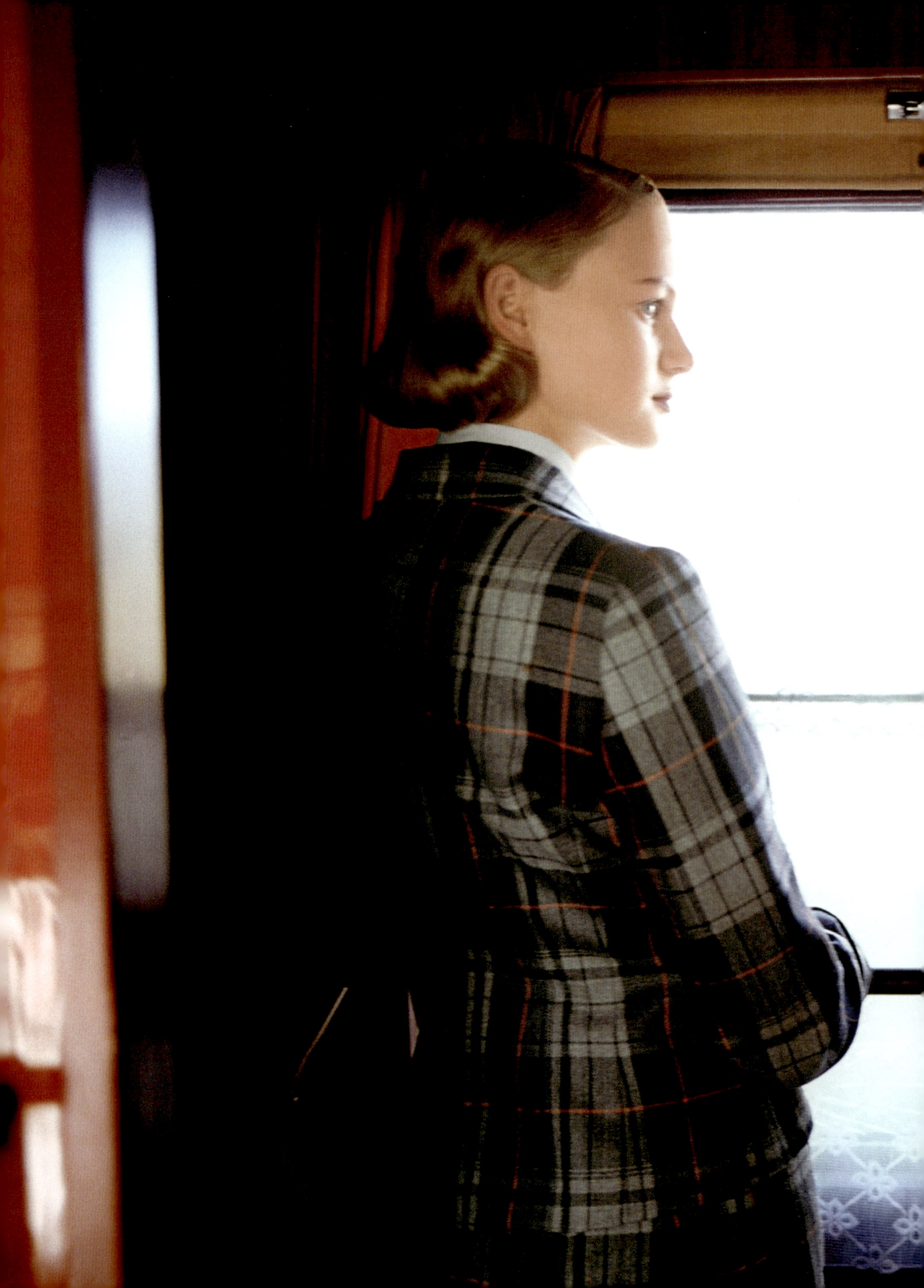

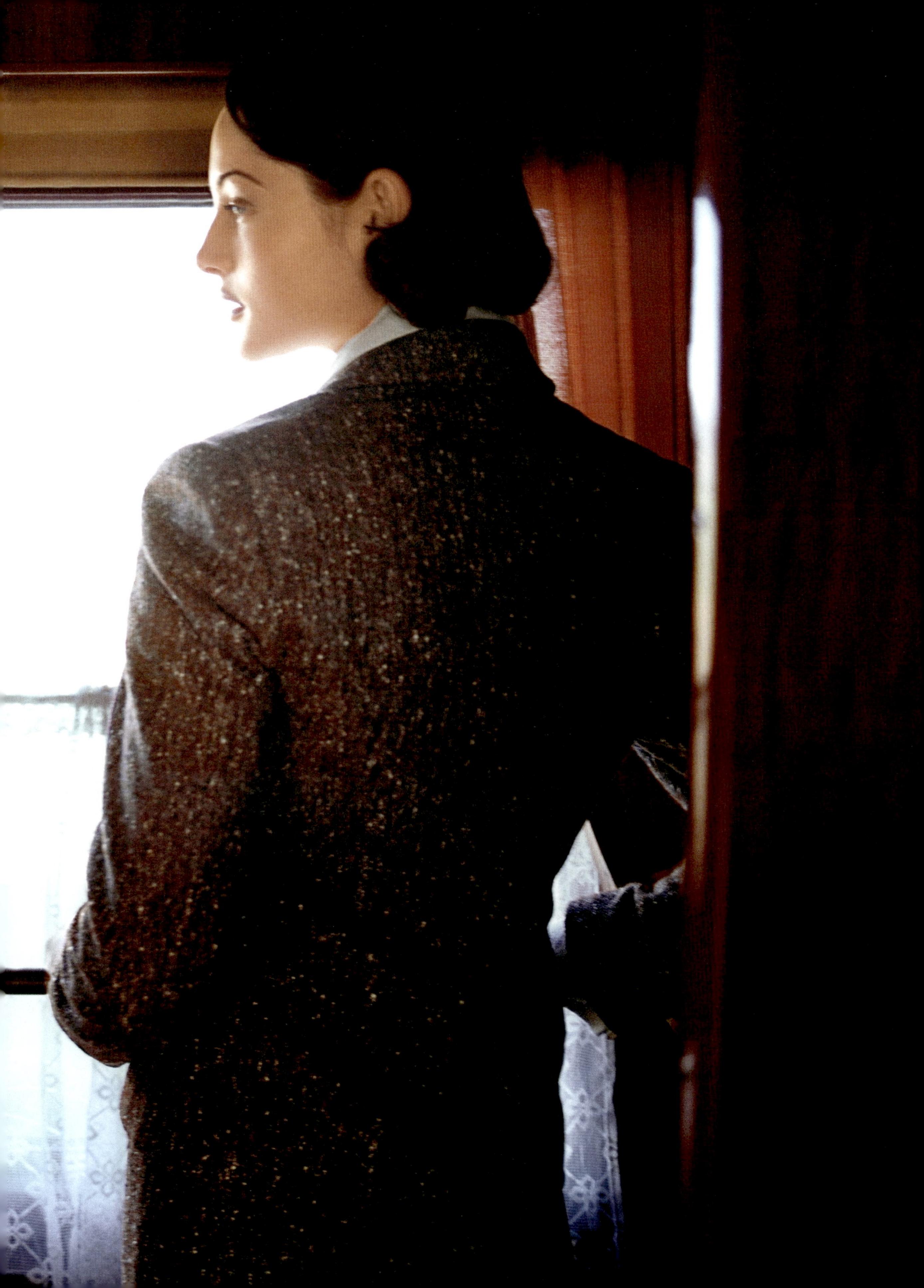

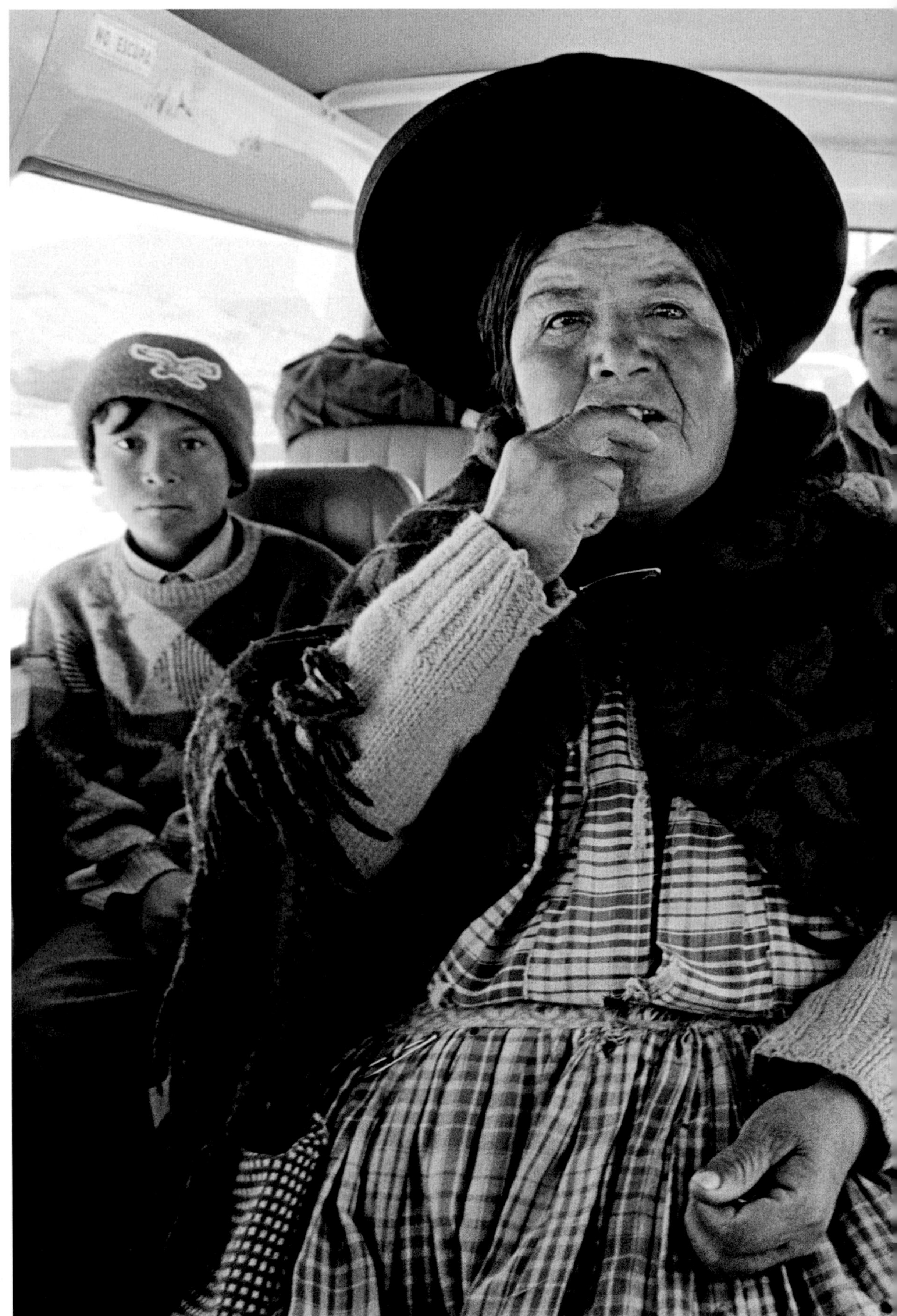

NO ESCUPA

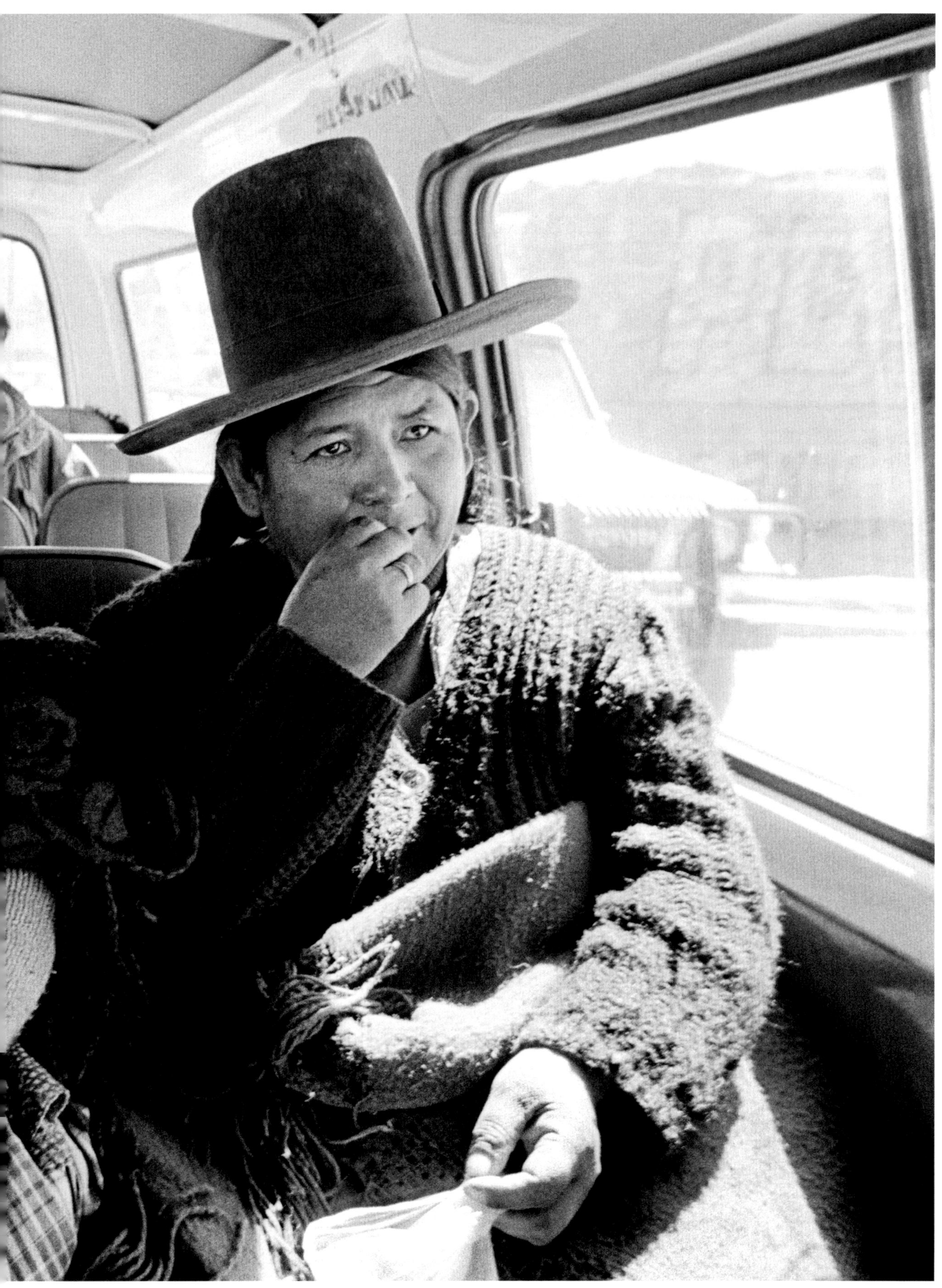

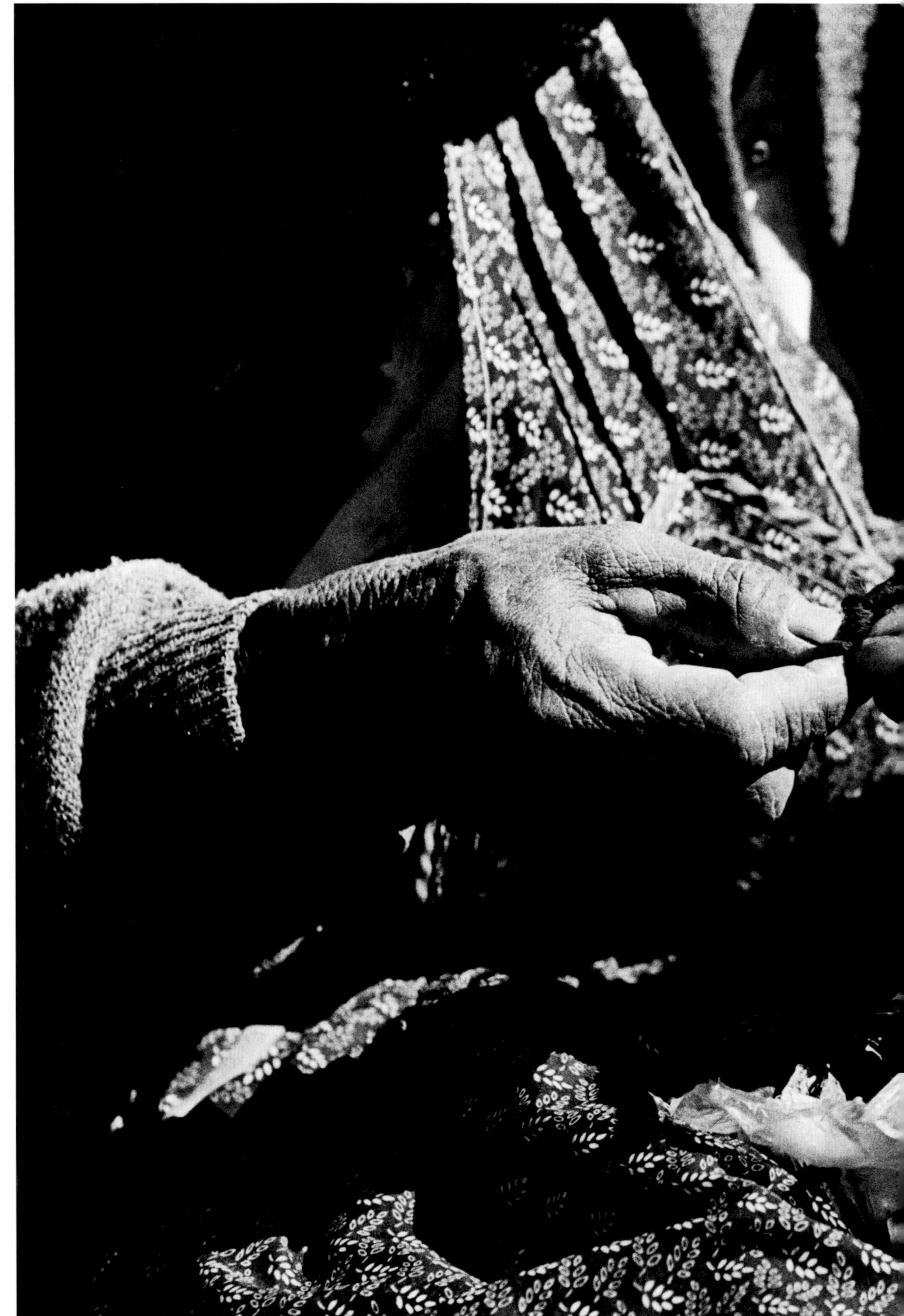

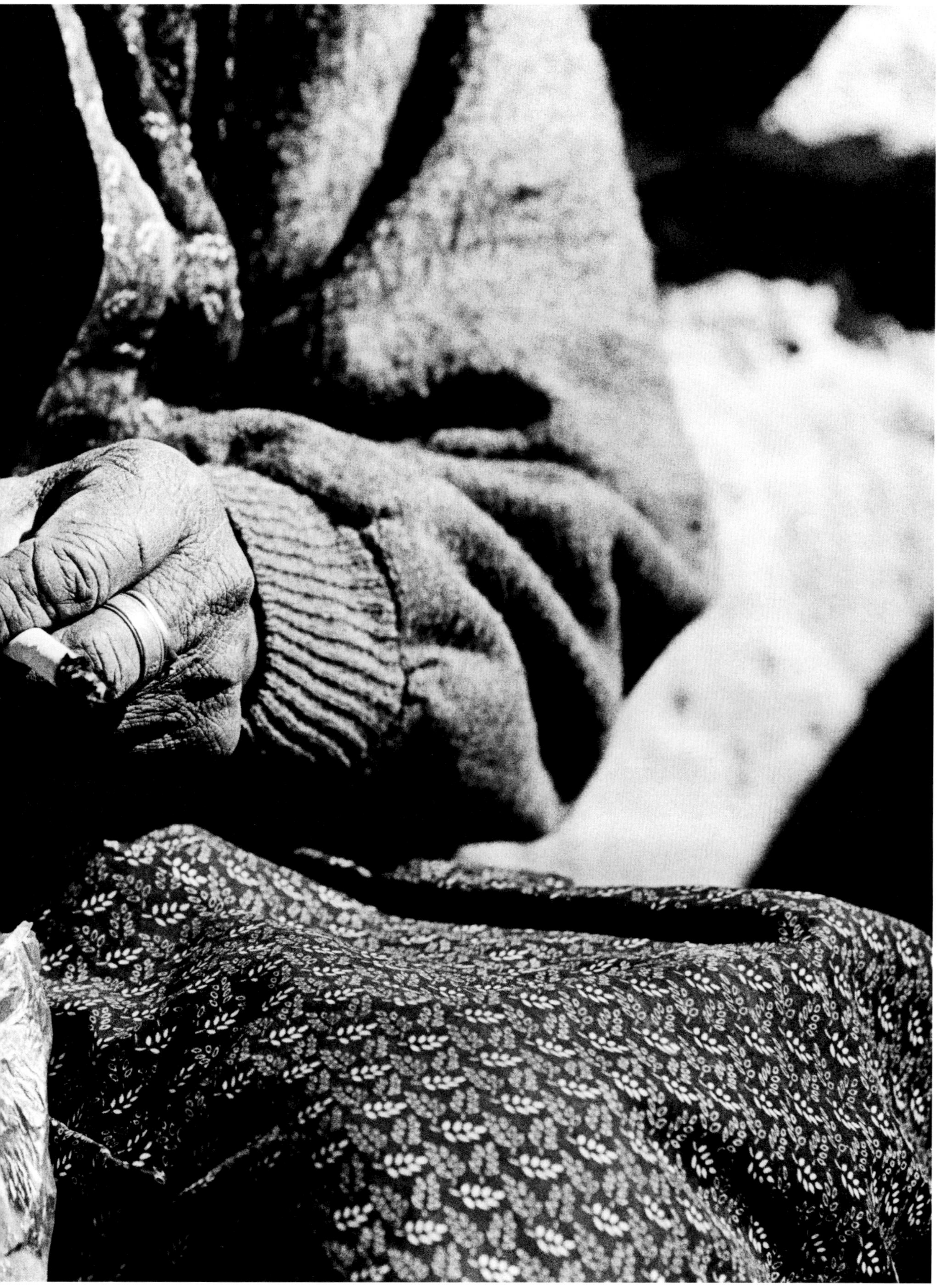

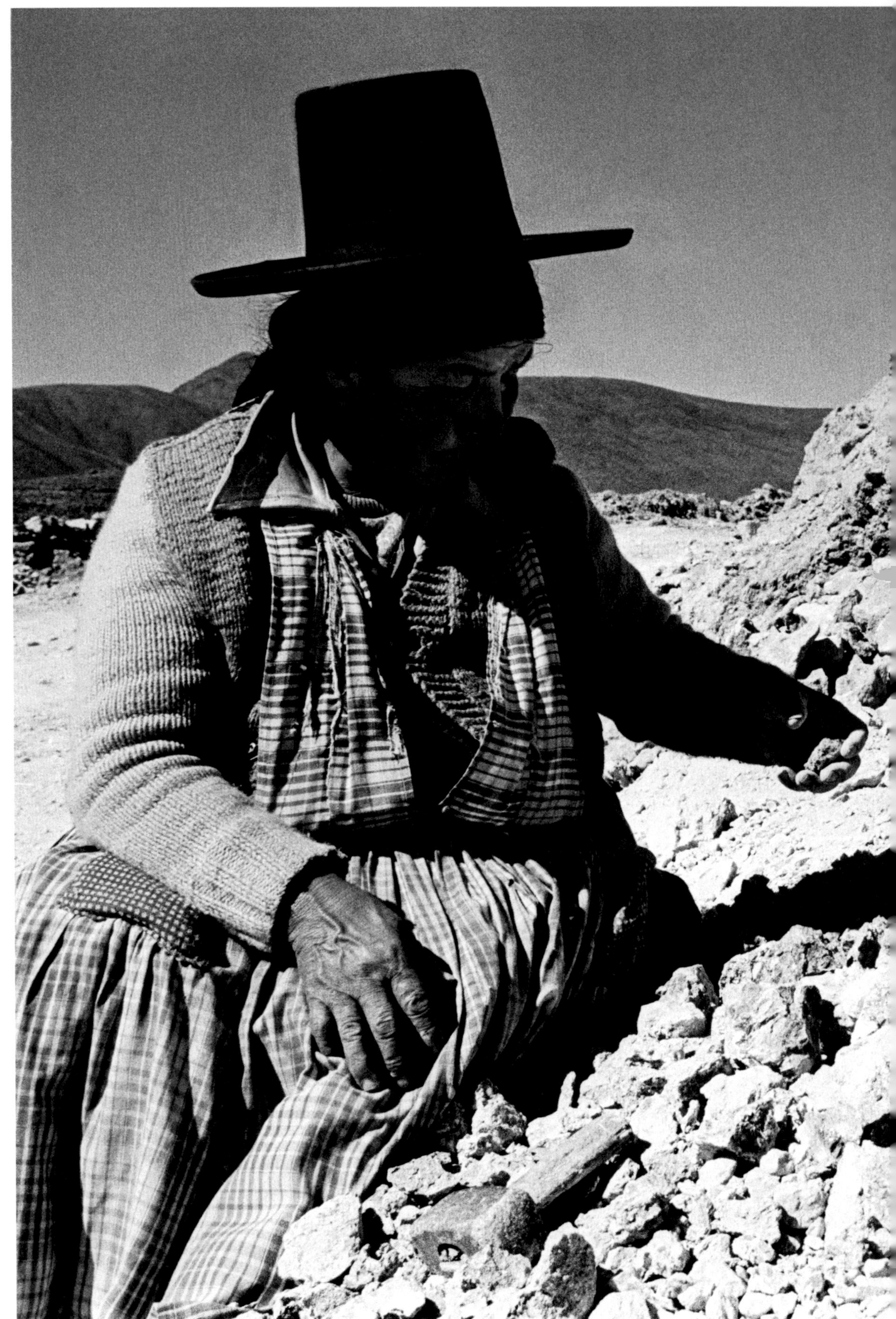

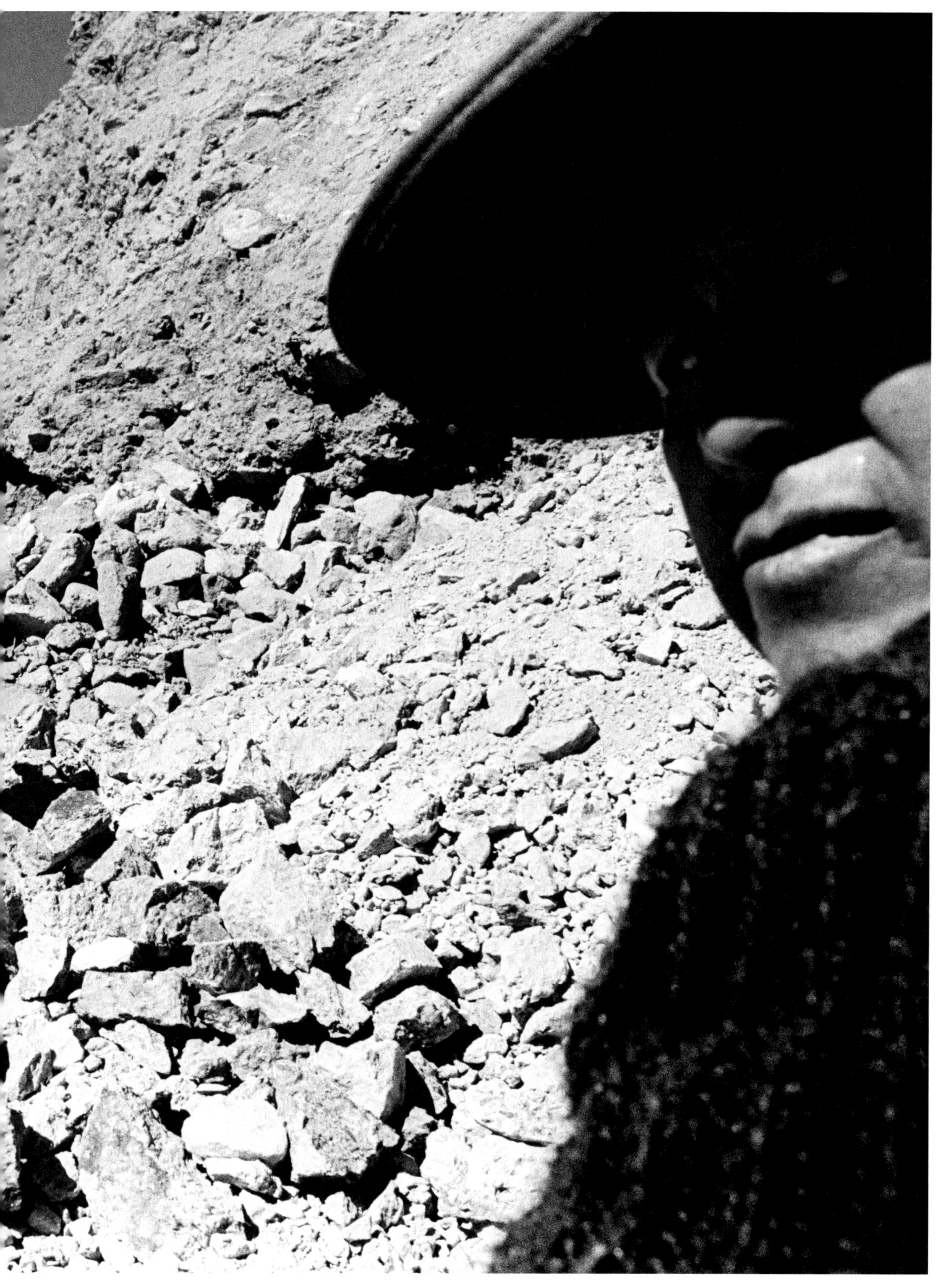

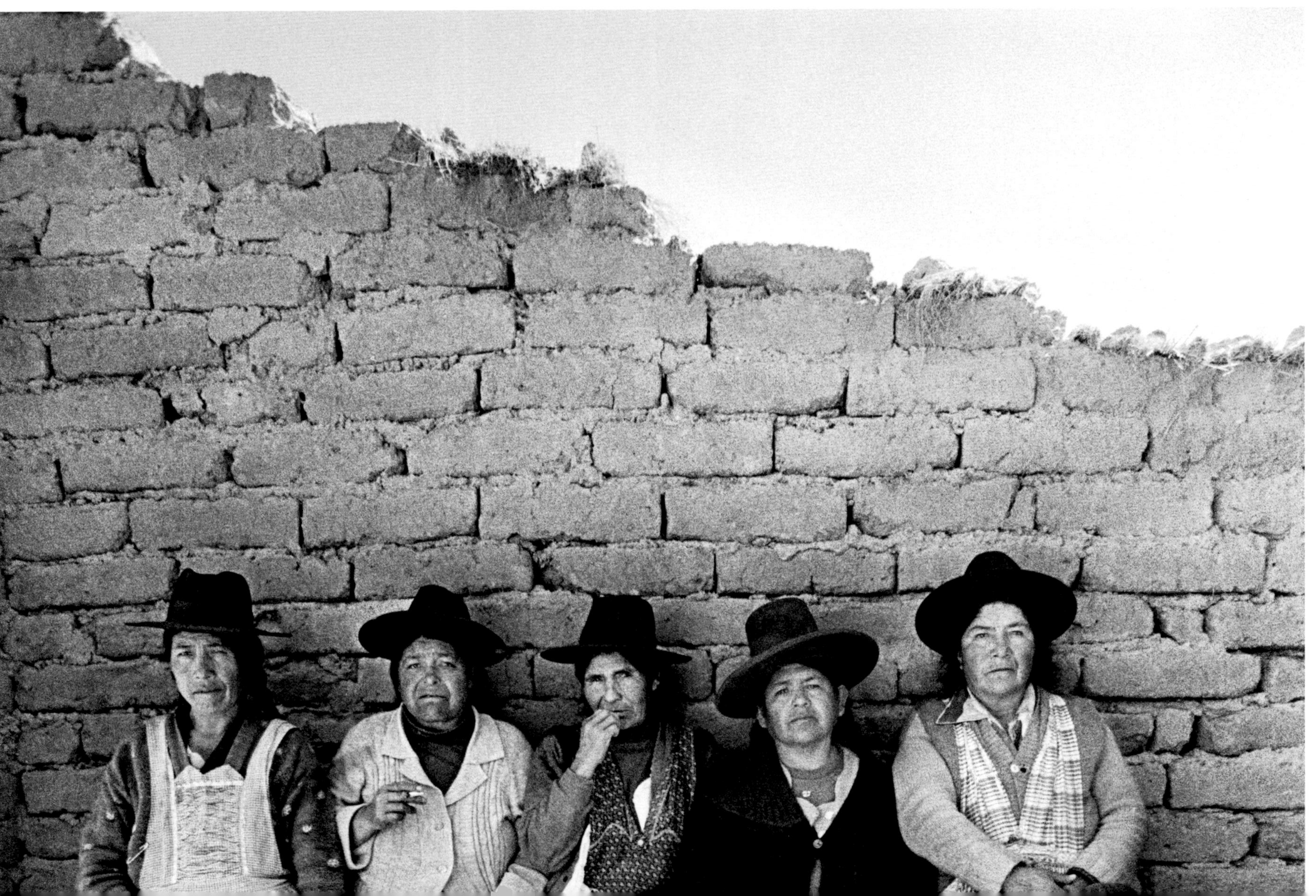

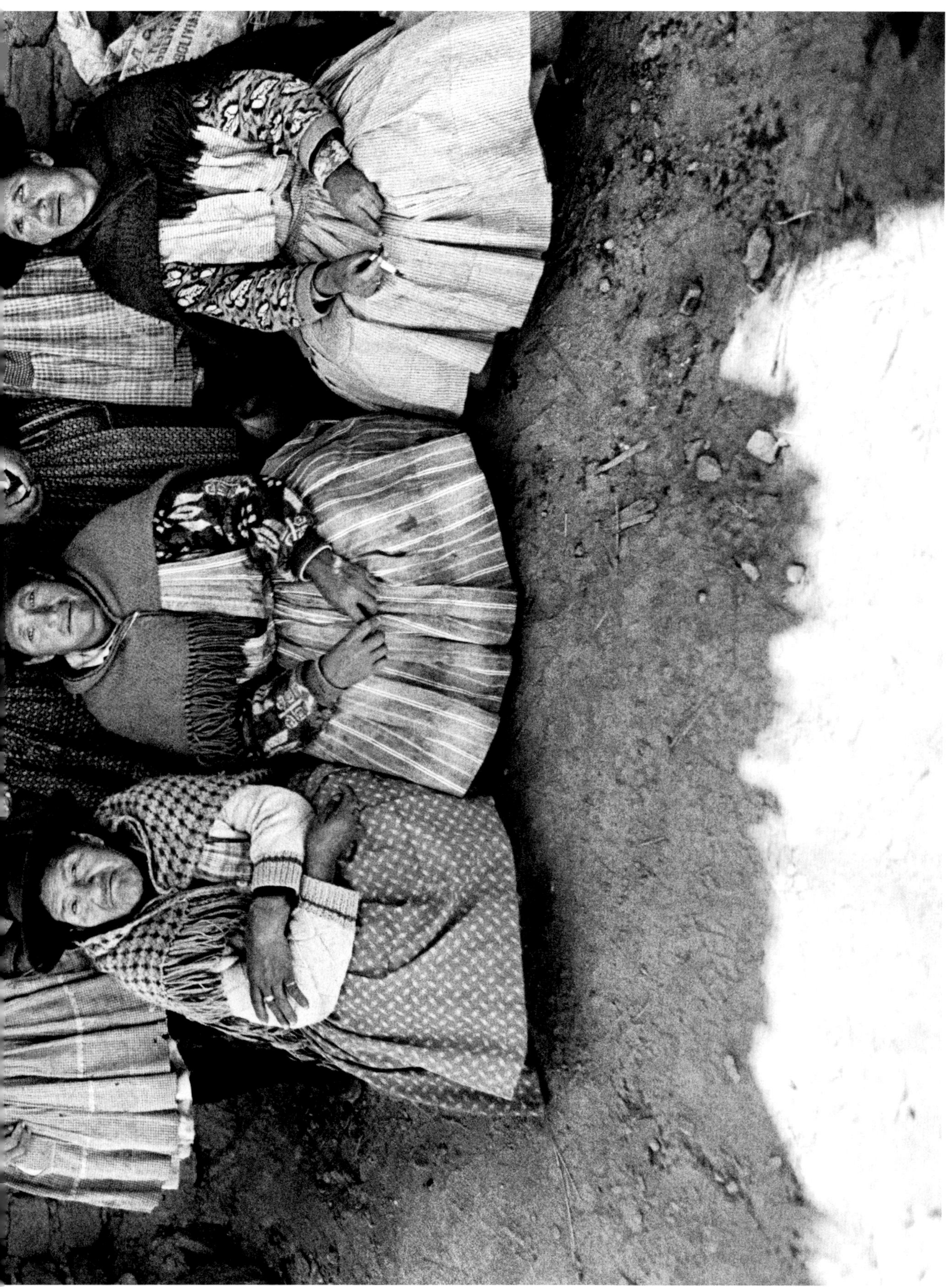

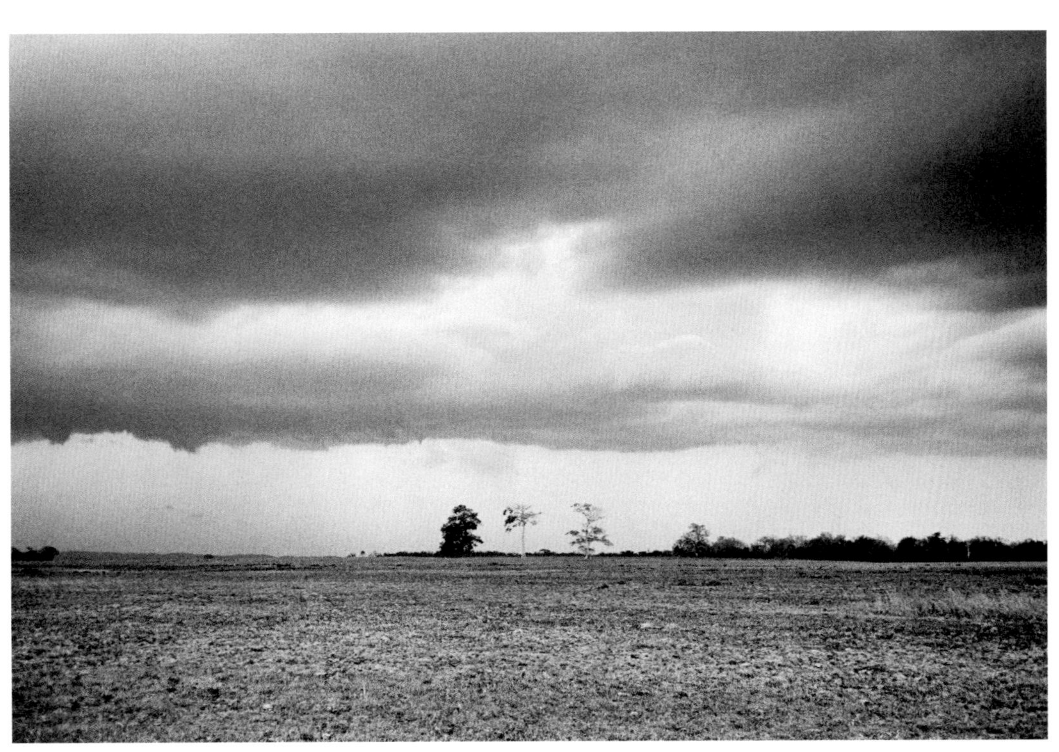

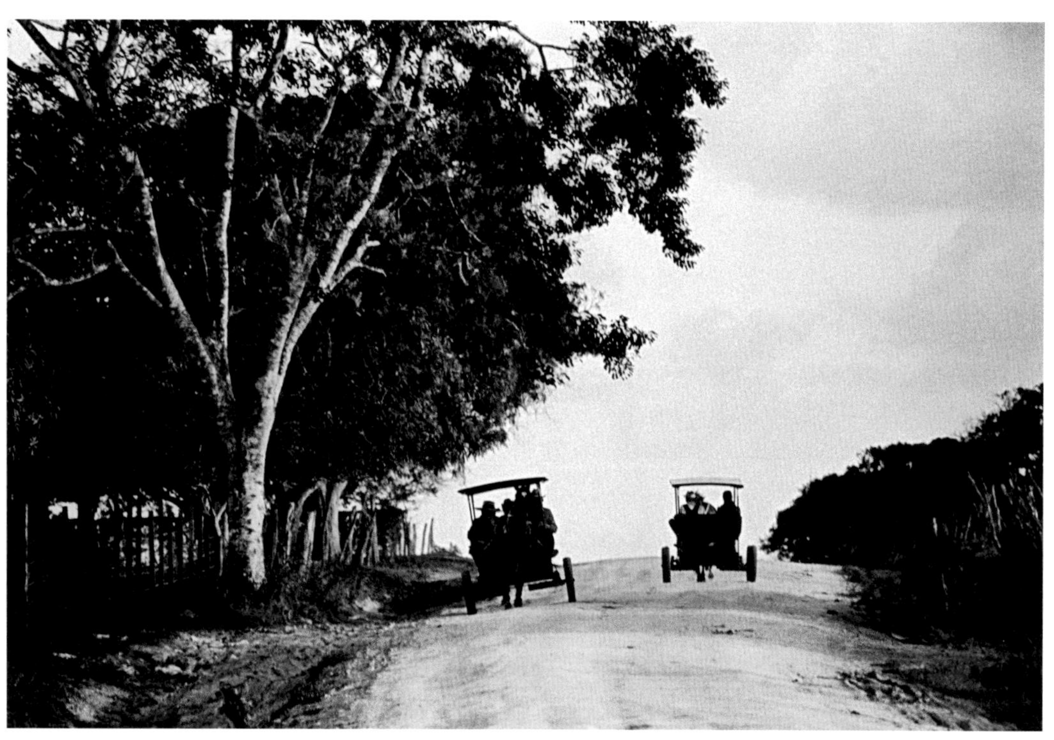

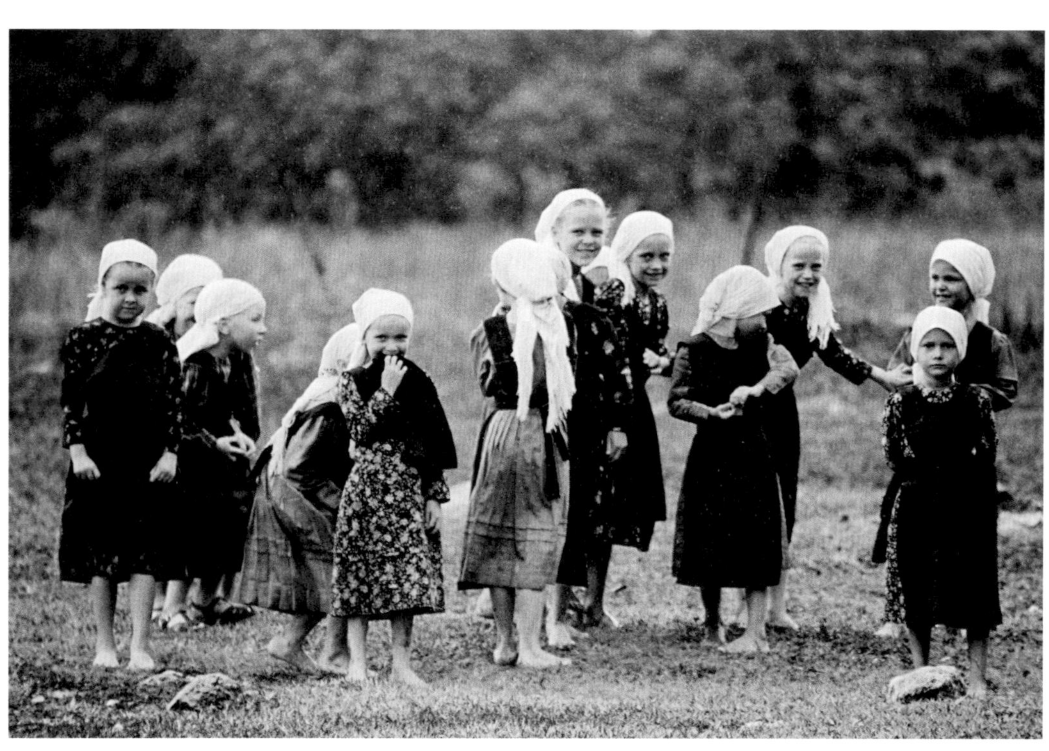

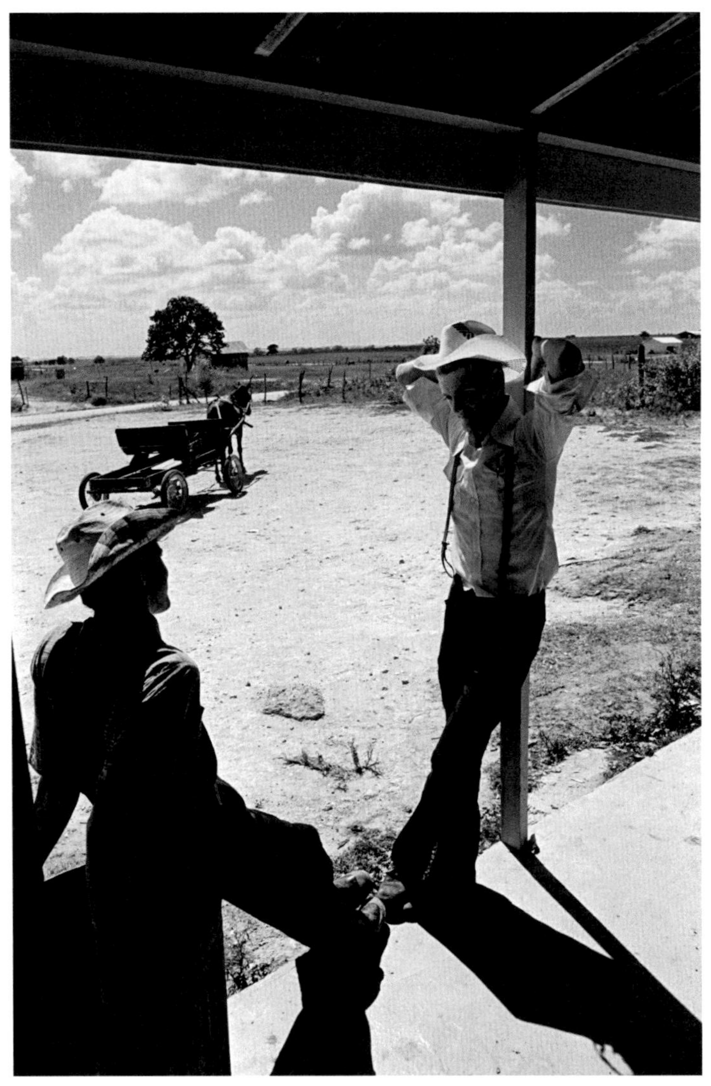

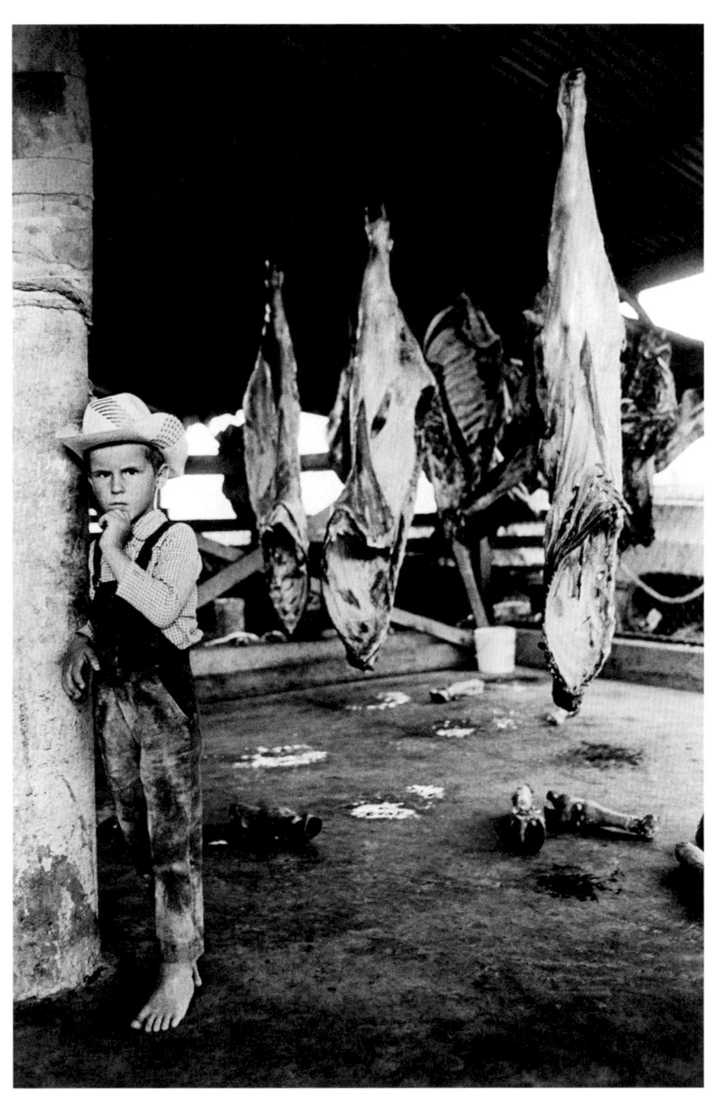

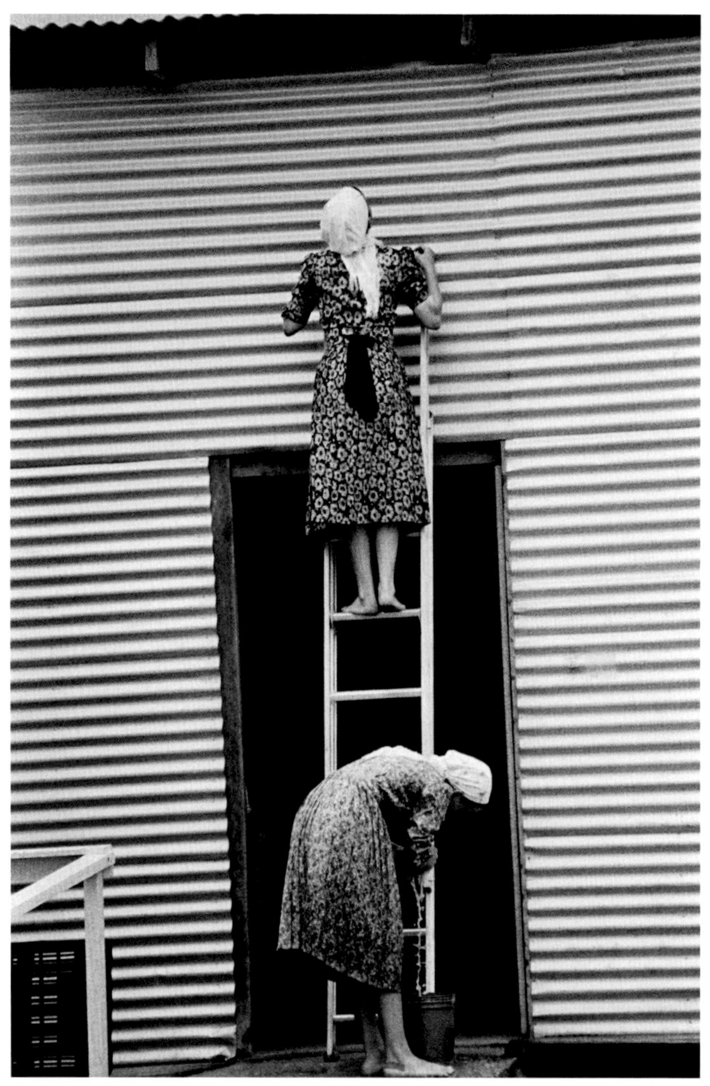

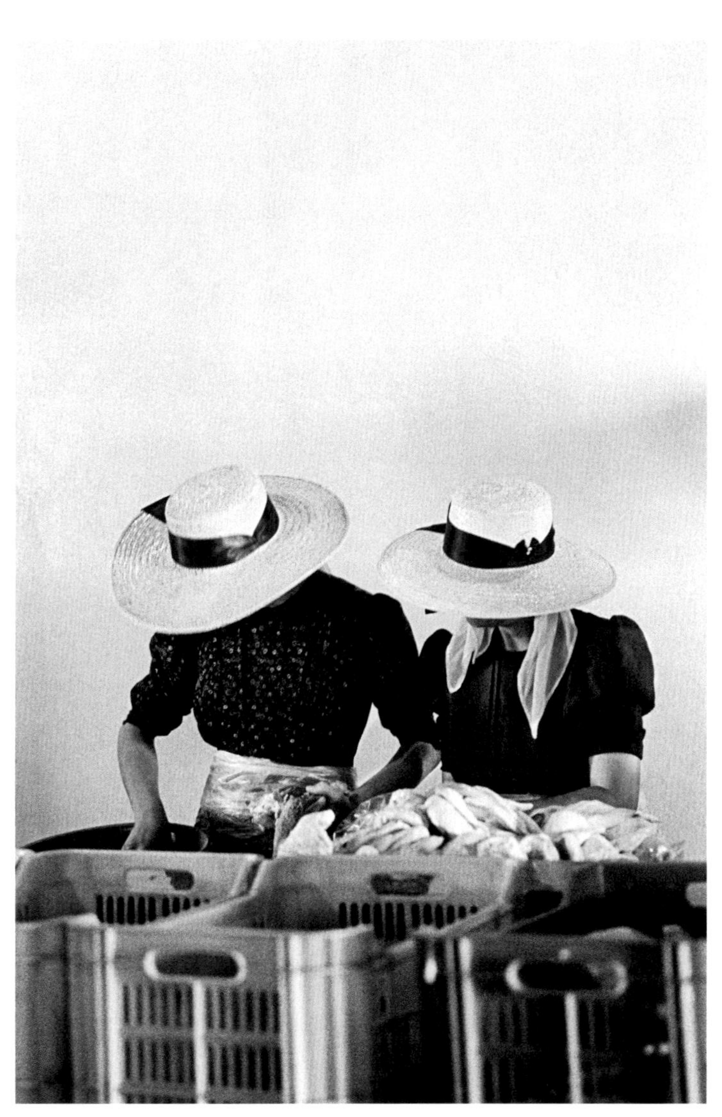

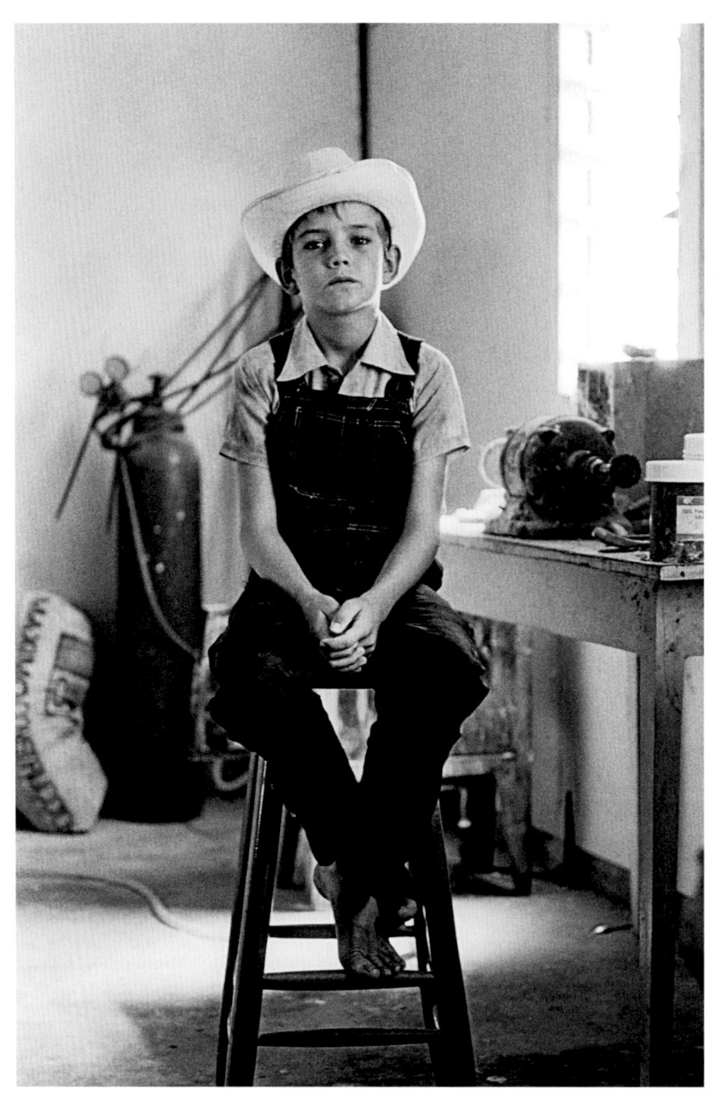

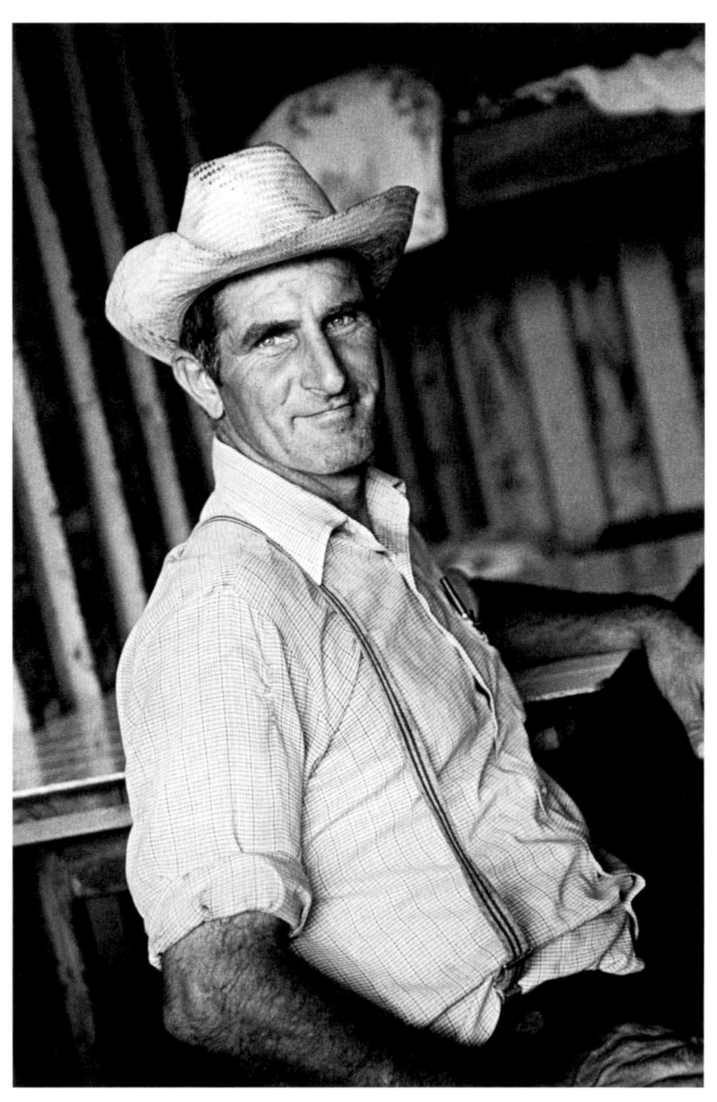

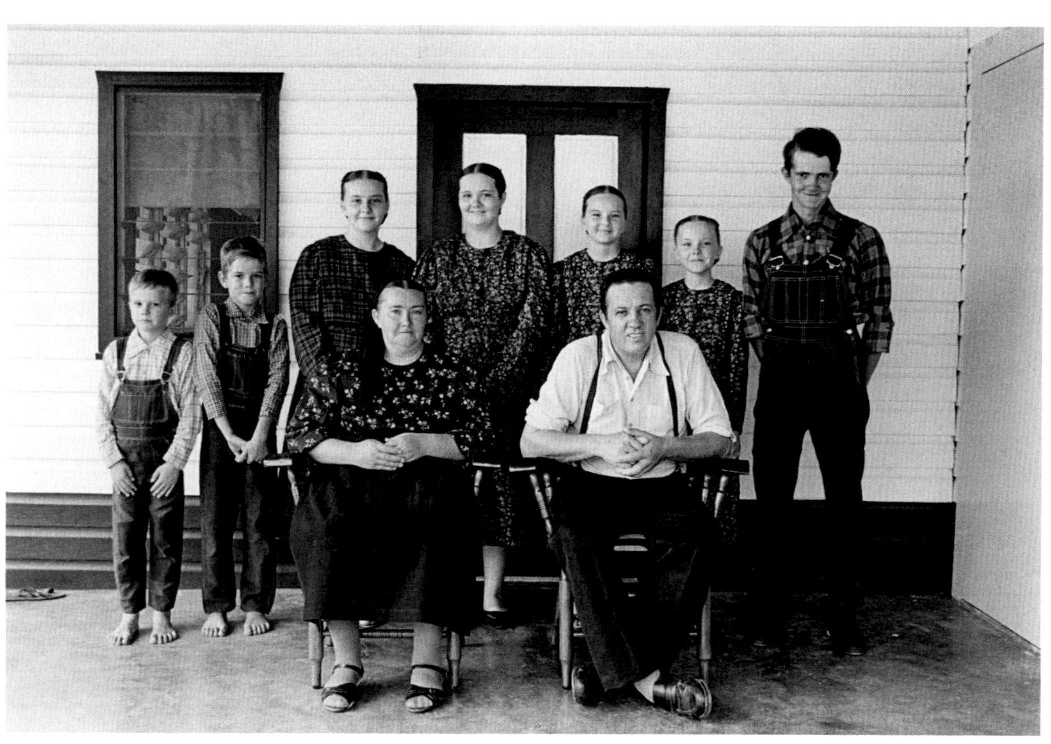

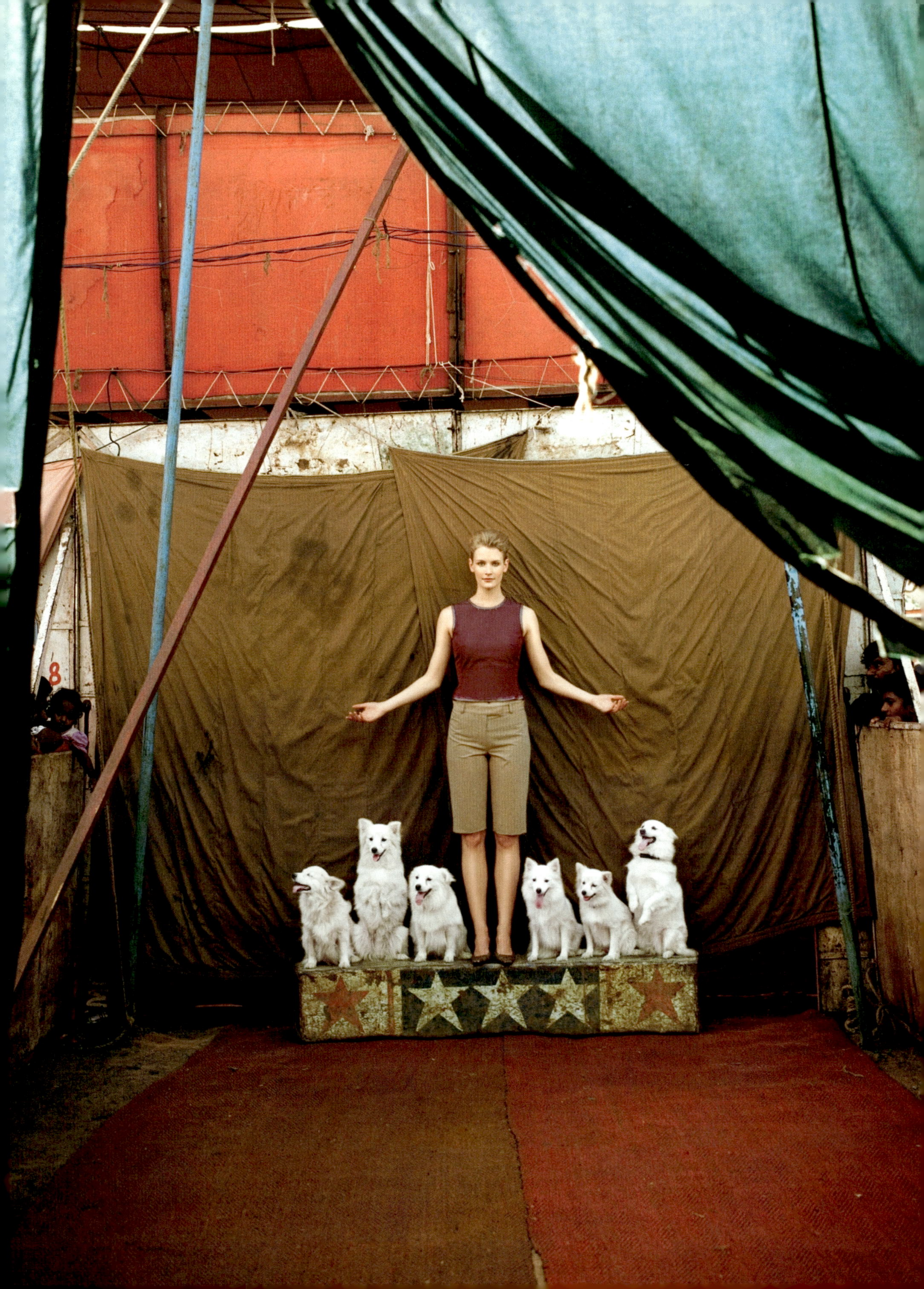

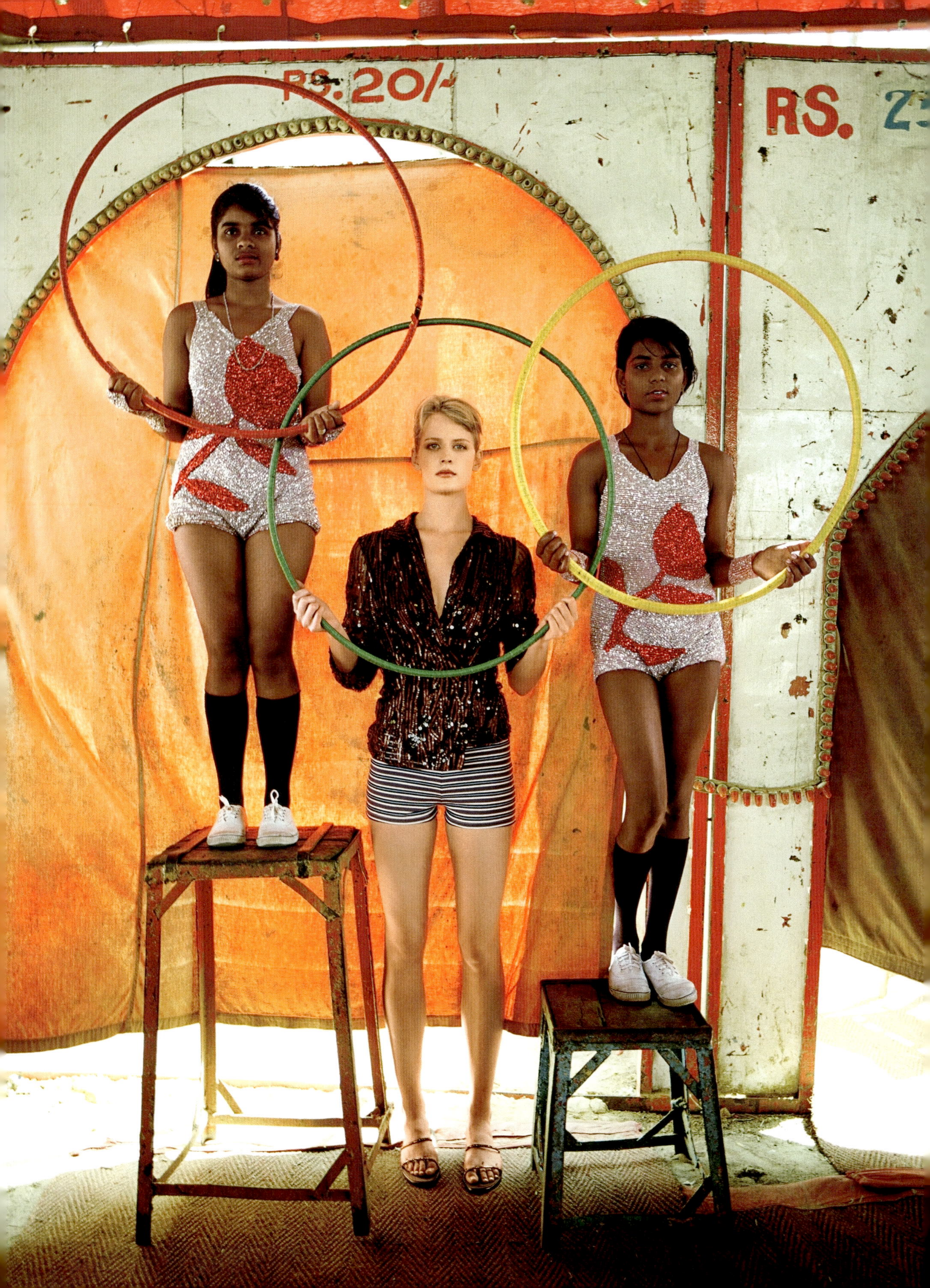

RS. 20/-
RS. 2

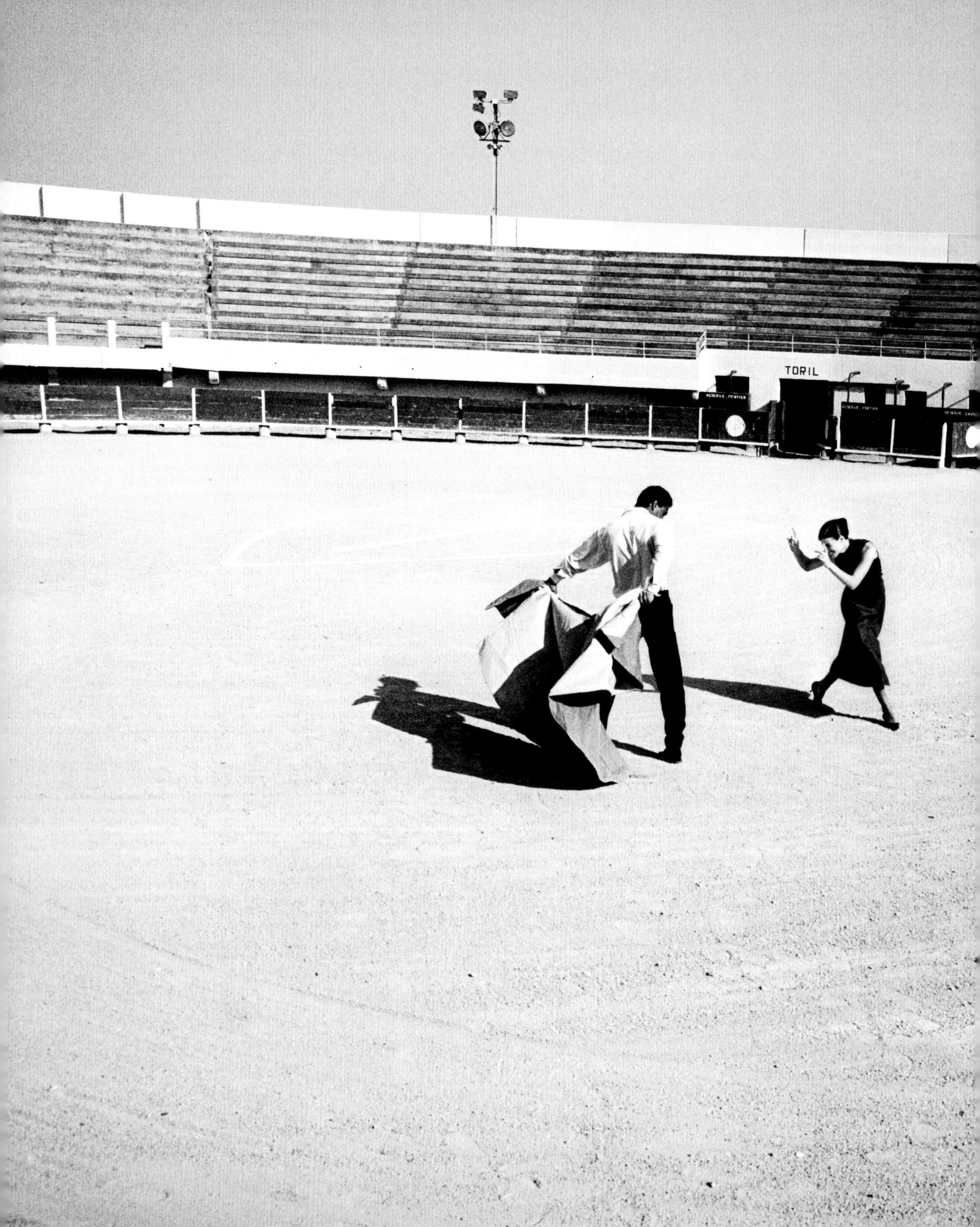

TORIL

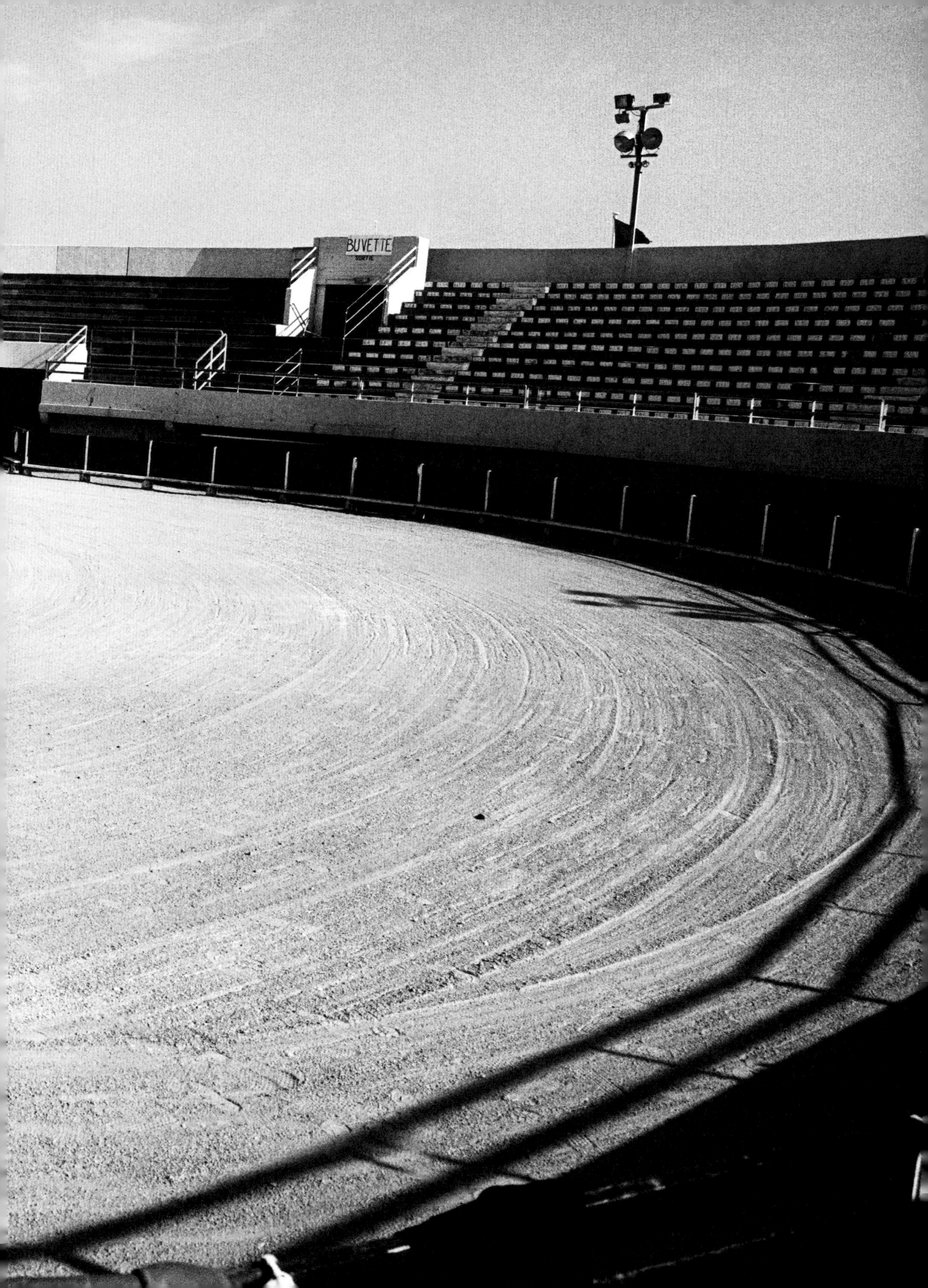

BUVETTE
SORTIE

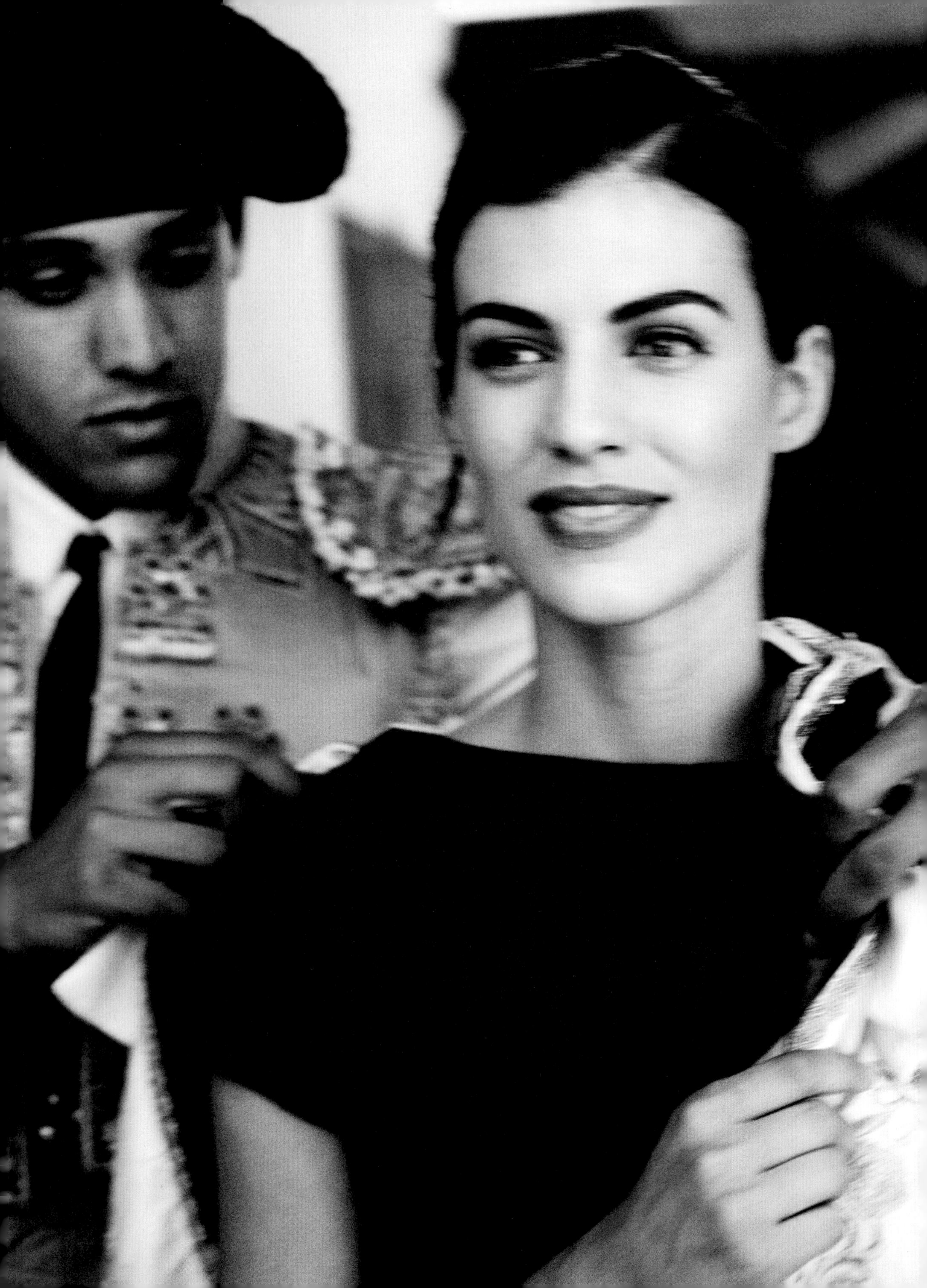

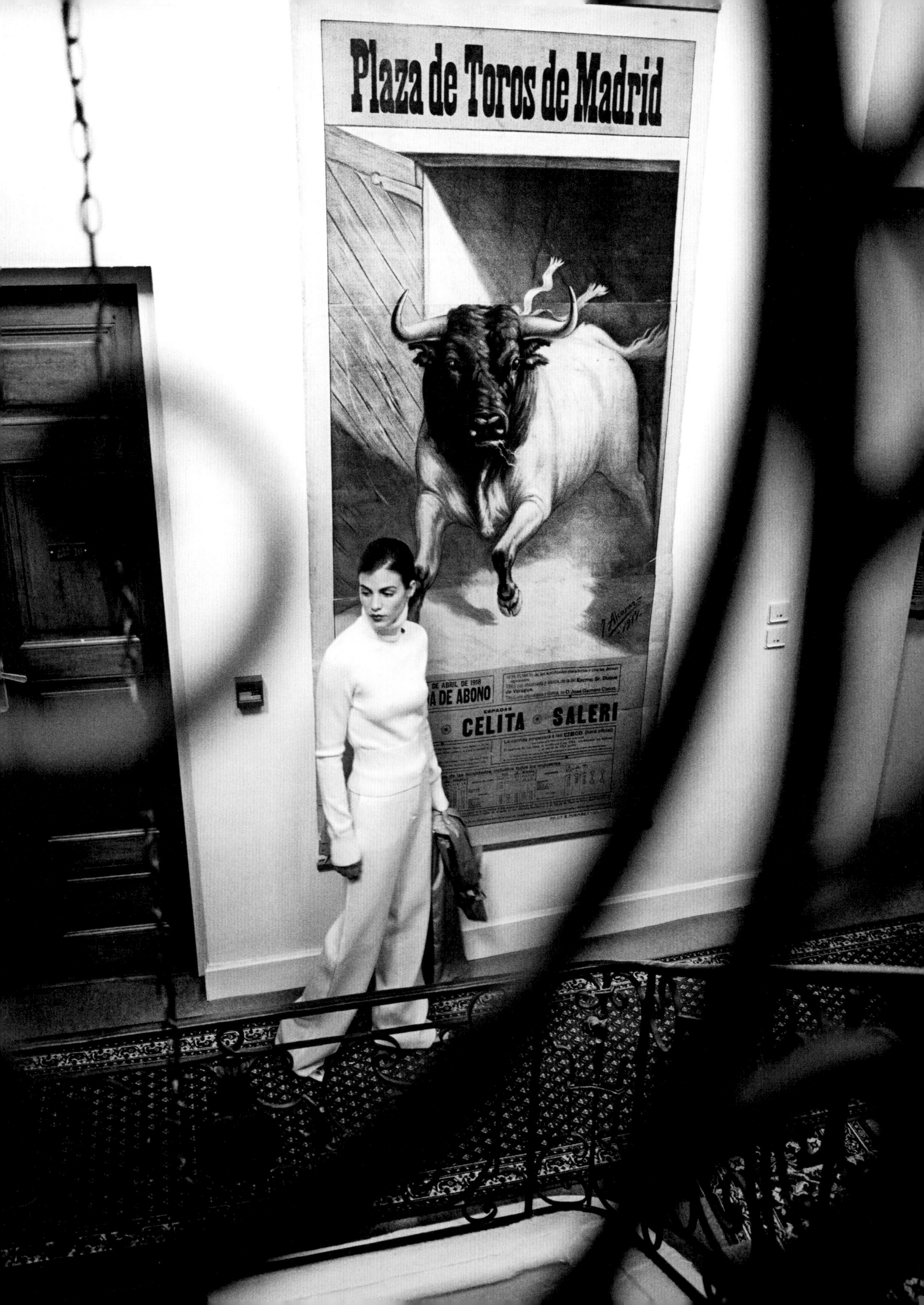

Plaza de Toros de Madrid
DE ABRIL DE 1918
DE ABONO
CELITA   SALERI

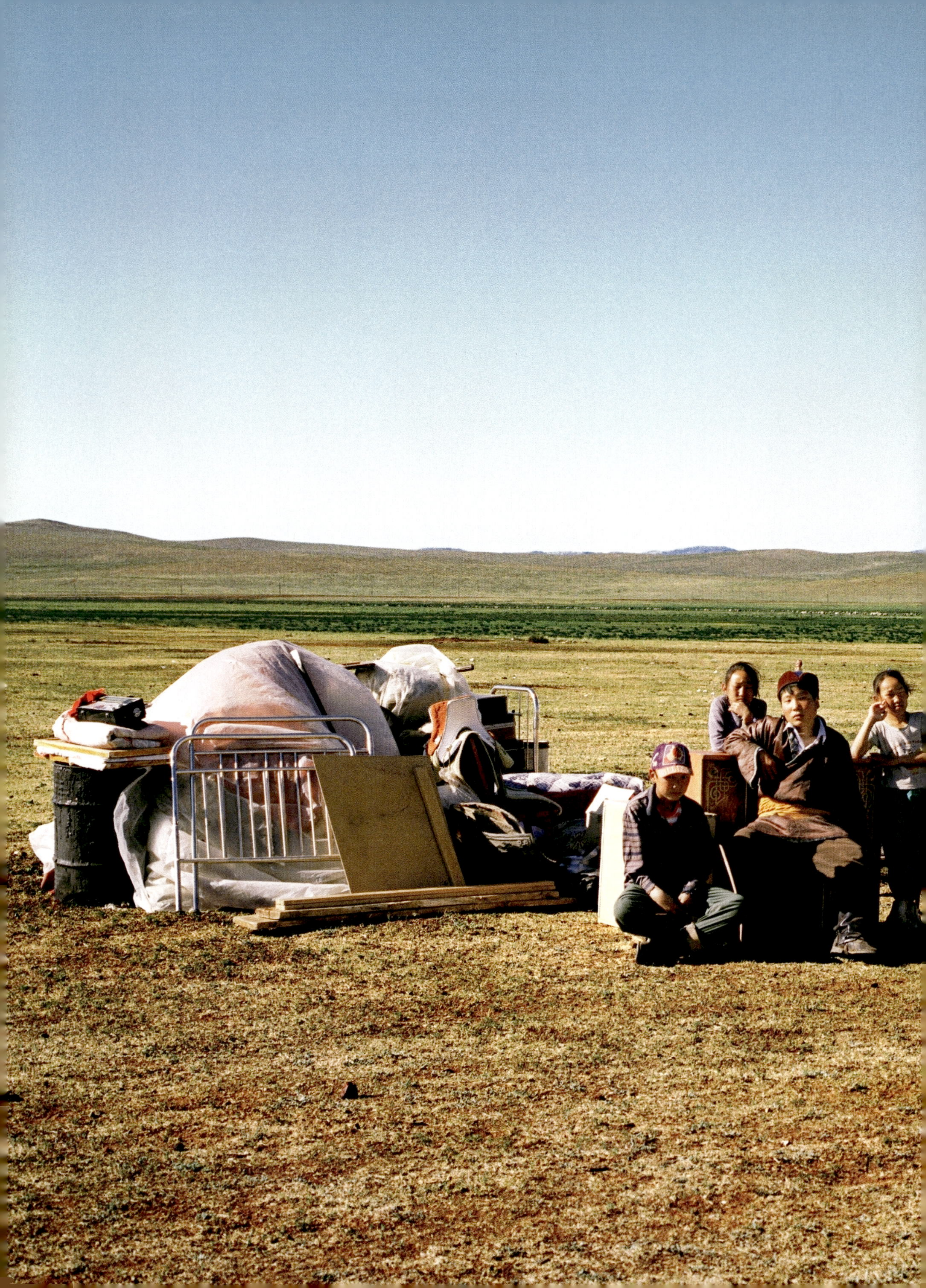

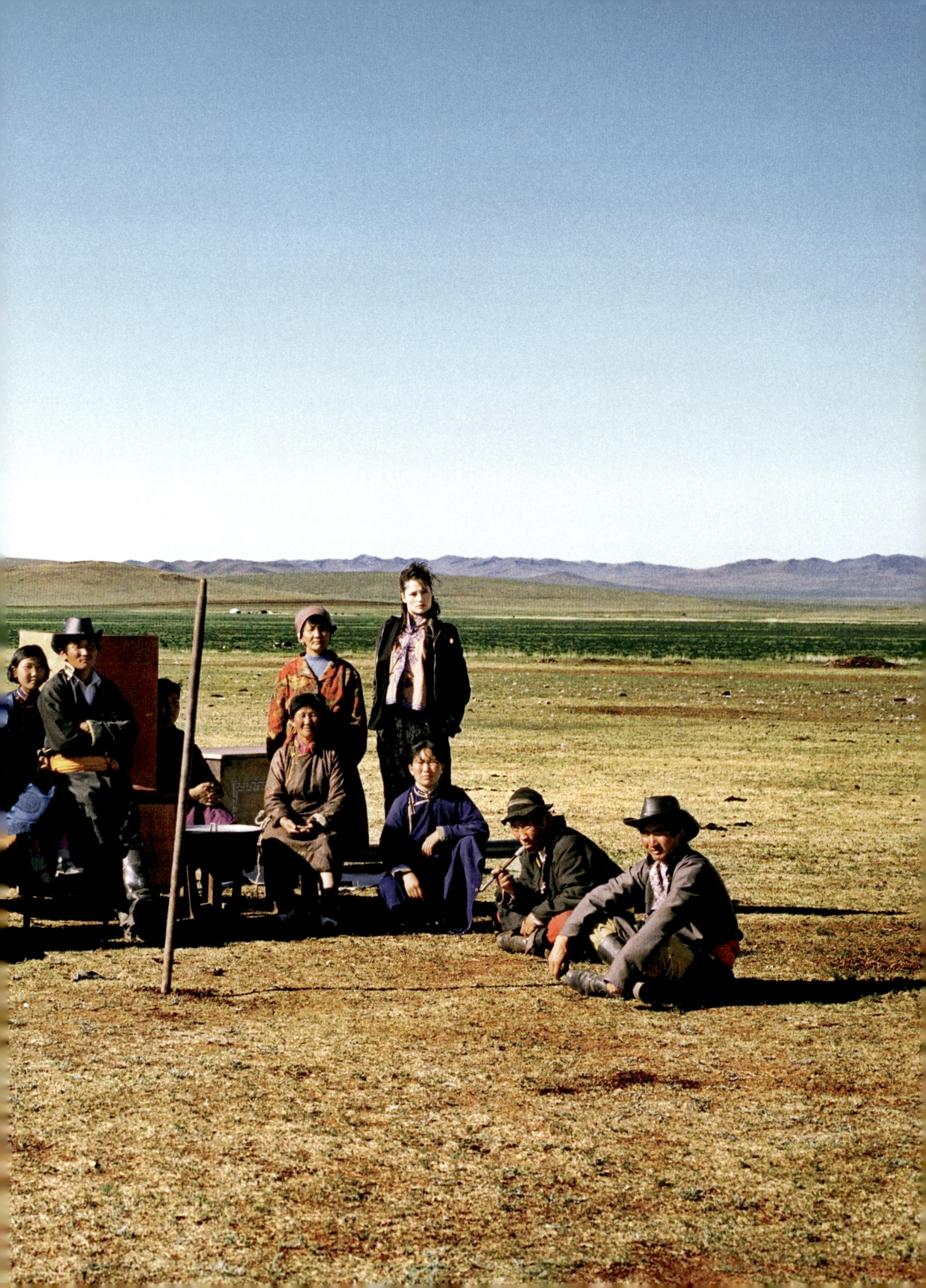

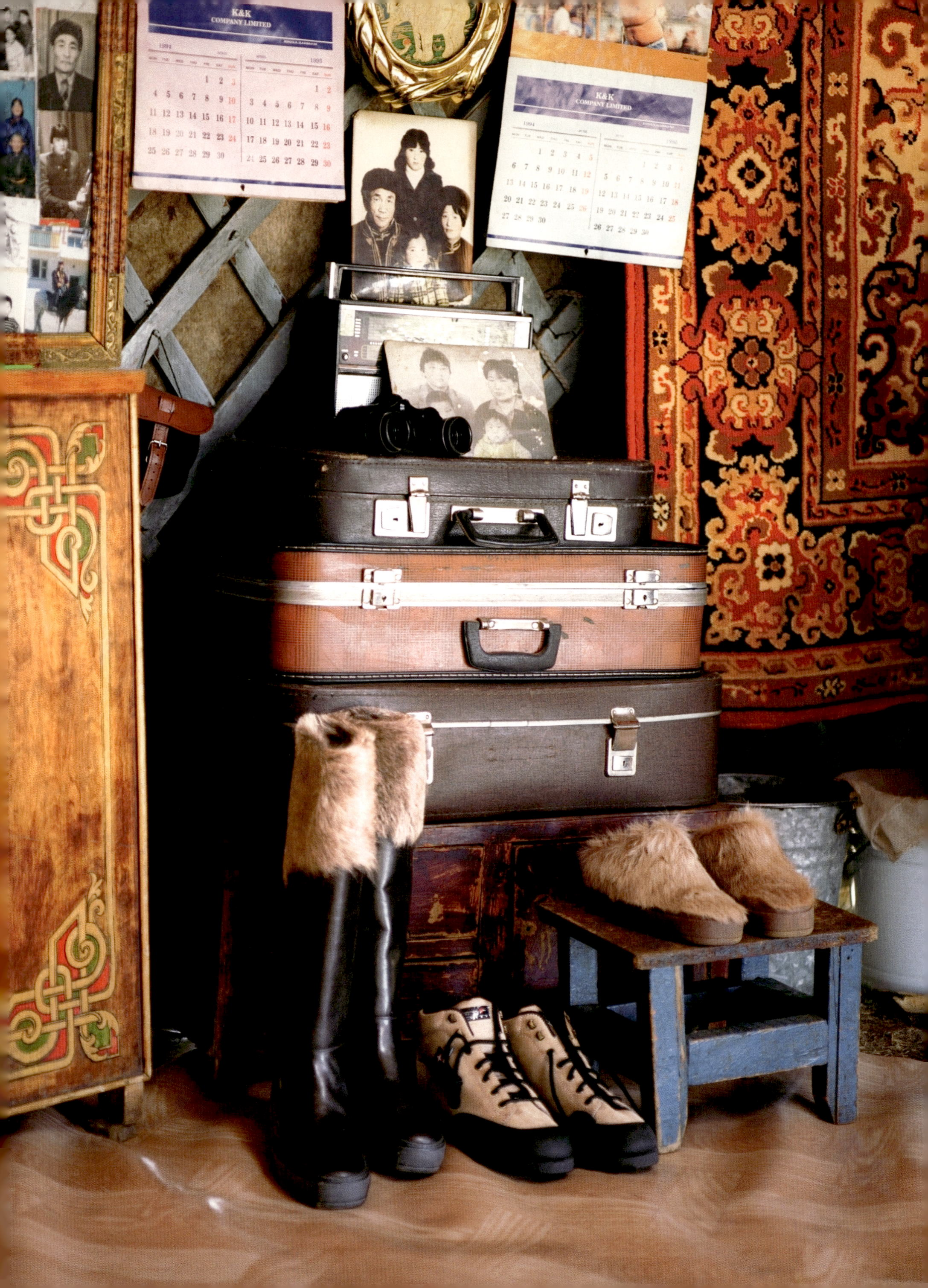

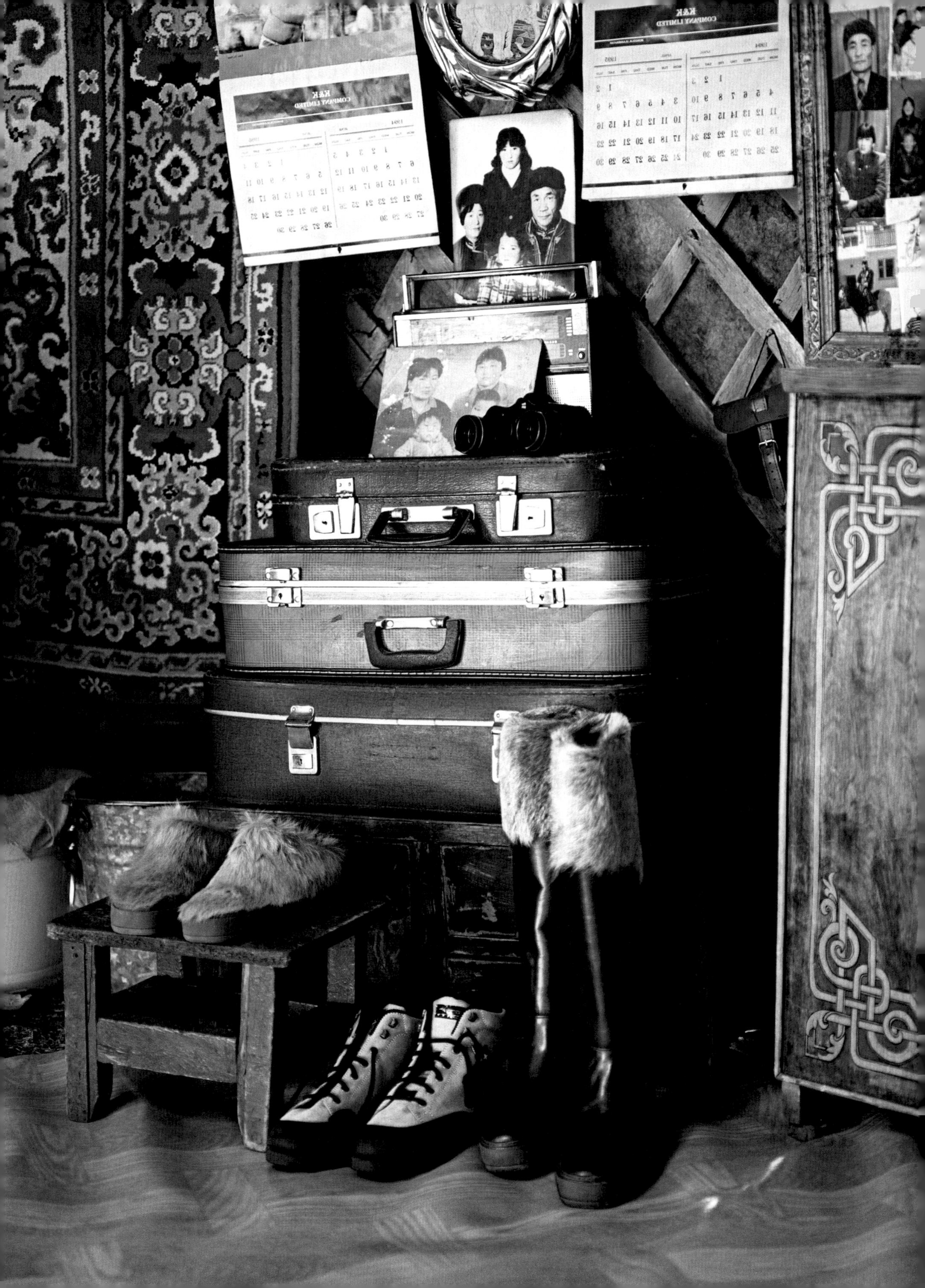

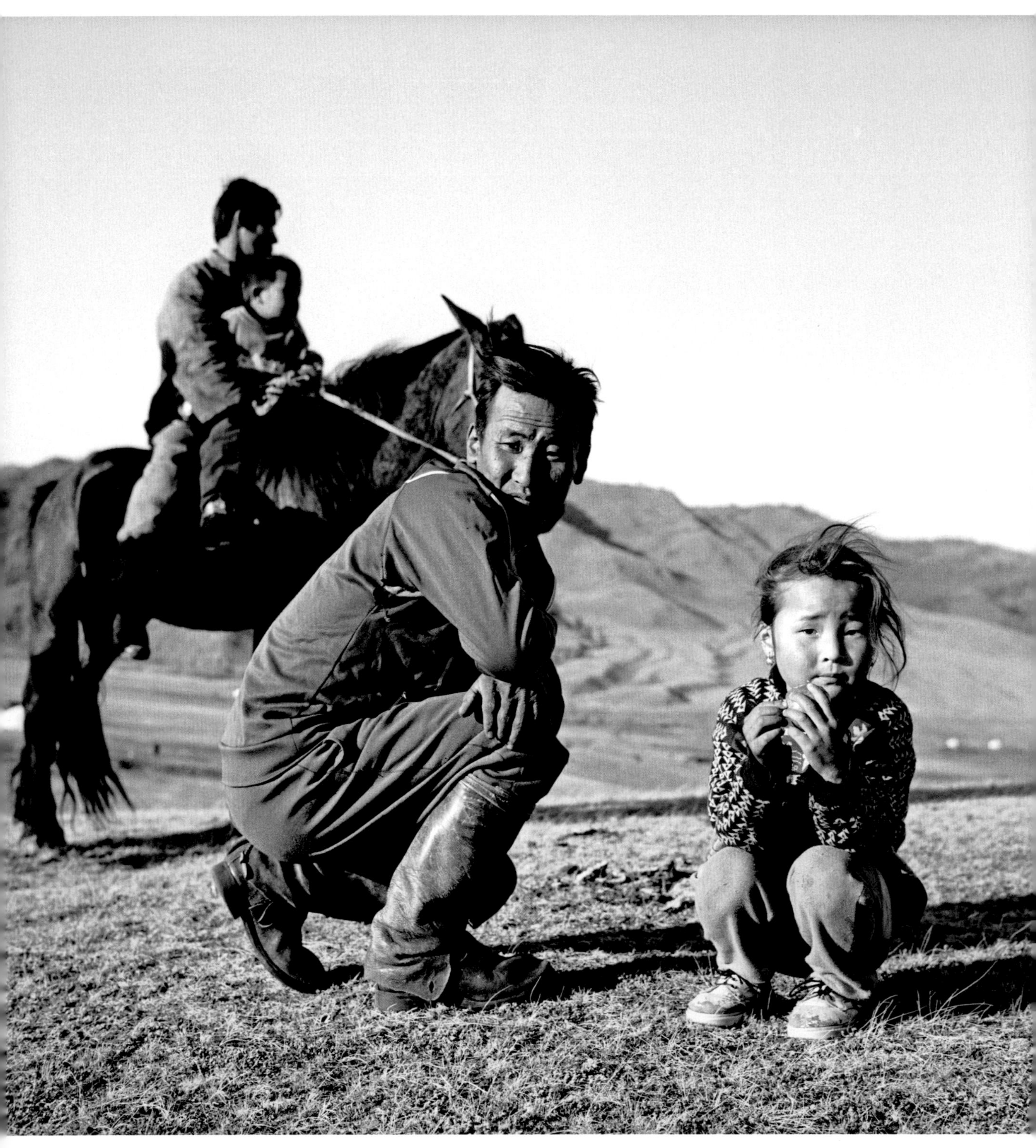

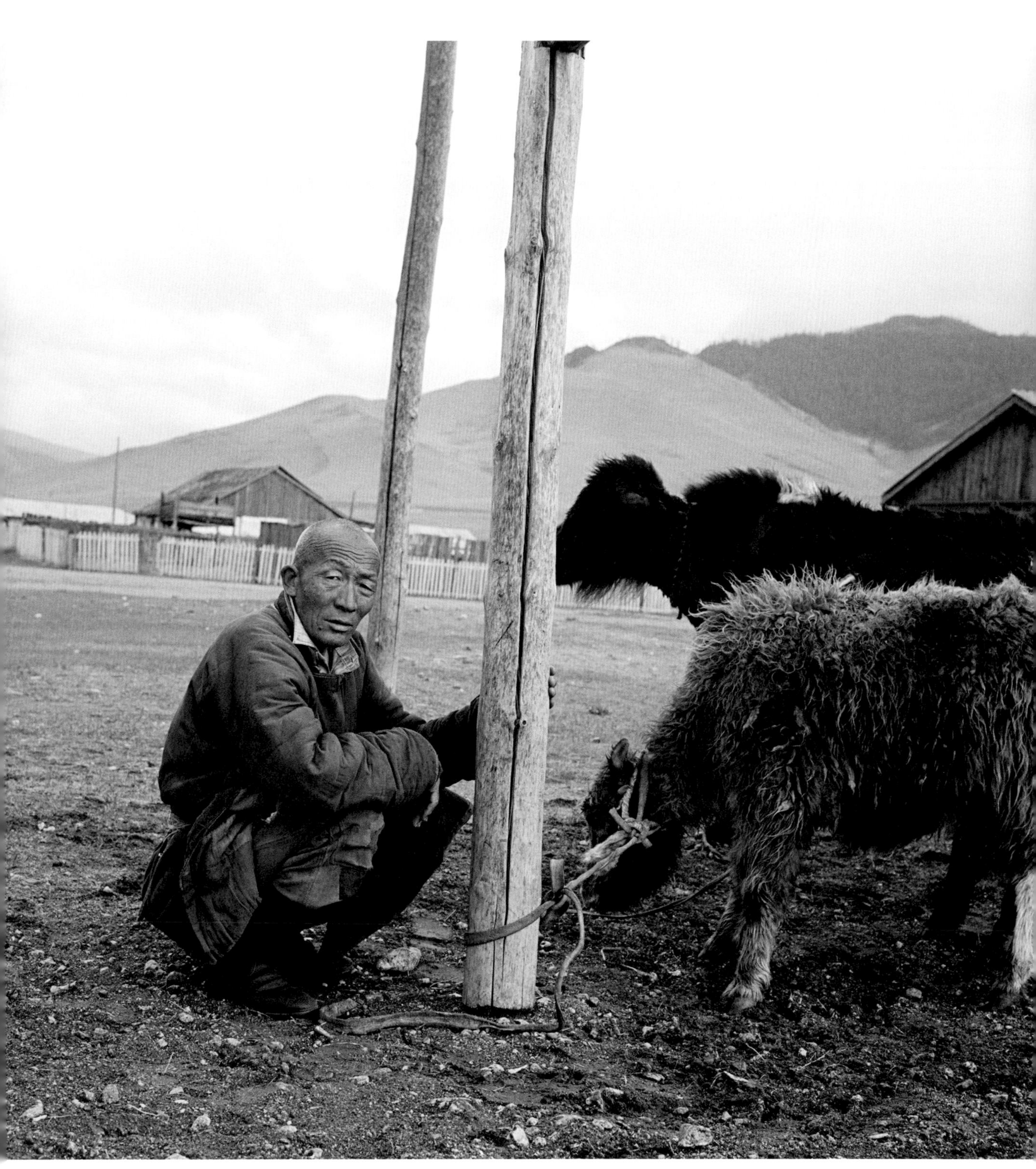

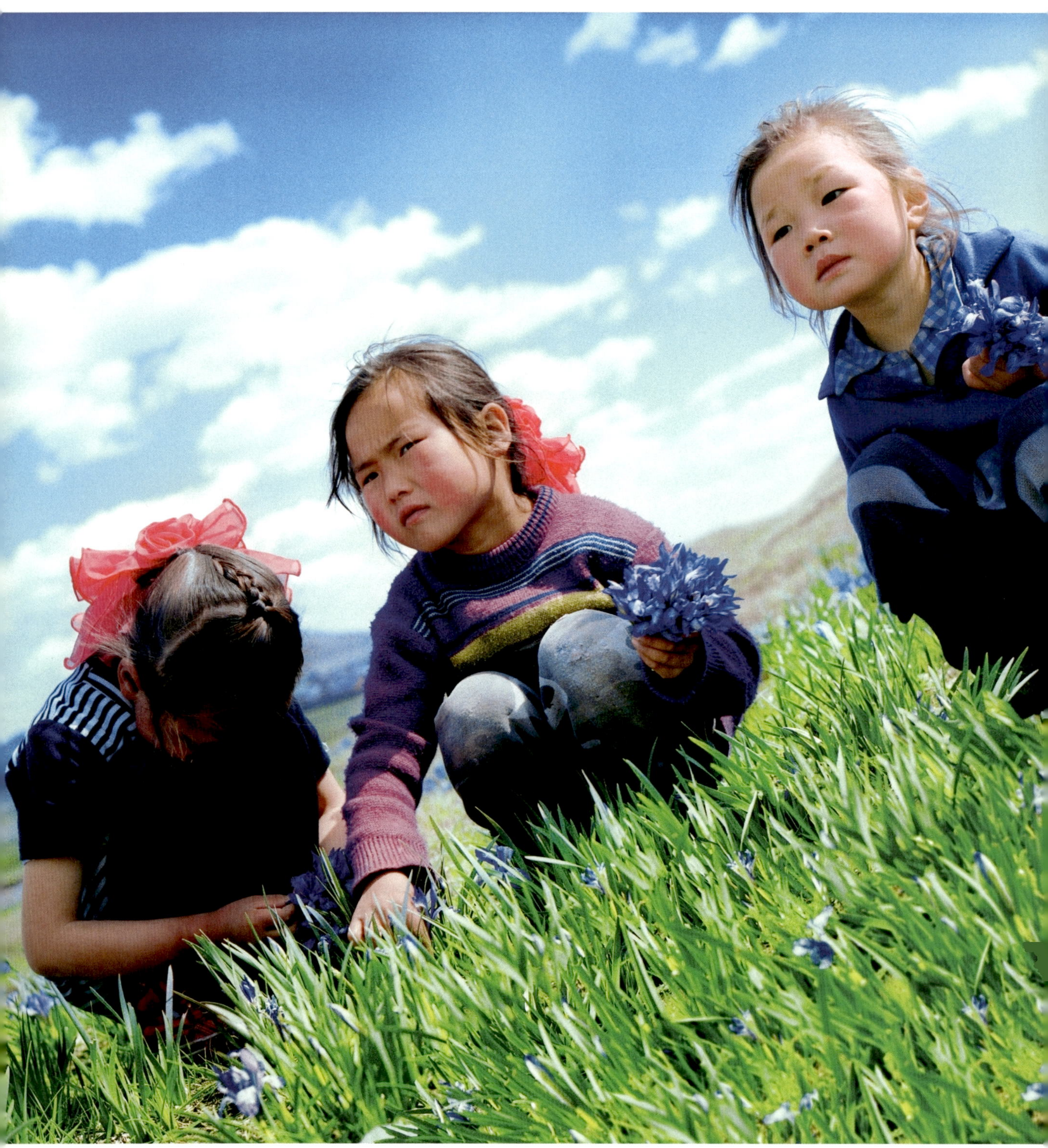

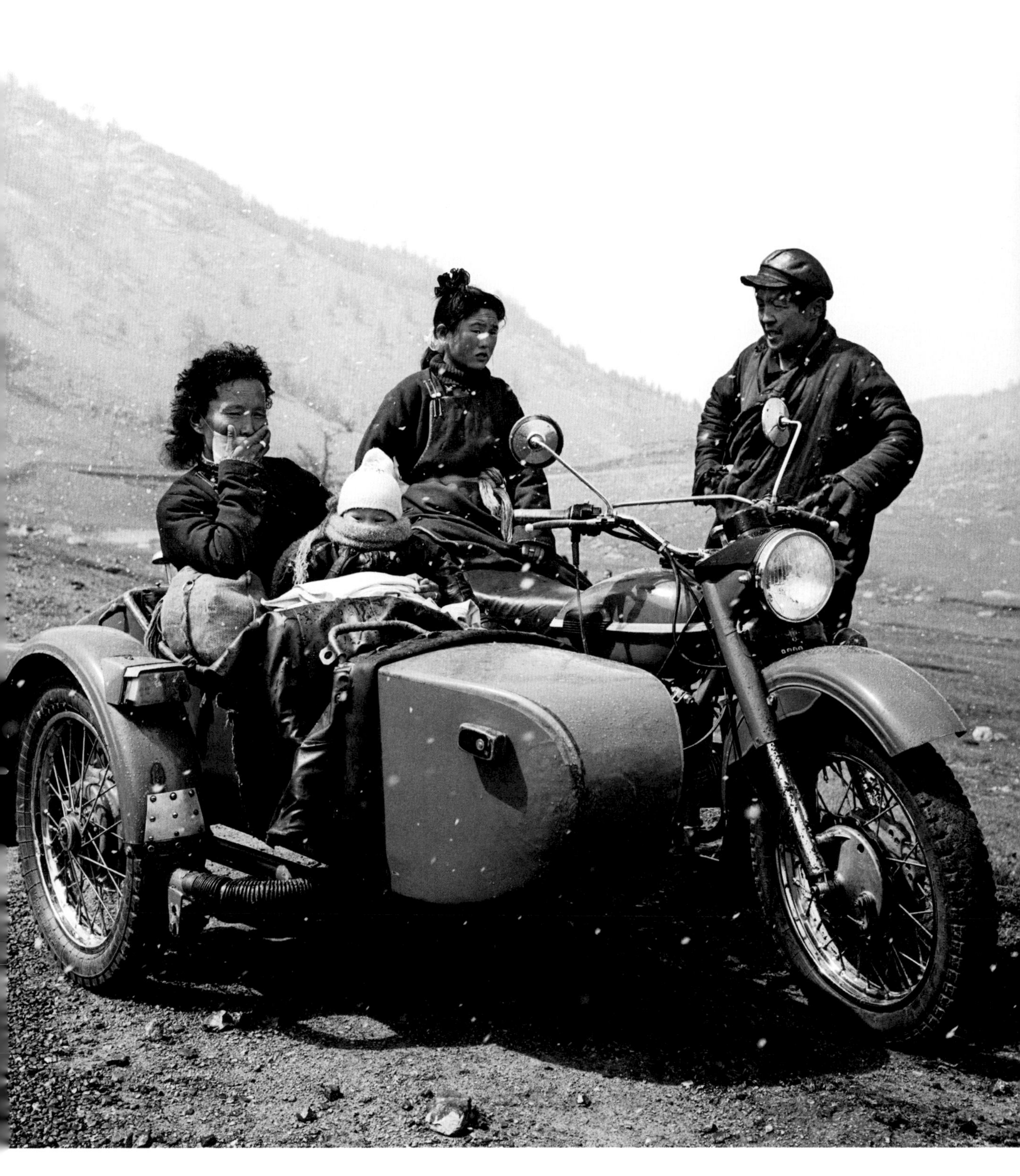

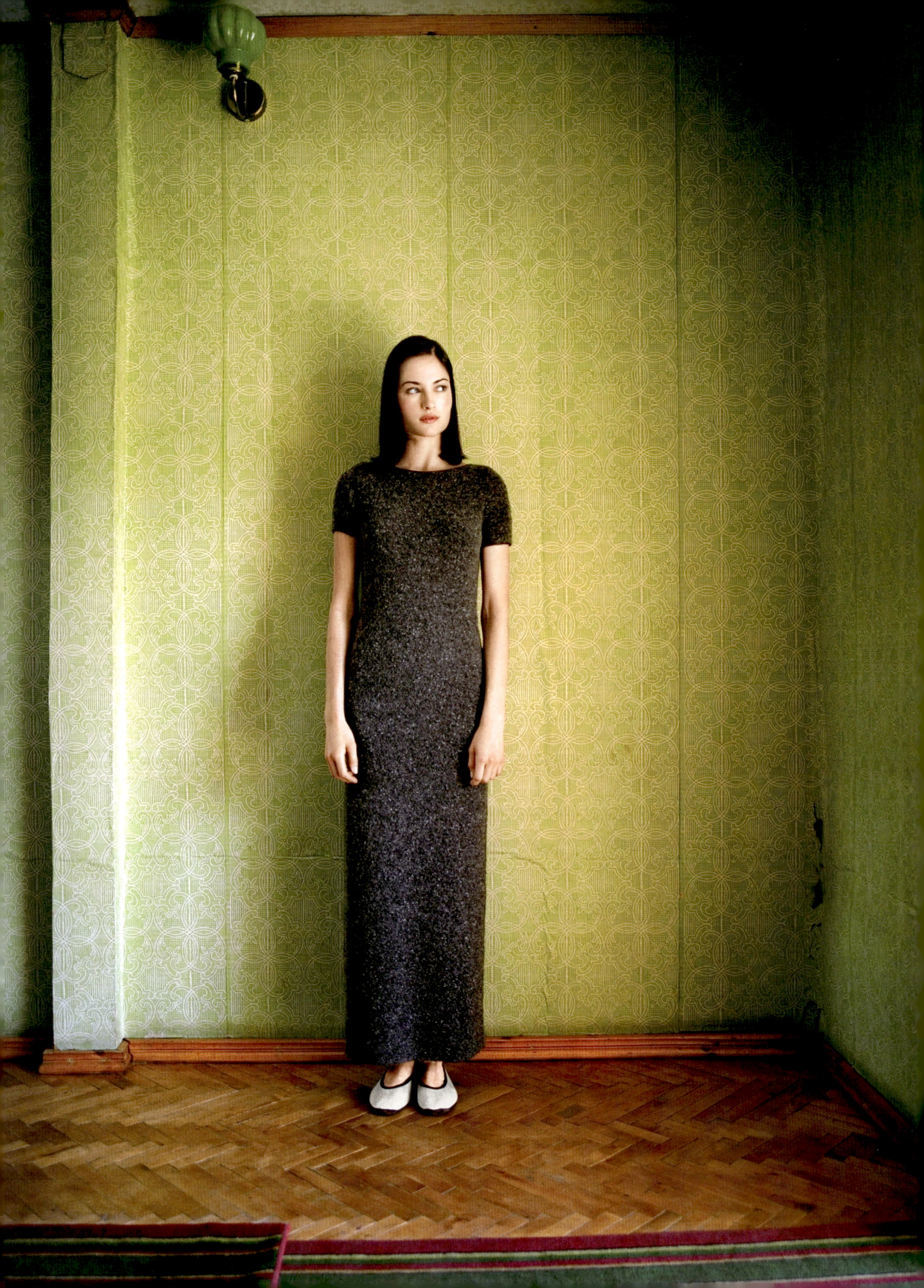

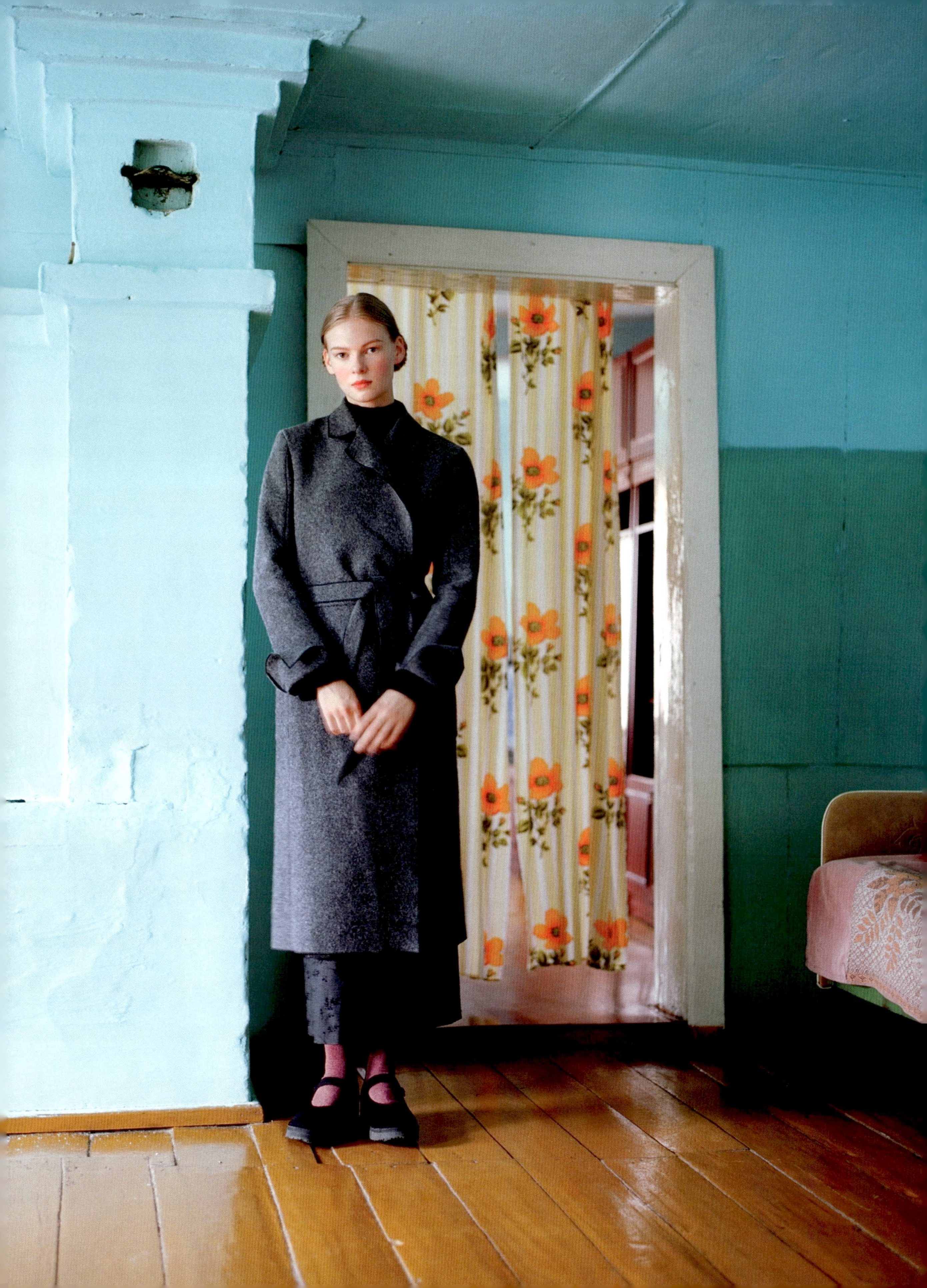

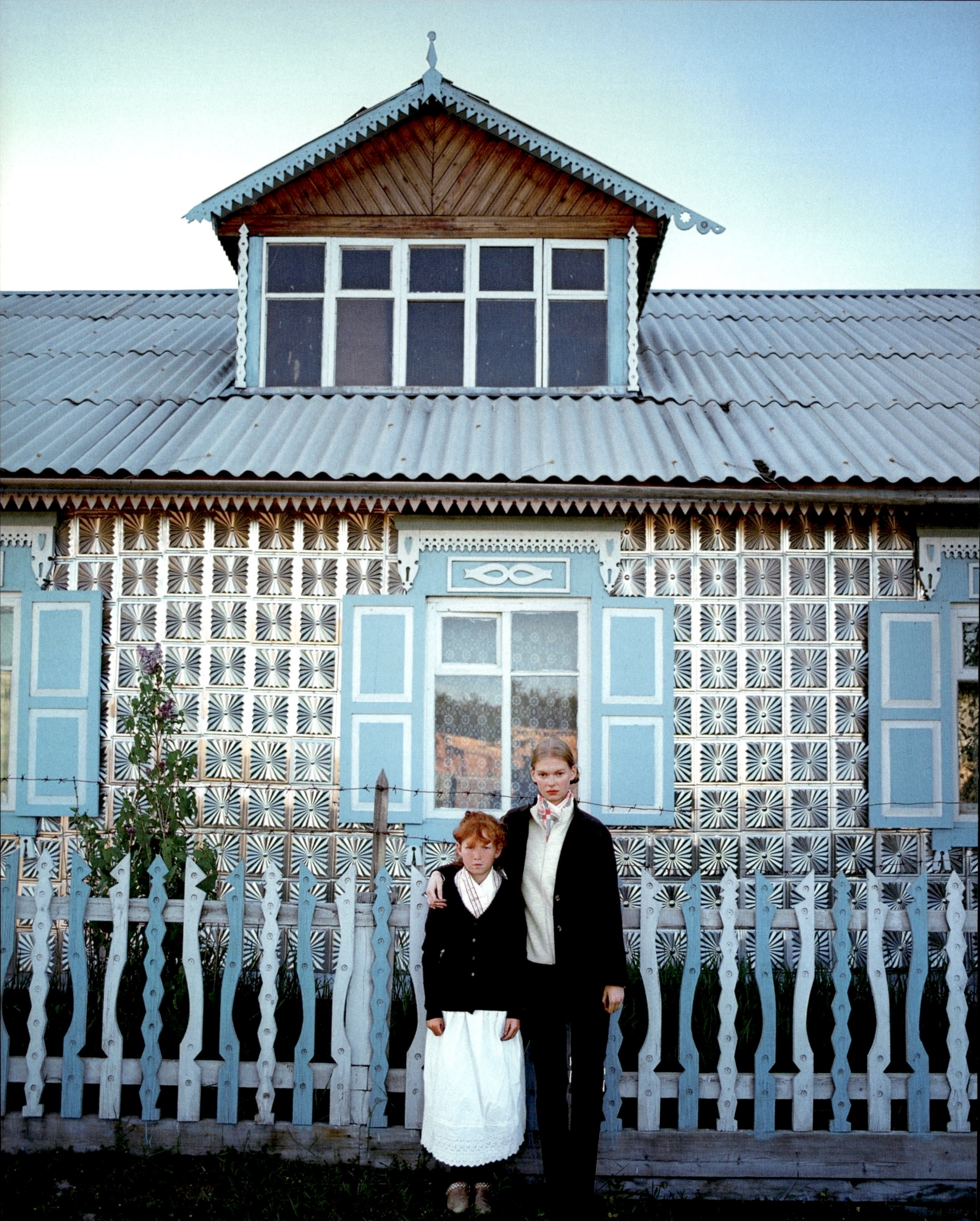

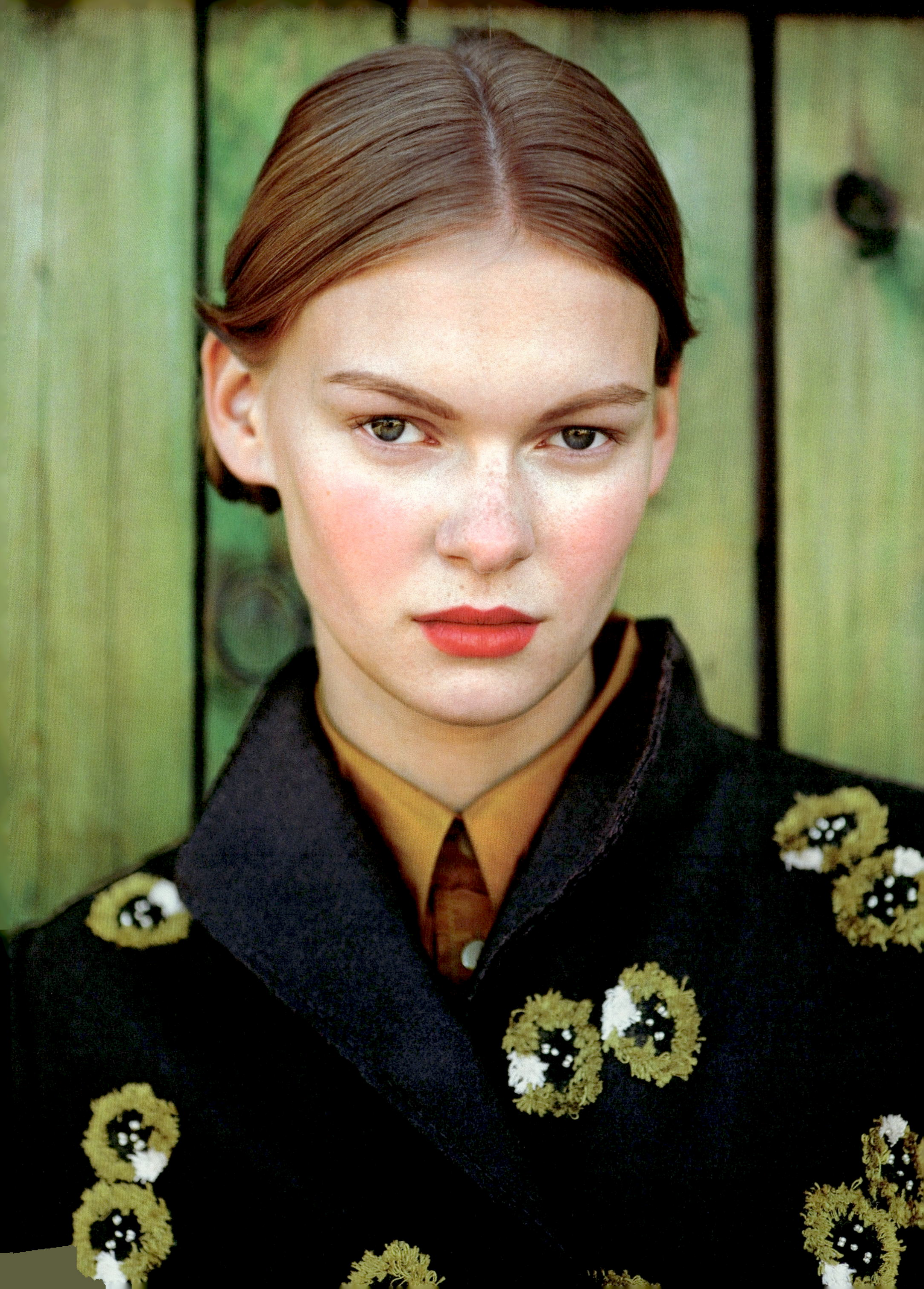

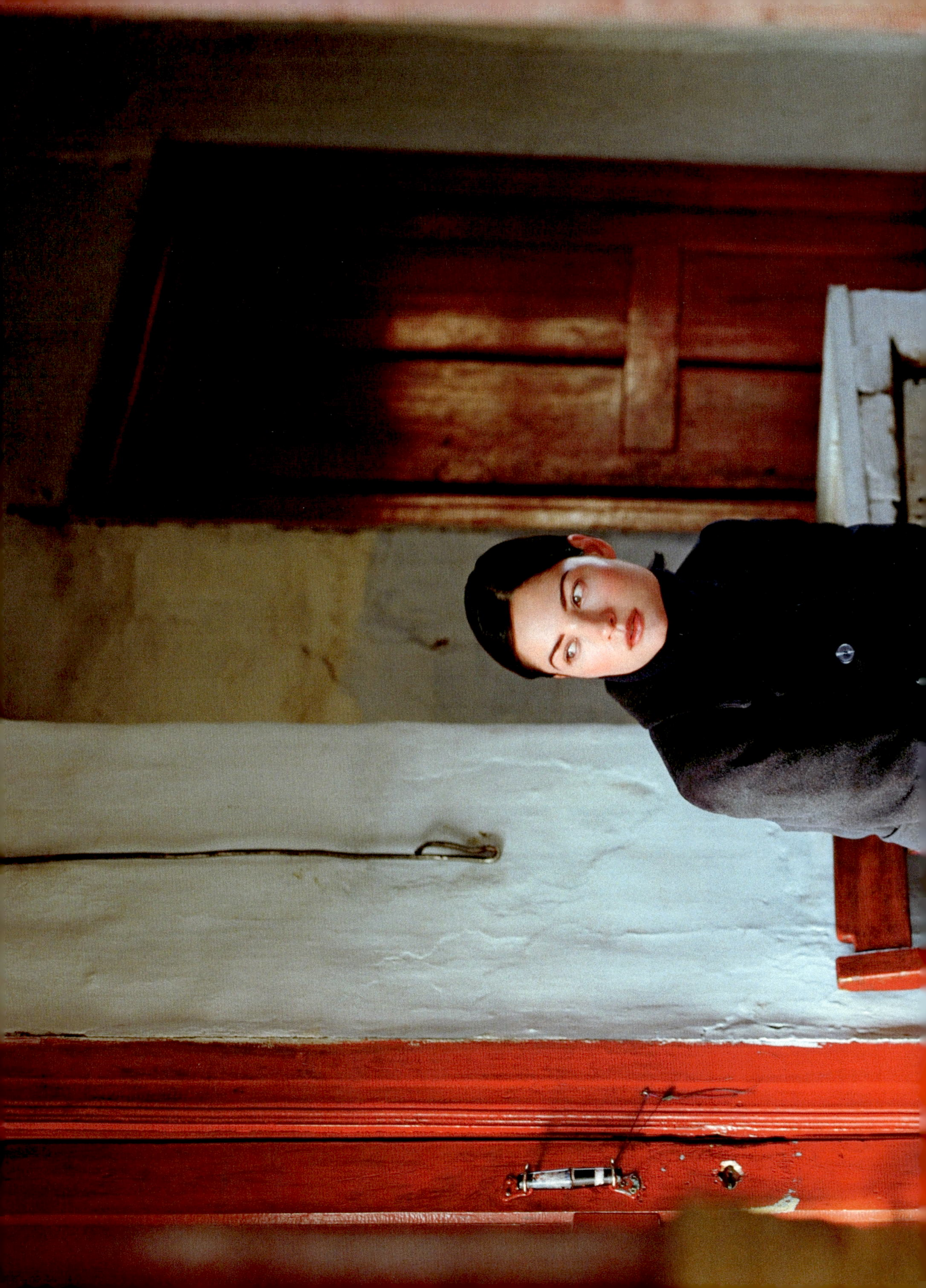

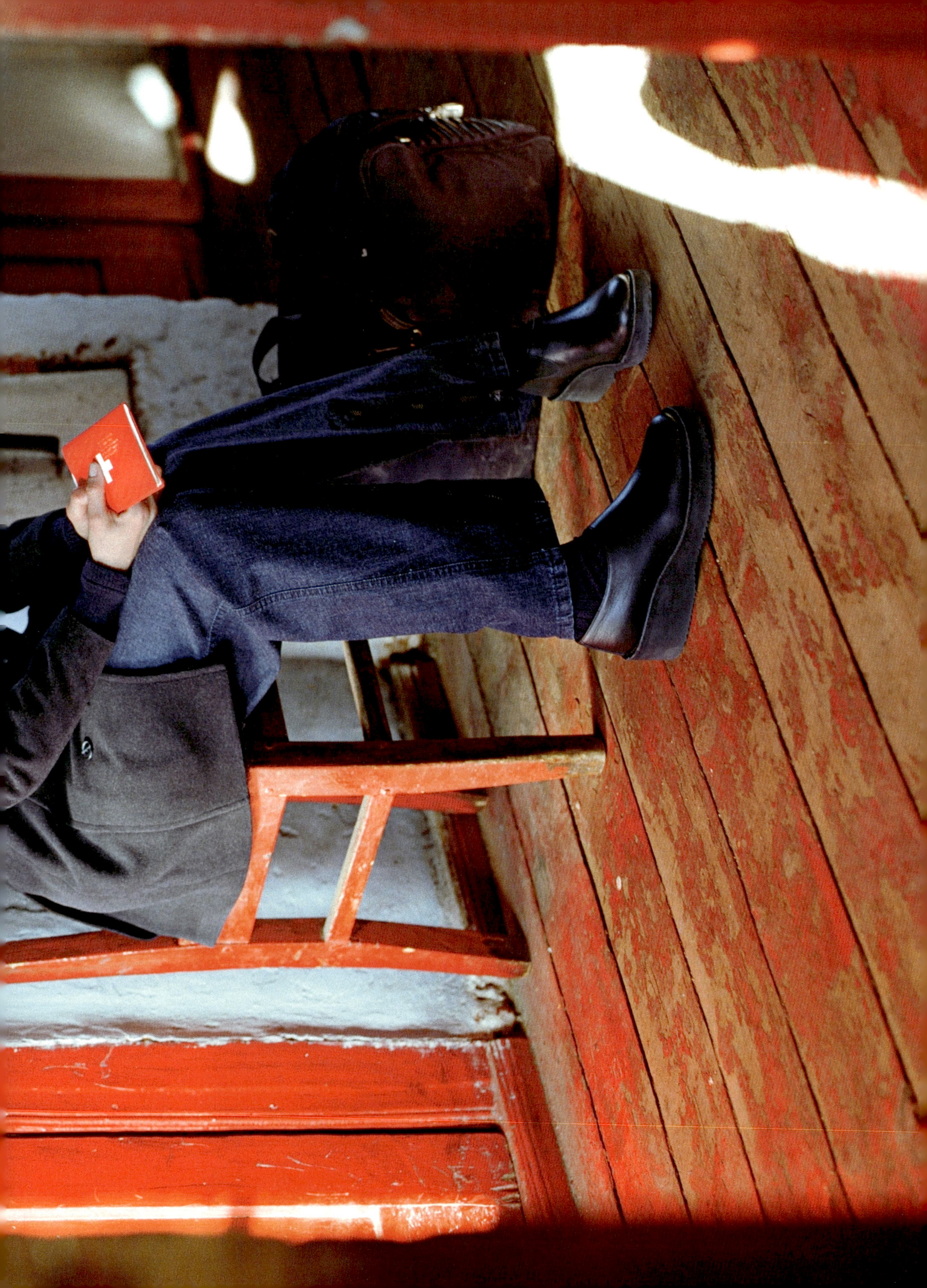

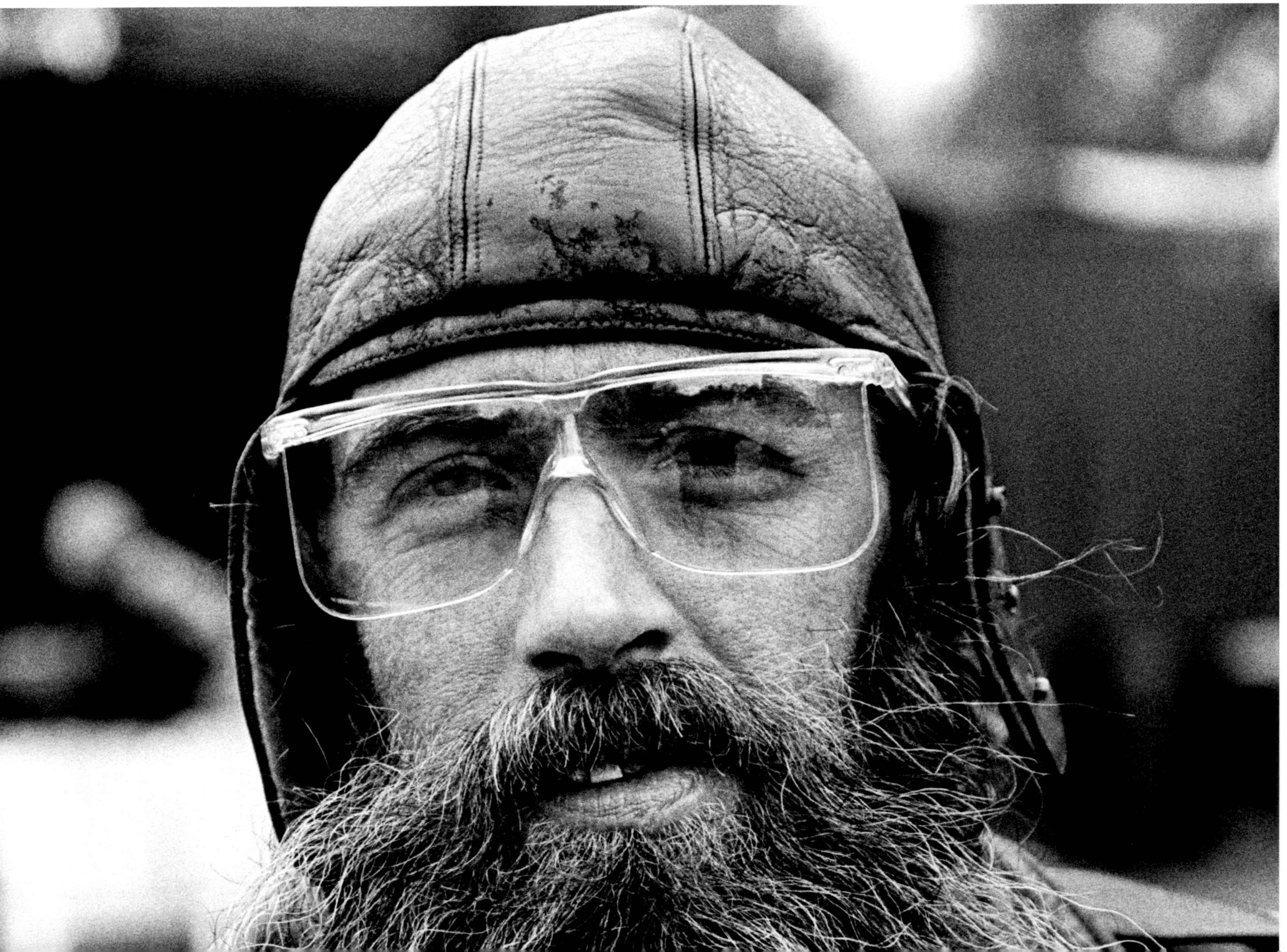

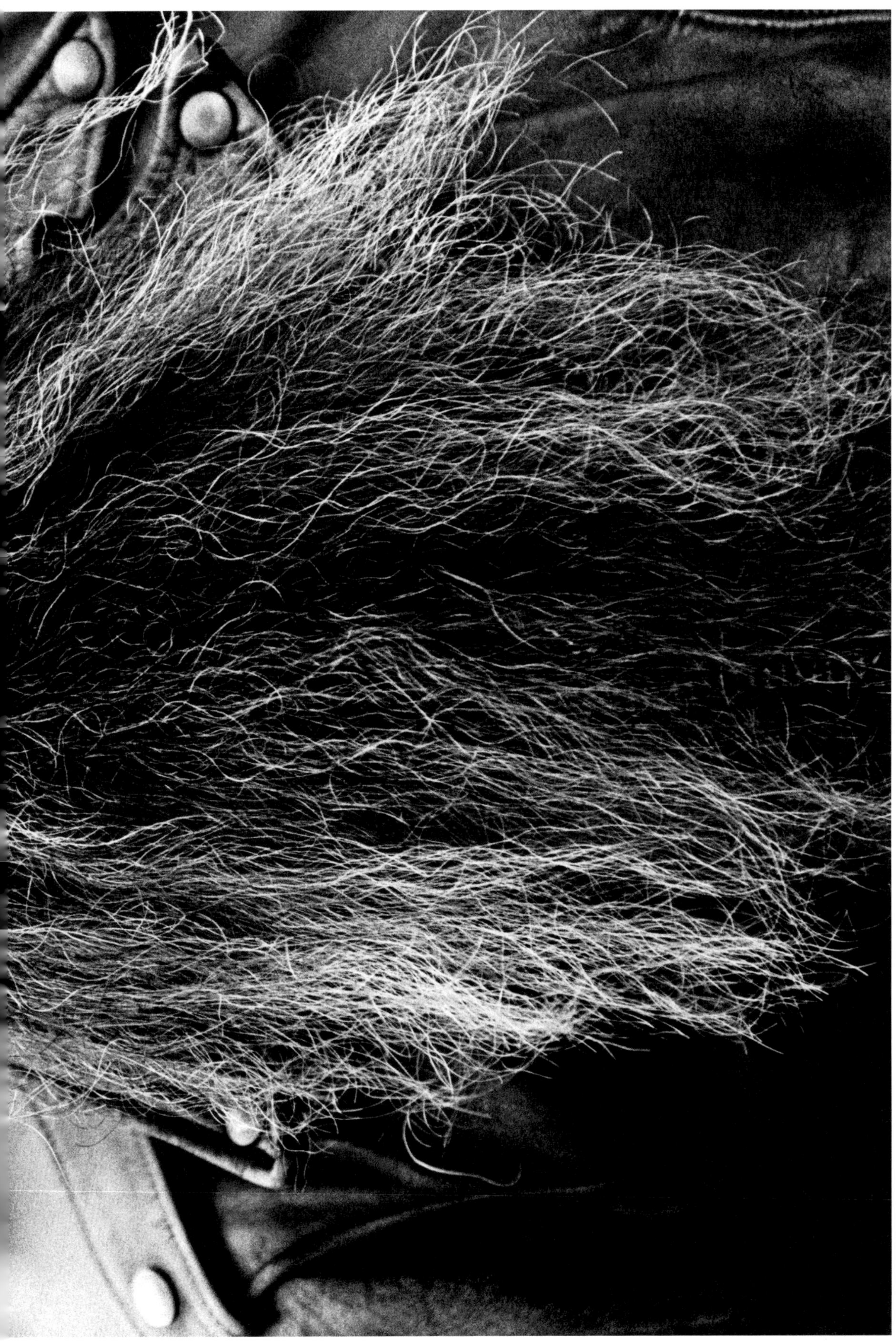

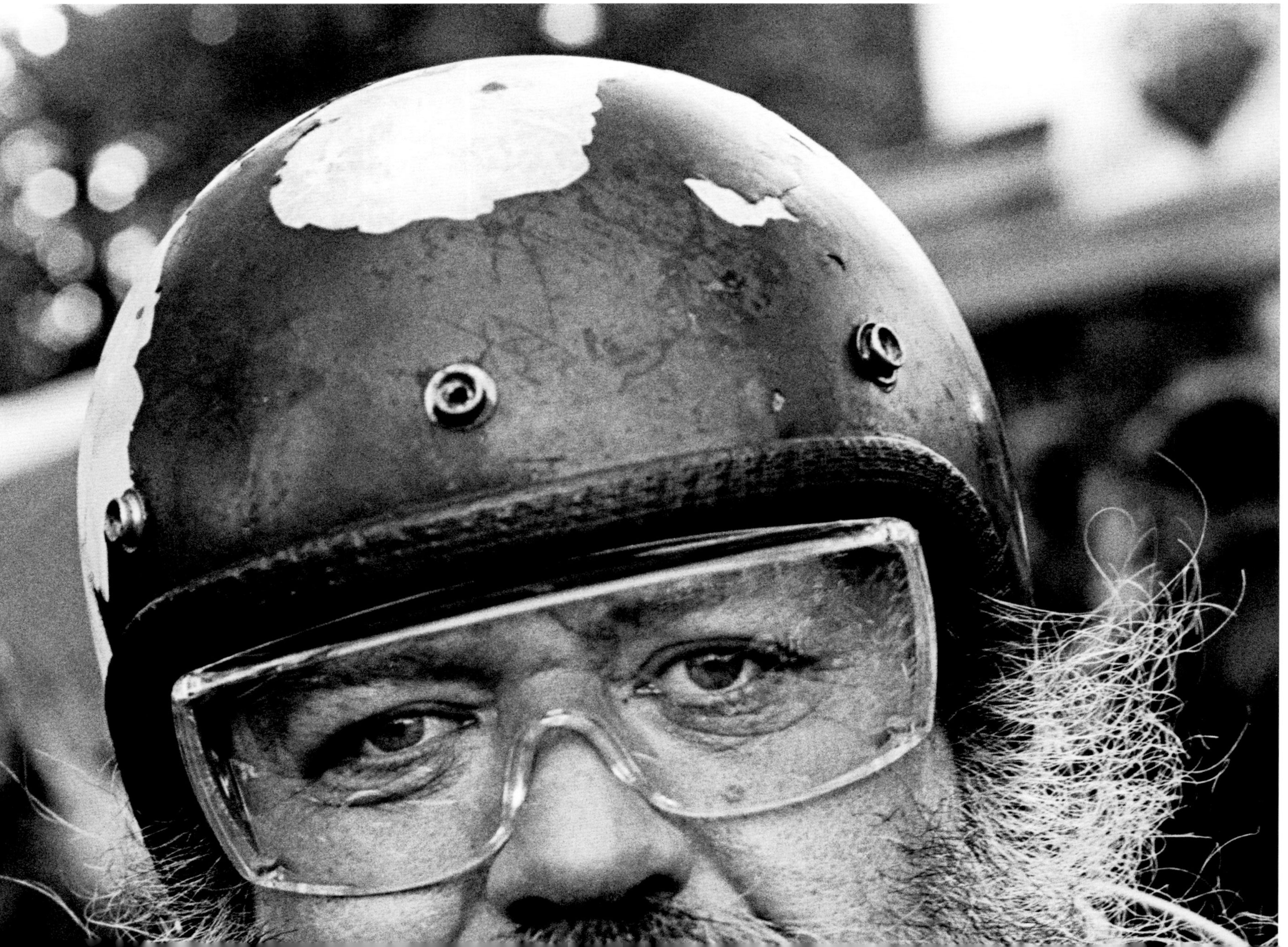

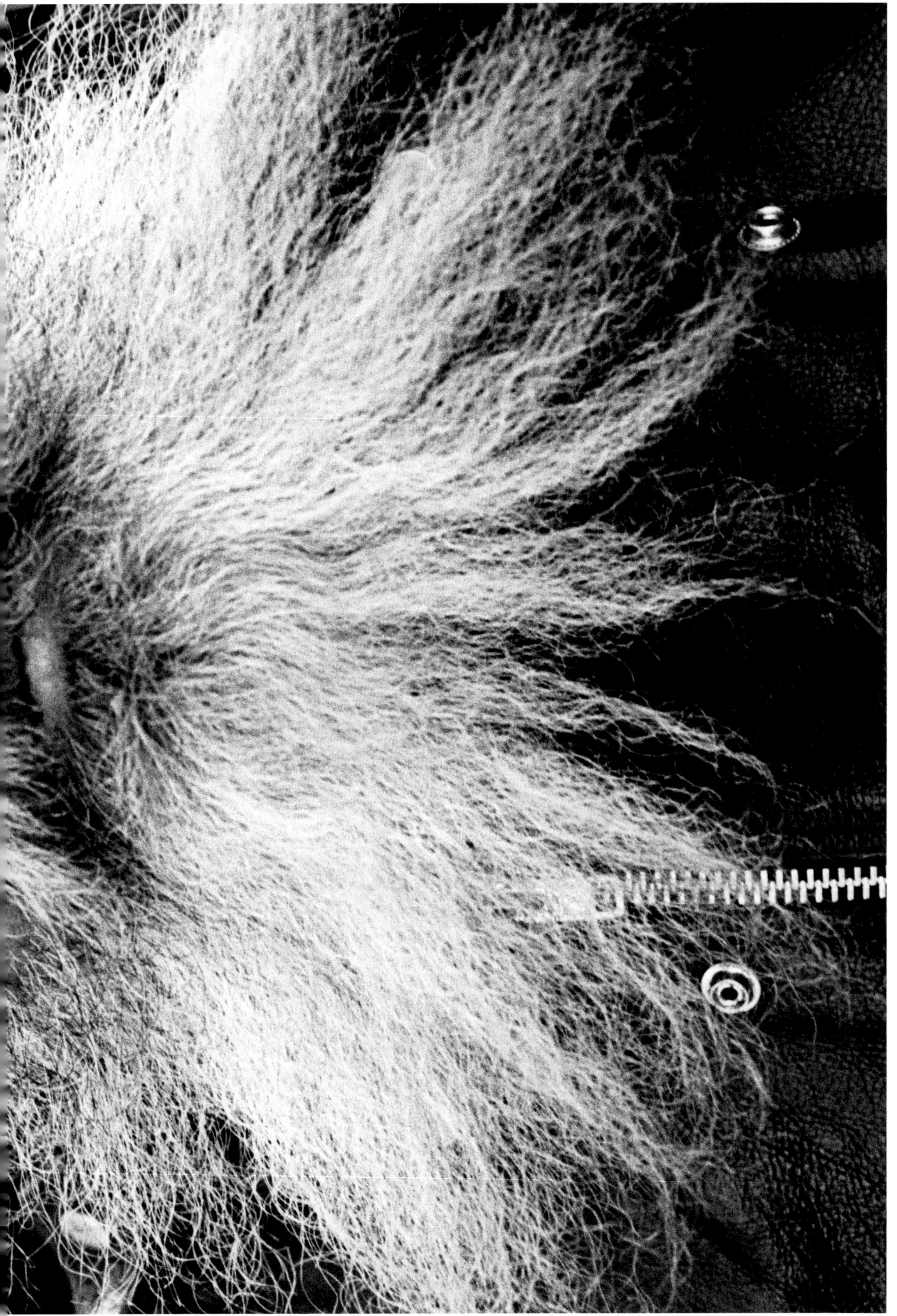

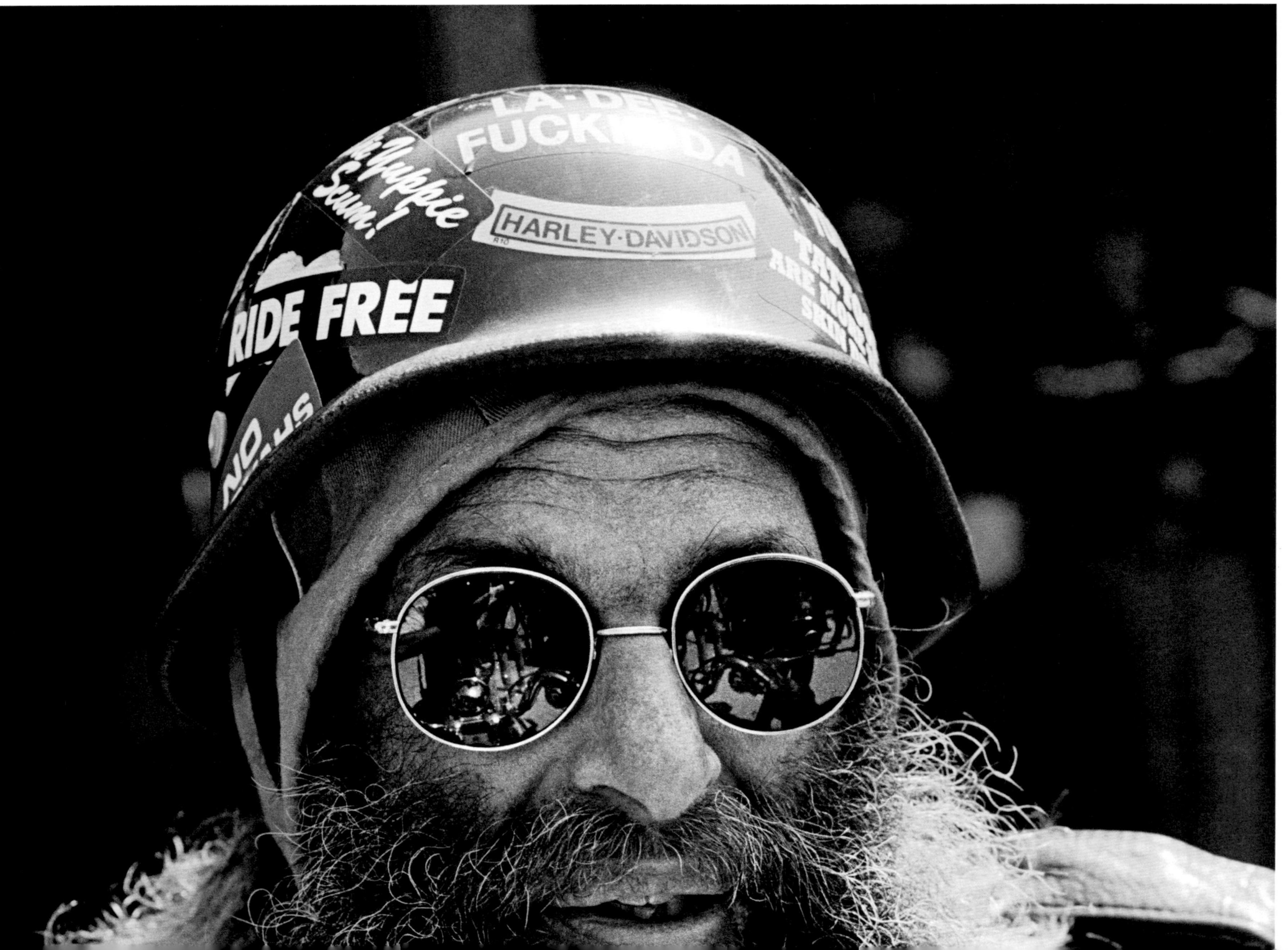
LA·DEE
FUCK DA
Yuppie
Scum!
HARLEY·DAVIDSON
RIDE FREE
NO US

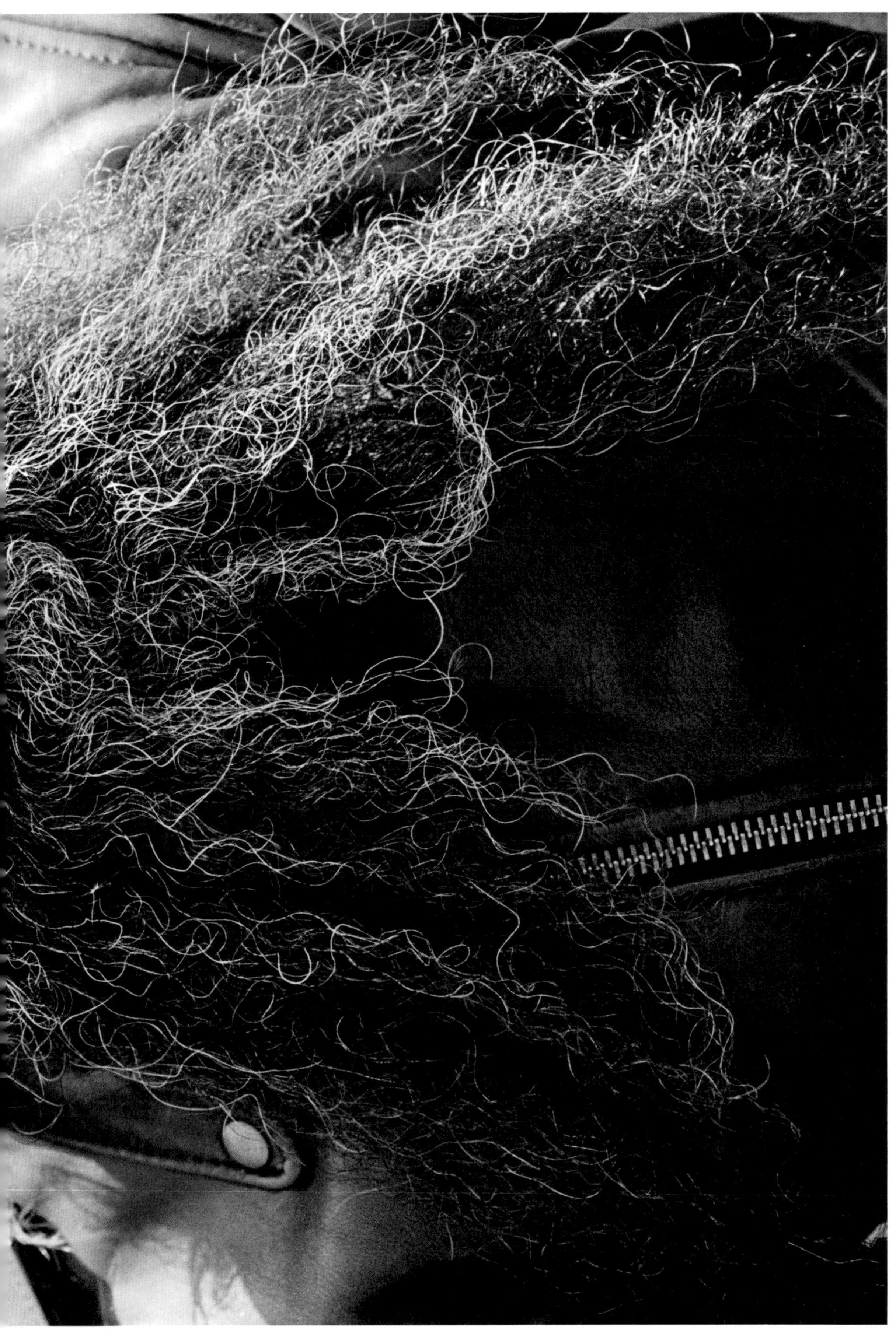

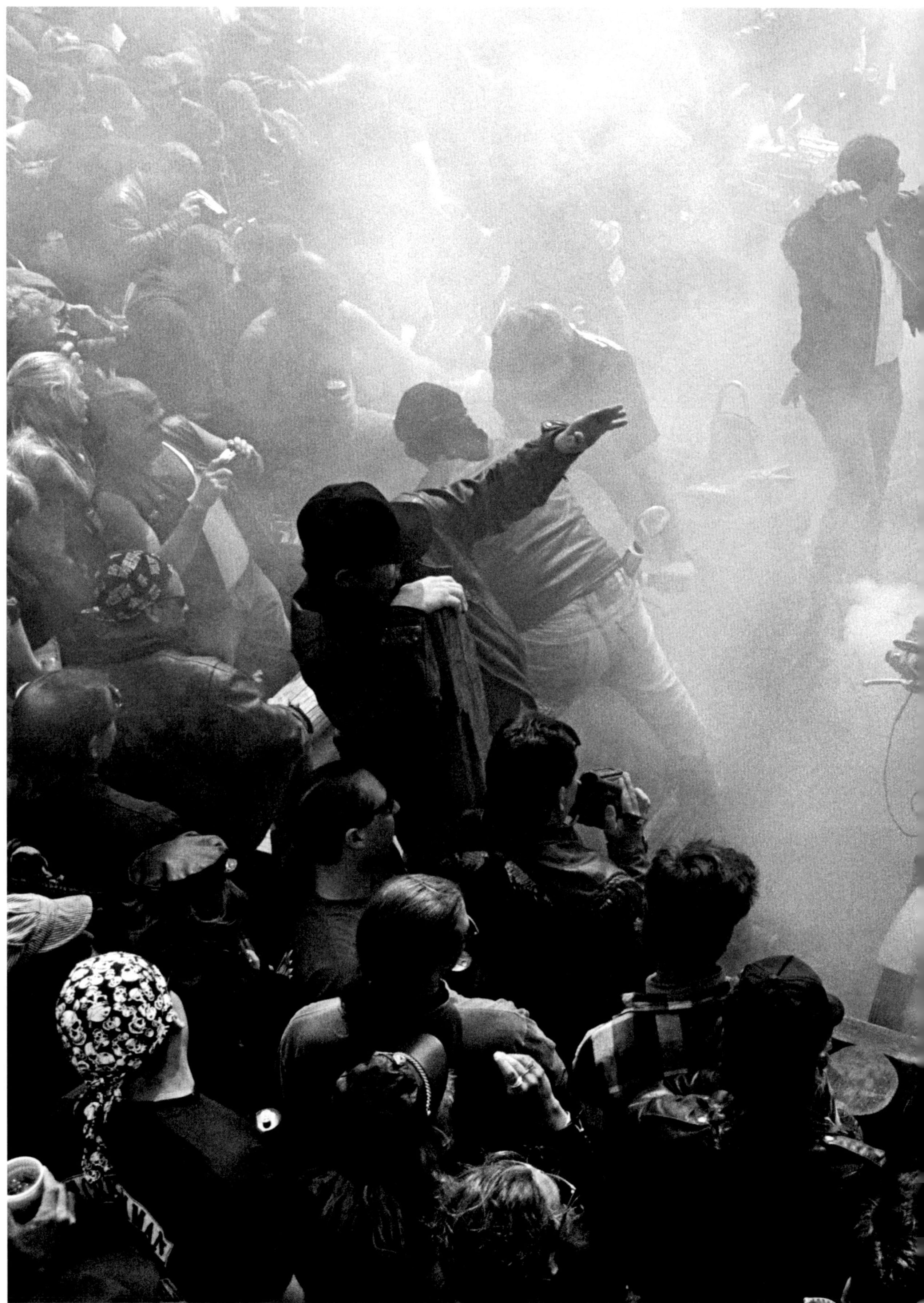

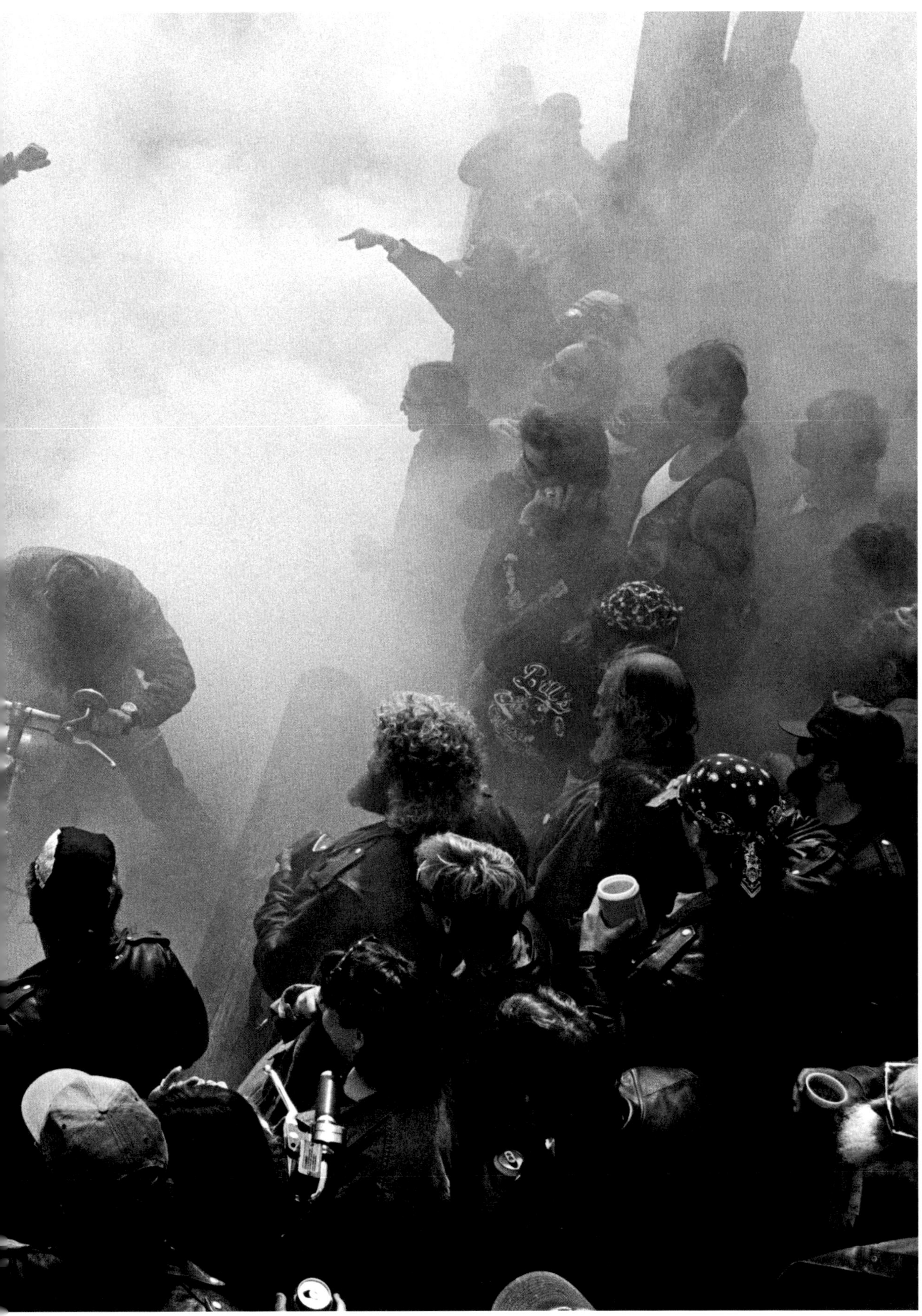

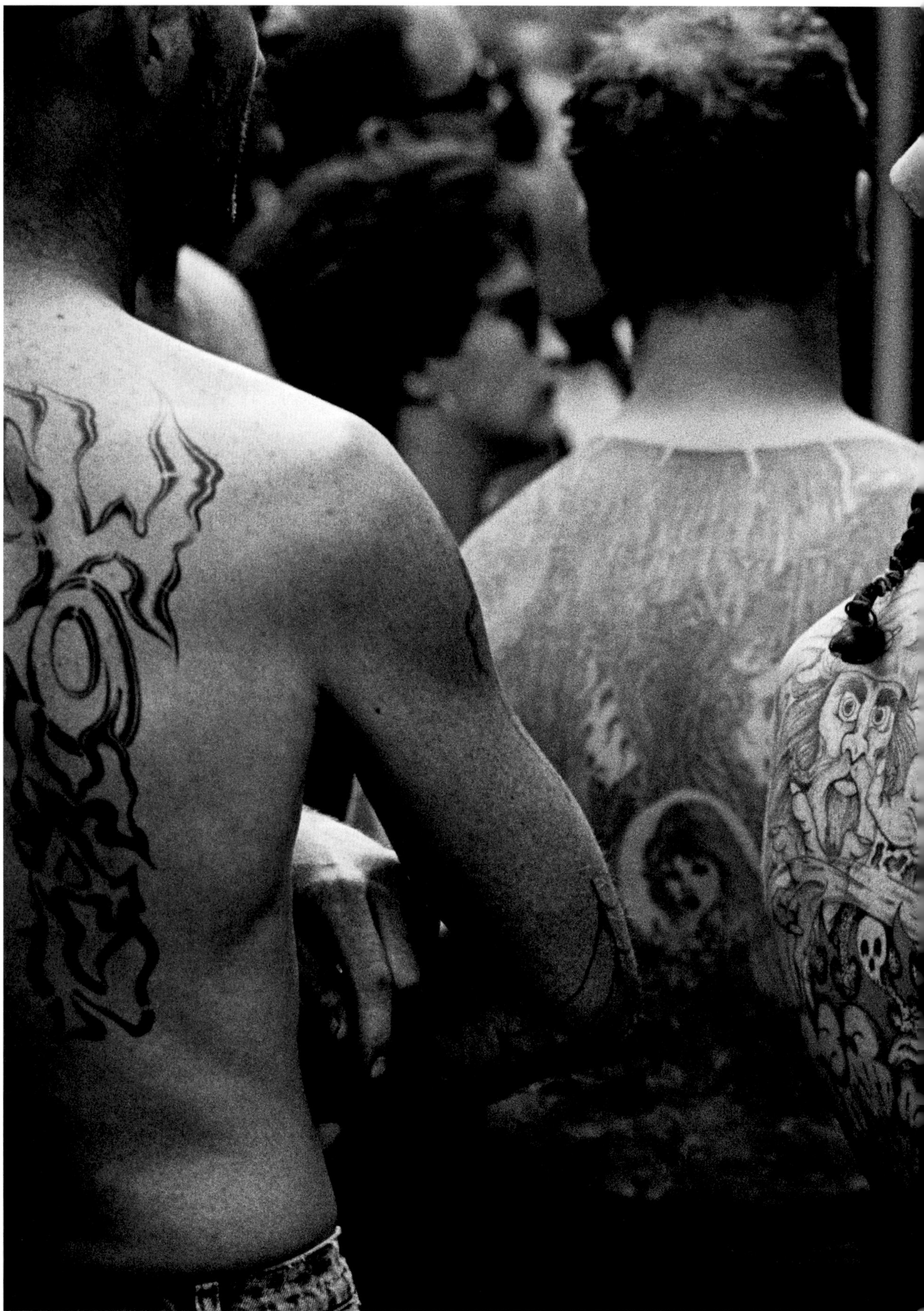

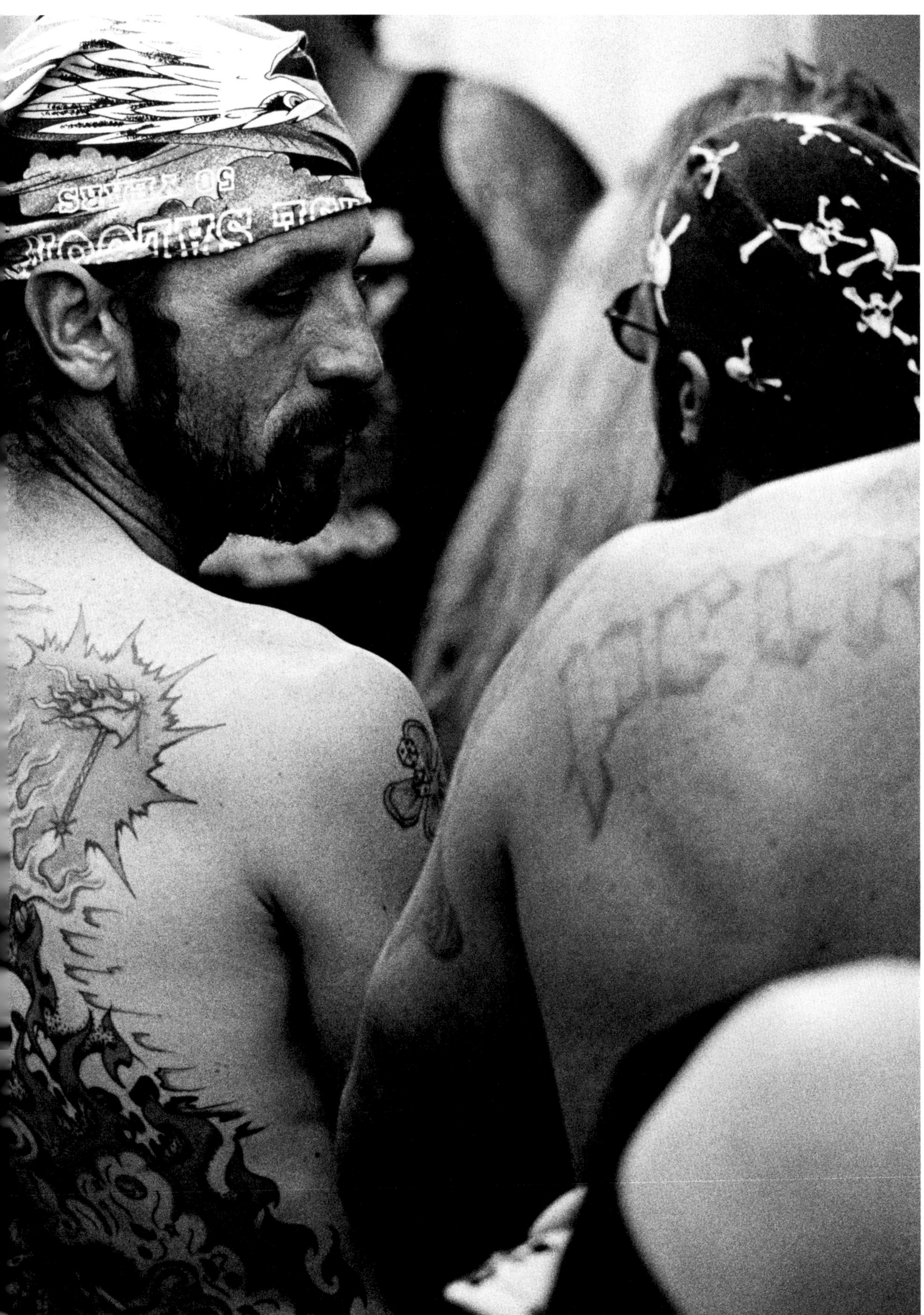

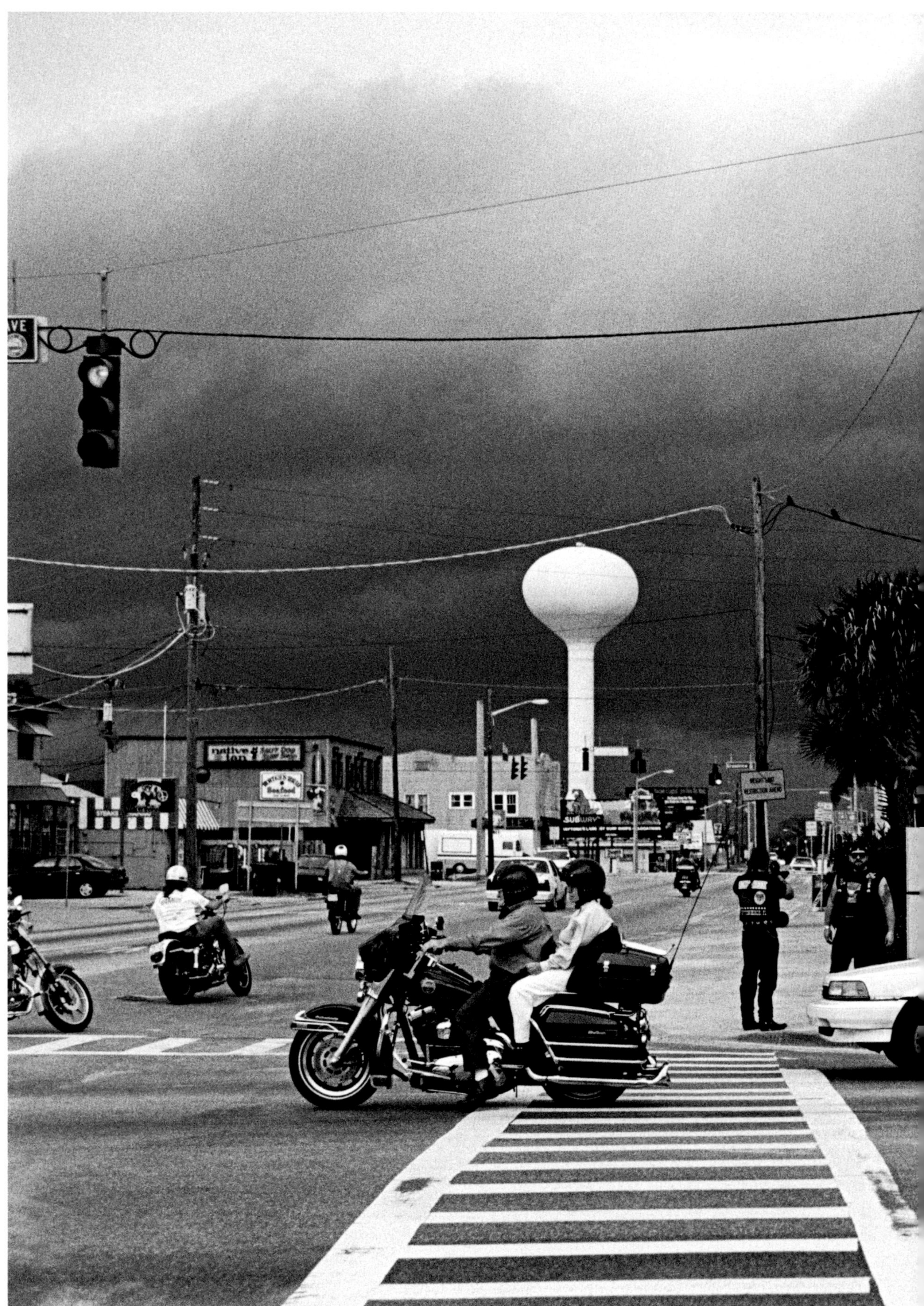

native
on
SUBWAY

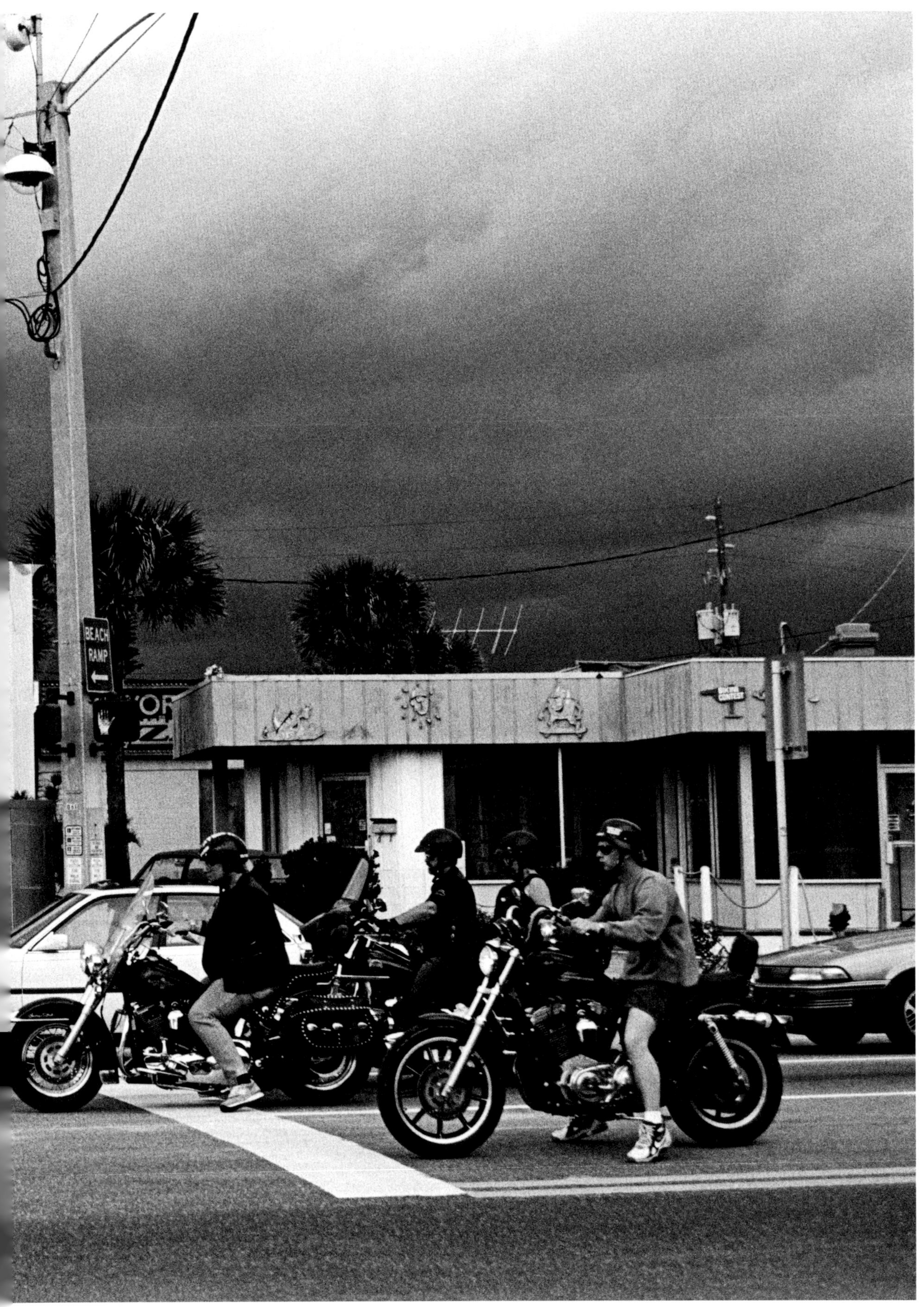

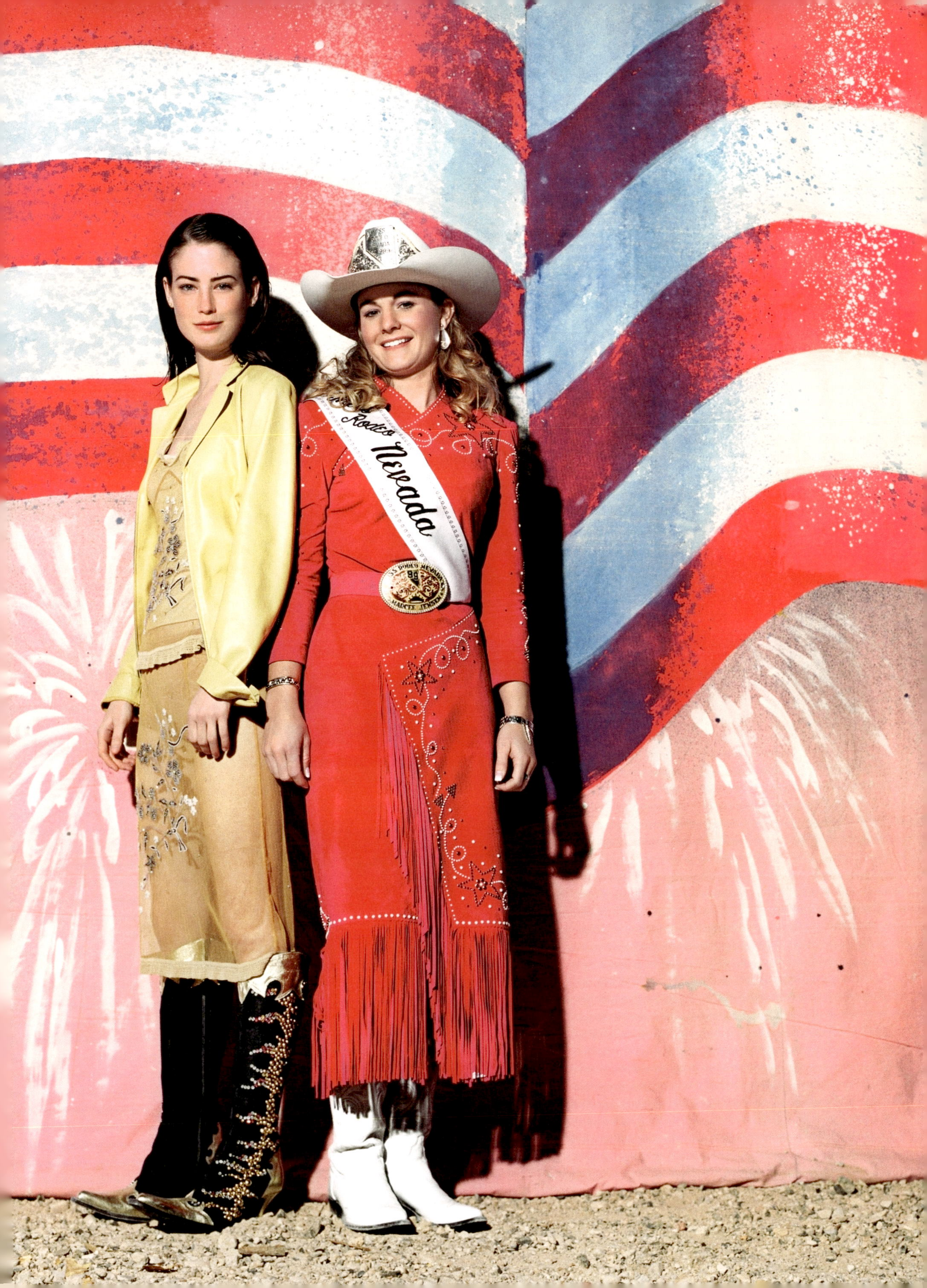
Rodeo
Nevada

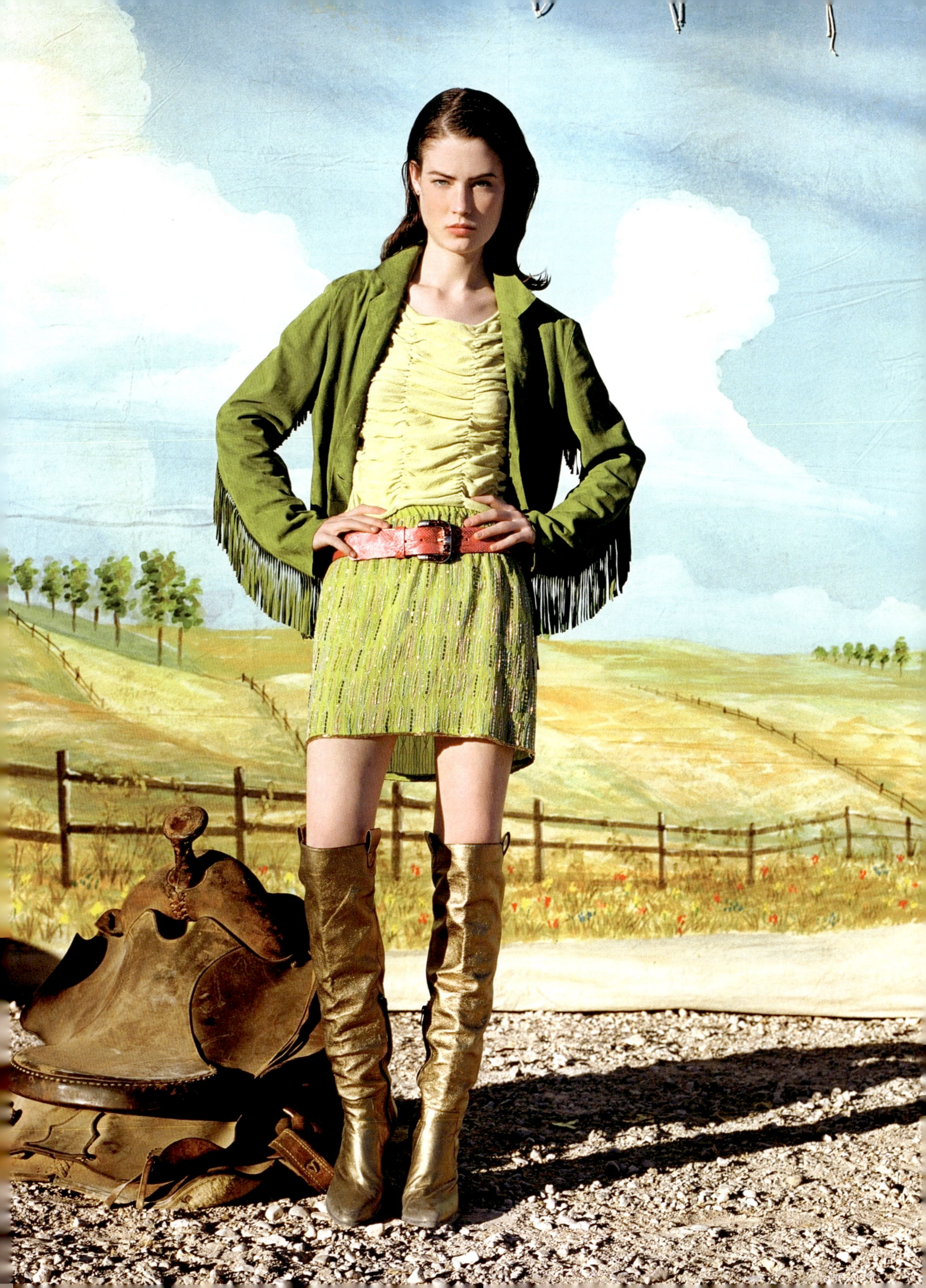

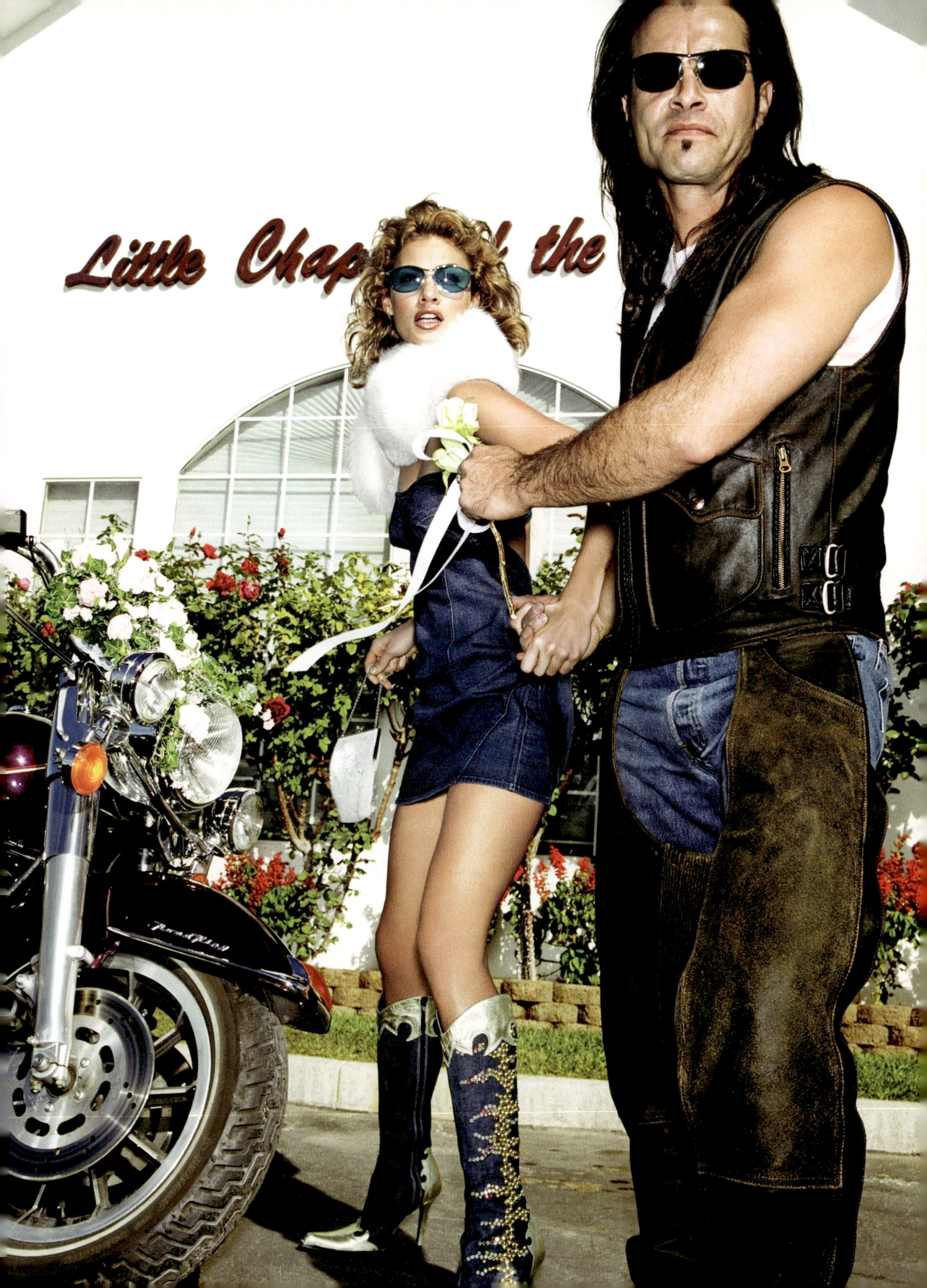

Little Chap   the

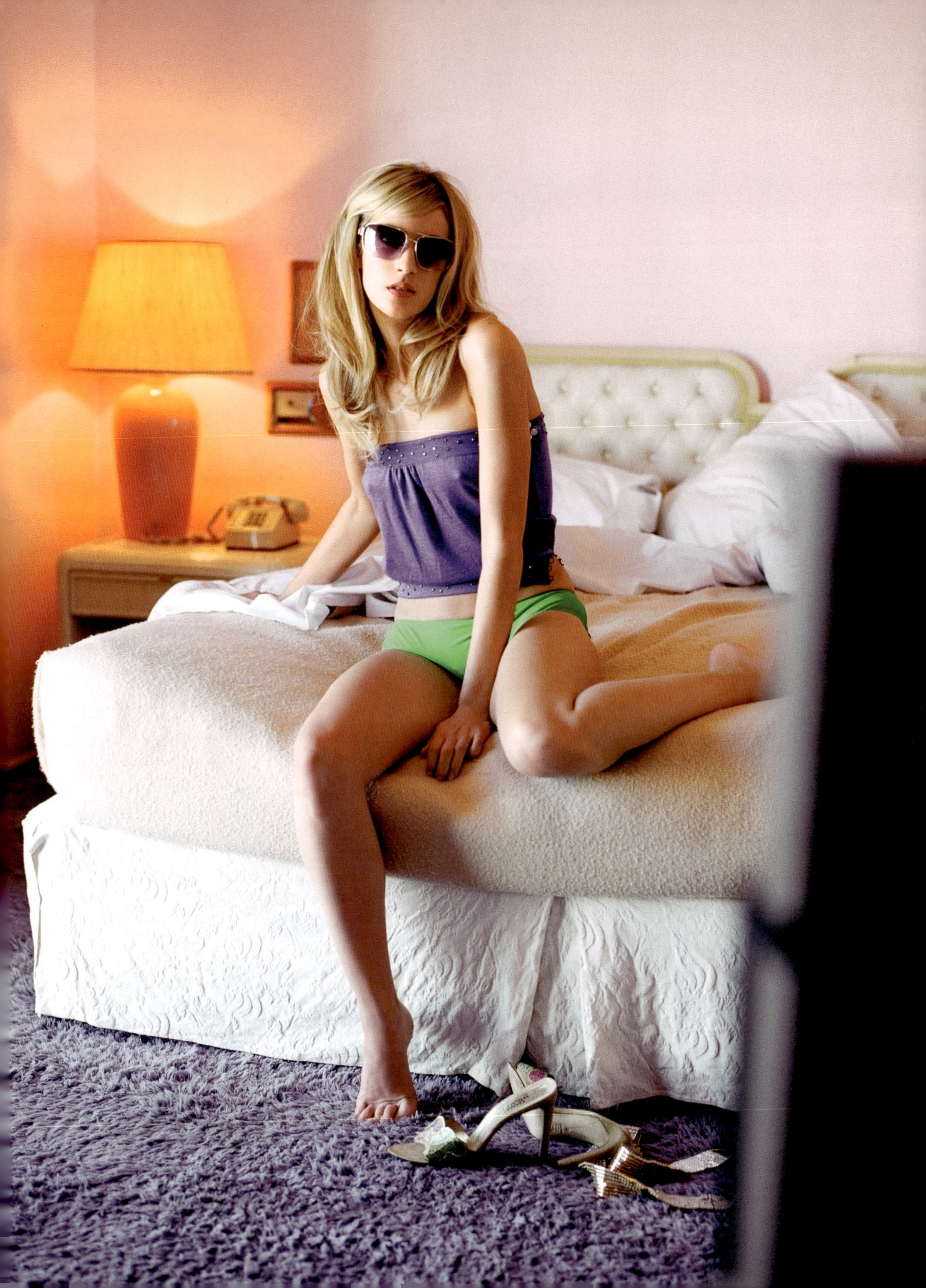

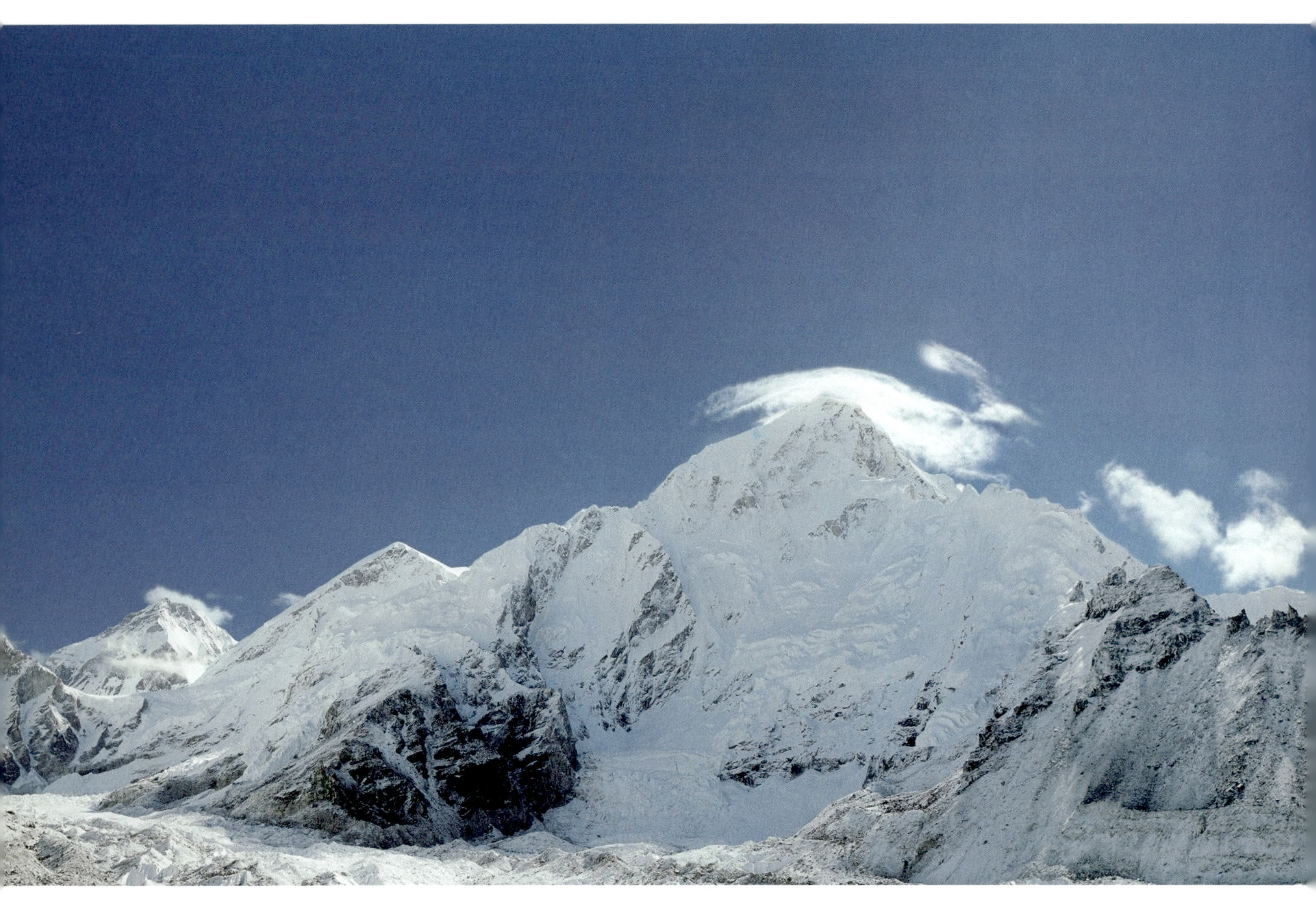

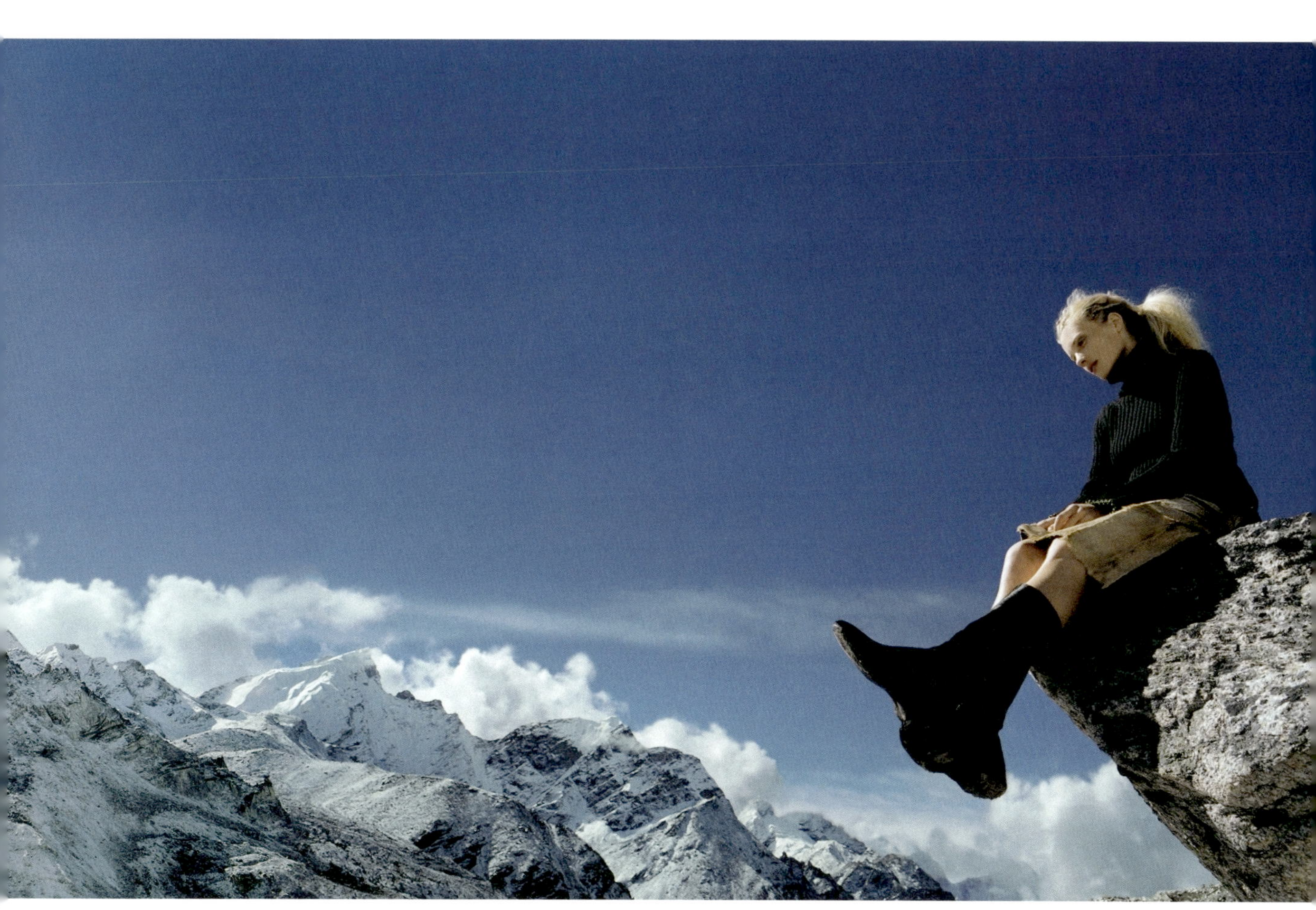

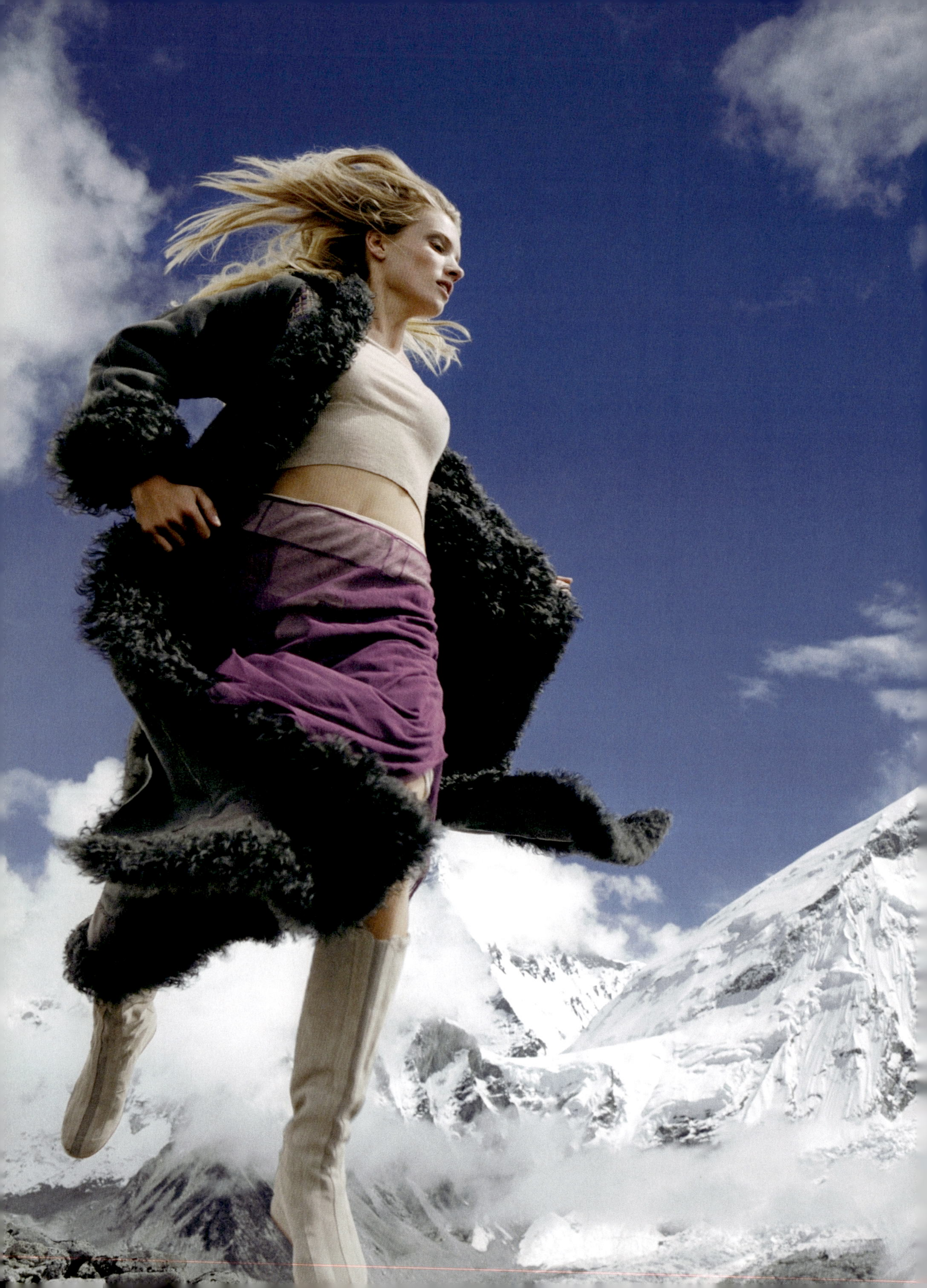

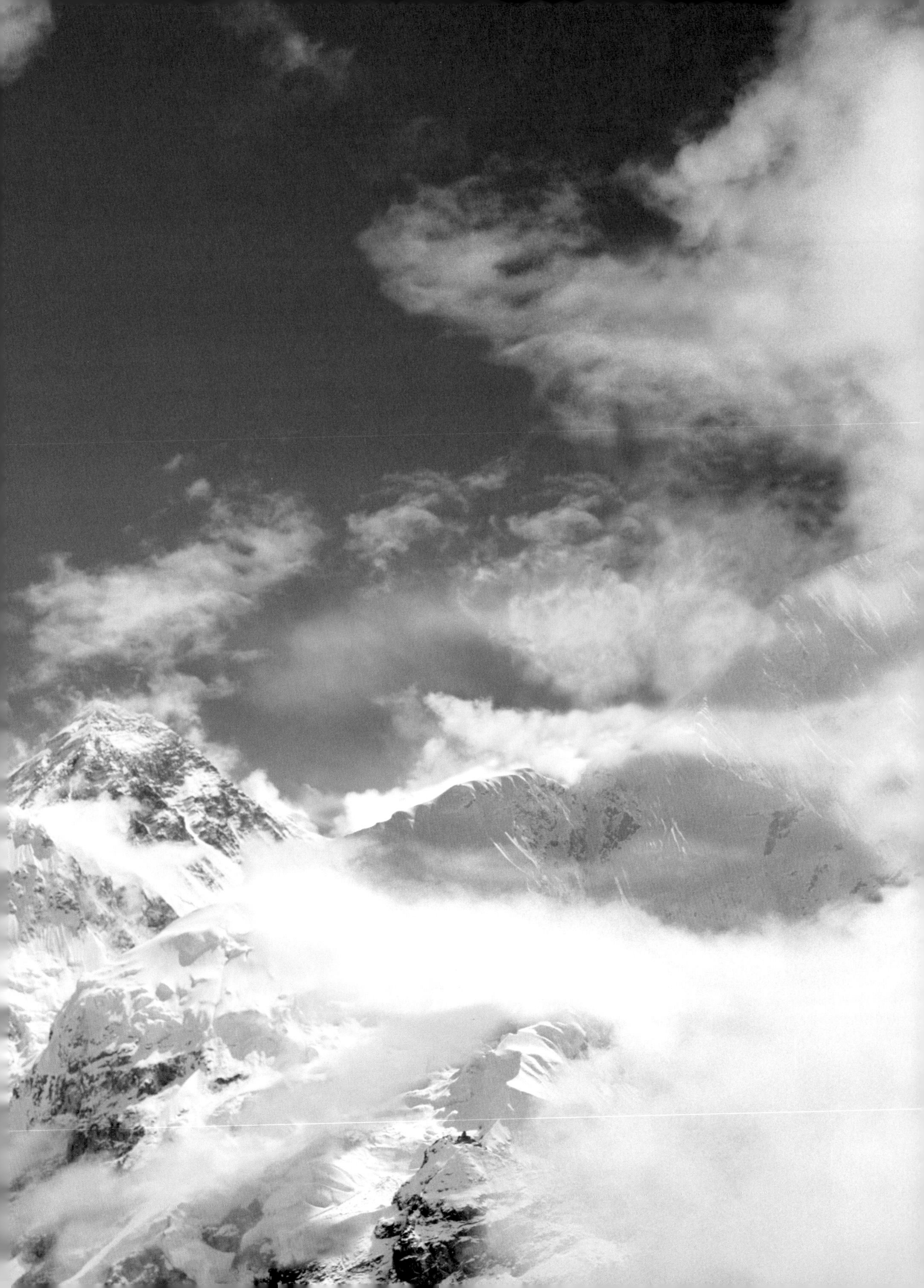

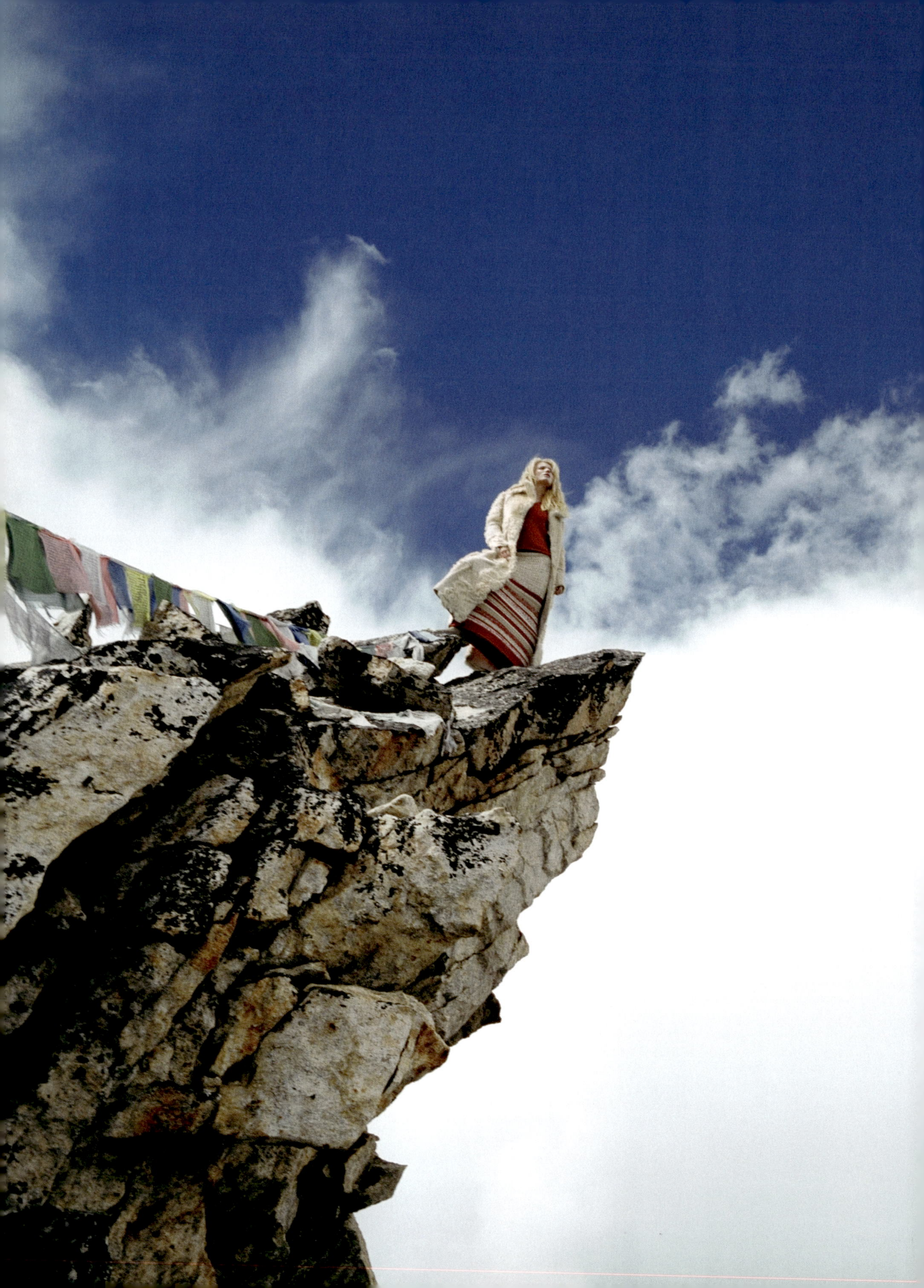

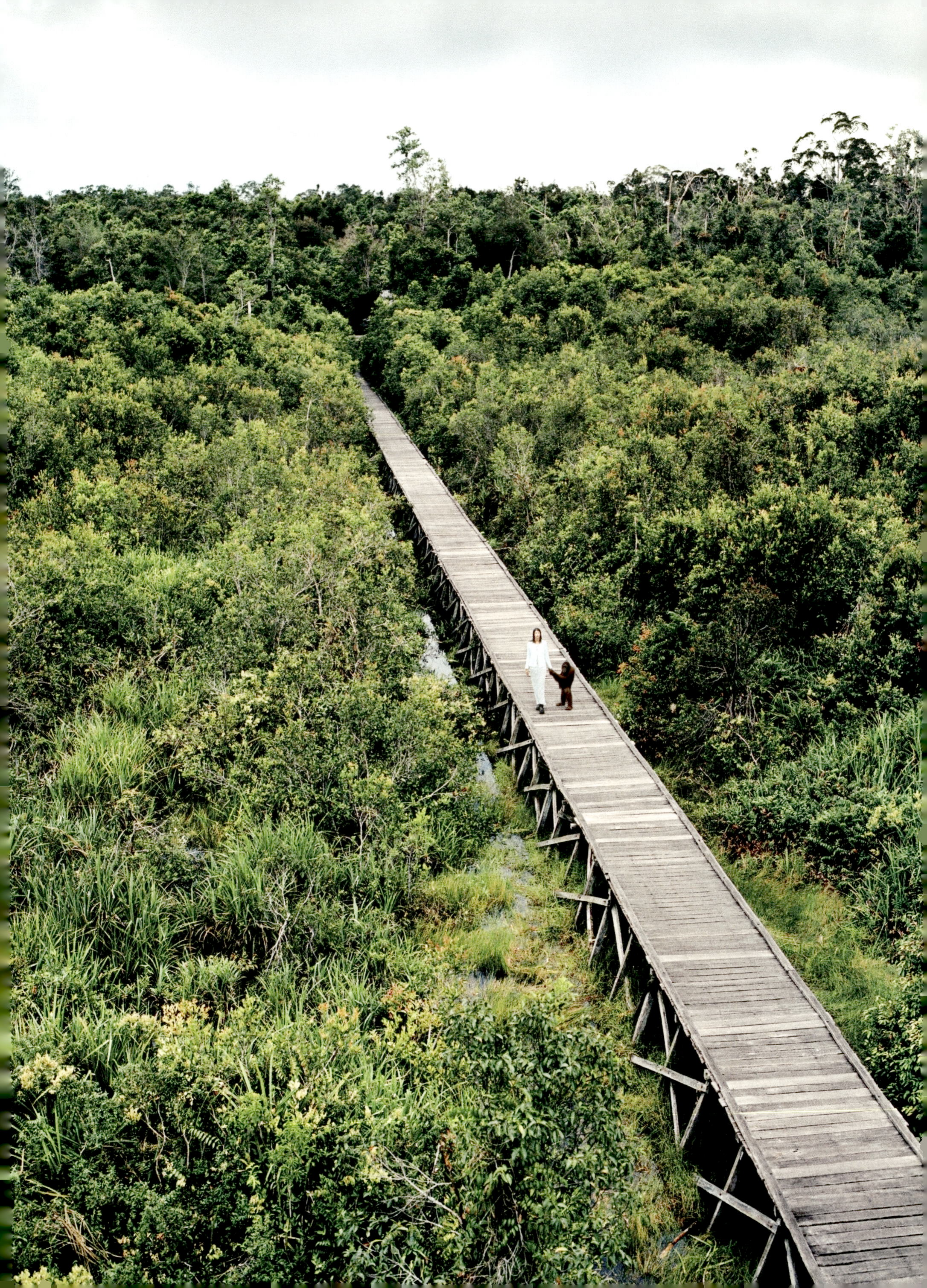

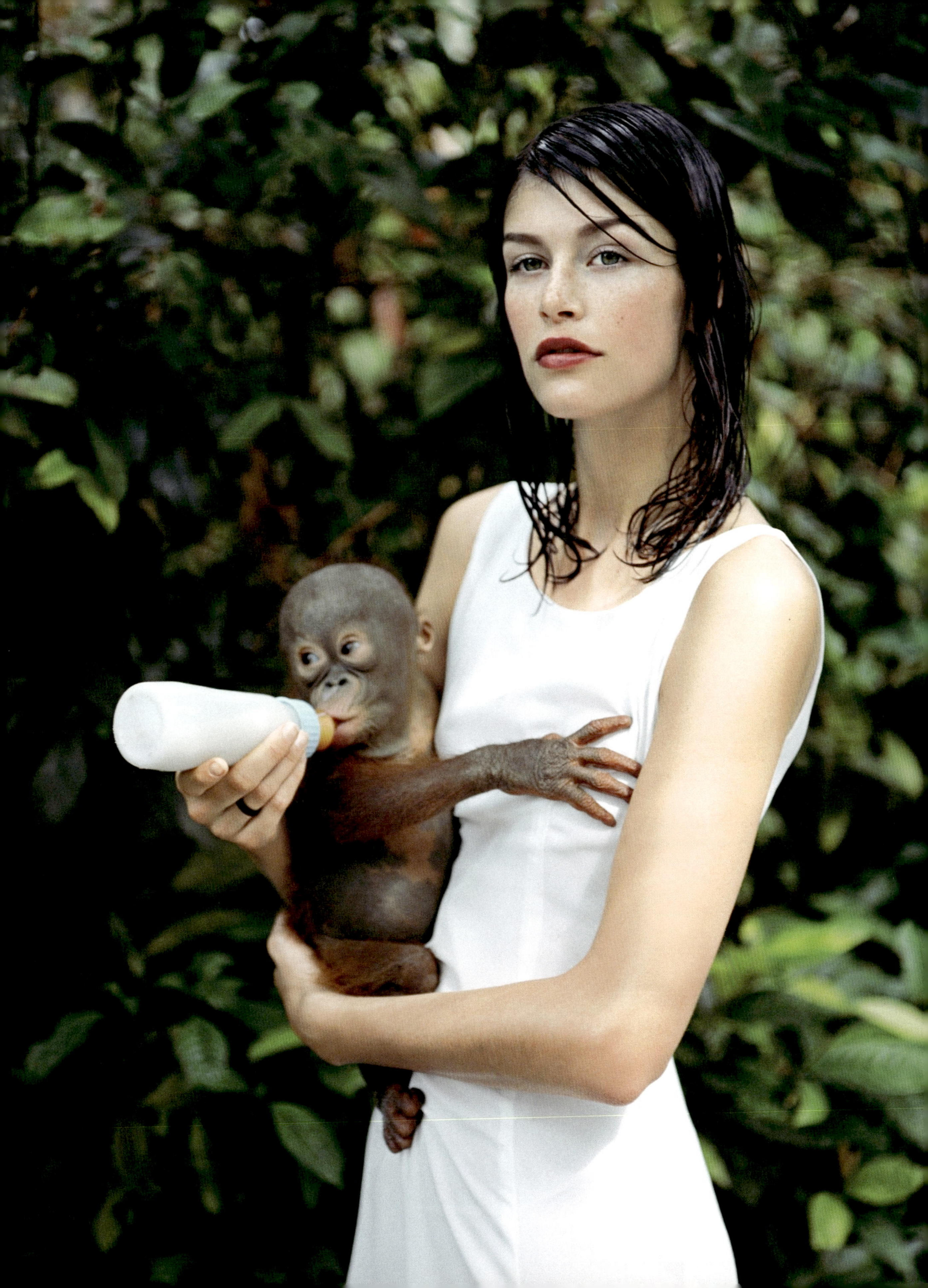

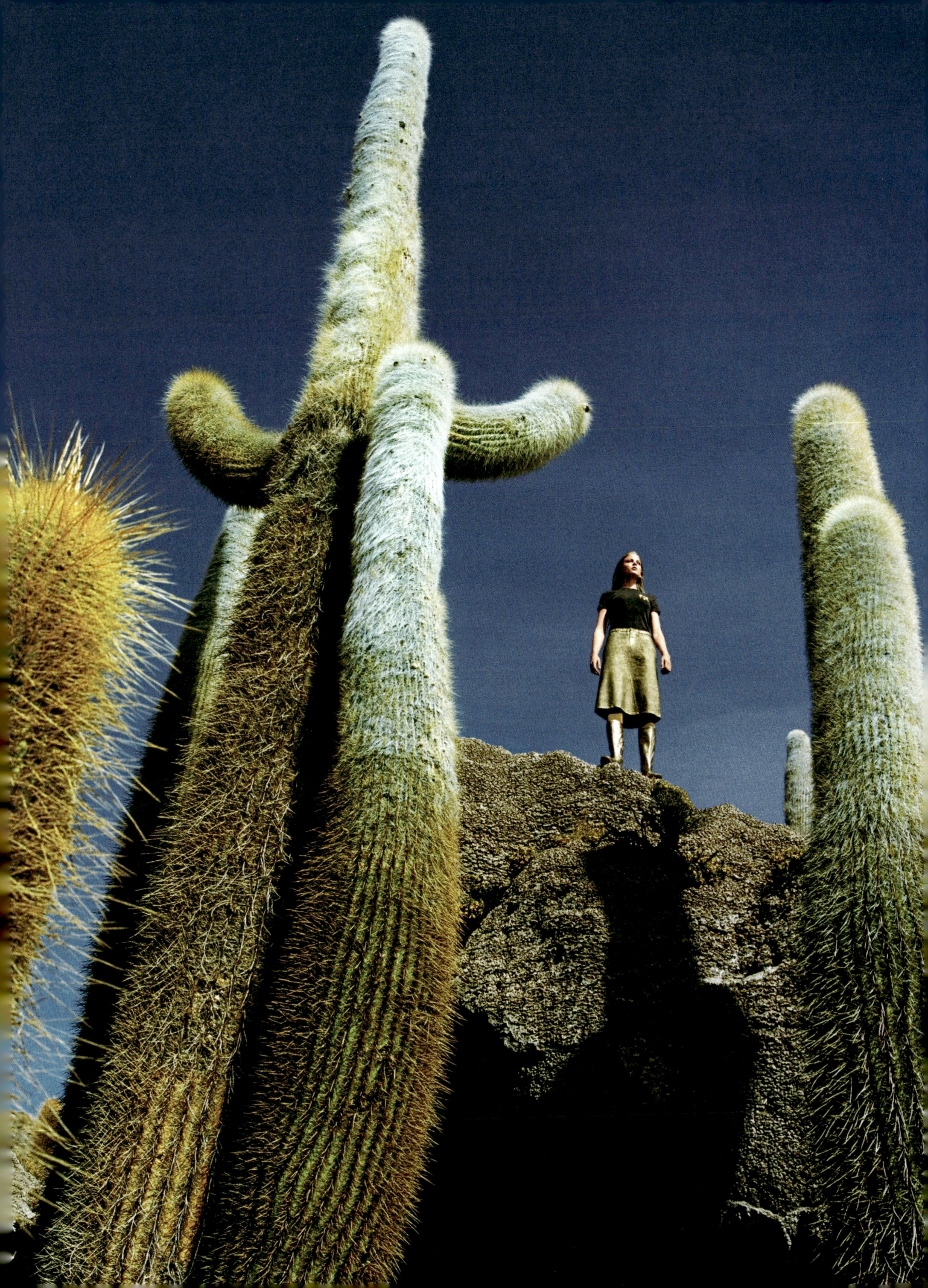

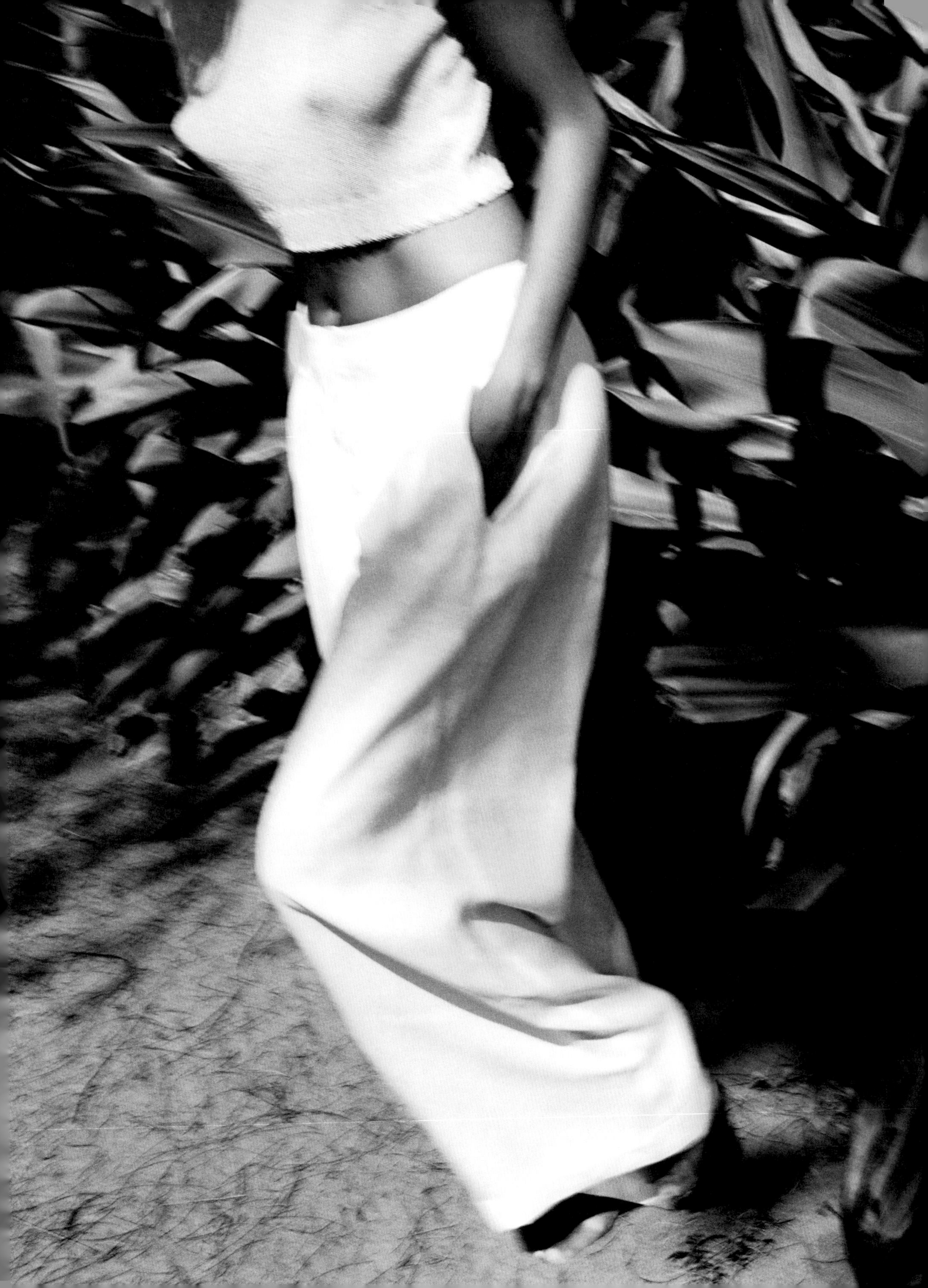

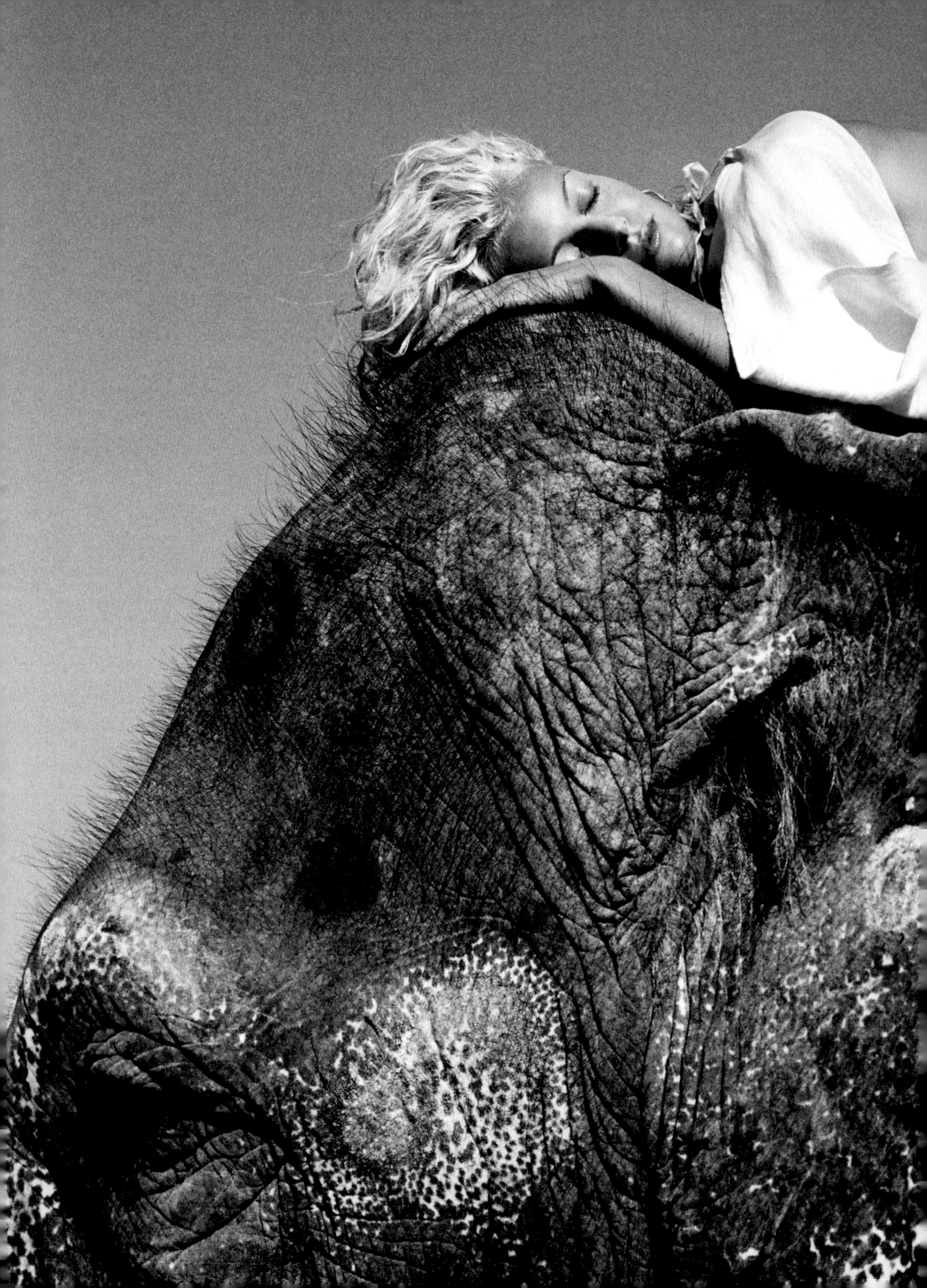

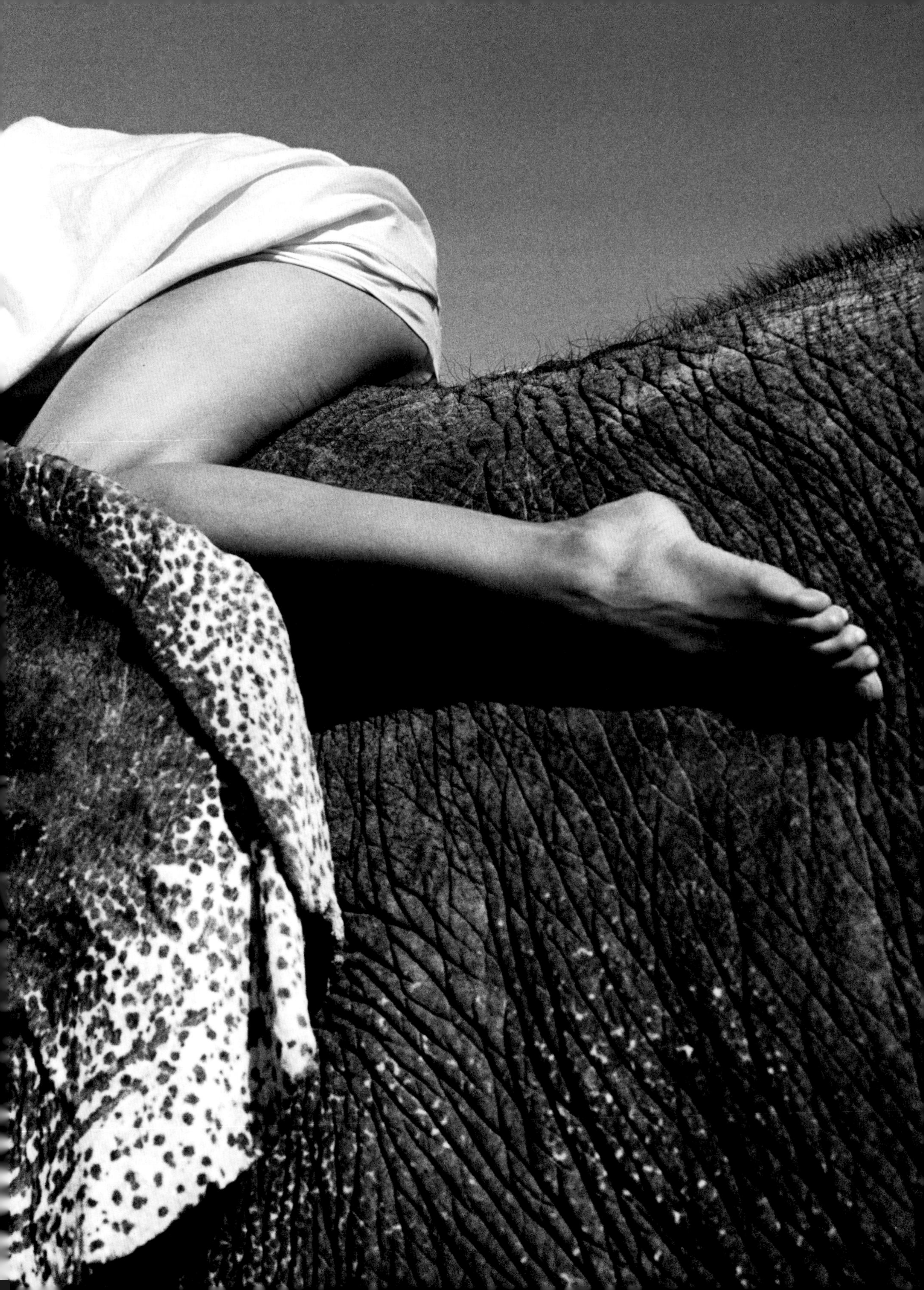

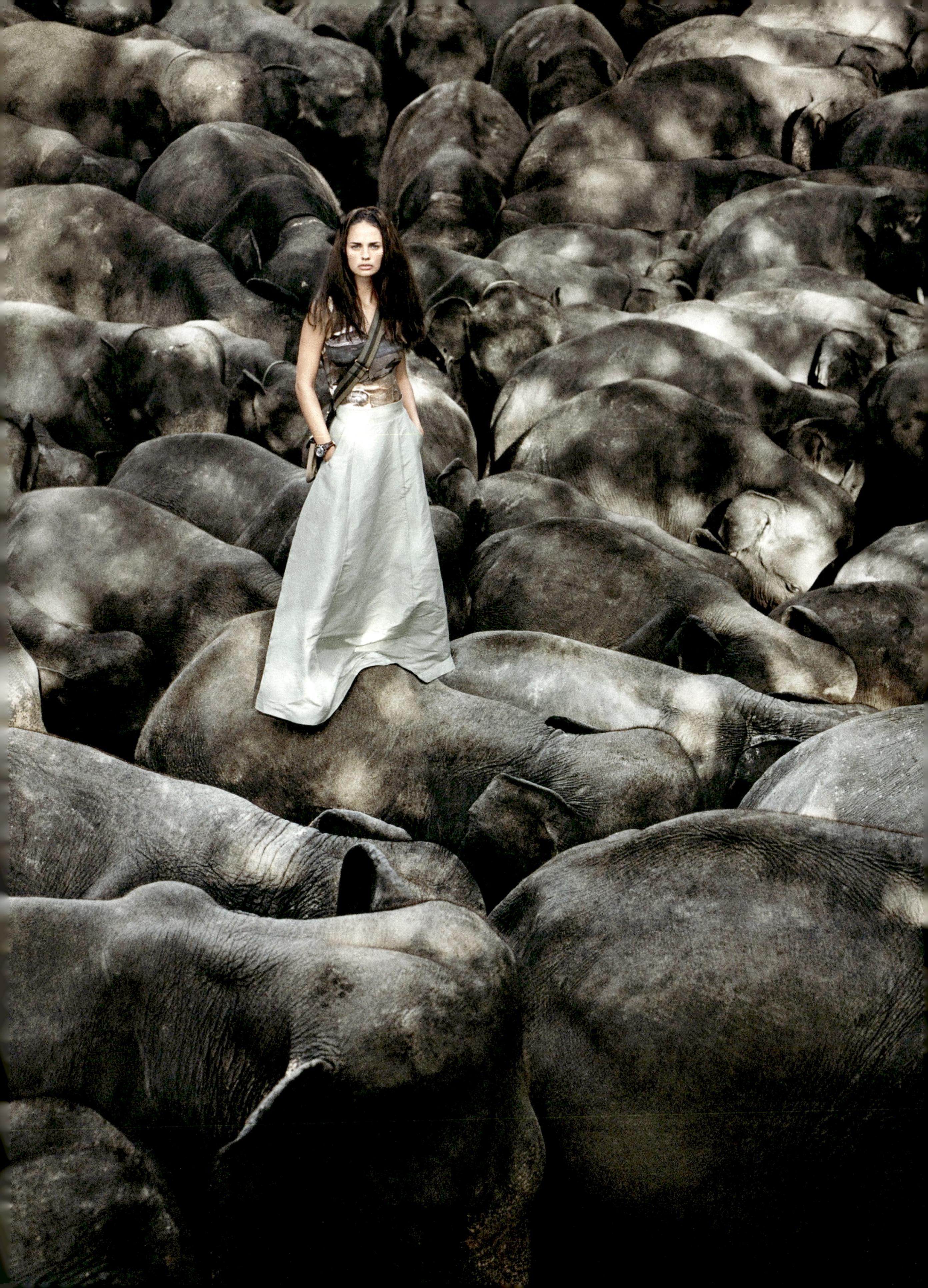

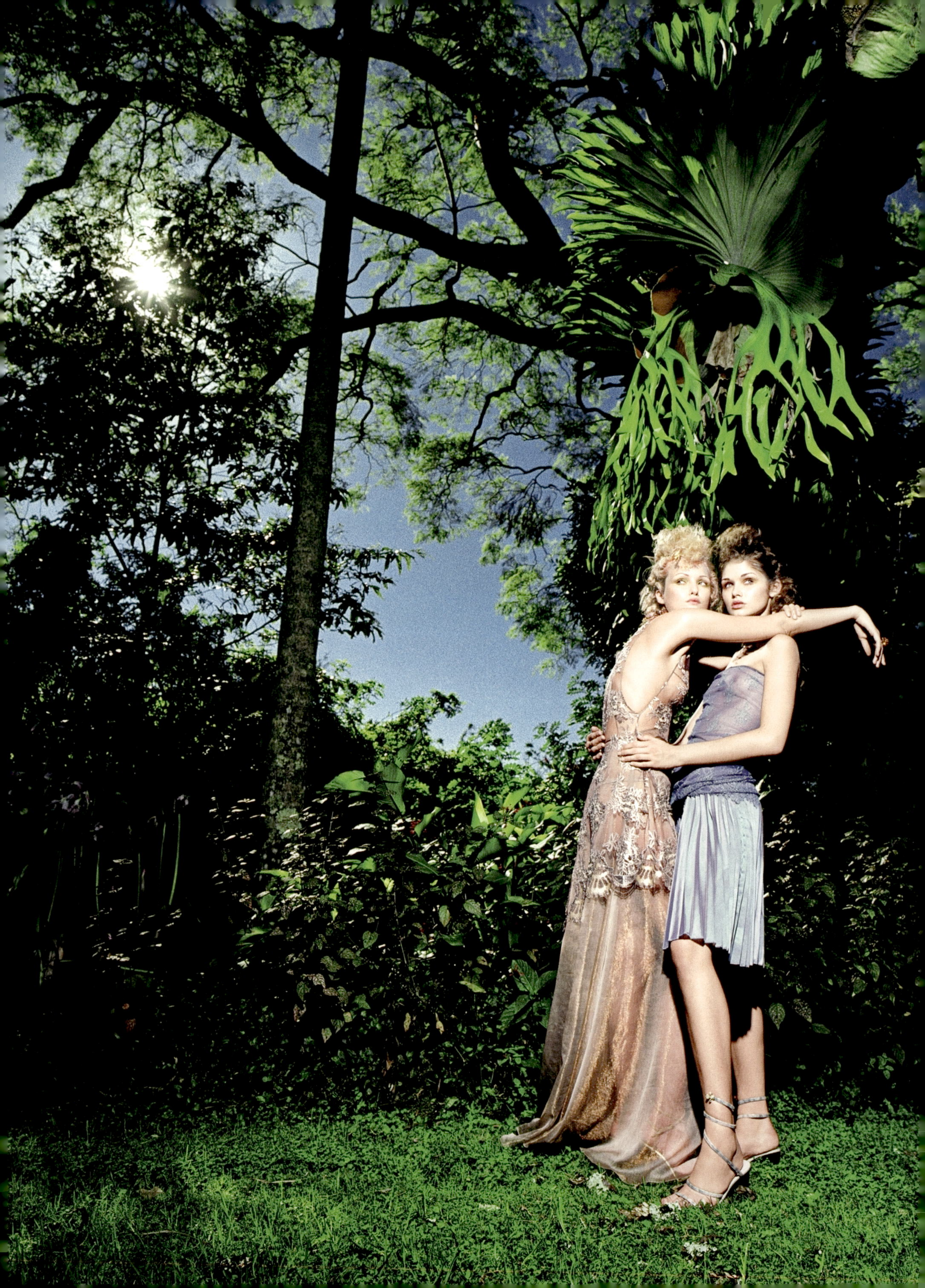

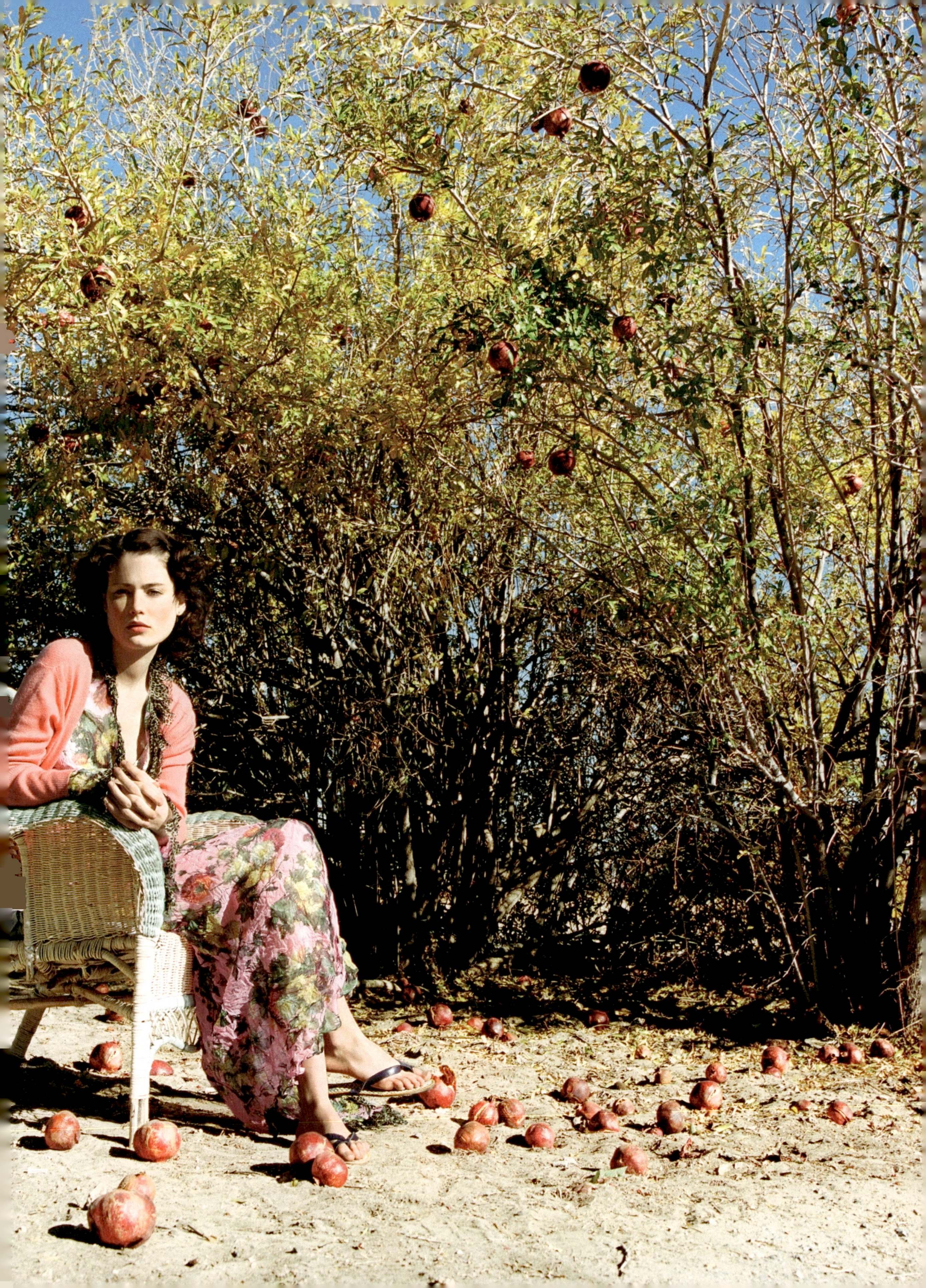

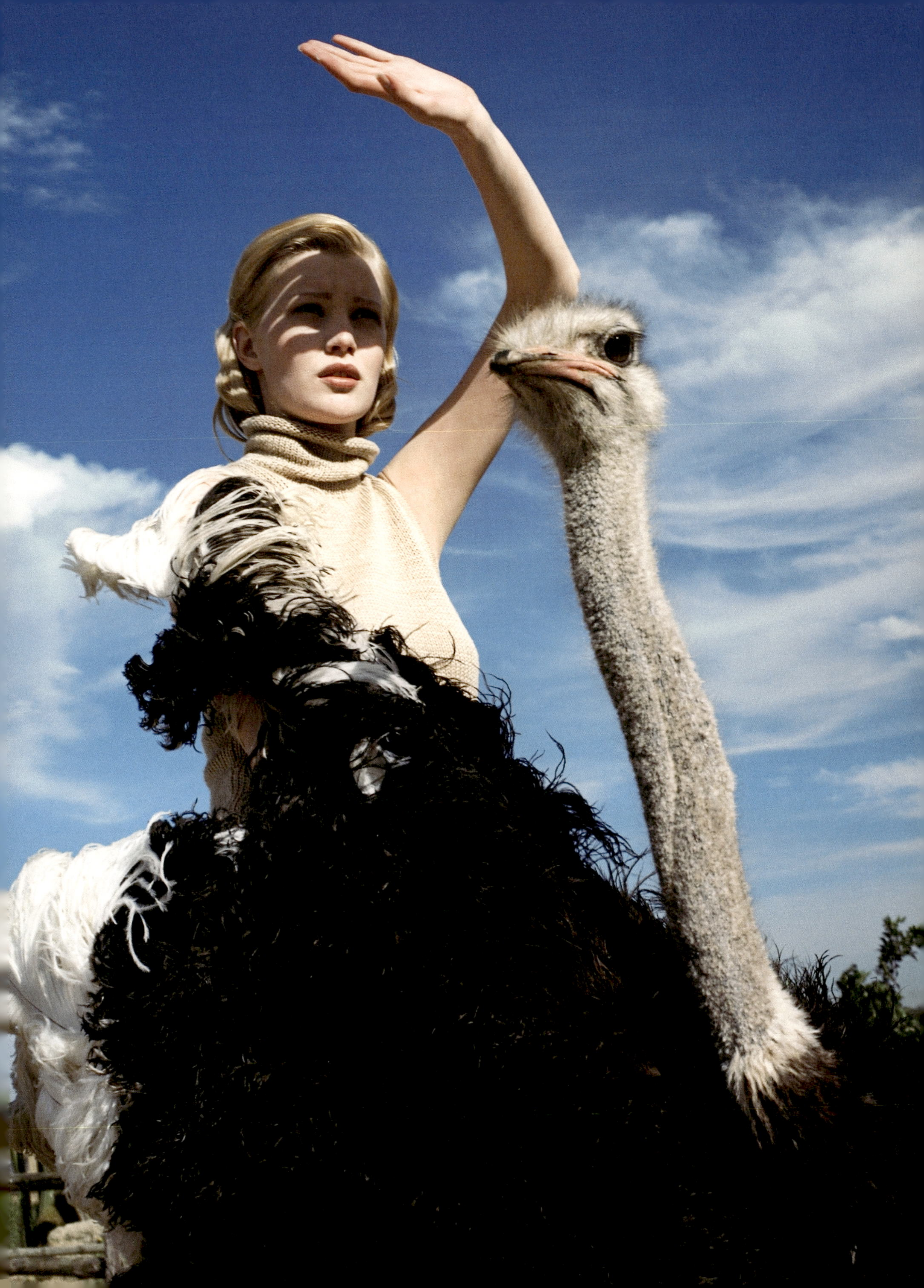

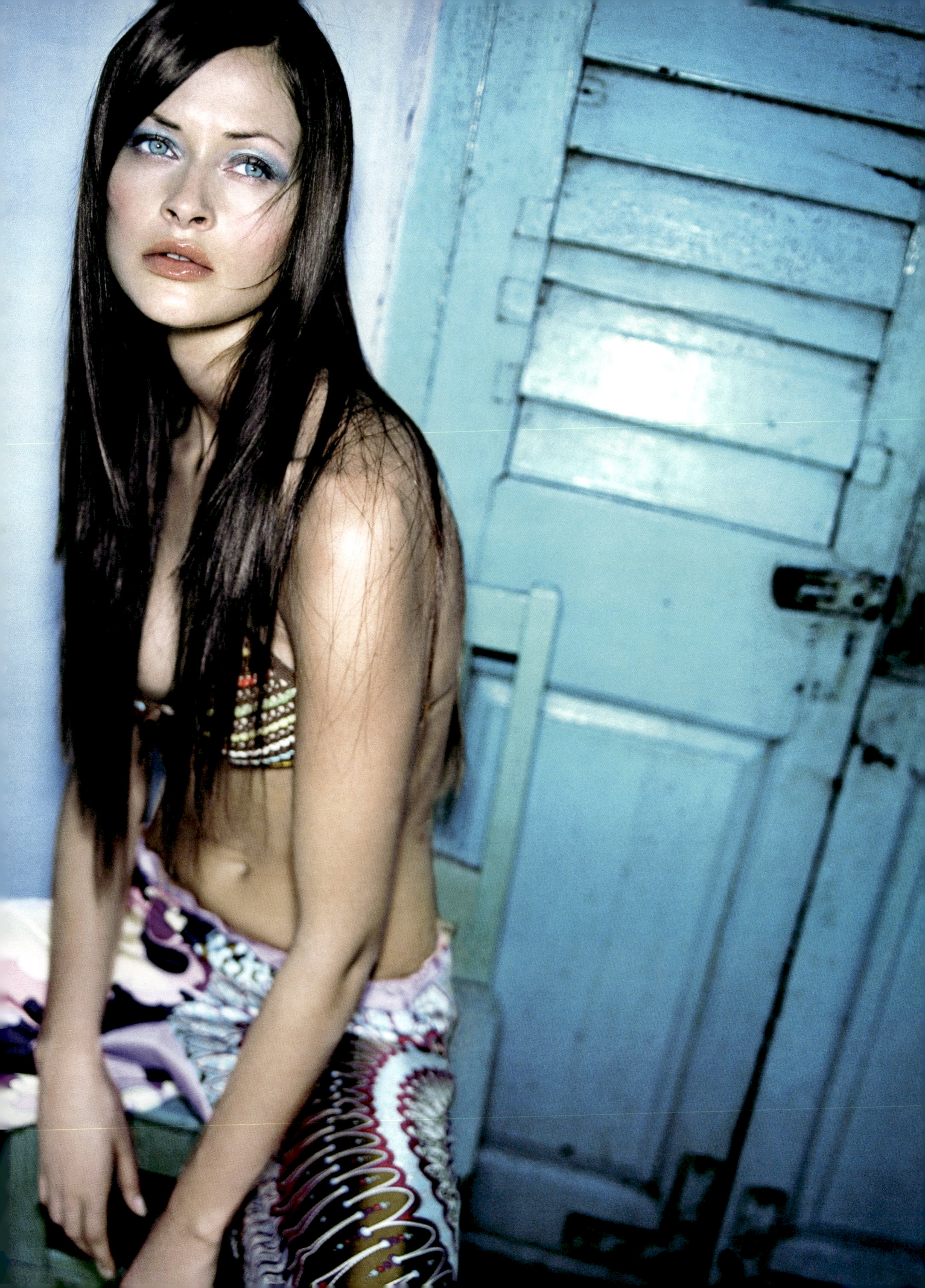

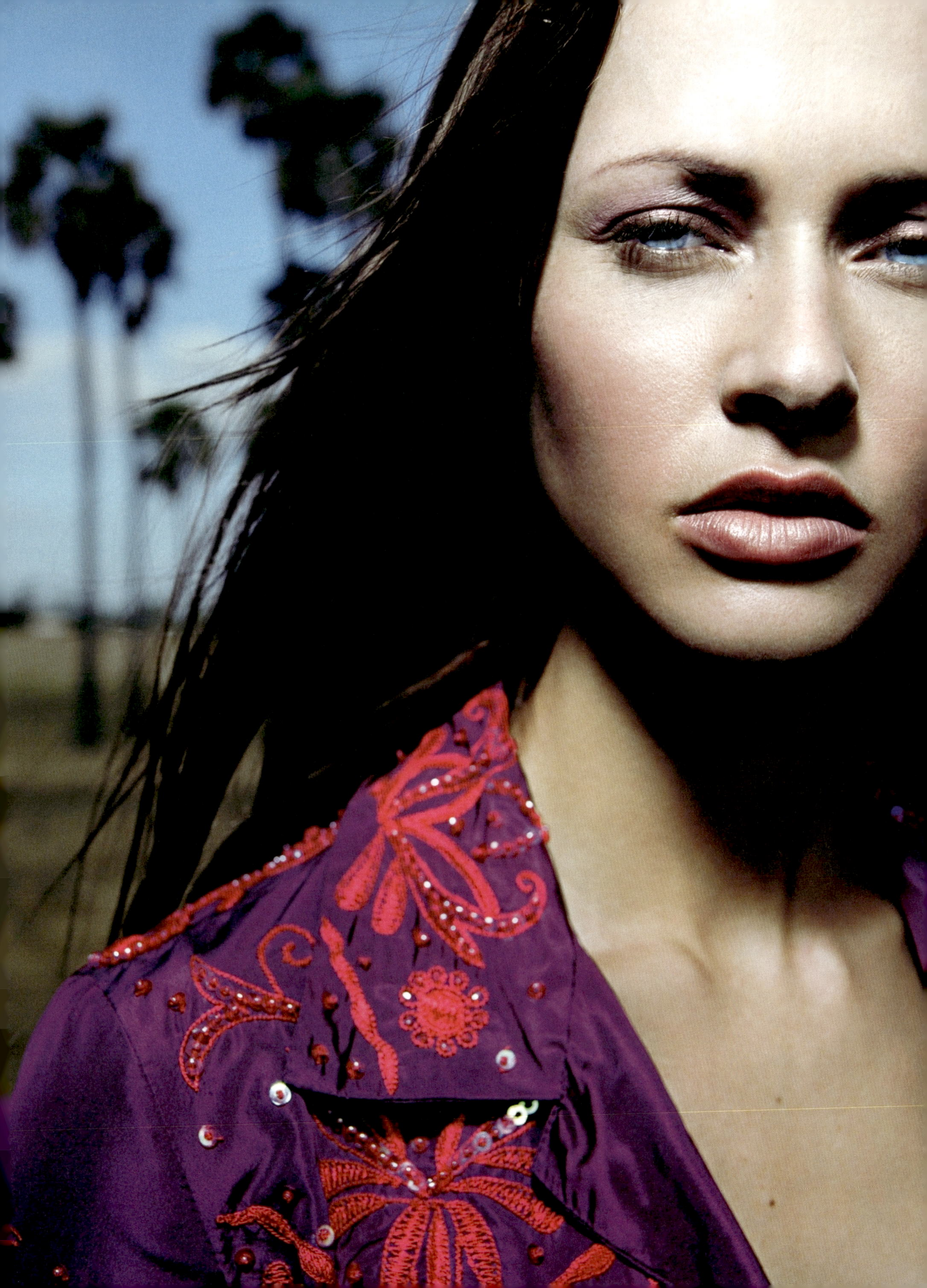

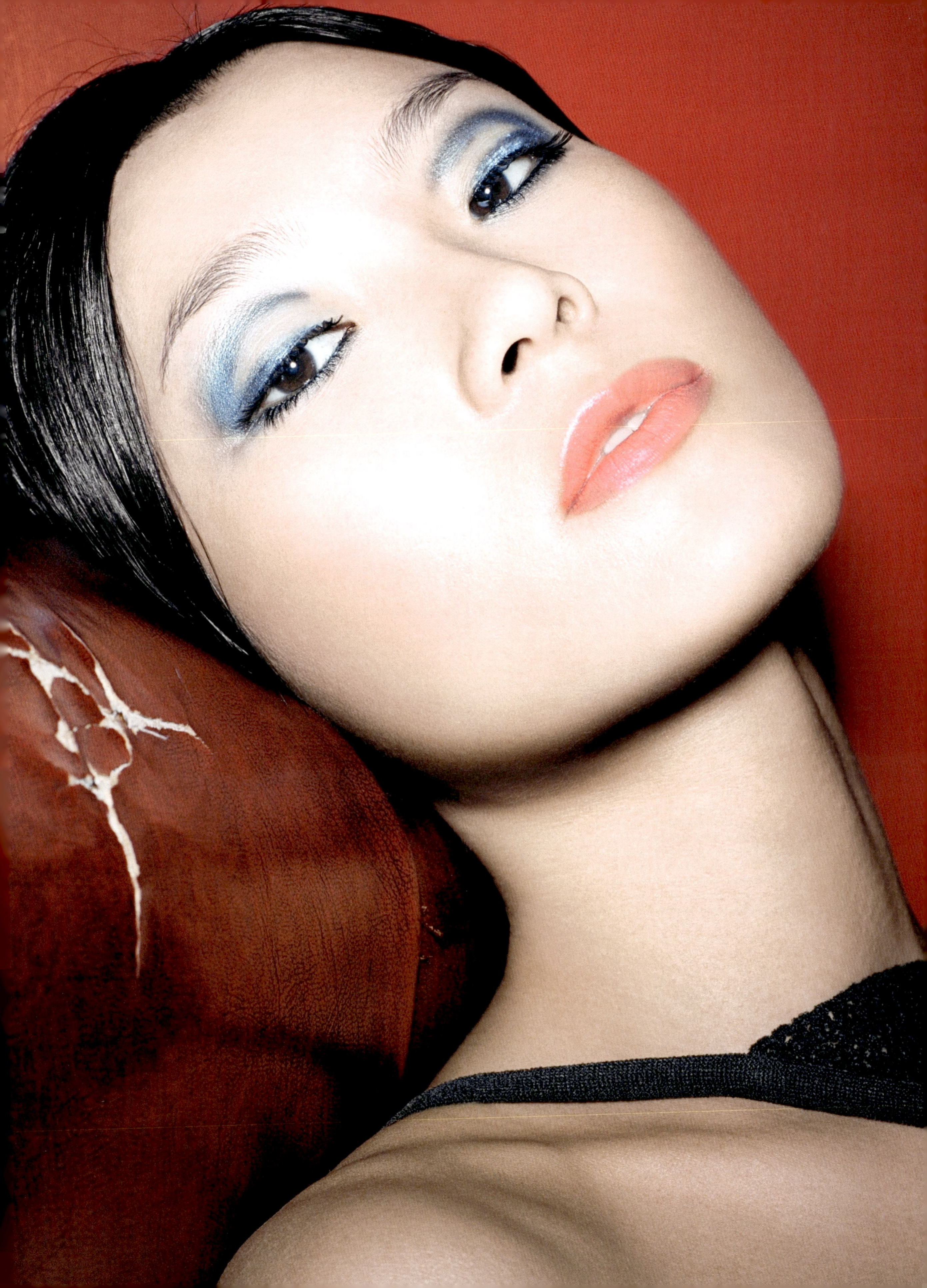

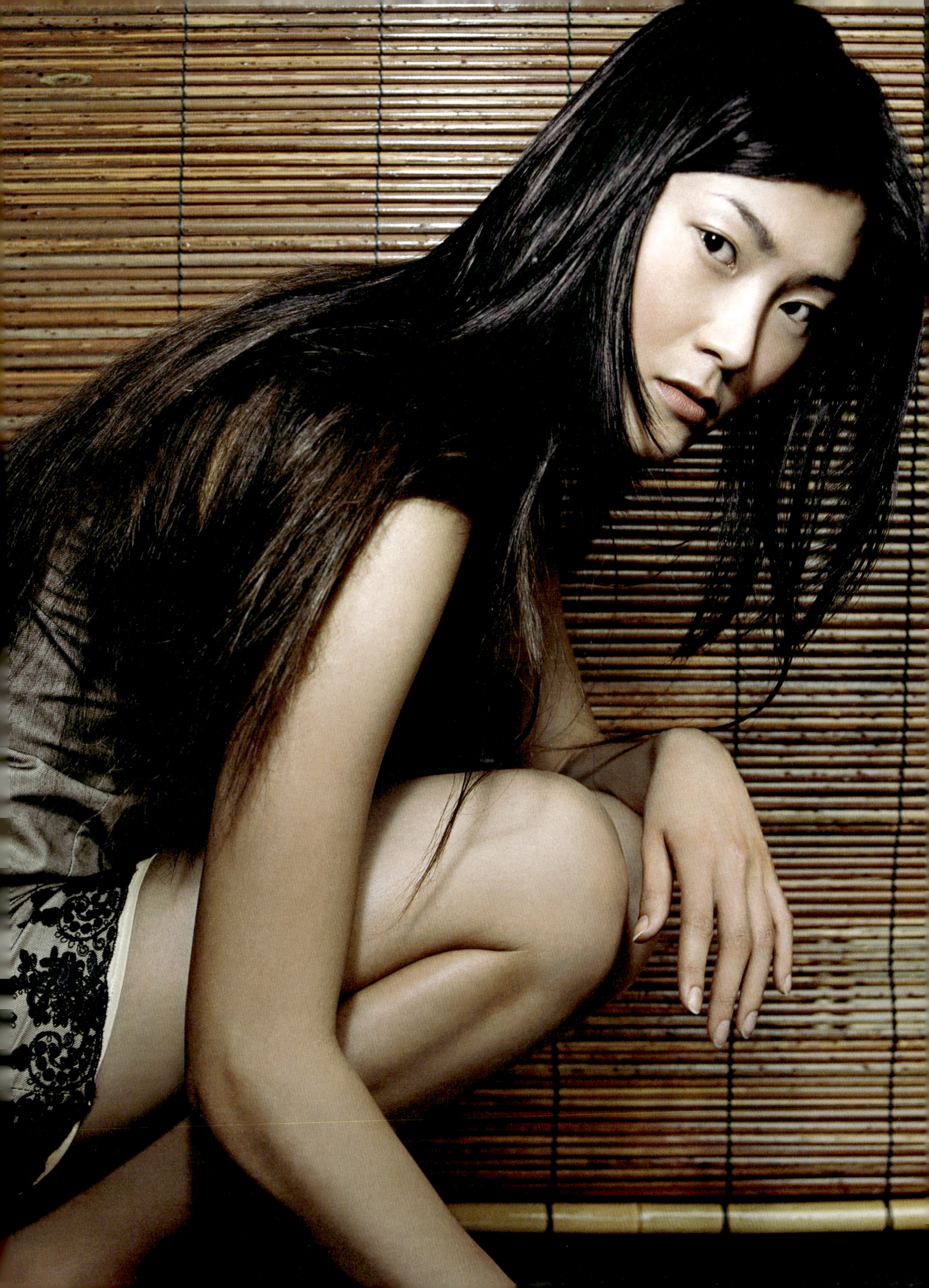

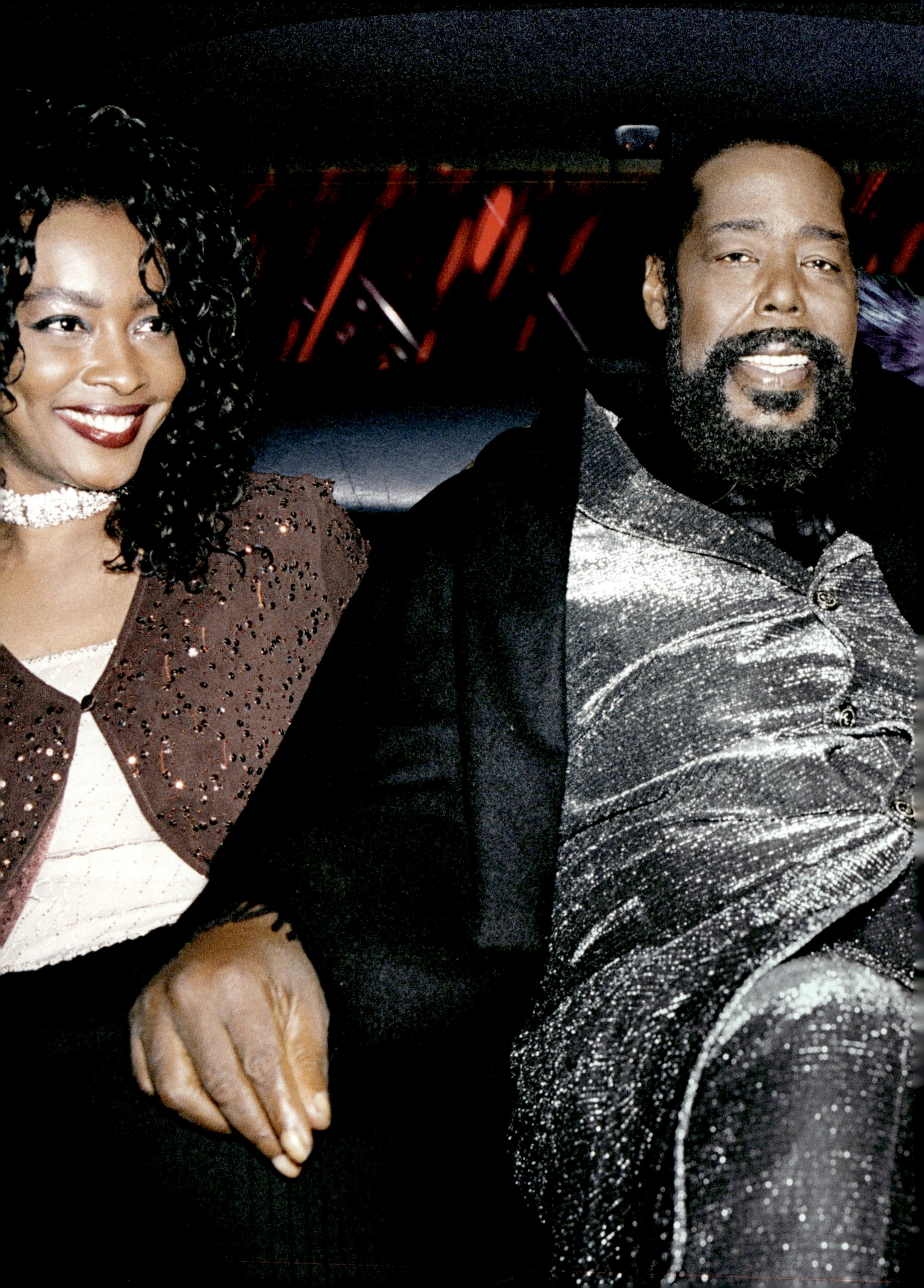

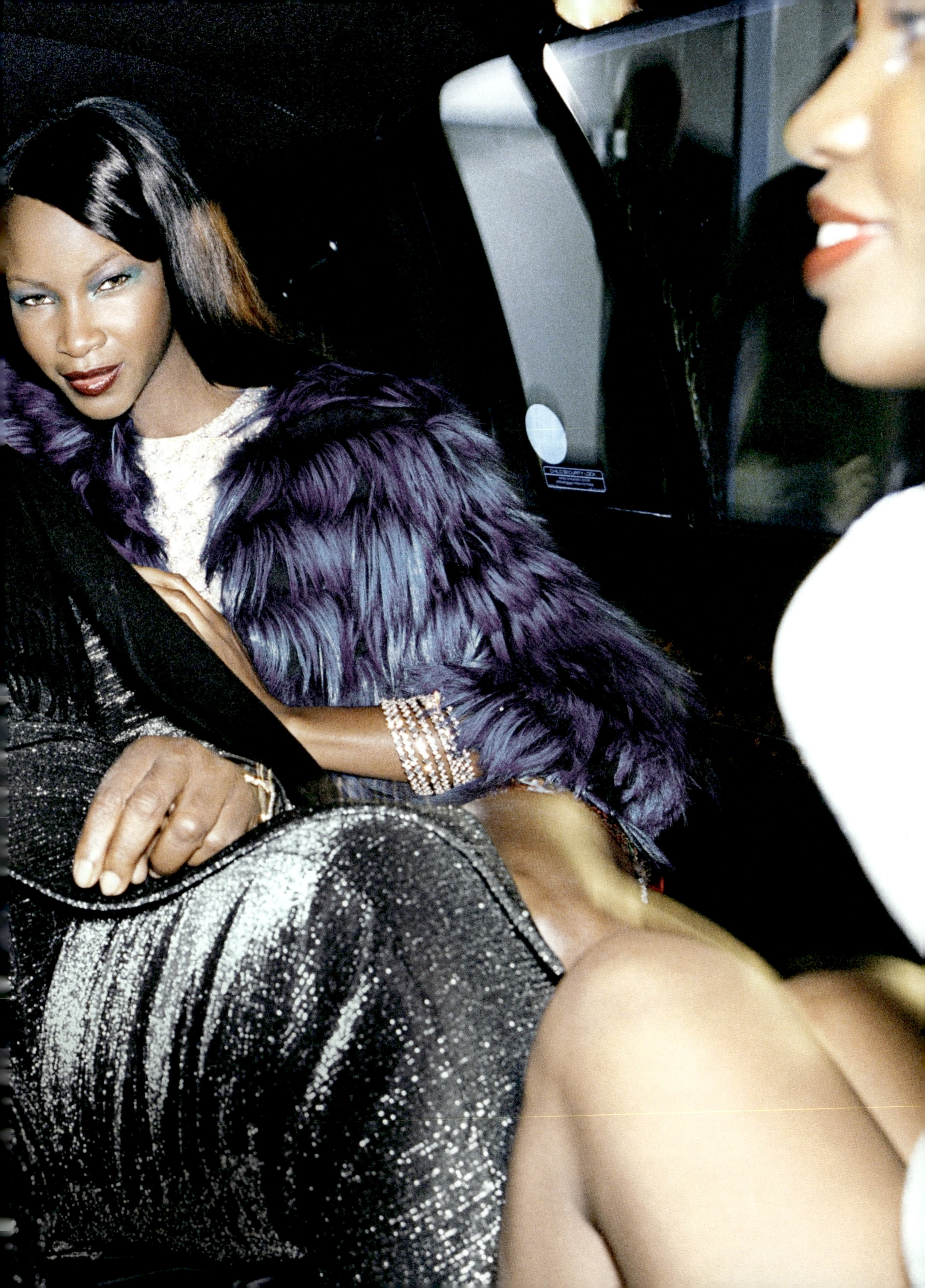

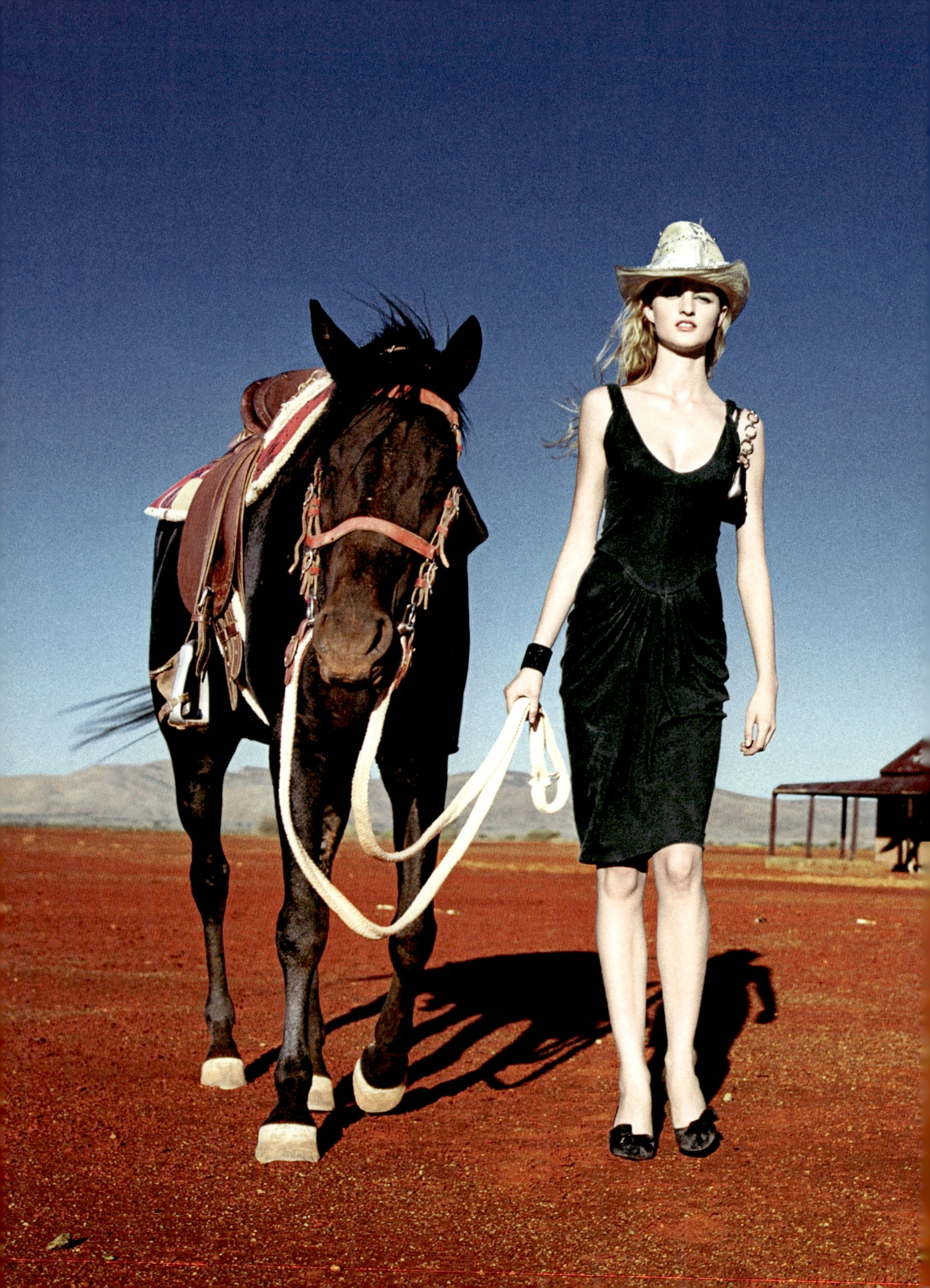

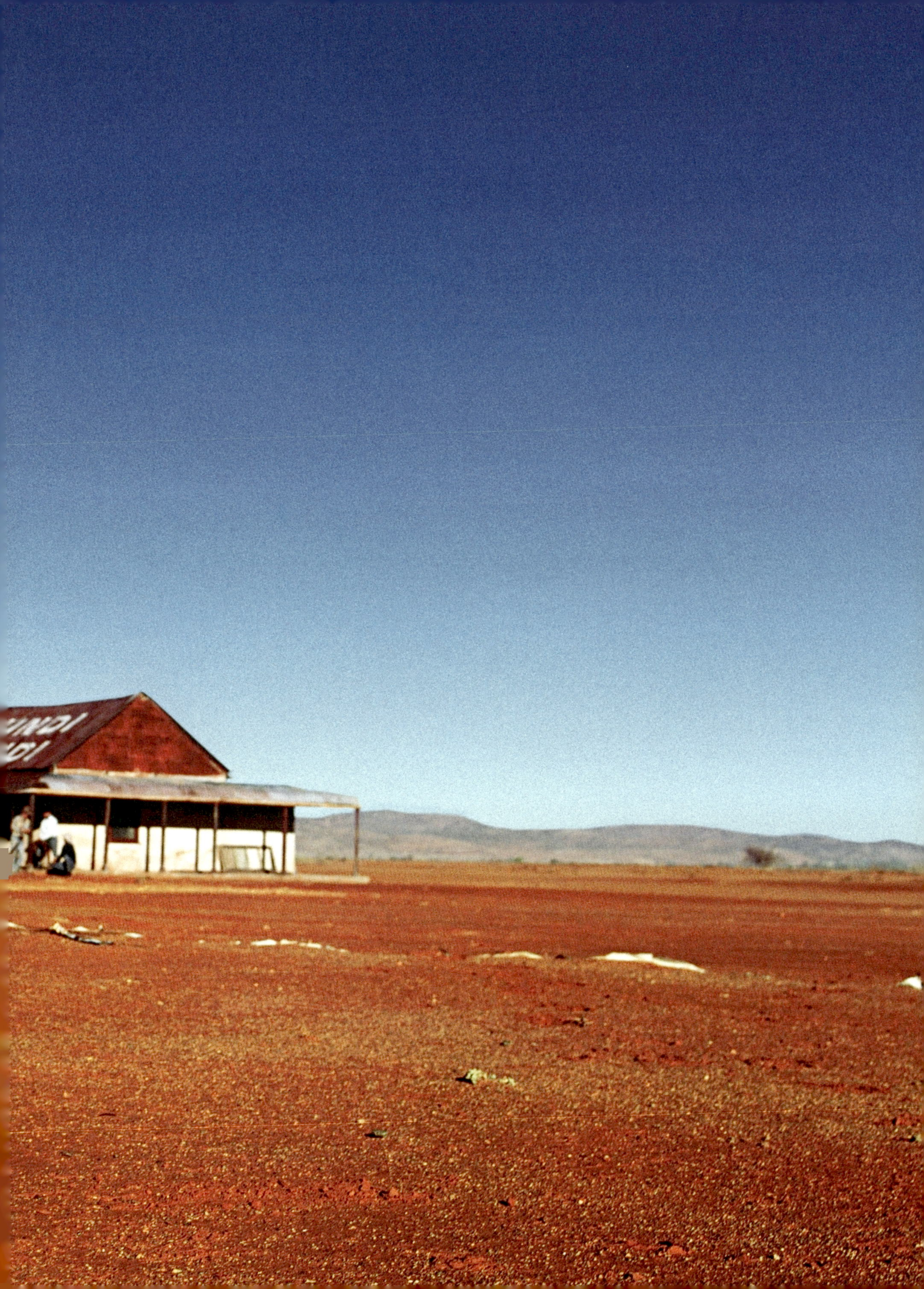

INDI
161

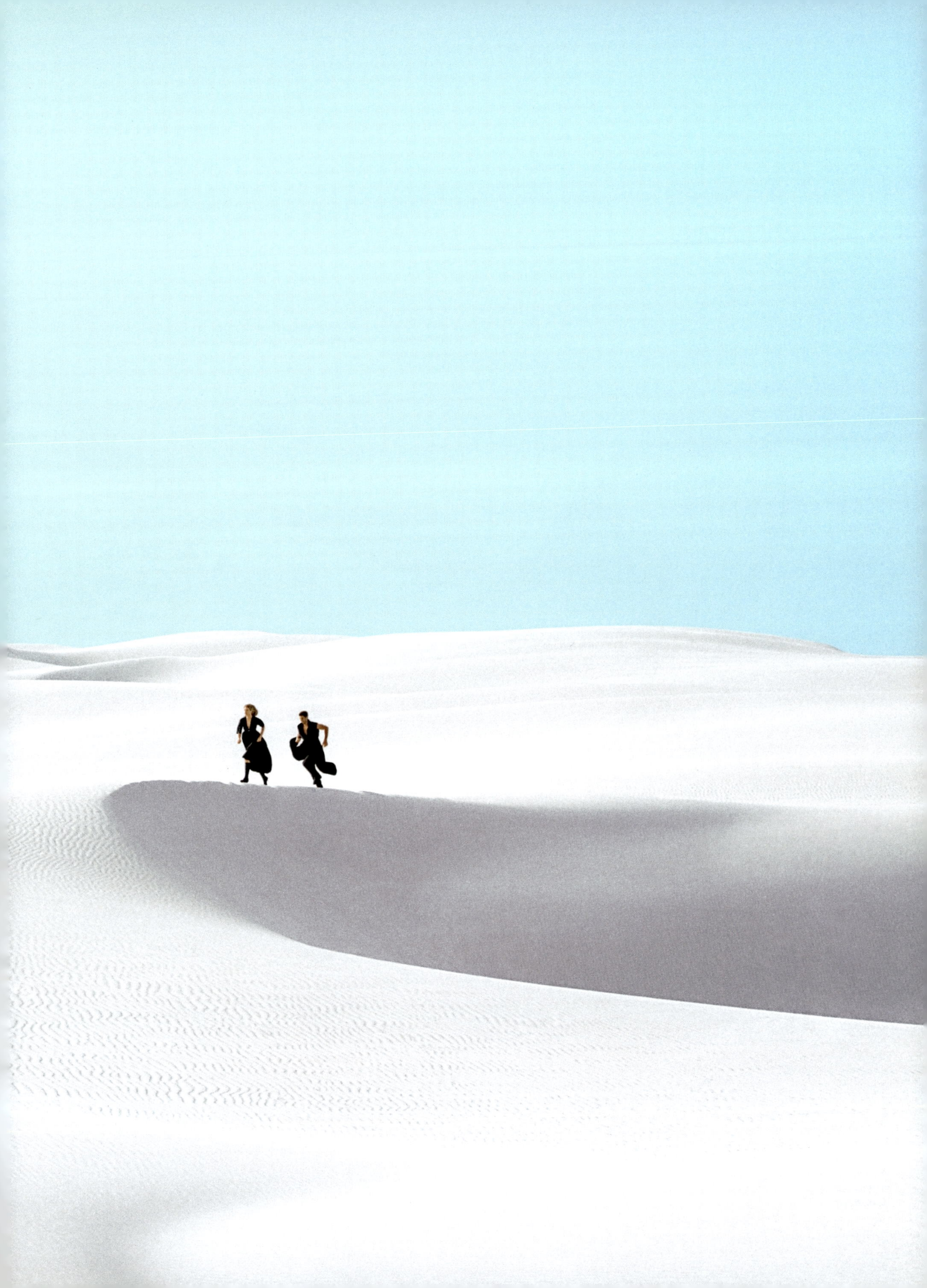

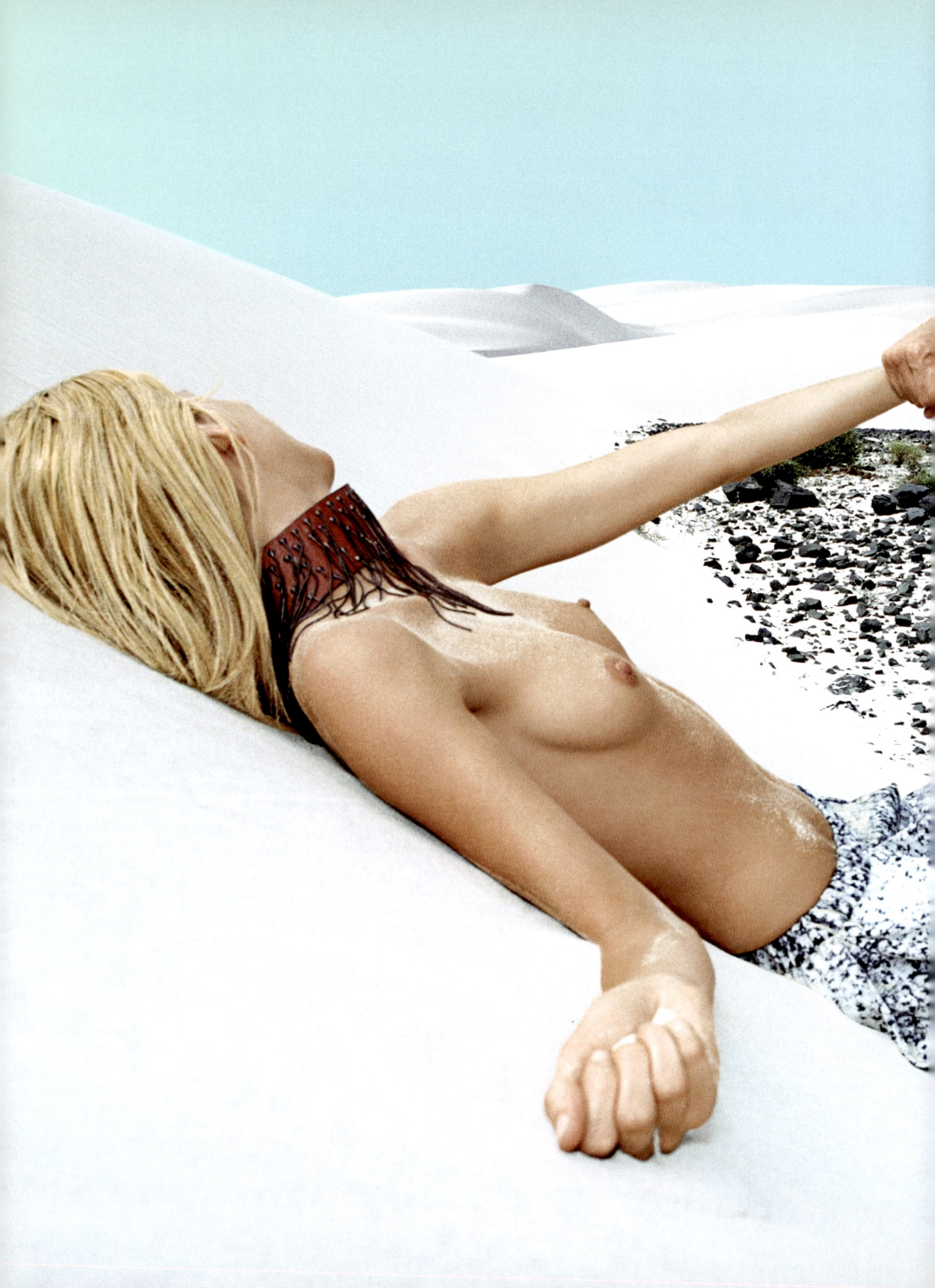

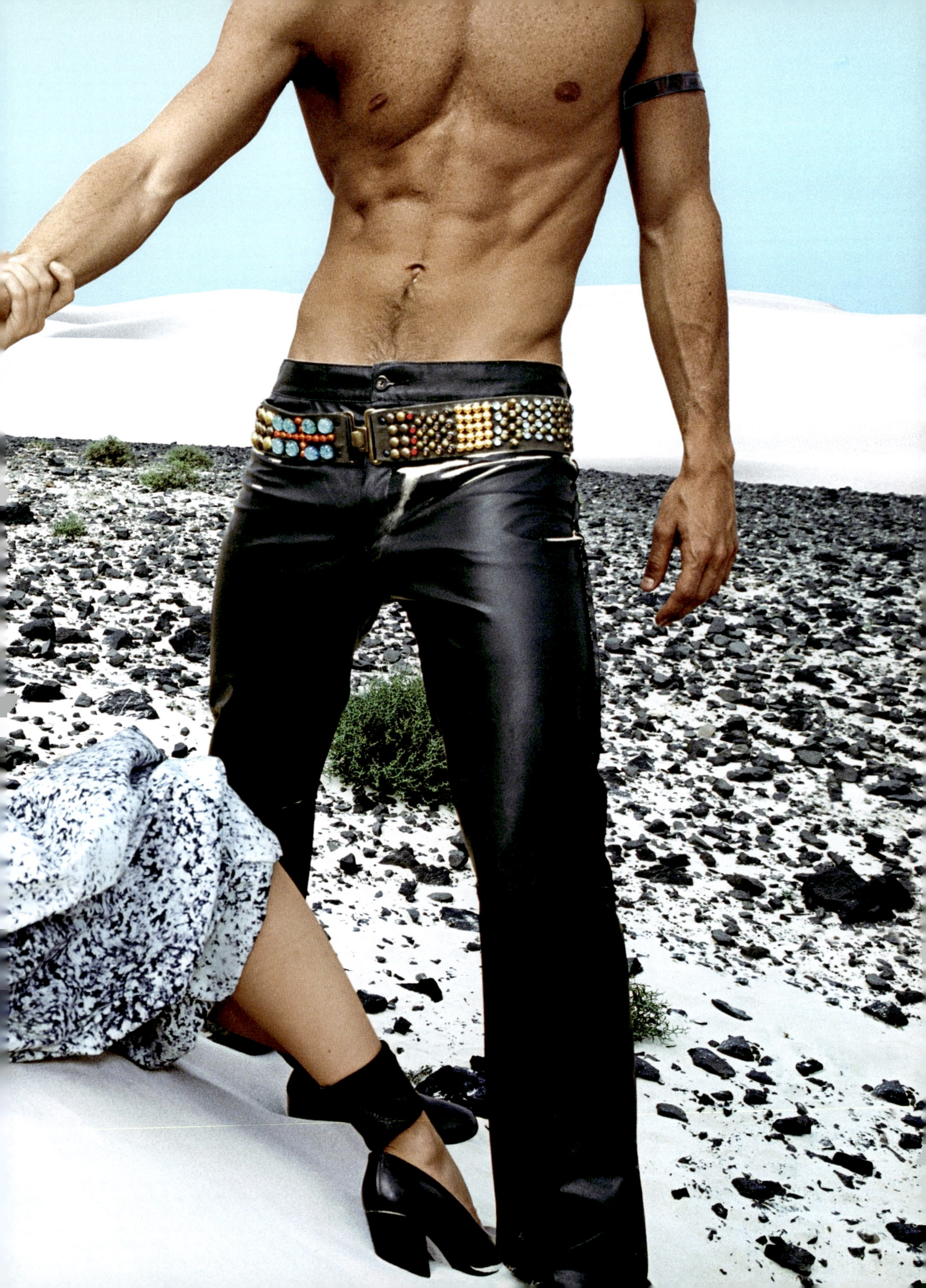

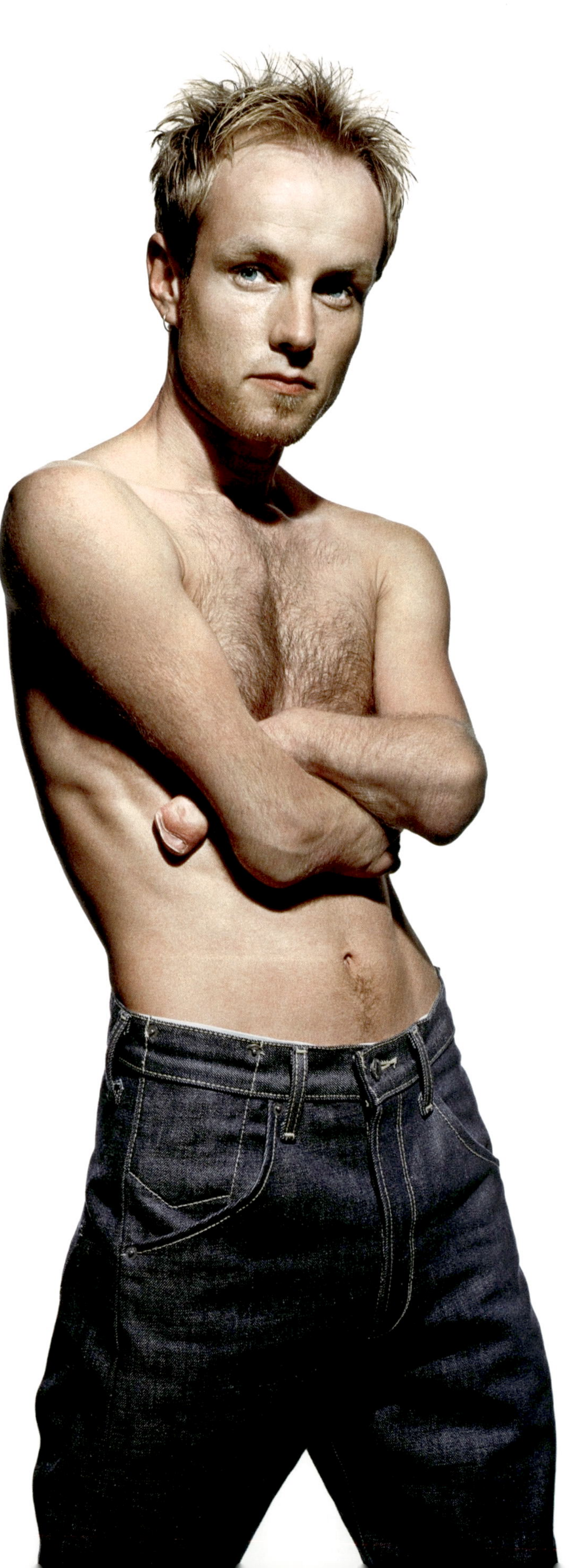

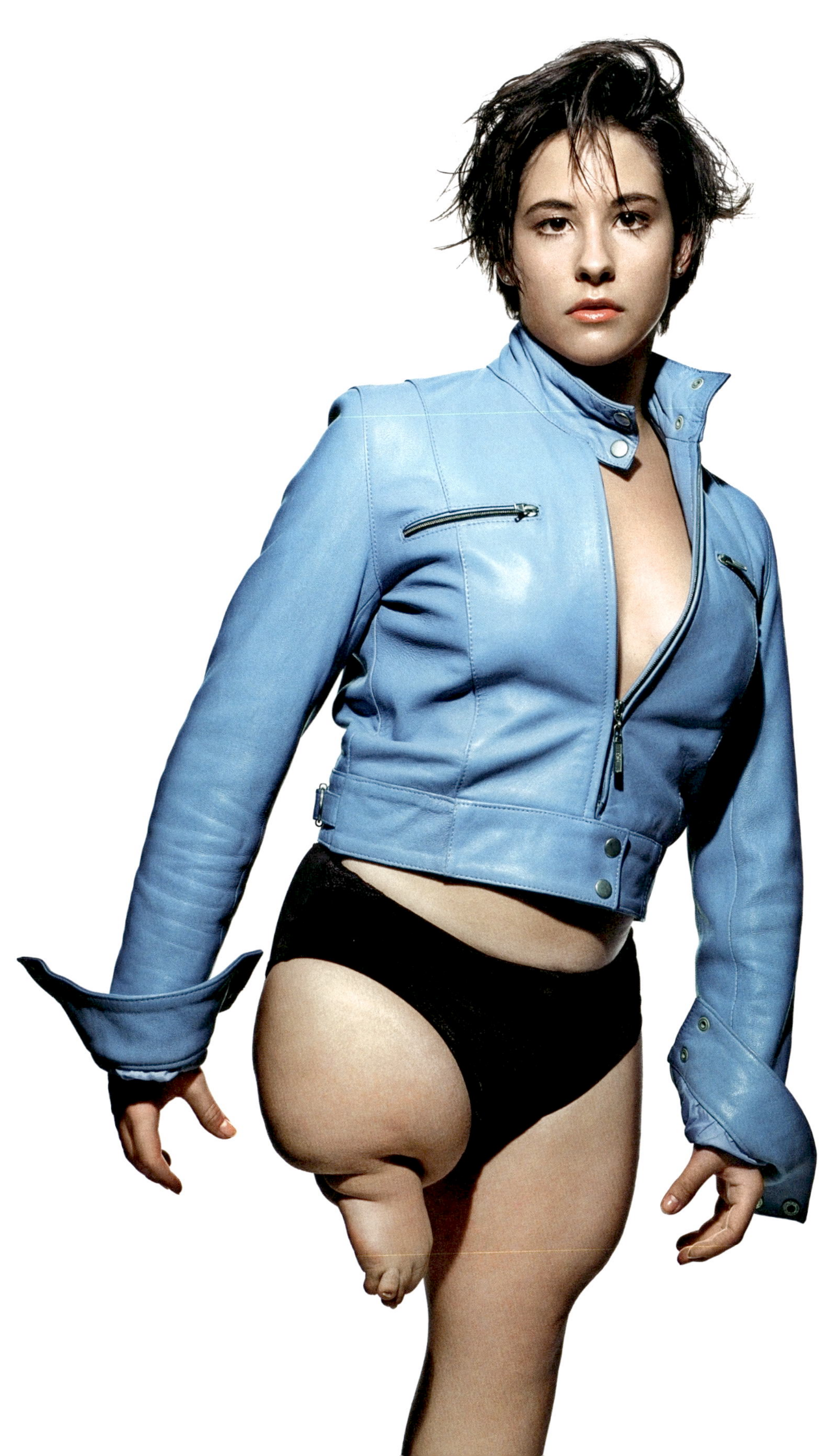

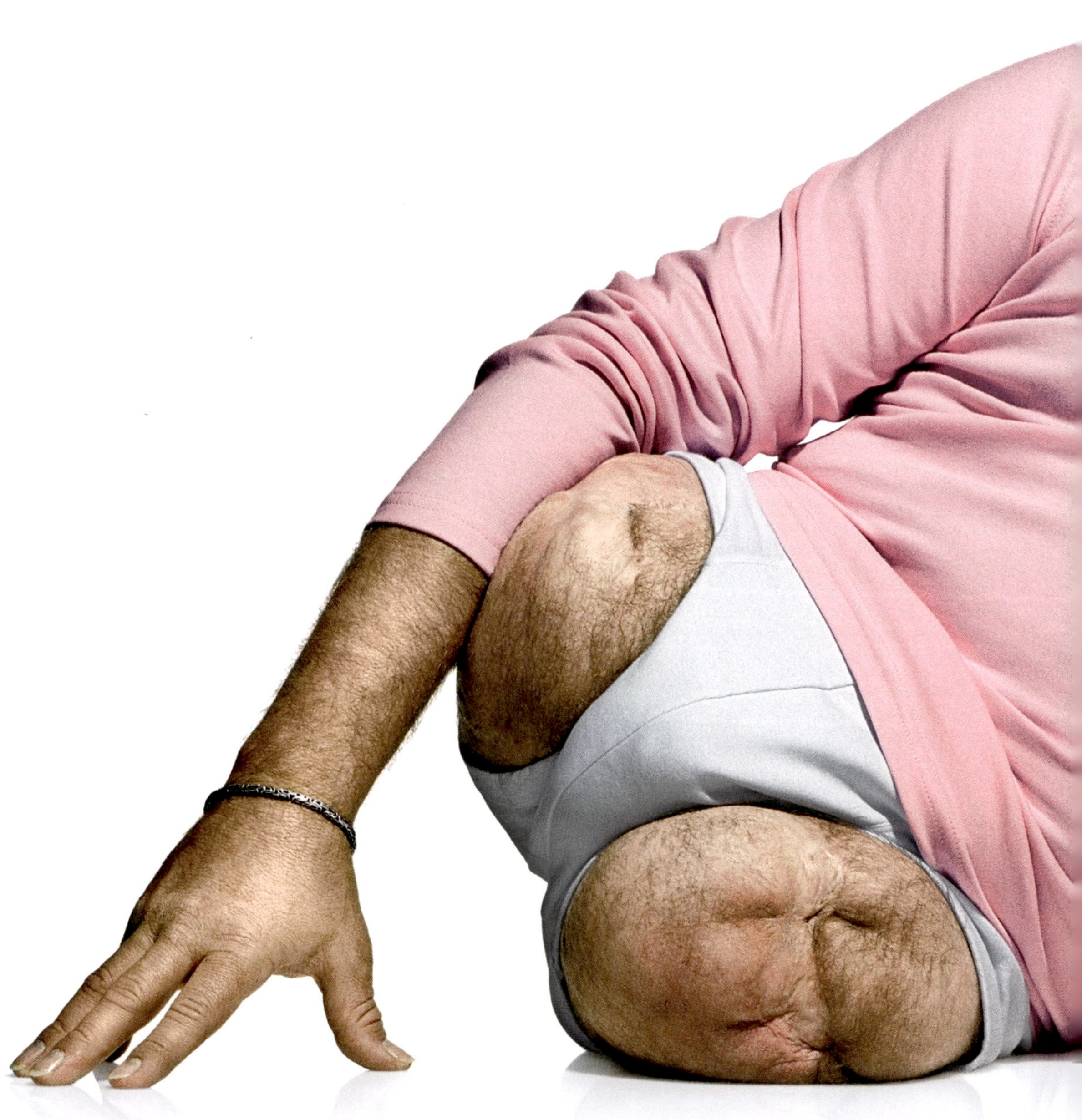

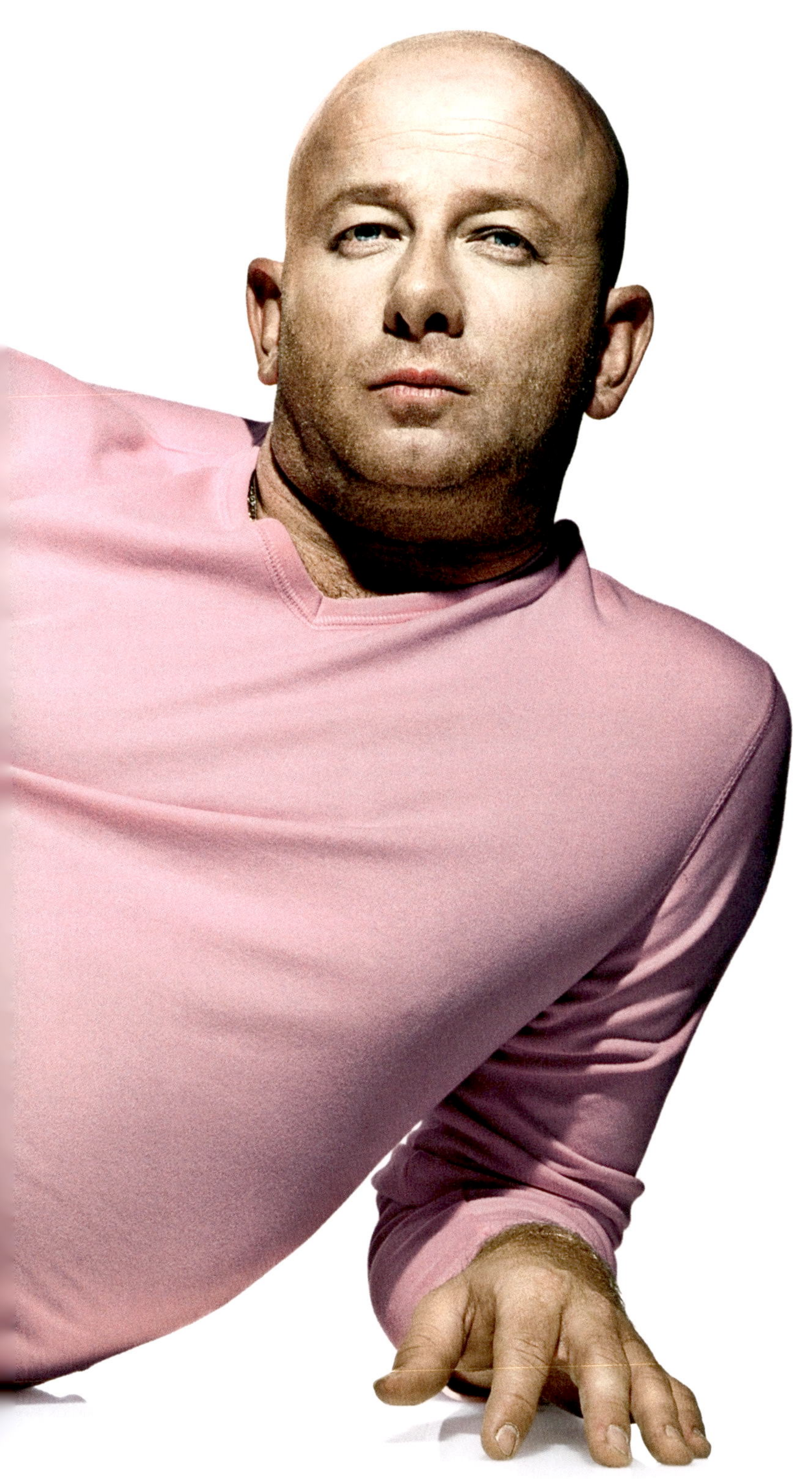

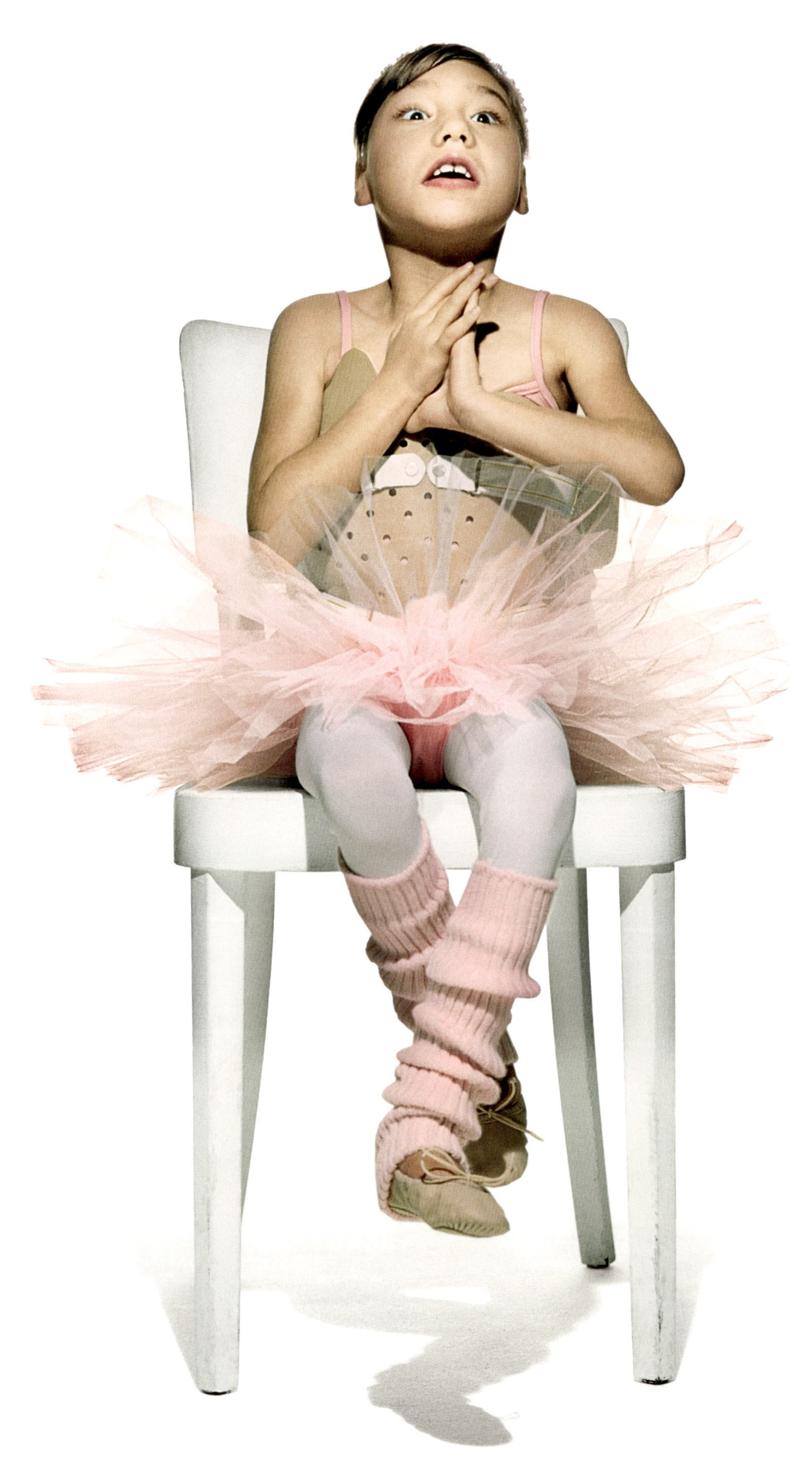

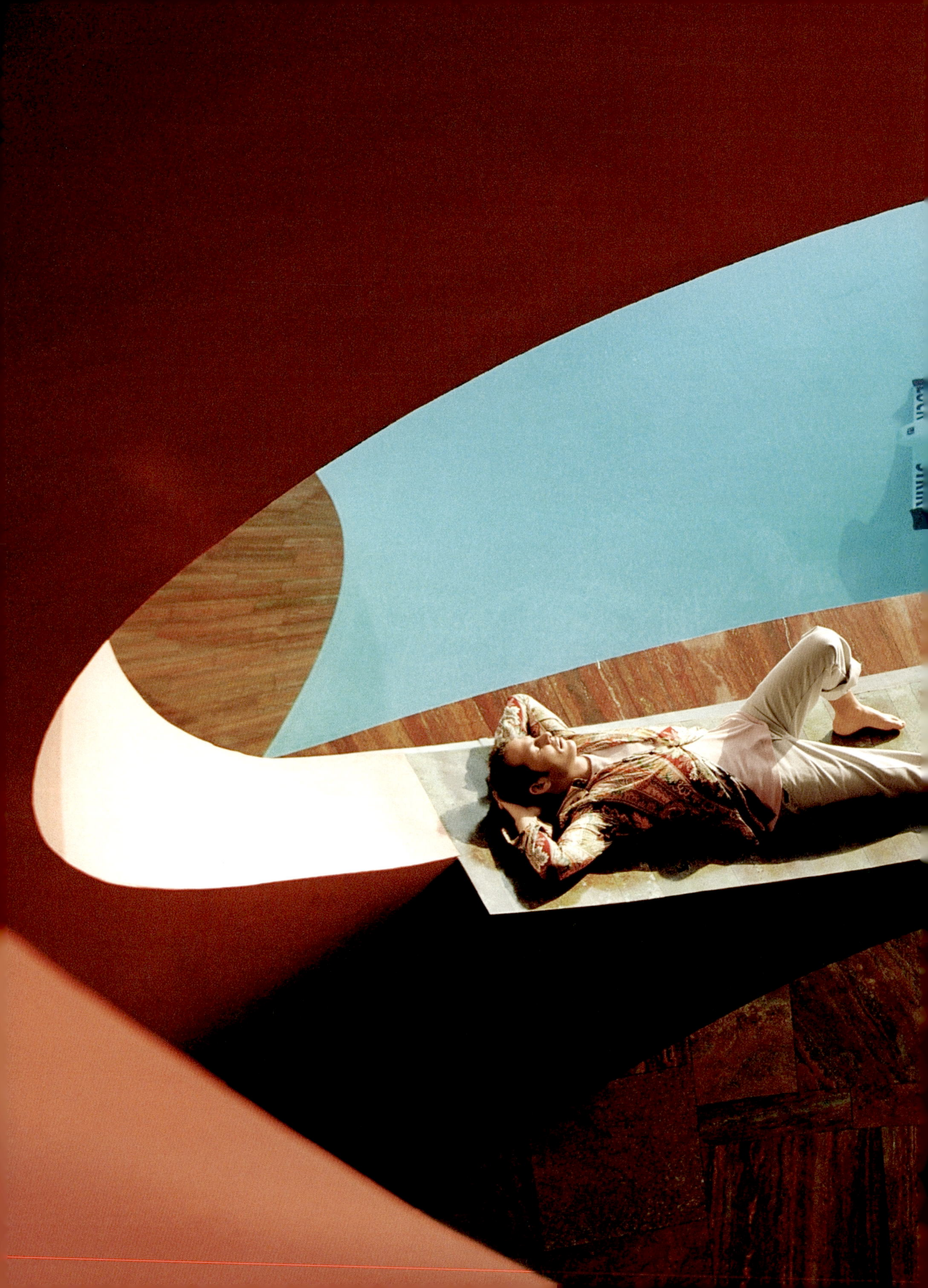

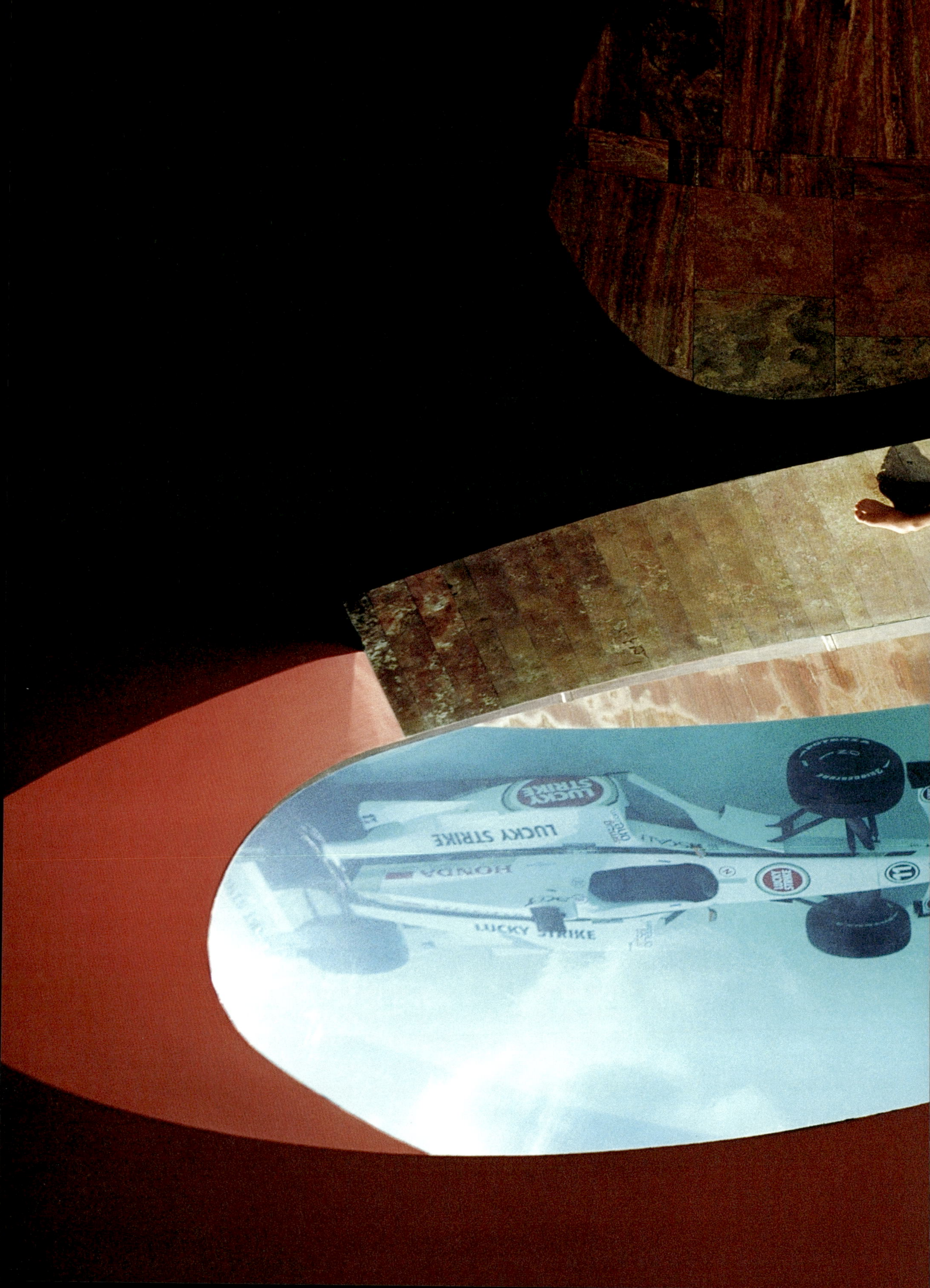

LUCKY STRIKE
LUCKY STRIKE
HONDA
LUCKY STRIKE
Bridgestone

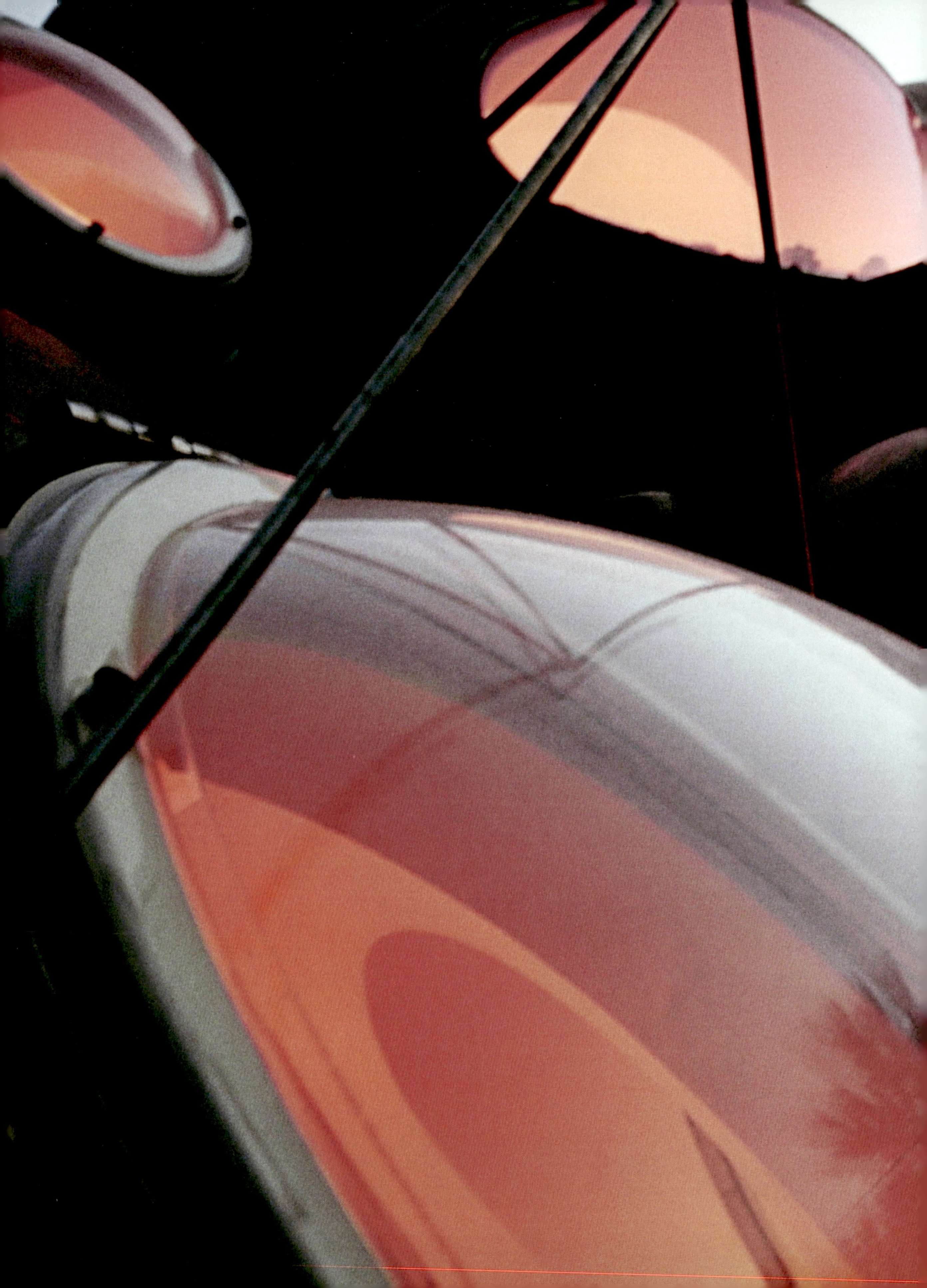

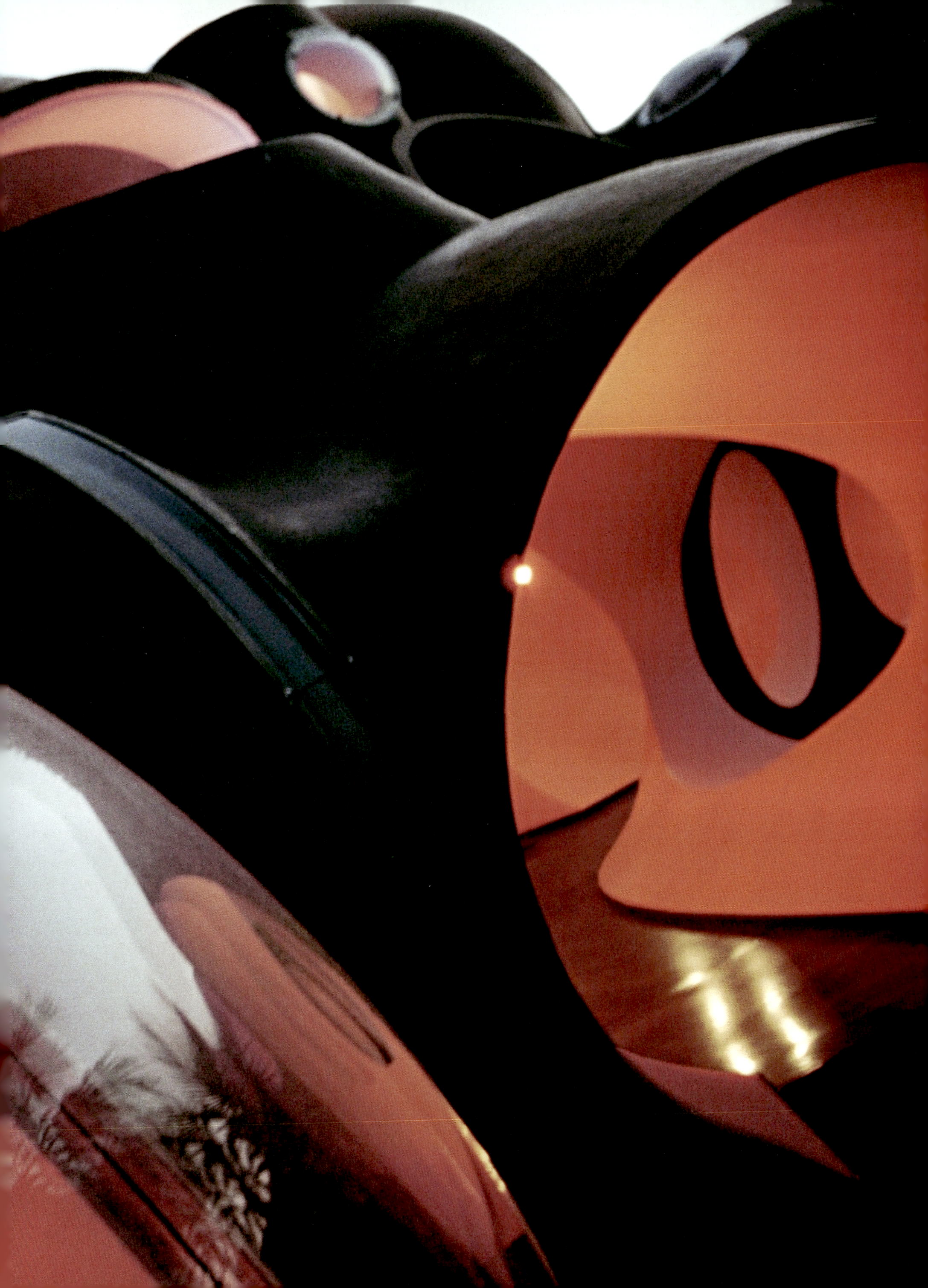

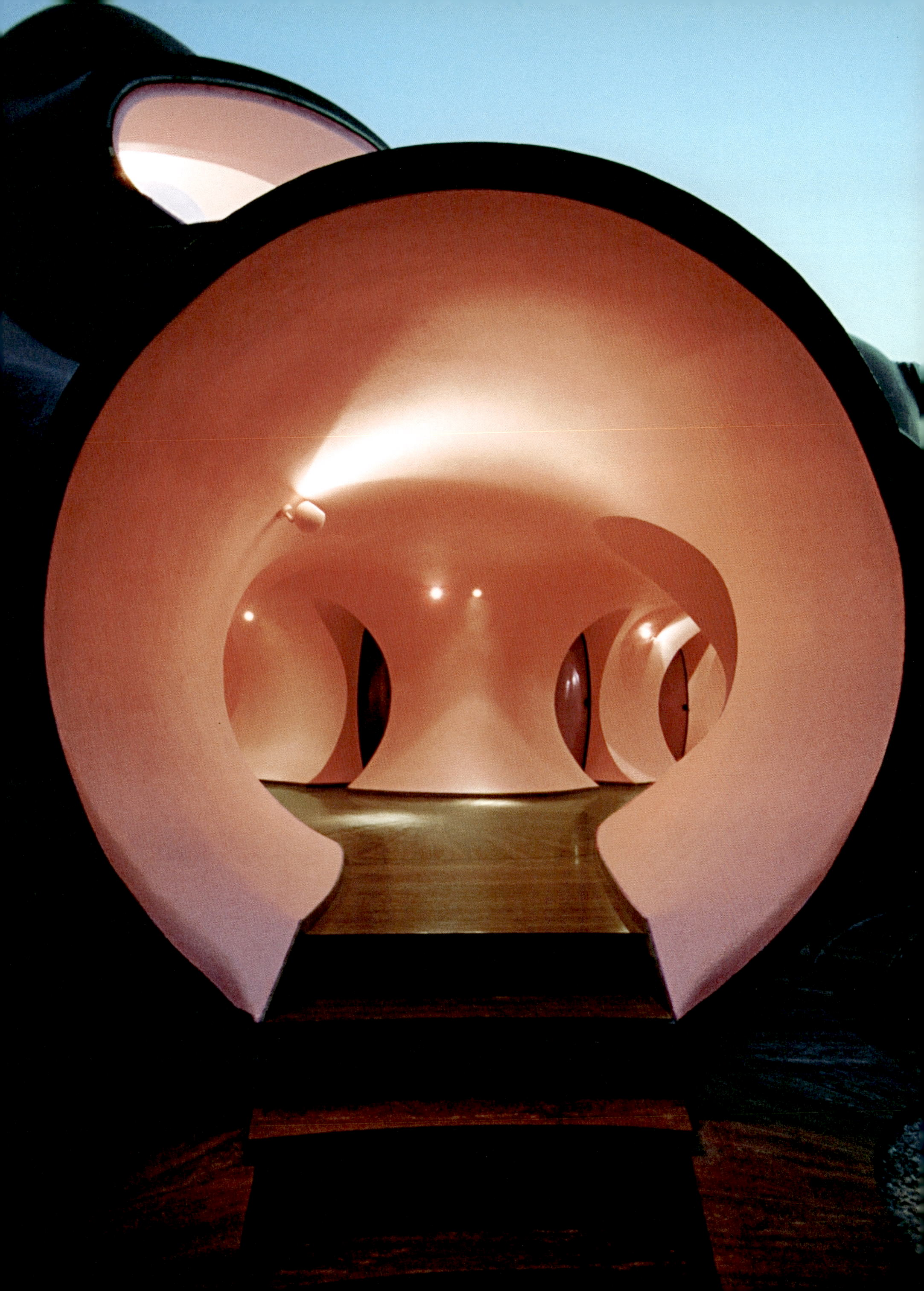

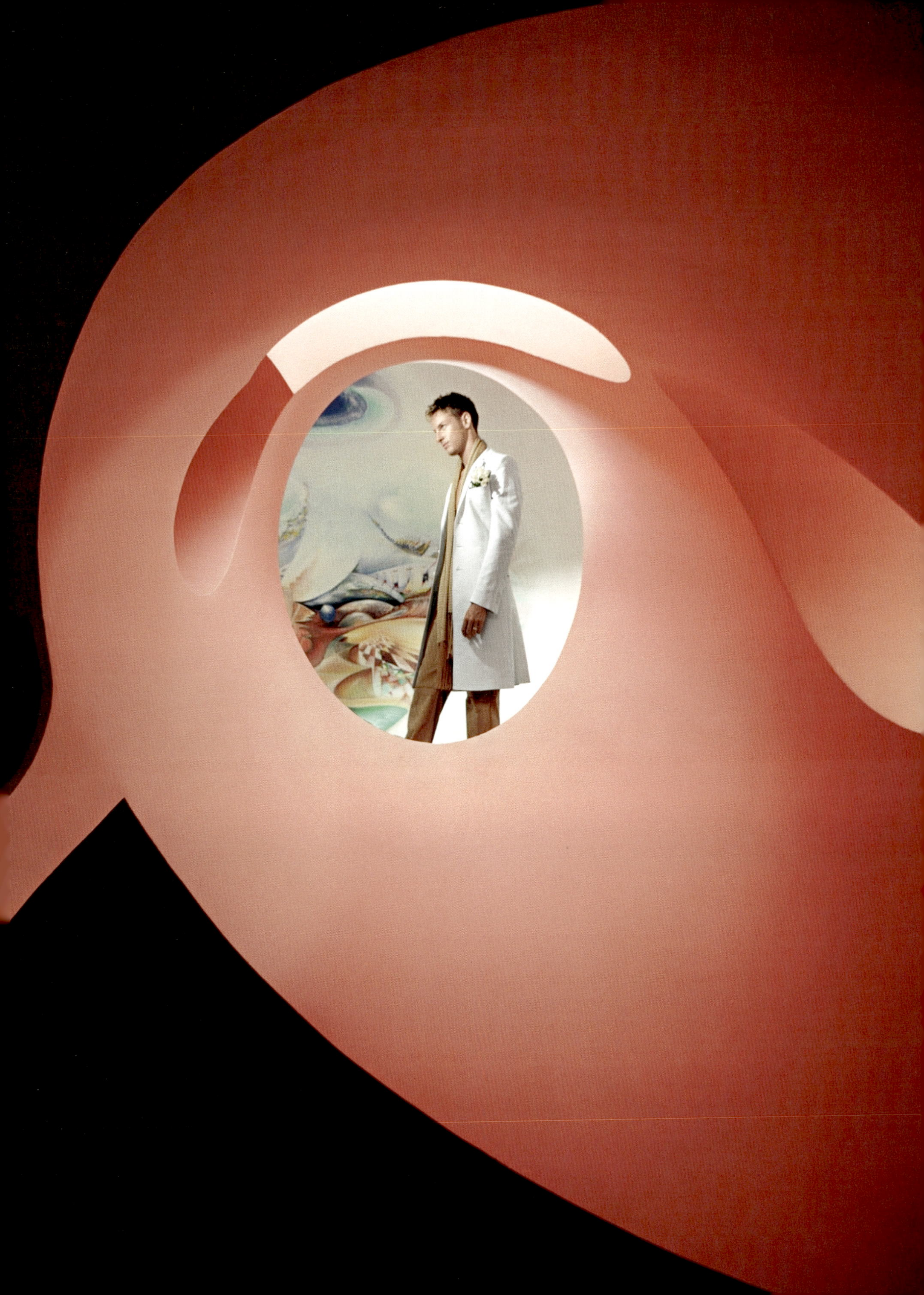

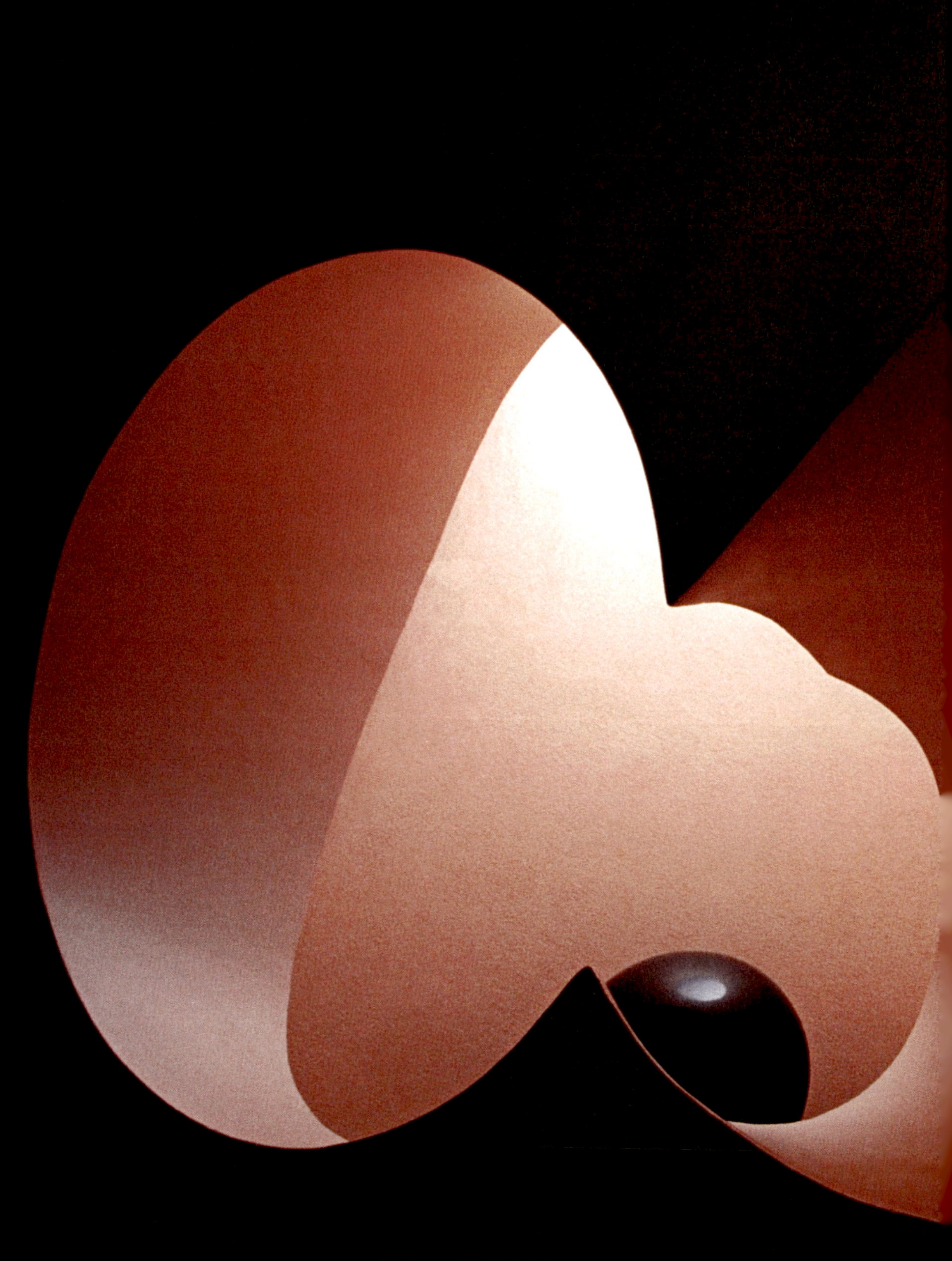

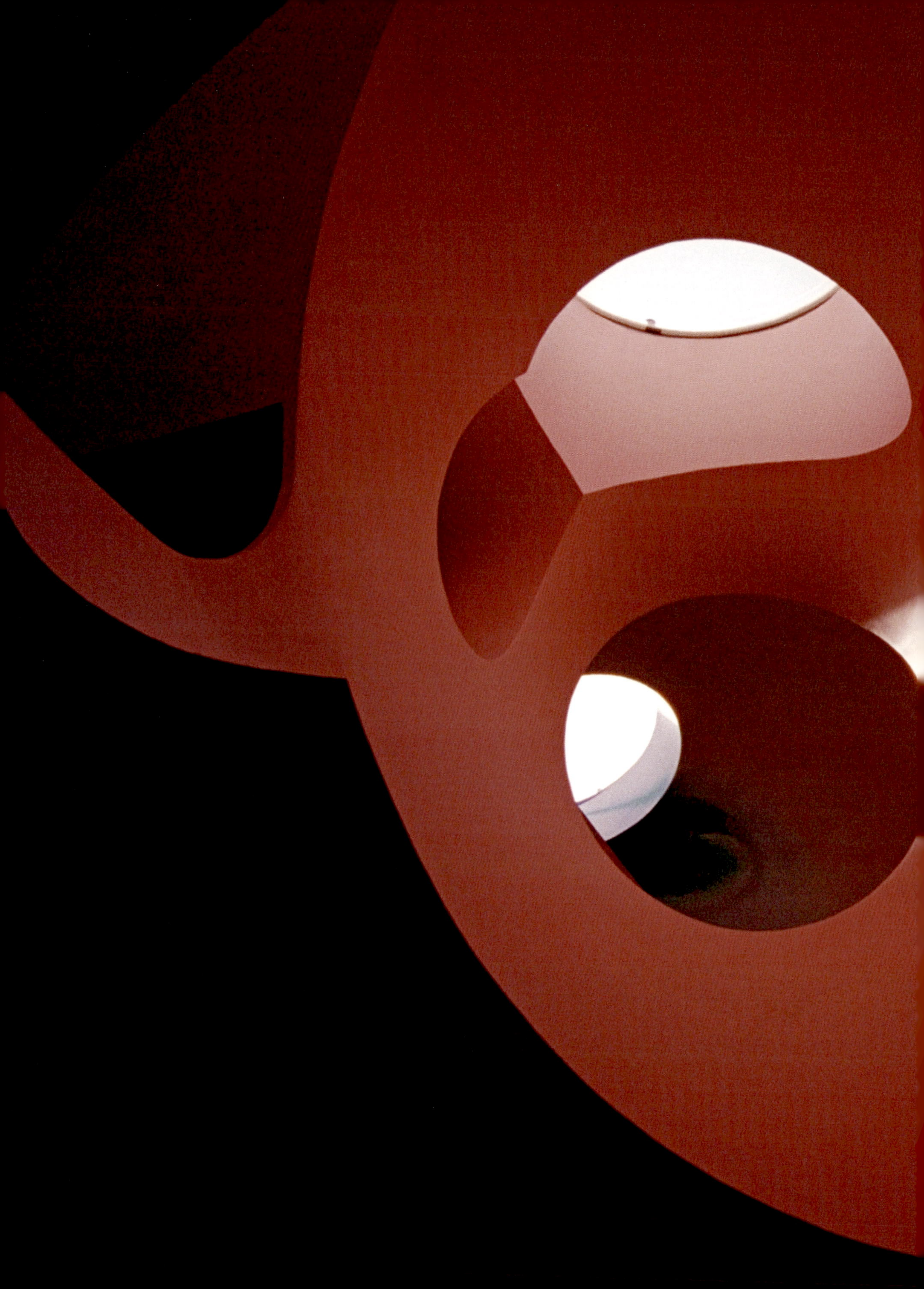

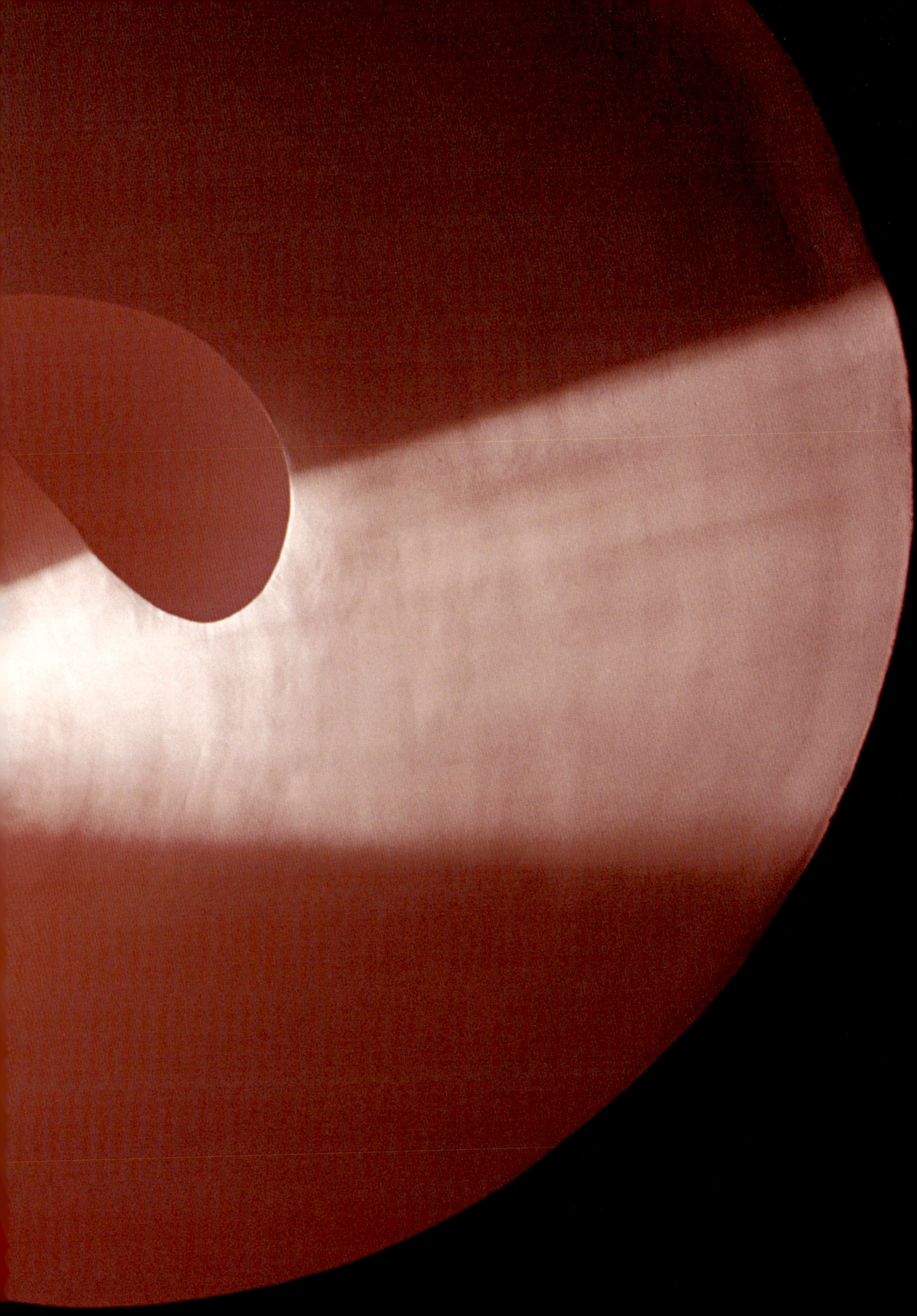

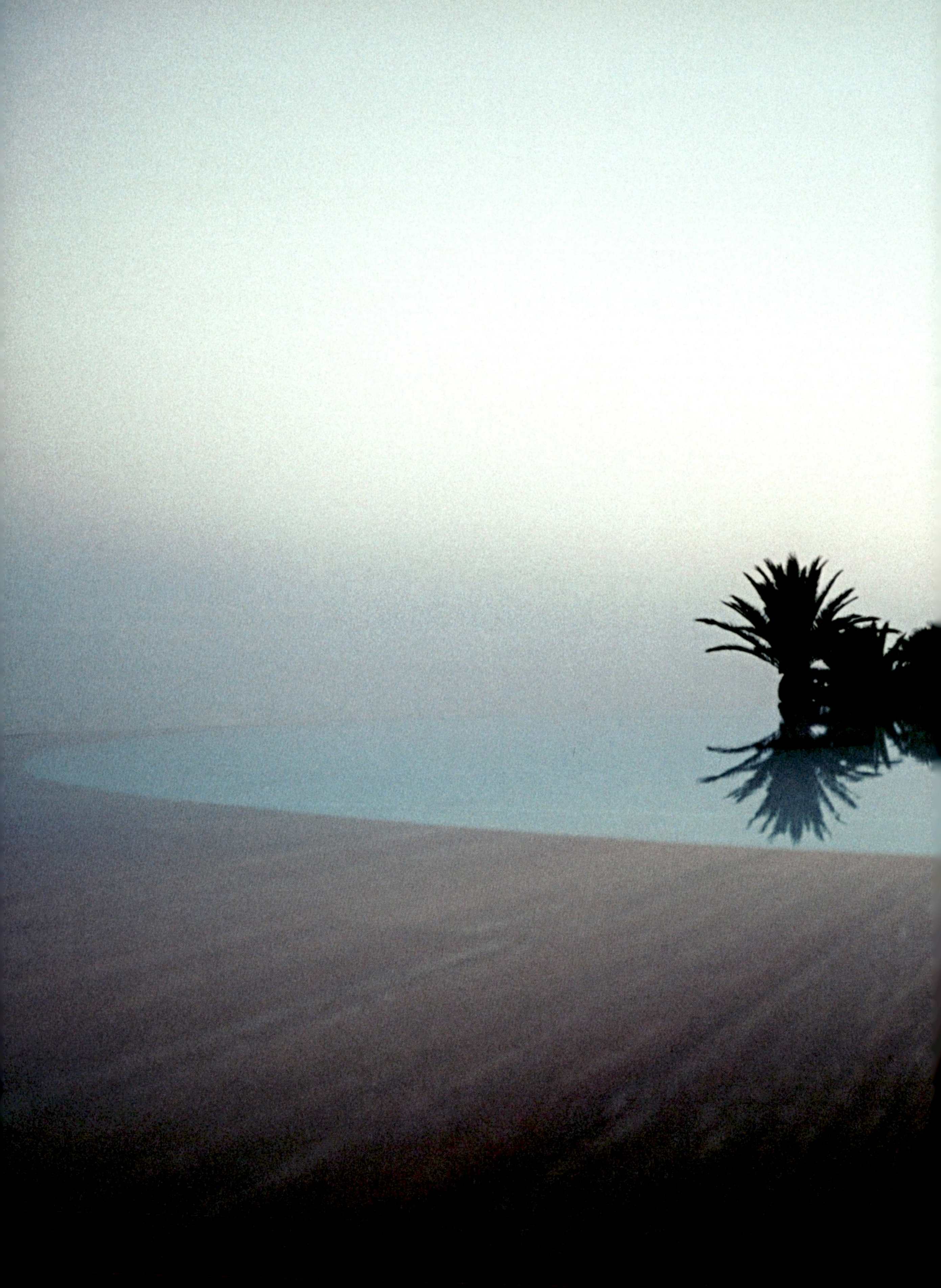

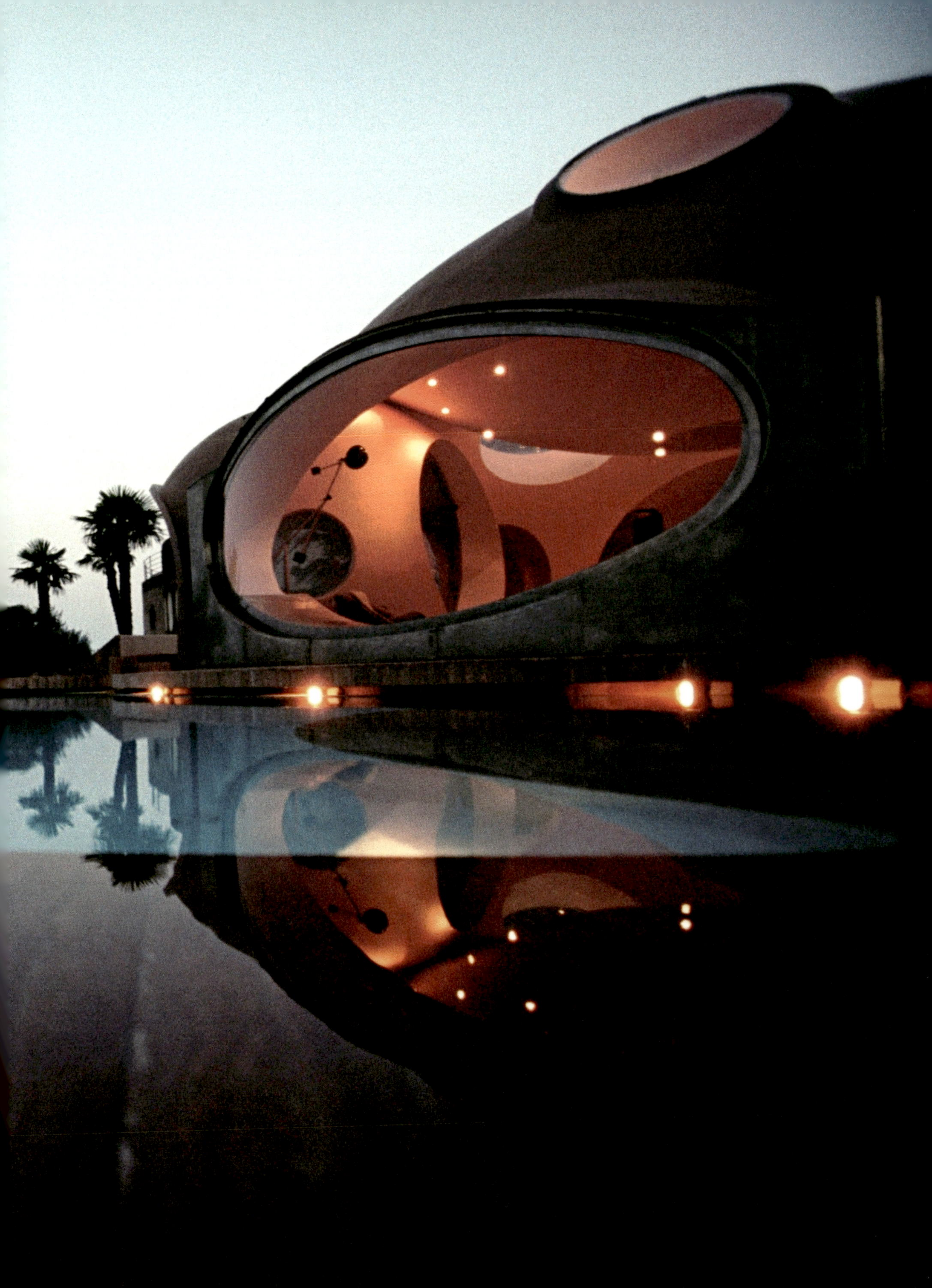

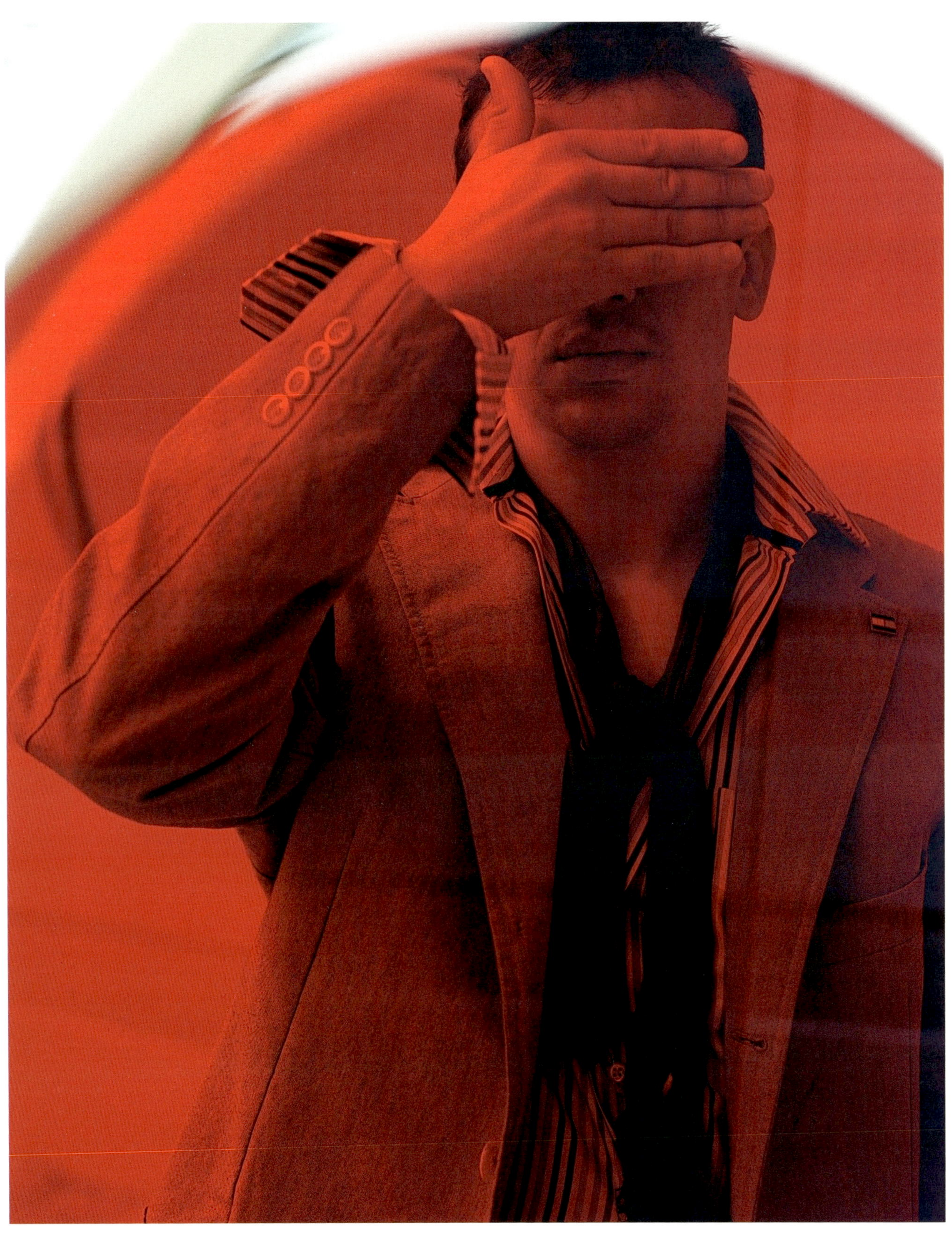

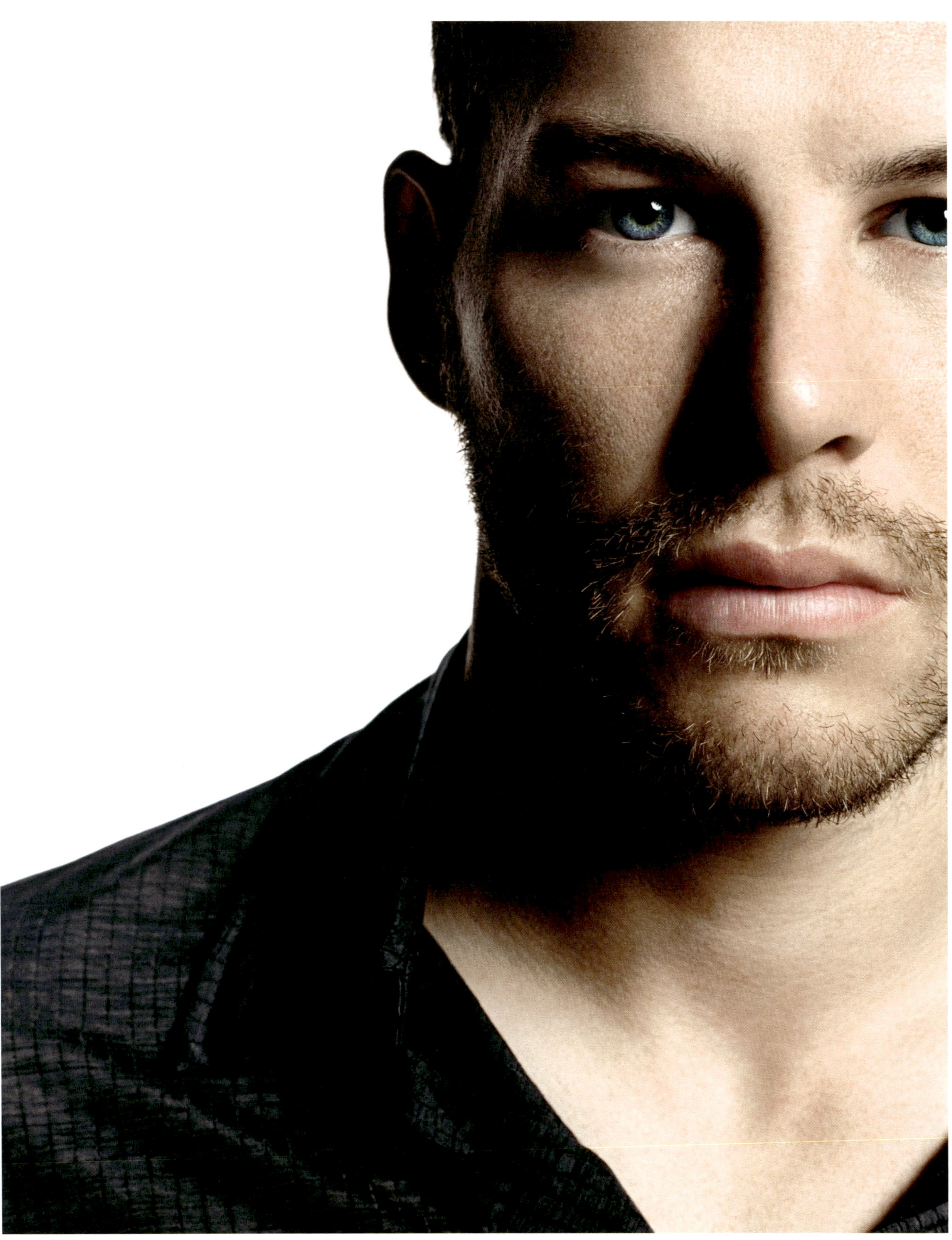

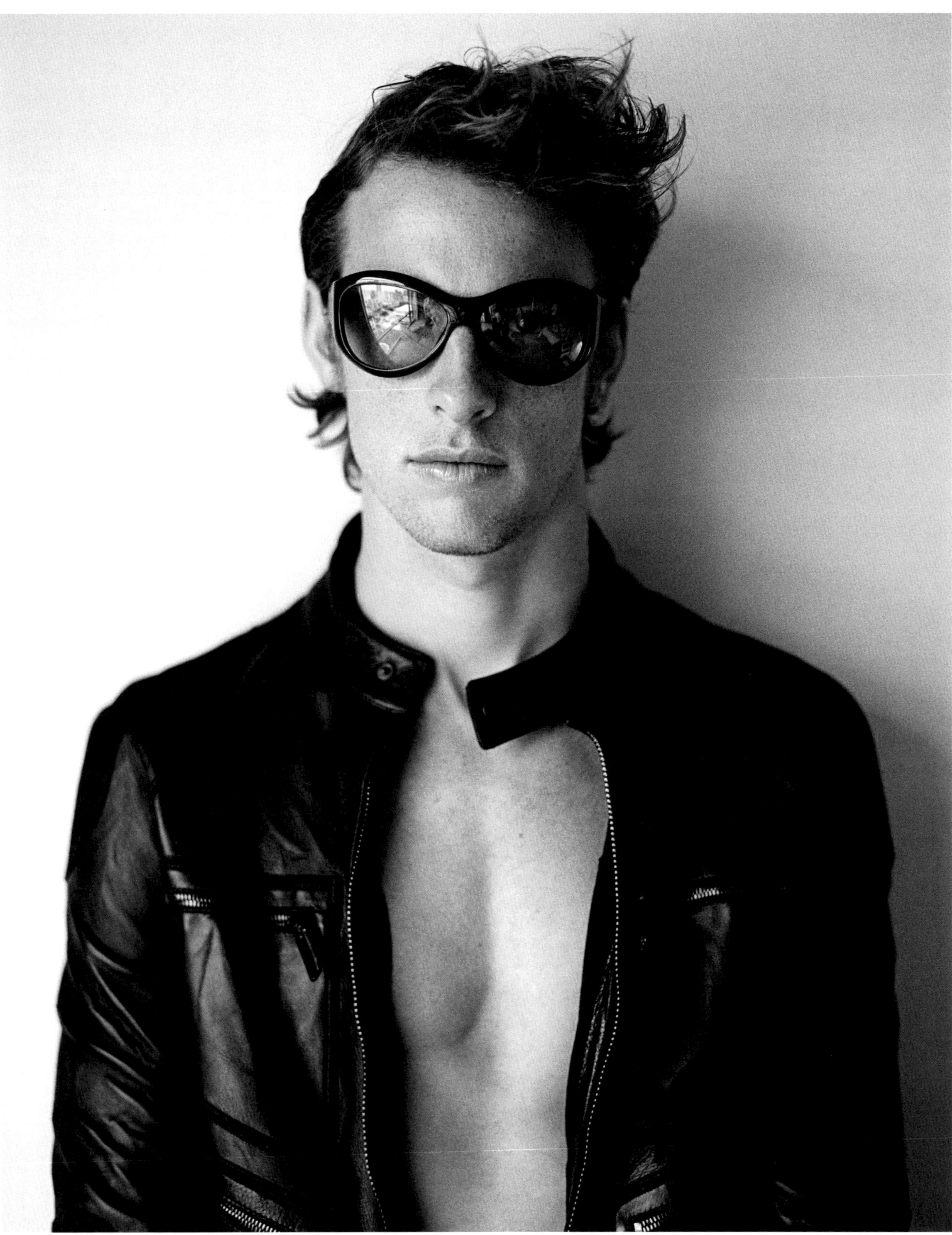

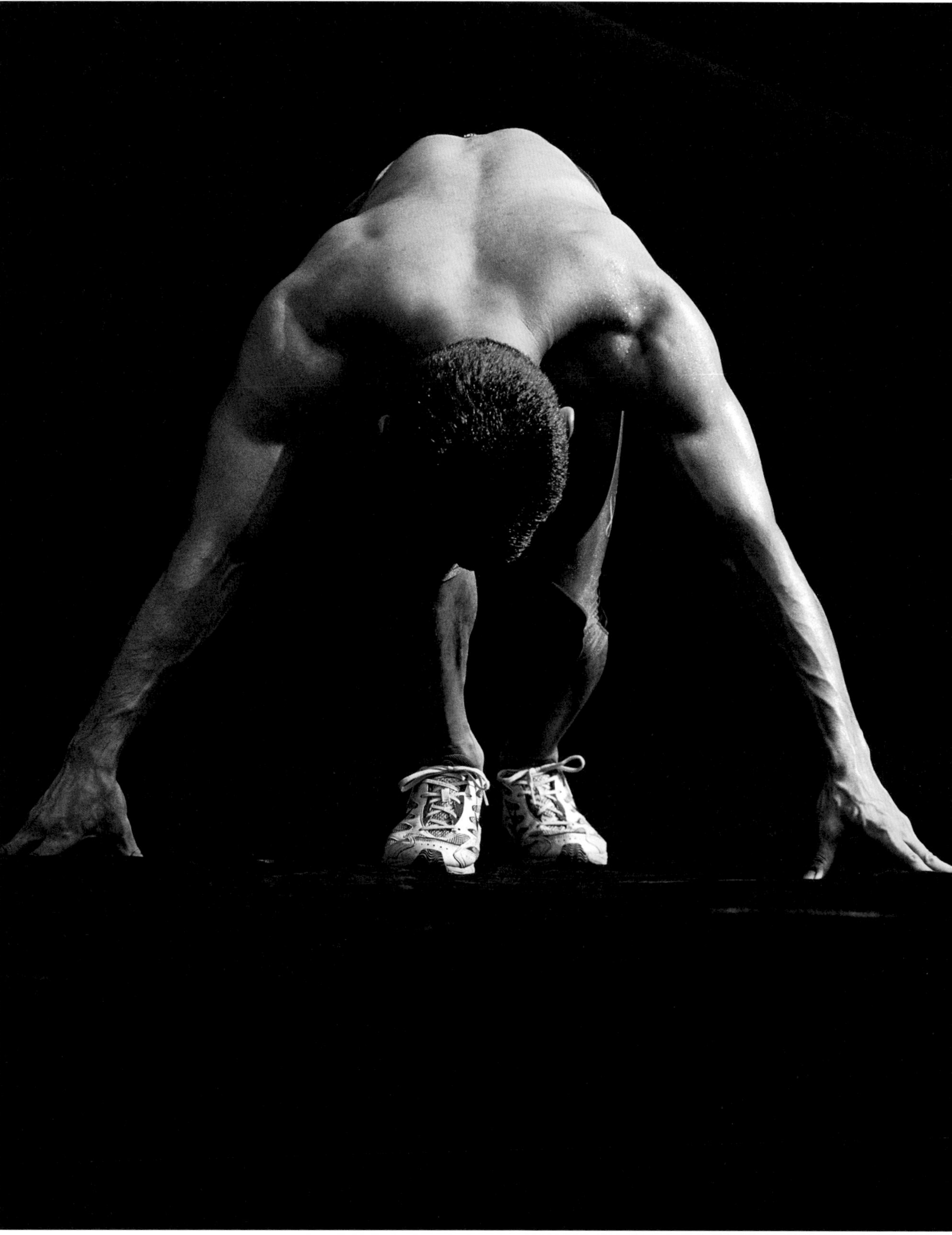

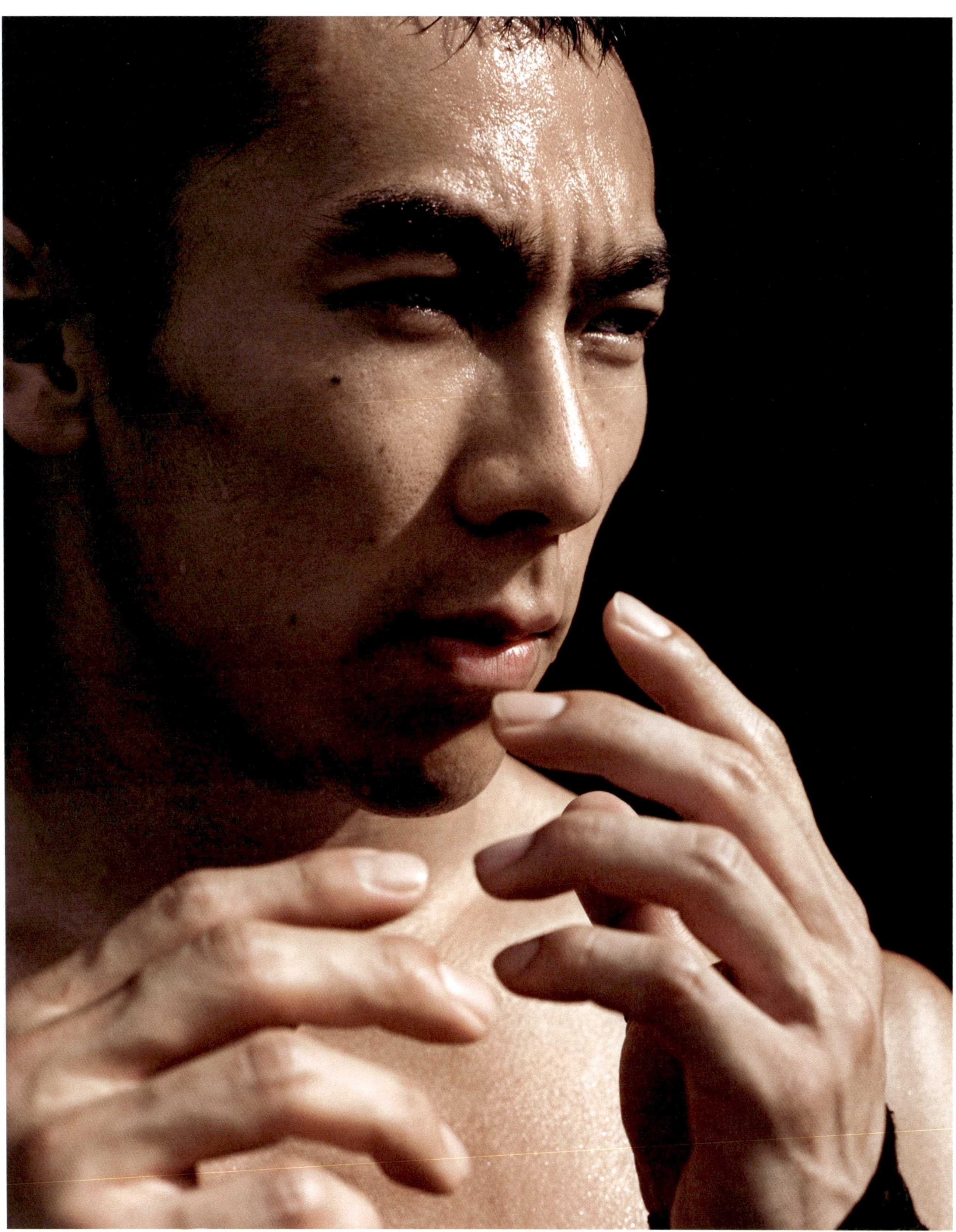

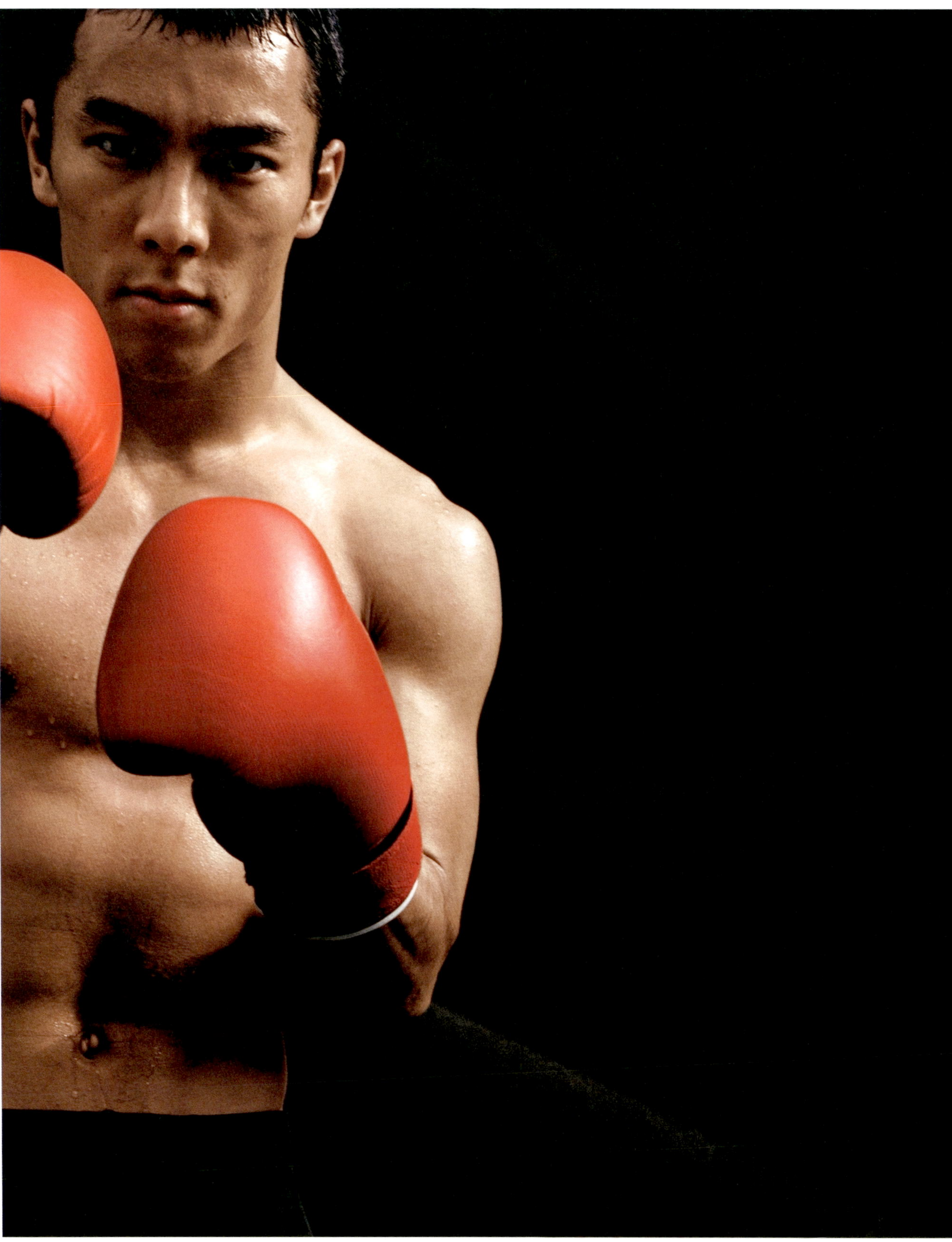

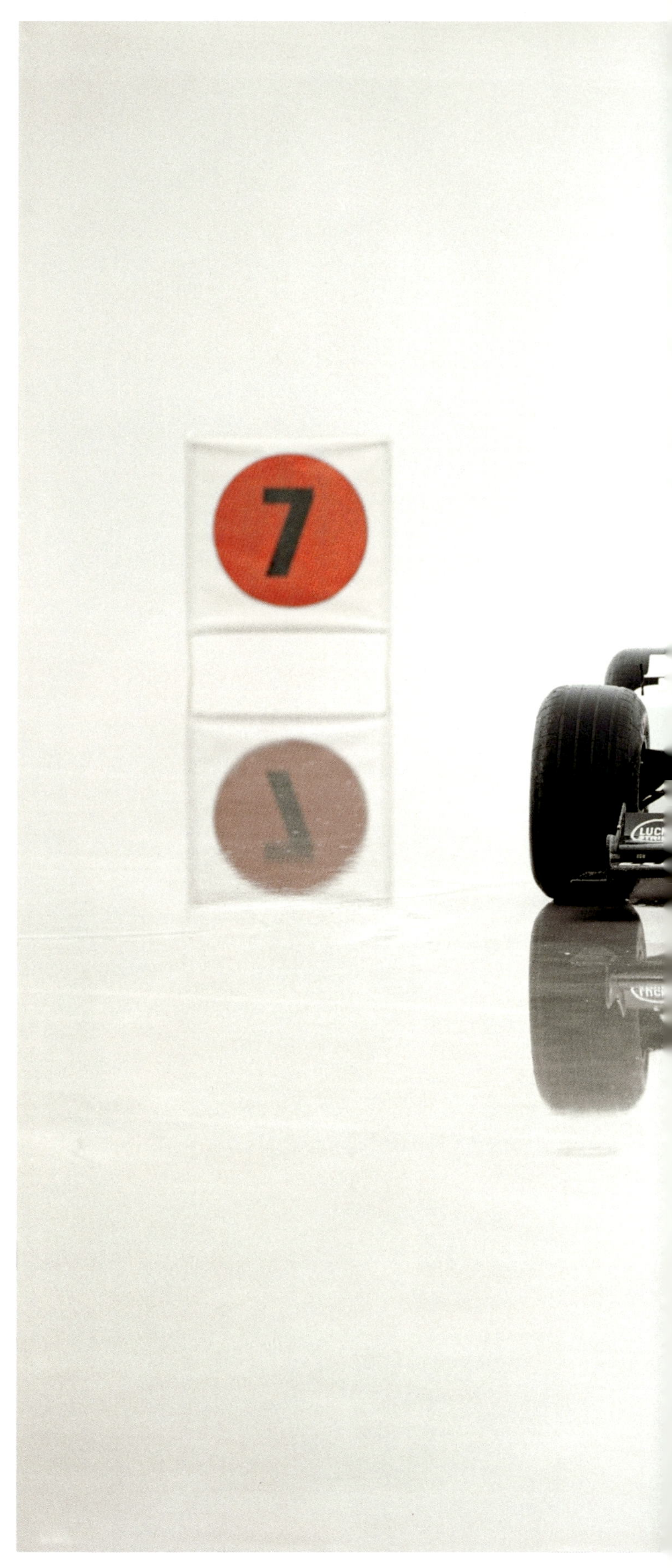
7

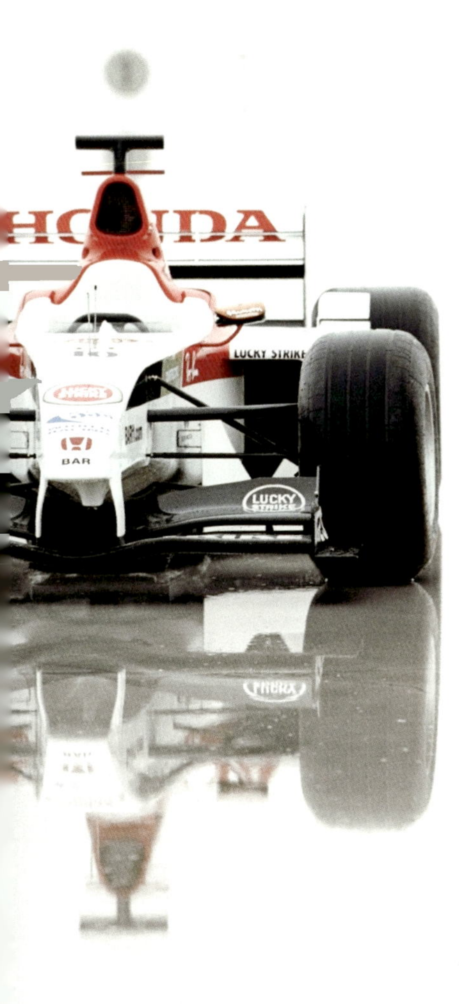
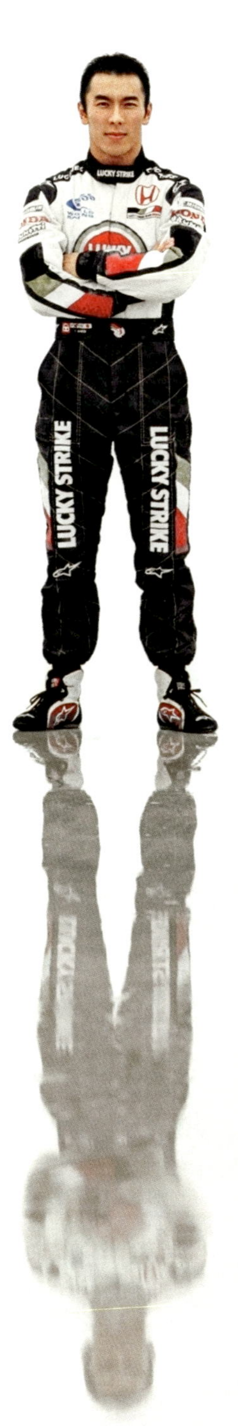

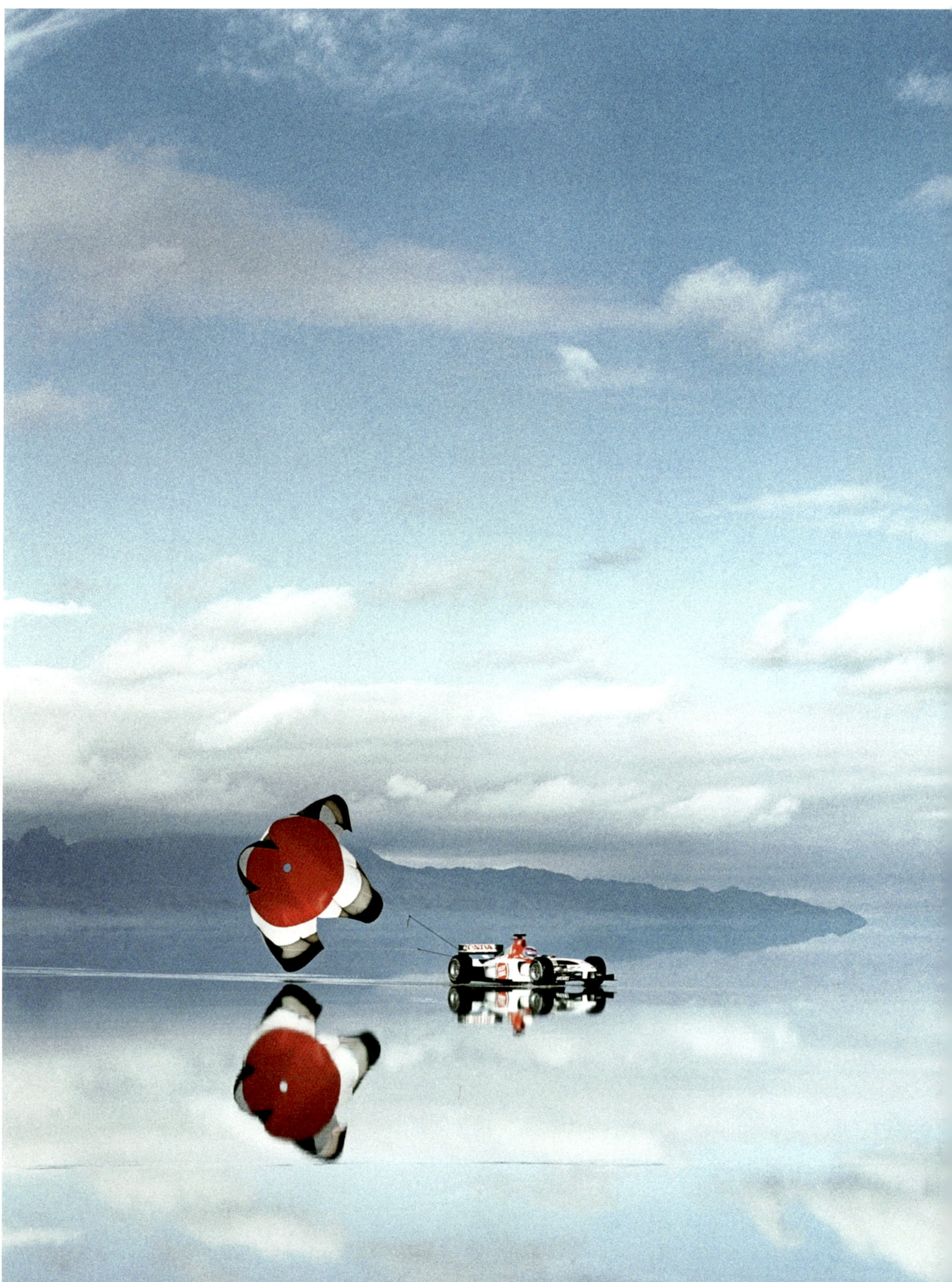

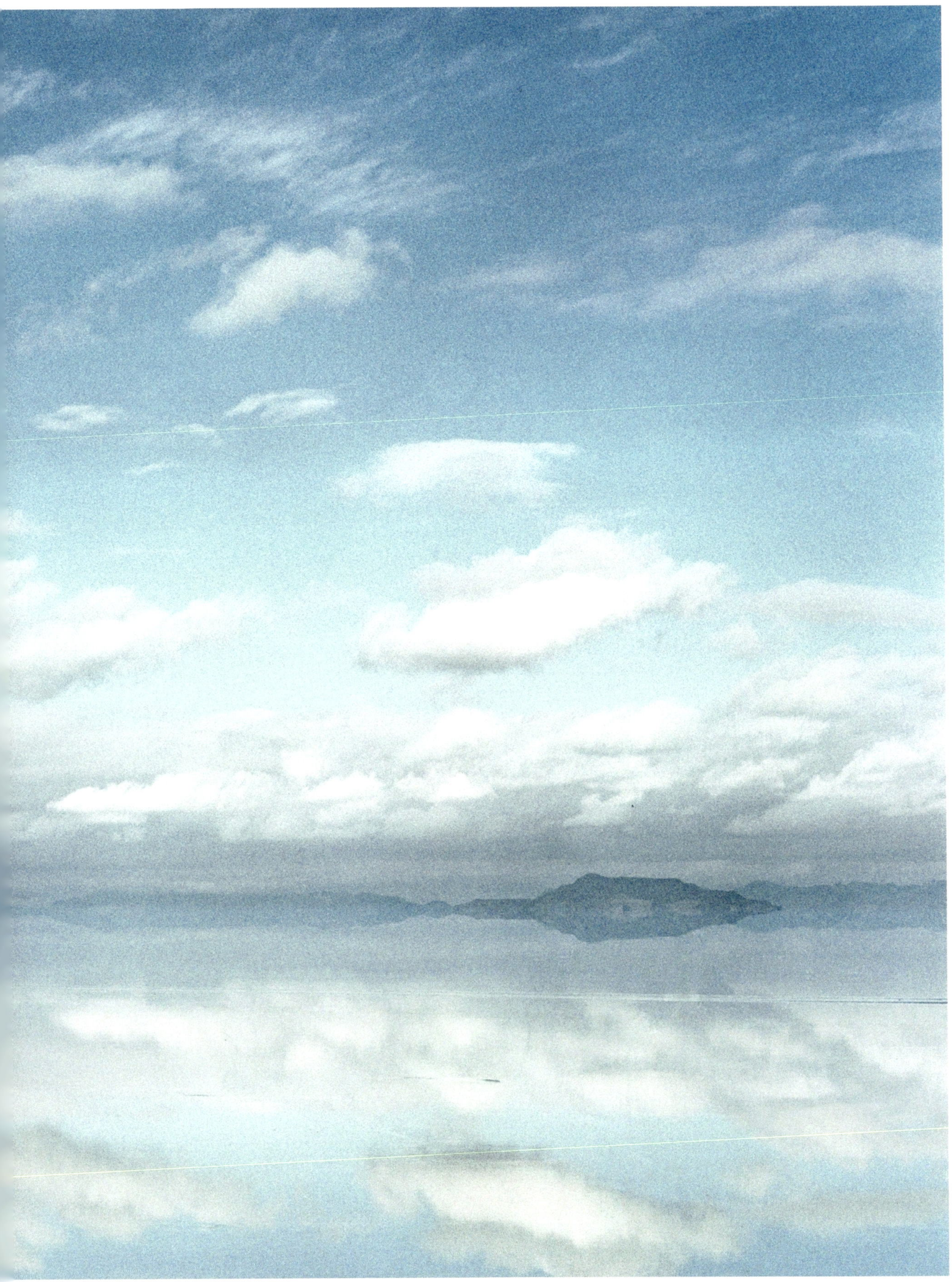

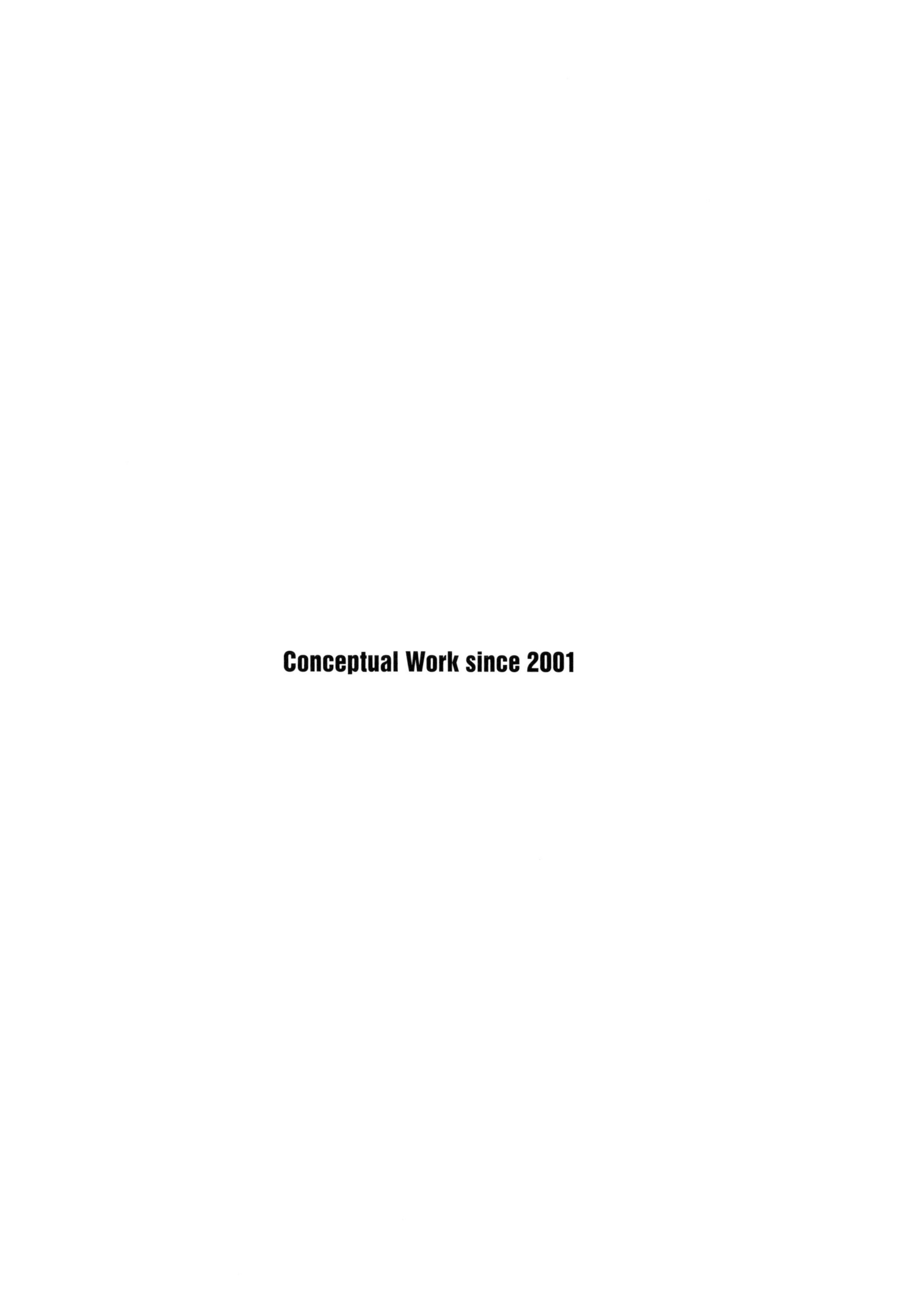

Conceptual Work since 2001

Moment of a Moment

Like the real world, the filmic world is sustained by the presumption that, as Husserl says, "the experience will constantly continue to flow by in the same constitutive style"; but the Photograph breaks the "constitutive style" (this is its astonishment); it is without future (this is its pathos, its melancholy); in it, no protensity, whereas the cinema is protensive, hence in no way melancholic. . . .
Roland Barthes, *Camera Lucida,* 1979-1980

Schmid's installation of photographs and moving pictures addresses the contrasting principles of movement and stasis. In its themes it counters Formula 1 with the notion of slowness, so that—with reference to the distinction between film and photography— it becomes clear that there is a secret connection between slowness and remembering, between speed and forgetting, as Milan Kundera once said. Even as it looms into sight every individual moment is already over and done with; in photography it is preserved and remembered.

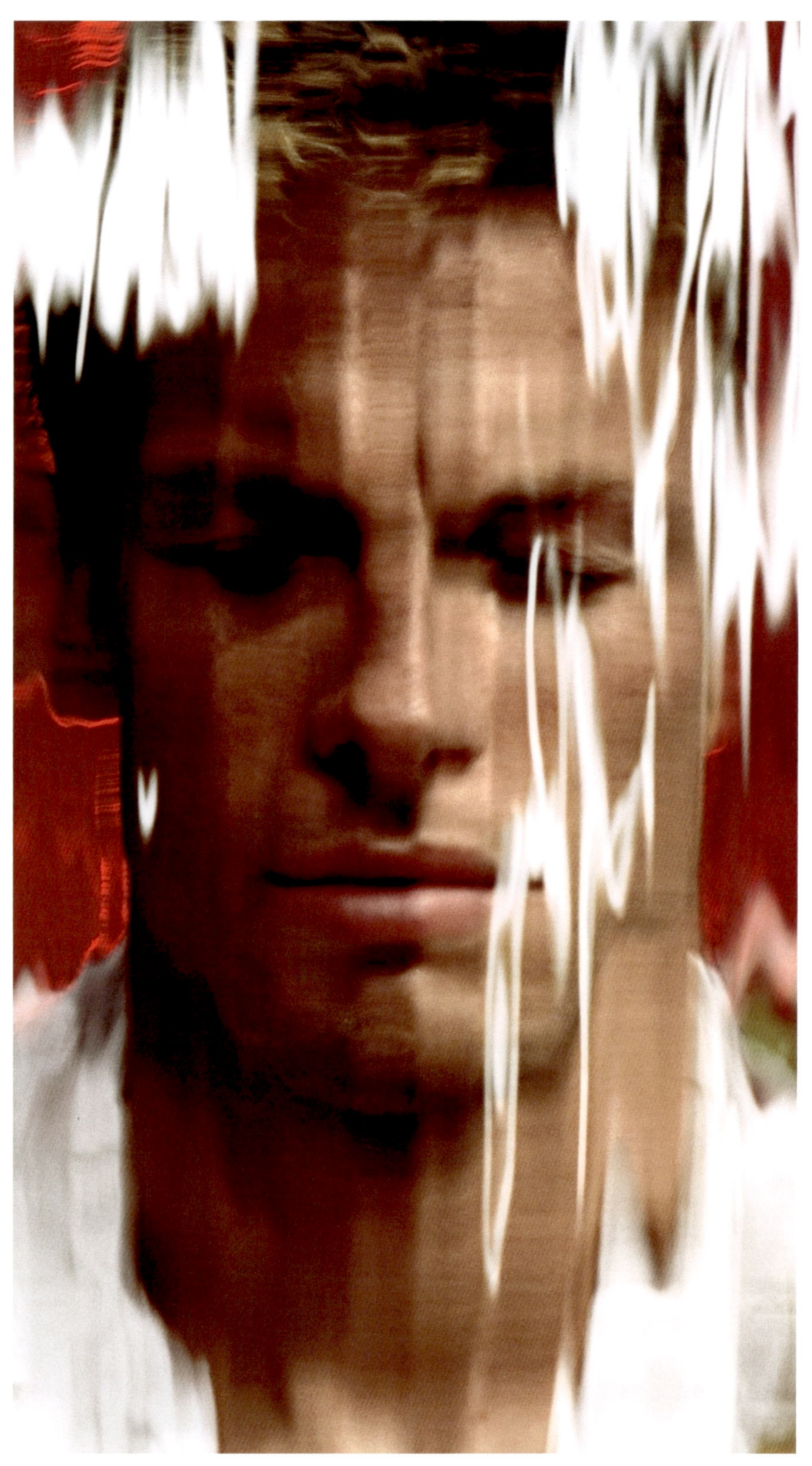

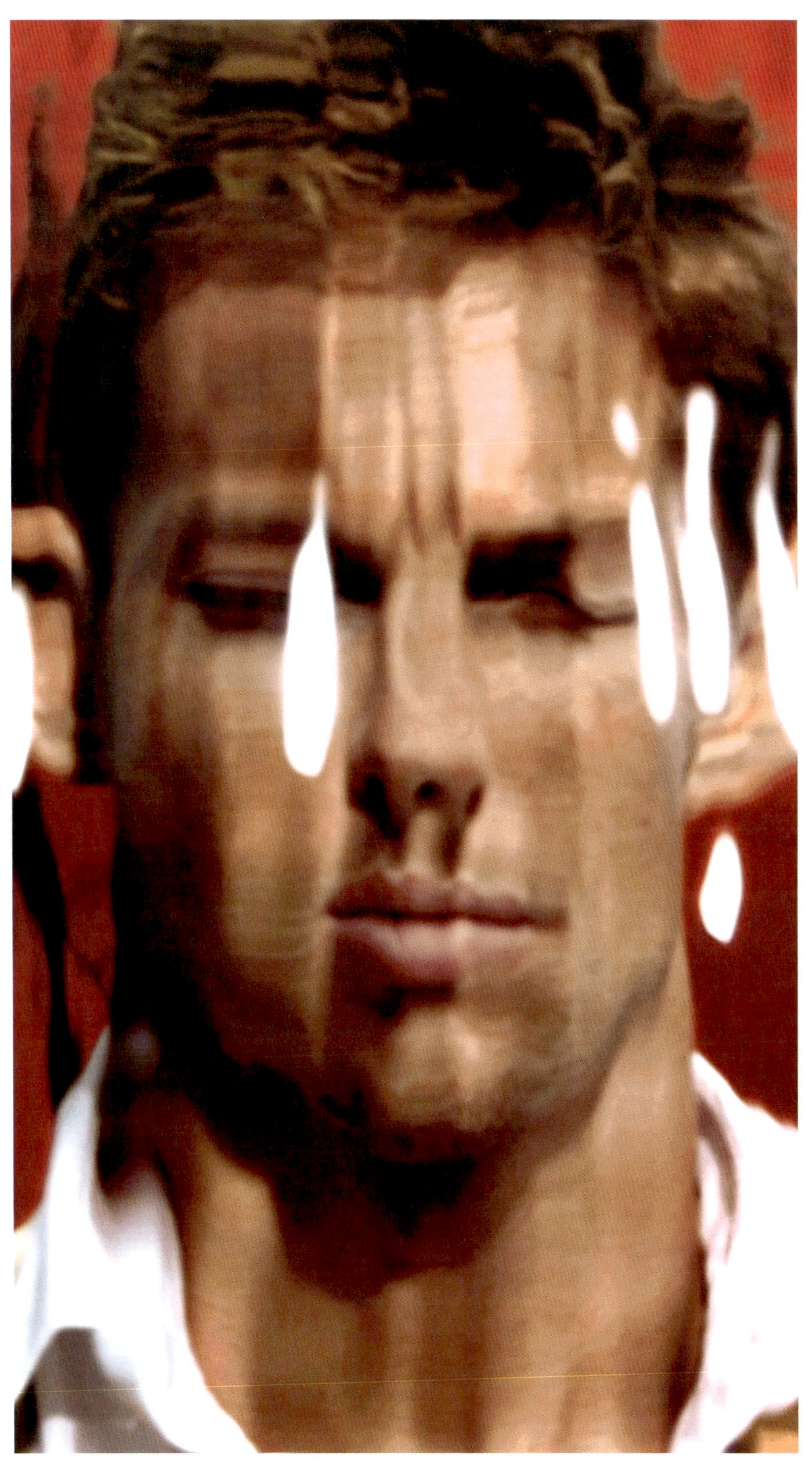

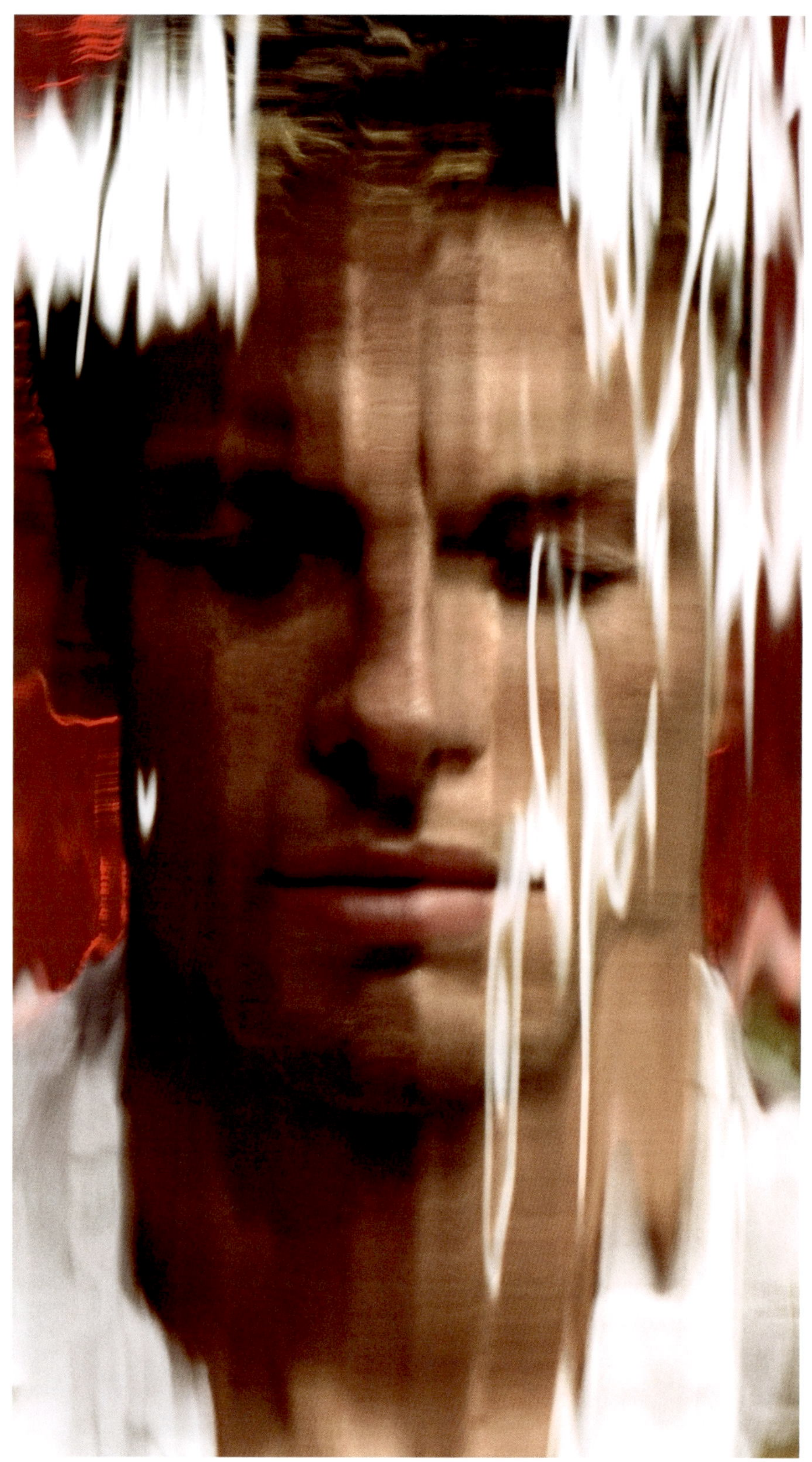

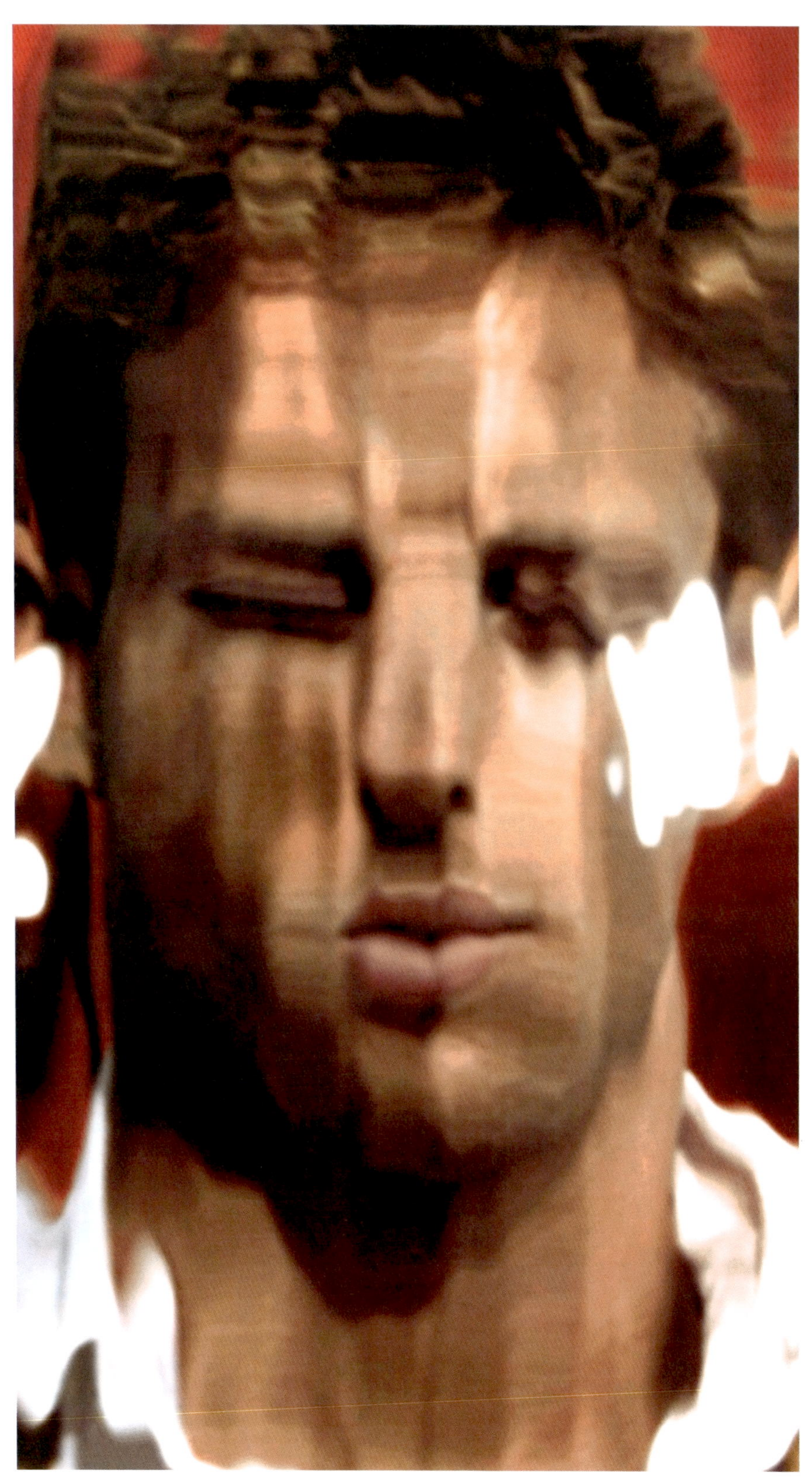

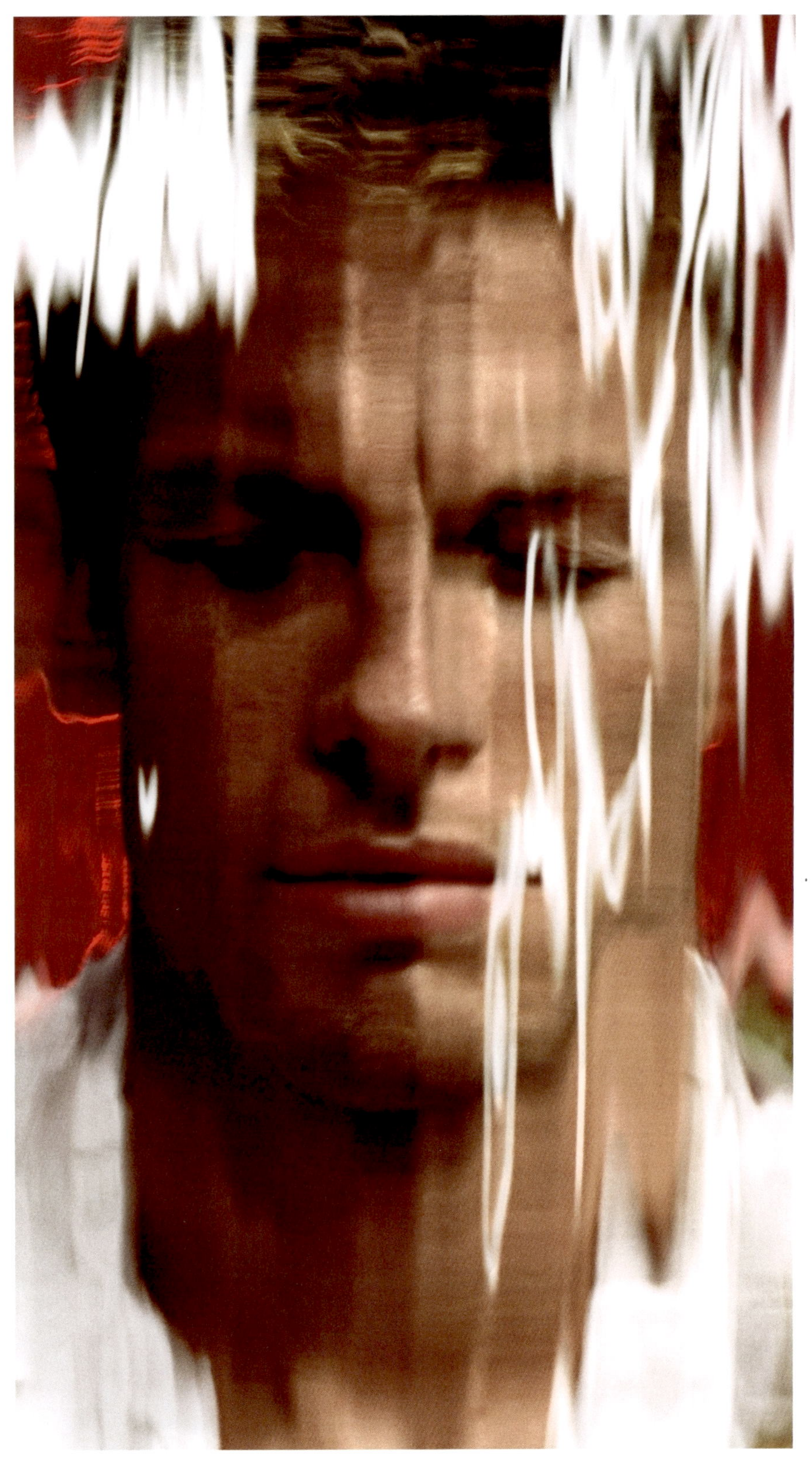

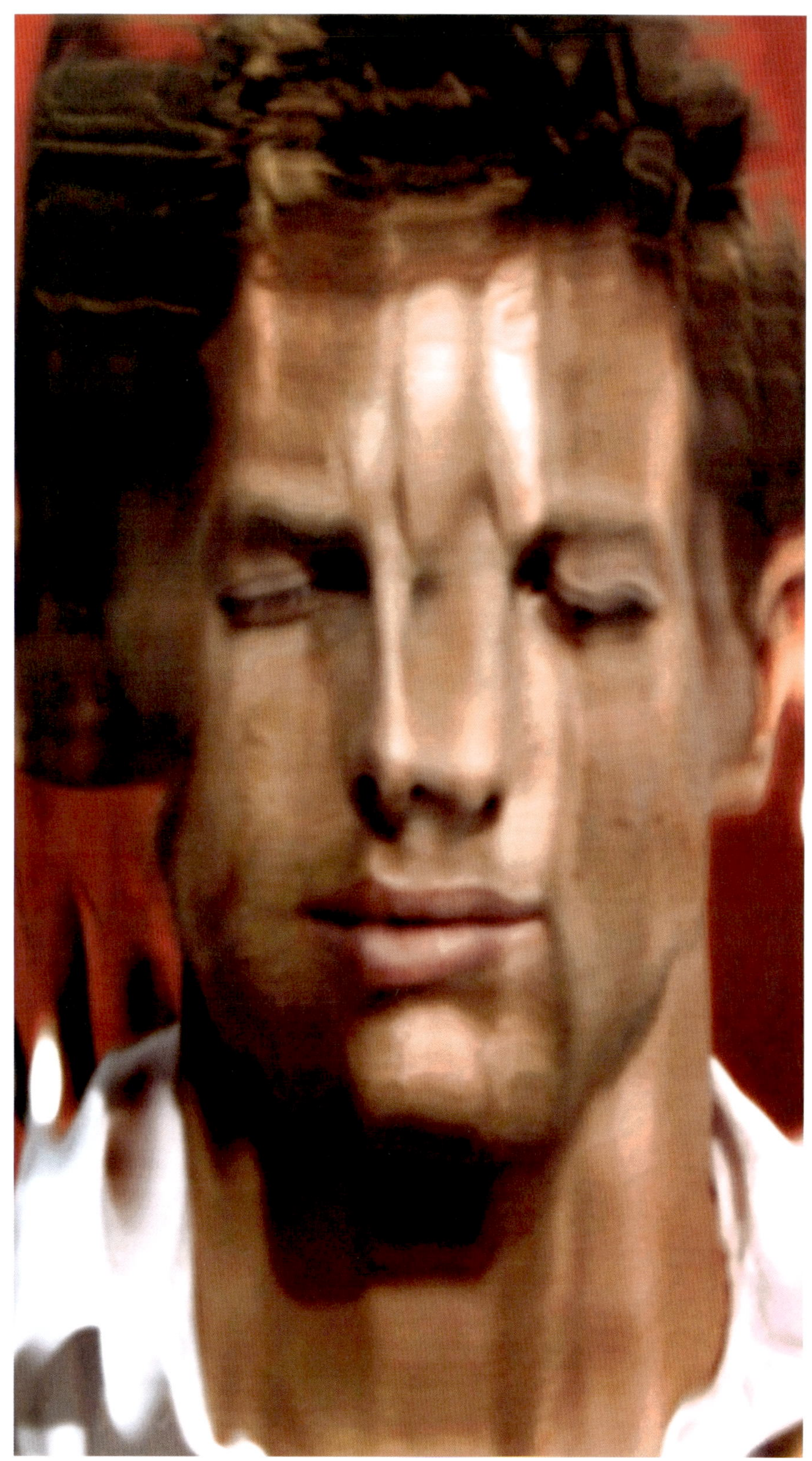

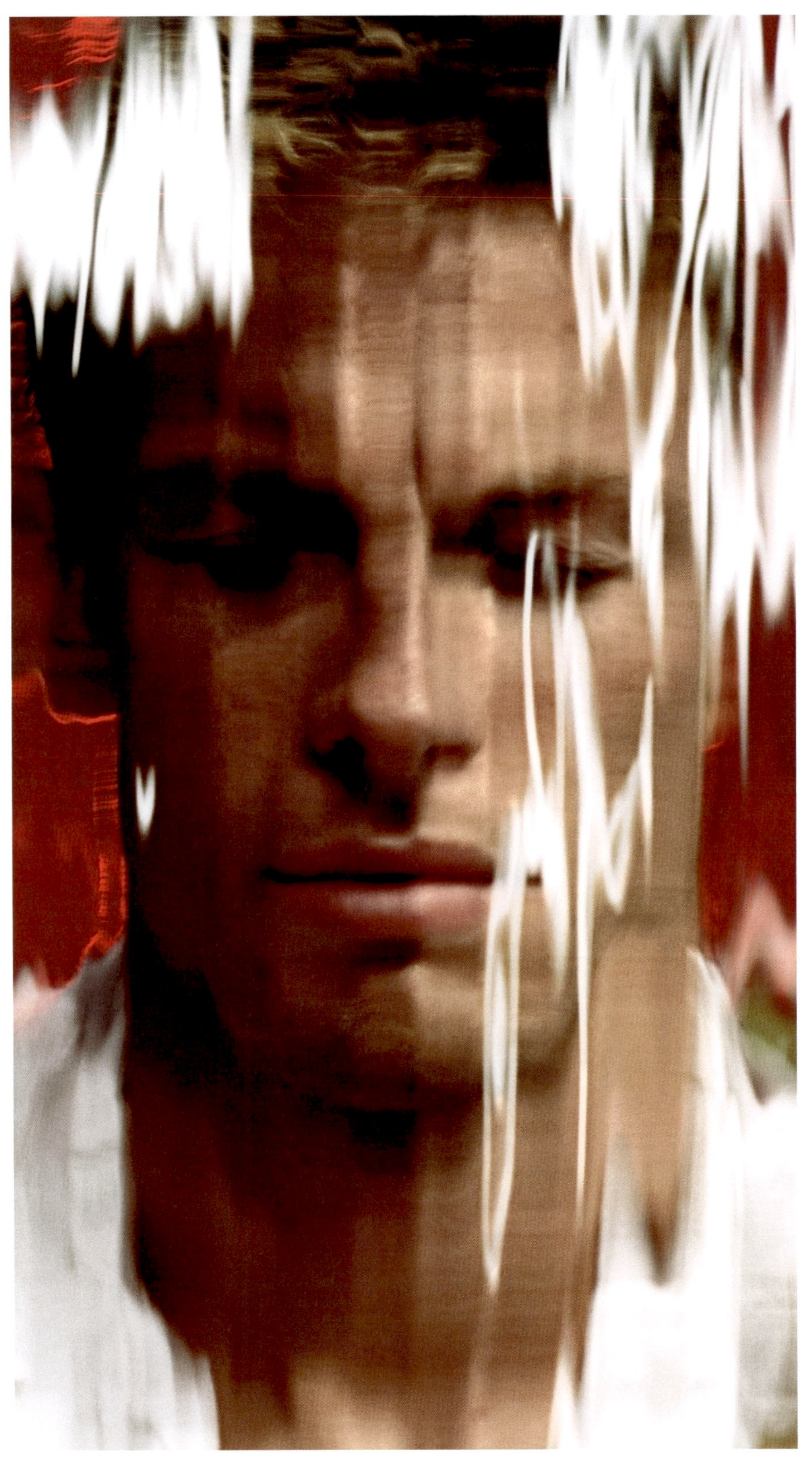

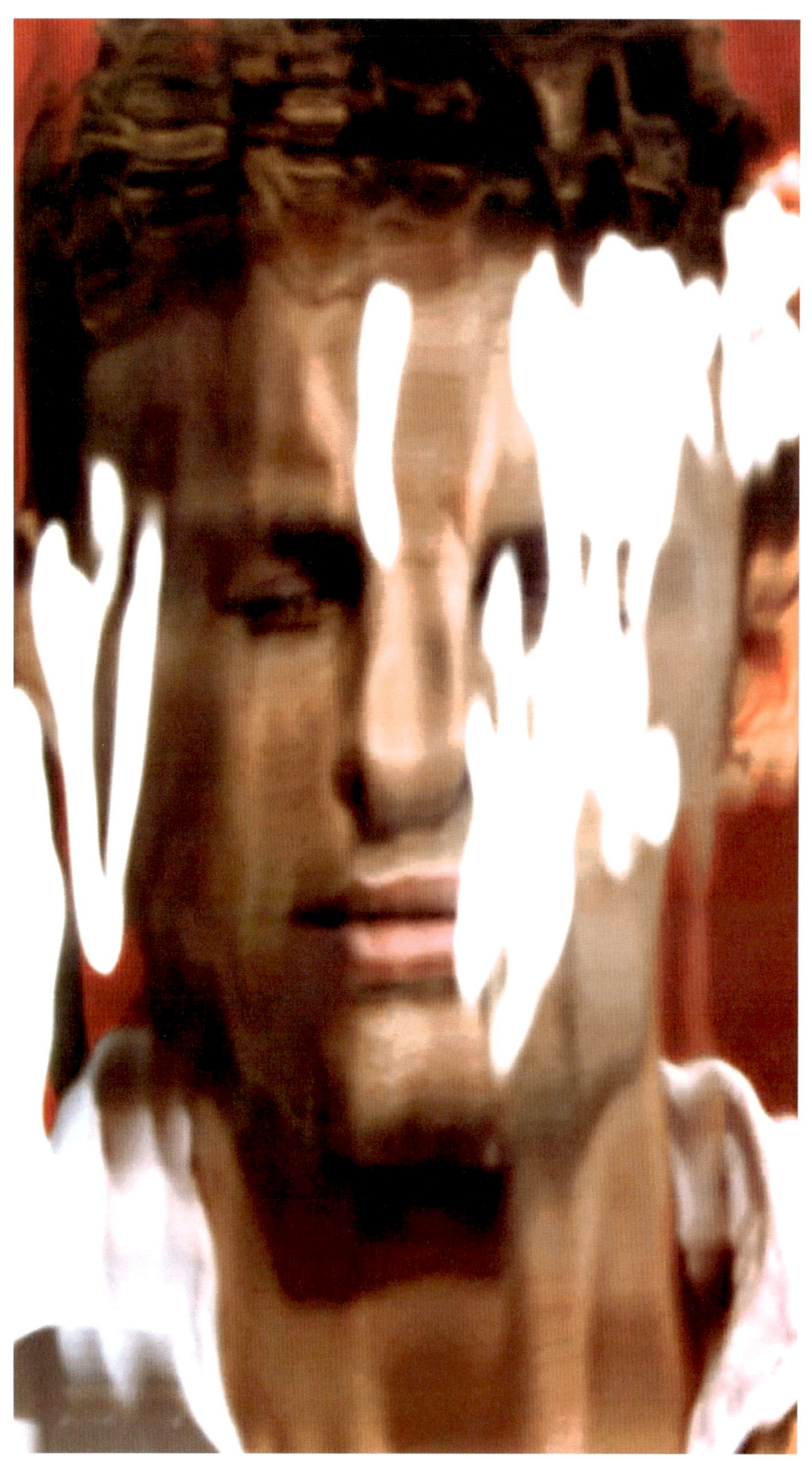

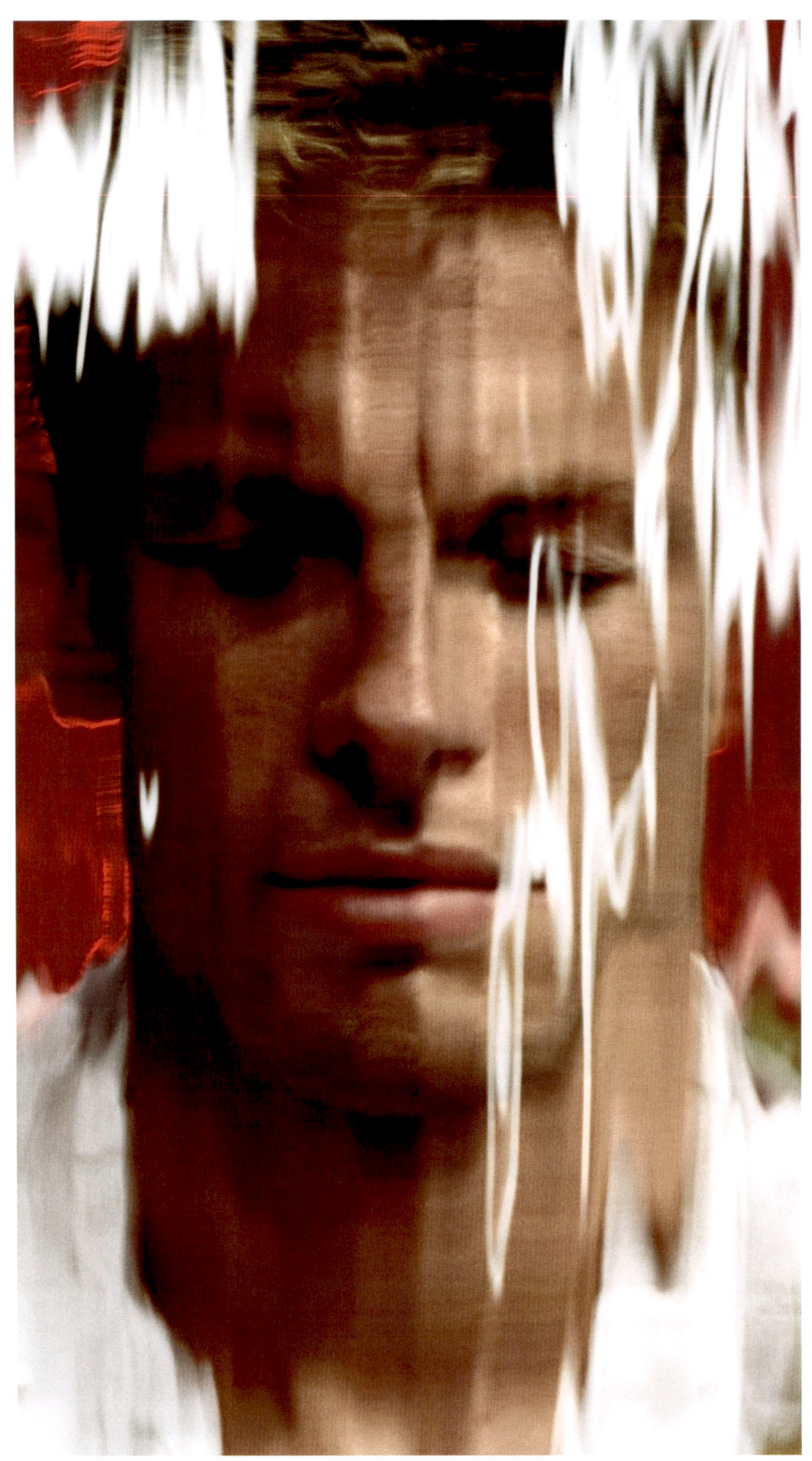

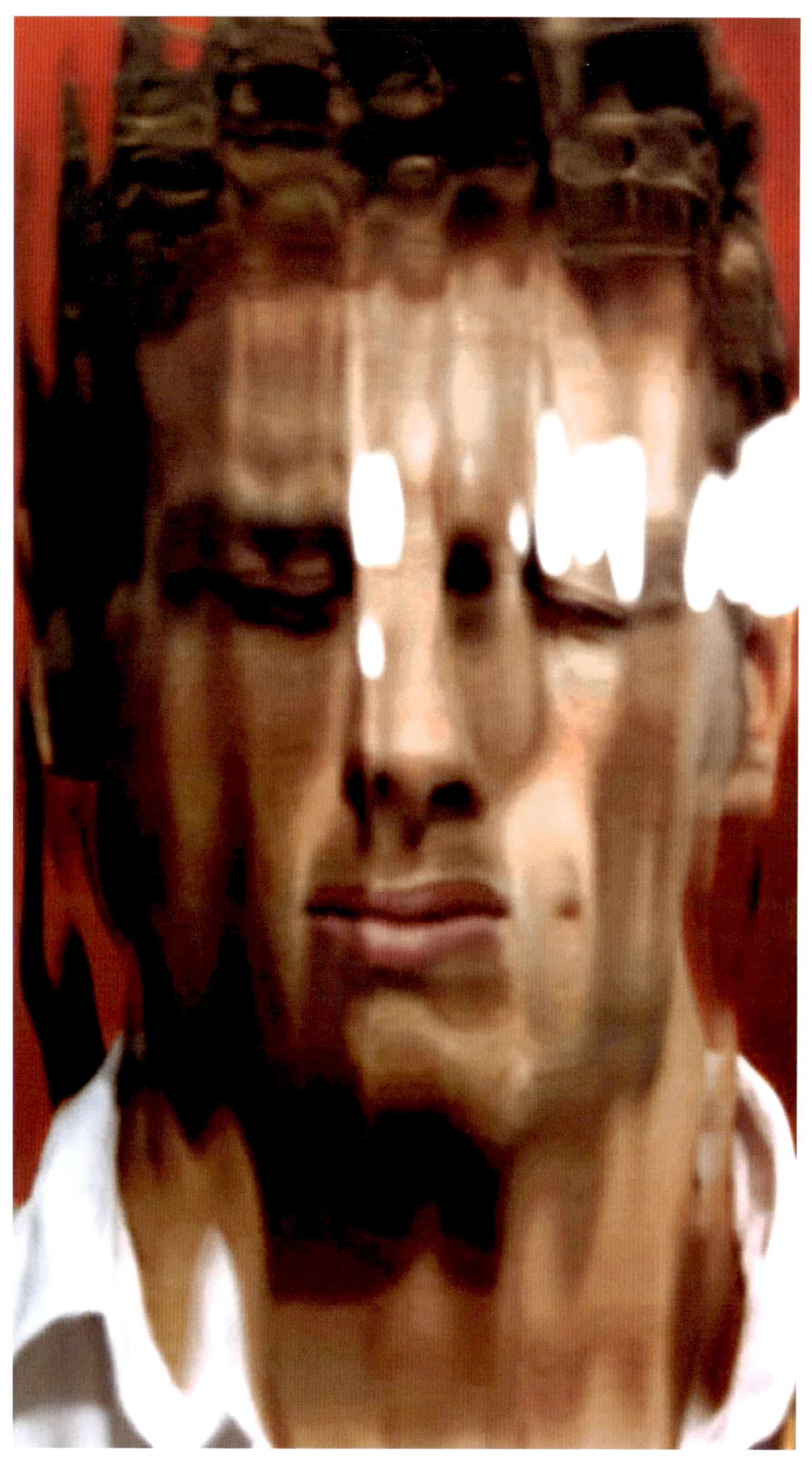

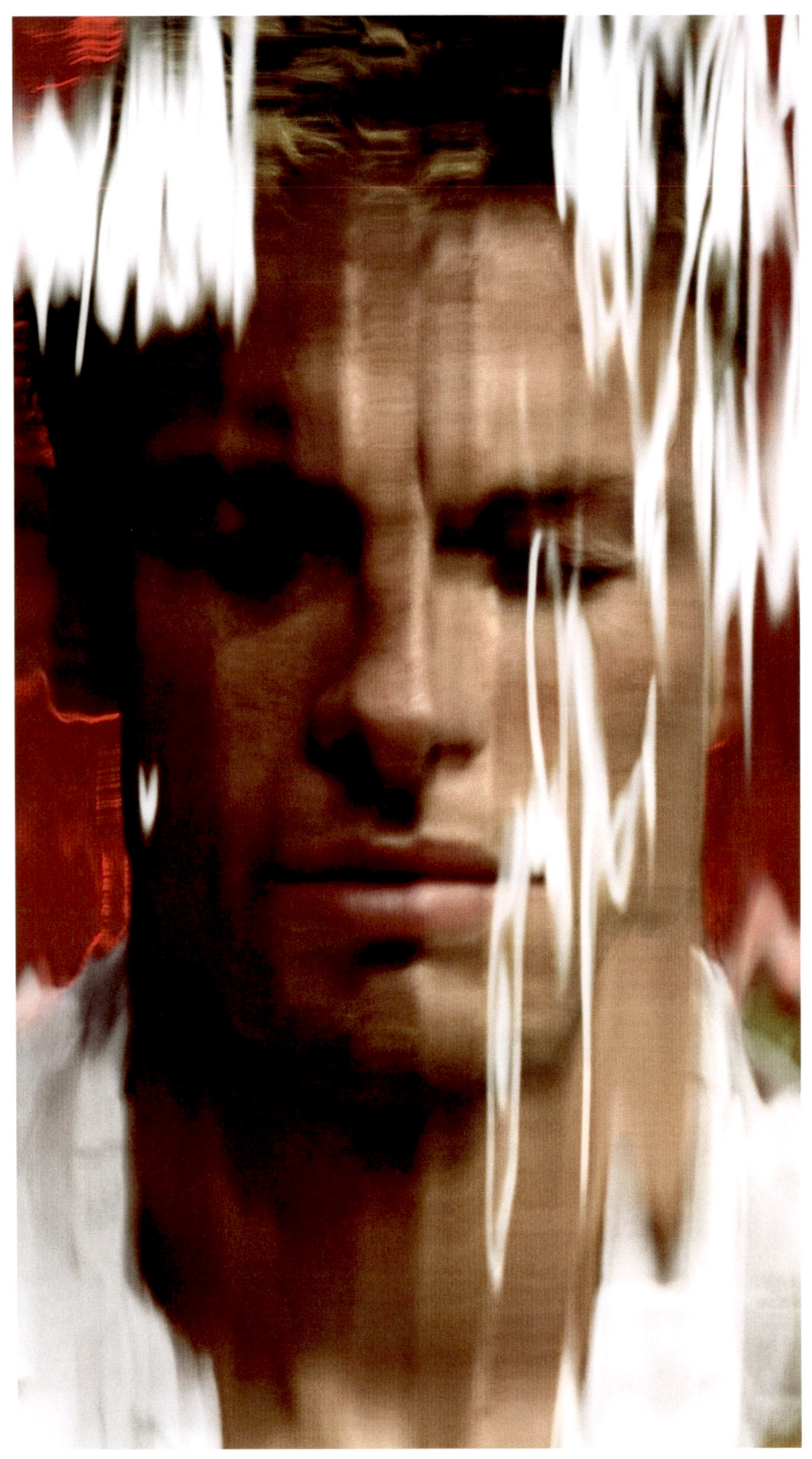

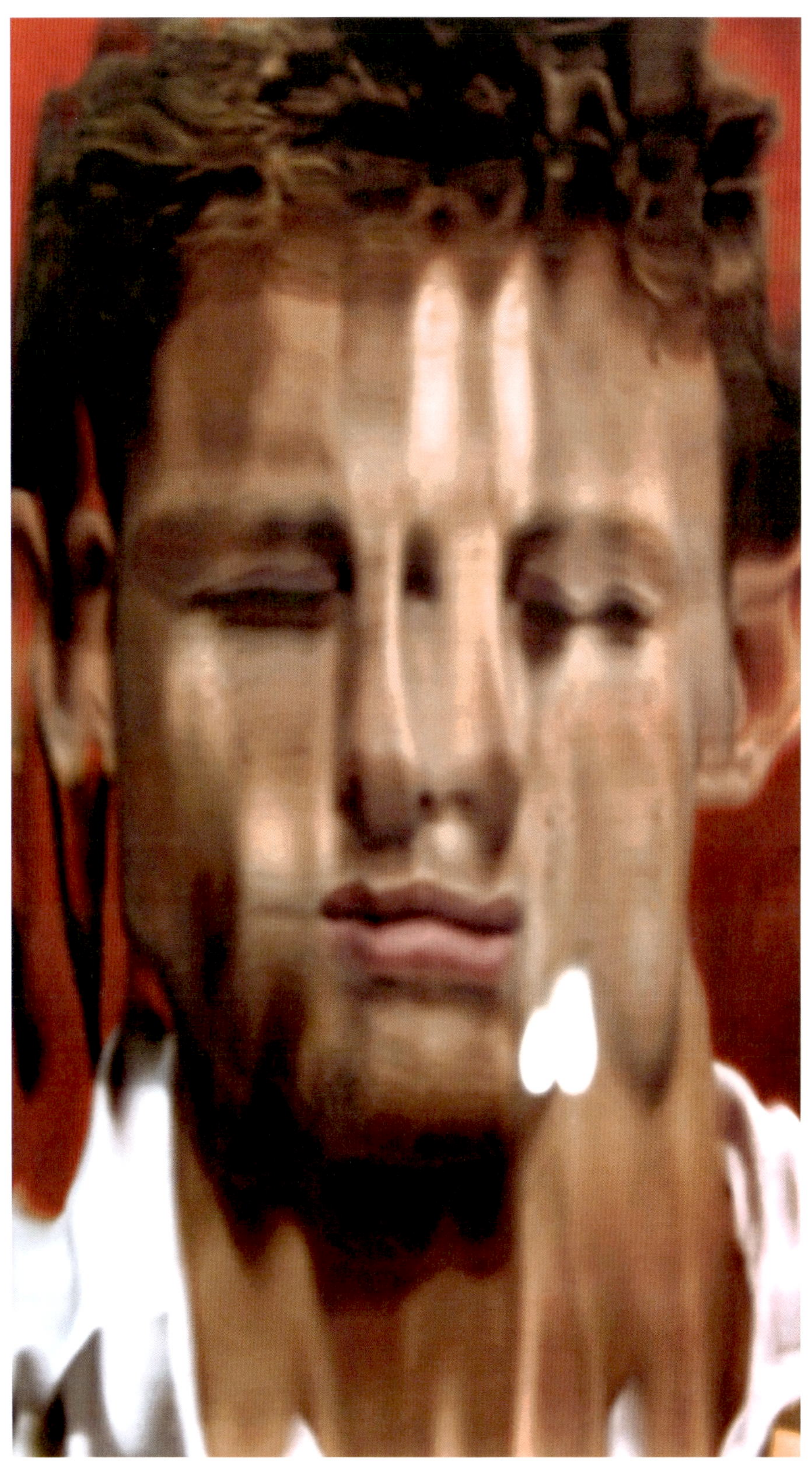

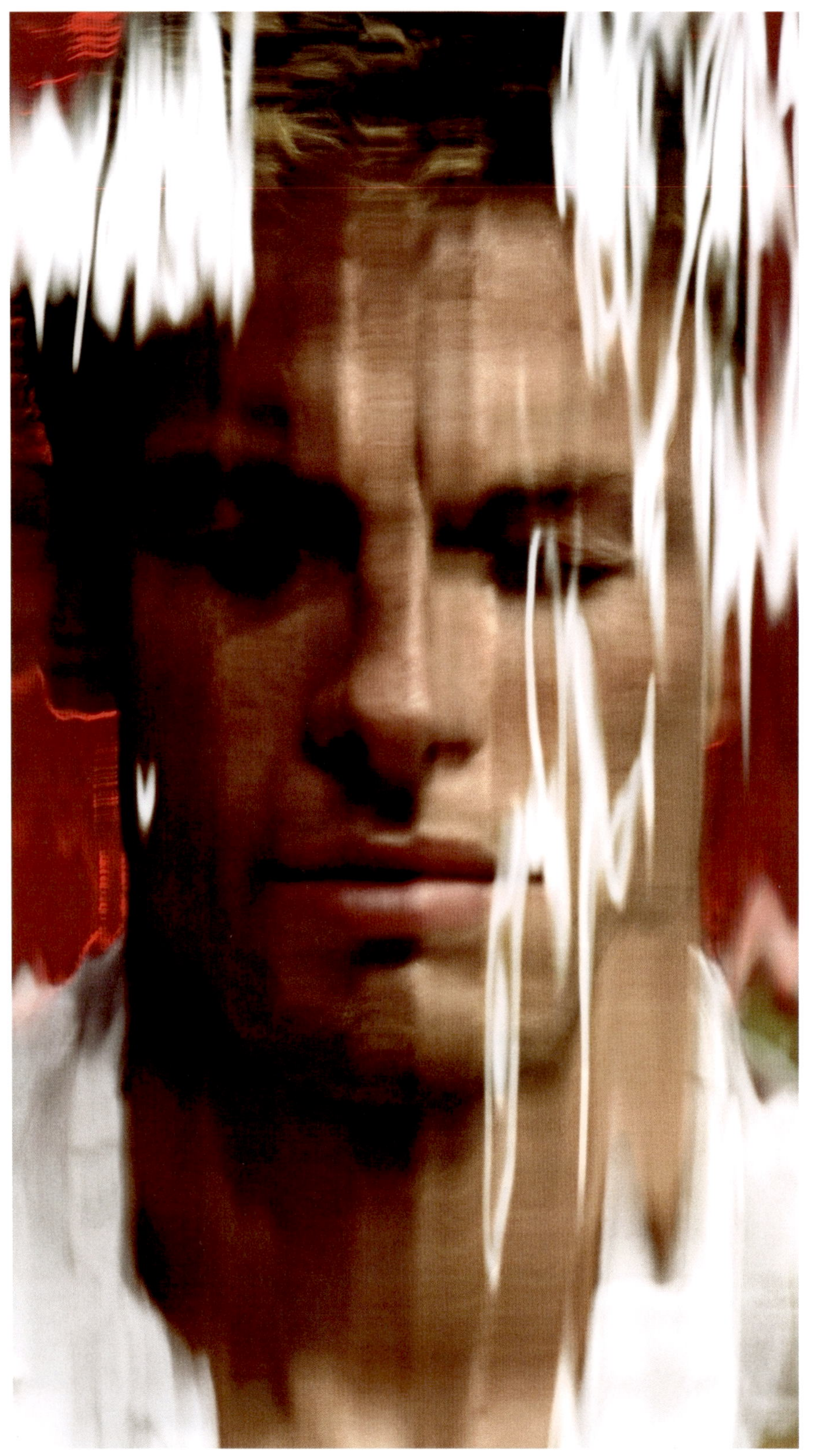

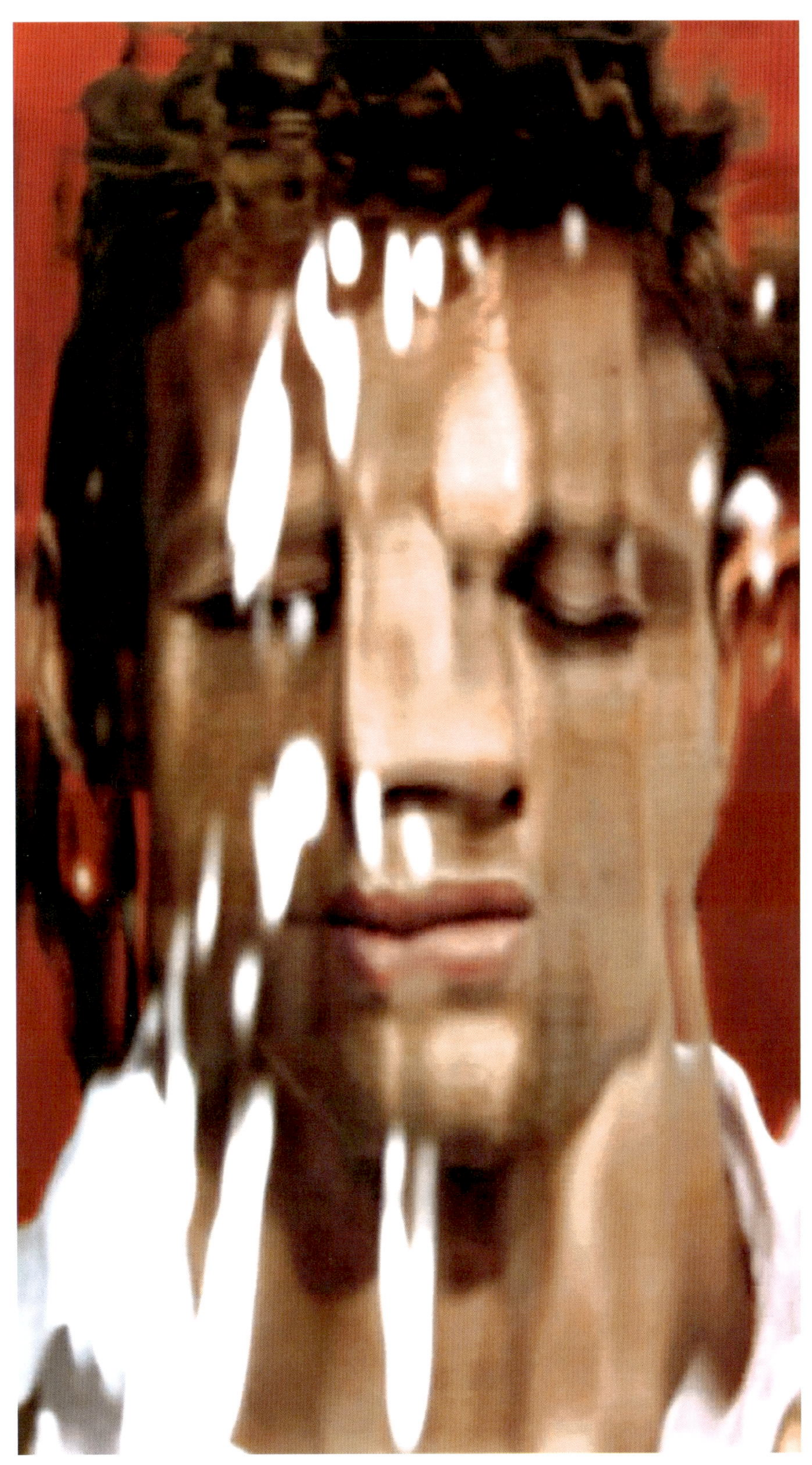

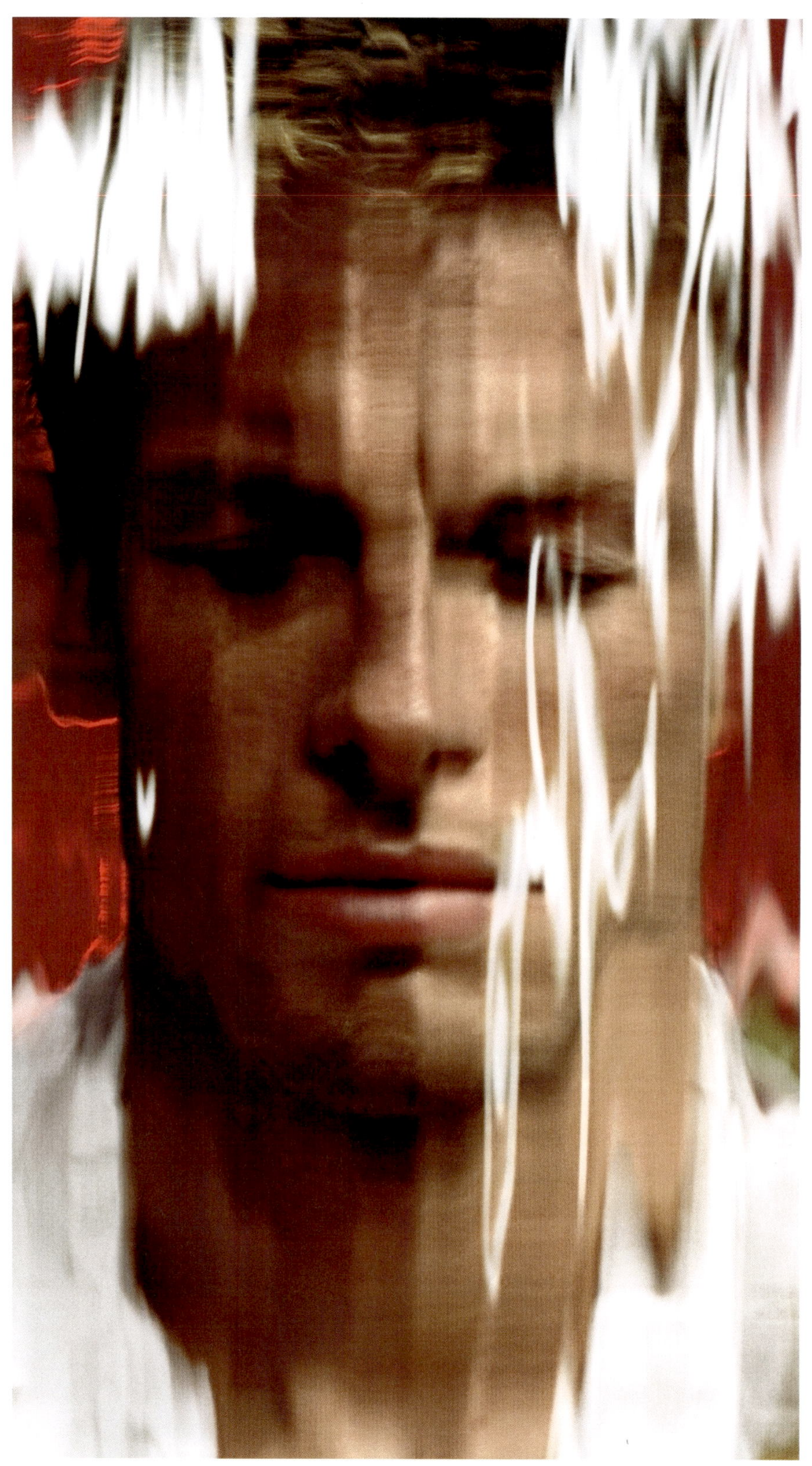

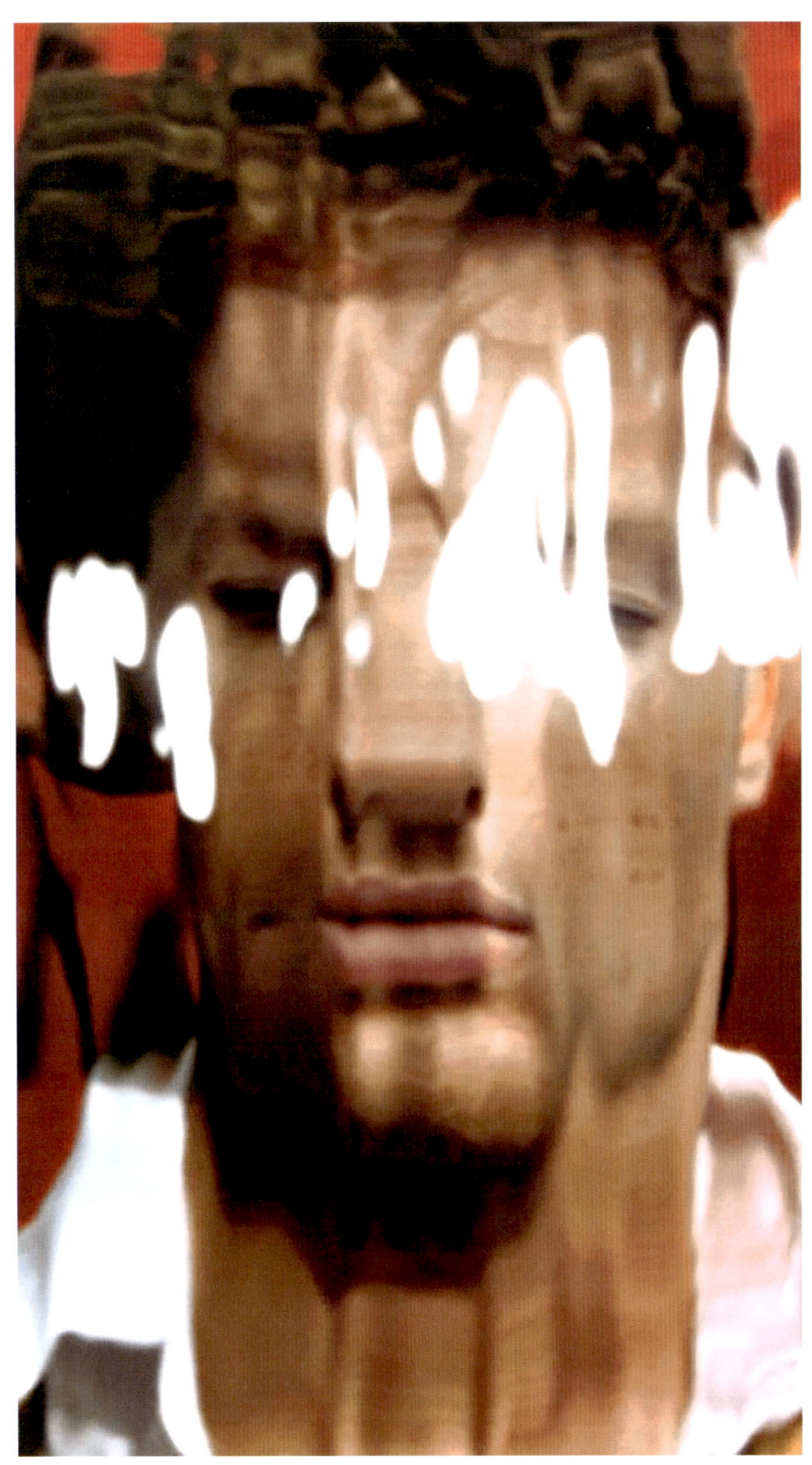

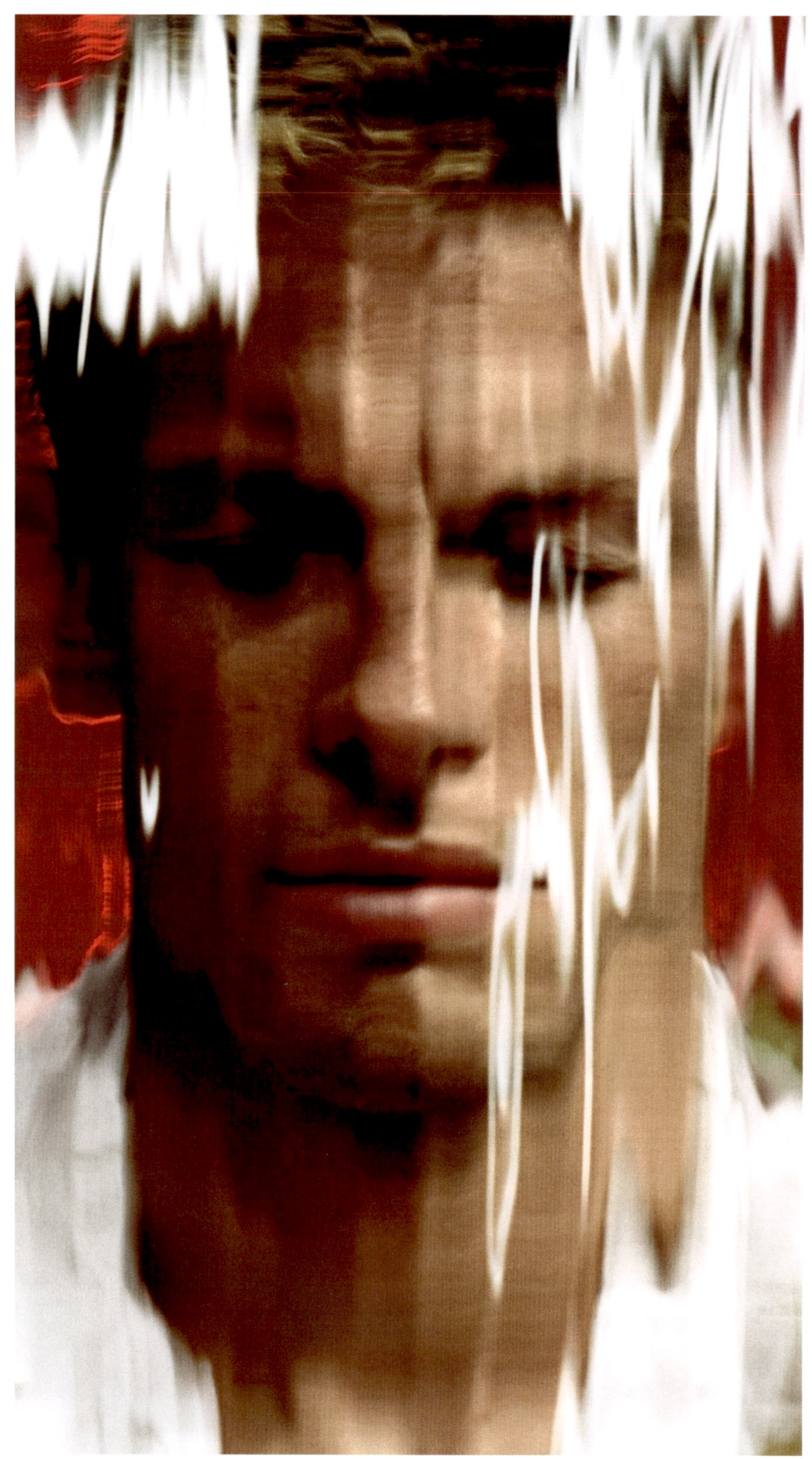

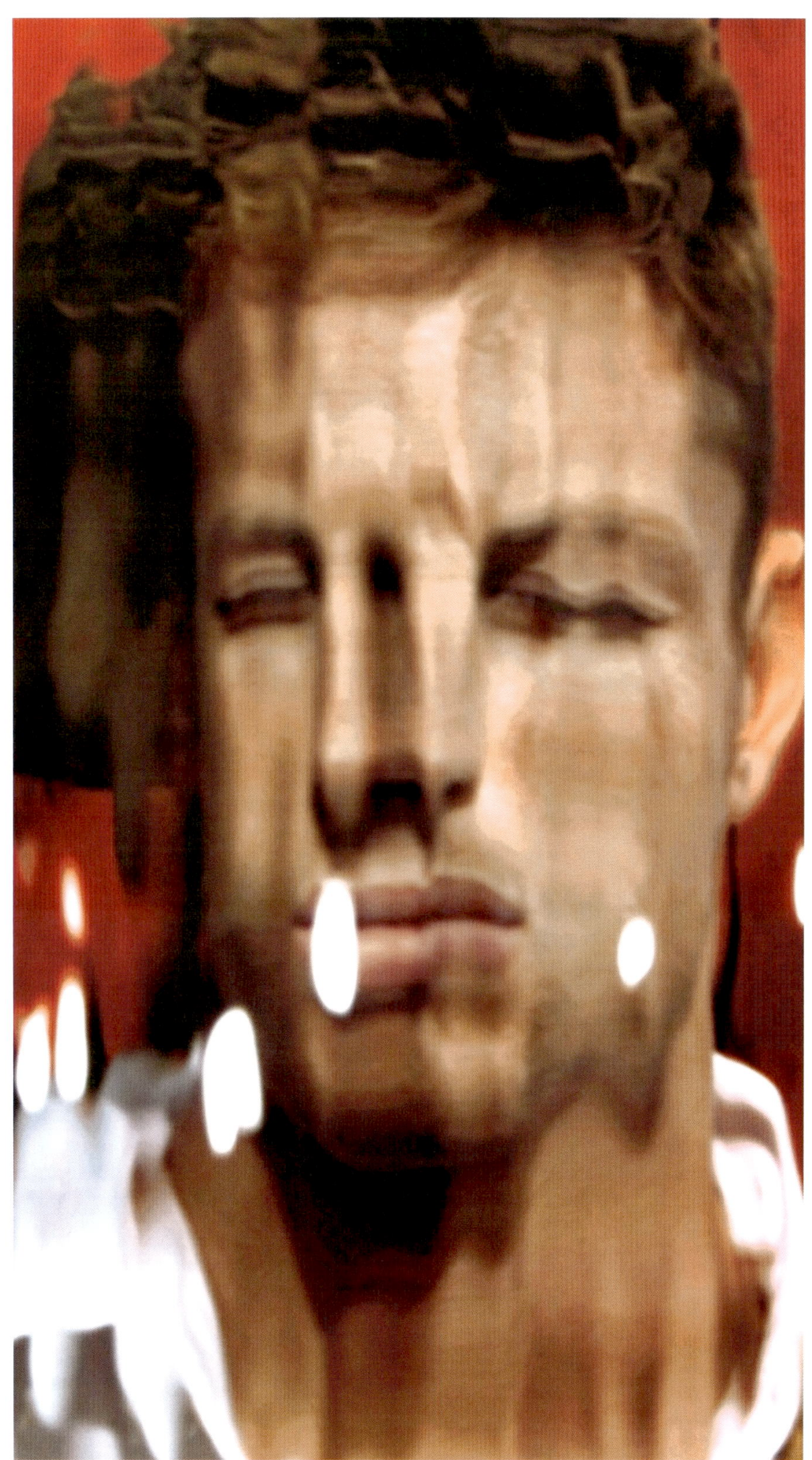

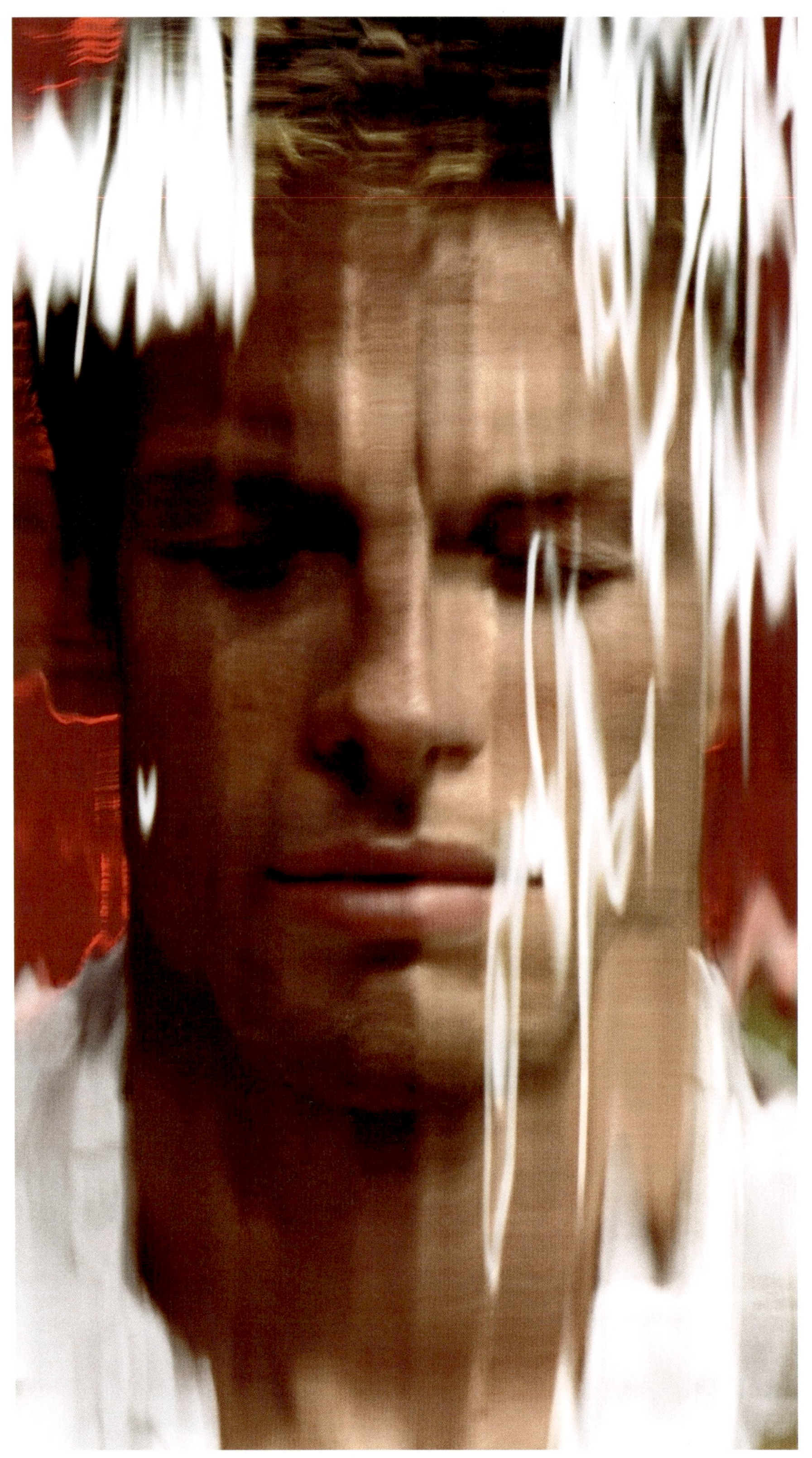

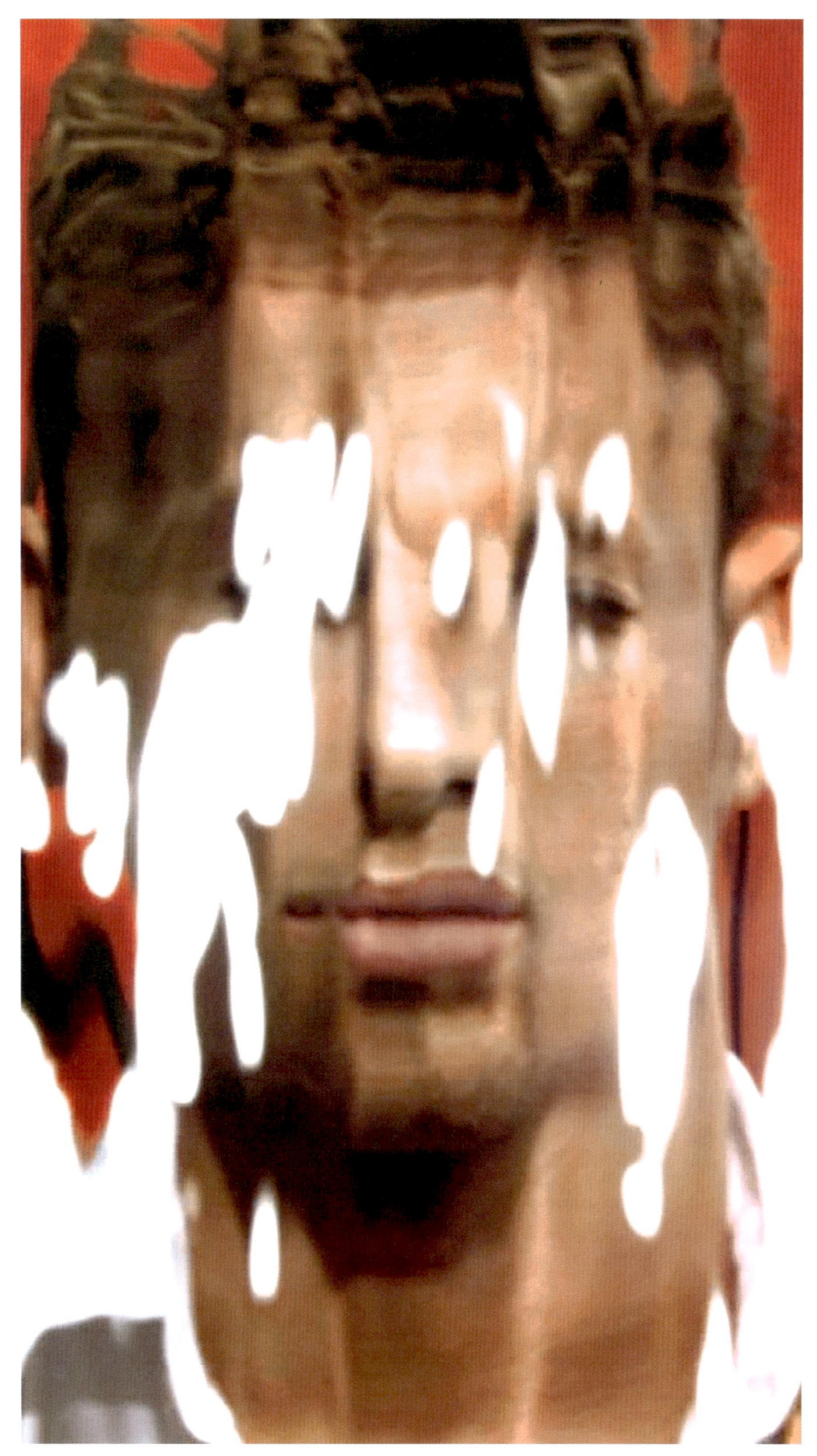

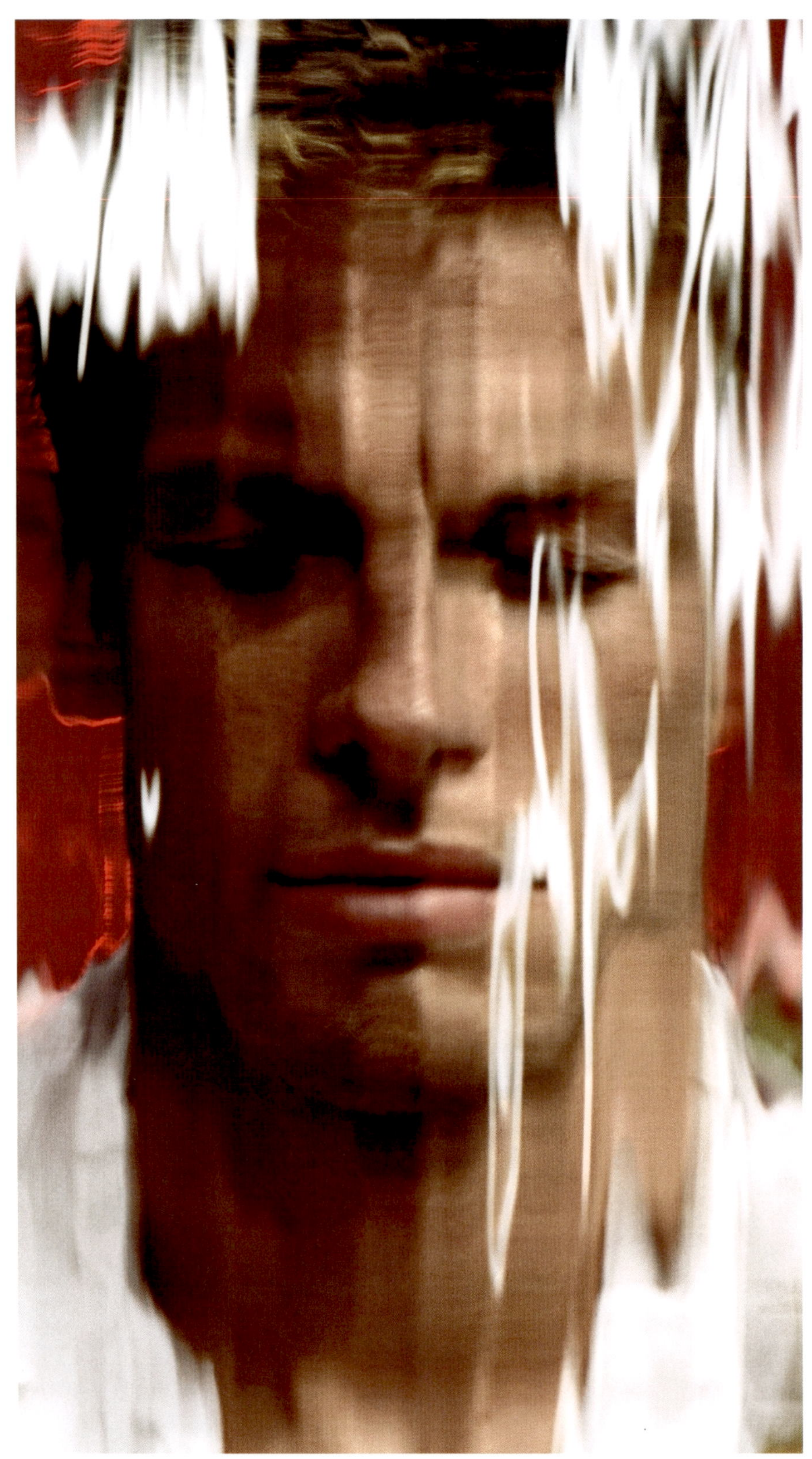

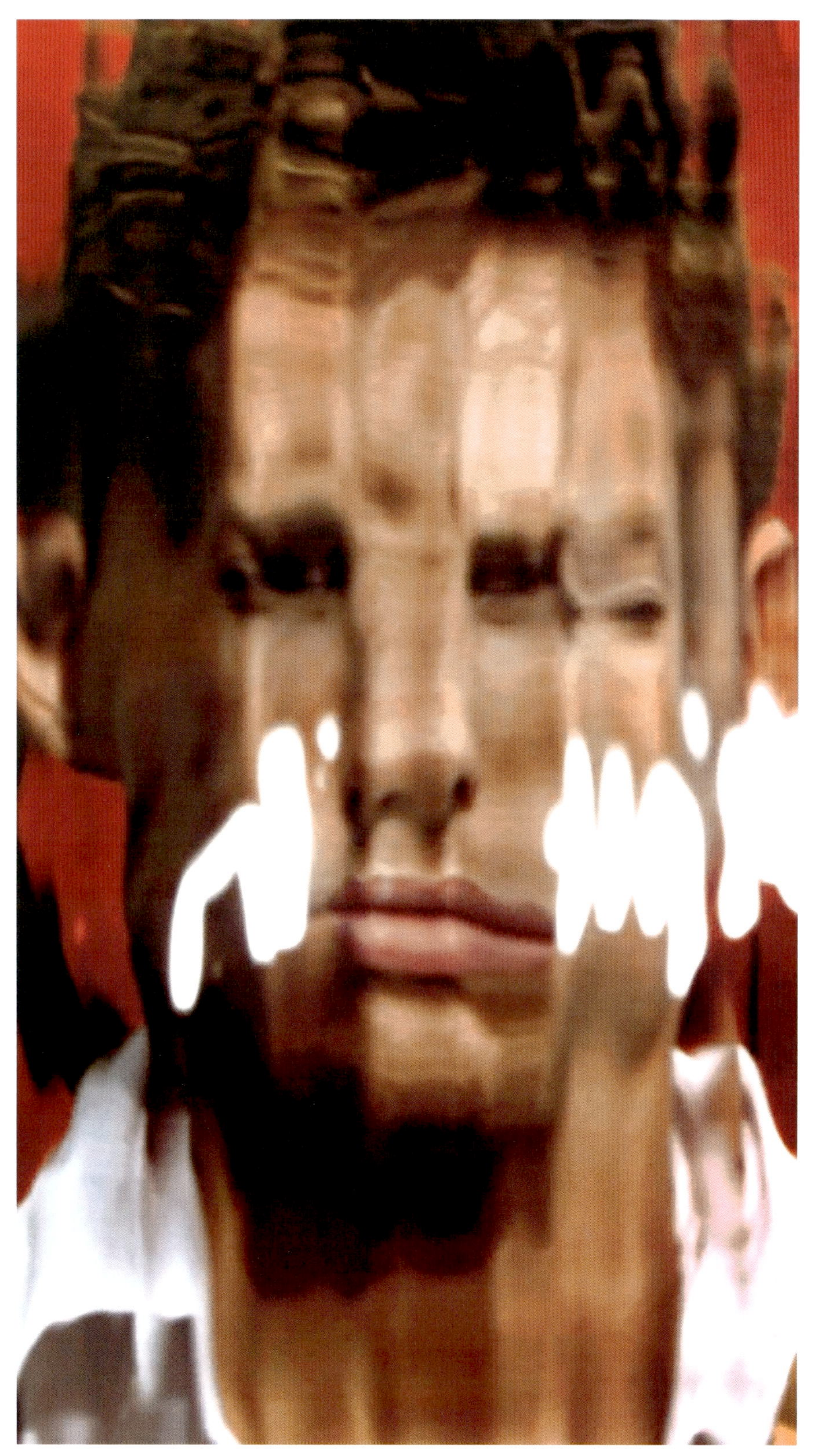

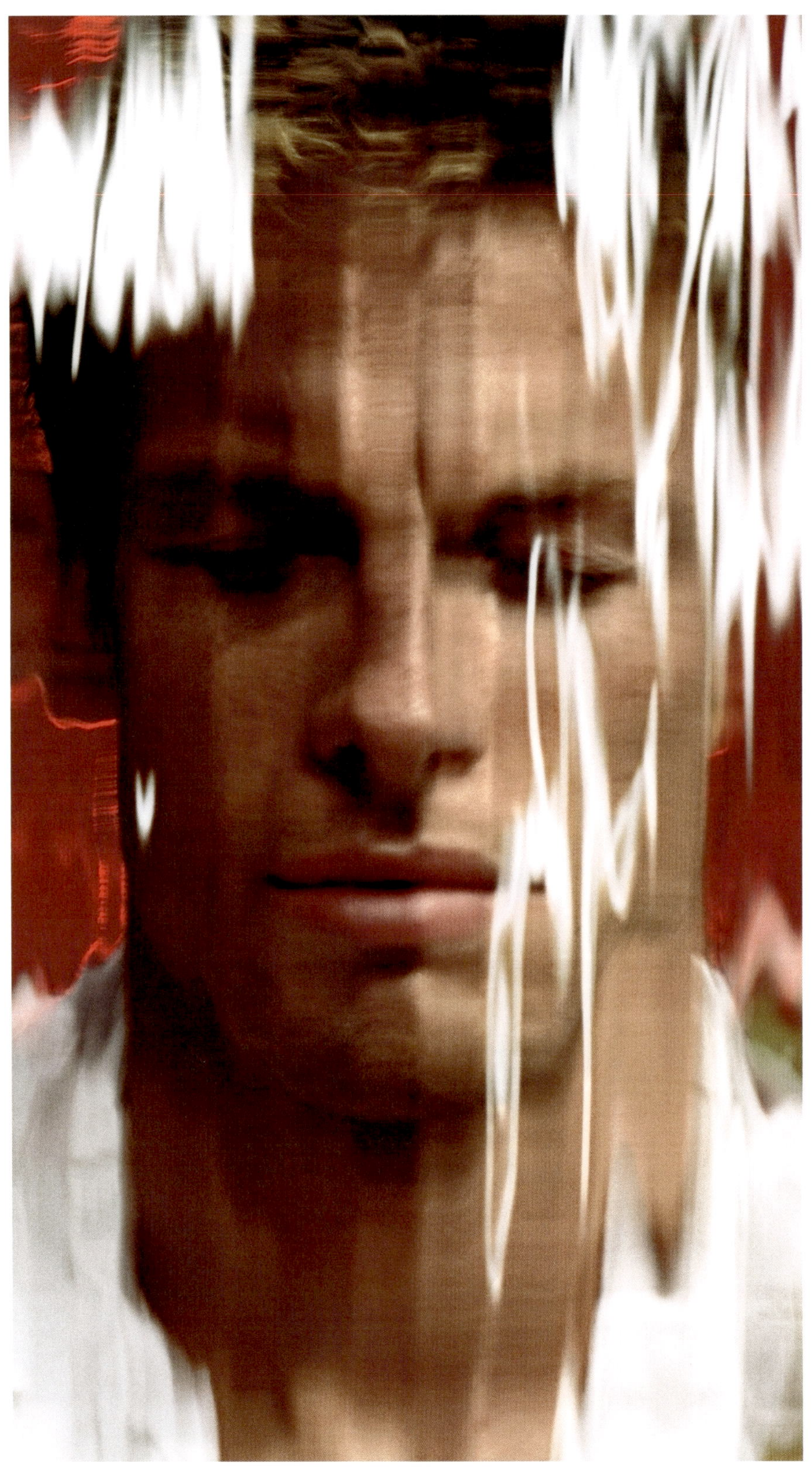

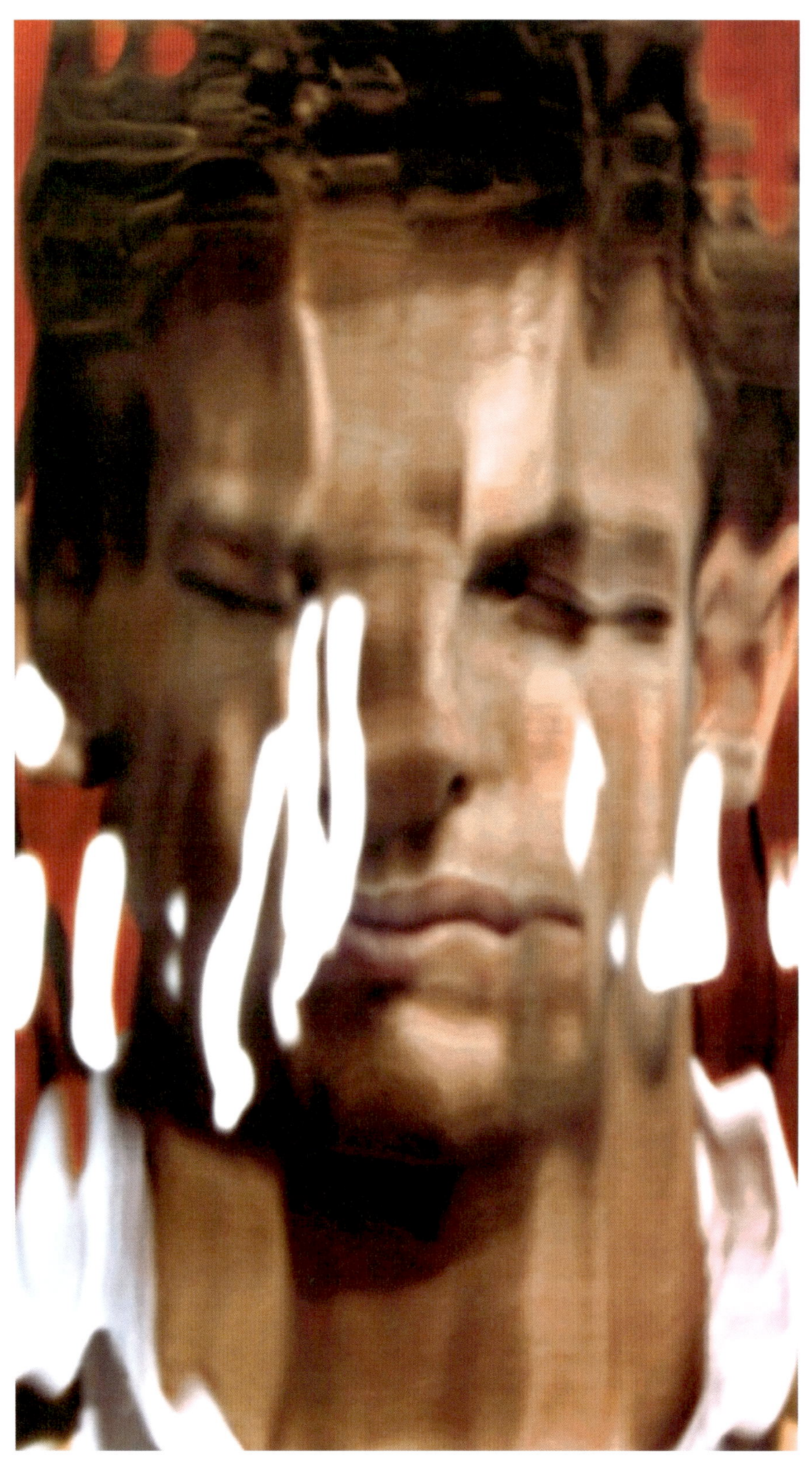

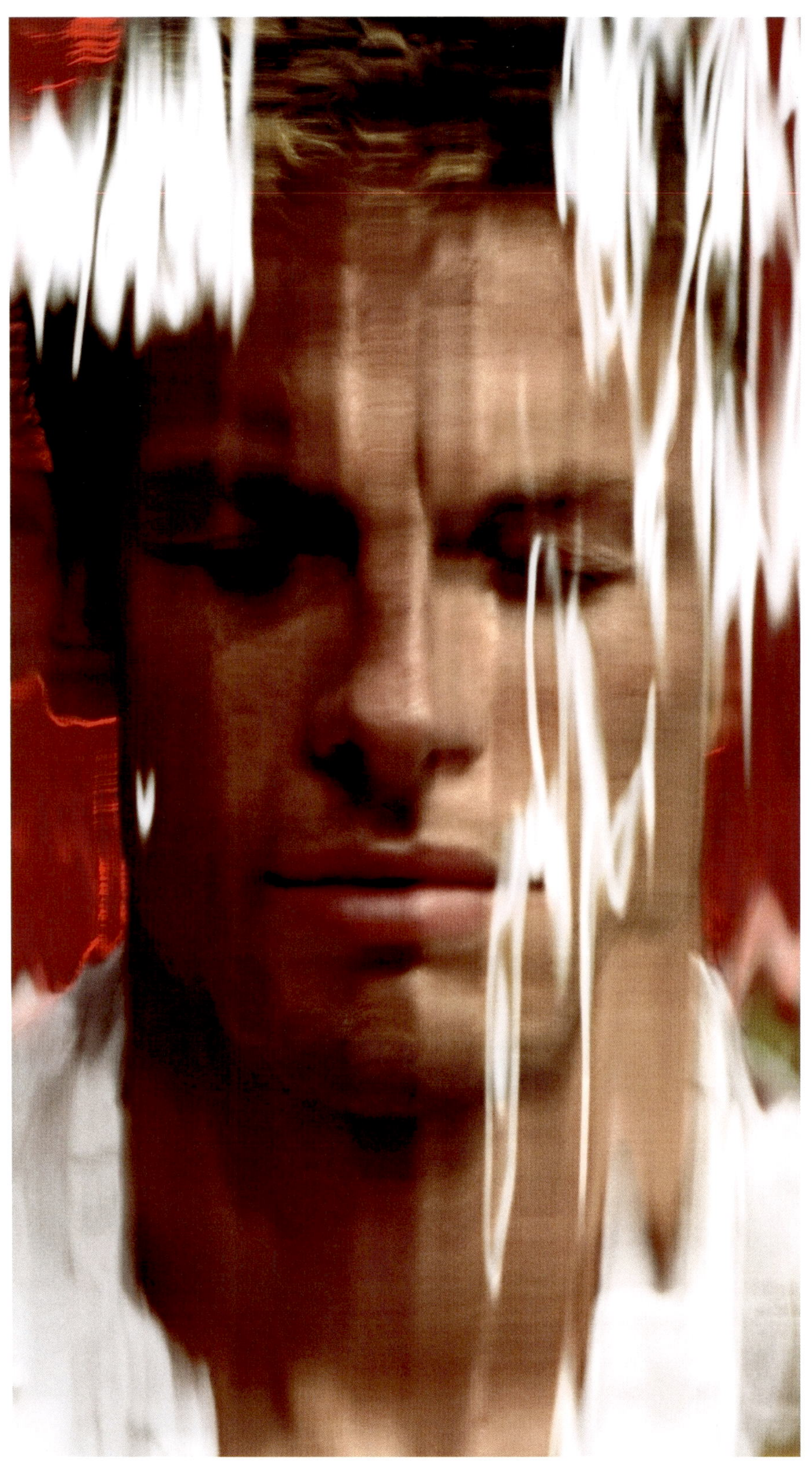

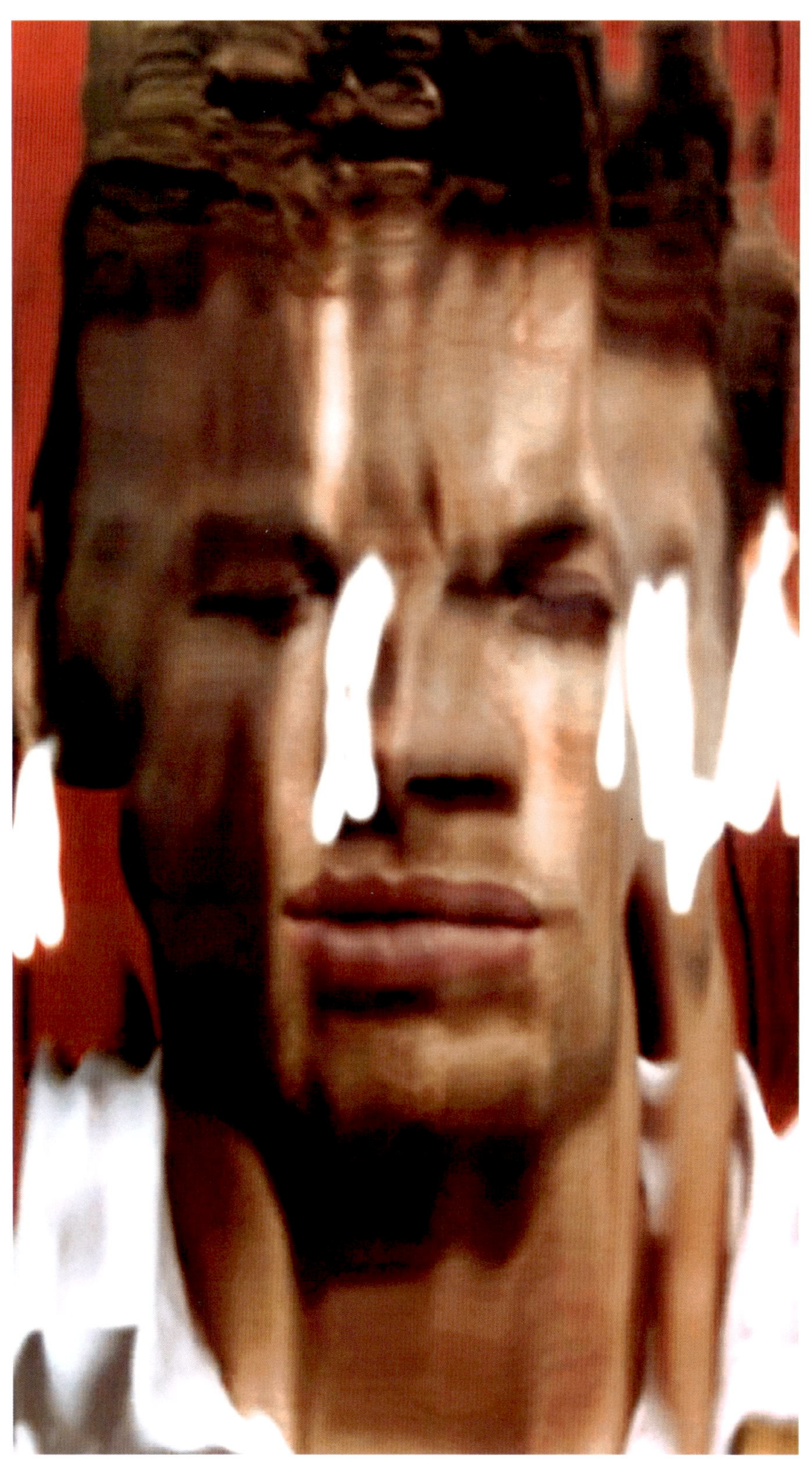

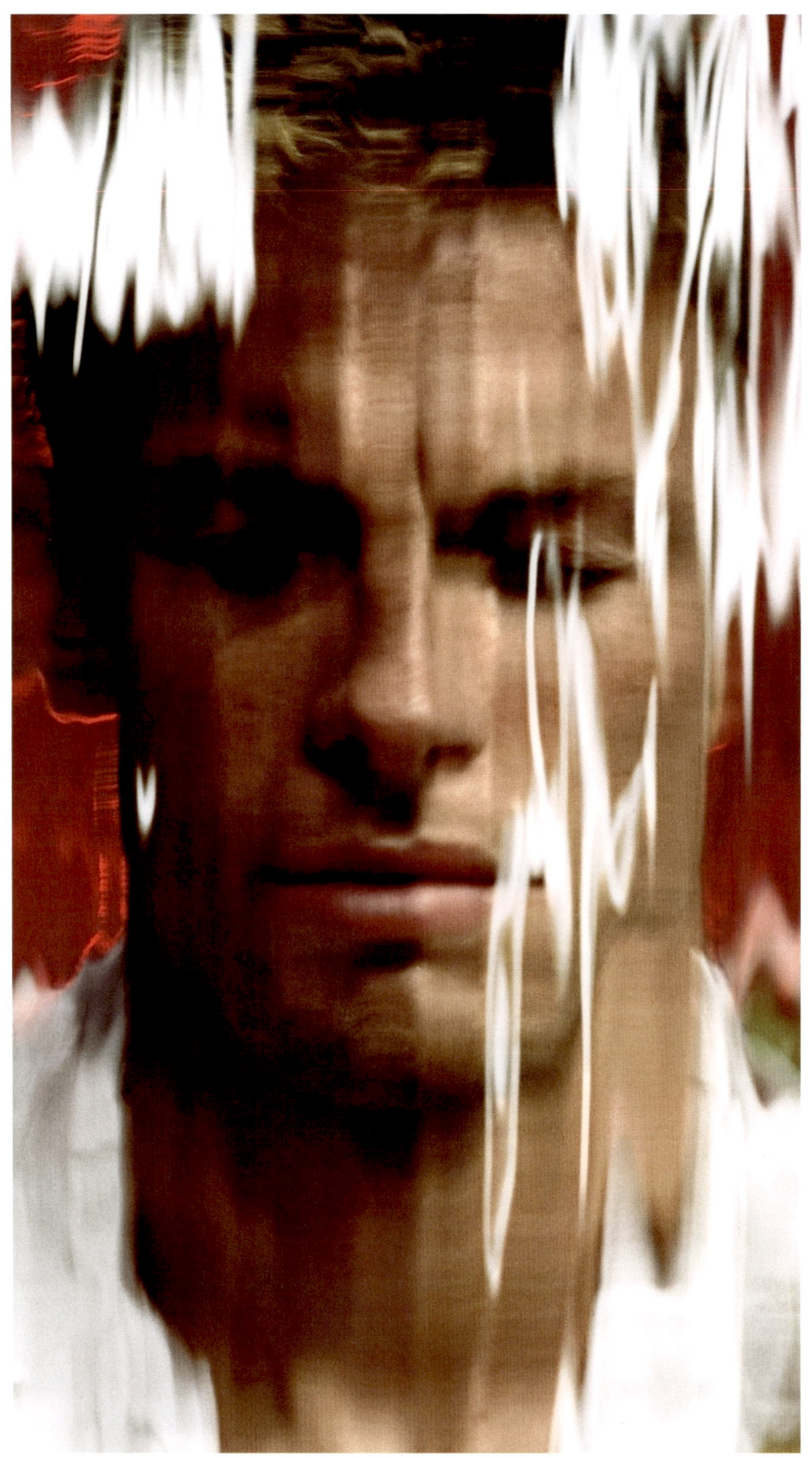

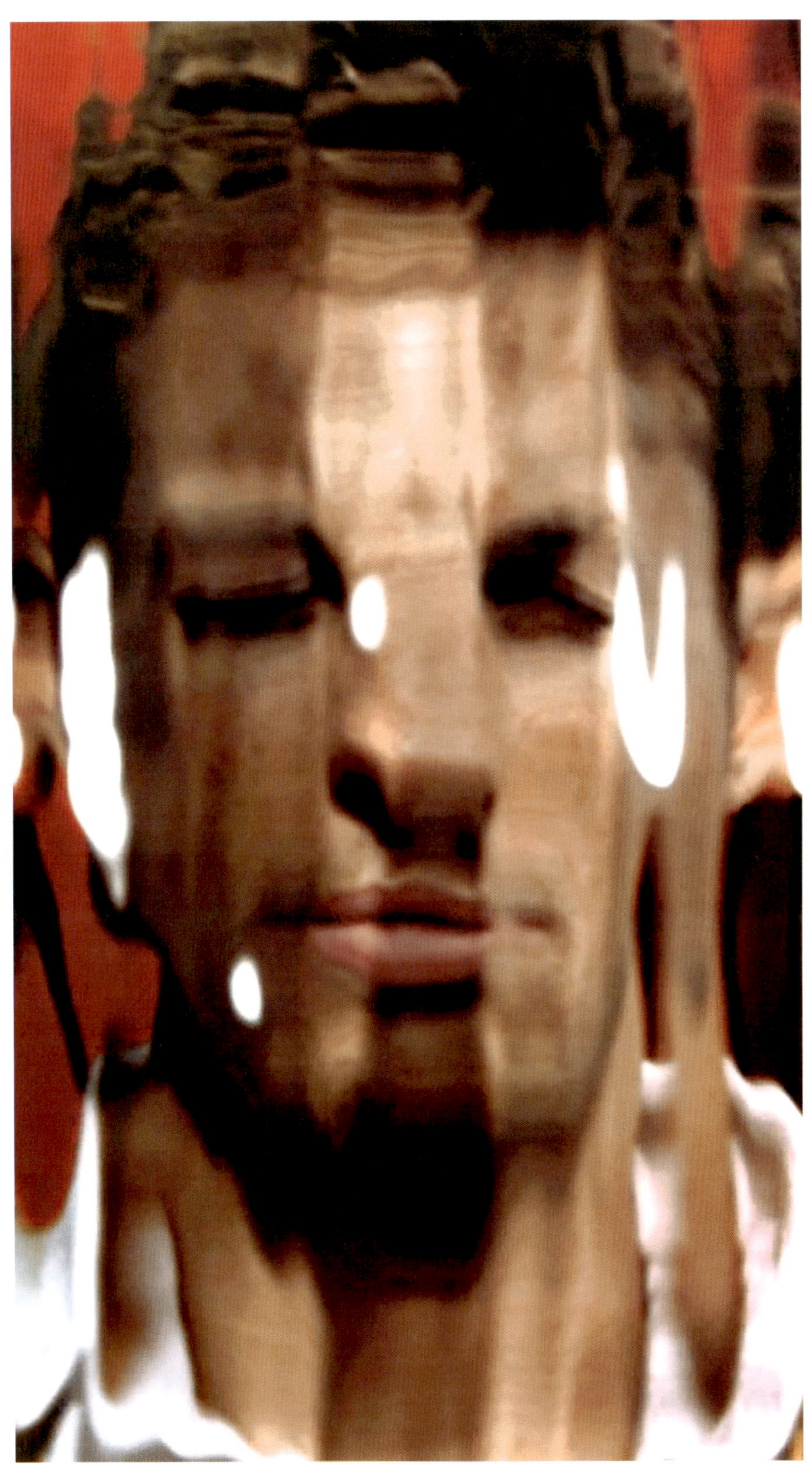

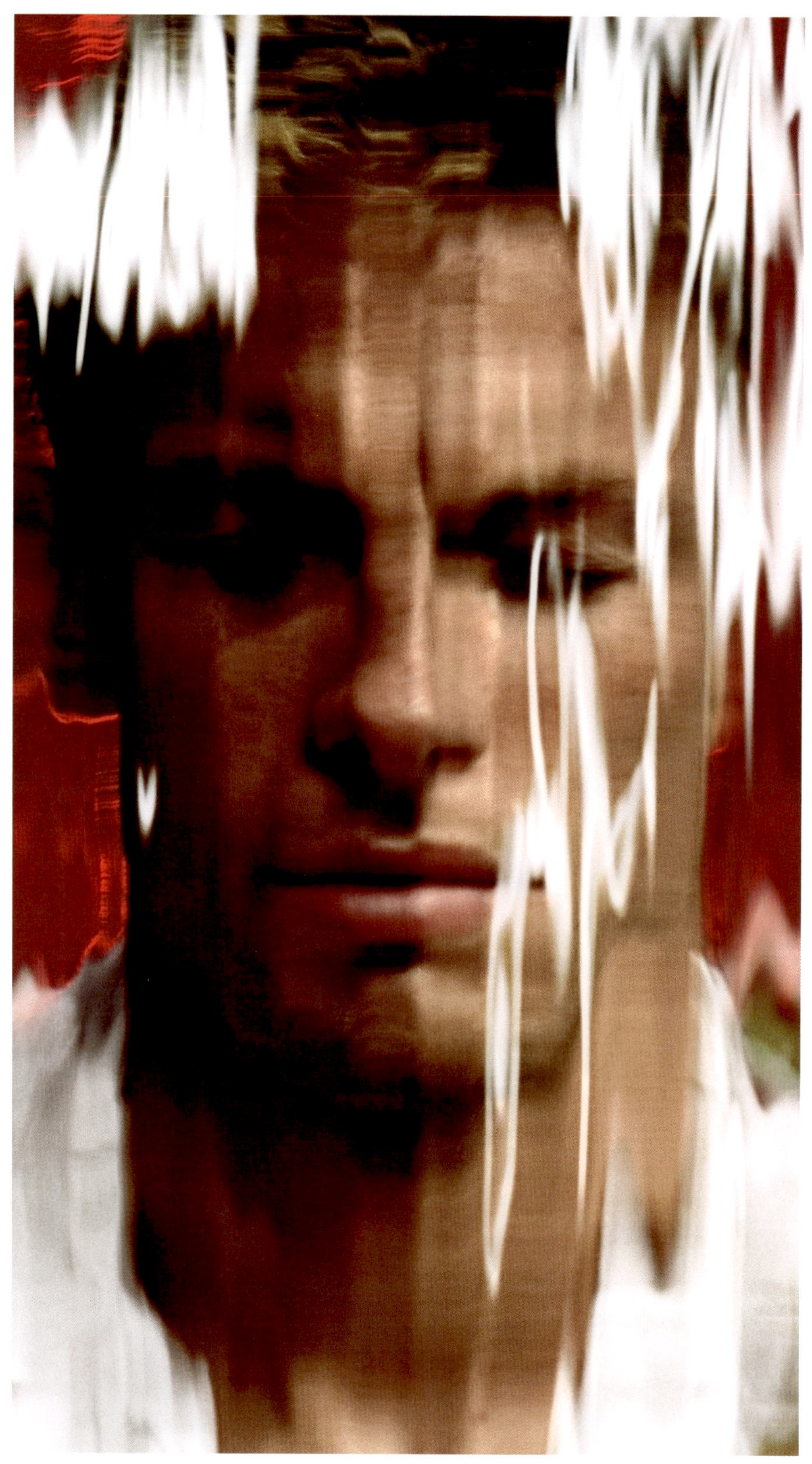

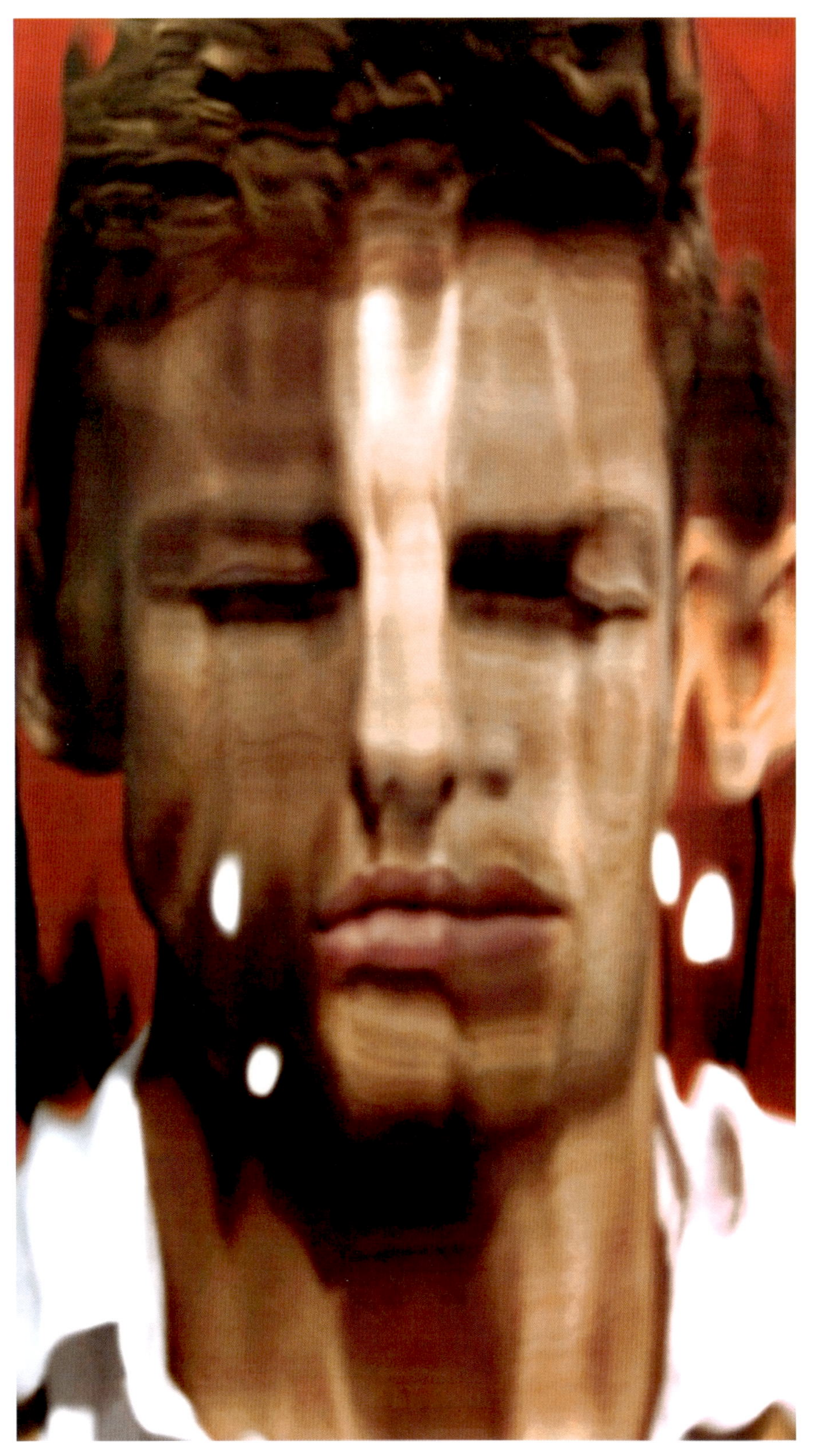

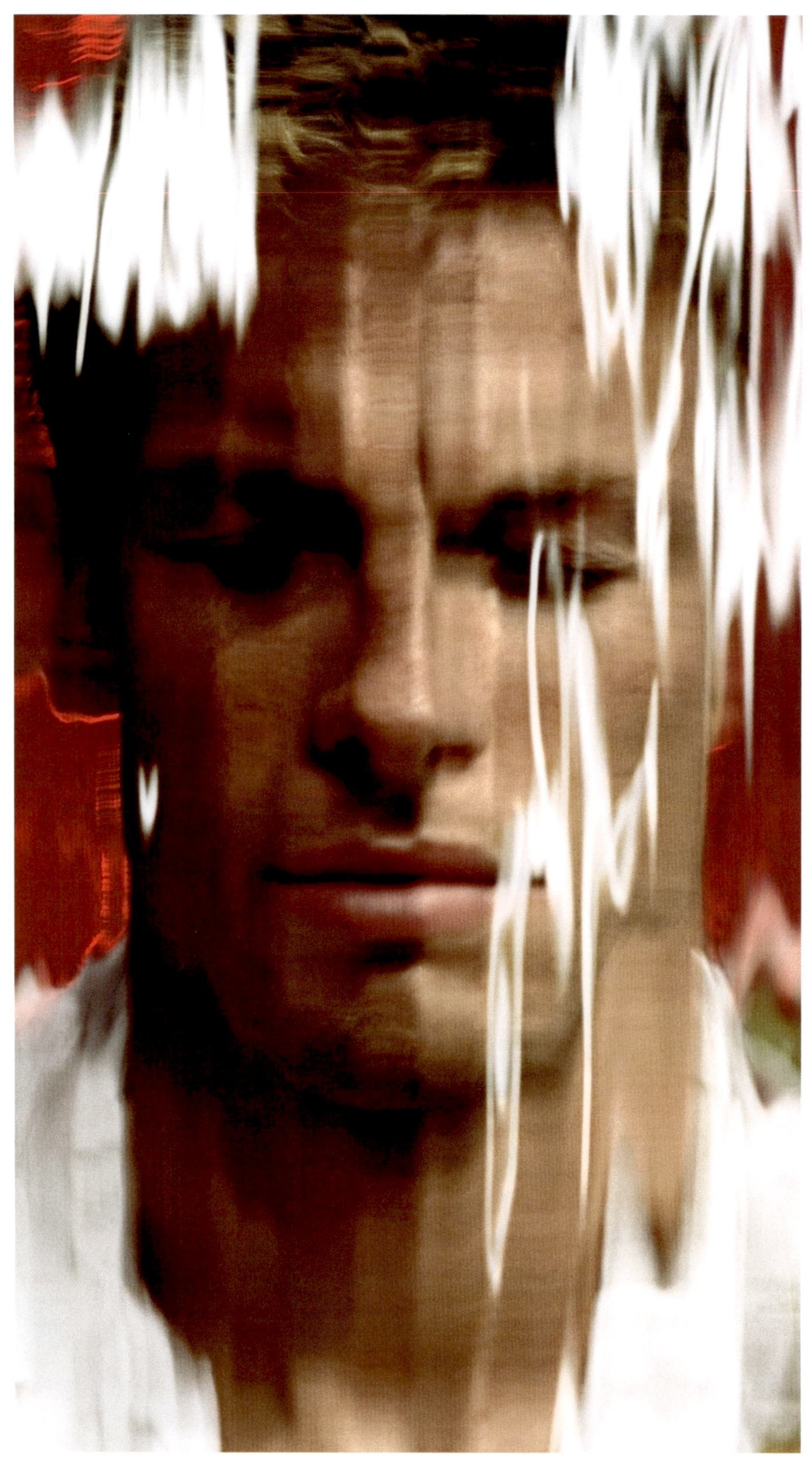

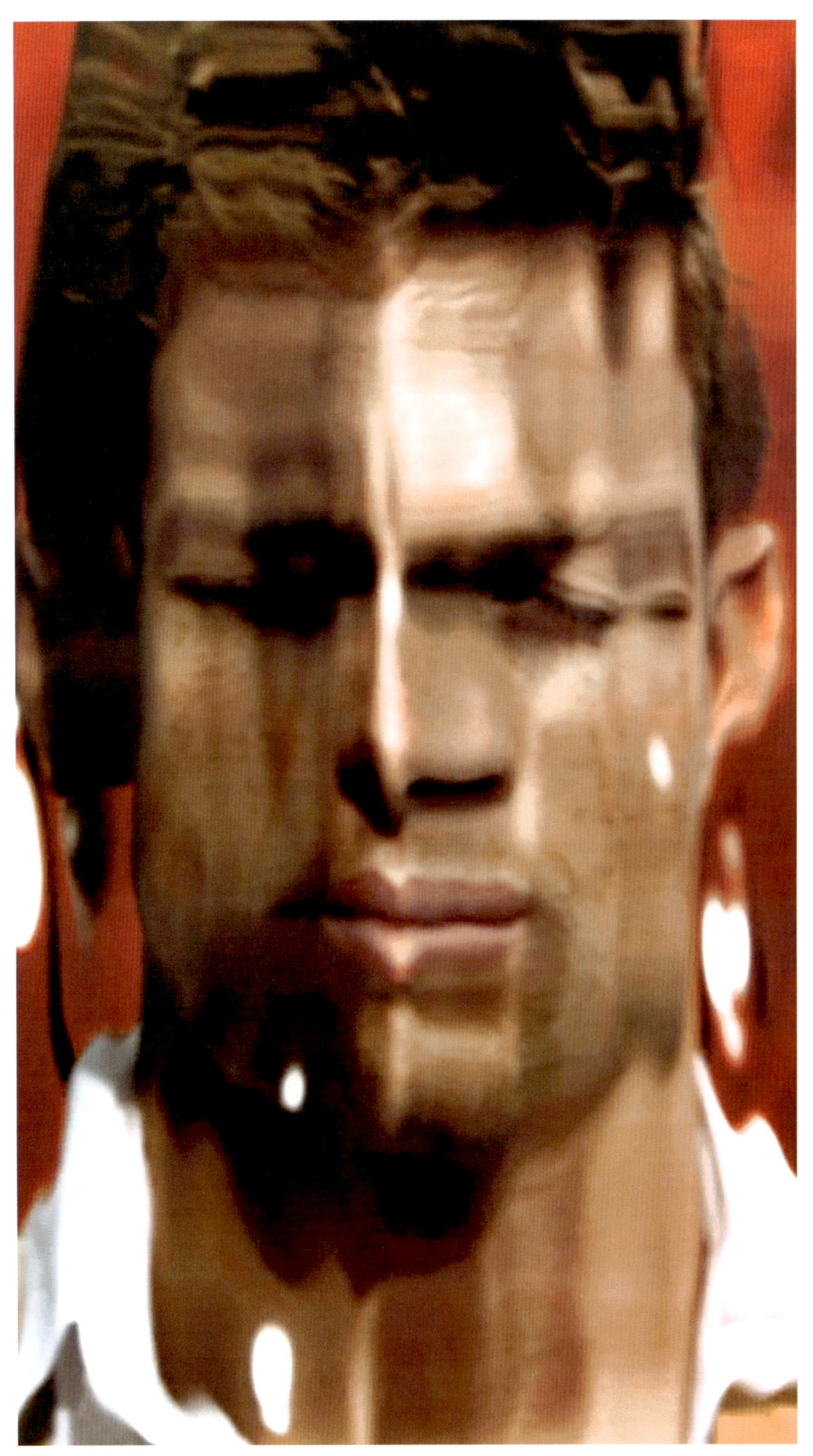

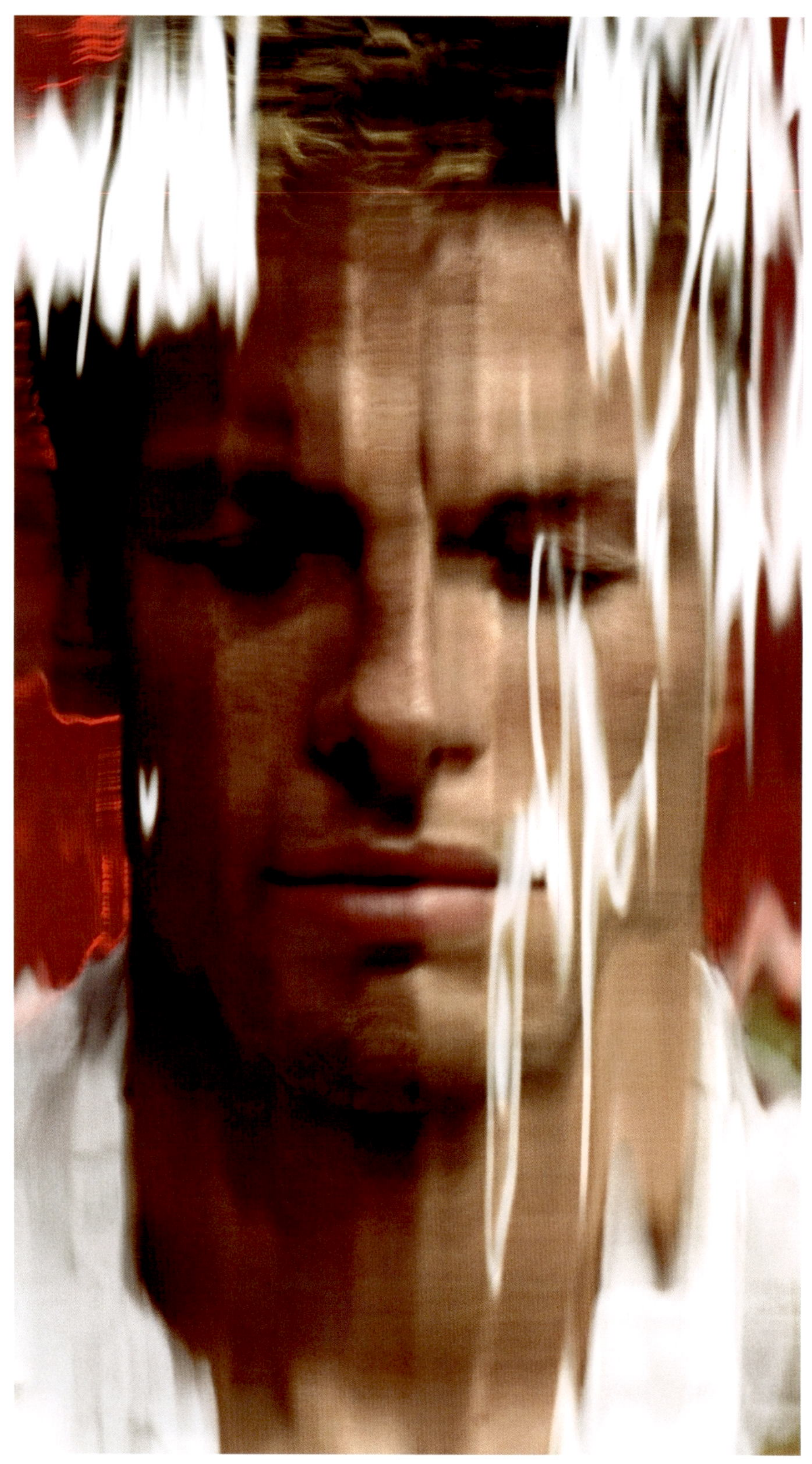

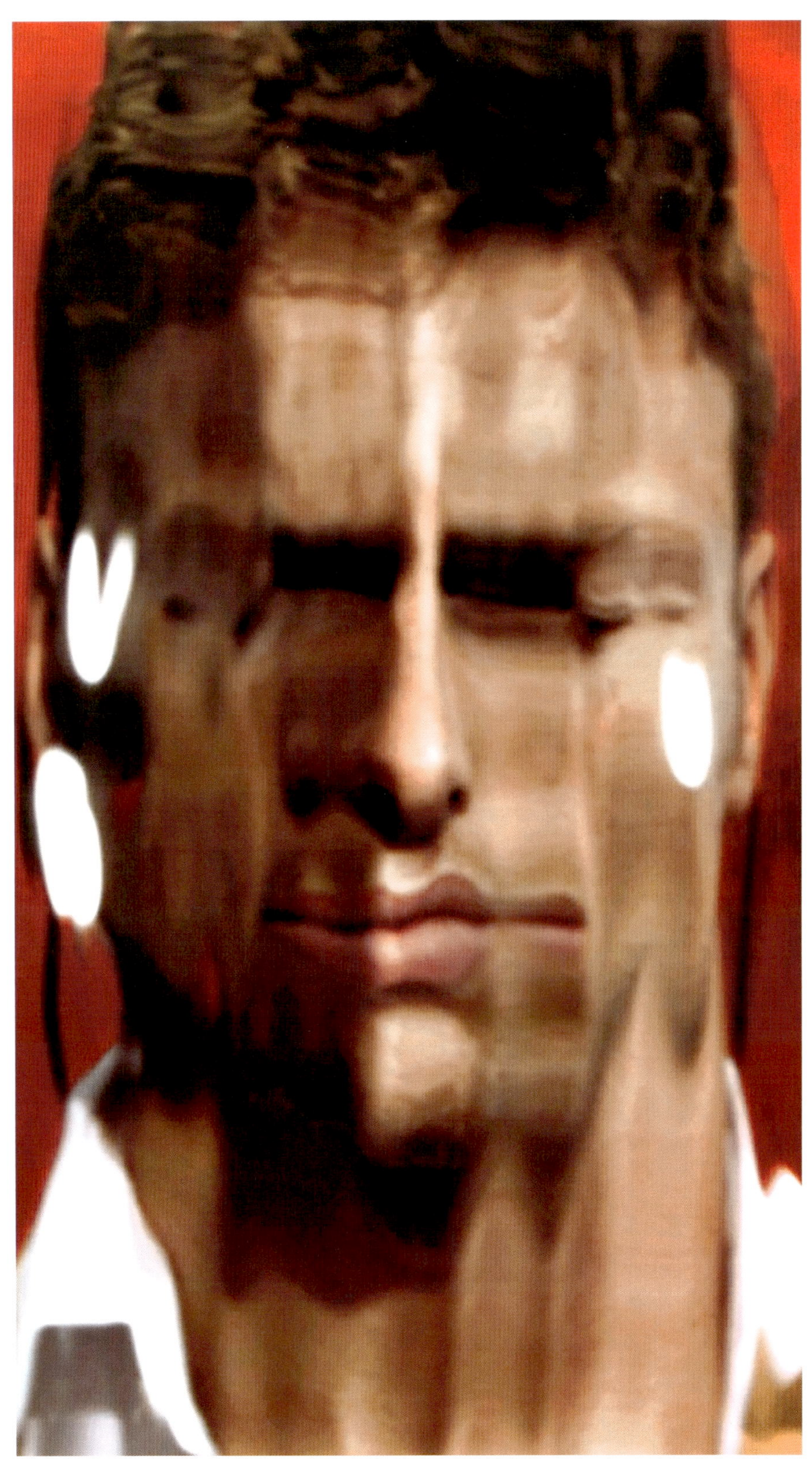

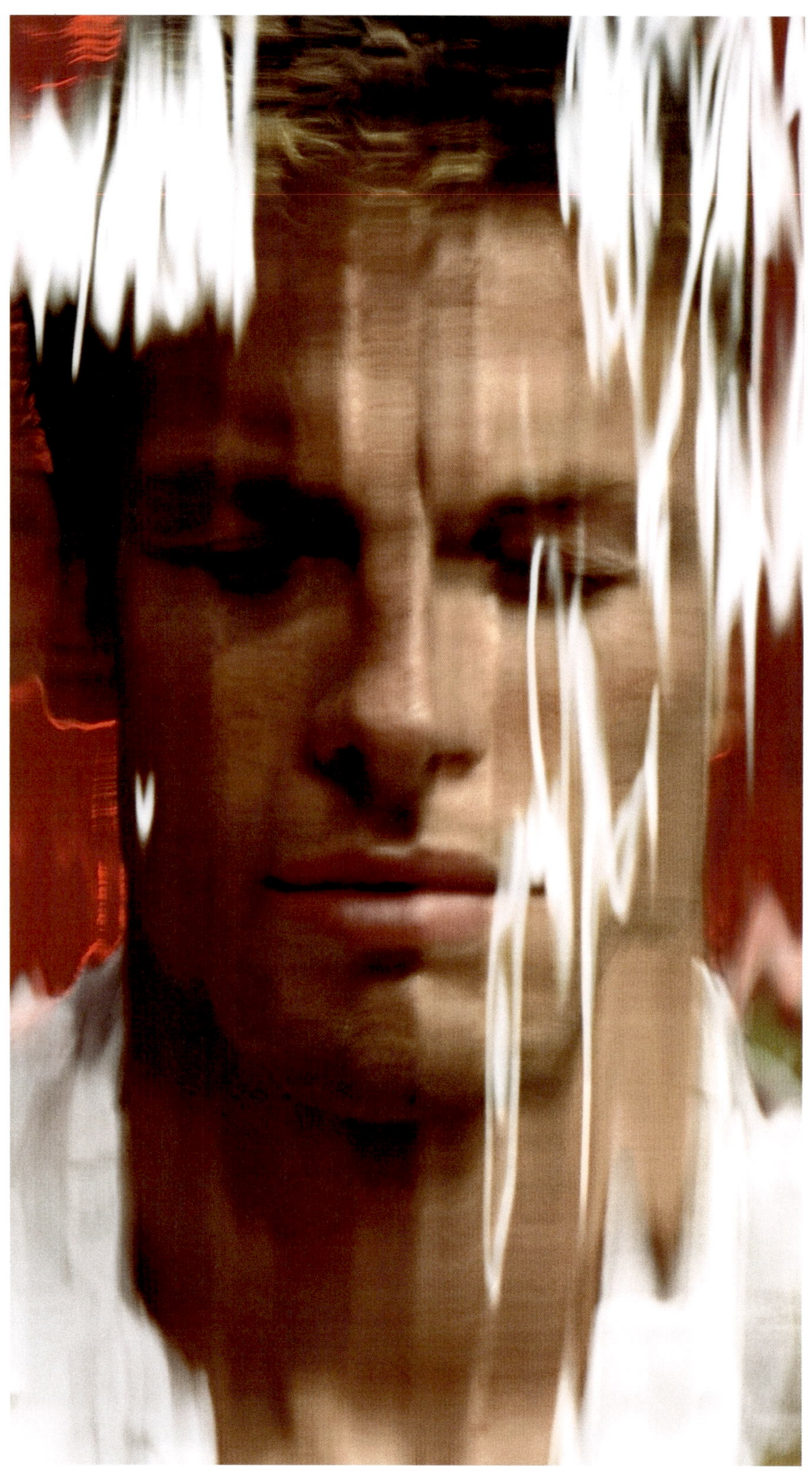

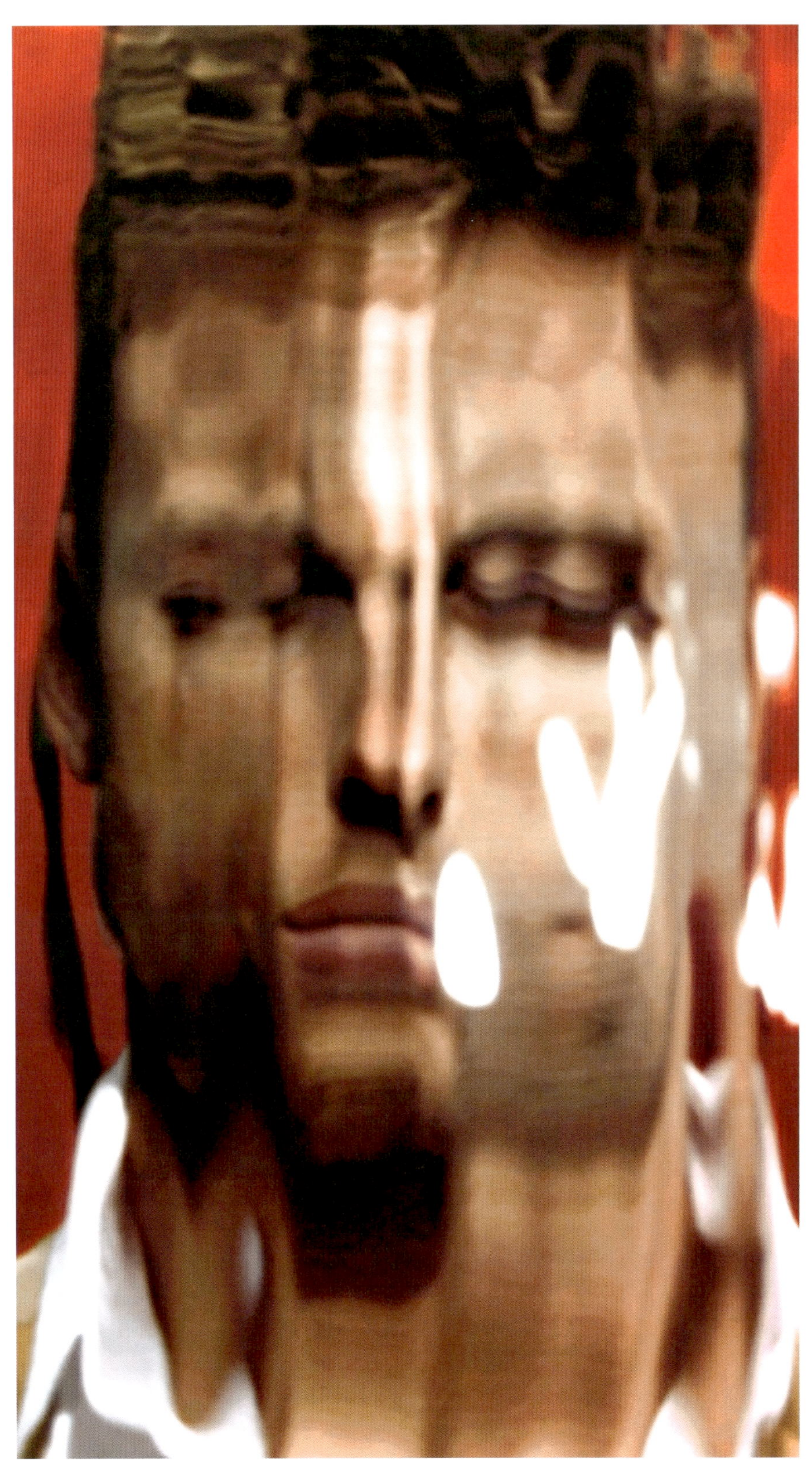

For Gods Only

The theatre relates to all the apparently special themes which pass and return …
connotation, hysteria, fiction, the imaginary, the scene, grace, the Orient,
violence, ideology …
Roland Barthes, *Roland Barthes par Roland Barthes*, 1977

For Barthes the stage and theatrical spectacles constitute a creative category that has
the capacity to contain within it the vast majority of all the transitory and poetic phenomena
found in a particular culture. The series *For Gods Only* reflects a similar view and
contemplates transience and transcendence in the context of a street opera performed
by a Chinese troupe in Singapore.

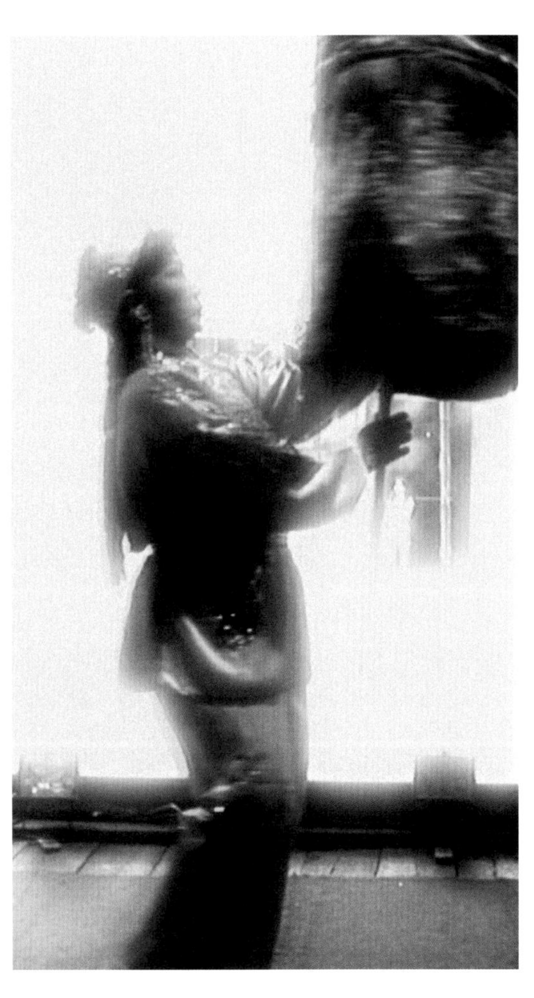
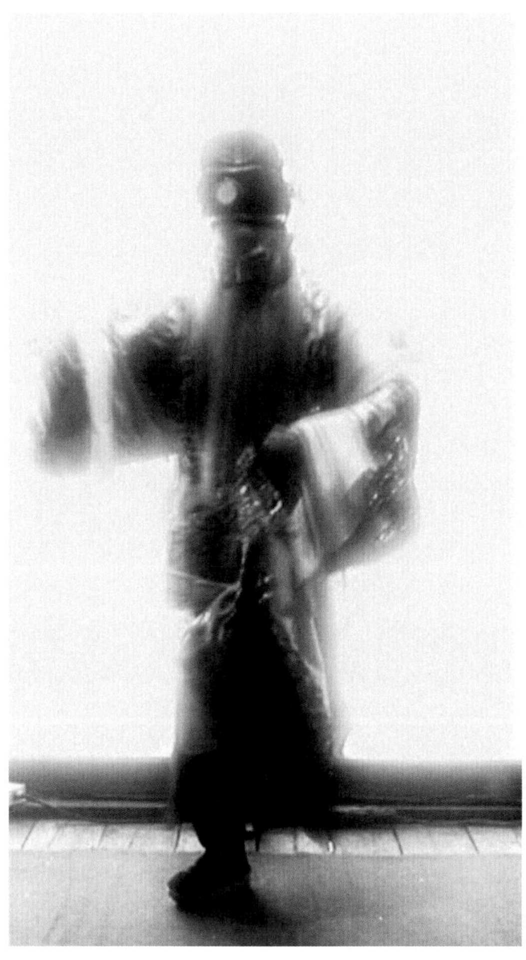
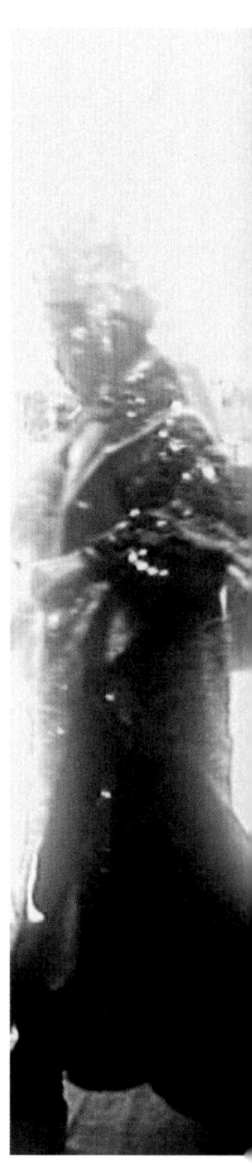

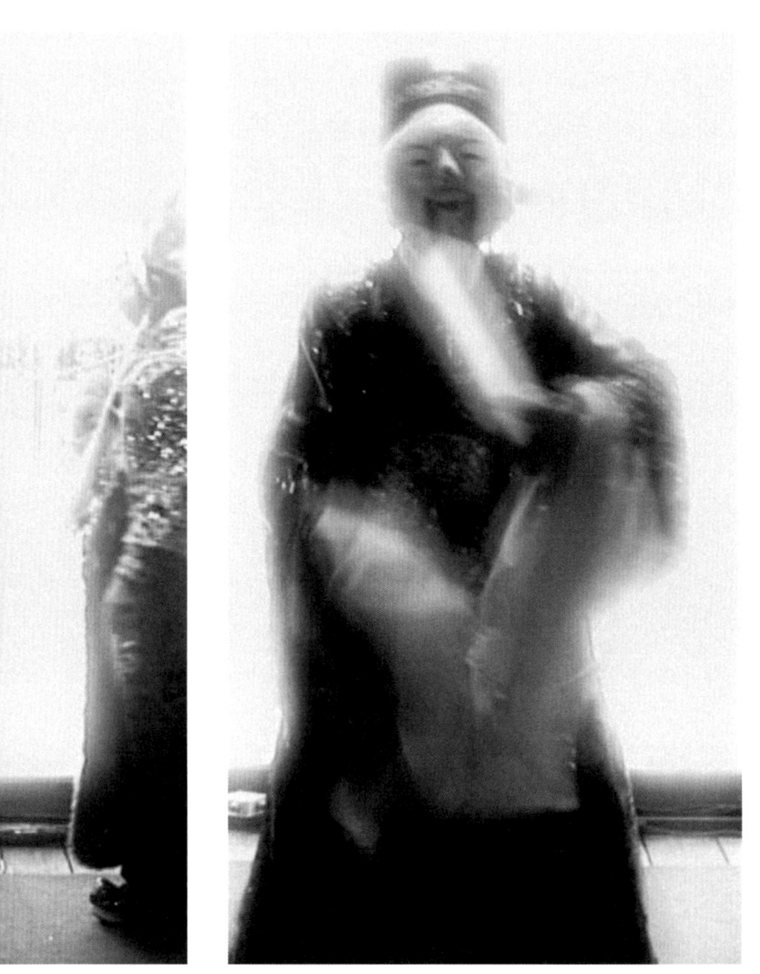
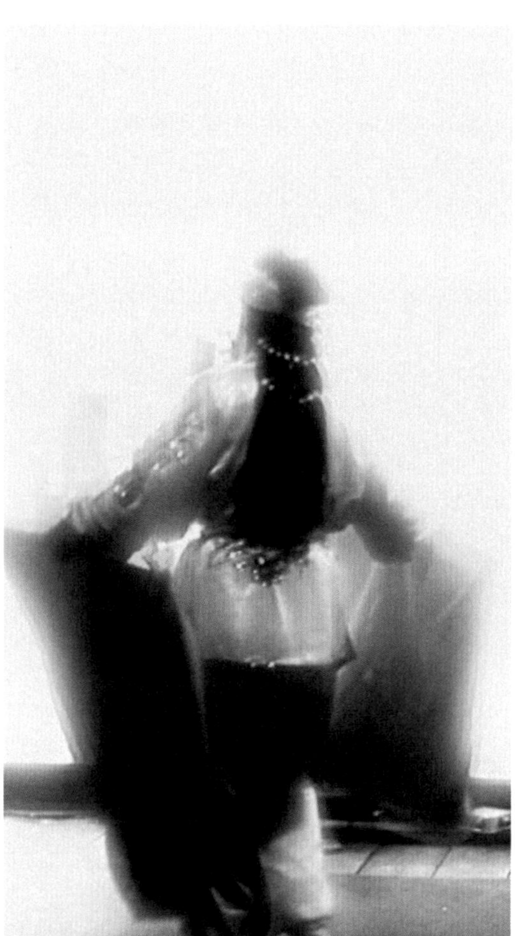

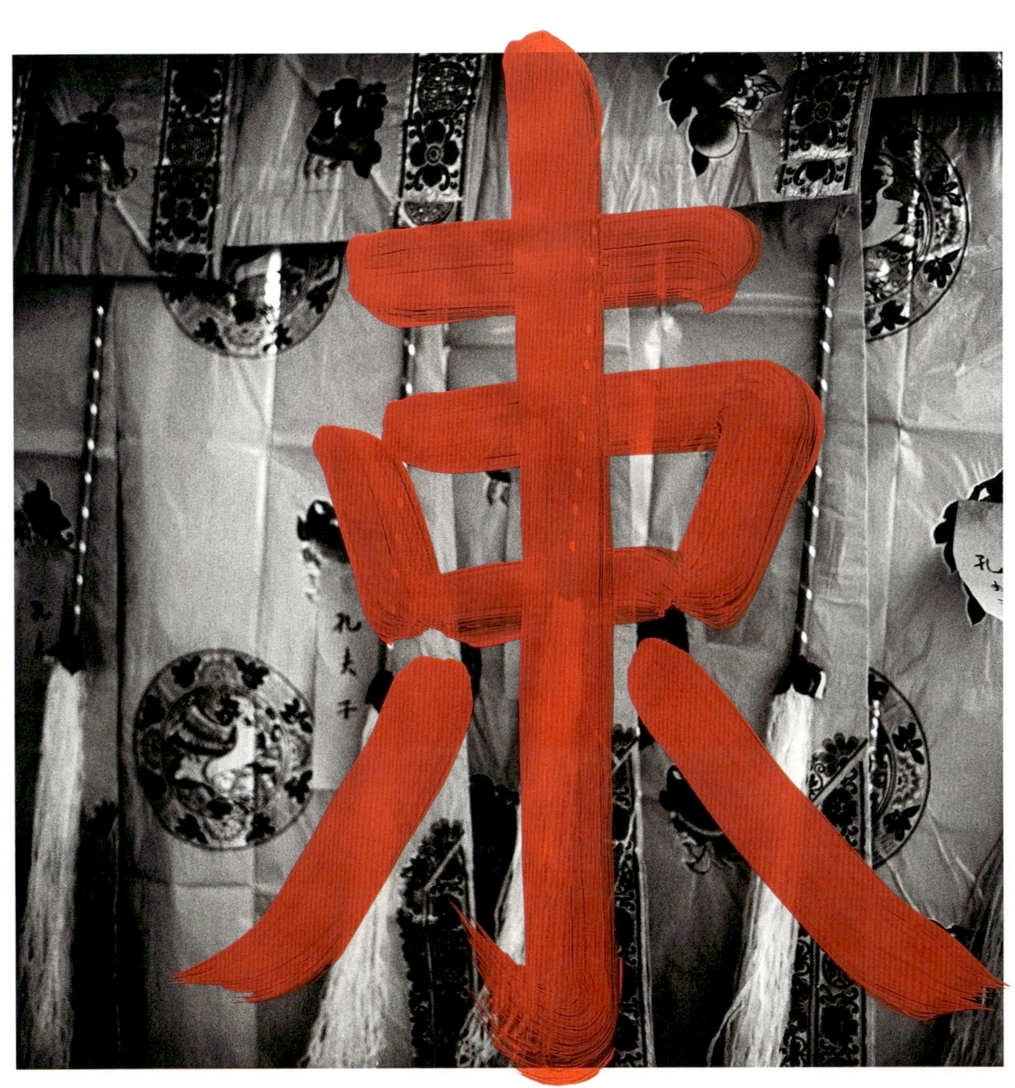

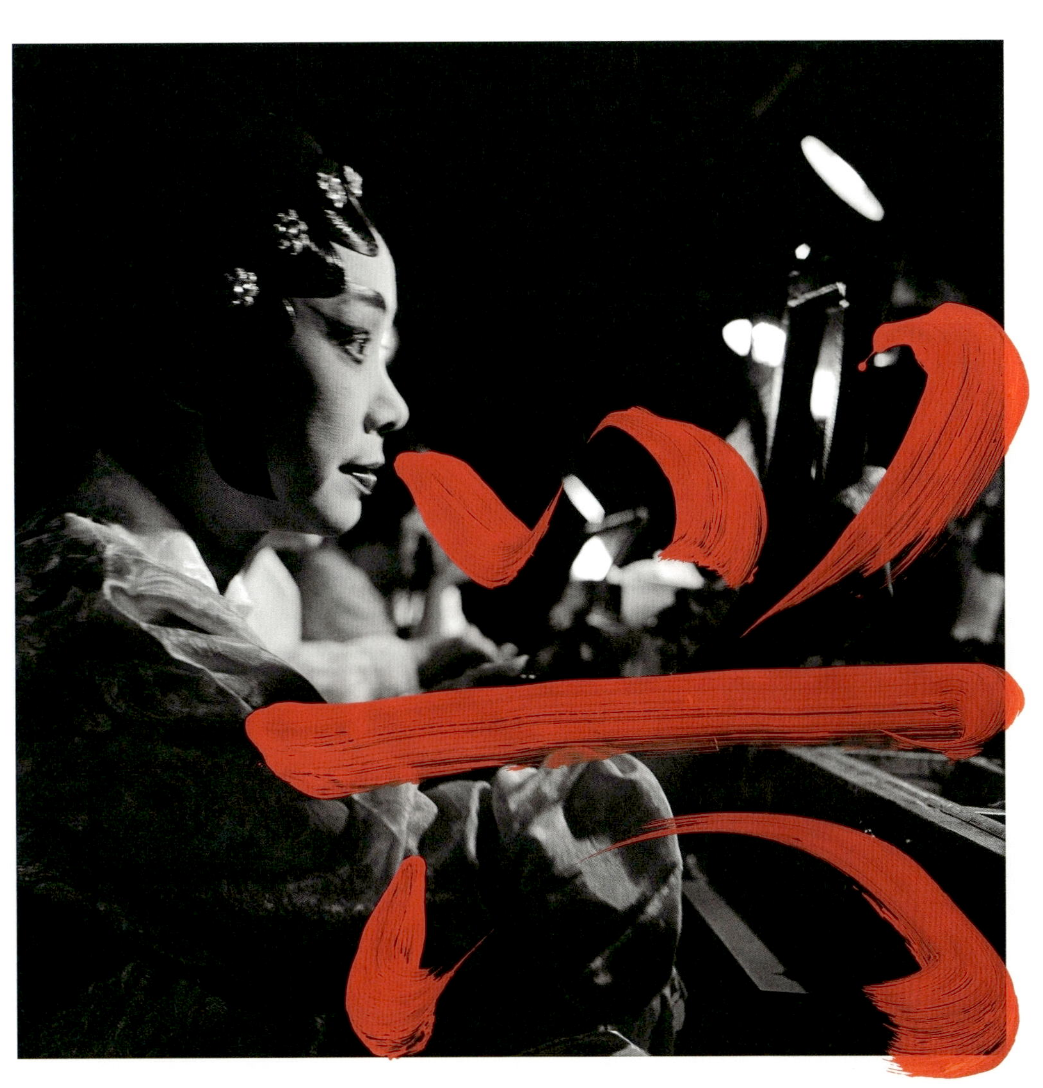

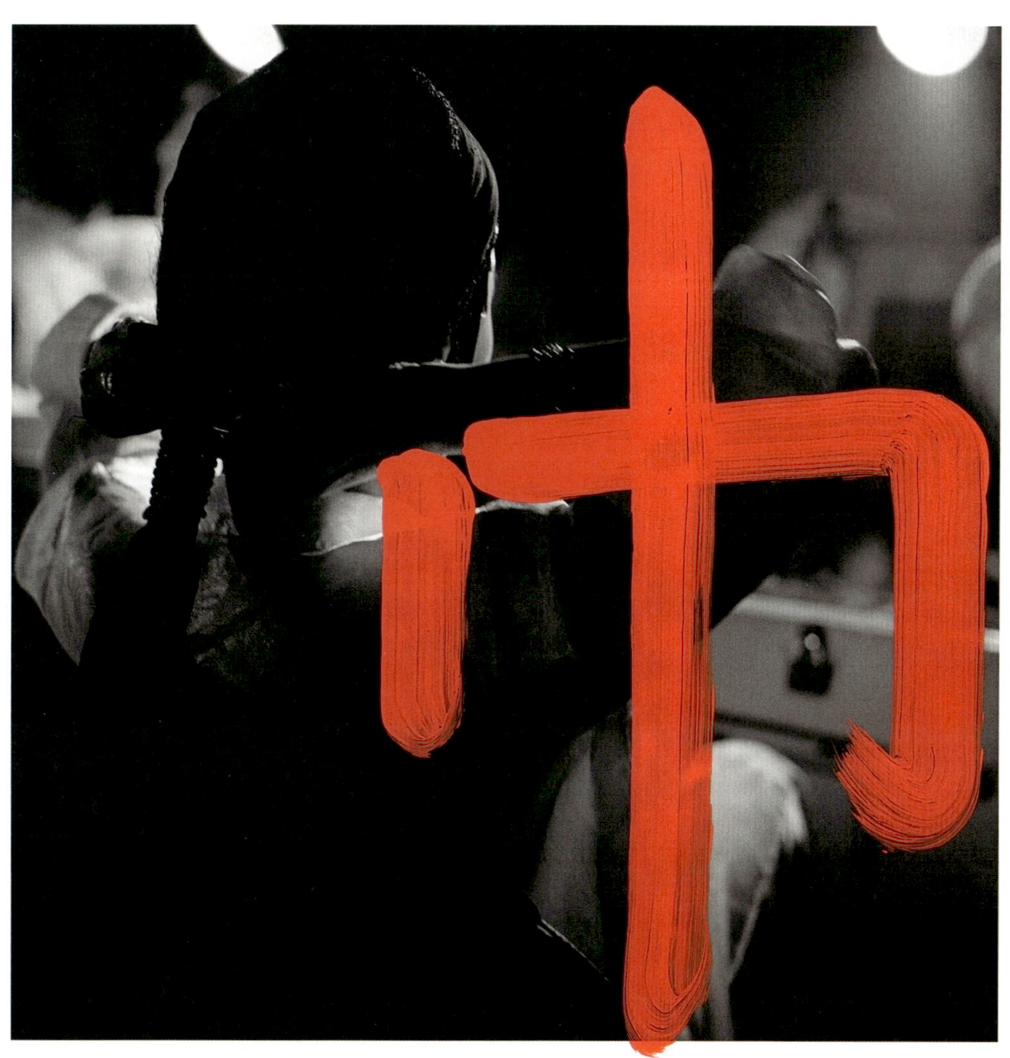

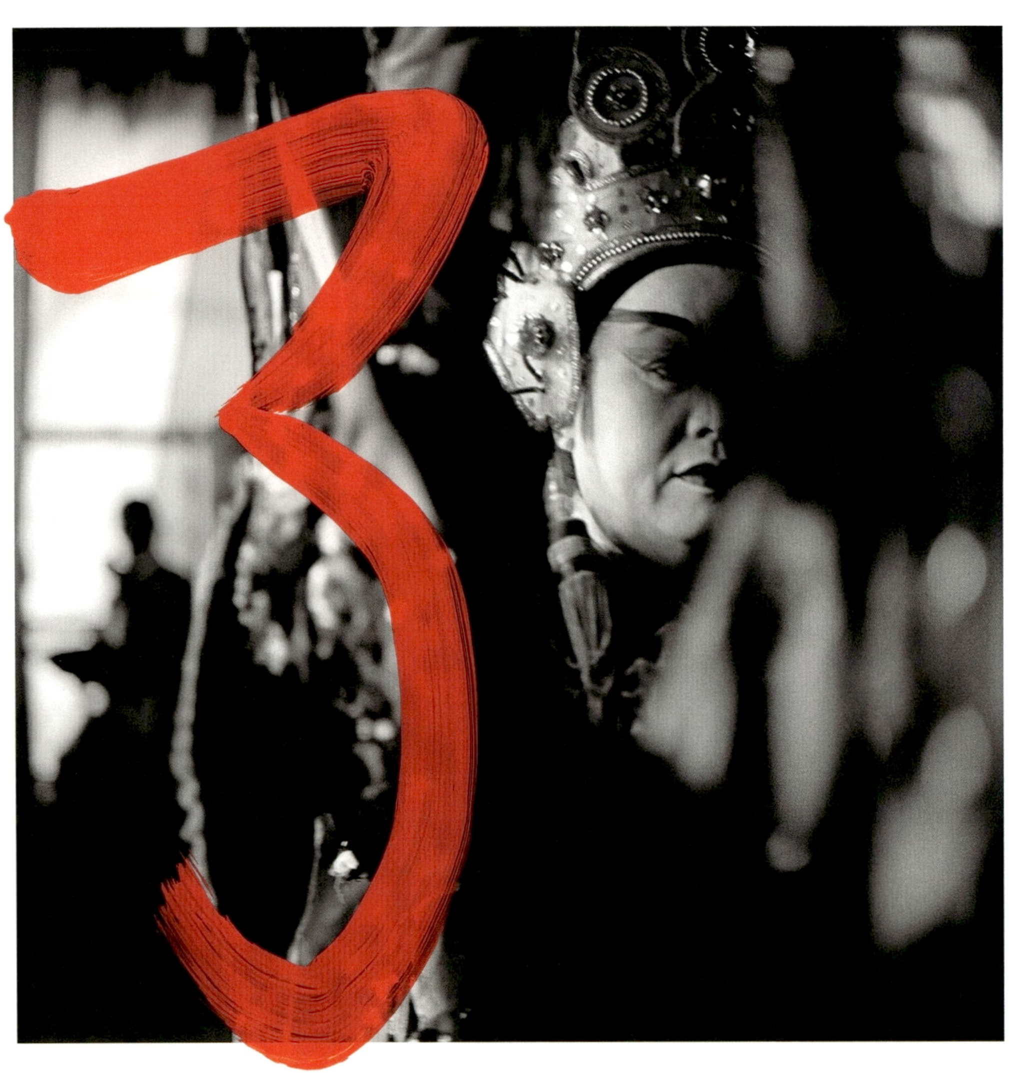

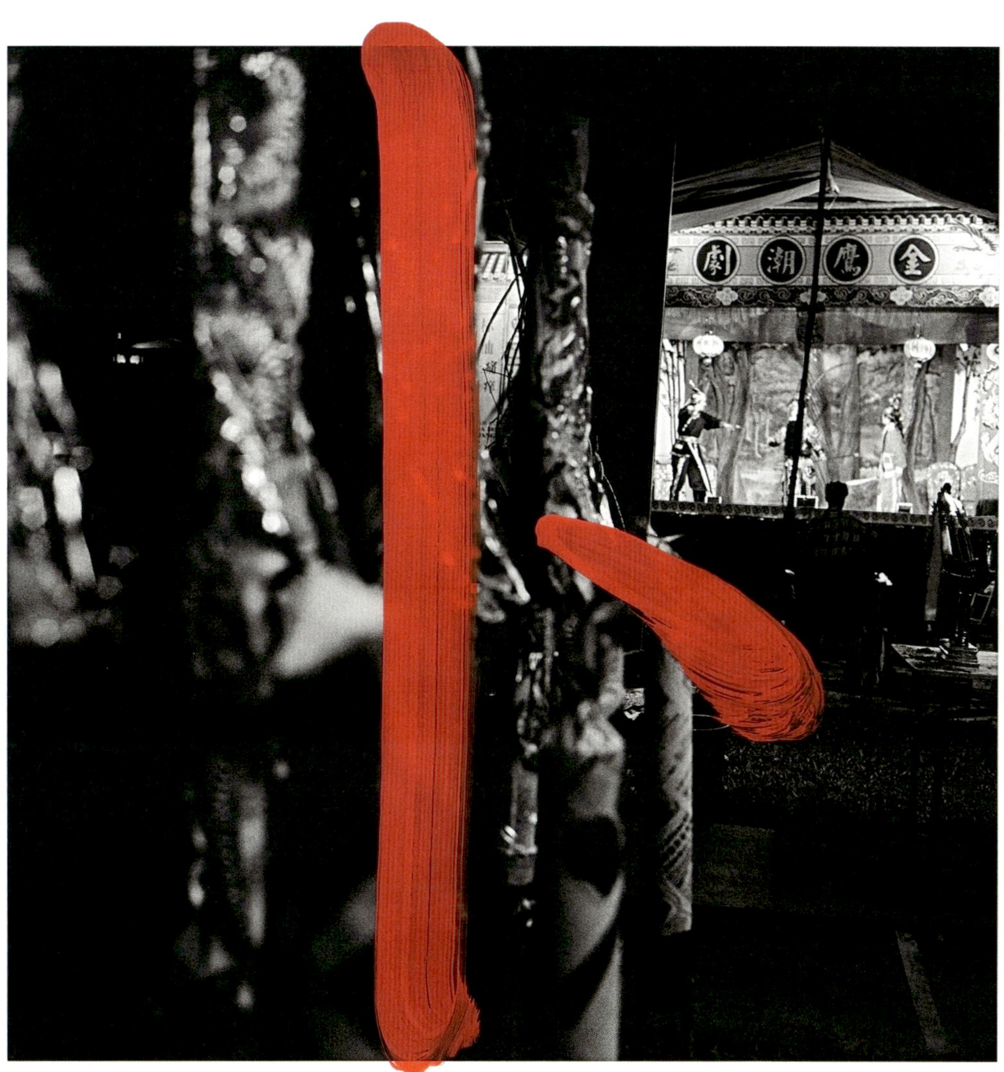

金鷹潮劇

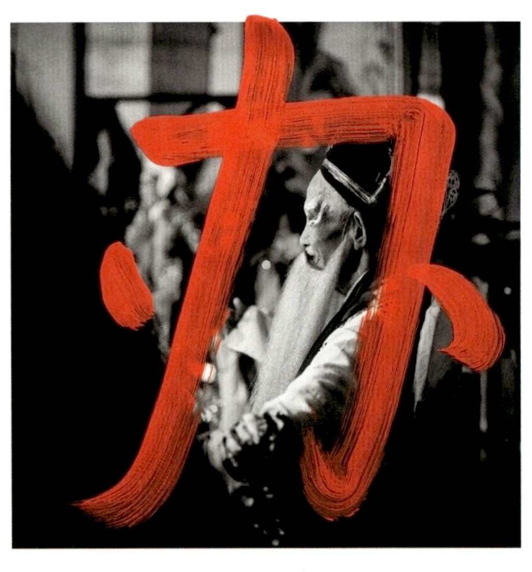

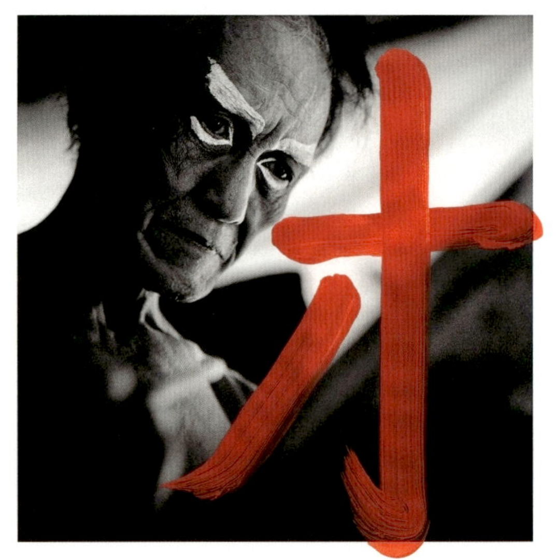

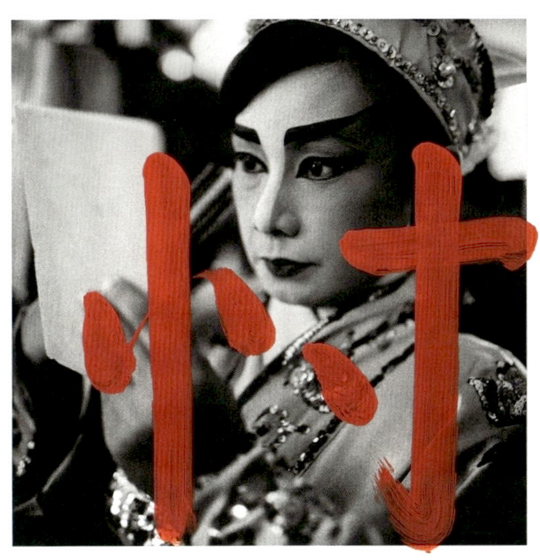

小村

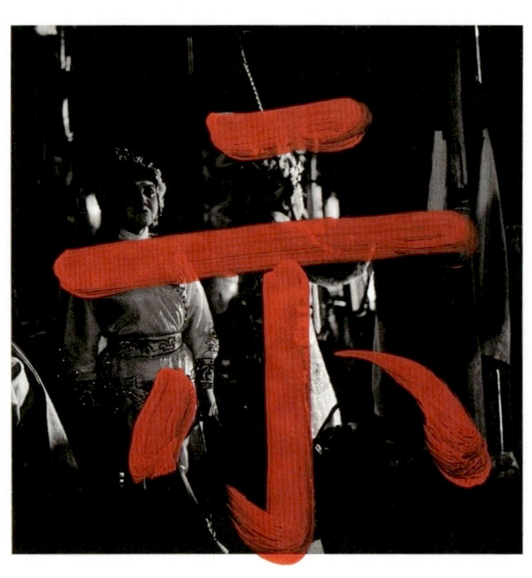
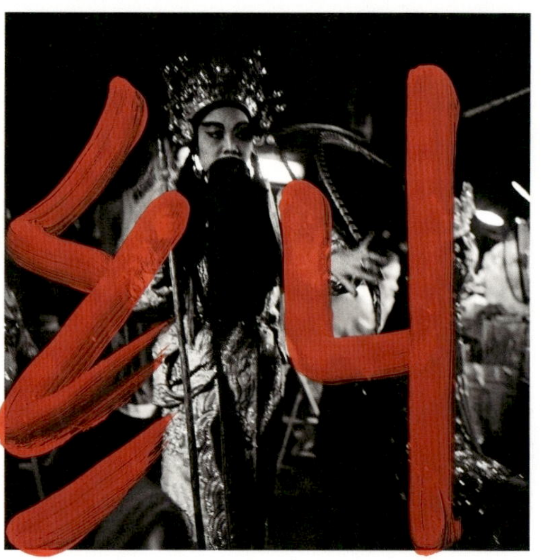

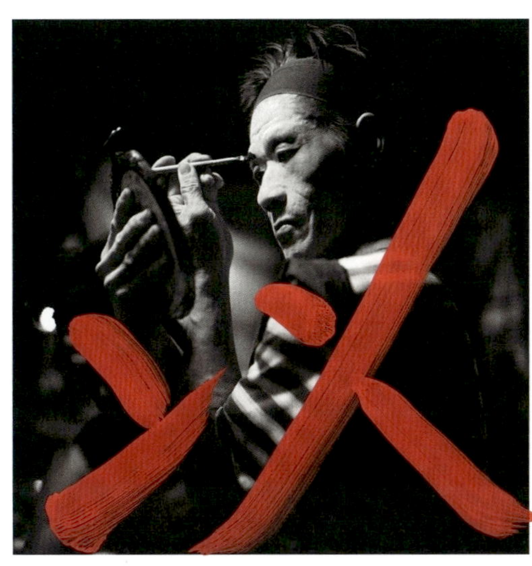

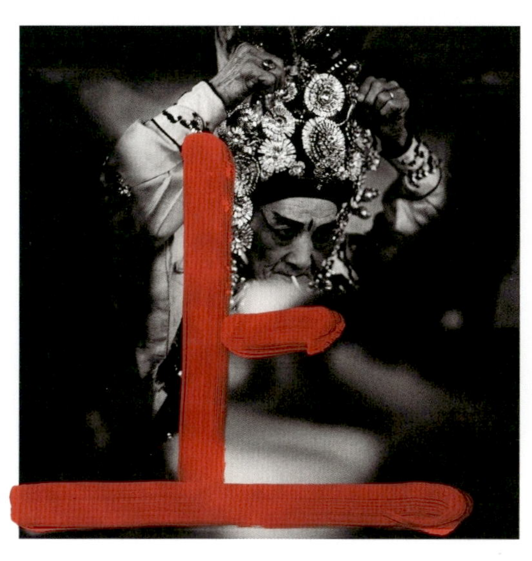
上

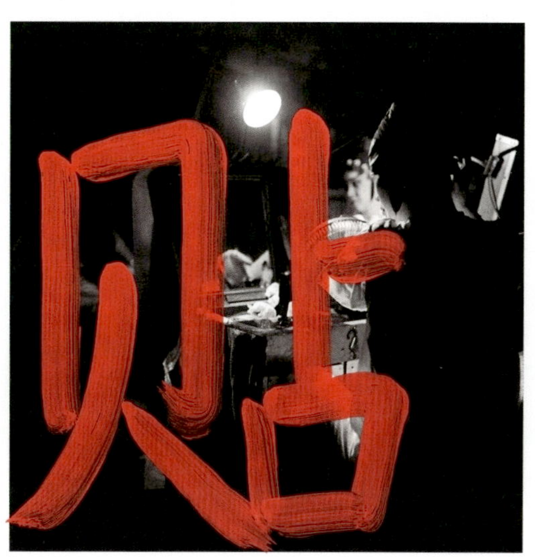
贴

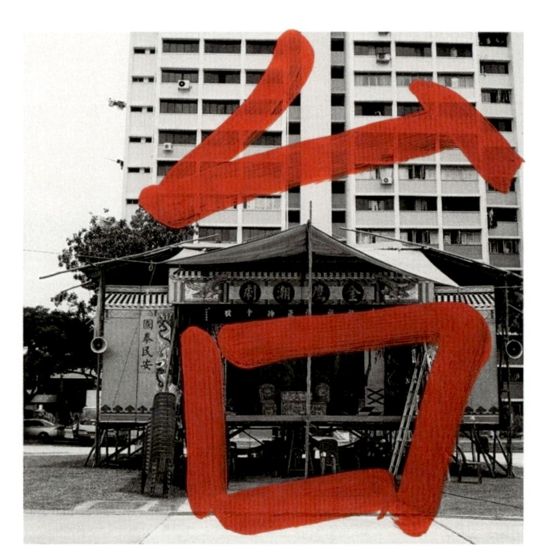

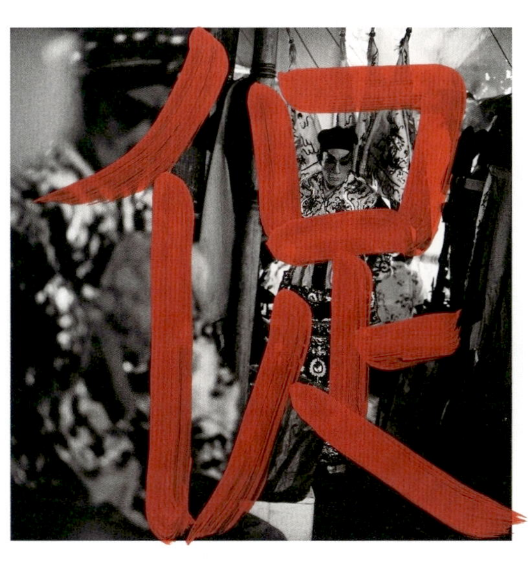 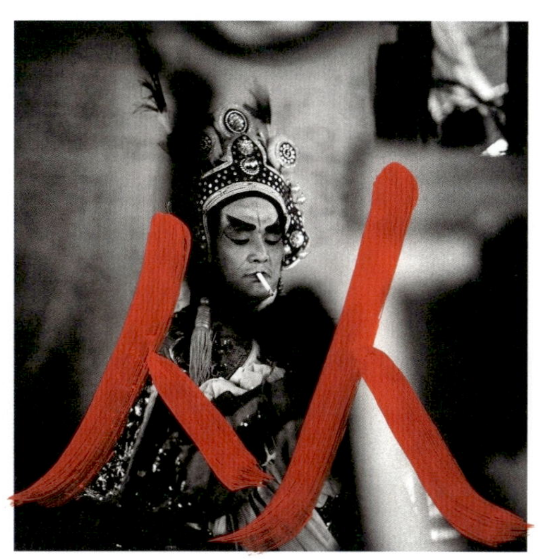

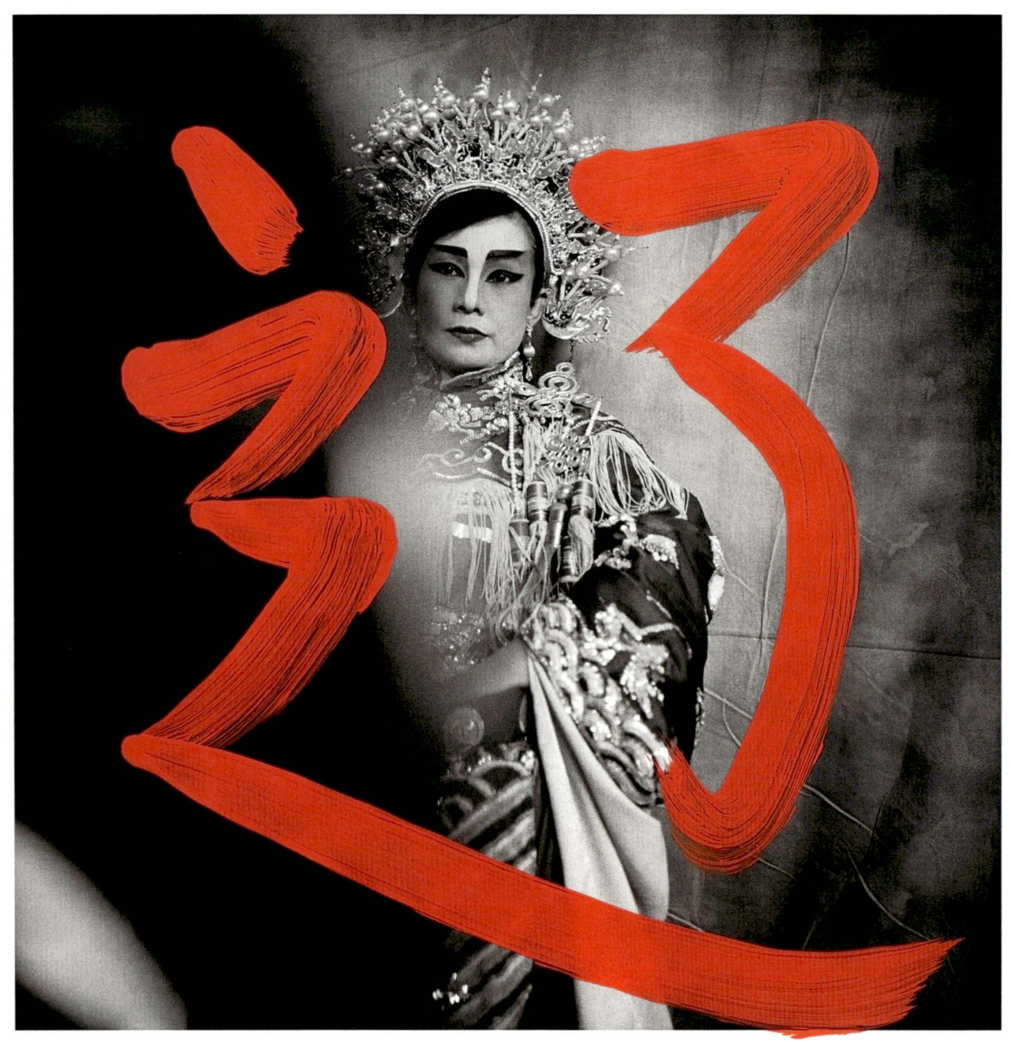

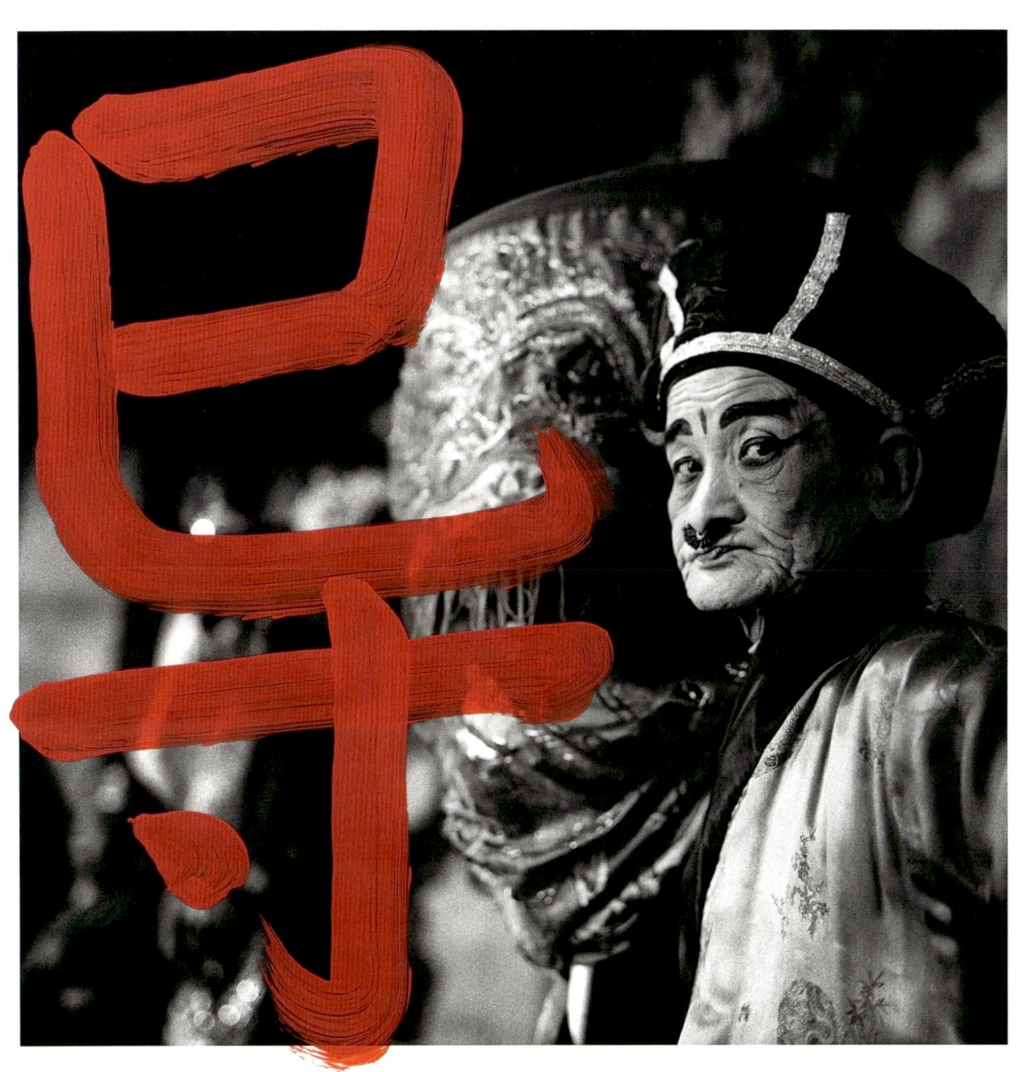

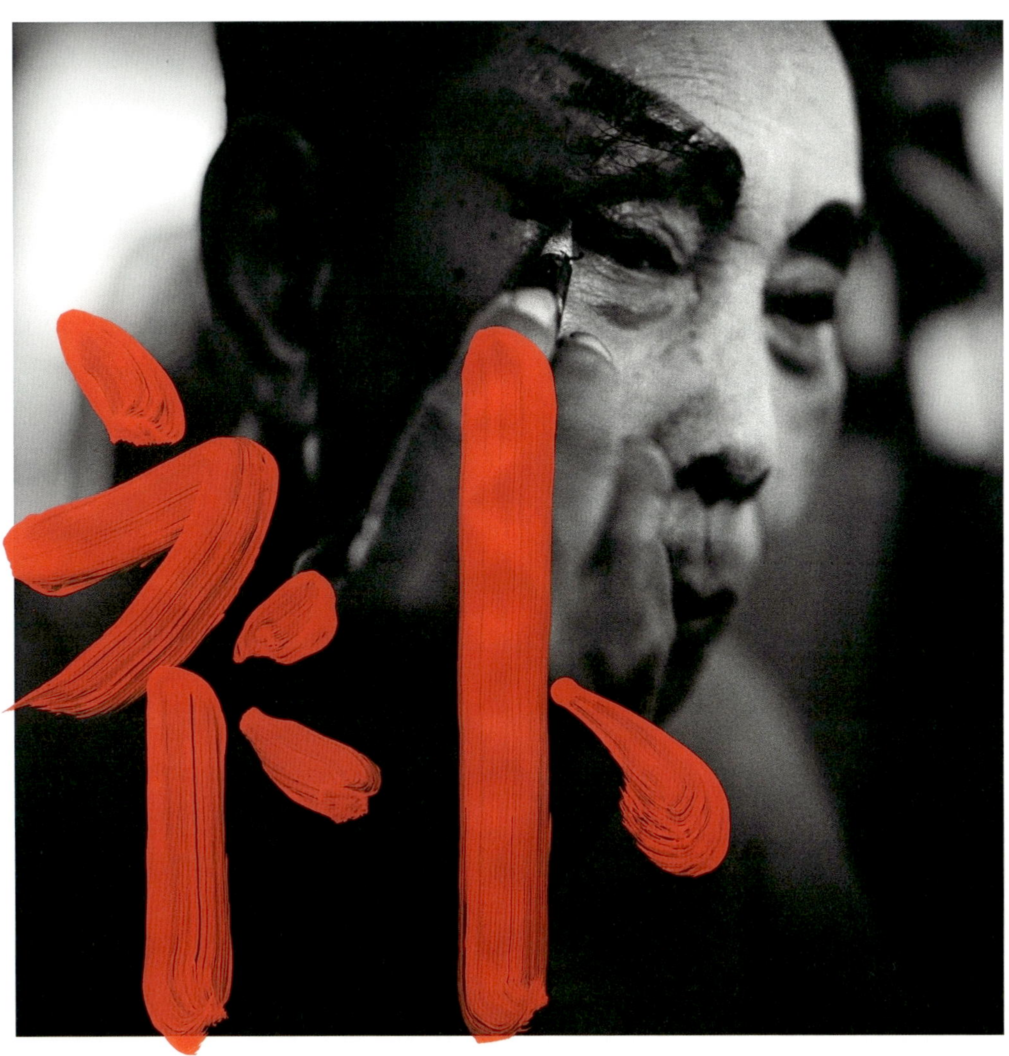

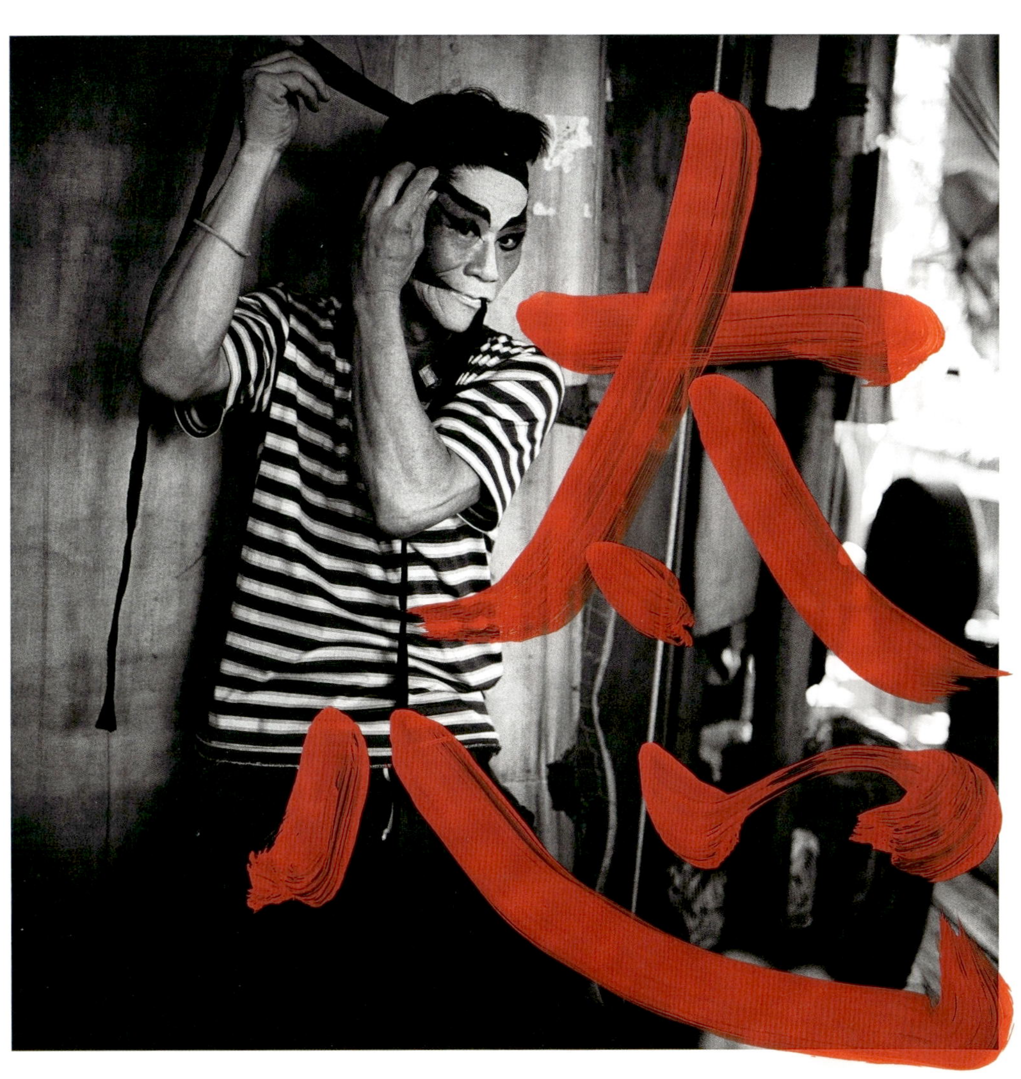

The Flow of Life

*A sort of umbilical cord links the body of the photographed thing to my gaze: light,
though impalpable, is here a carnal medium, a skin I share with anyone who has
been photographed.*
Roland Barthes, *Camera Lucida,* 1979-1980

The installation *The Flow of Life* conveys in spatial terms the physical energy of the referent,
as Barthes calls the "photographed thing." The glances of the pilgrims flooding past Hannes
Schmid's camera give them a strikingly immediate presence. This impression is heightened
by the moving pictures and the quiet soundtrack that draw viewers into the scene and sweep
them up in the crowd.

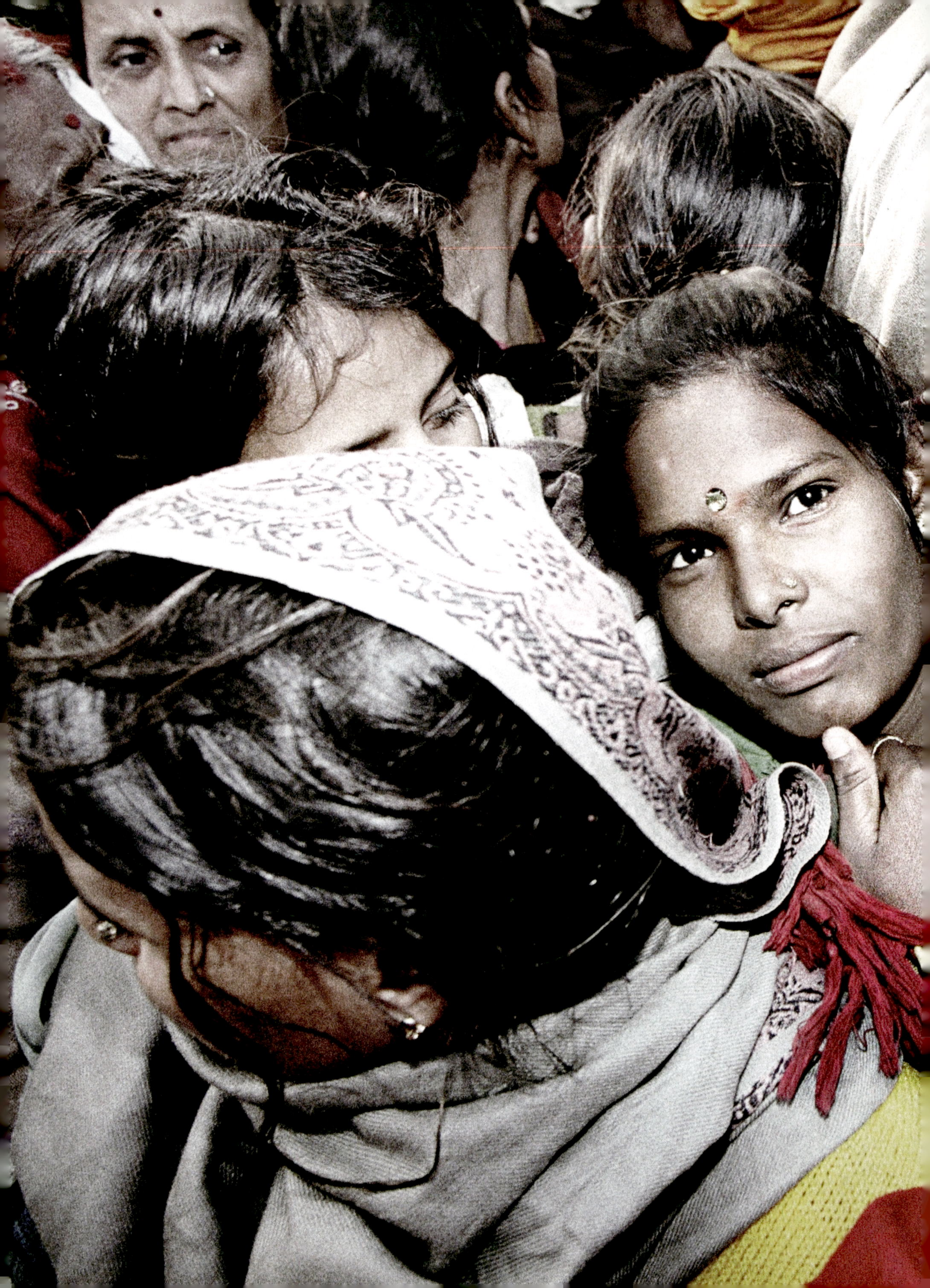

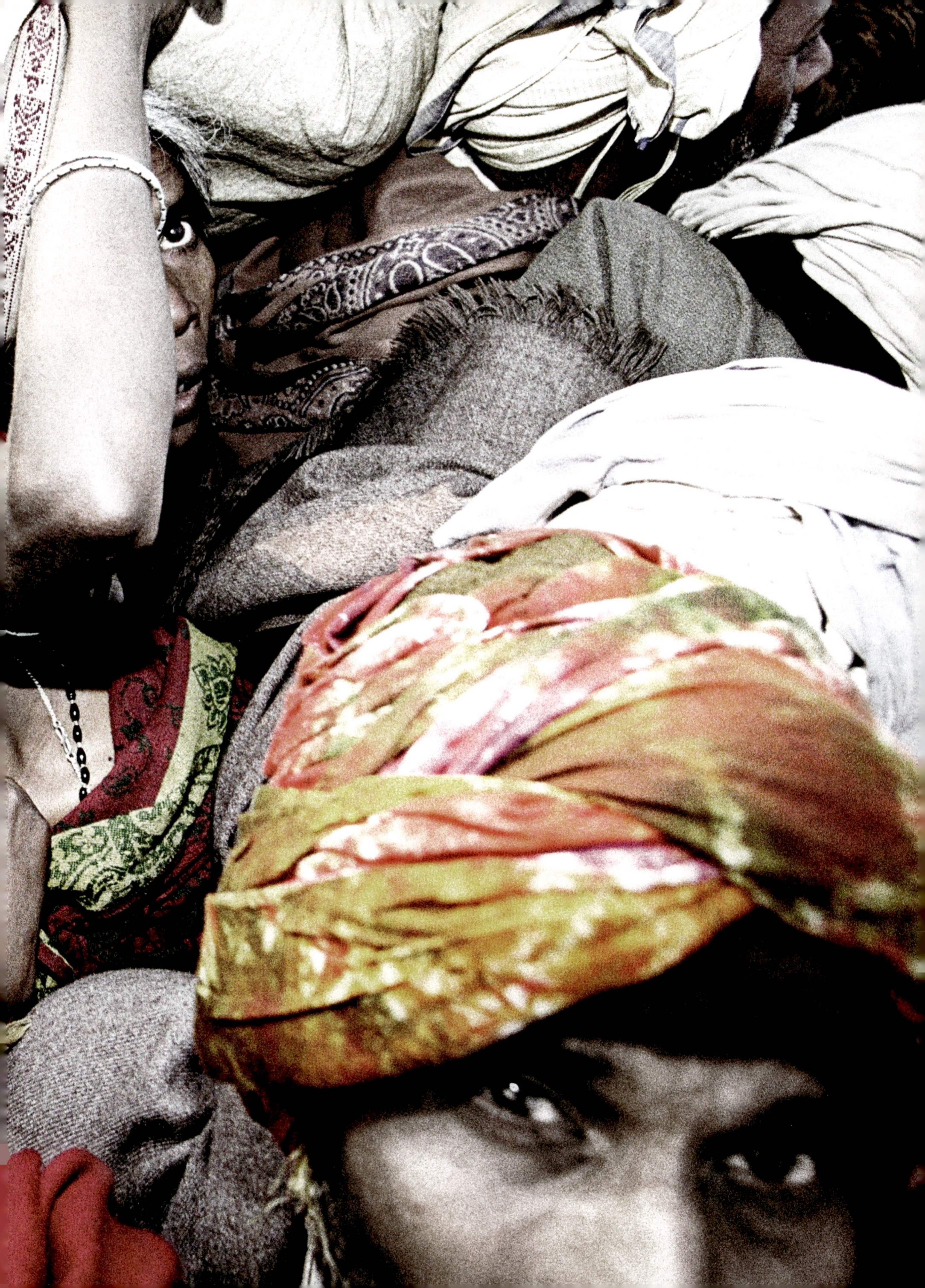

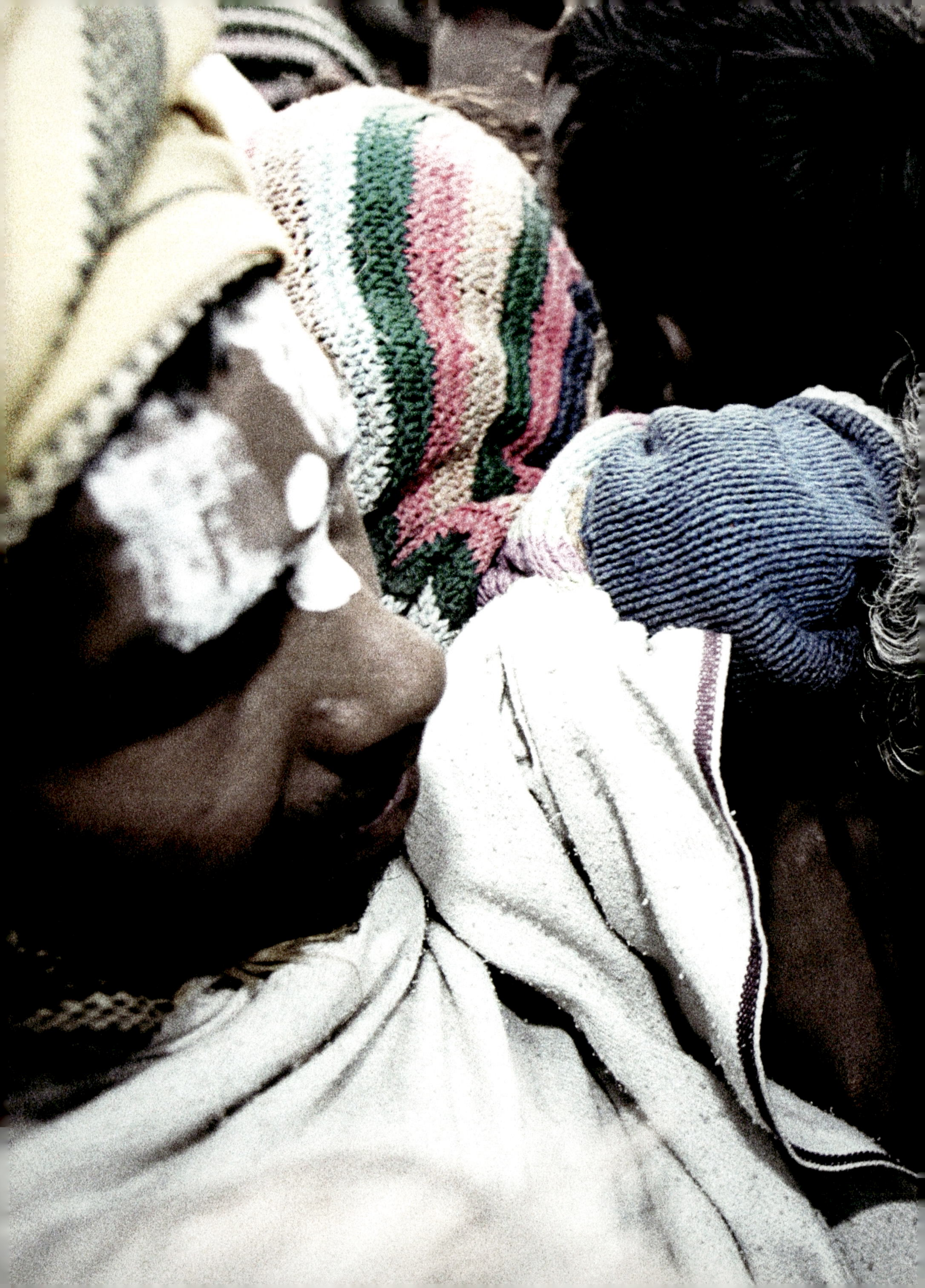

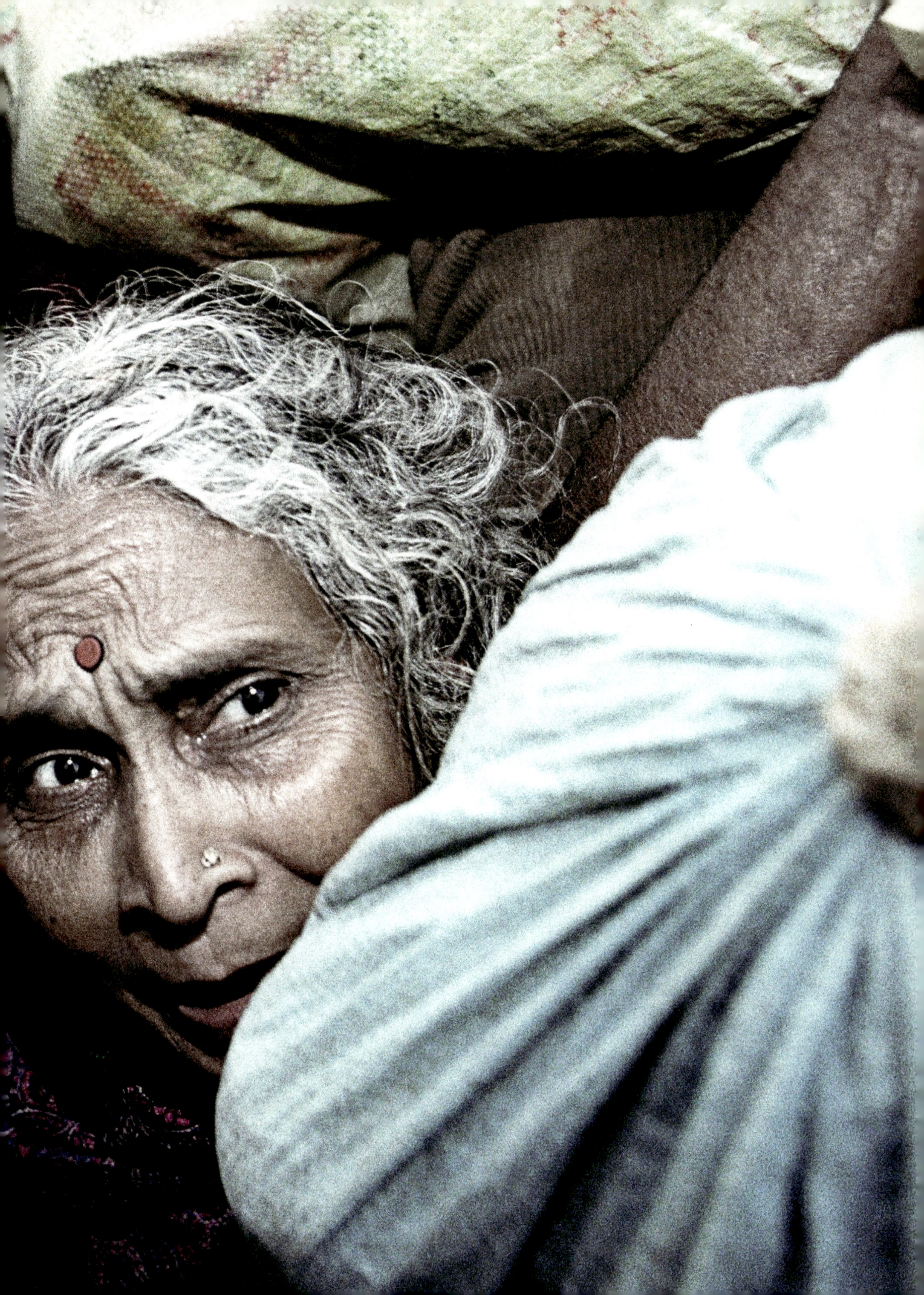

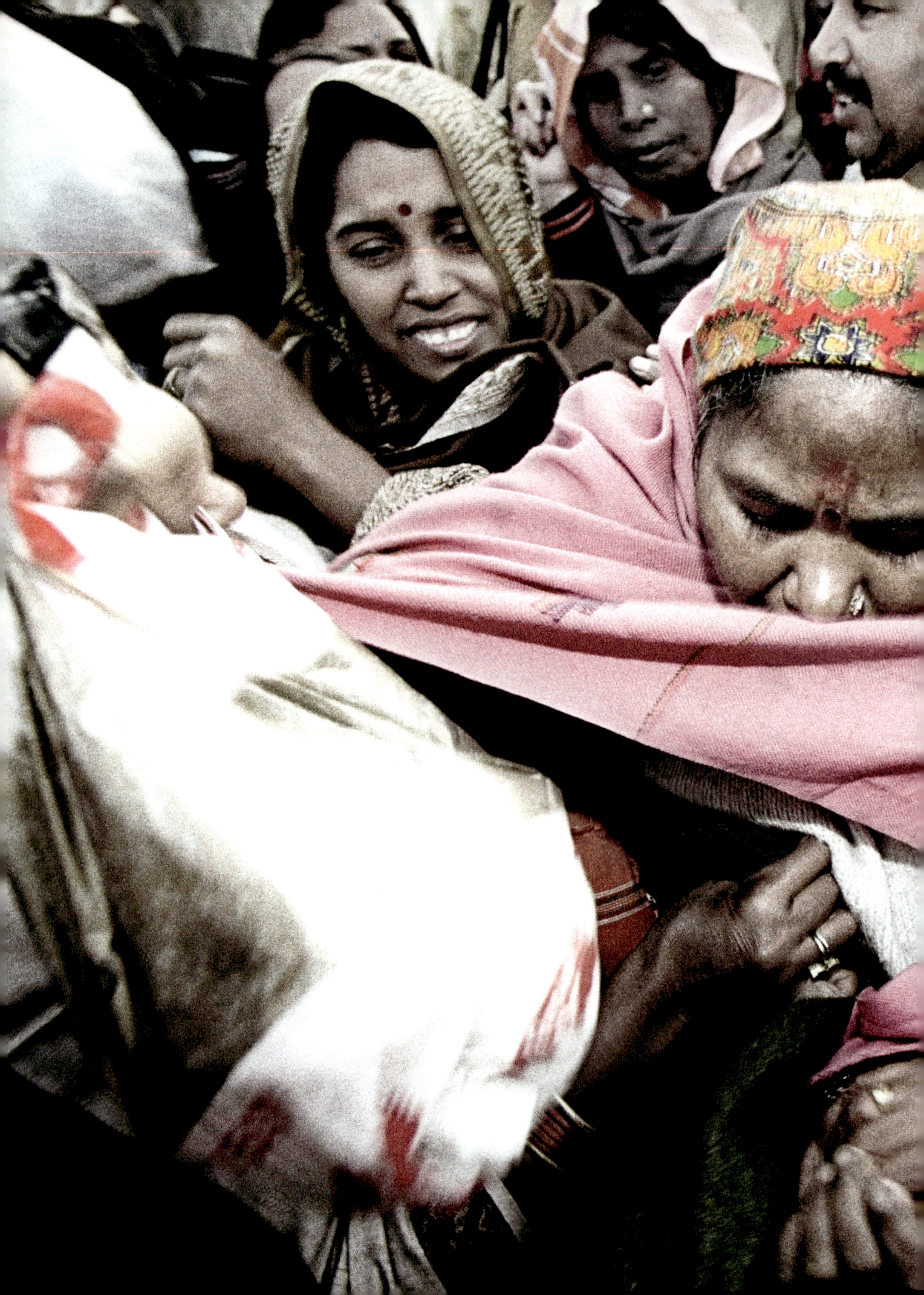

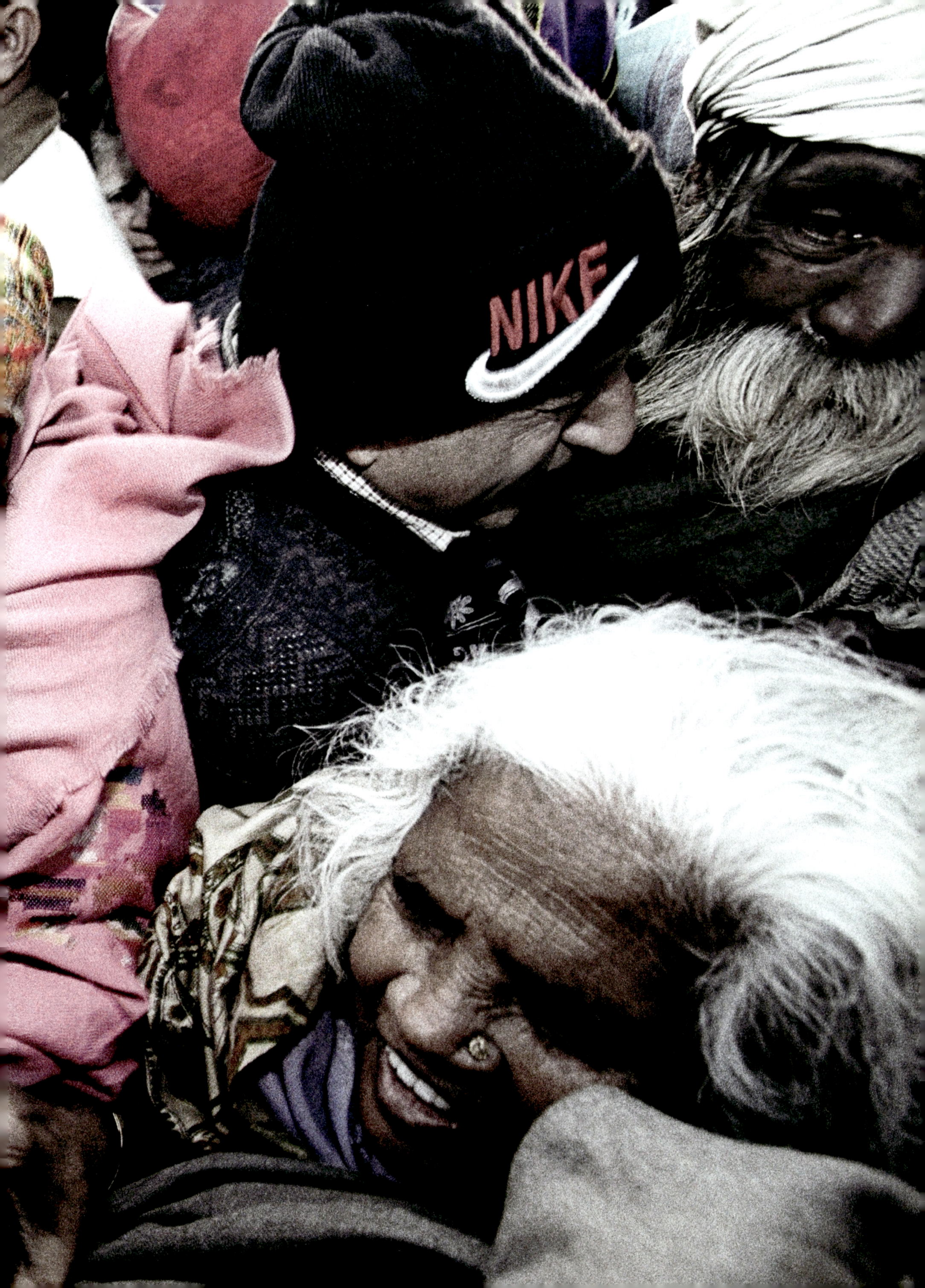

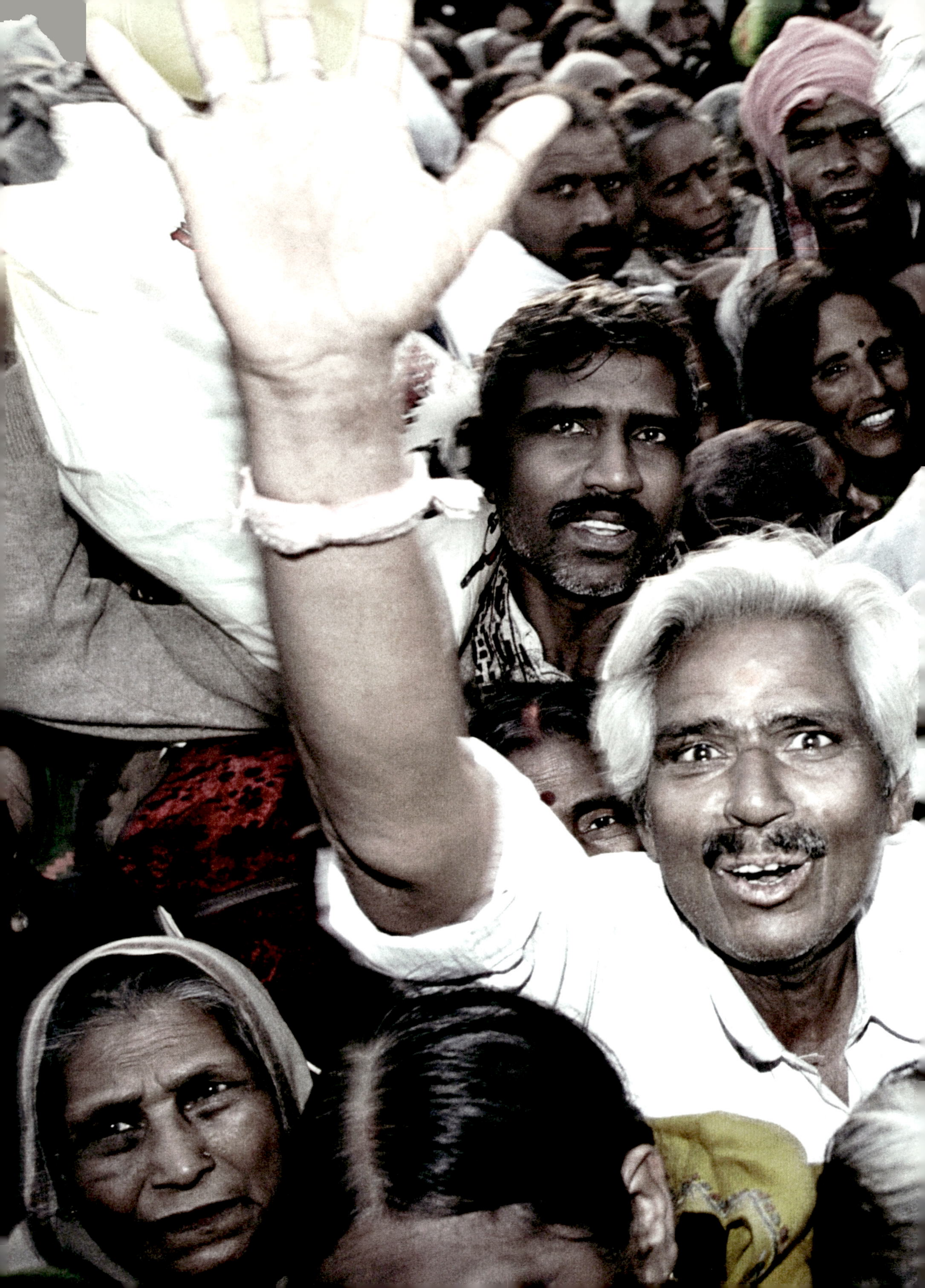

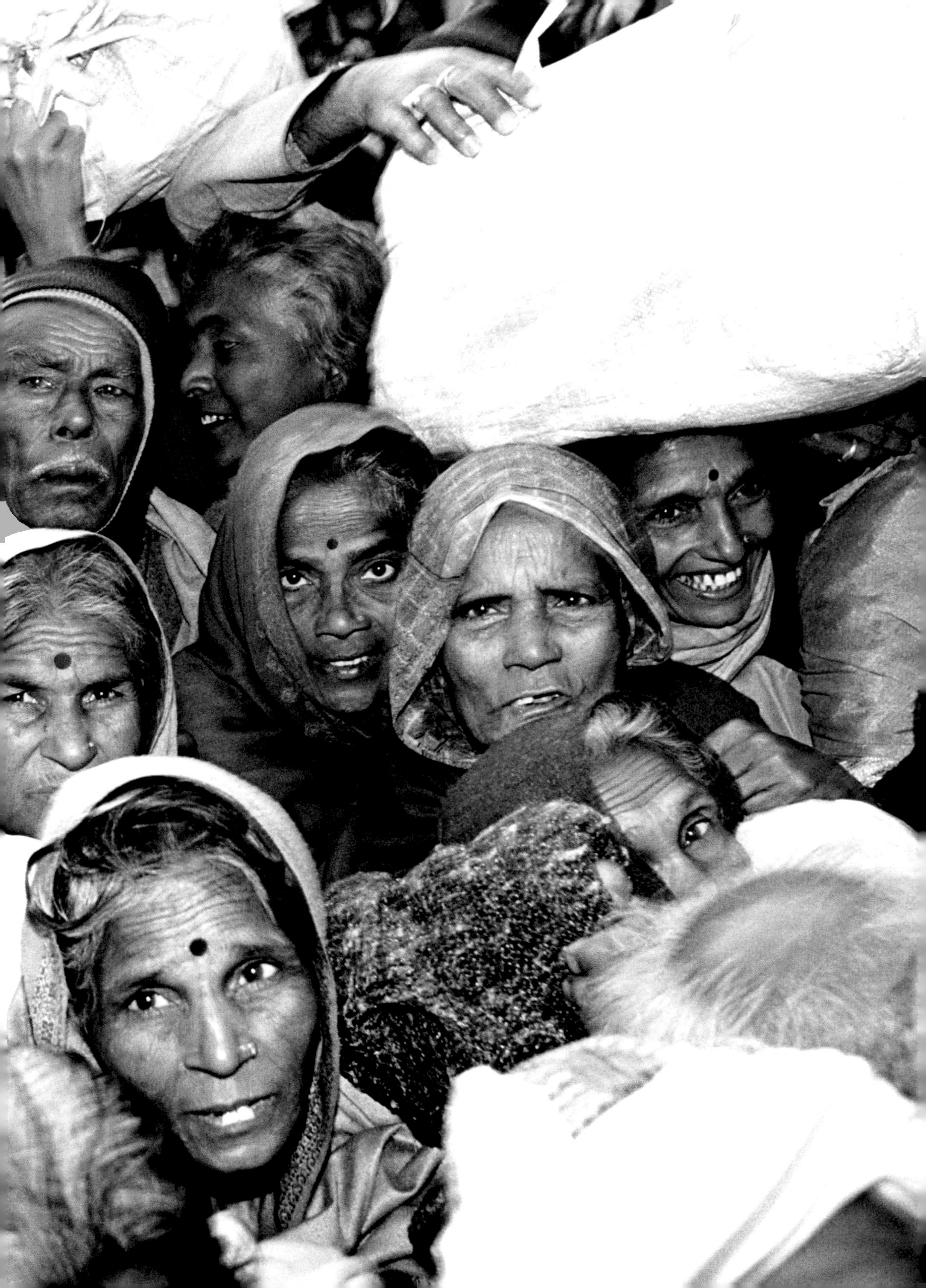

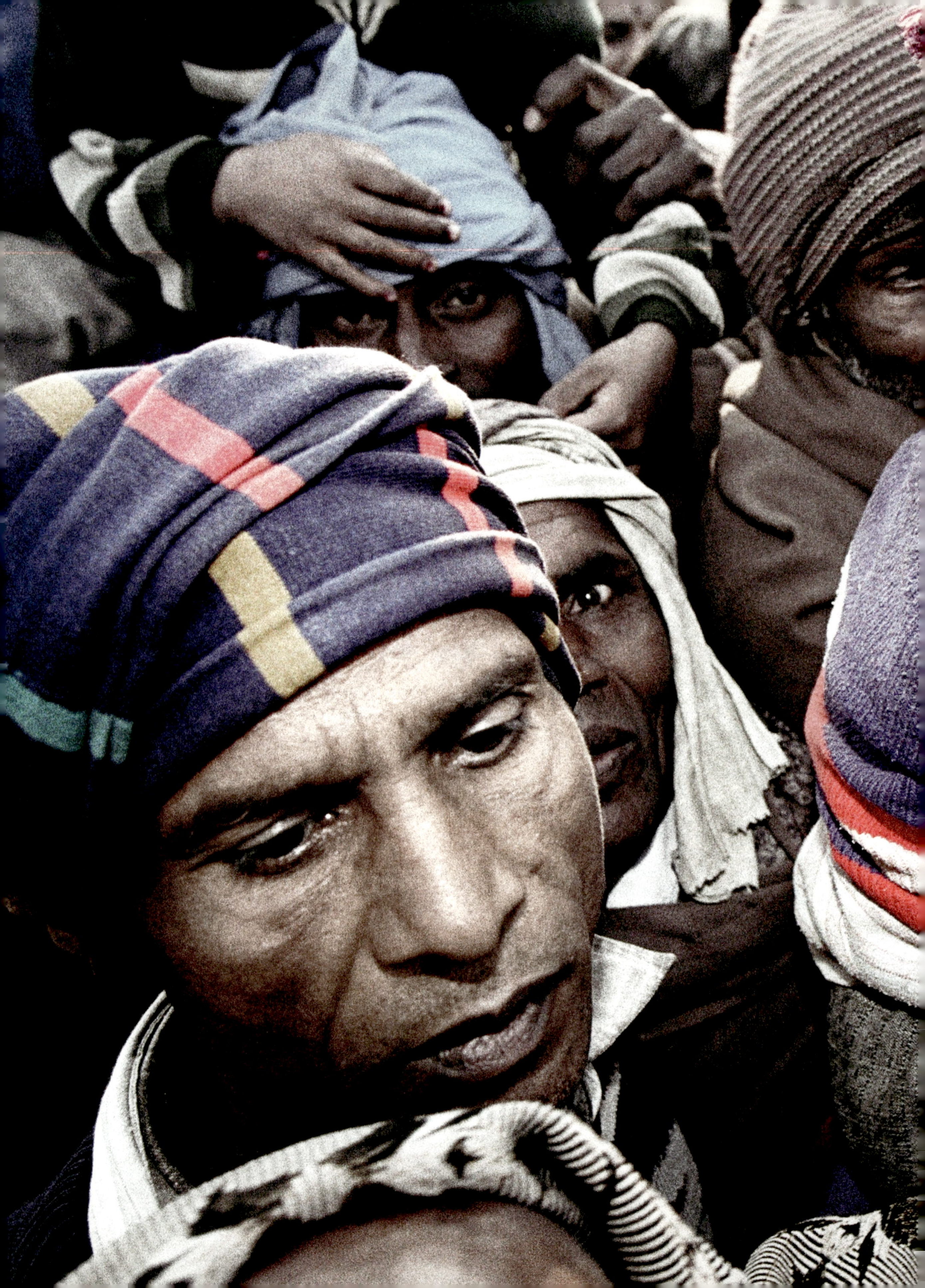

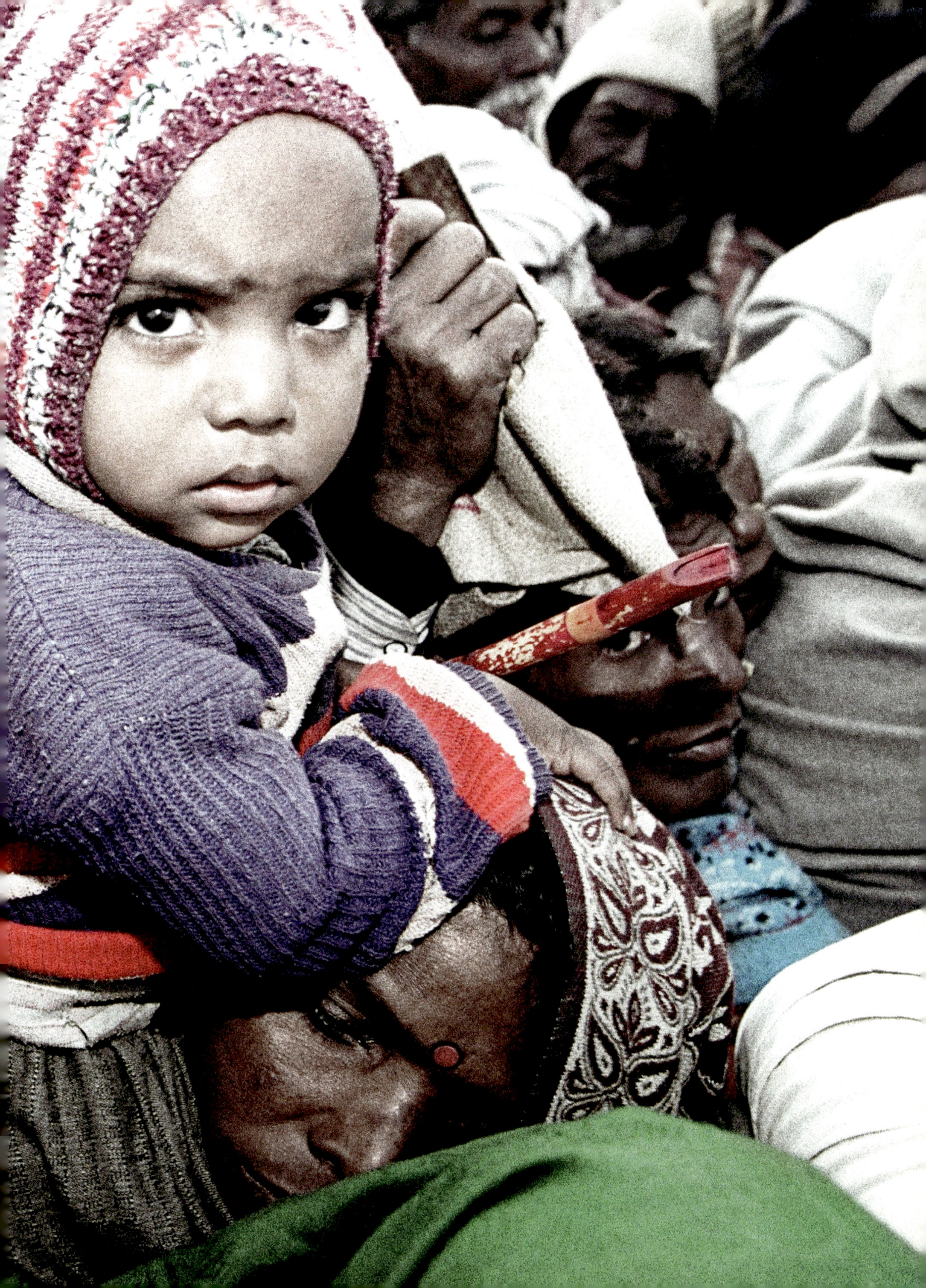

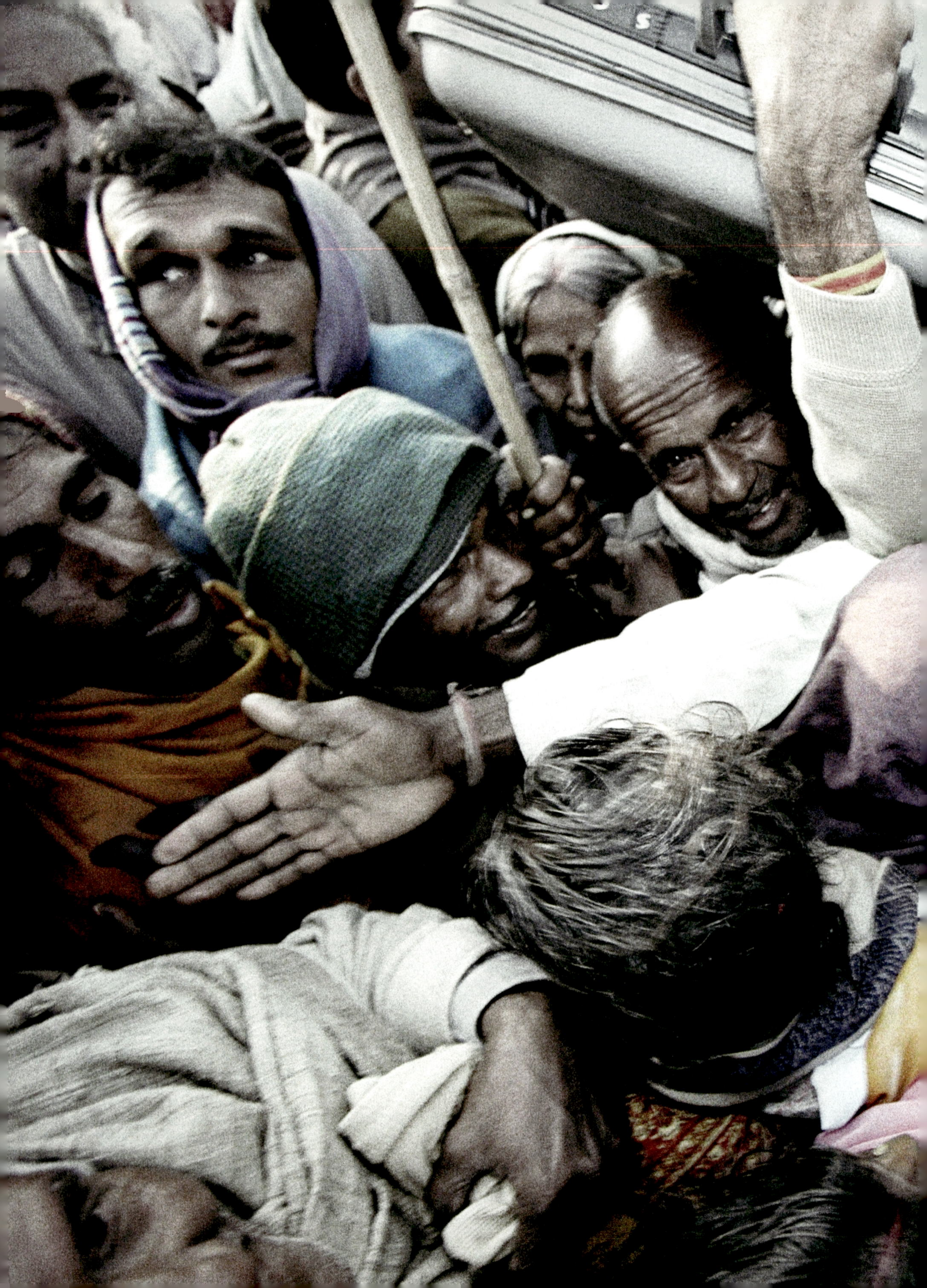

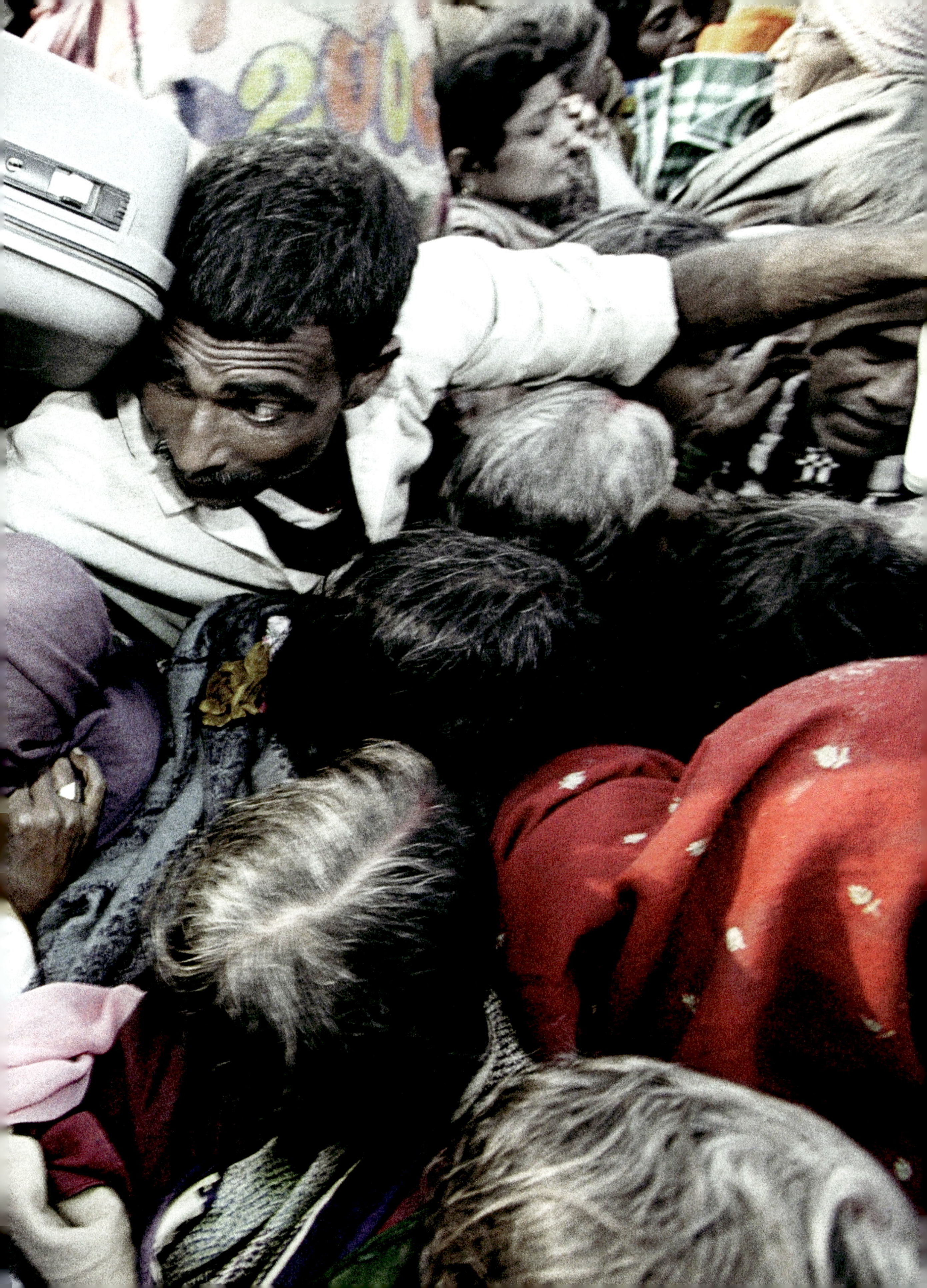

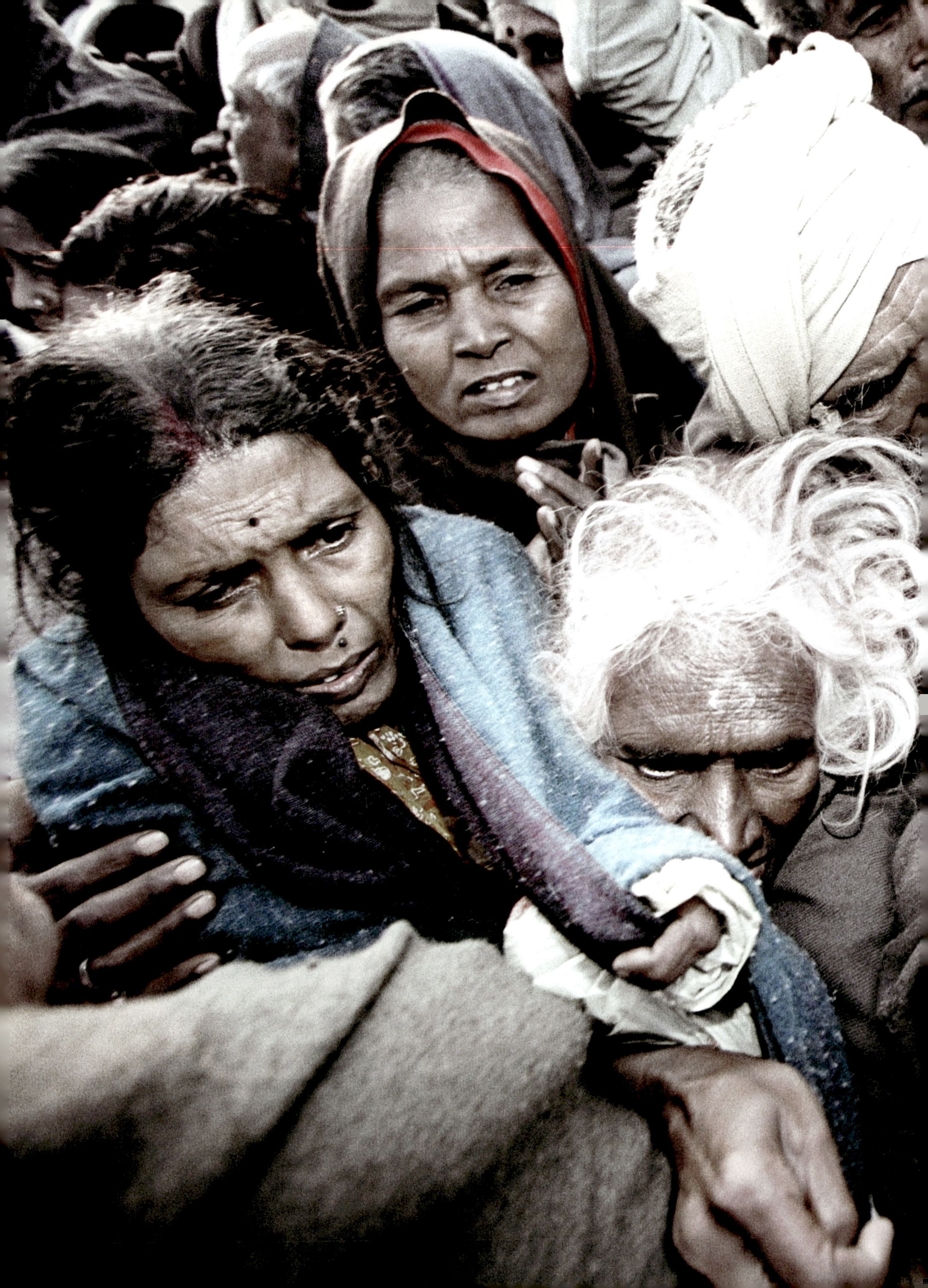

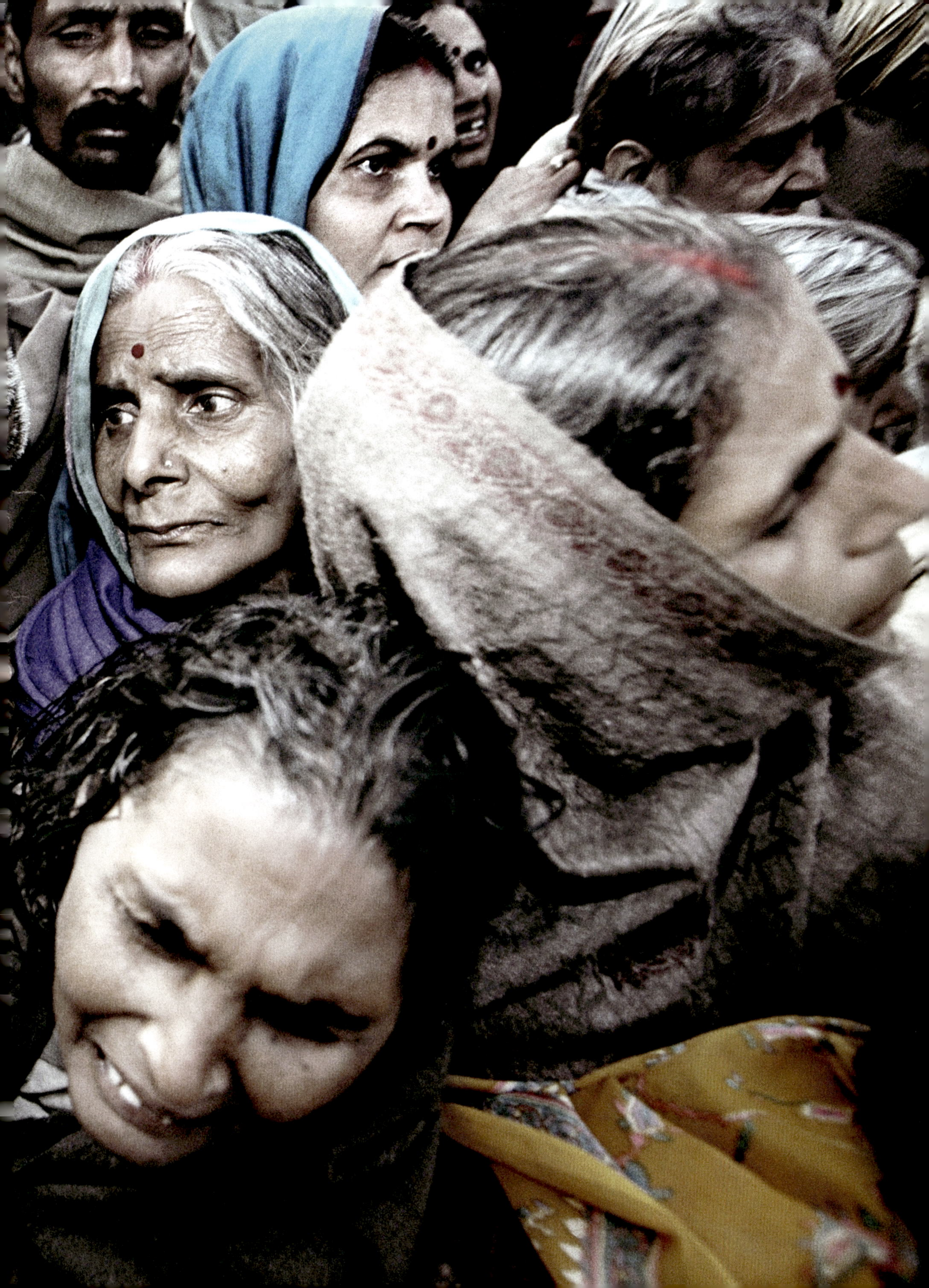

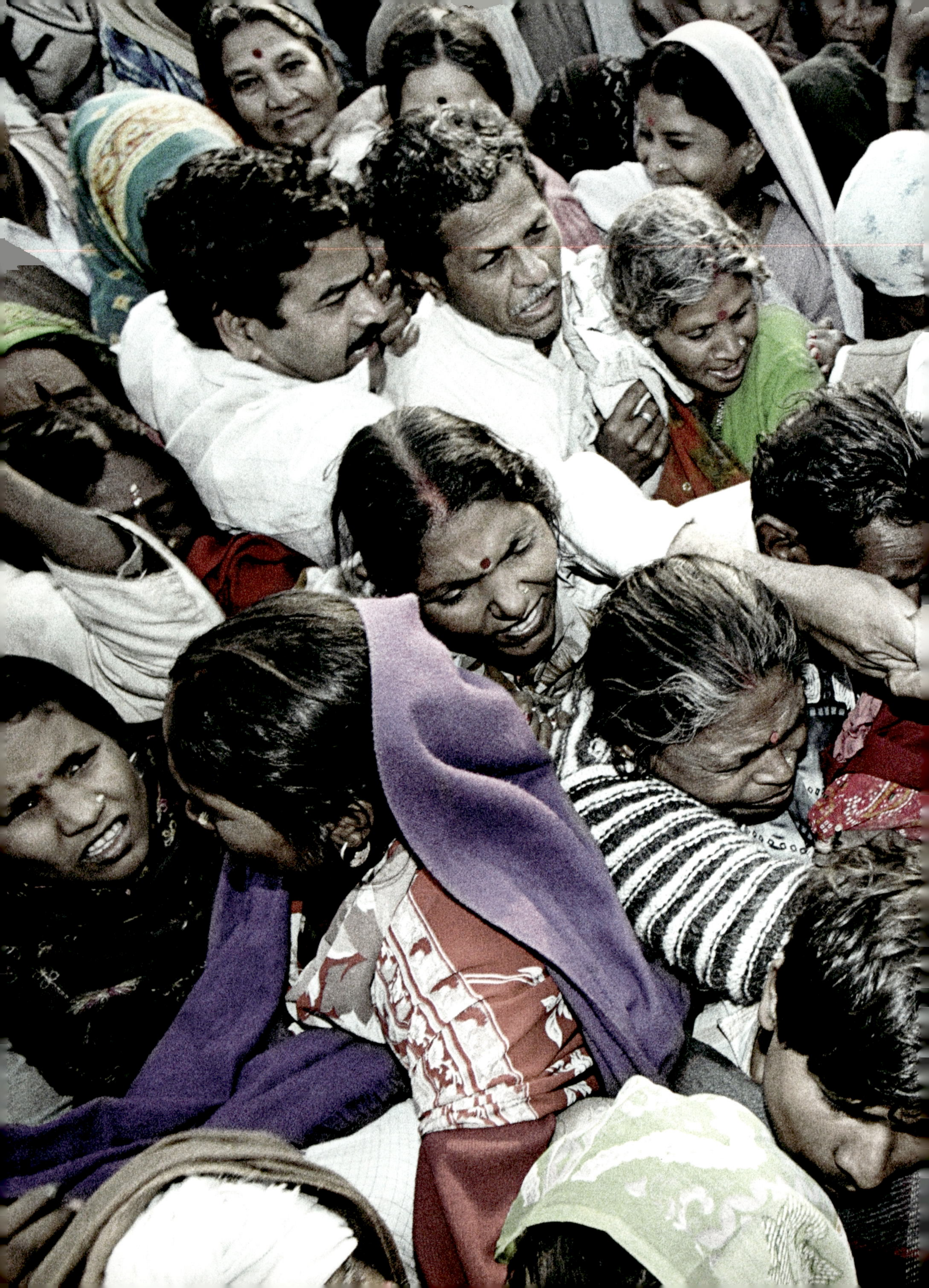

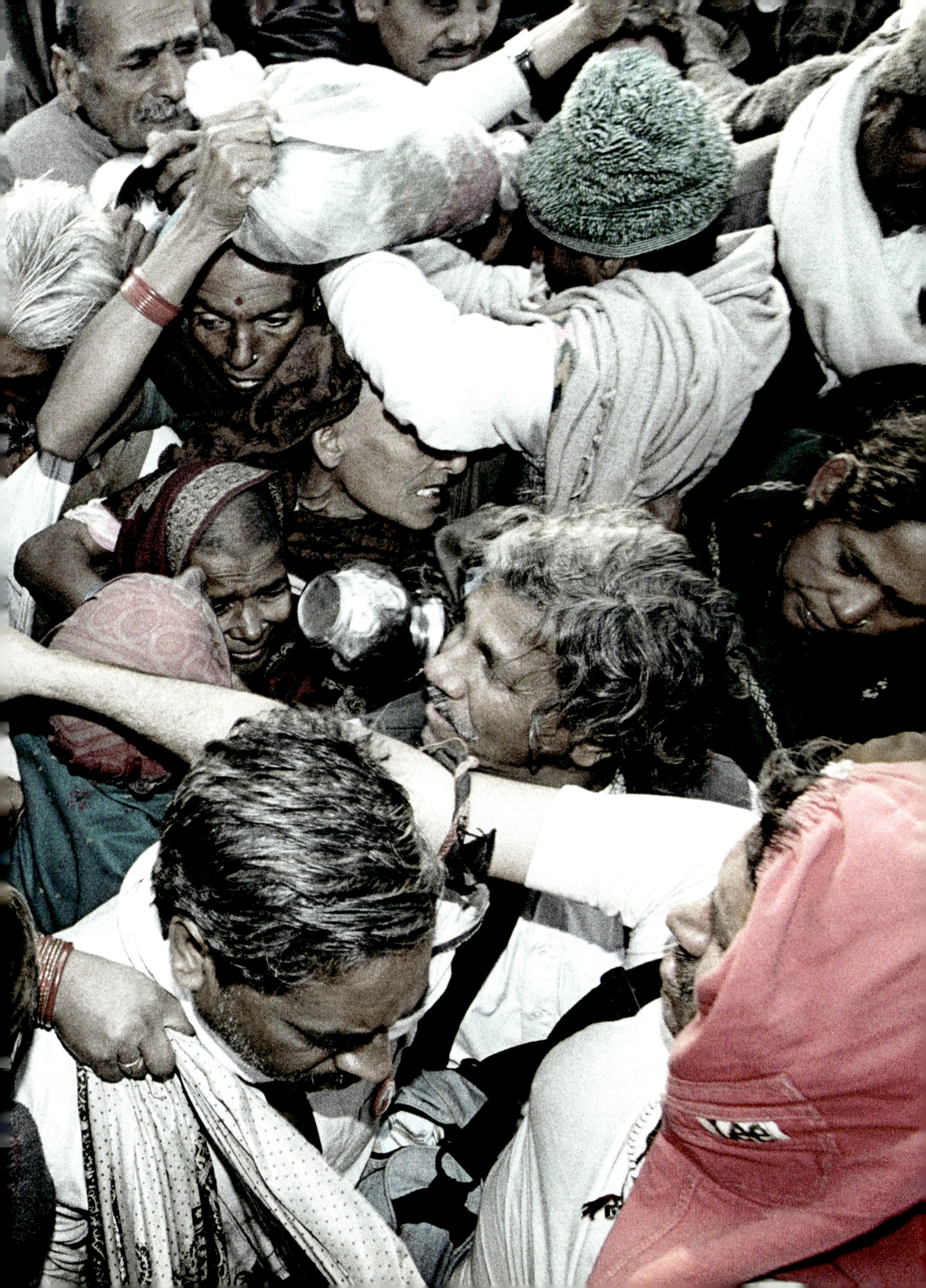

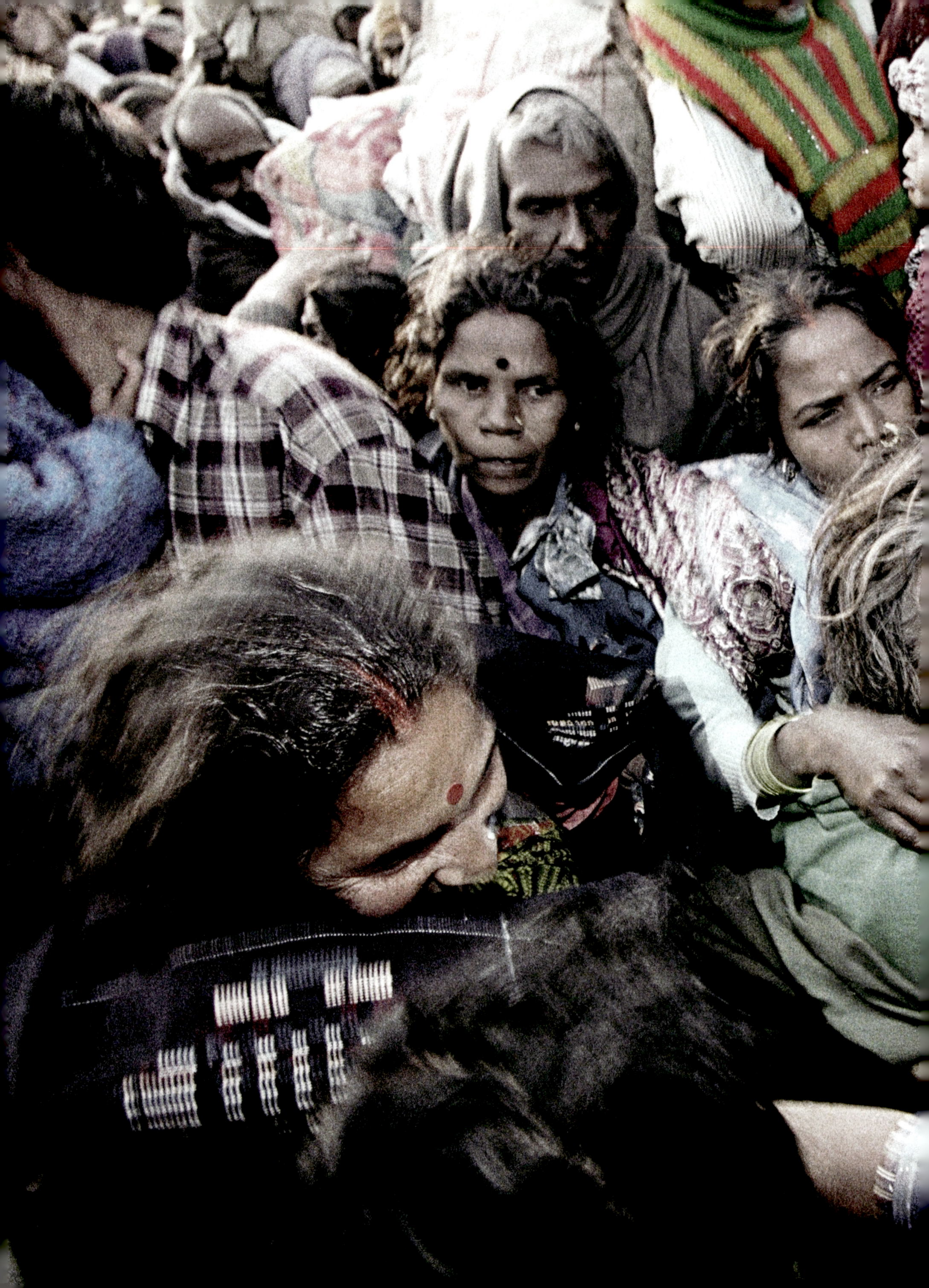

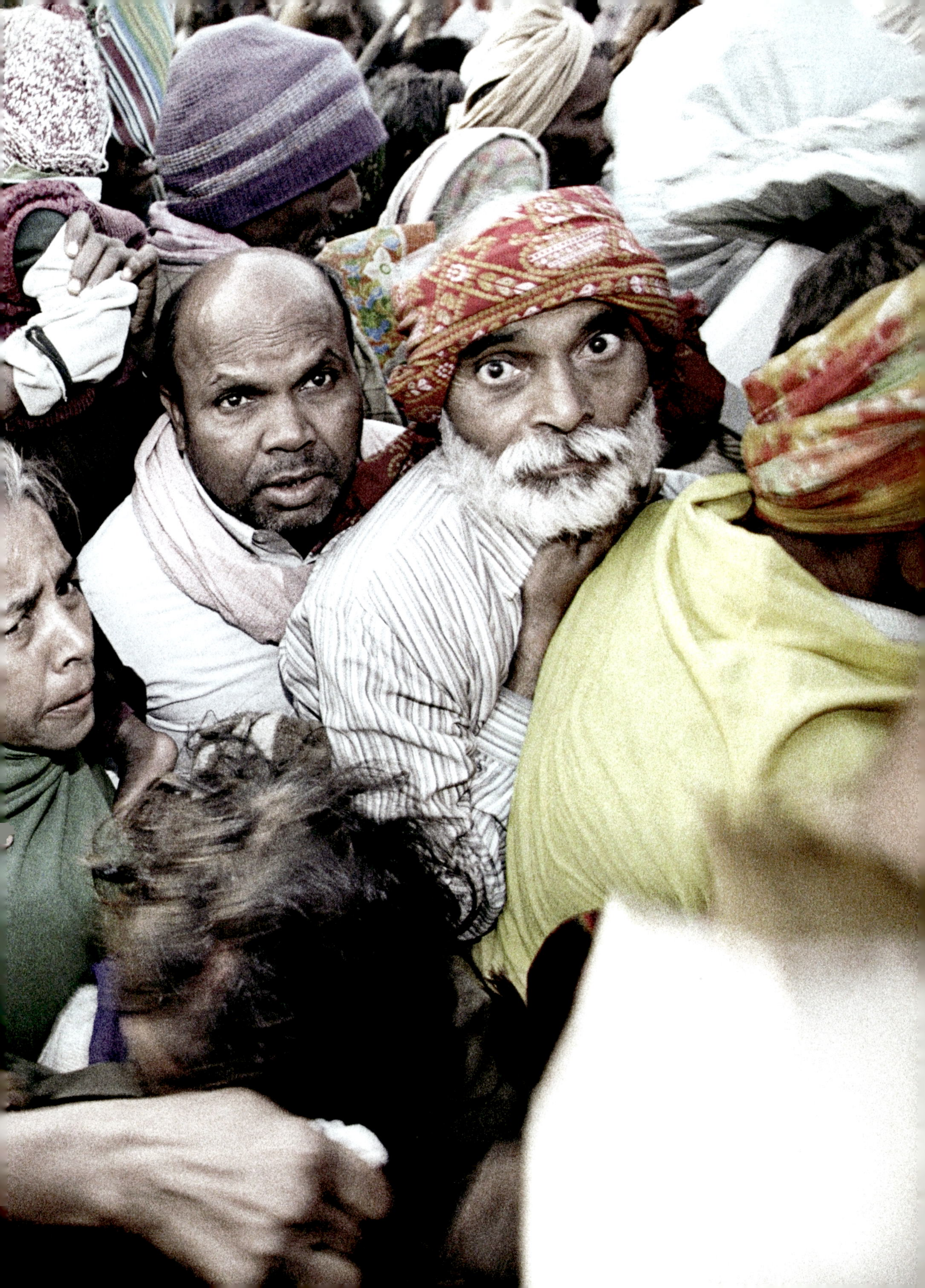

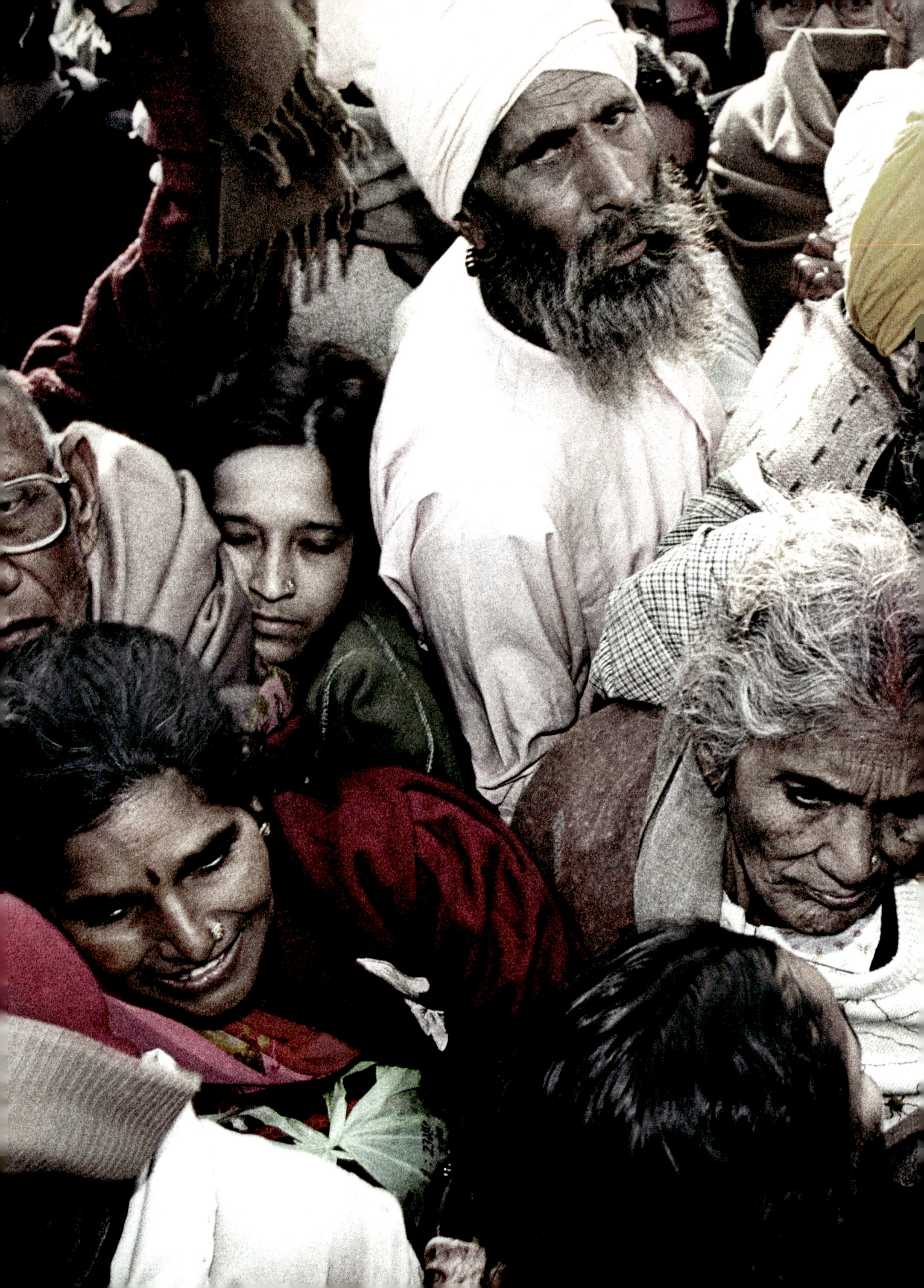

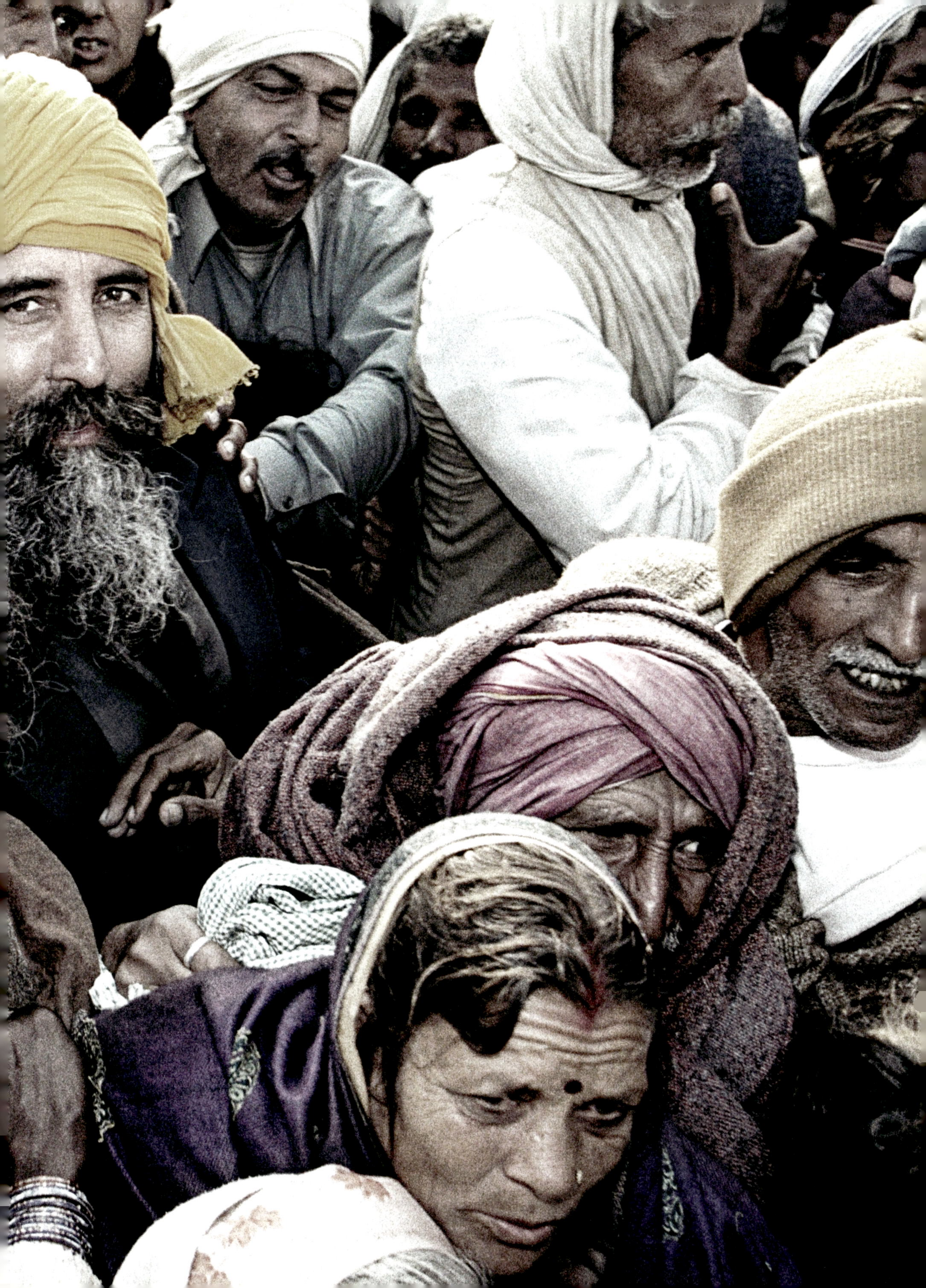

Divas+Heroes

In front of the lens, I am at the same time: the one I think I am, the one I want others to think I am, the one the photographer thinks I am, and the one he makes use of to exhibit his art. In other words, a strange action: I do not stop imitating myself. . . .
Roland Barthes, *Camera Lucida,* 1979-1980

Schmid's *Divas+Heroes* is a series of portraits of rock stars. The colors and the style of these images dates them to the late 1970s and 1980s. They tread a fine line between intimacy and star worship. Where does the private persona begin and end? Where does it suddenly become public? These and similar questions resonate in these images of the stars, however familiar some of the settings. The bizarre nature of any pose for a camera, as Barthes puts it, is seen in these pictures. Extra-large enlargements and echoes of the allures of stardom turn Schmid's series into a backdrop against which the drama of self and public perception is played out.

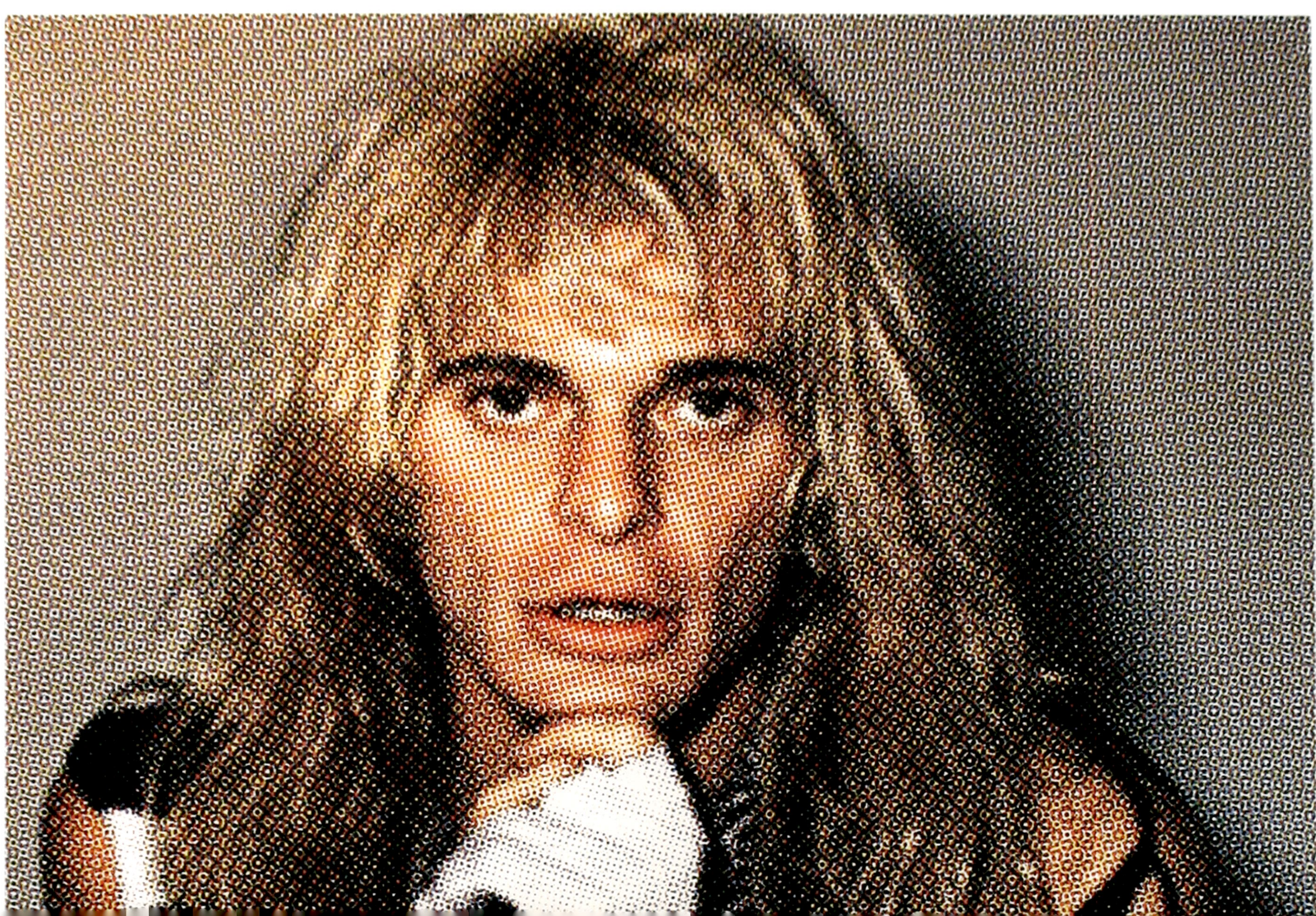

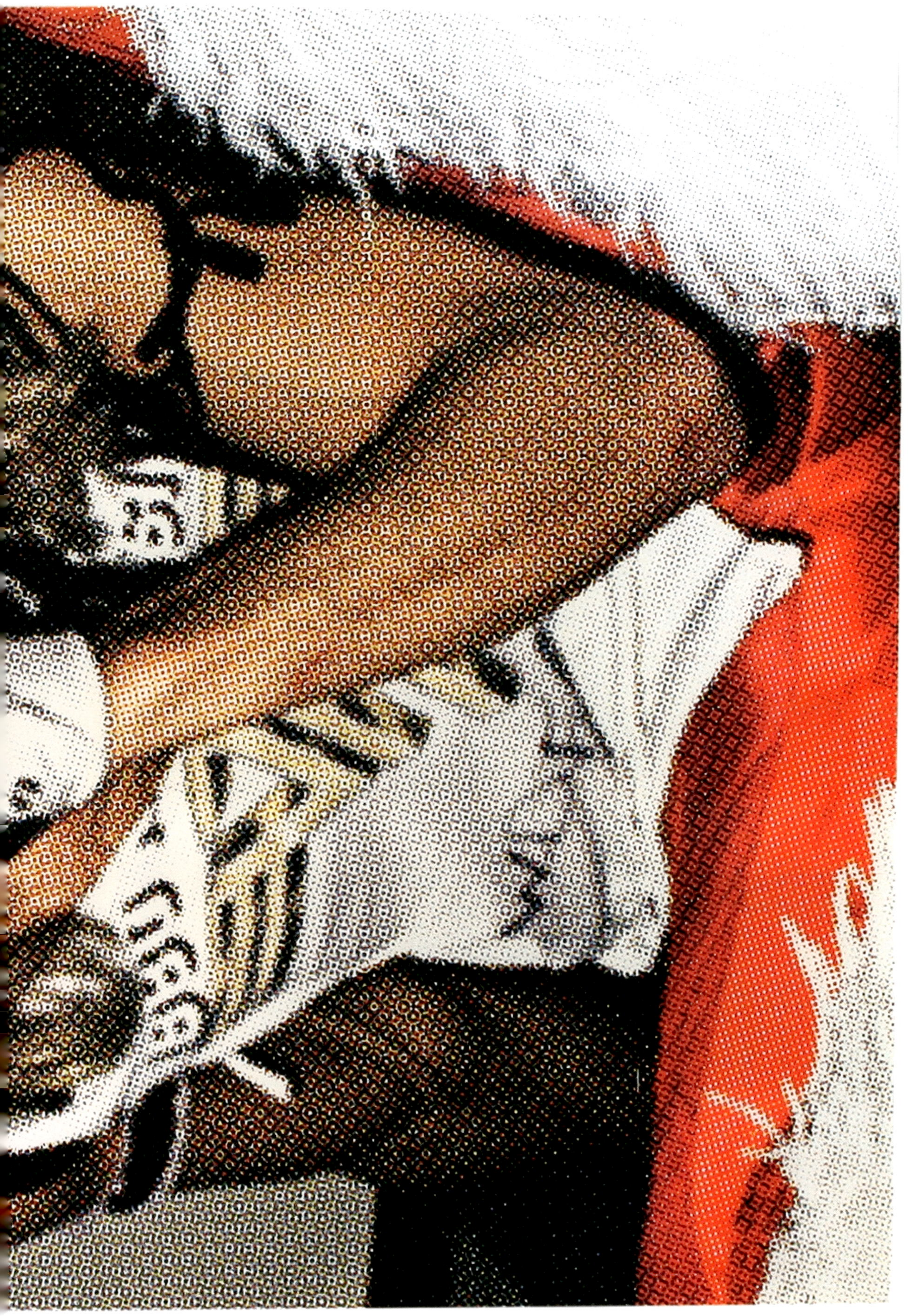

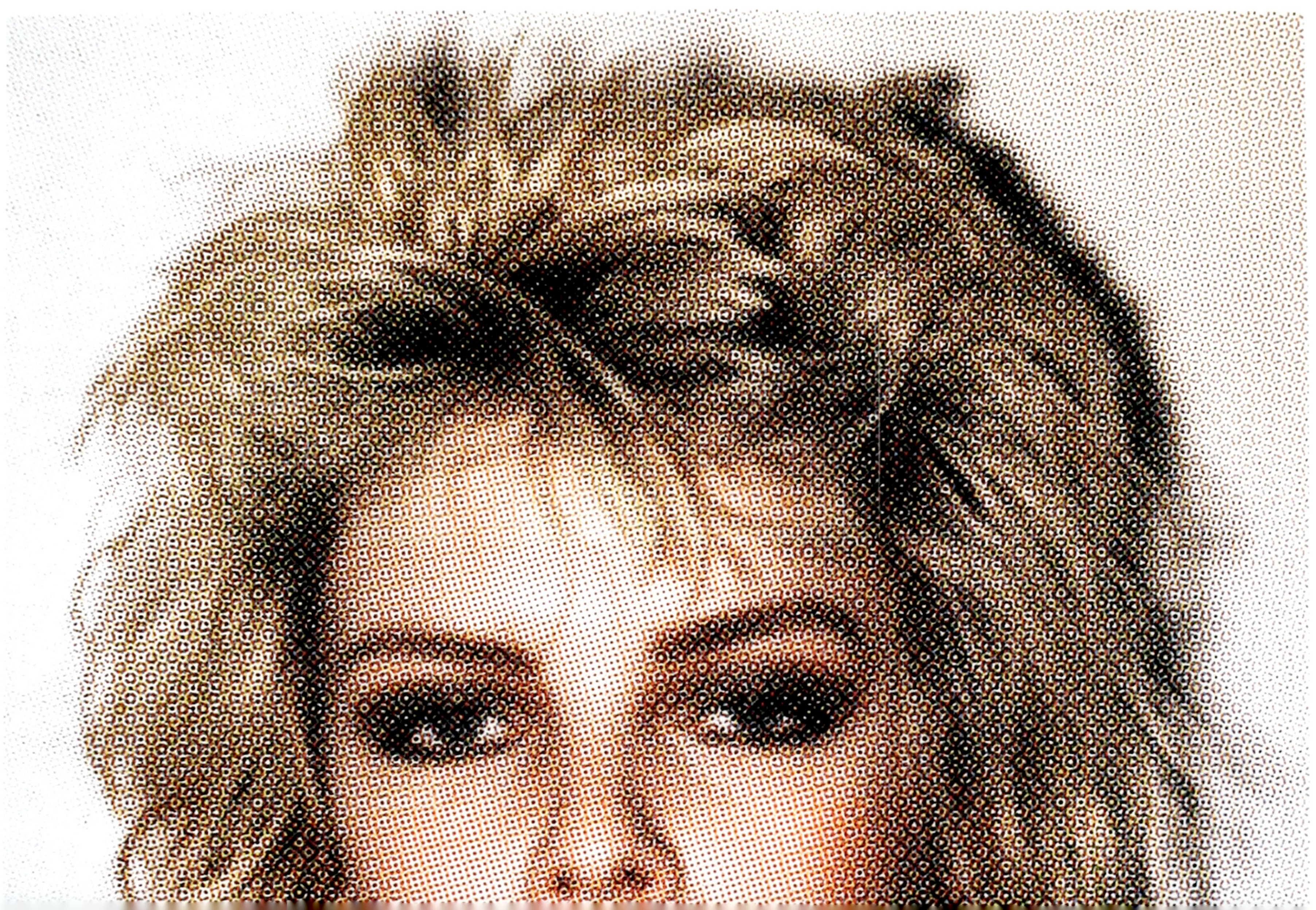

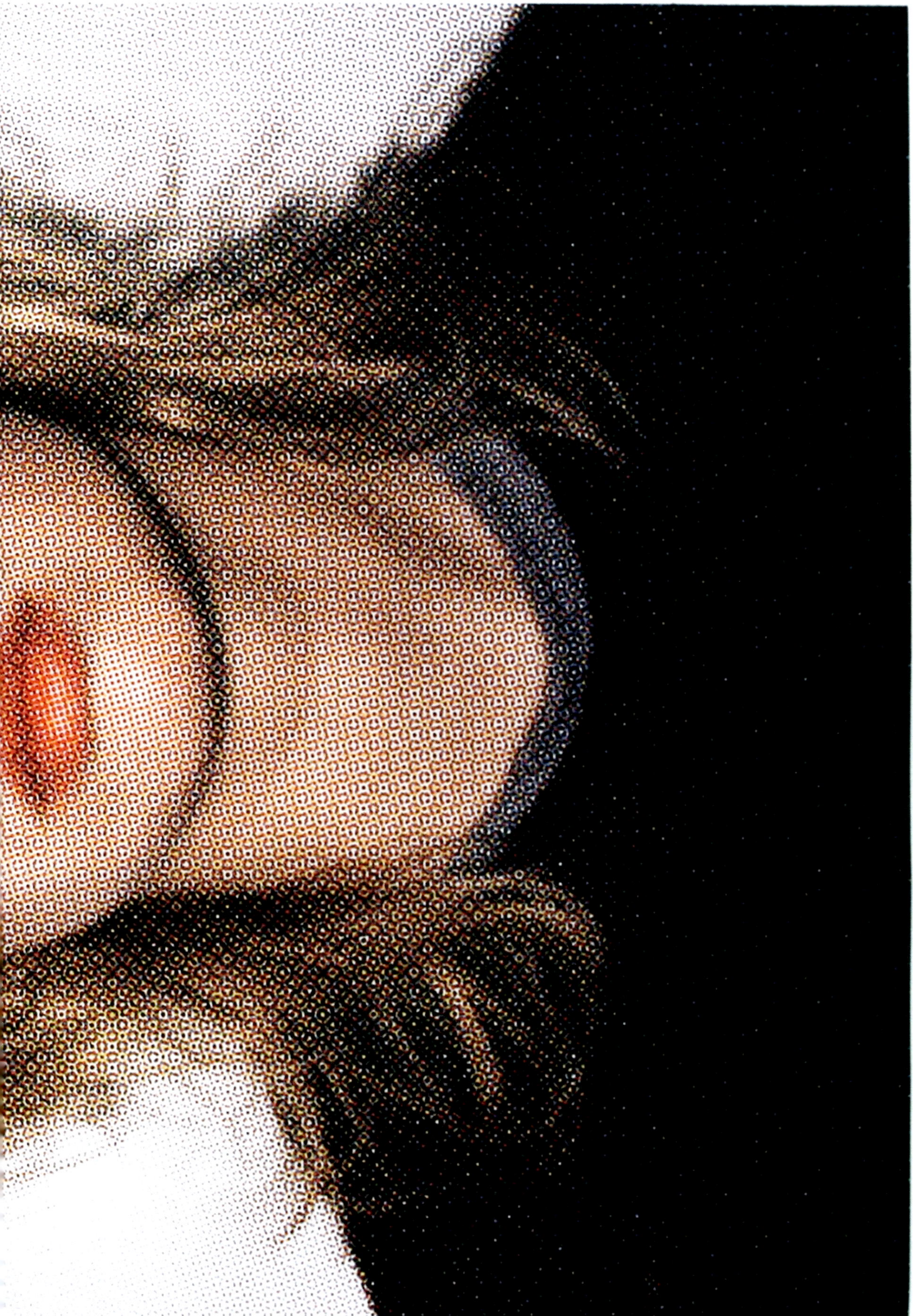

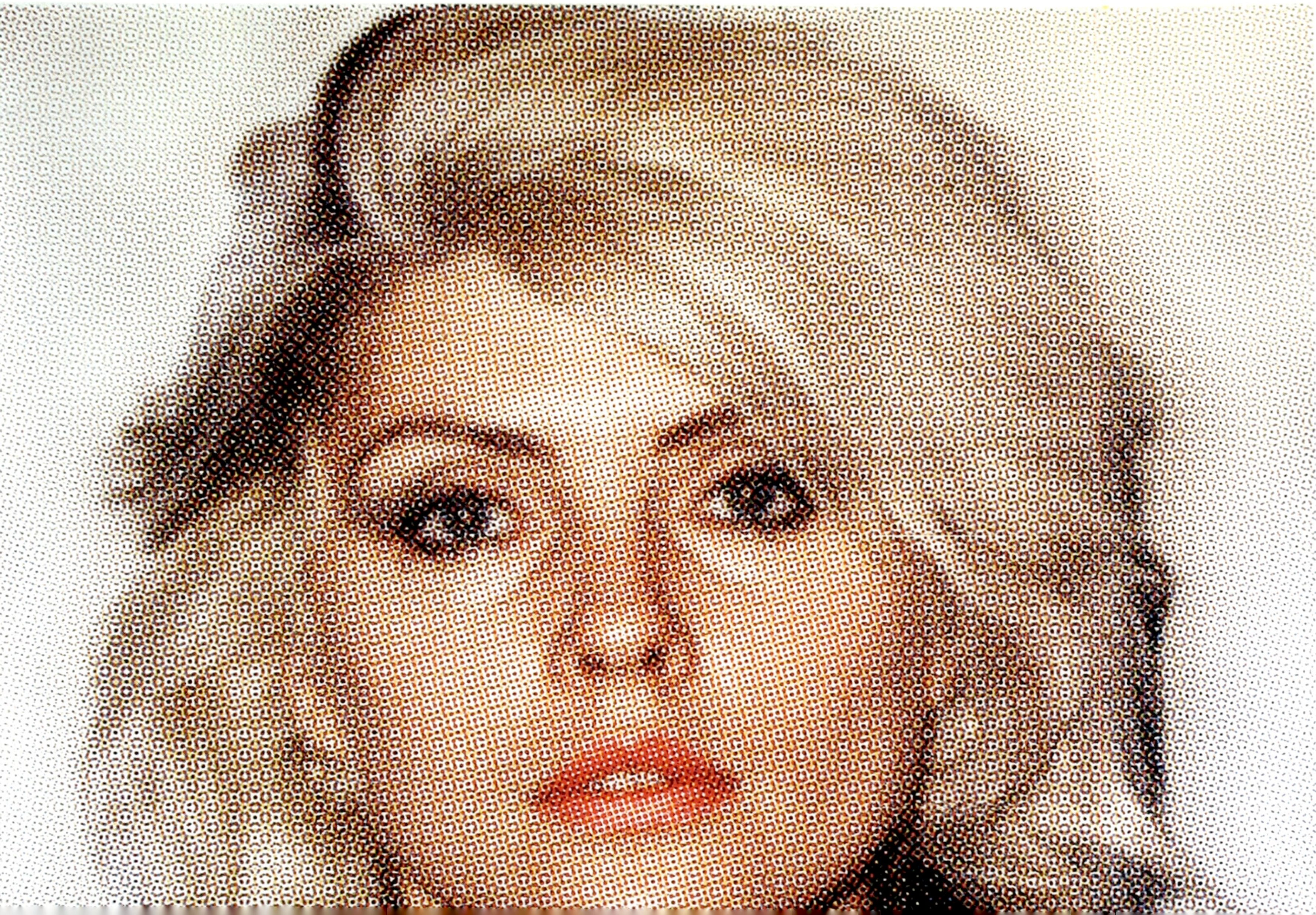

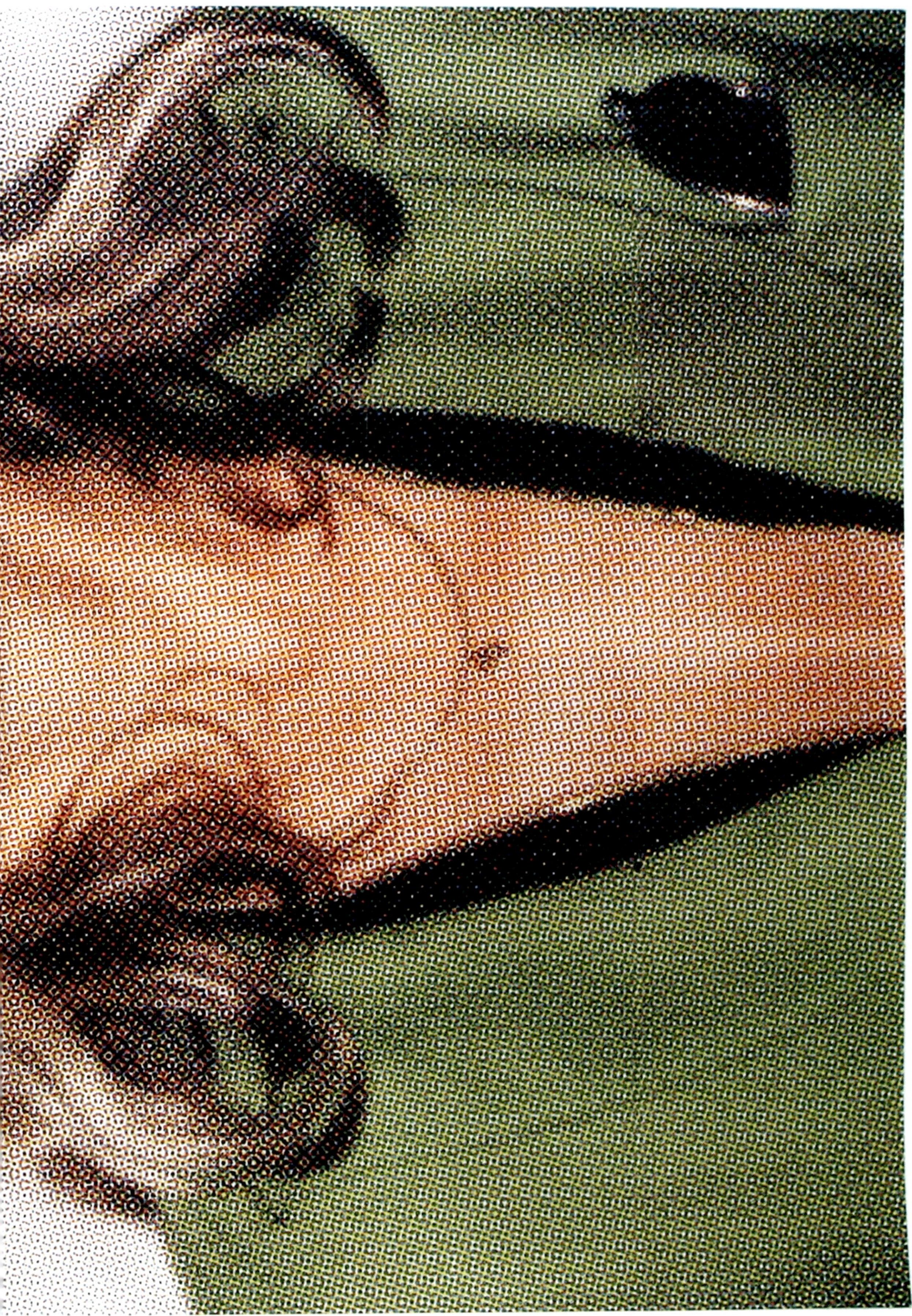

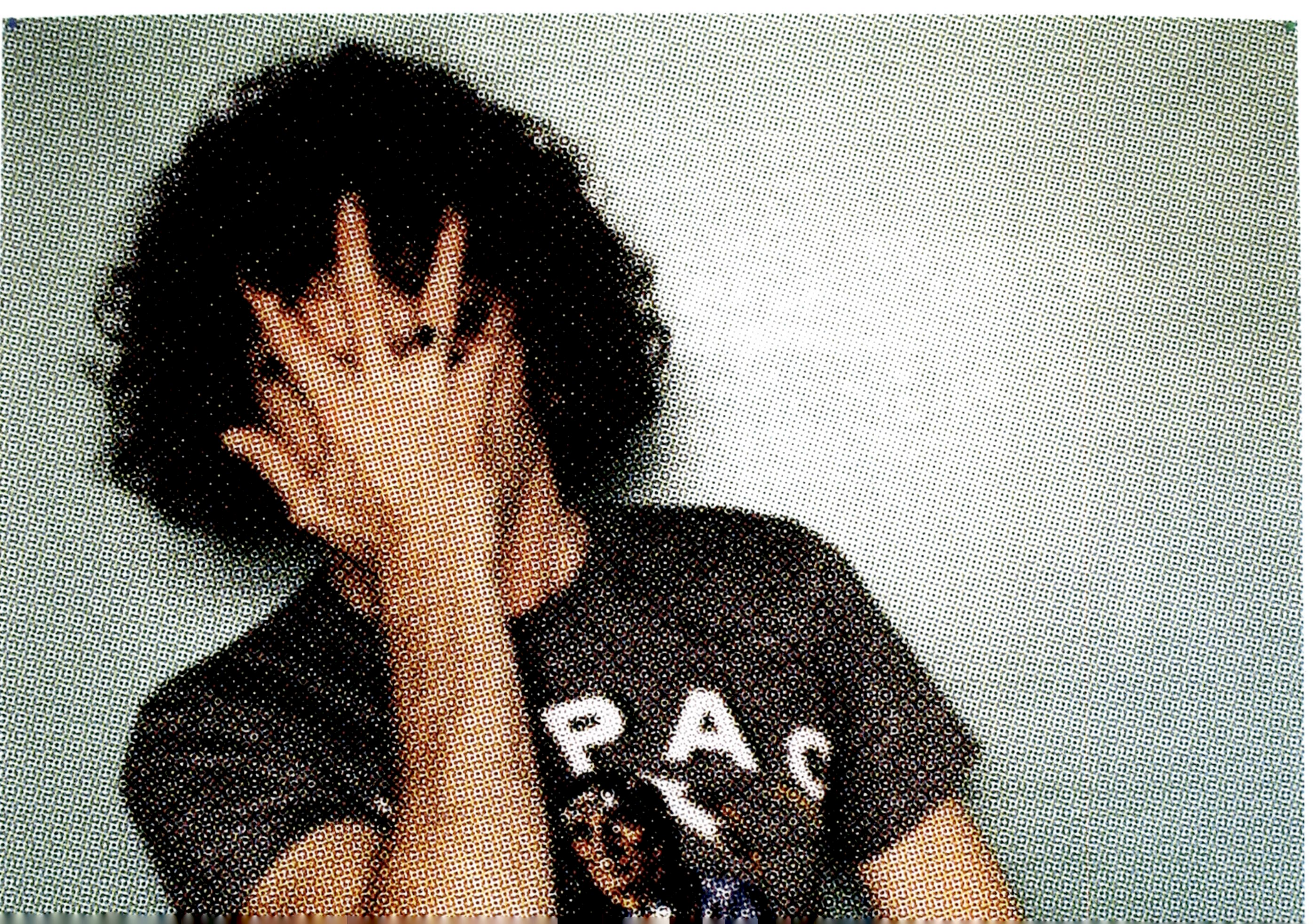

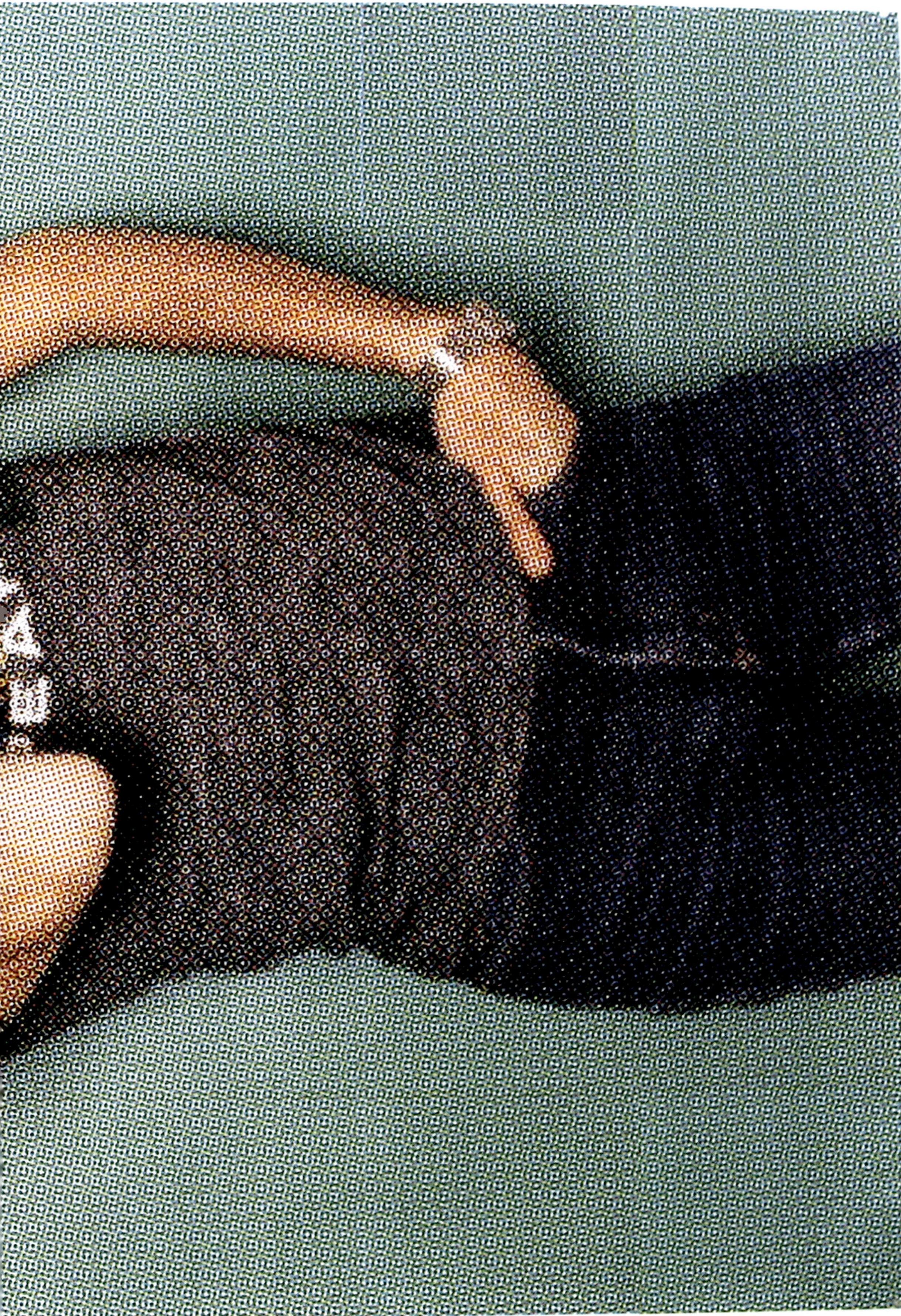

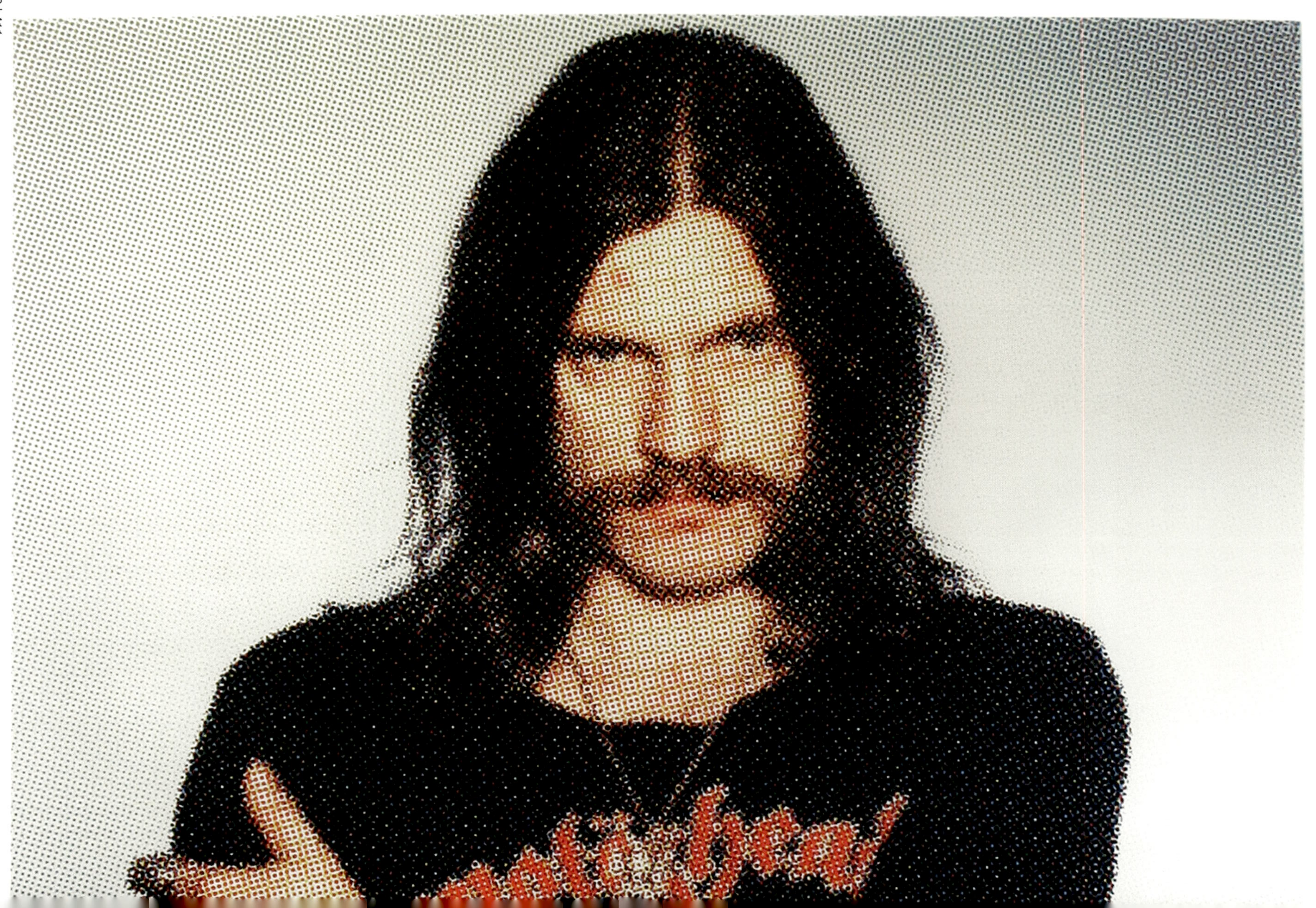

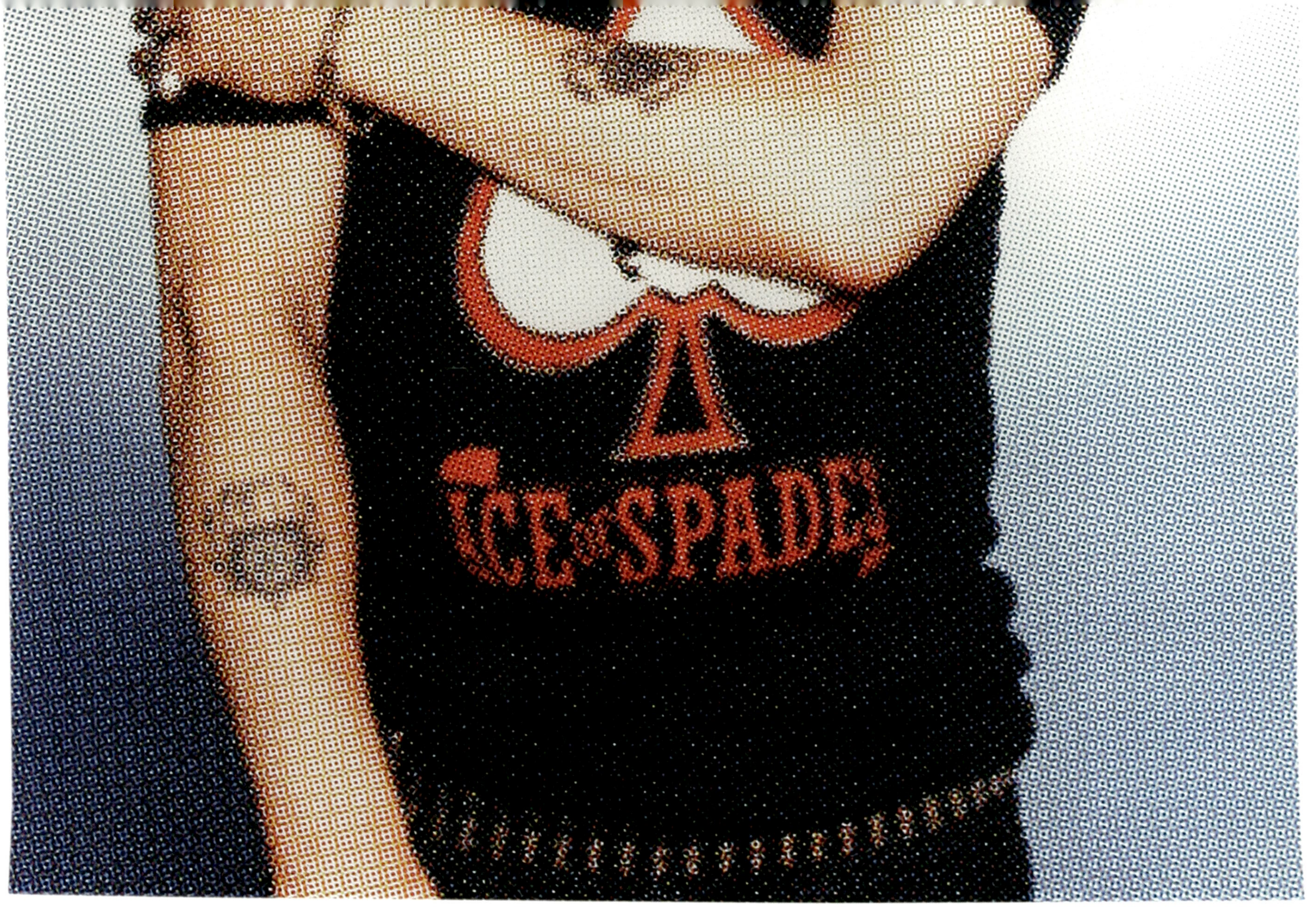
ACE OF SPADES

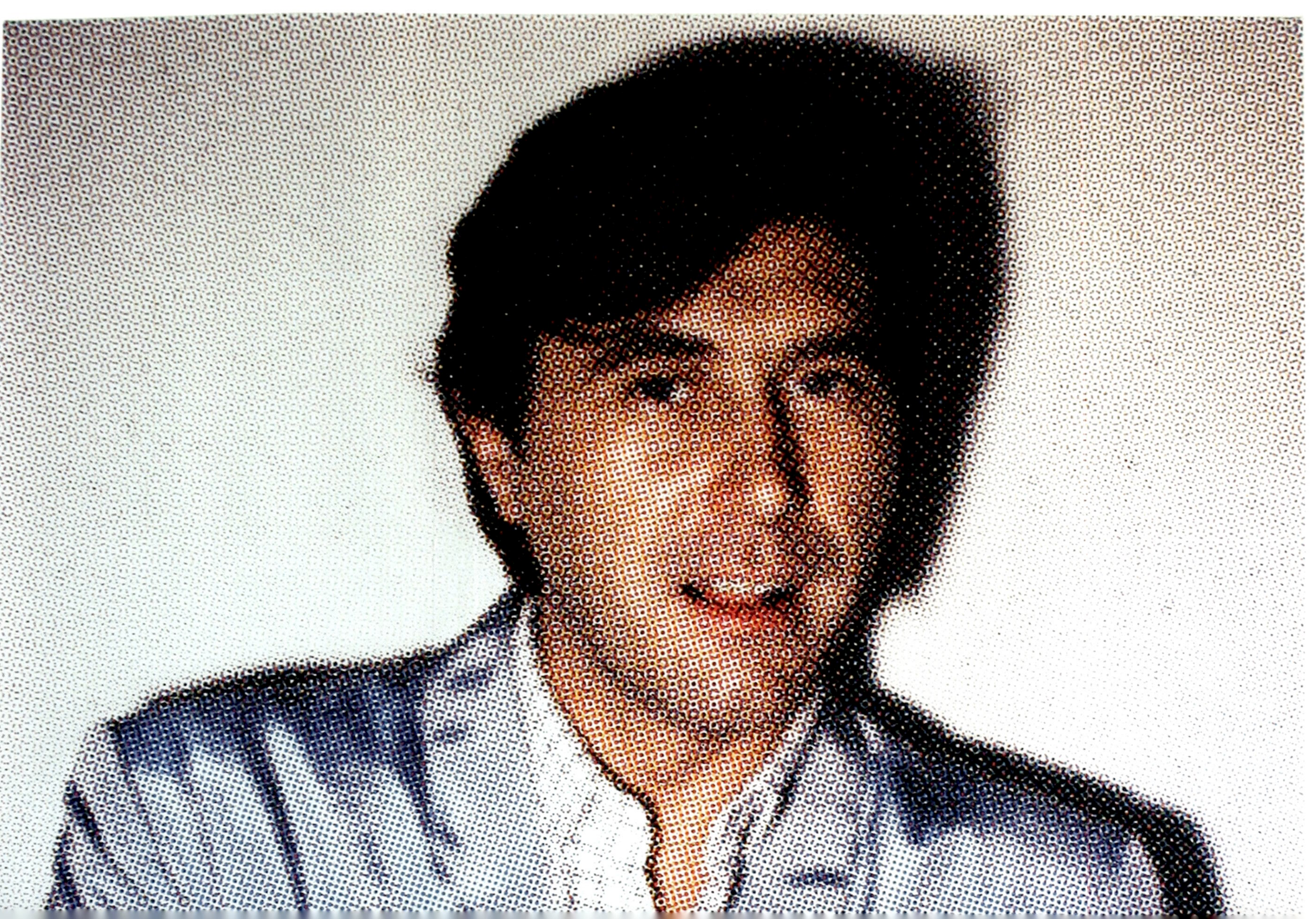

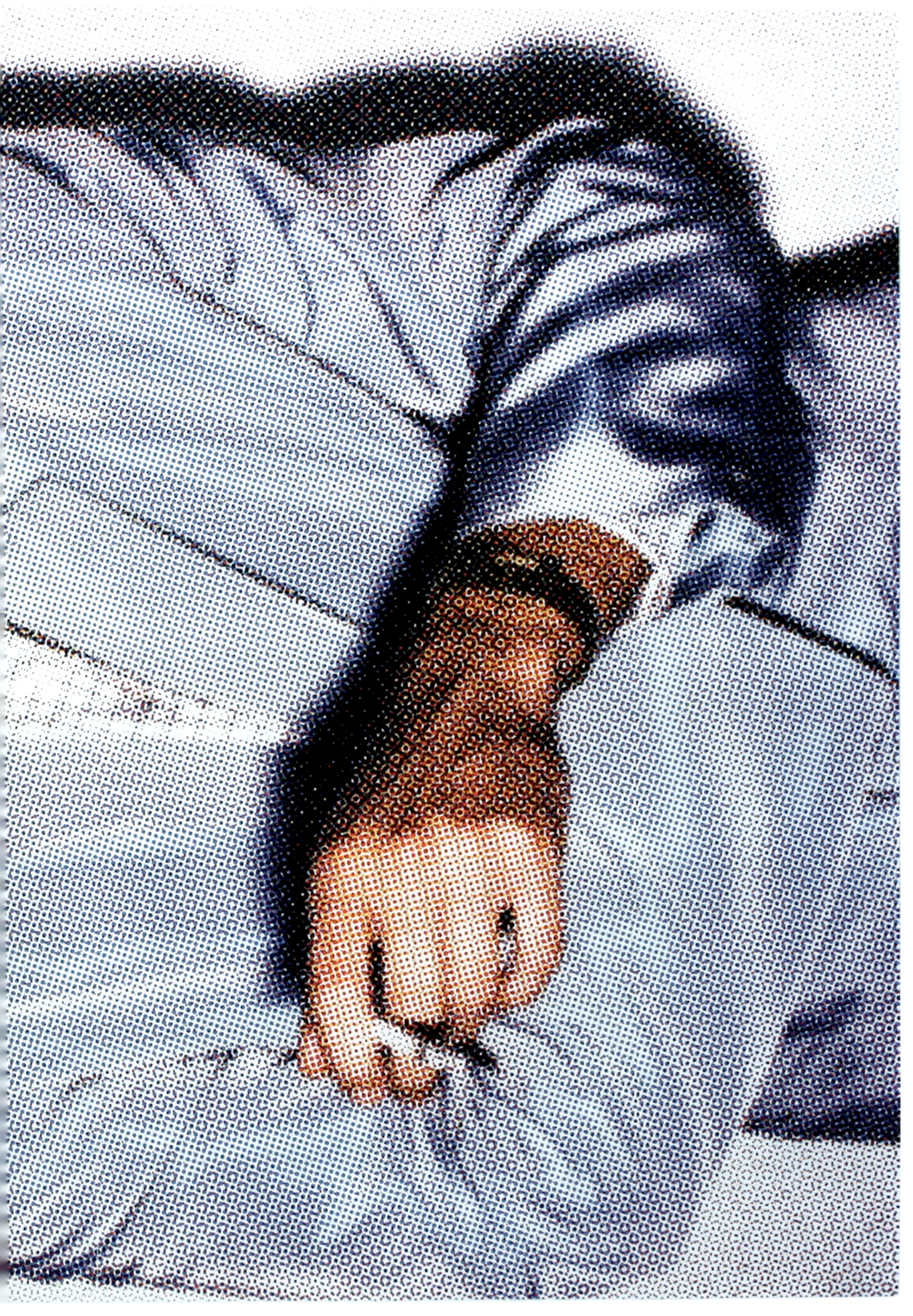

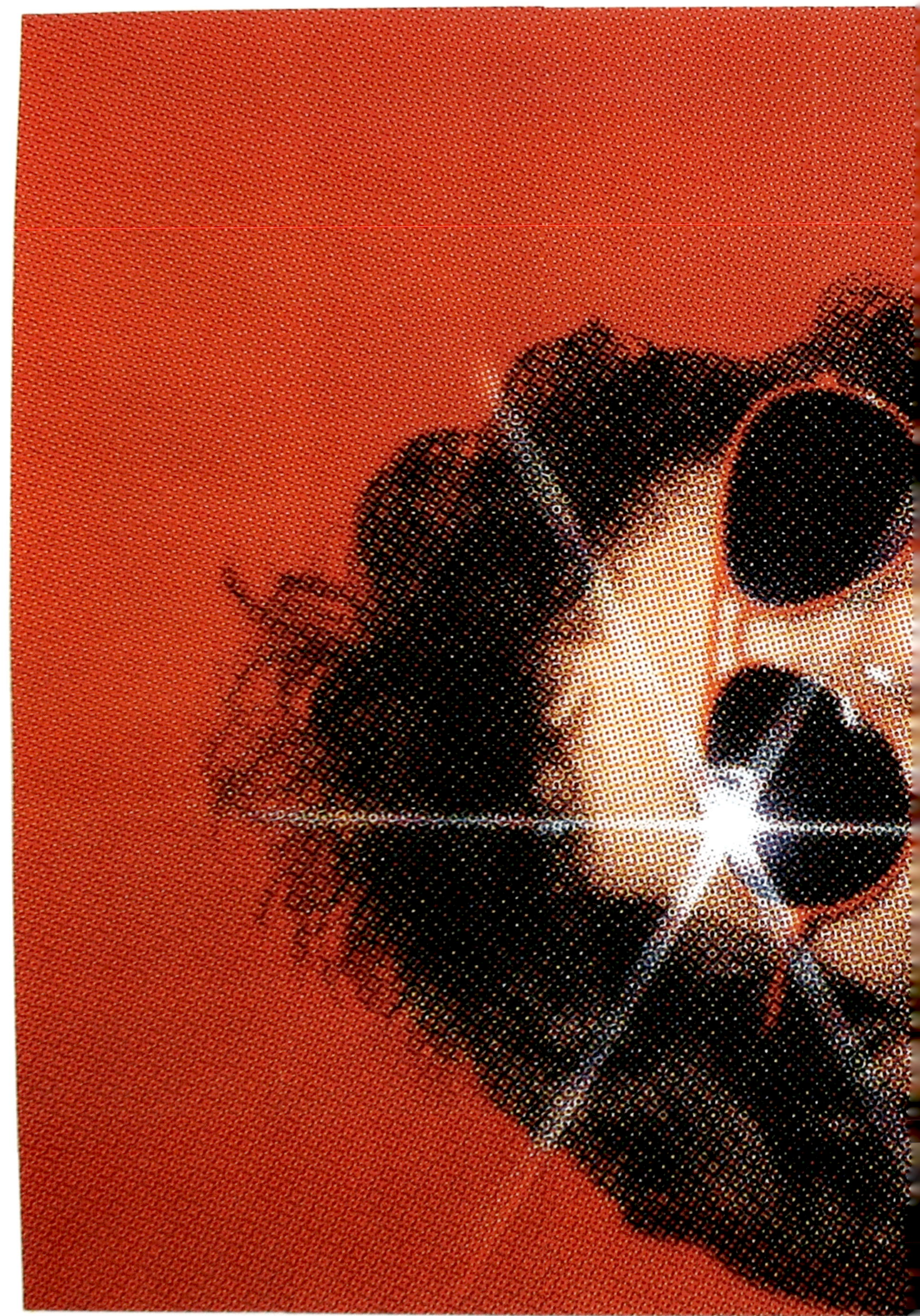

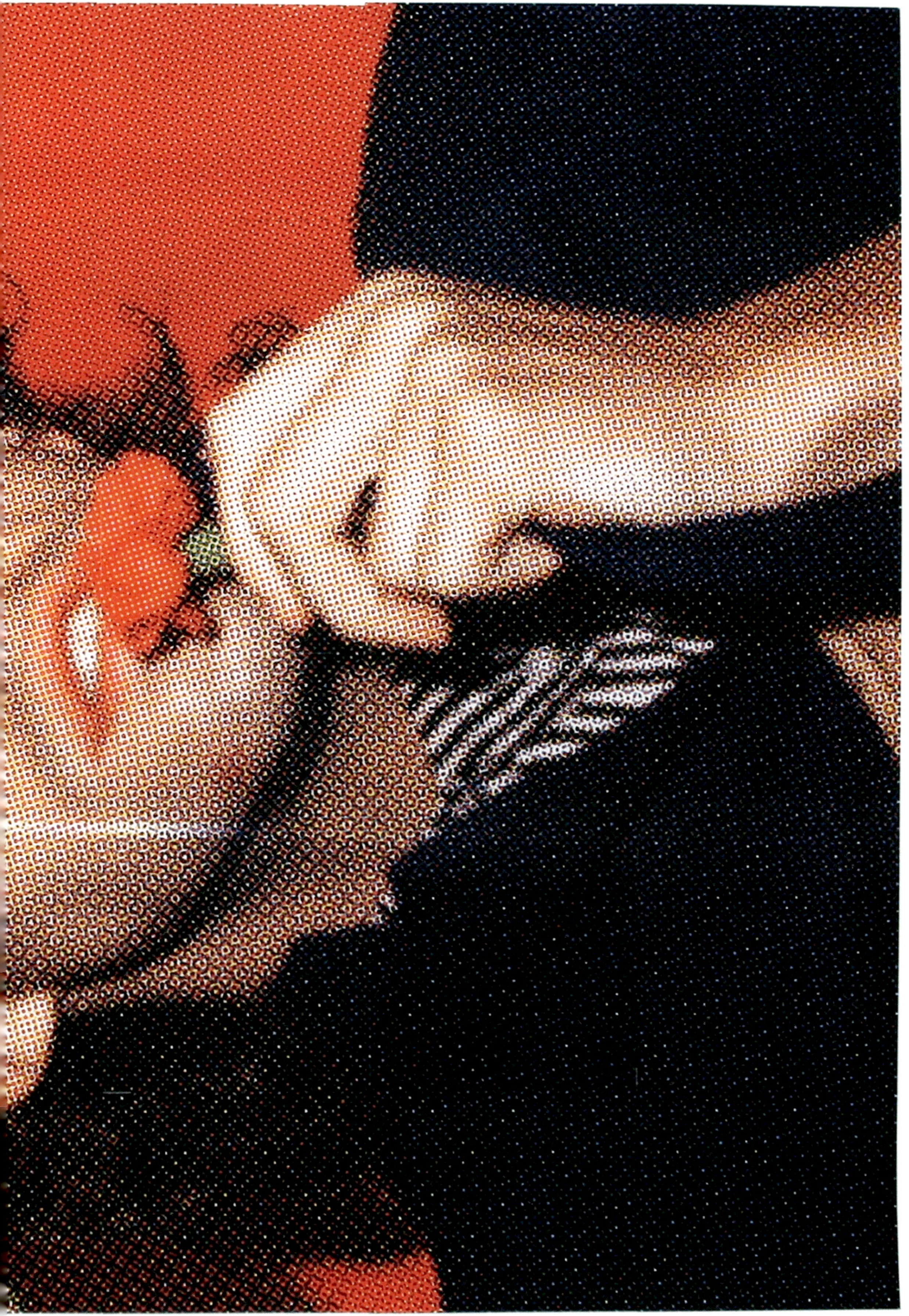

Dani & Lani

Now, once I feel myself observed by the lens, everything changes: I constitute myself in the process of "posing," I instantaneously make another body for myself, I transform myself in advance into an image. This transformation is an active one: I feel that the Photograph creates my body or mortifies it, according to its caprice. . . .
Roland Barthes, *Camera Lucida,* 1979-1980

The series *Dani & Lani* encapsulates the transformation that ensues through photography. Whereas the body, in the pose of a warrior, exudes self-confidence, the trousers and shirt communicate a sense of defeat. Clothes maketh the man, but here the effects are seen in the medium of clothing in the context of a culture that cannot survive much longer like this. In this series the nature of photography—always to represent and to reproduce the past—is turned on its head and instead conveys a memory of tomorrow. In the light of the masquerade, Schmid dares to countenance a possible "could be . . . ," a hypothesis of another essence of photographic images, for what we see is only ever a fragment of space and time.

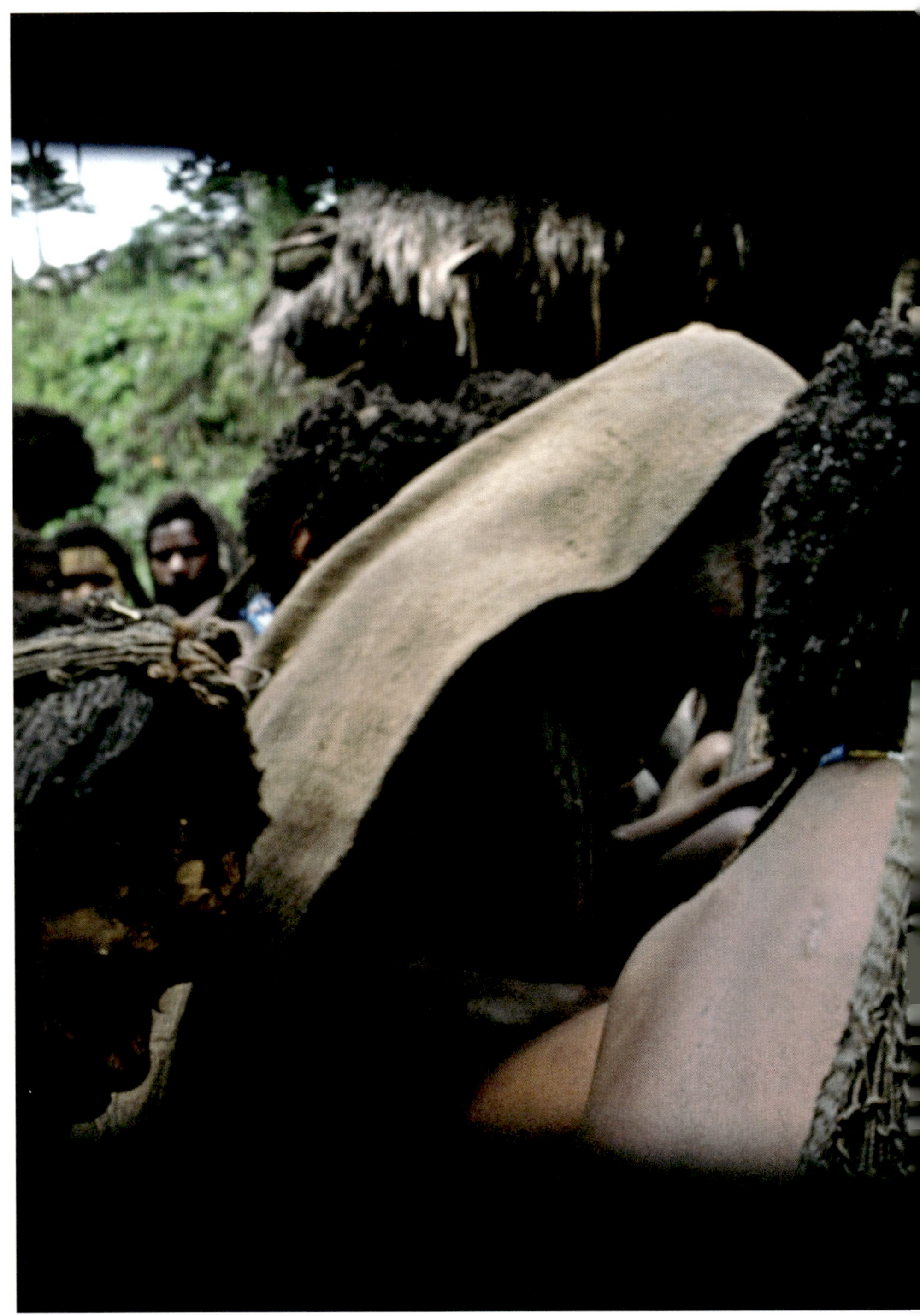

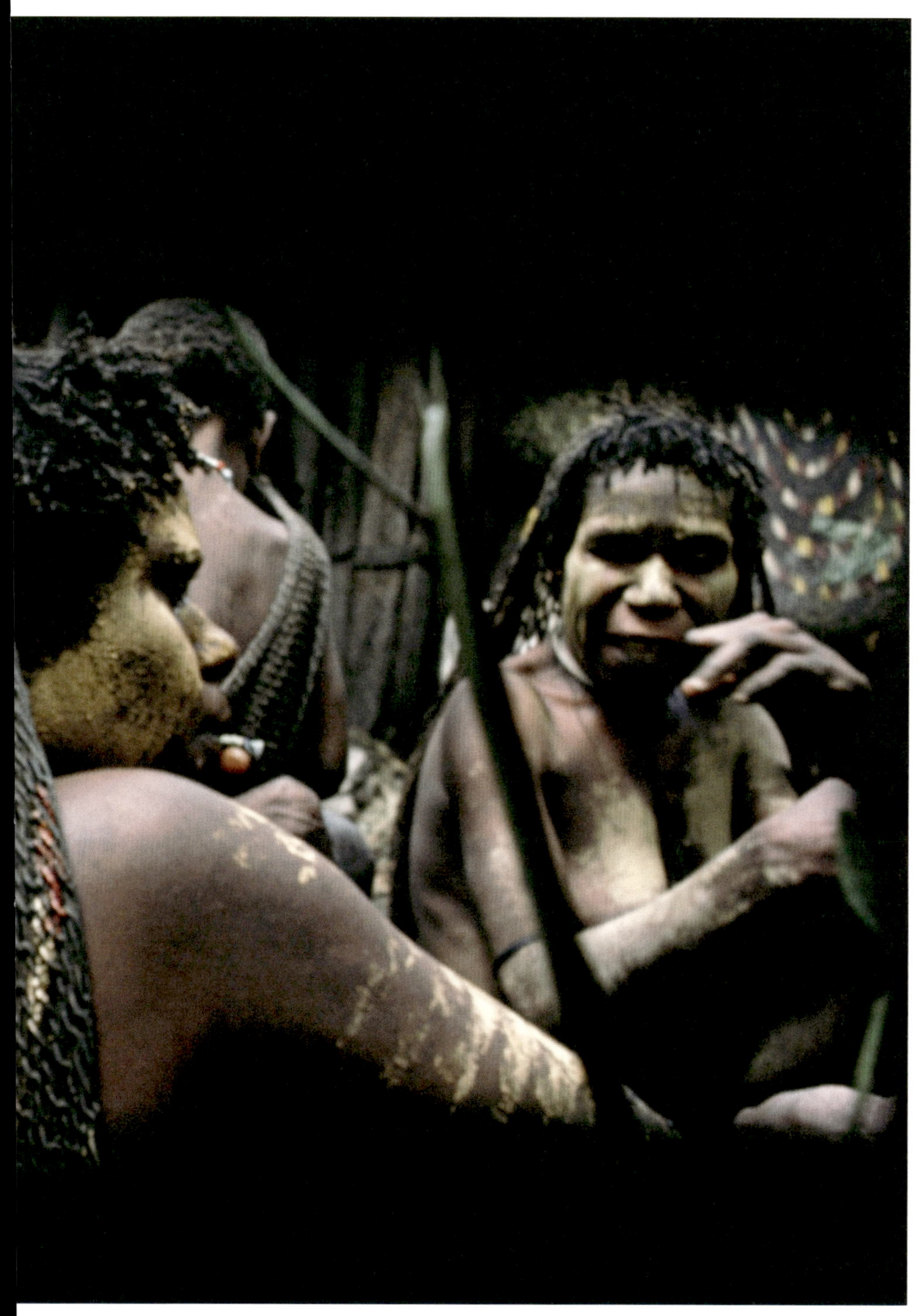

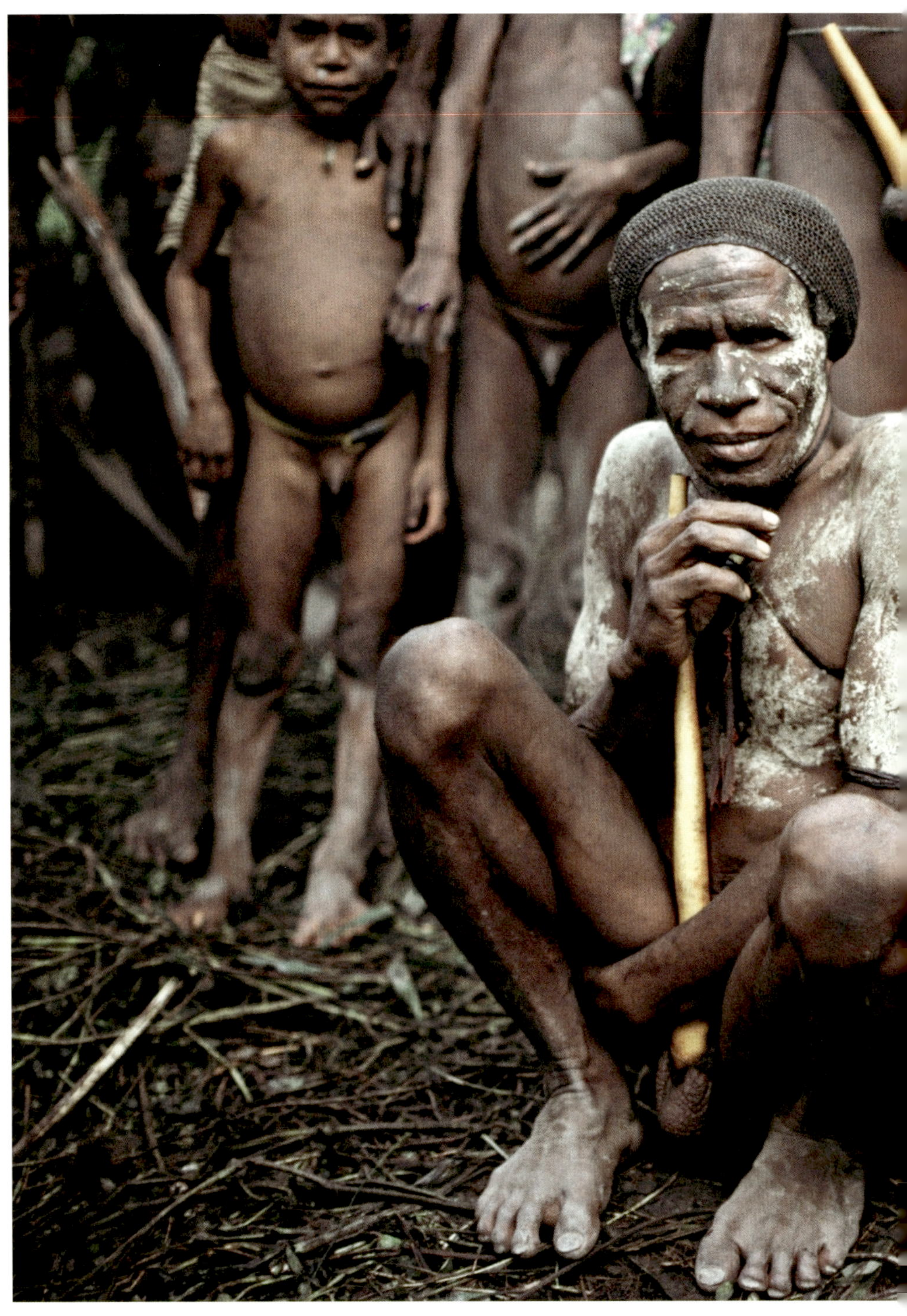

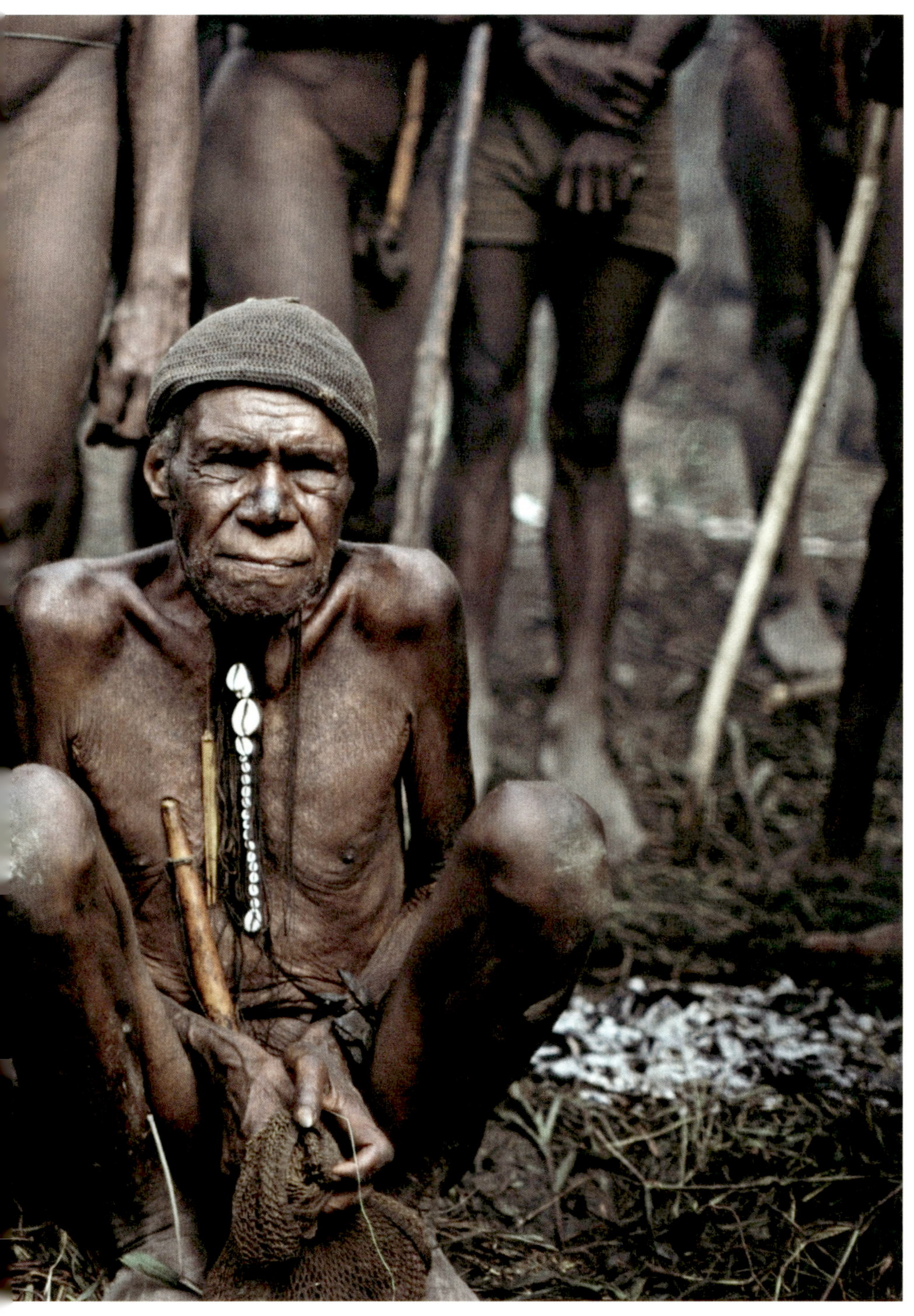

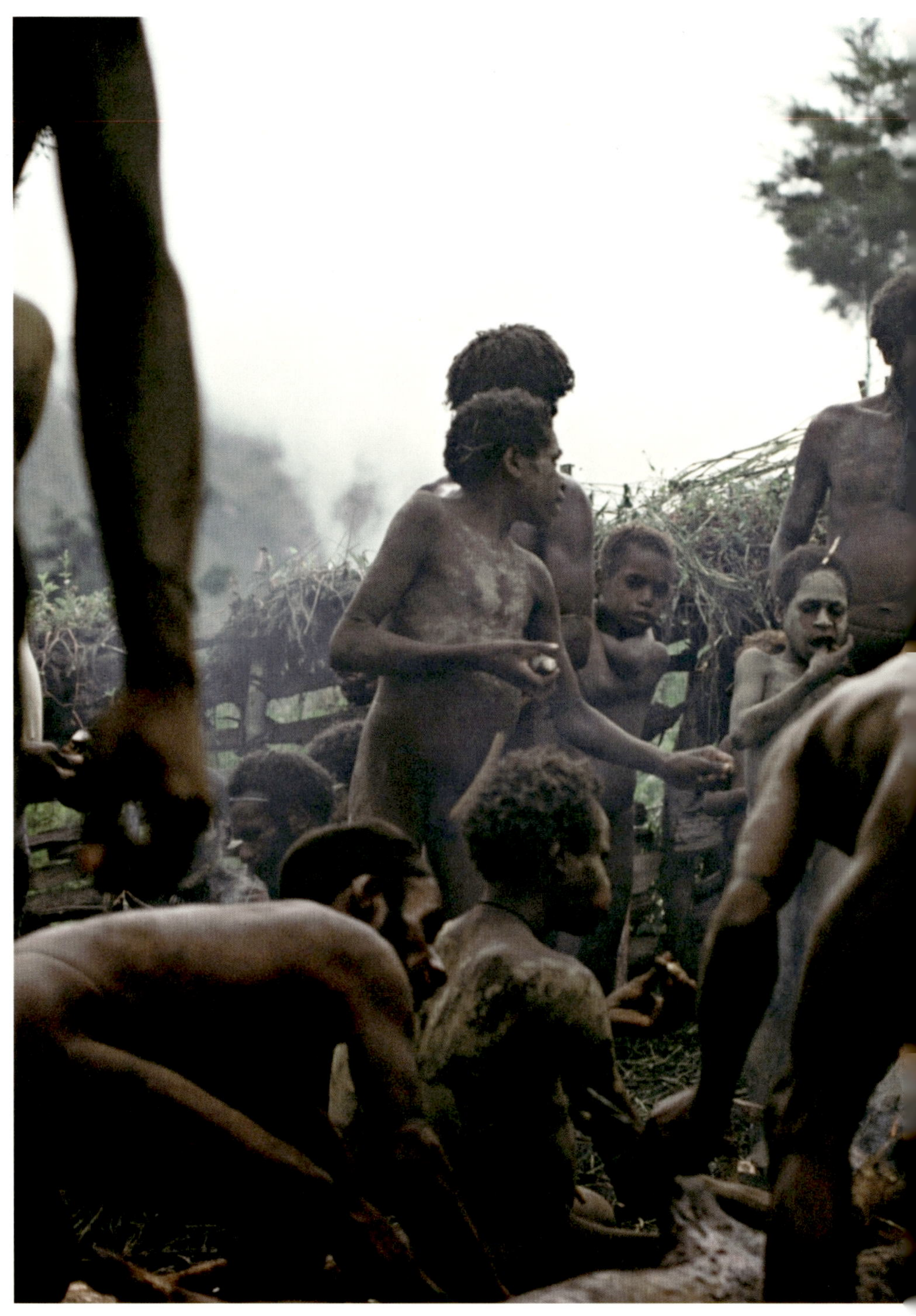

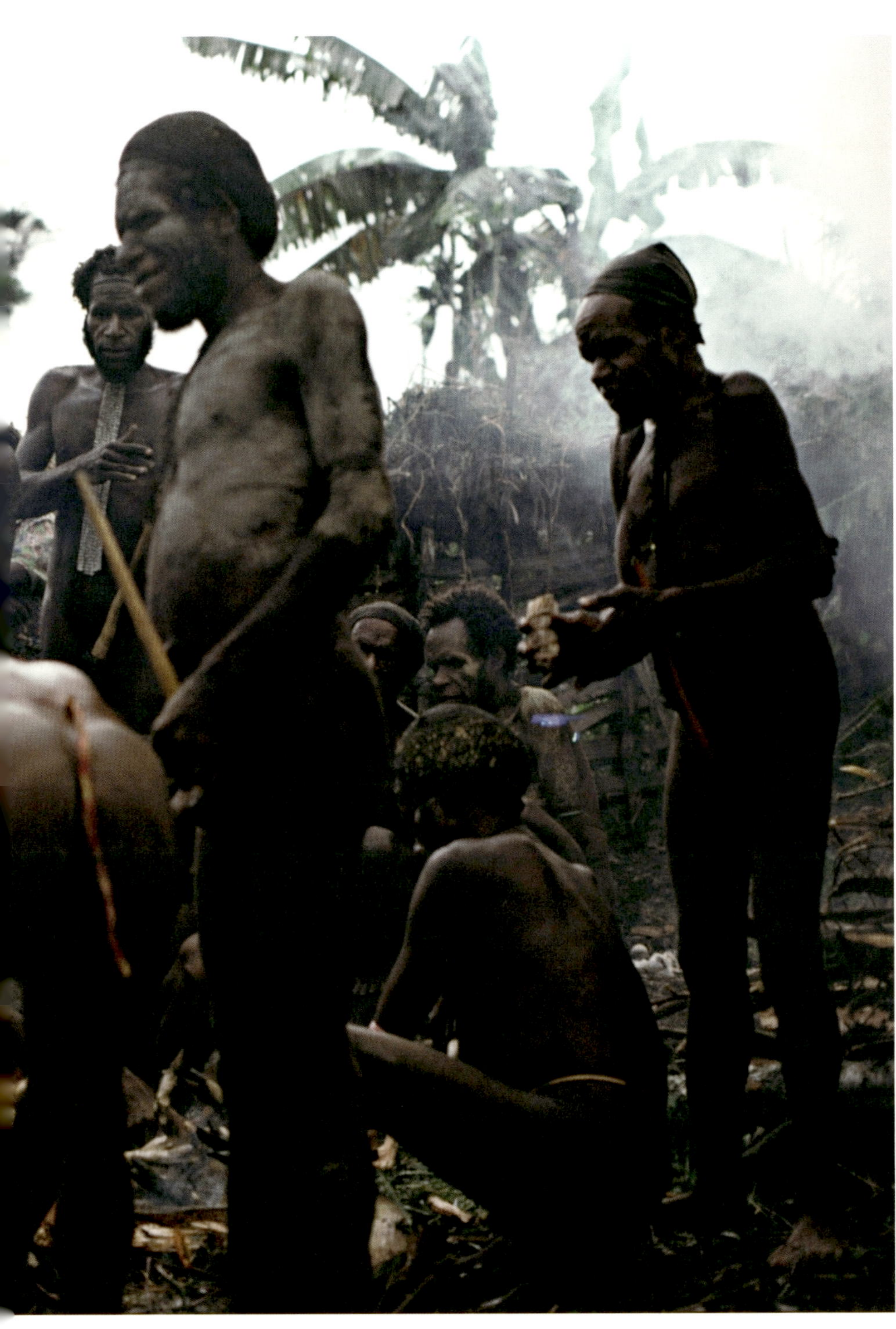

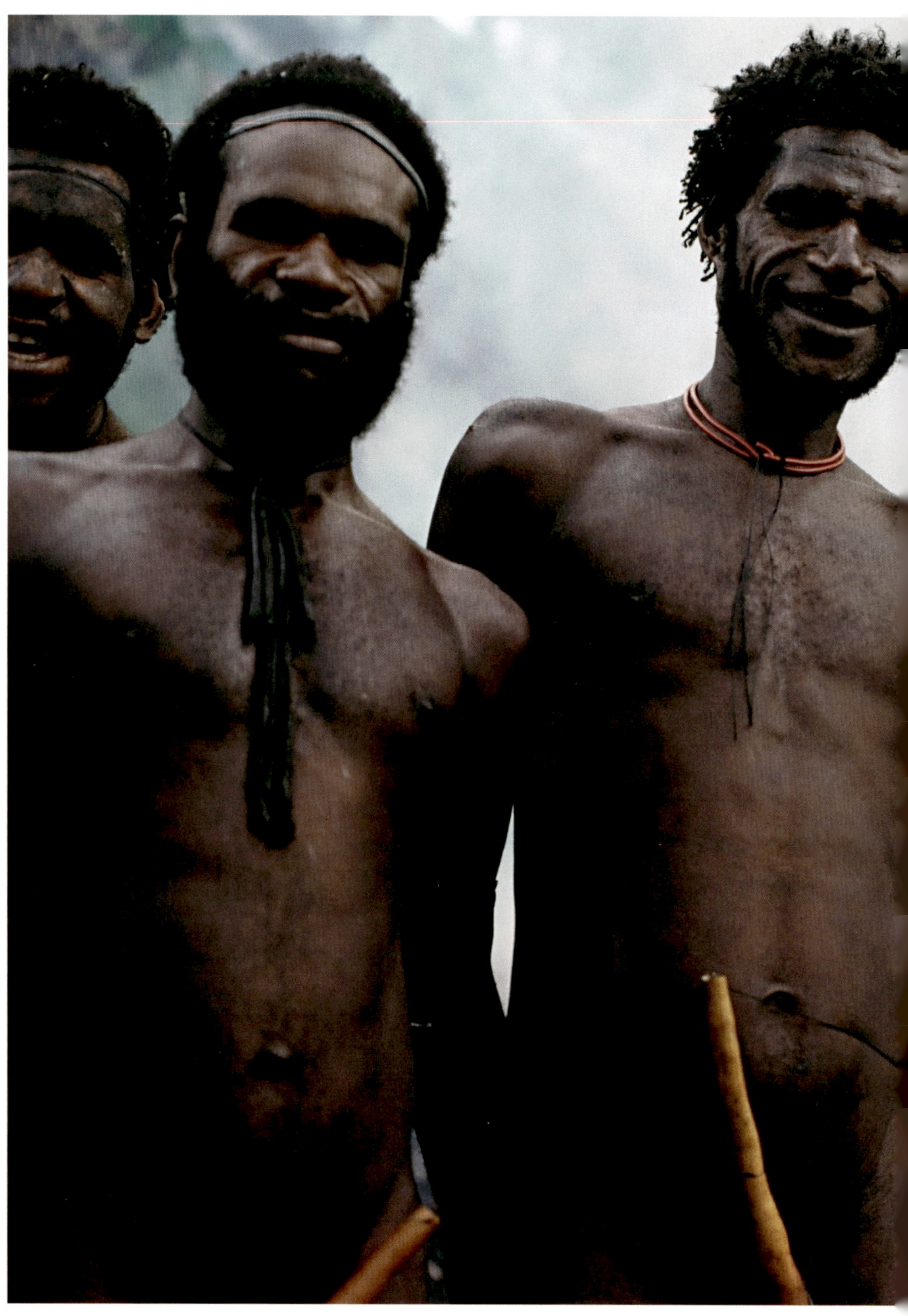

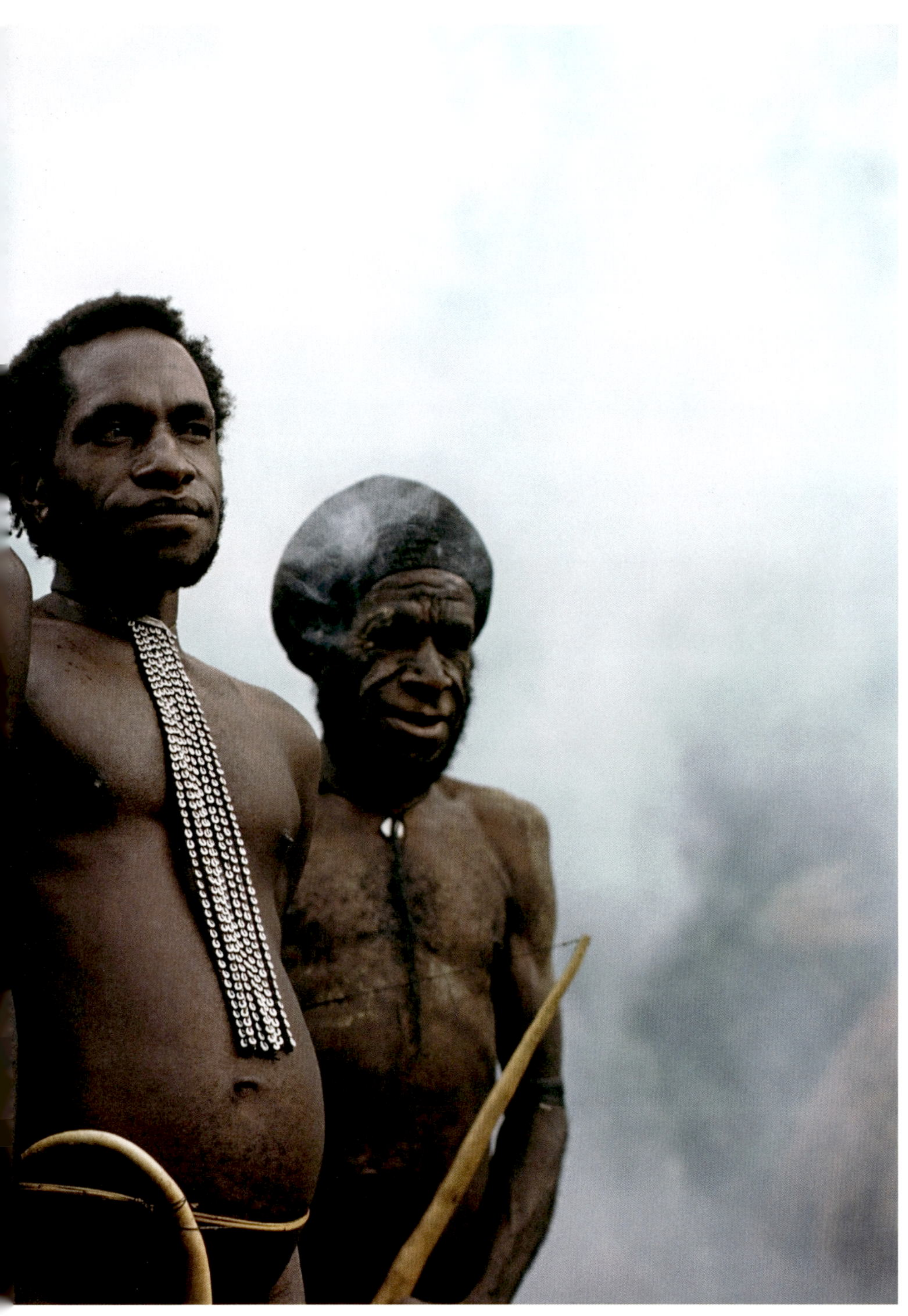

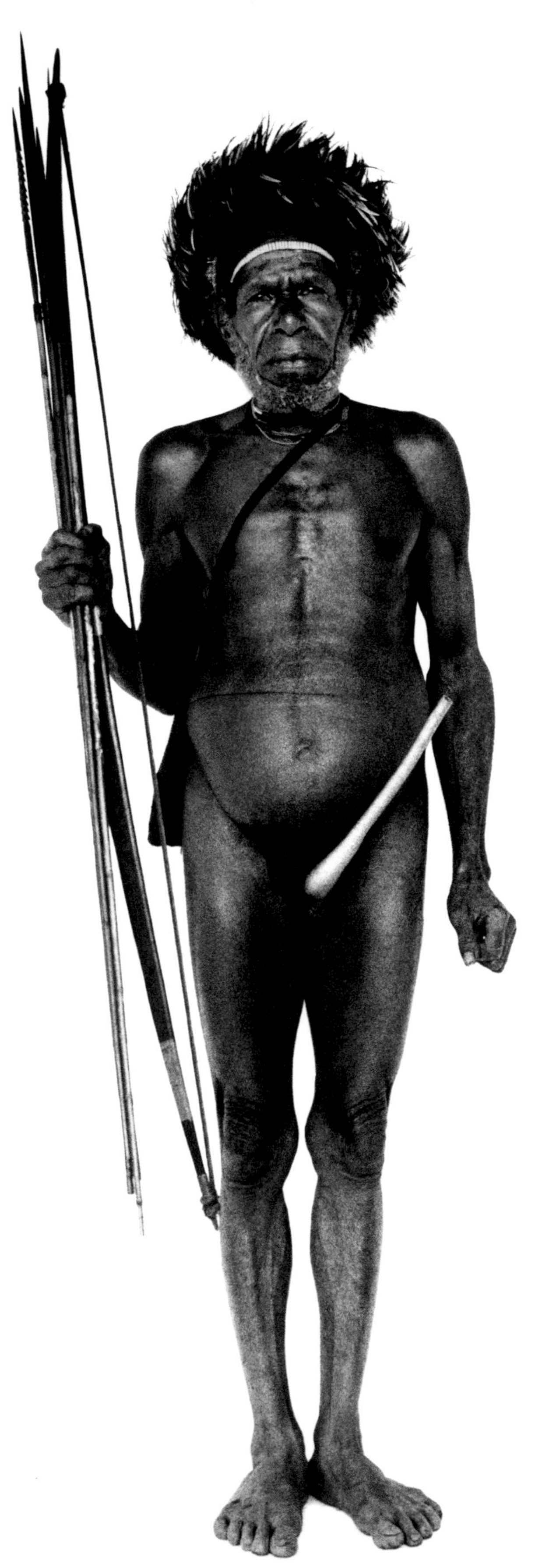

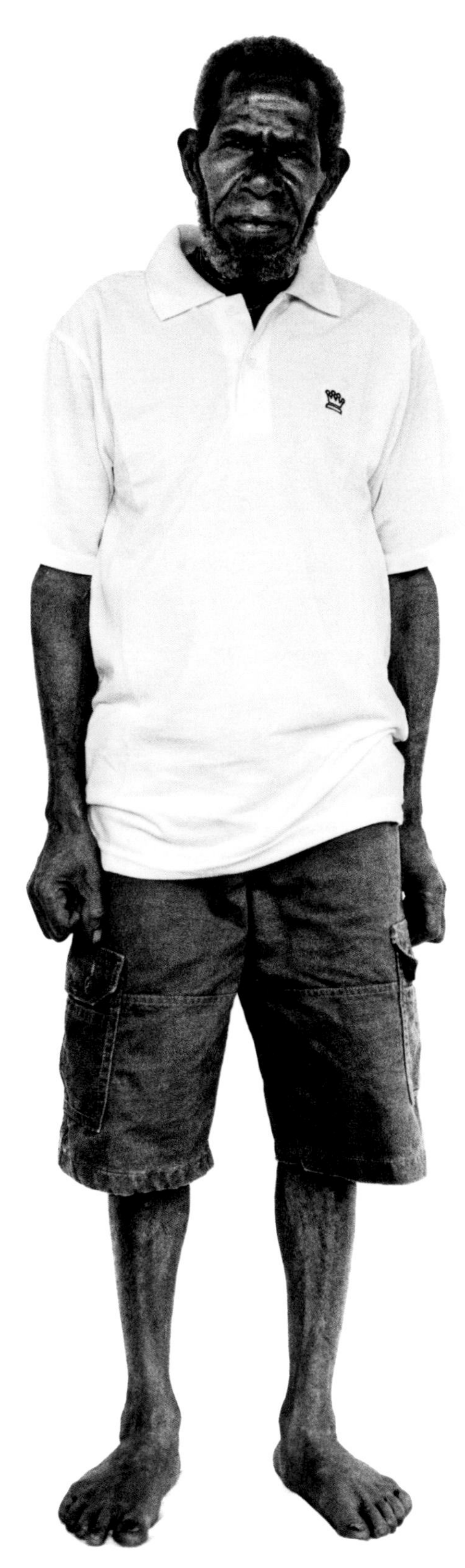

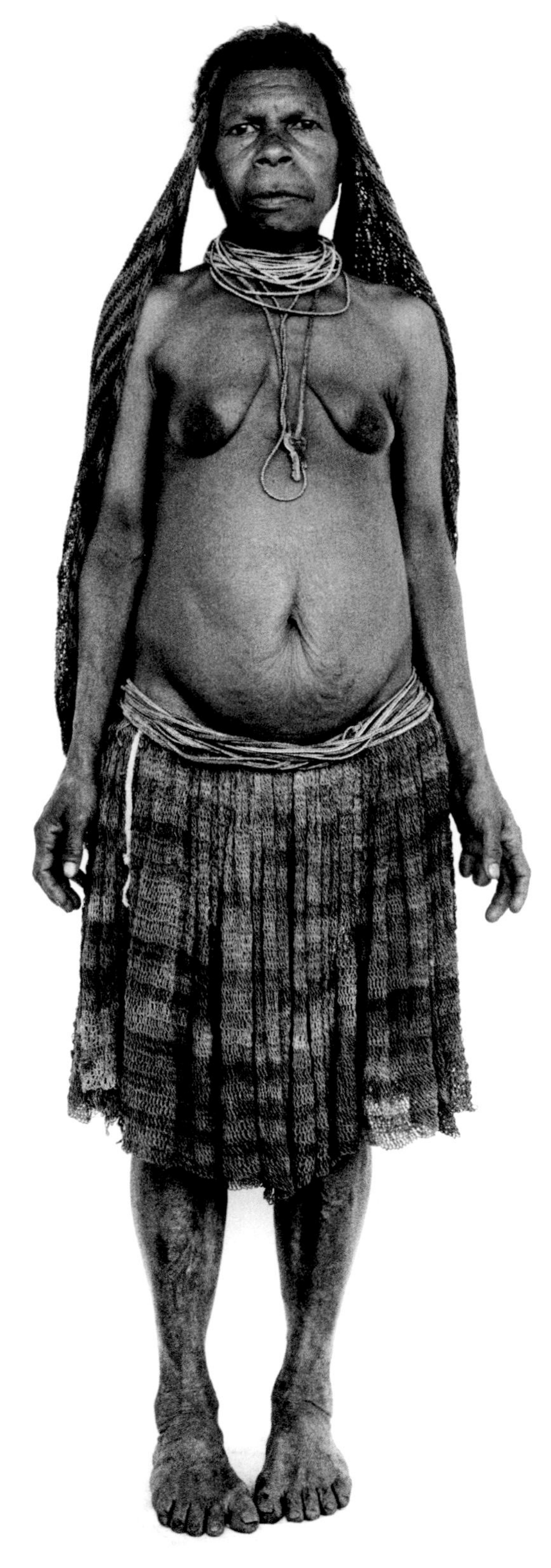

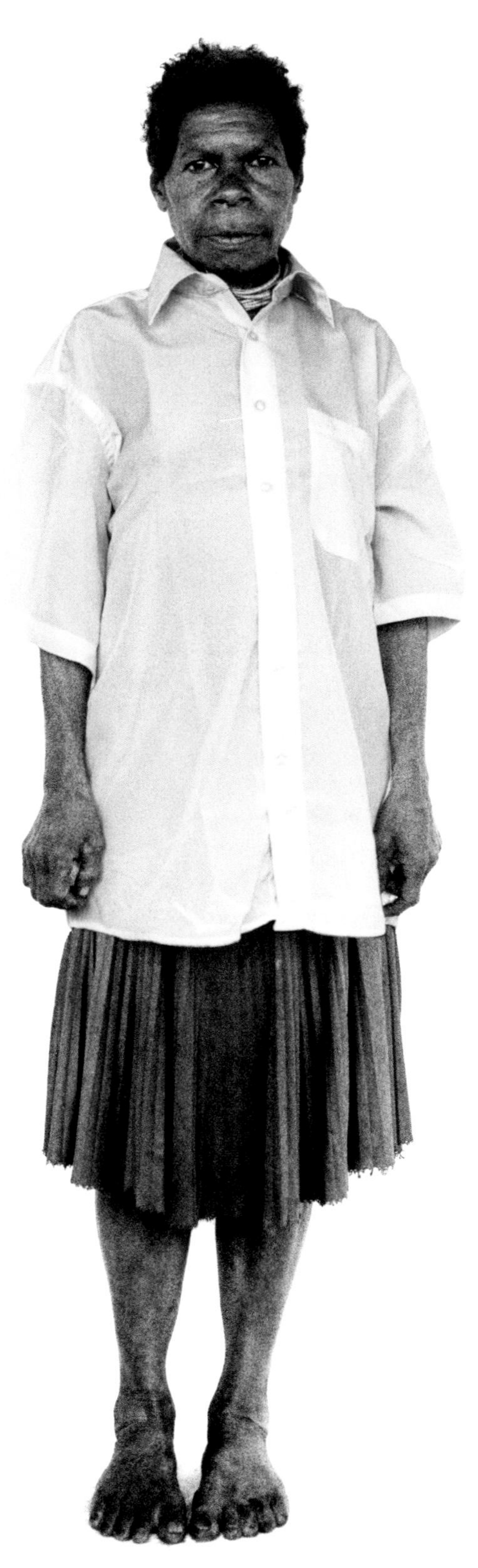

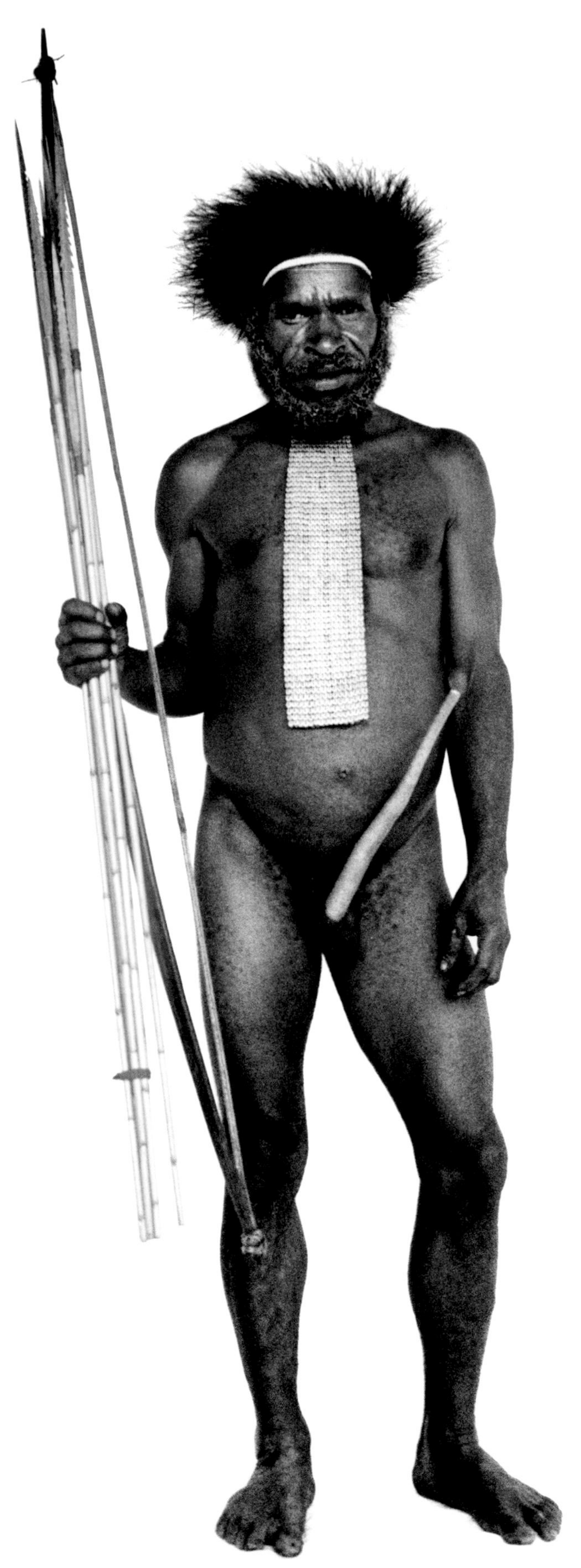

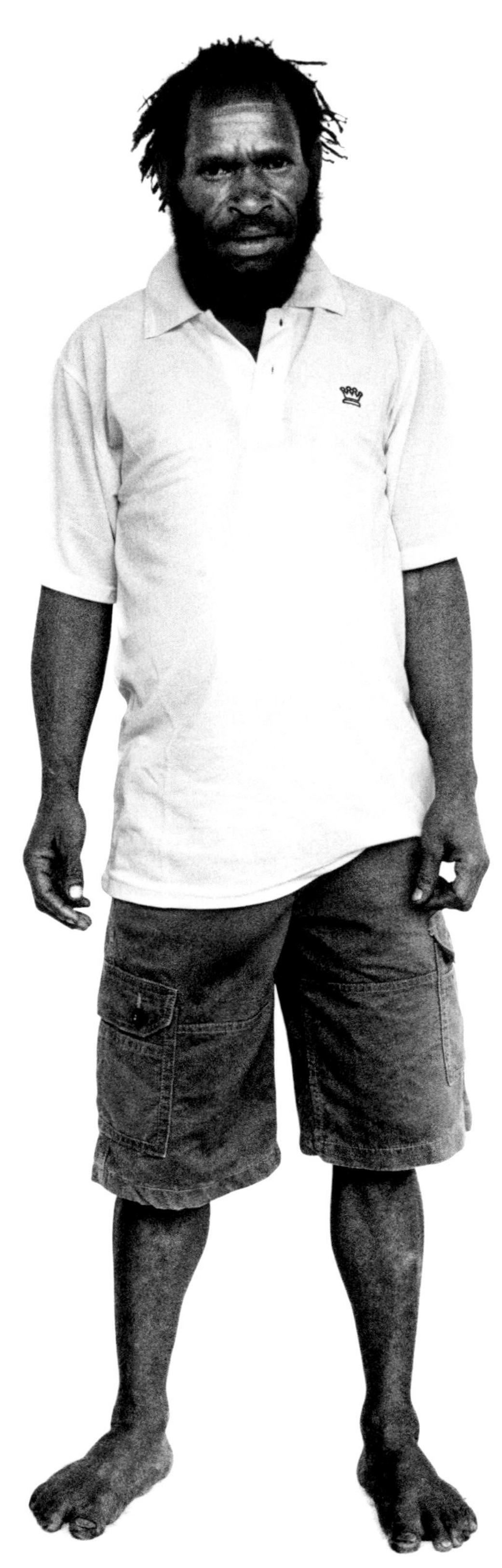

Cowboys

Photographs

The photograph itself is in no way animated (I do not believe in "lifelike" photographs), but it animates me: this is what creates every adventure.
Roland Barthes, *Camera Lucida*, 1979-1980

Barthes uses the word "adventure" to describe the attraction that a particular photograph may have for him. Whether one succumbs to that attraction or not depends on one's eye. More than either his literary or movie predecessors, the photo-cowboy is a visual daredevil, for he stands perfectly still while the smooth, calm surface of the photograph reflects fantasies and longings with a touch of freedom.

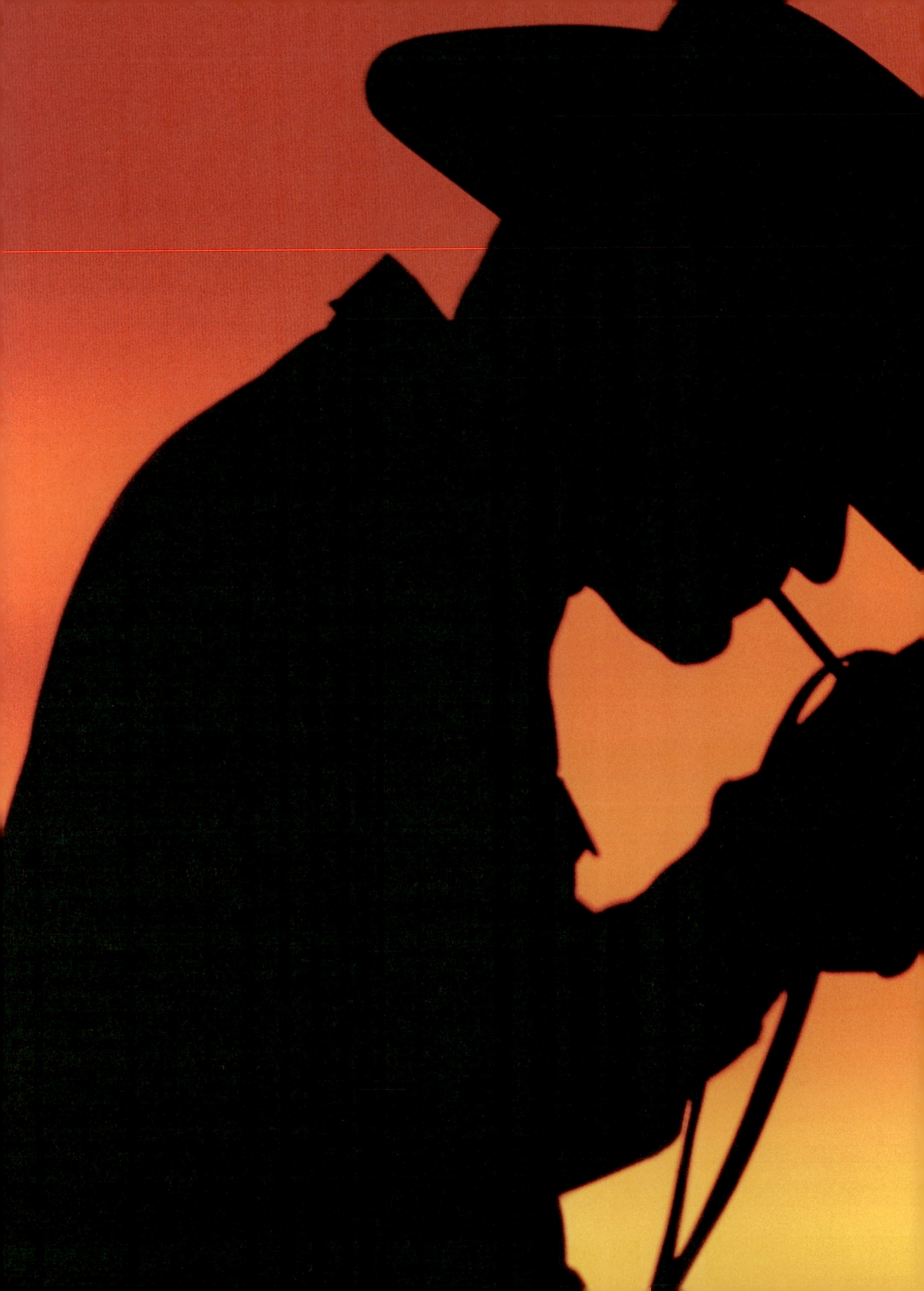

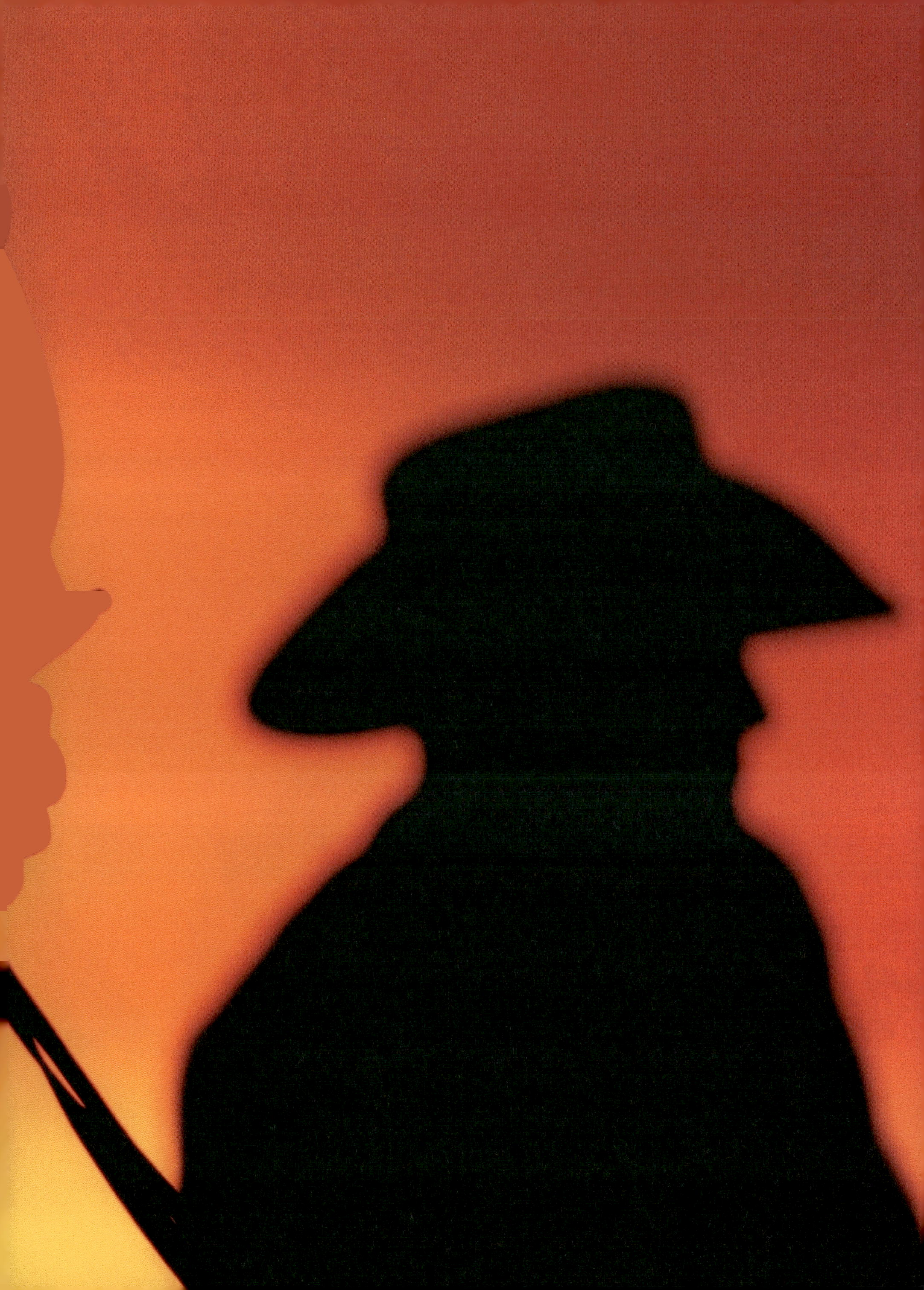

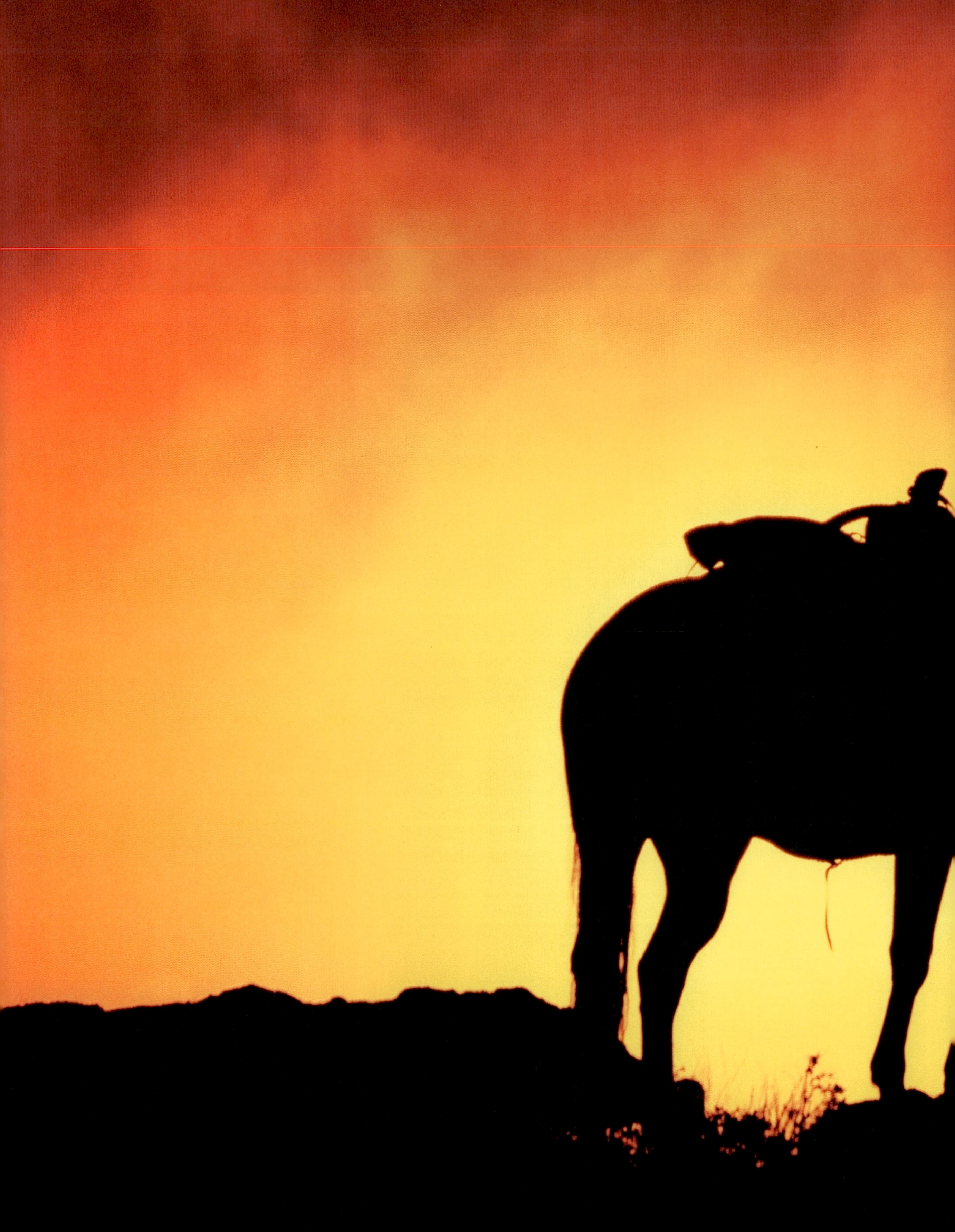

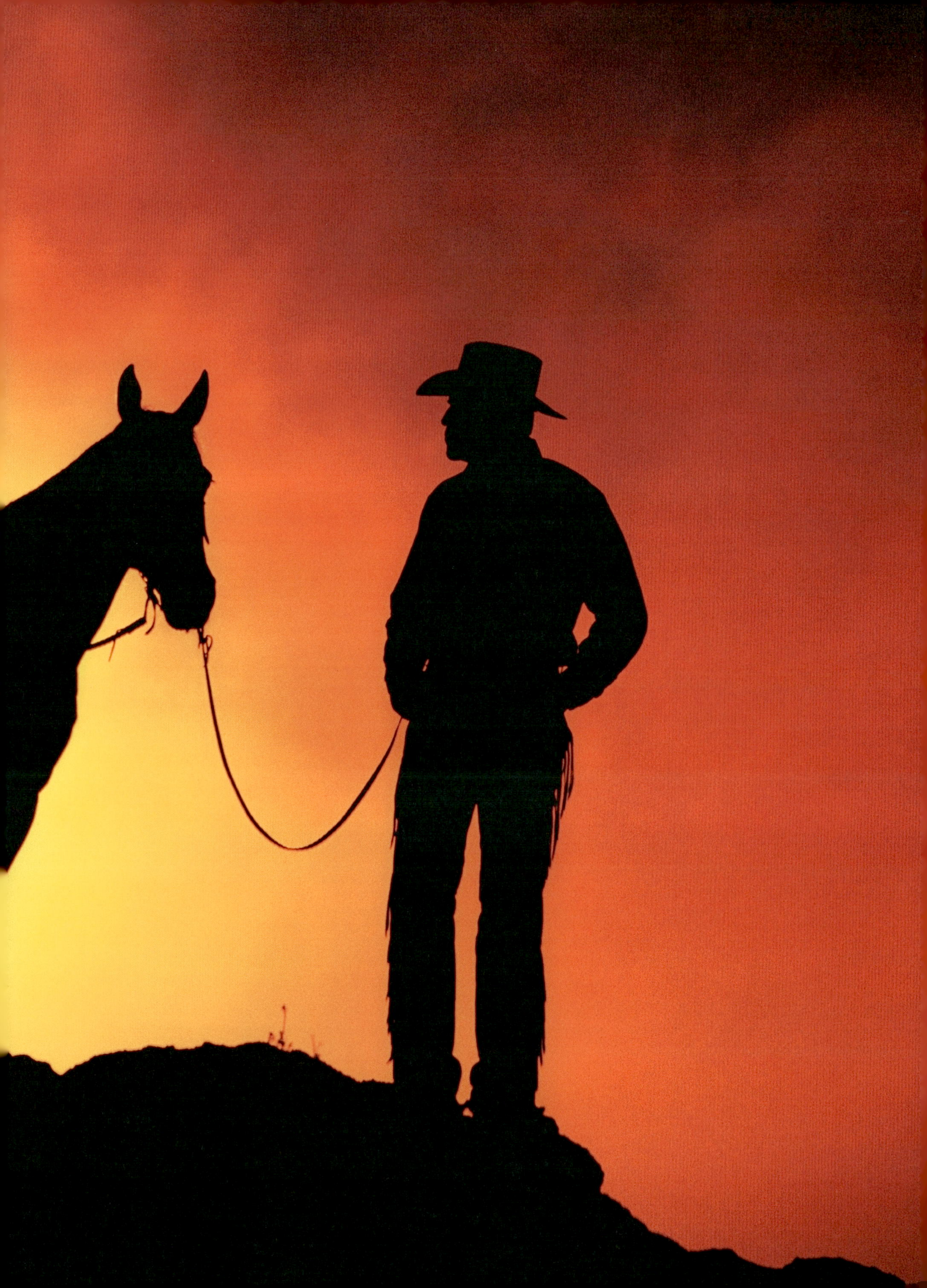

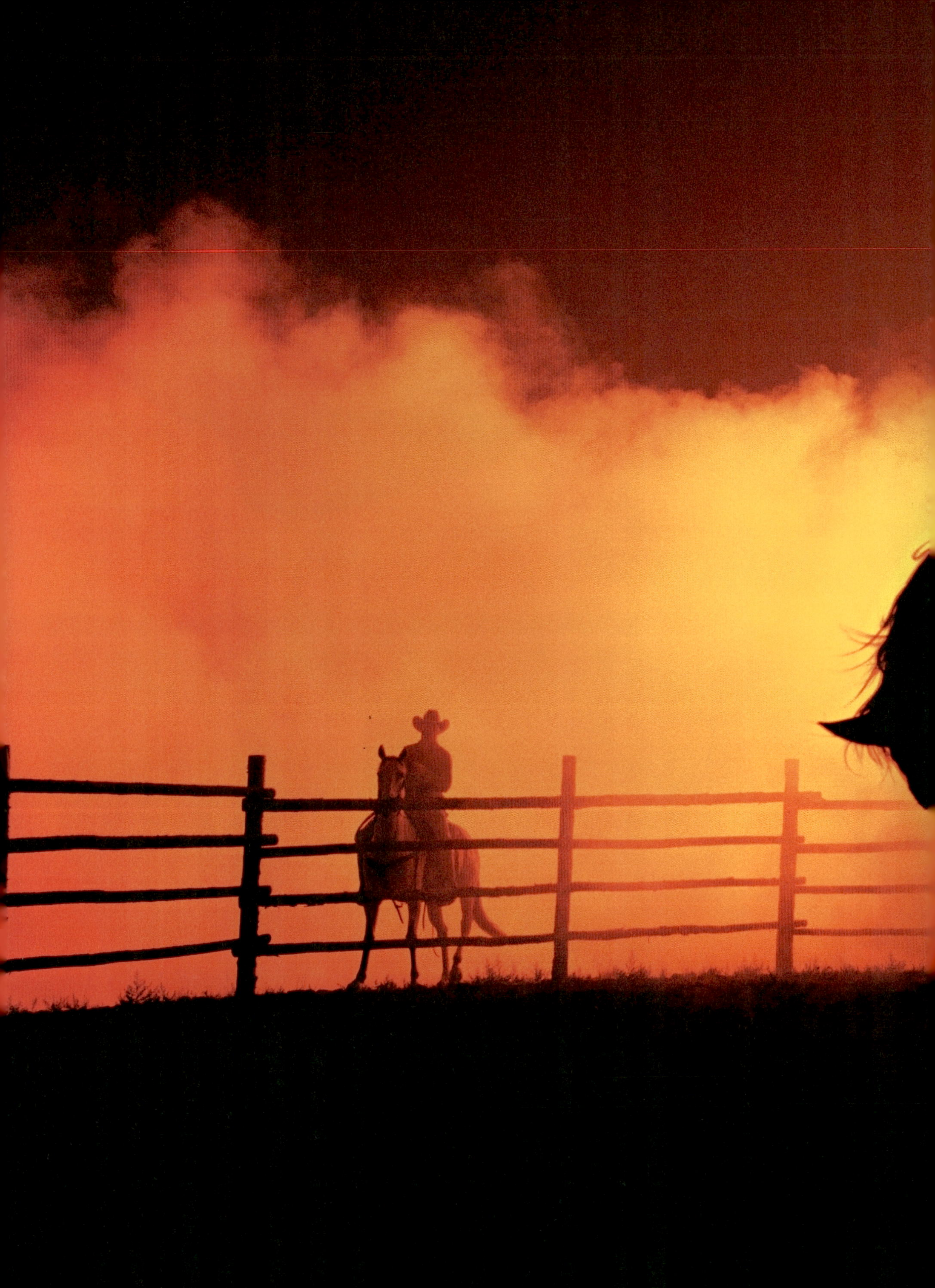

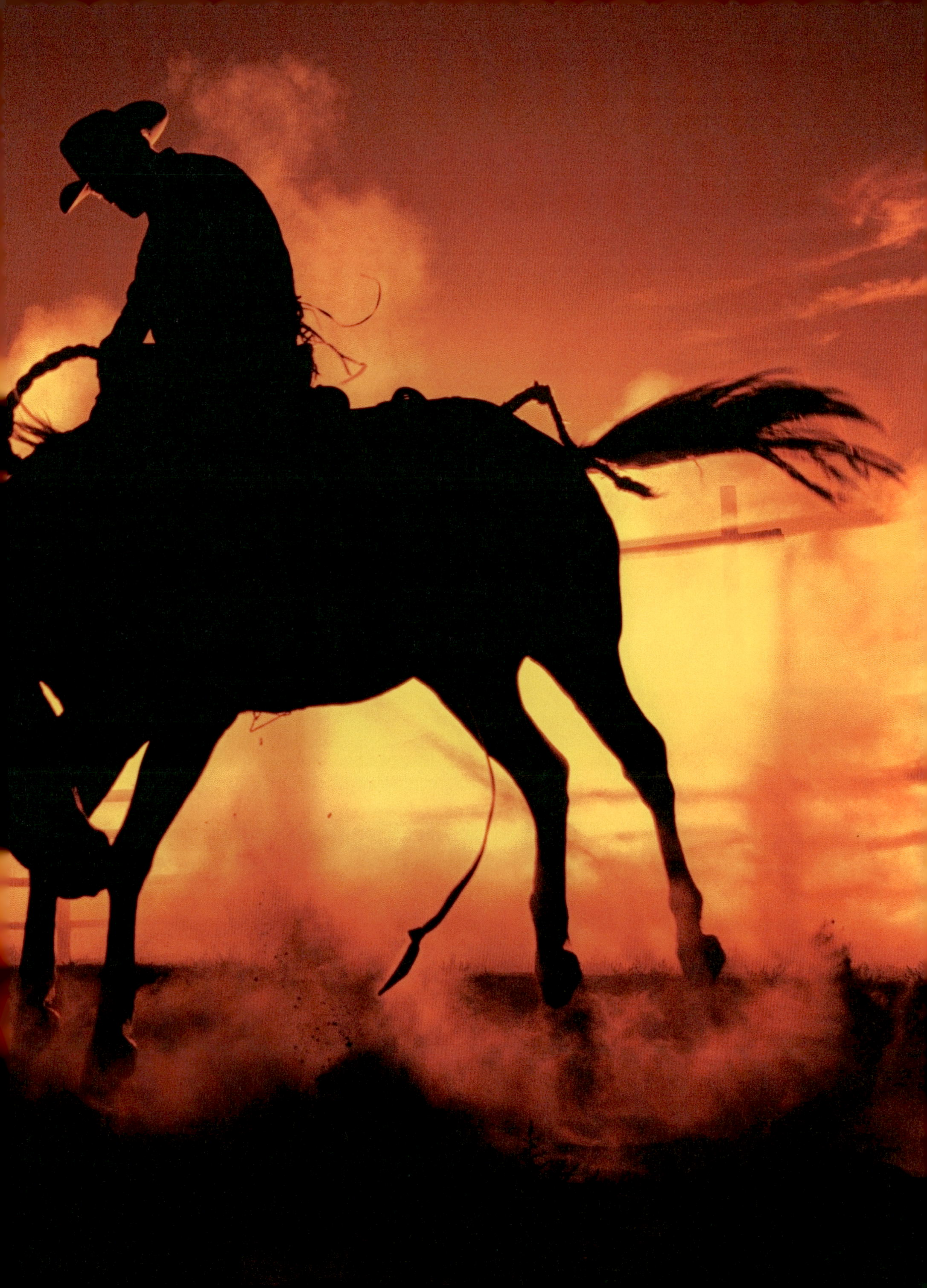

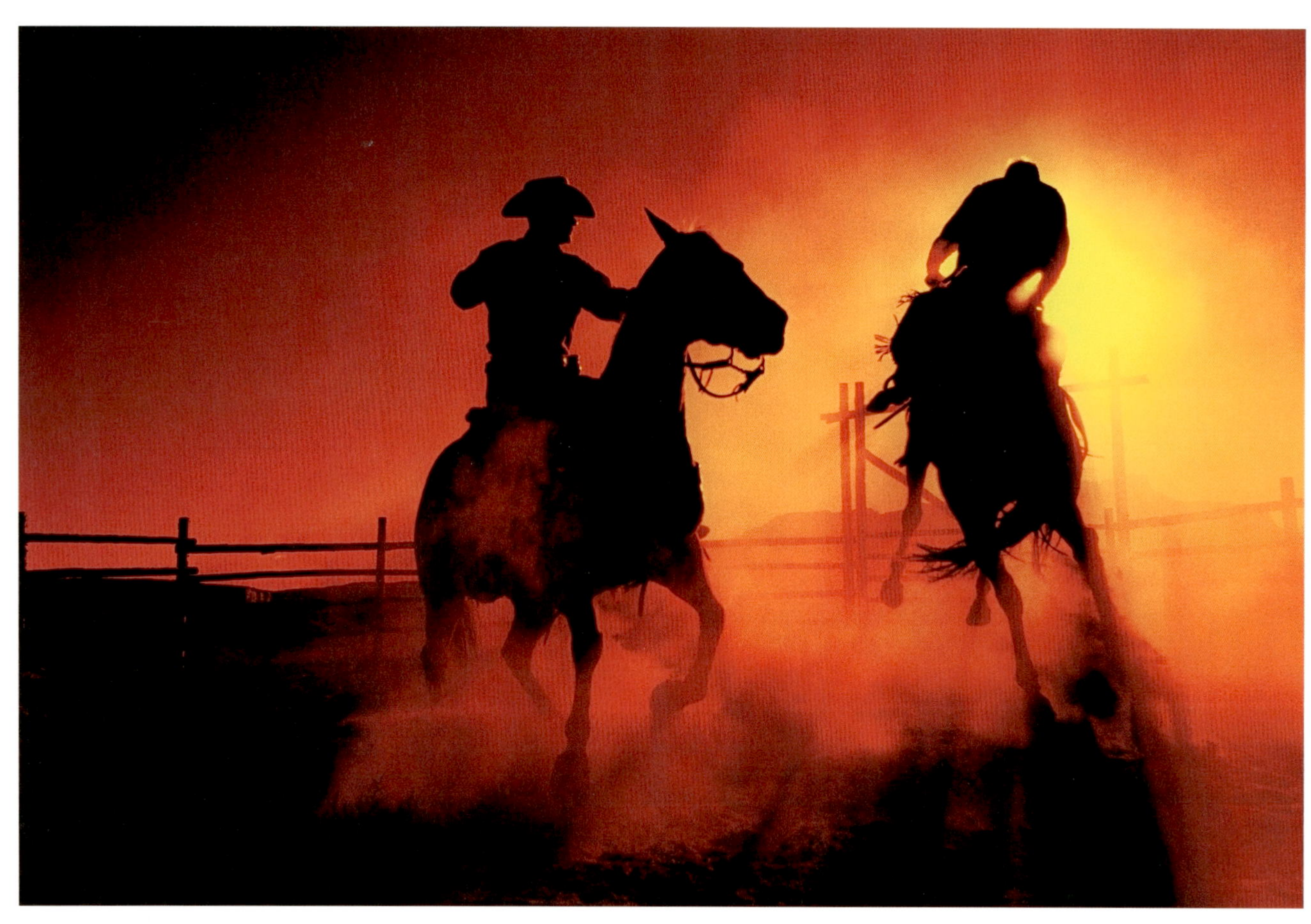

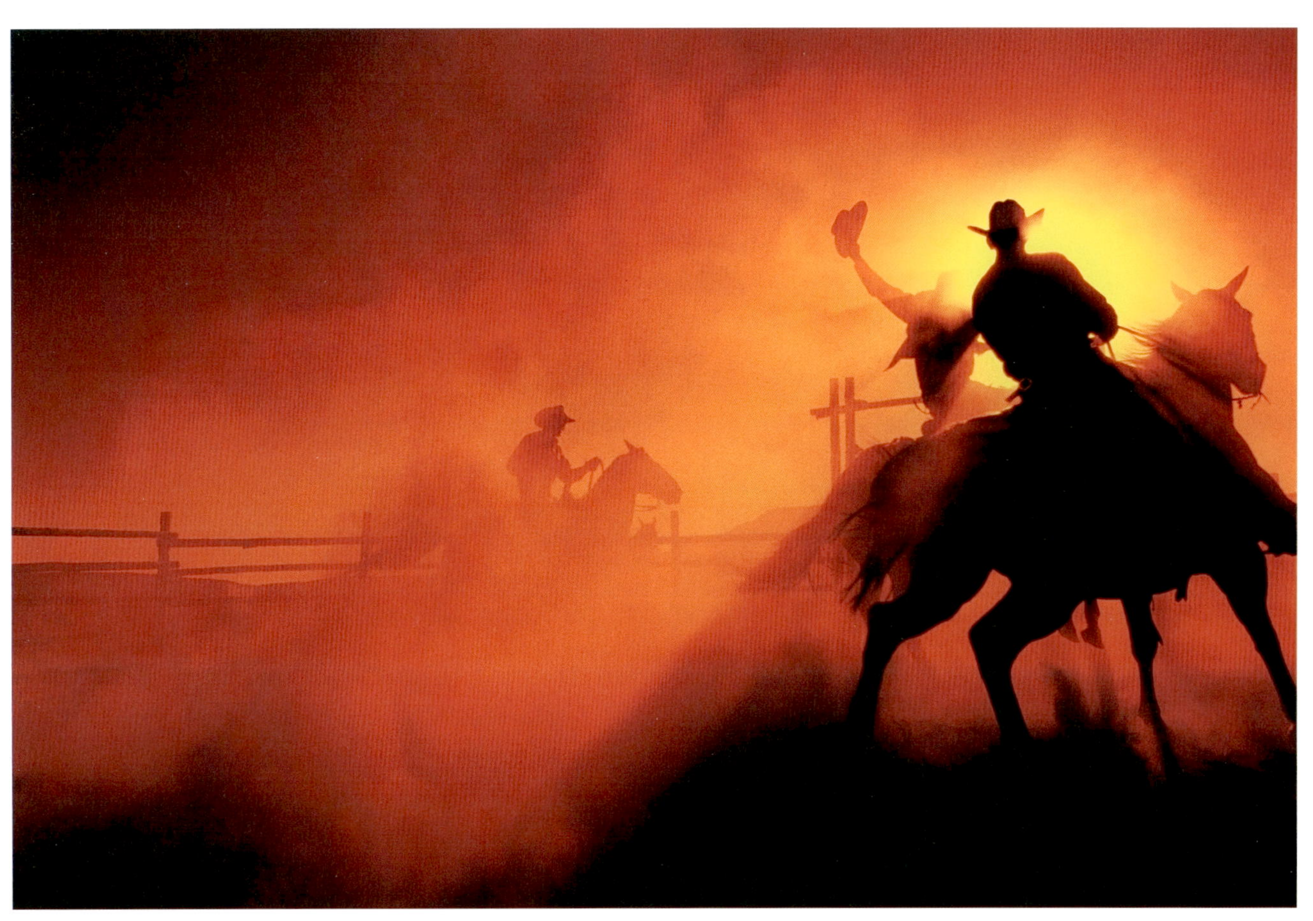

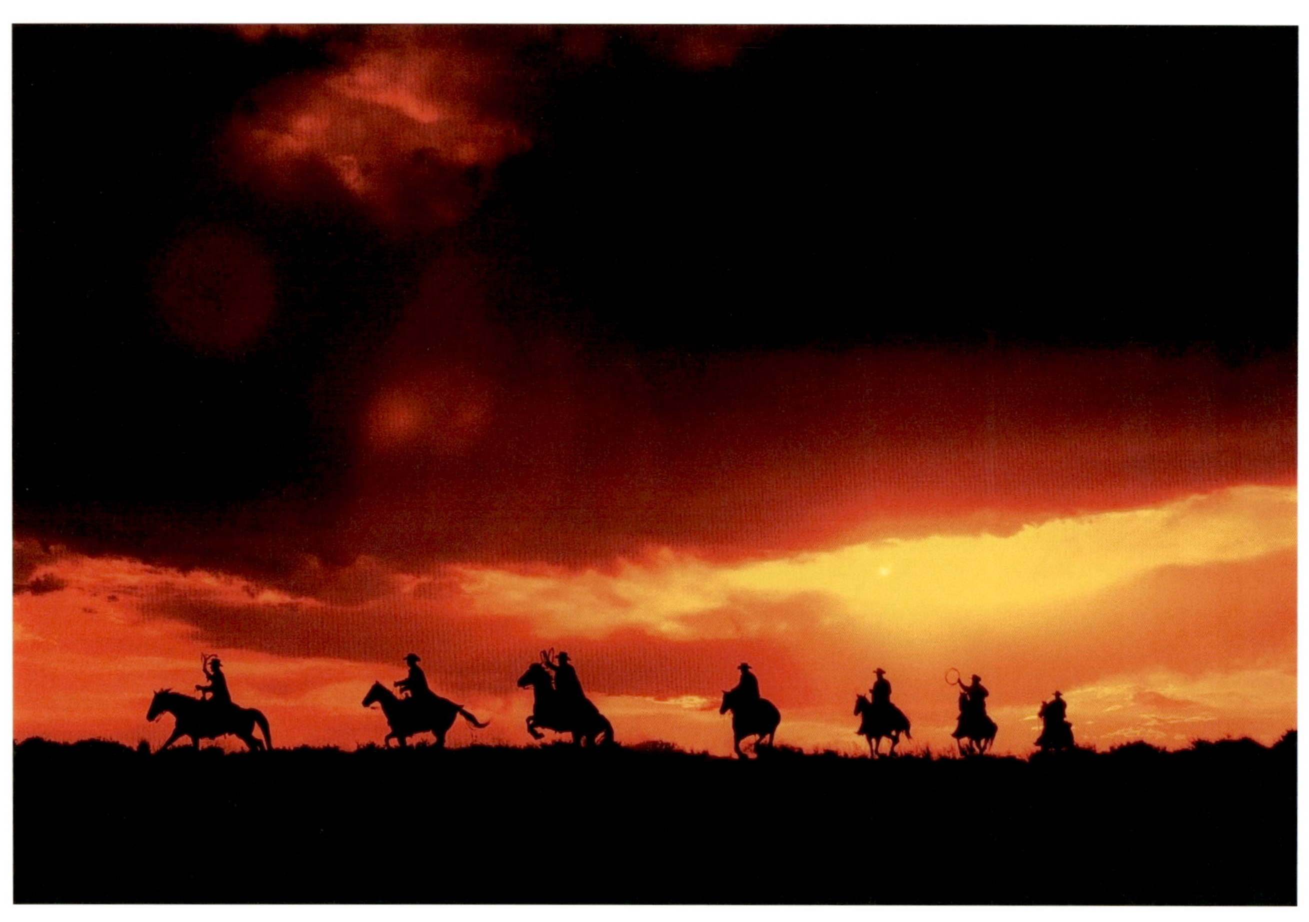

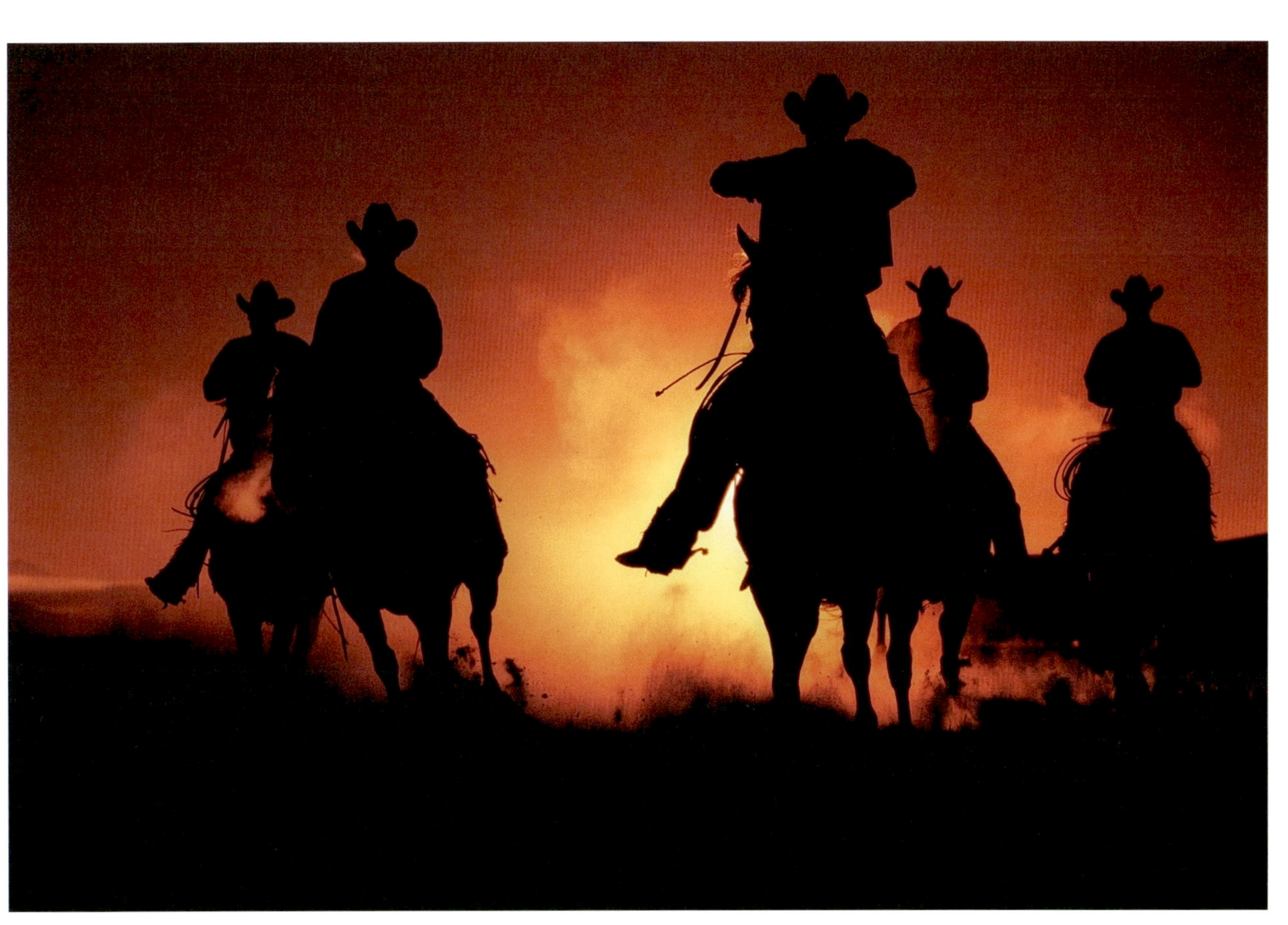

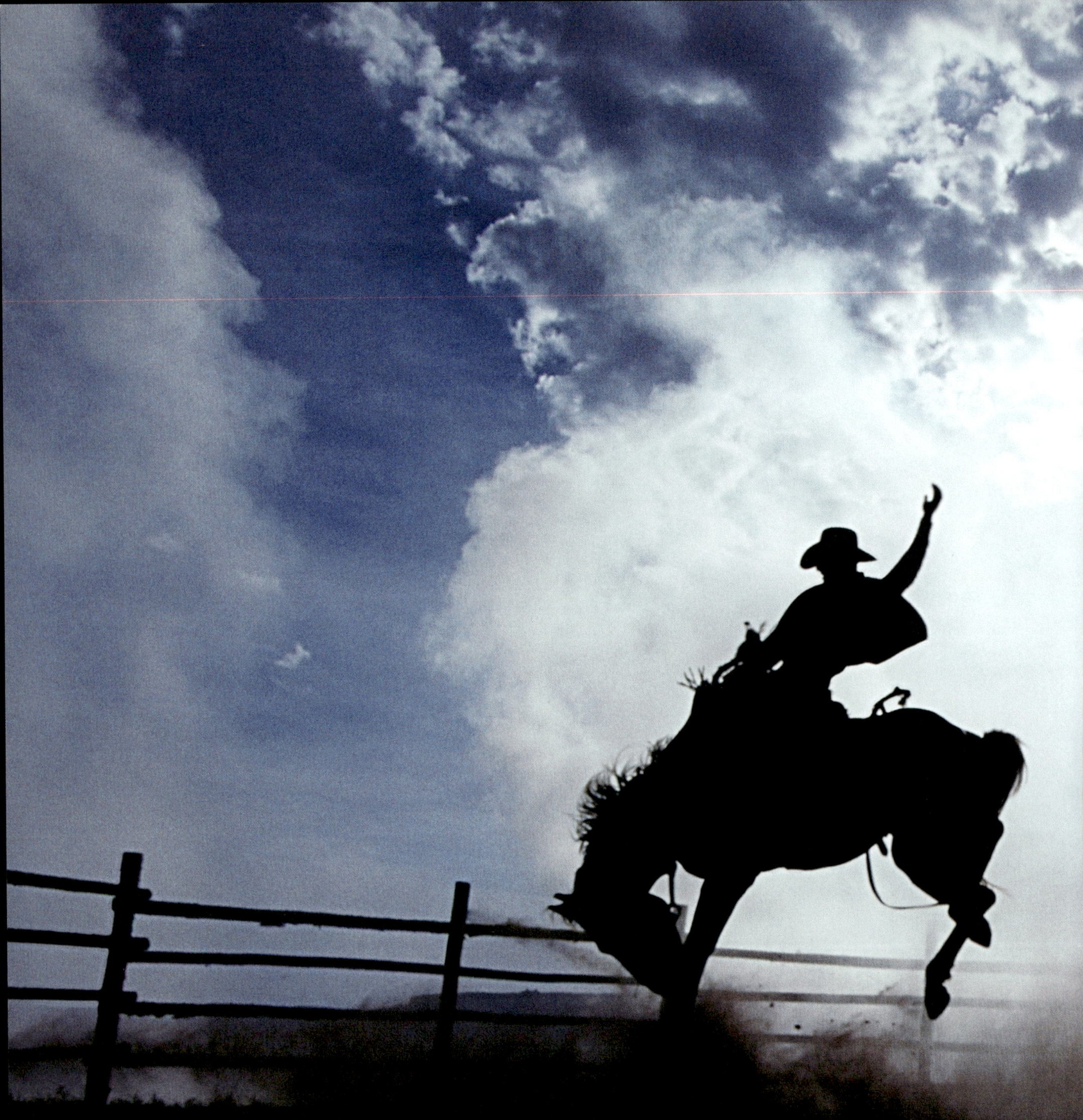

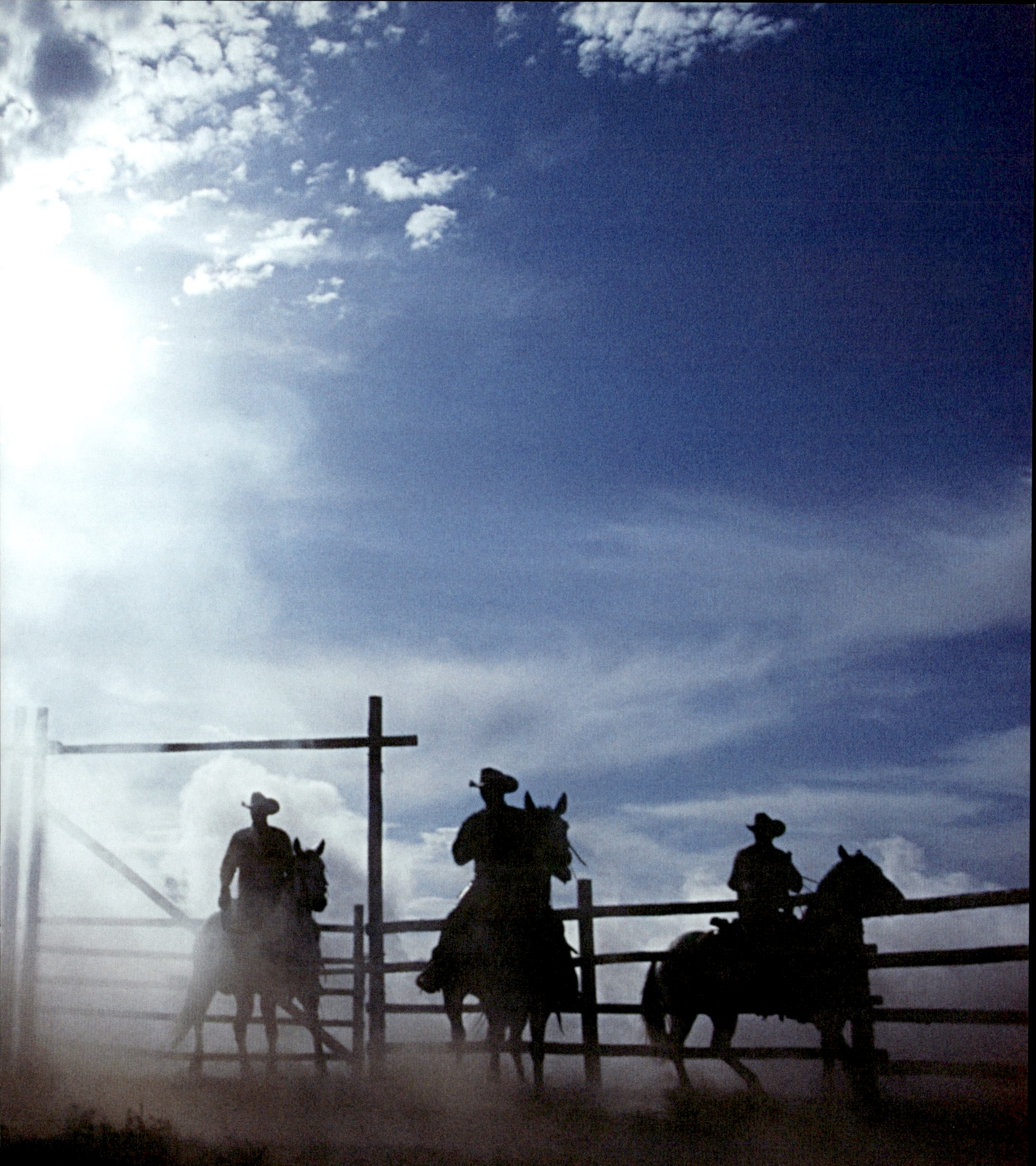

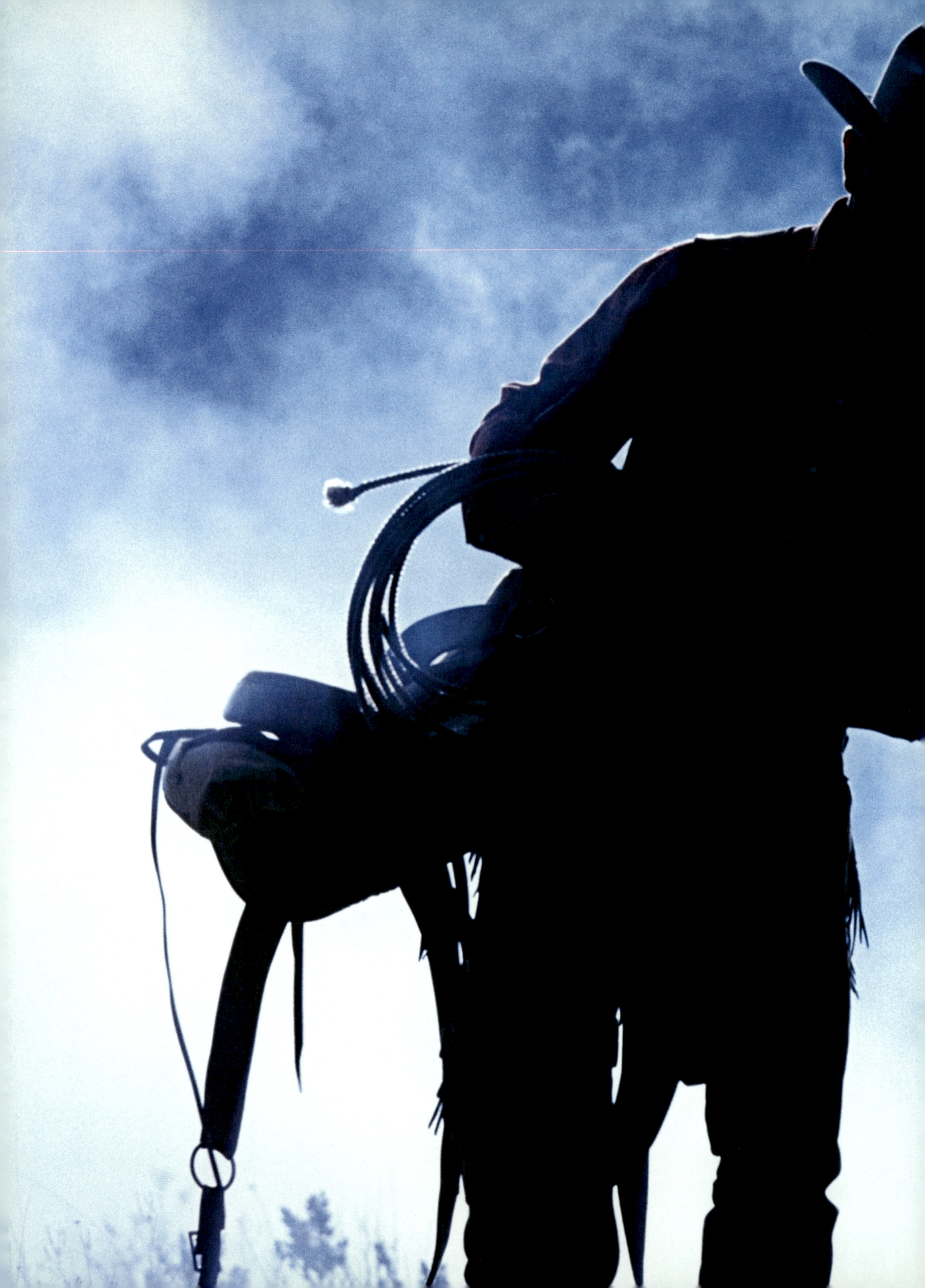

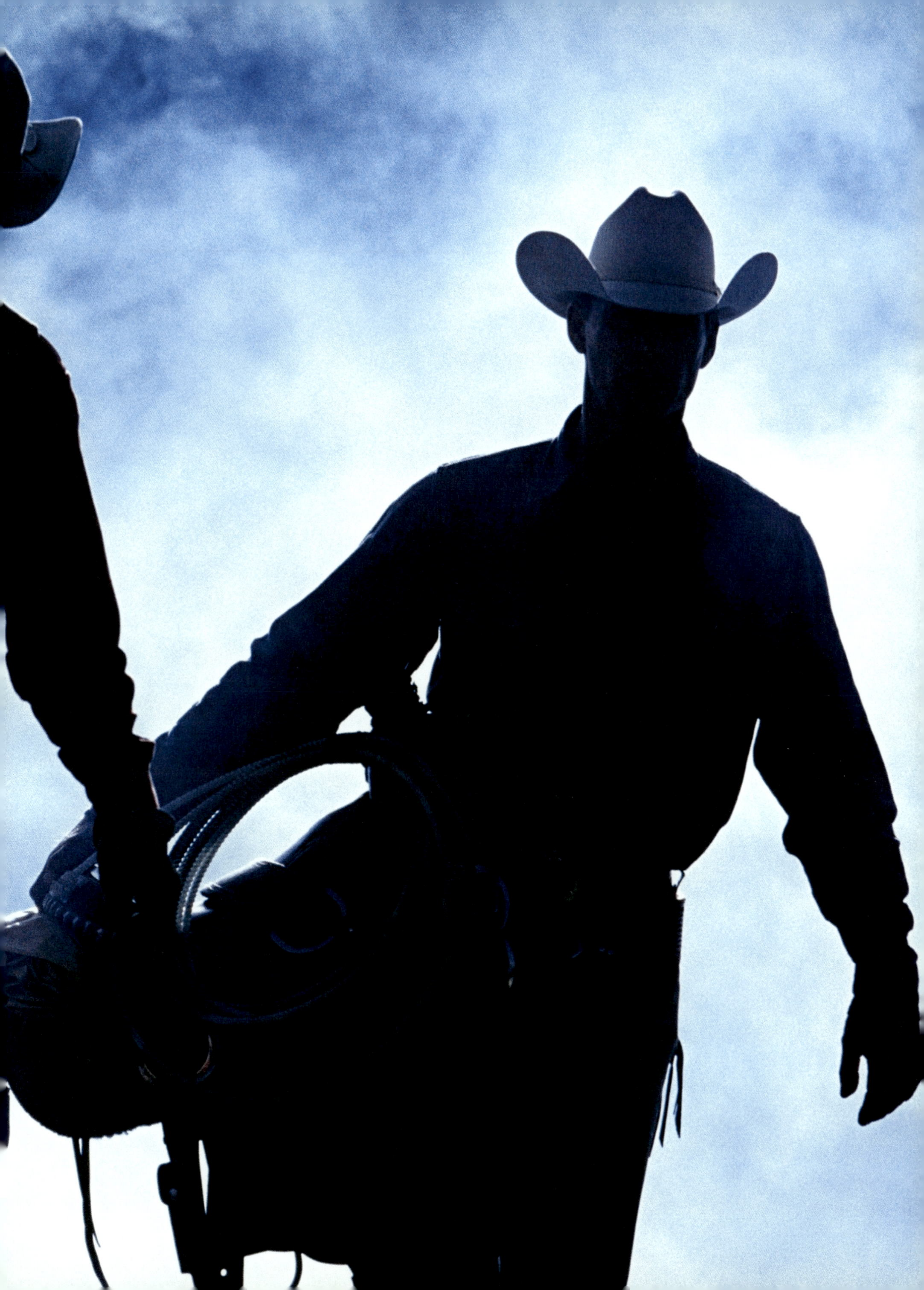

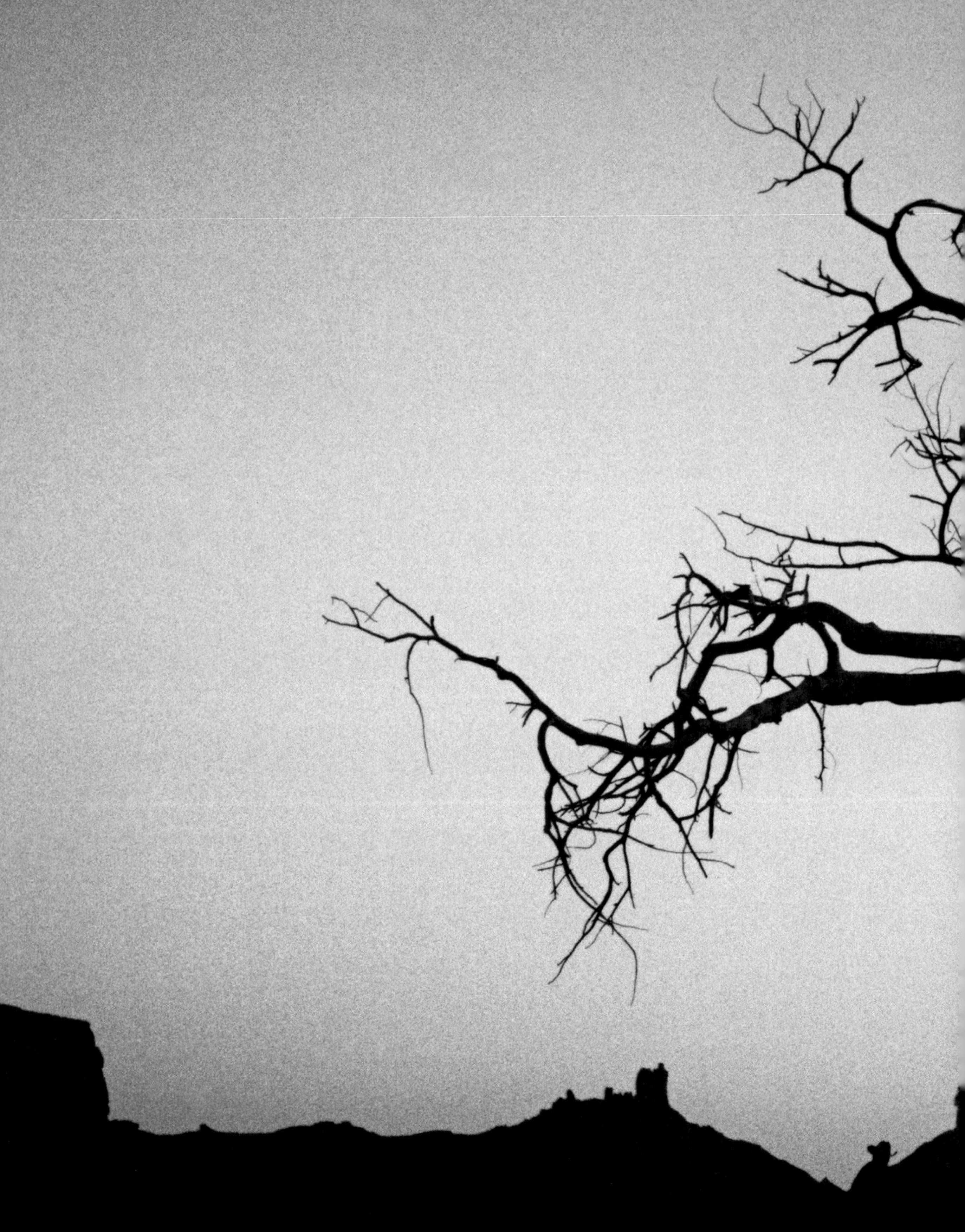

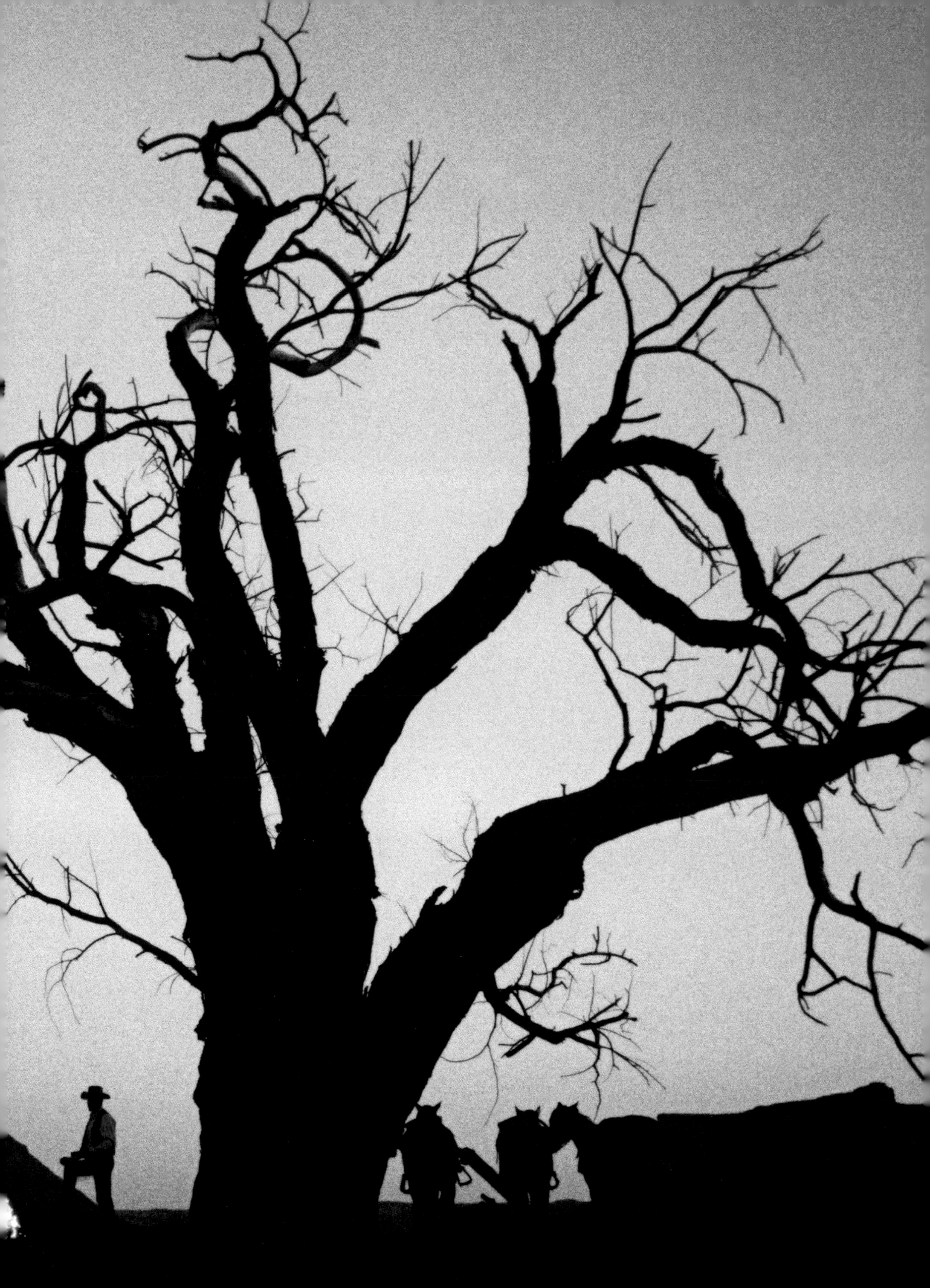

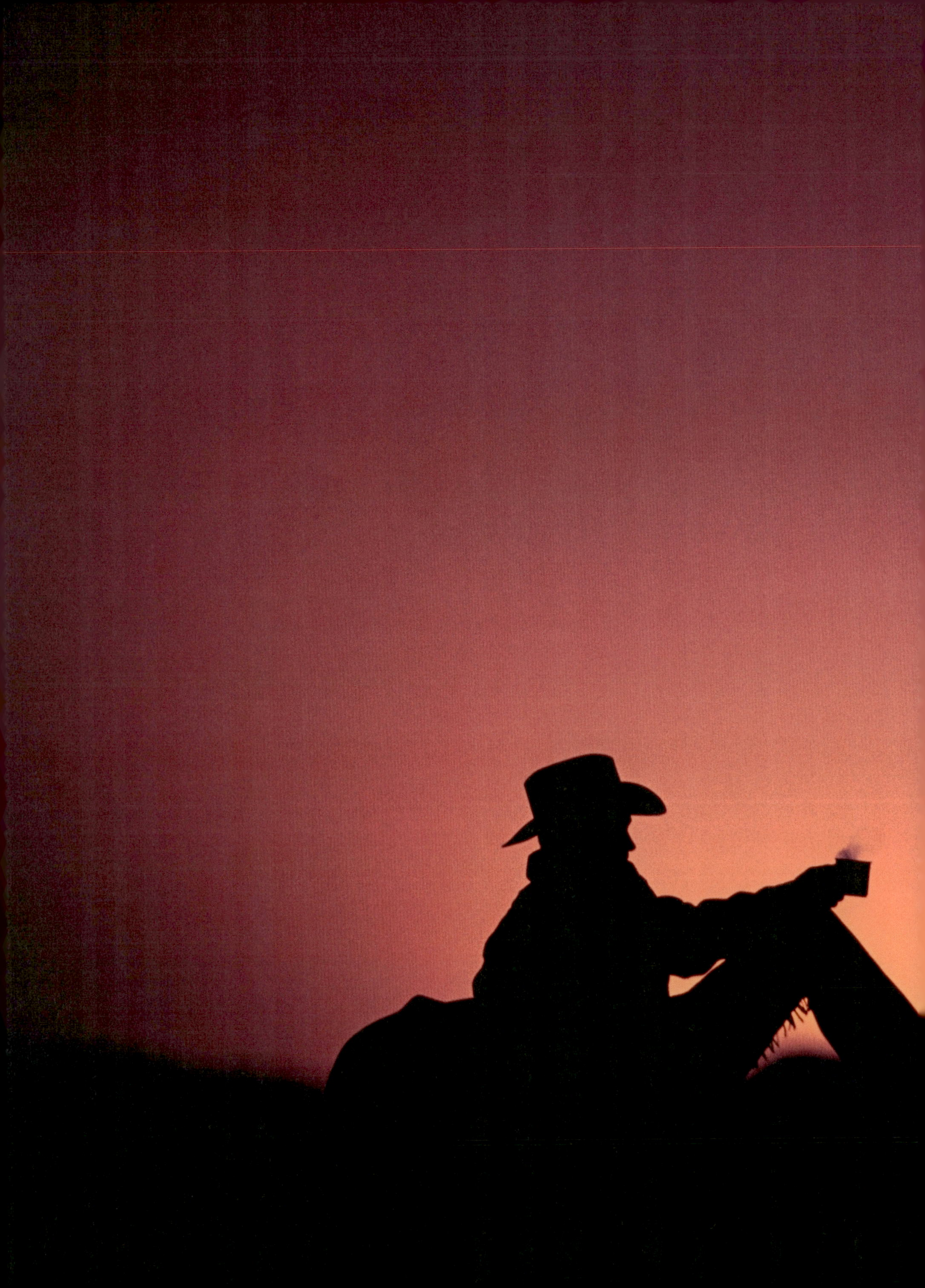

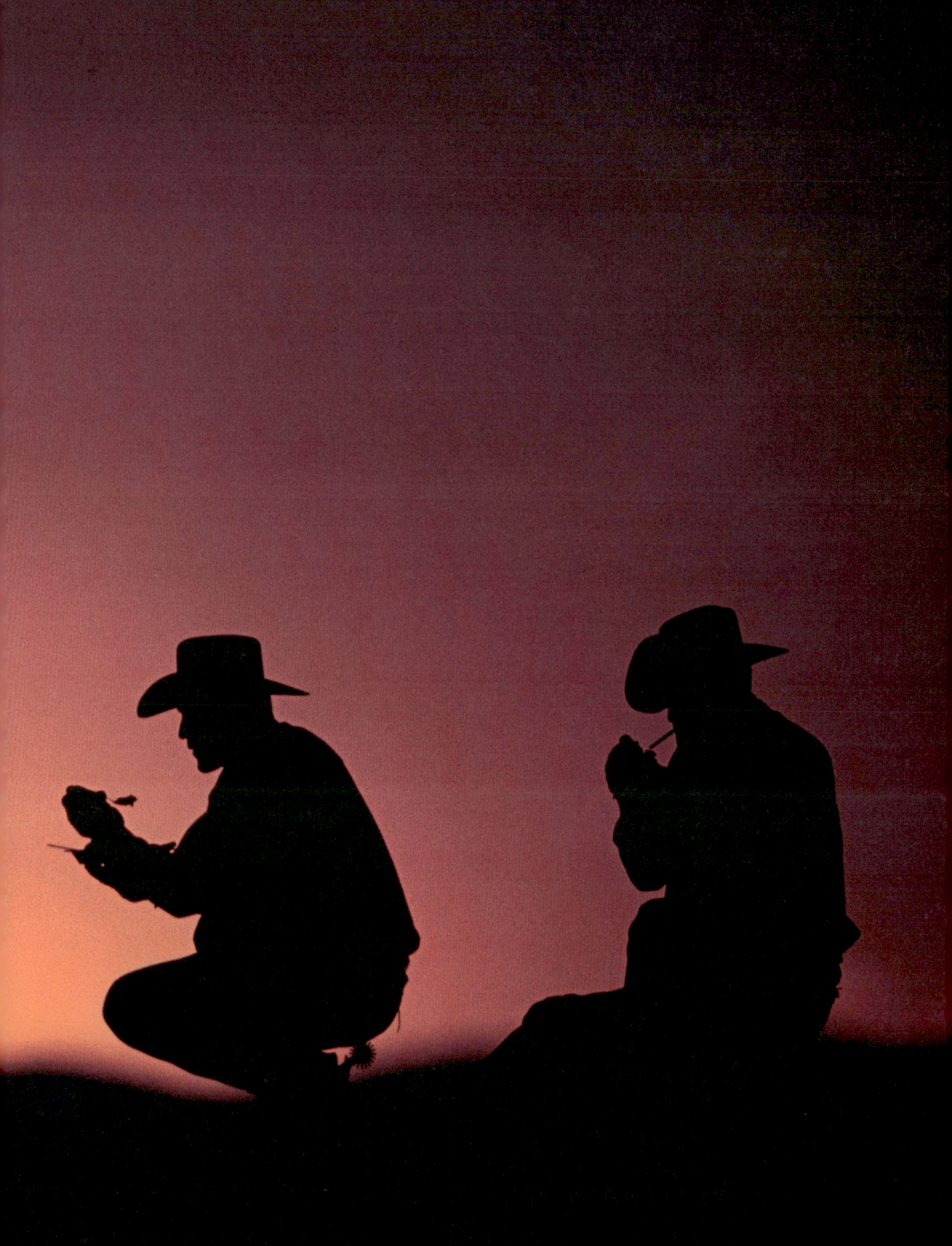

Cowboys

Oils

Yet it is not (it seems to me) by Painting that Photography touches art, but by Theater.
Roland Barthes, *Camera Lucida*, 1979-1980

Hannes Schmid's Cowboys, in photographs and paintings, refer on various levels to what photography is and can do: it is technical, reproducible, and can come in all sizes and shapes. Oddly enough, these qualities are most apparent in the painted images. For the painted Cowboys do not hide their photographic origins, on the contrary, these compositions still only encompass a limited view, with the same field of vision as the camera. Distortions and areas of blurred focus are registered and replicated in the paintings. It is only the temporality of the images that changes. The paintings are one-offs, in which the drama of the artificiality of the original scenario comes to the fore once again.

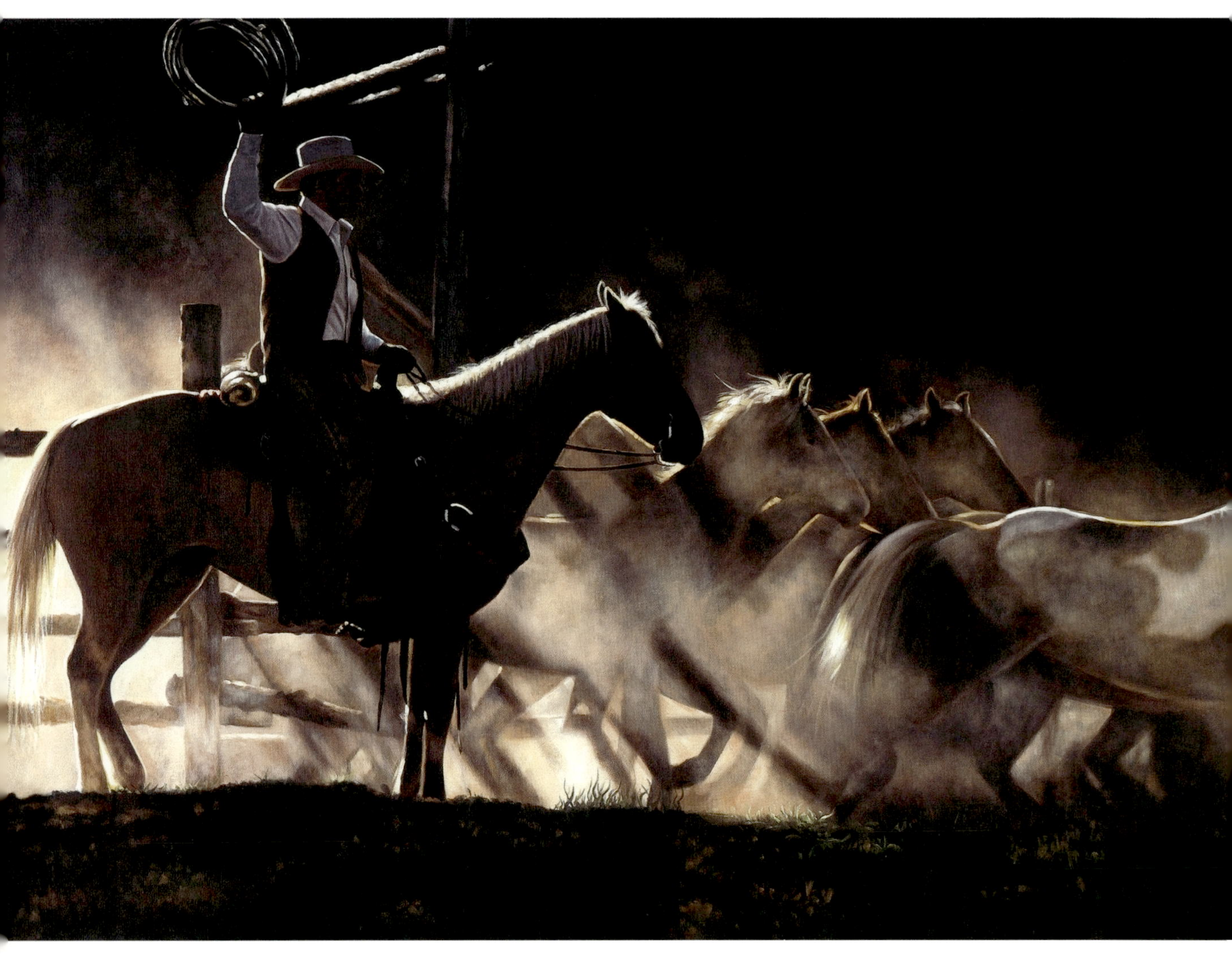

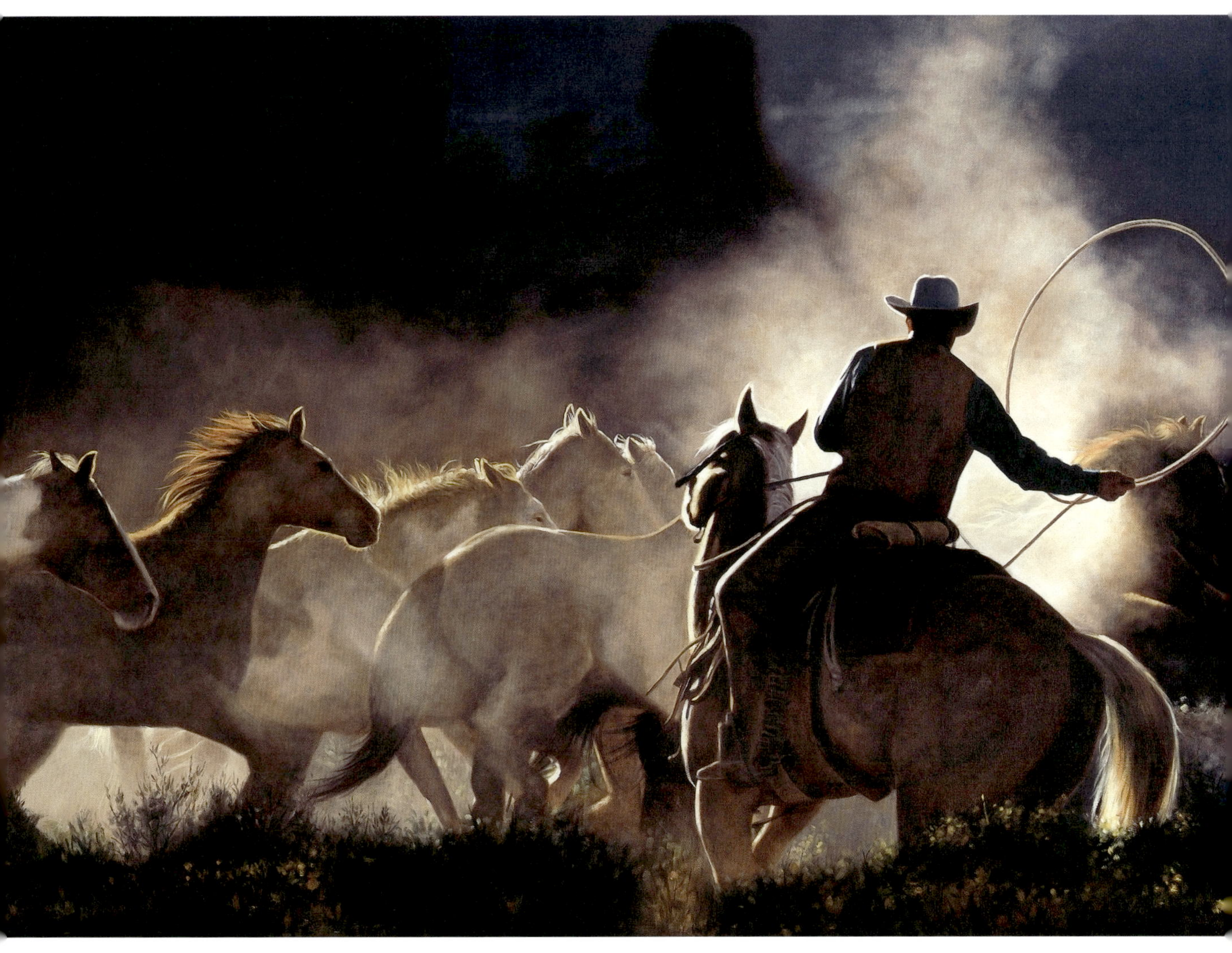

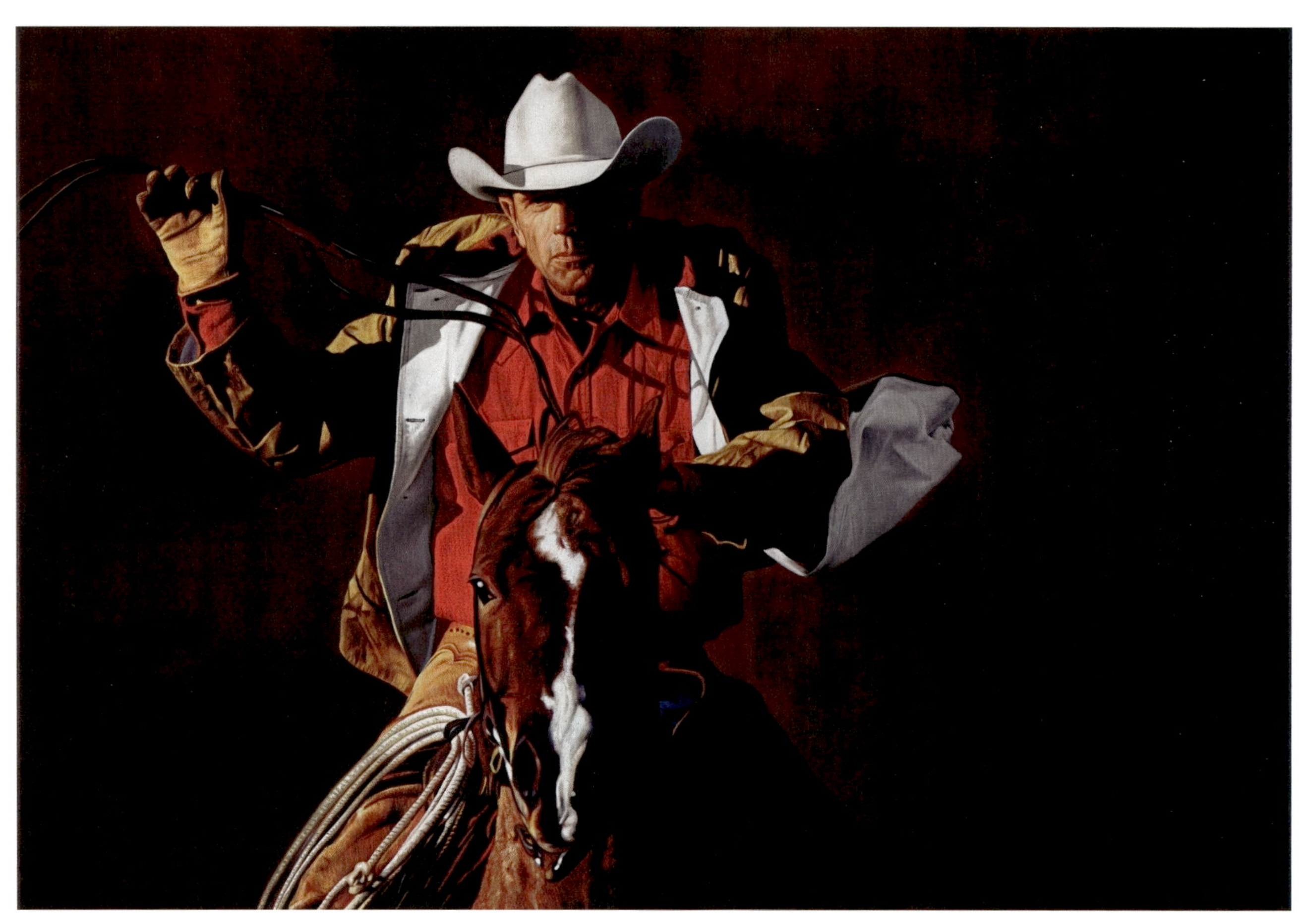

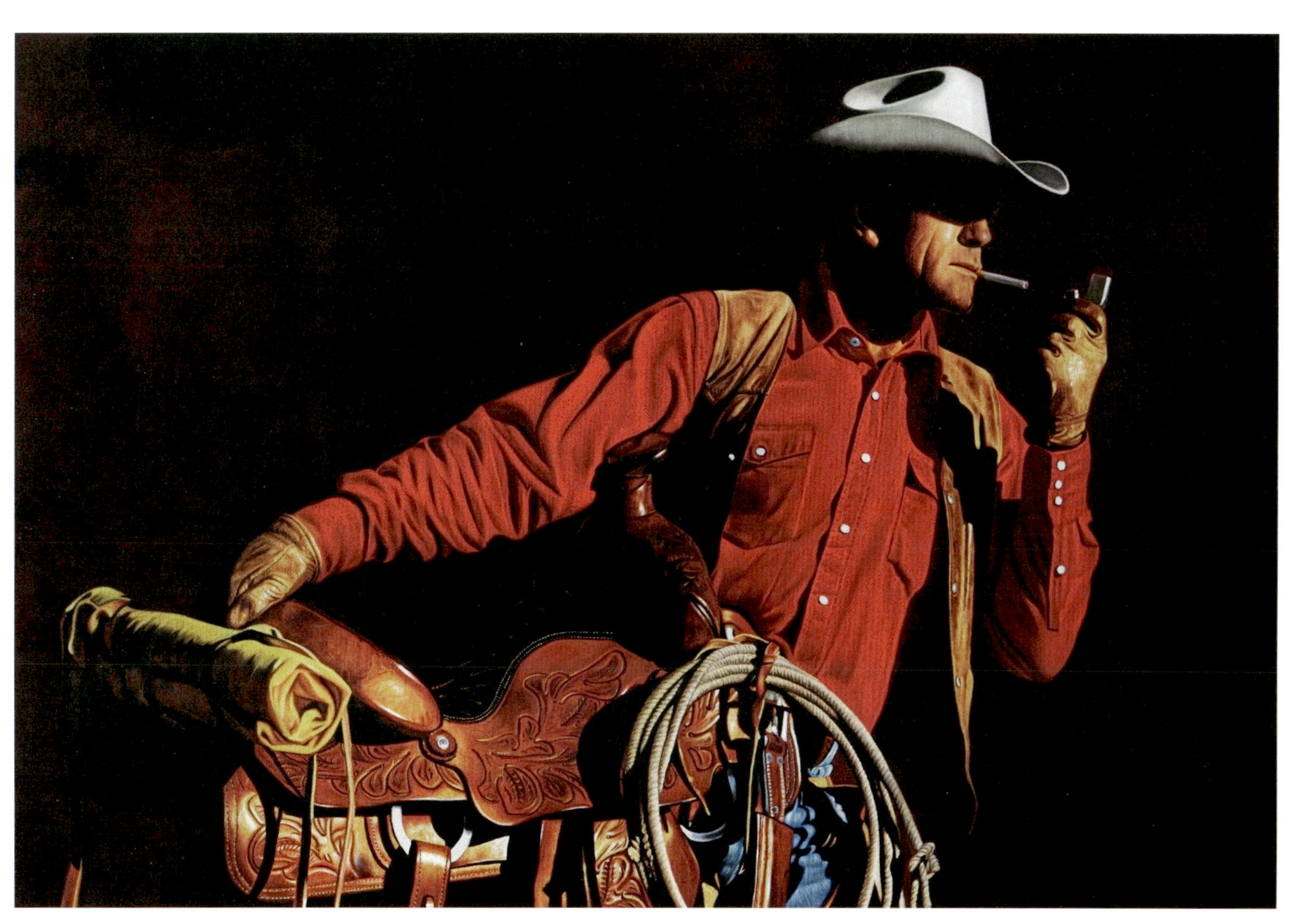

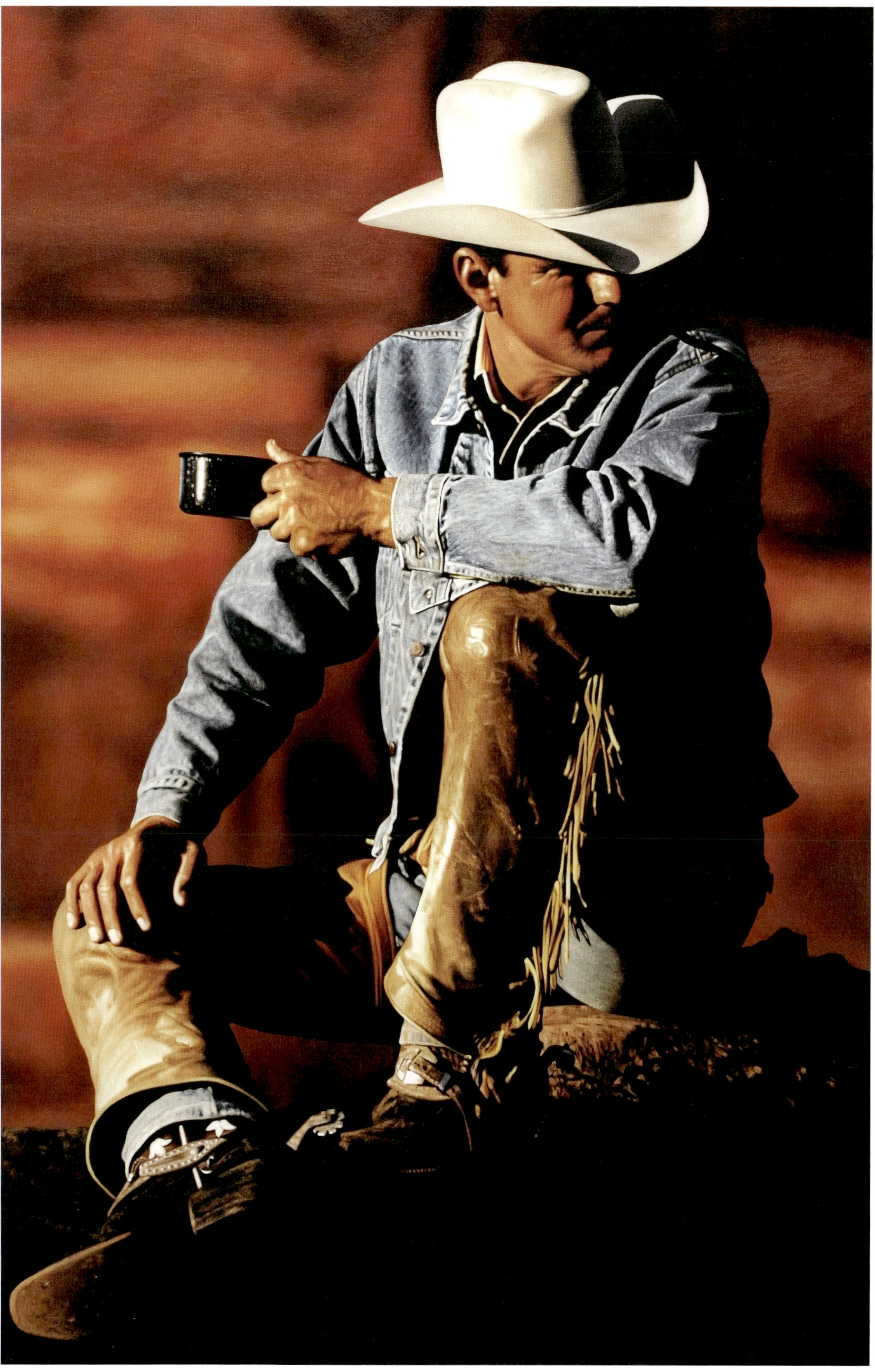

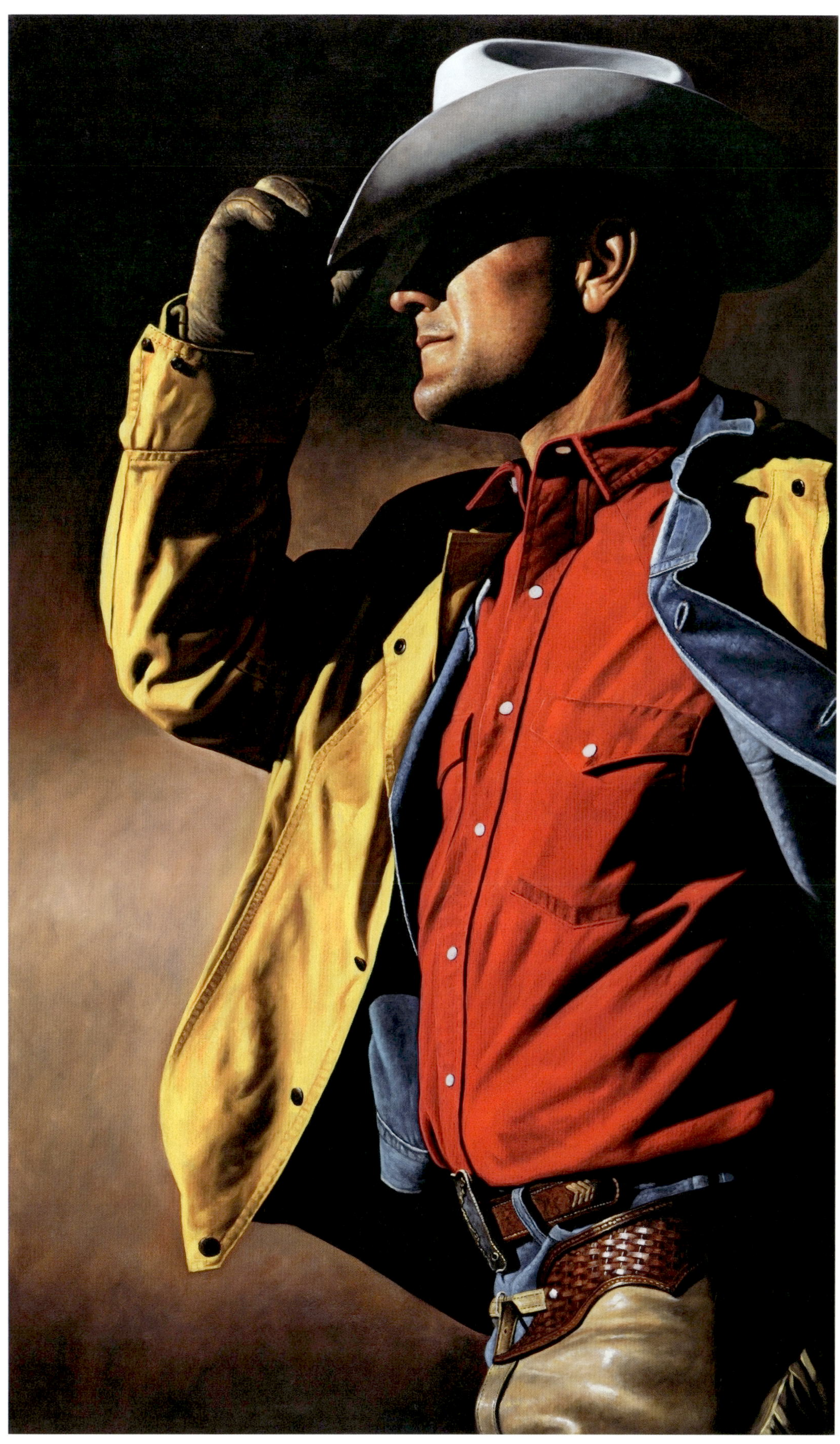

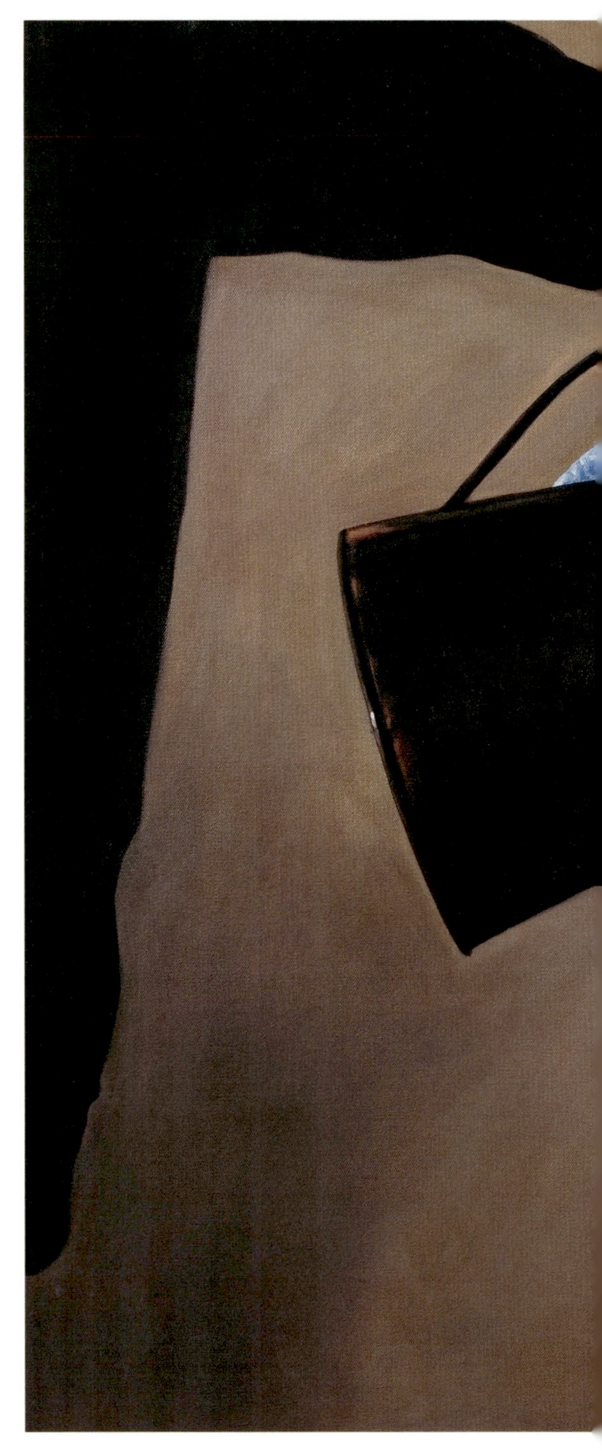

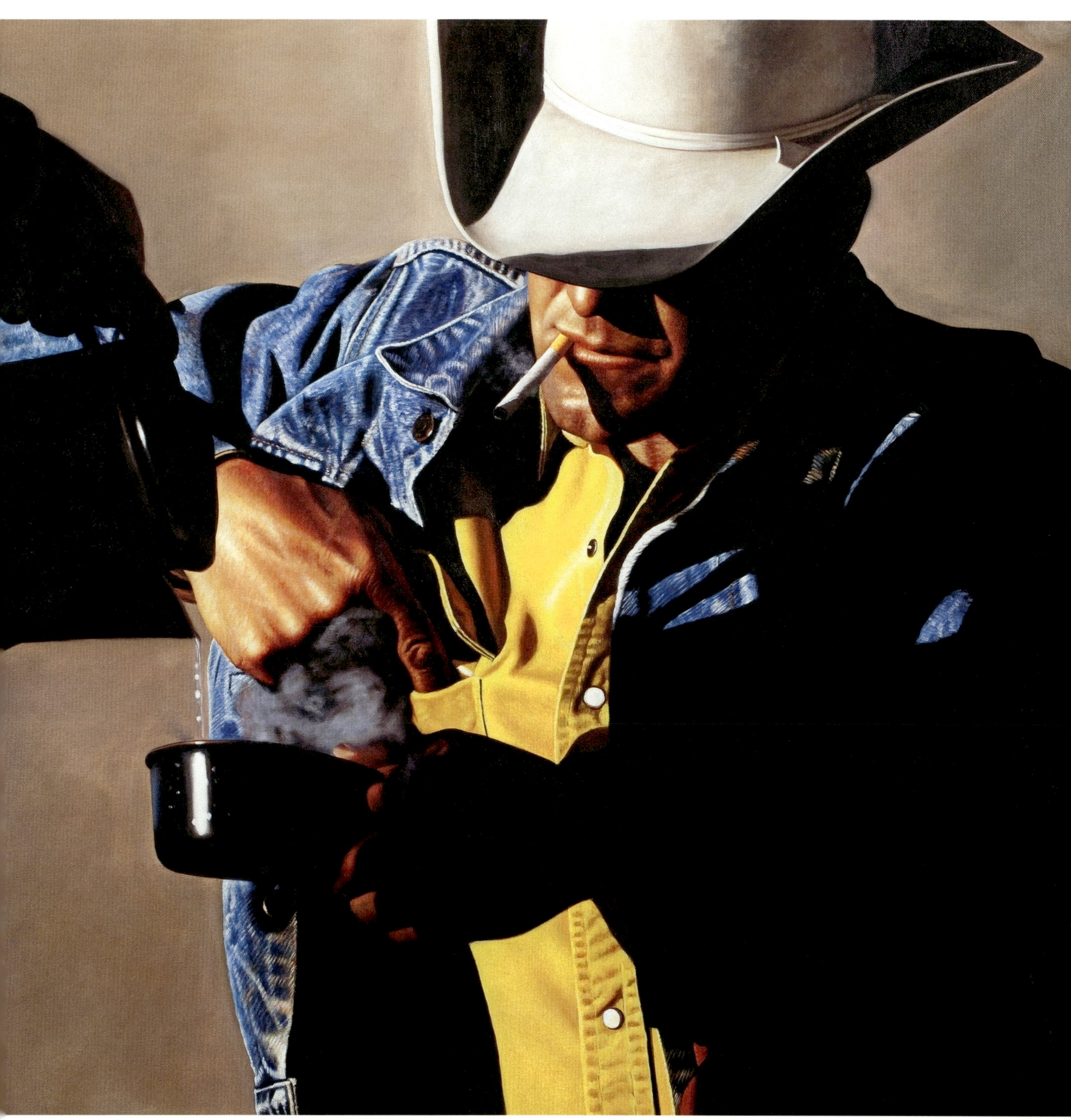

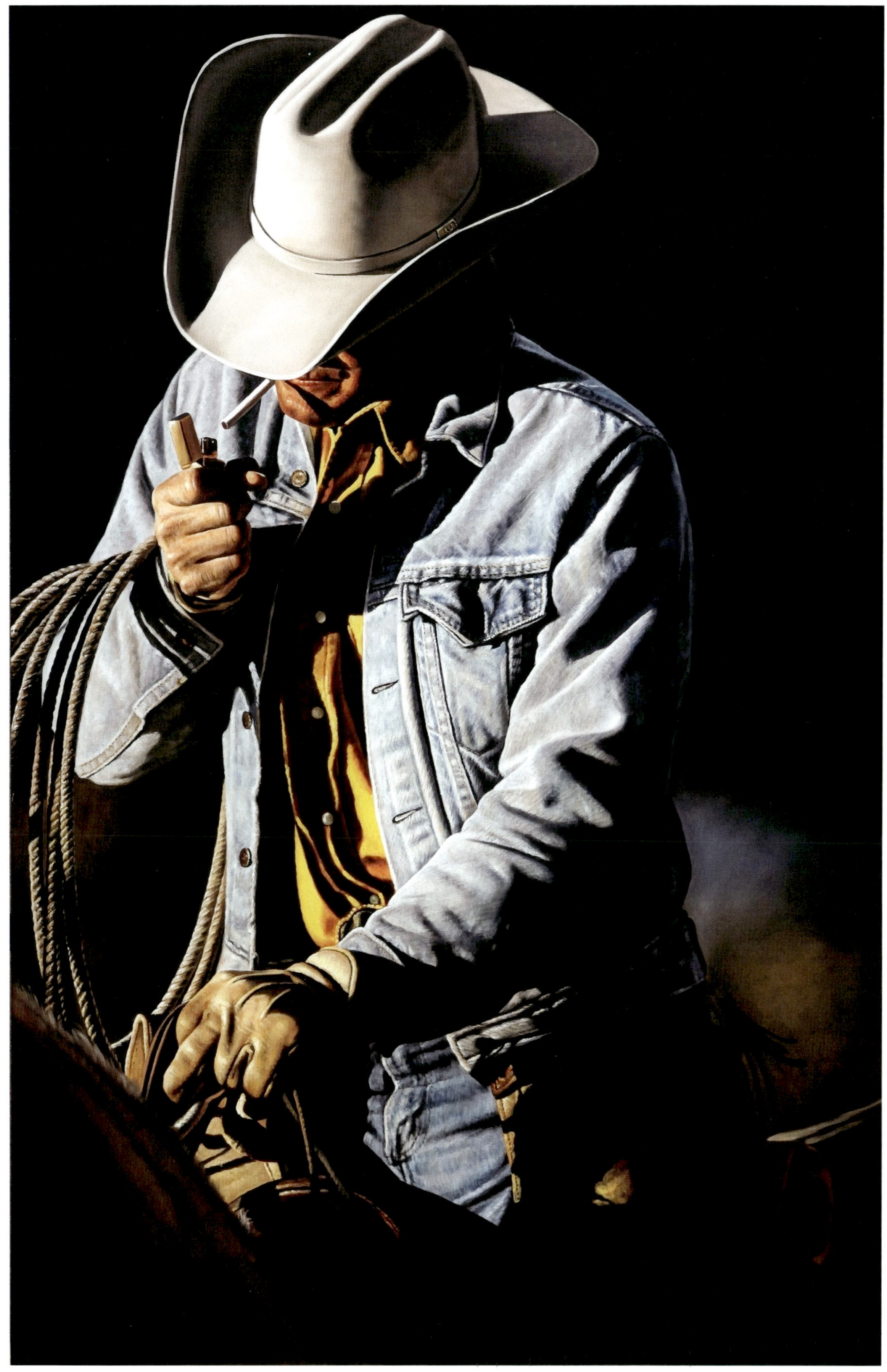

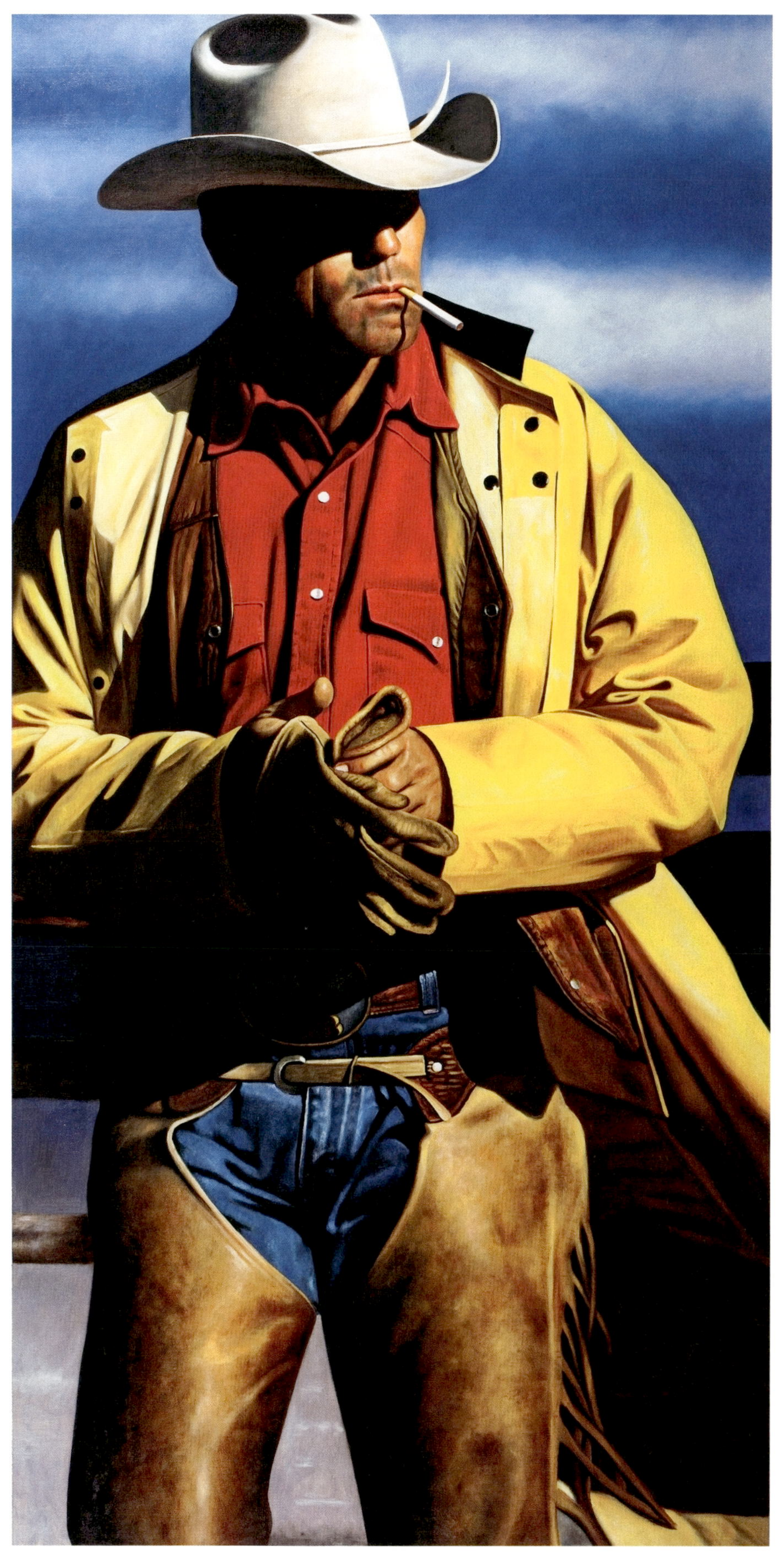

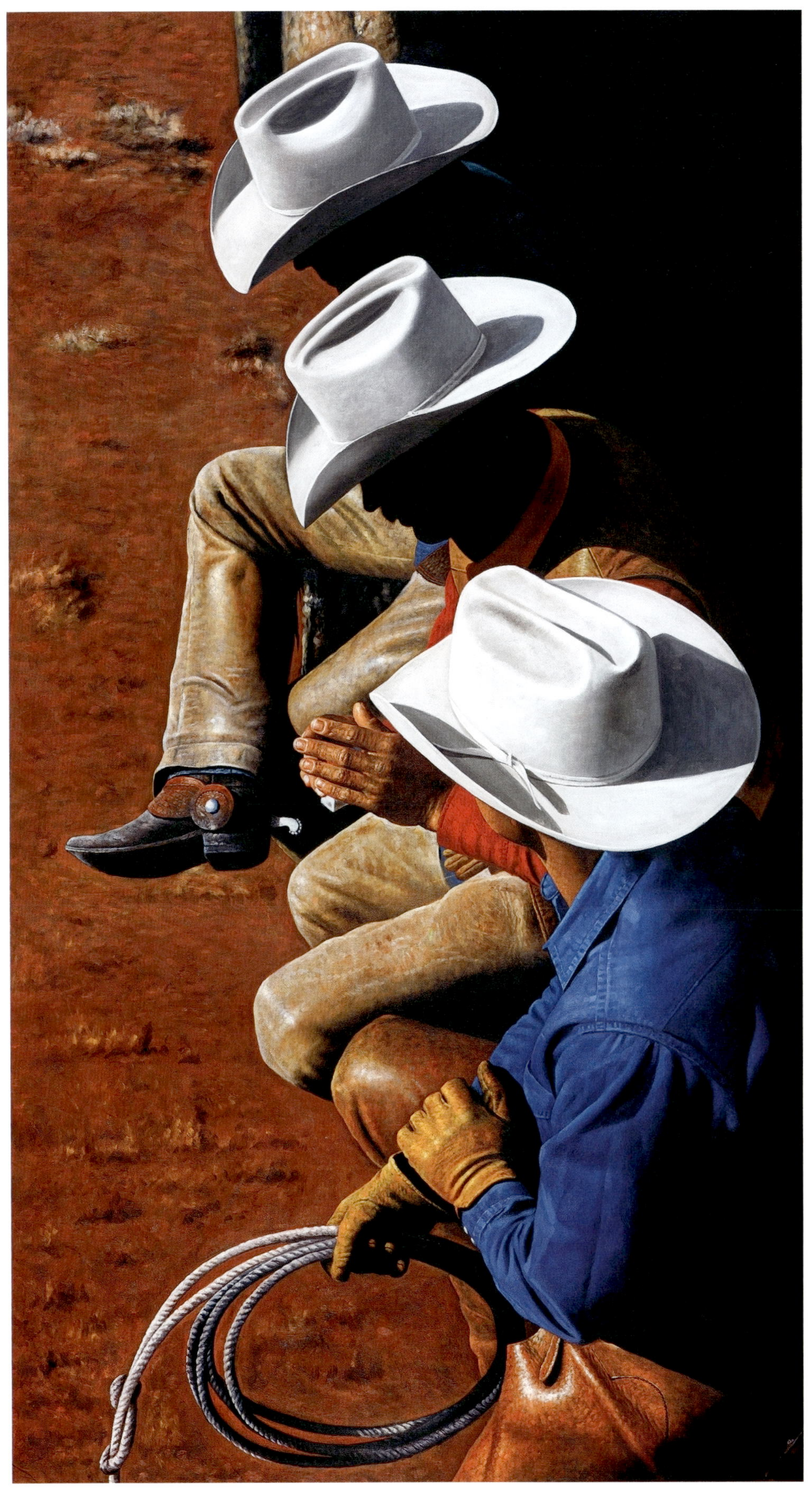

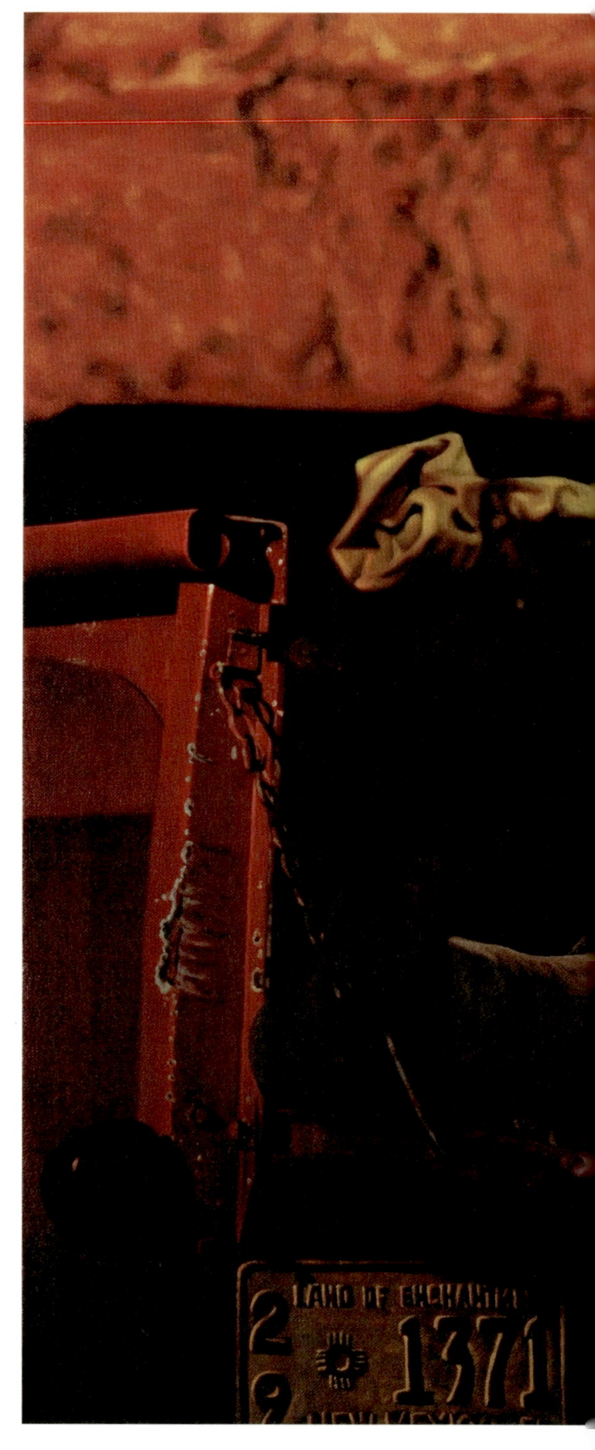
LAND OF ENCHANTMENT
2
9
1371
NEW MEXICO

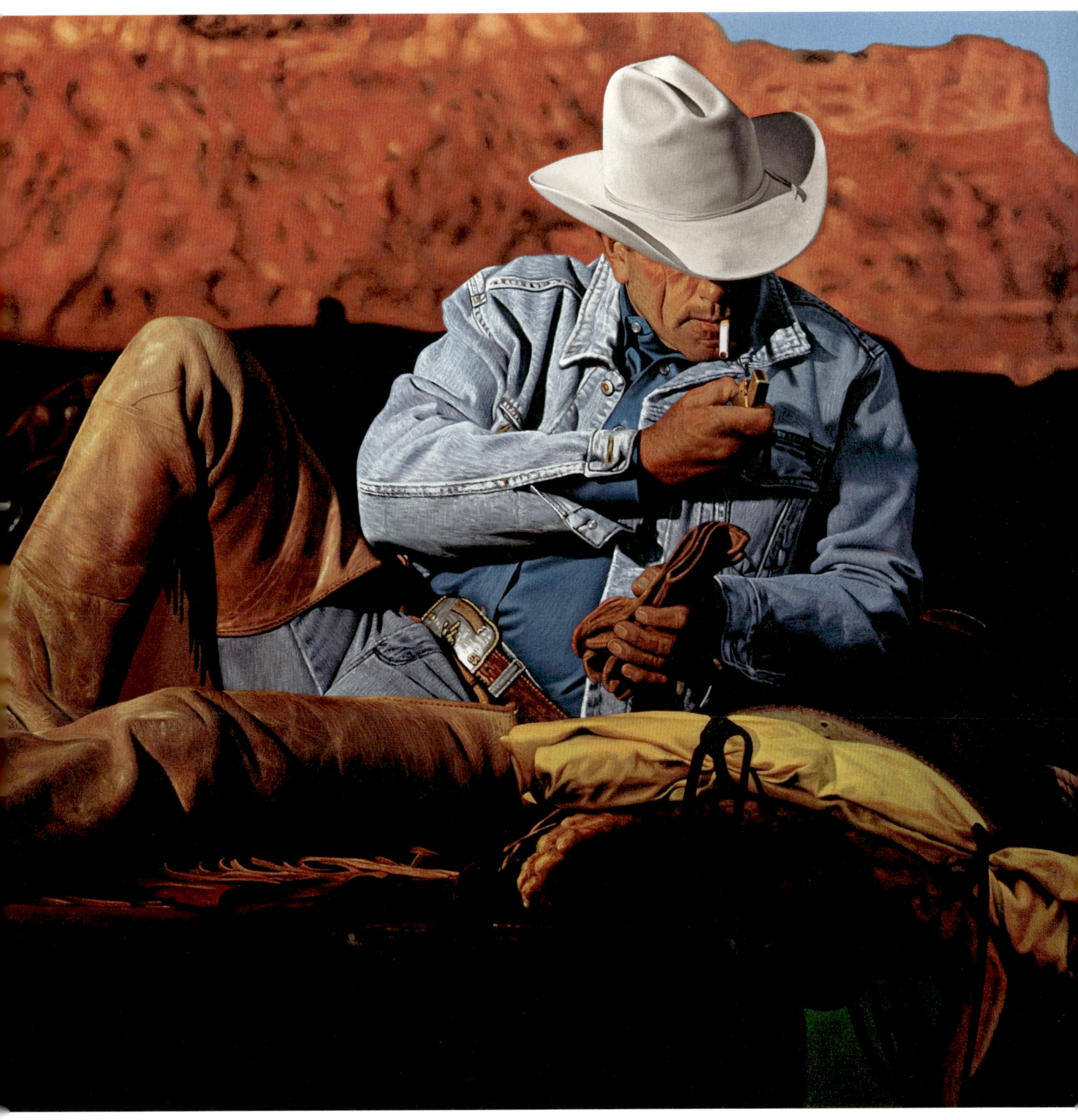

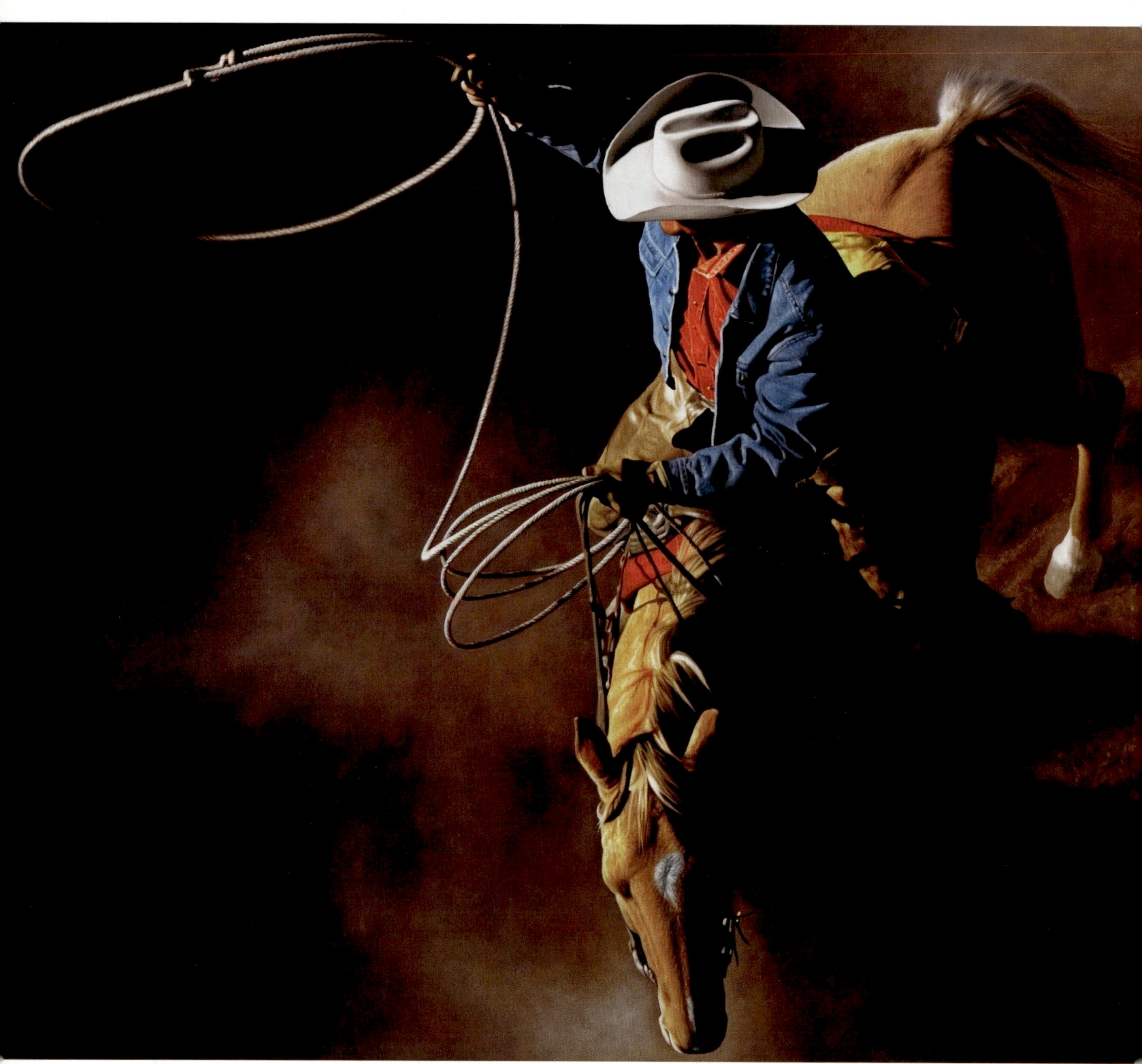

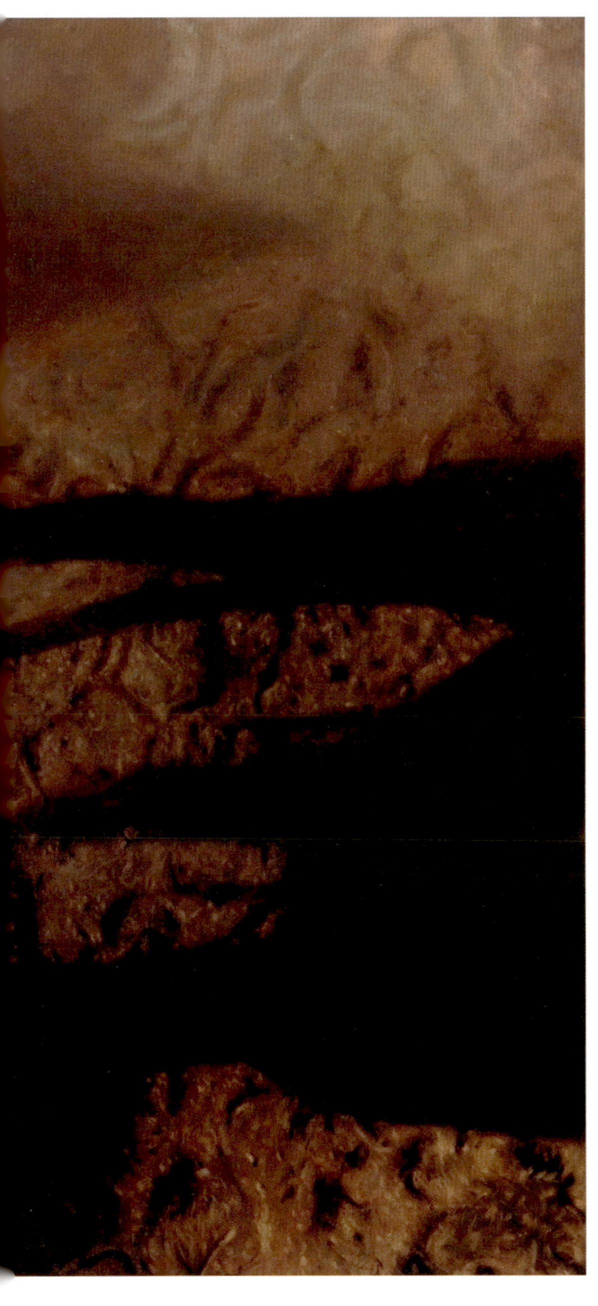

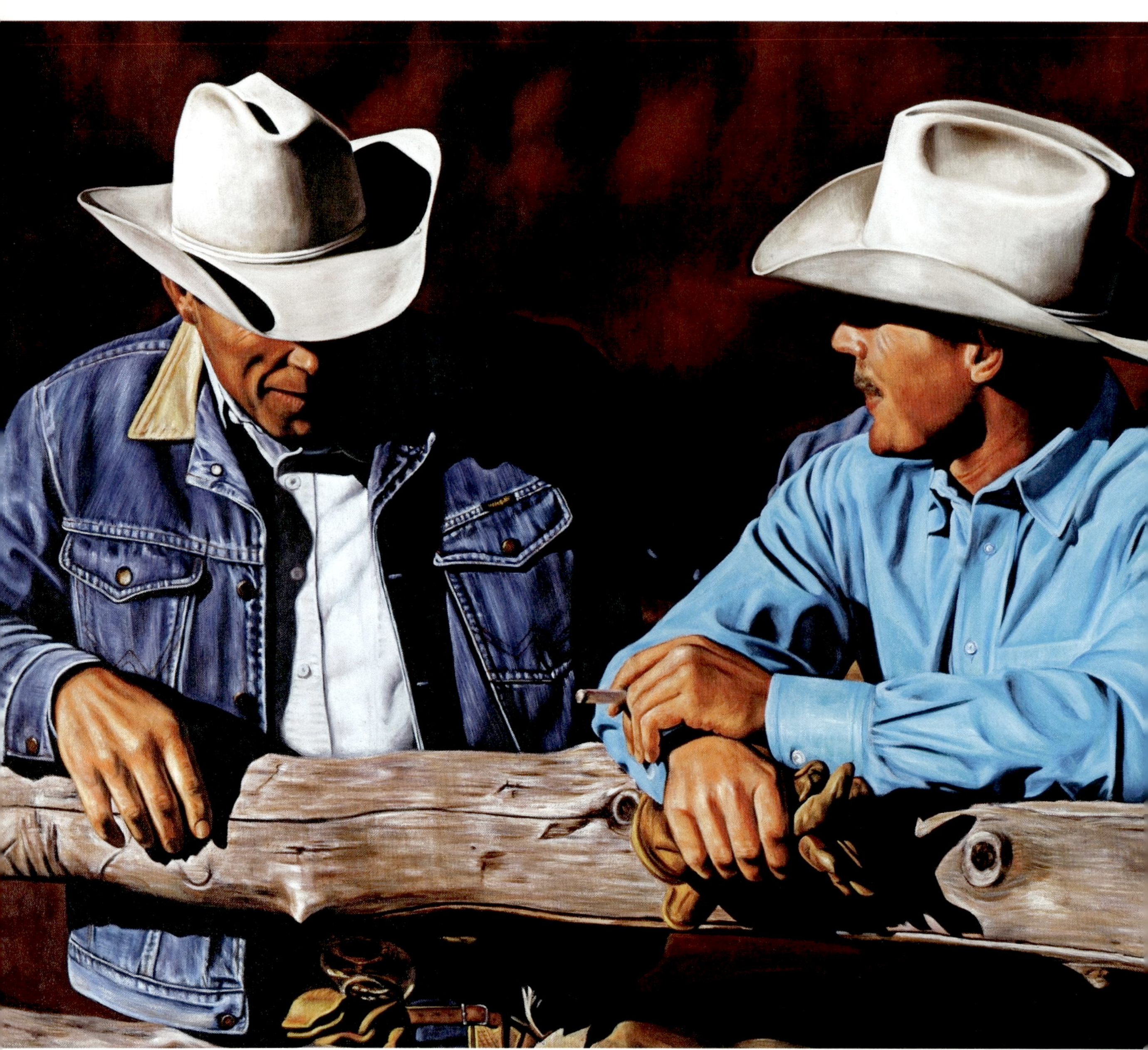

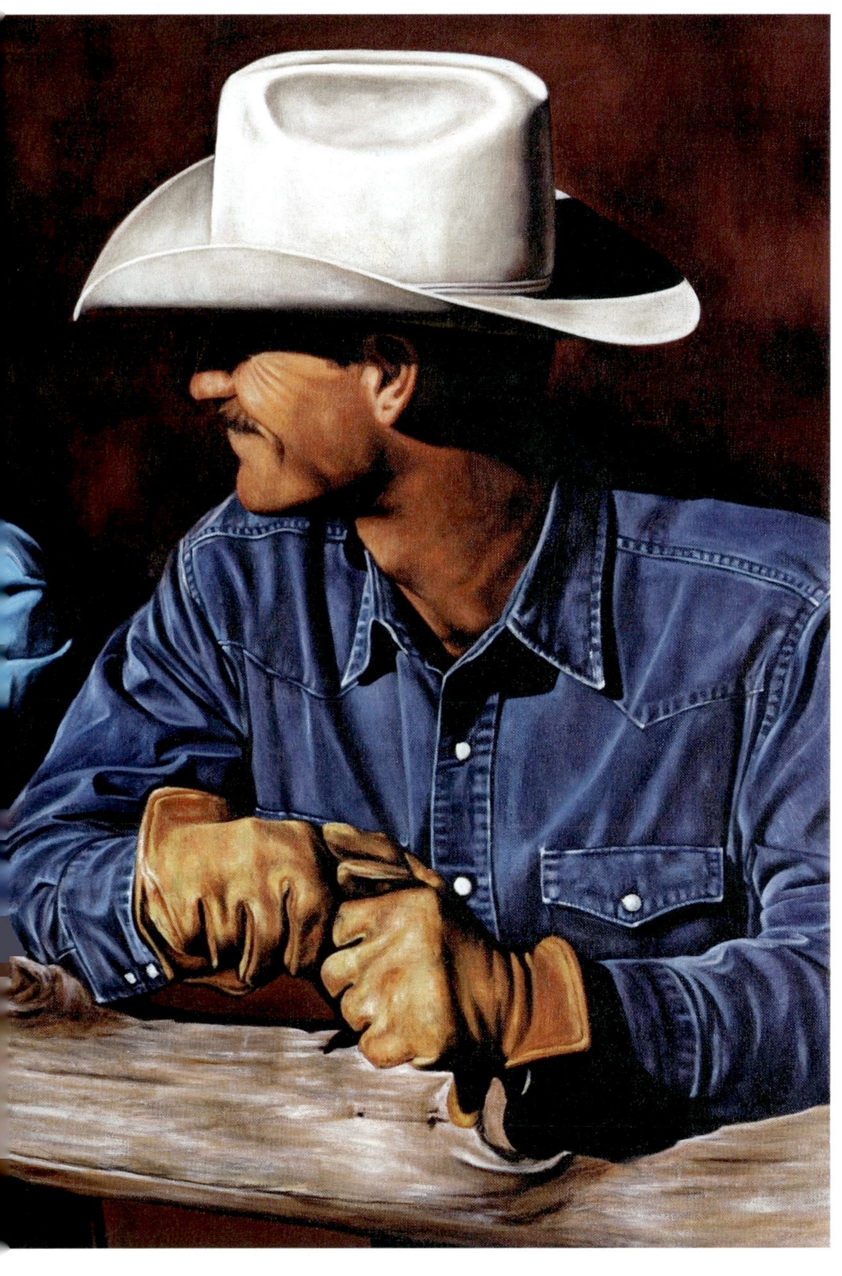

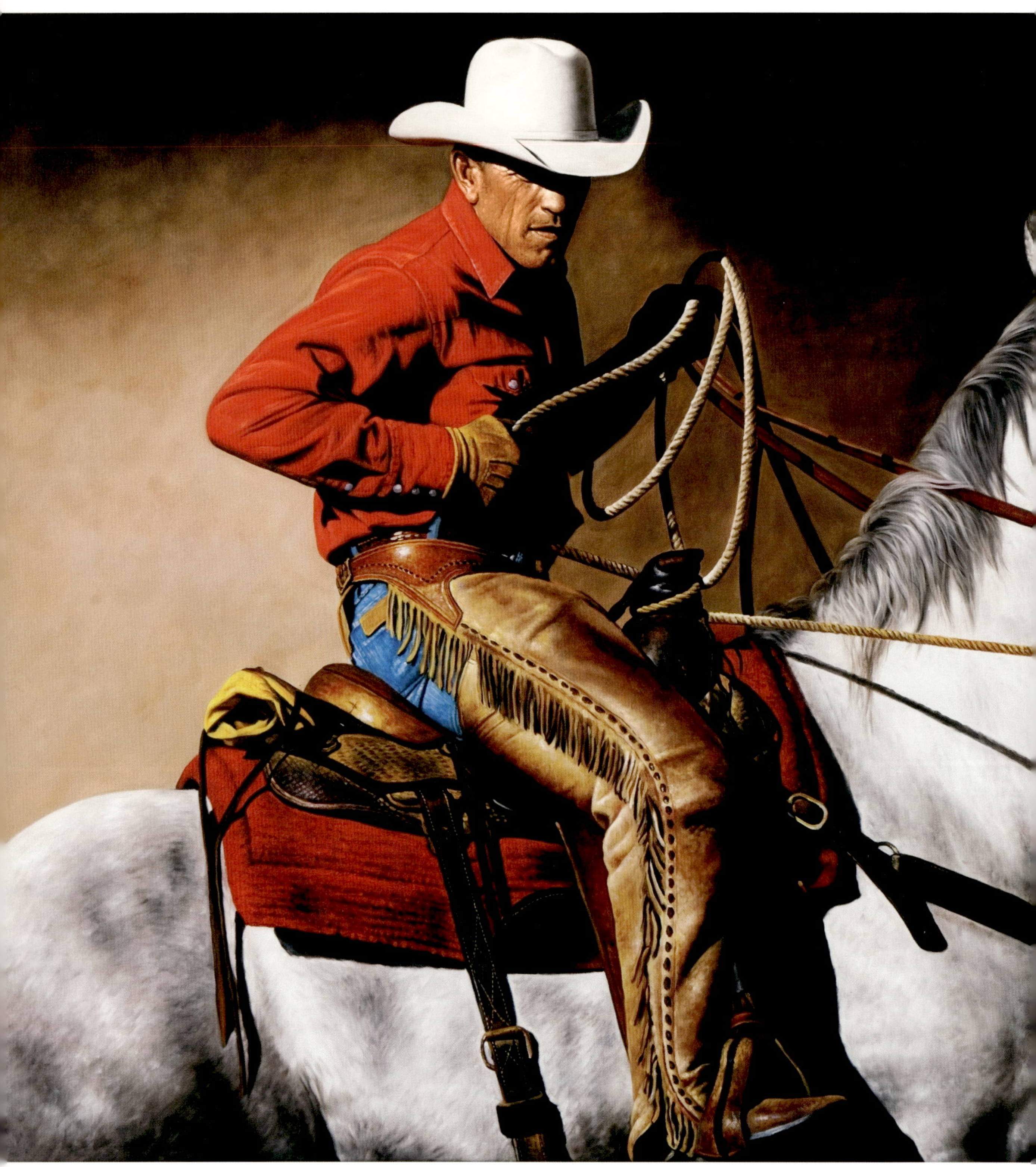

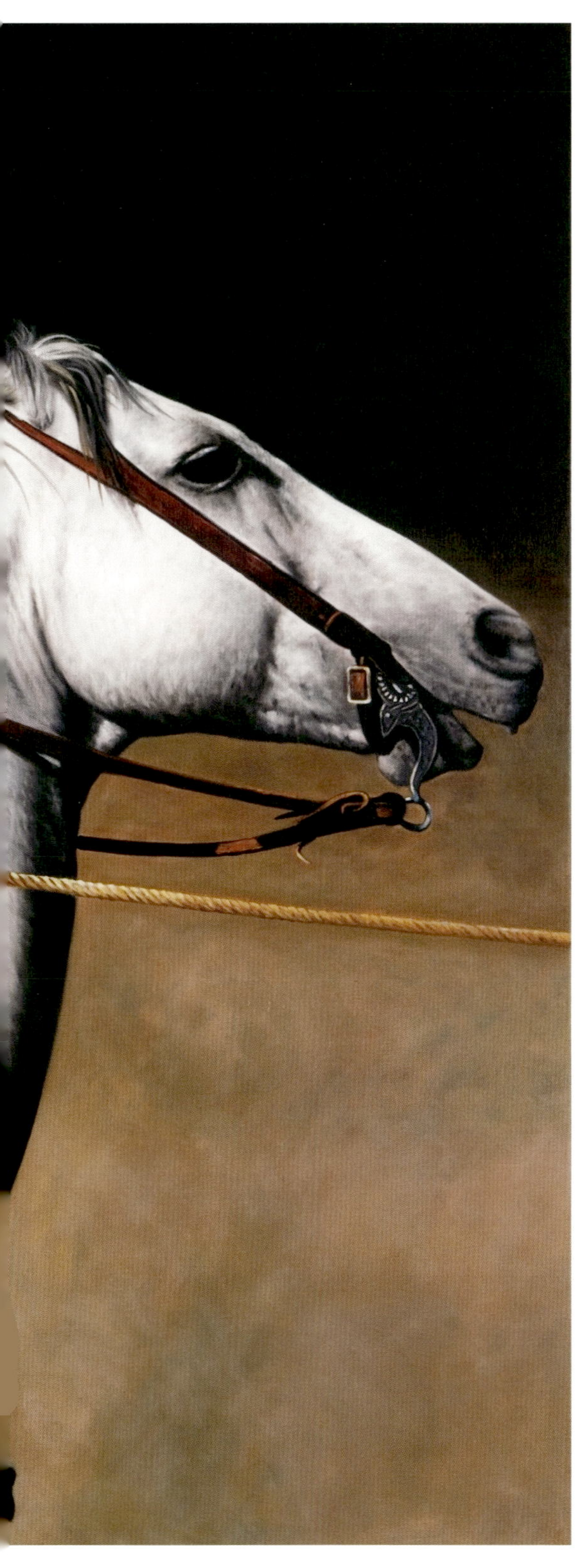

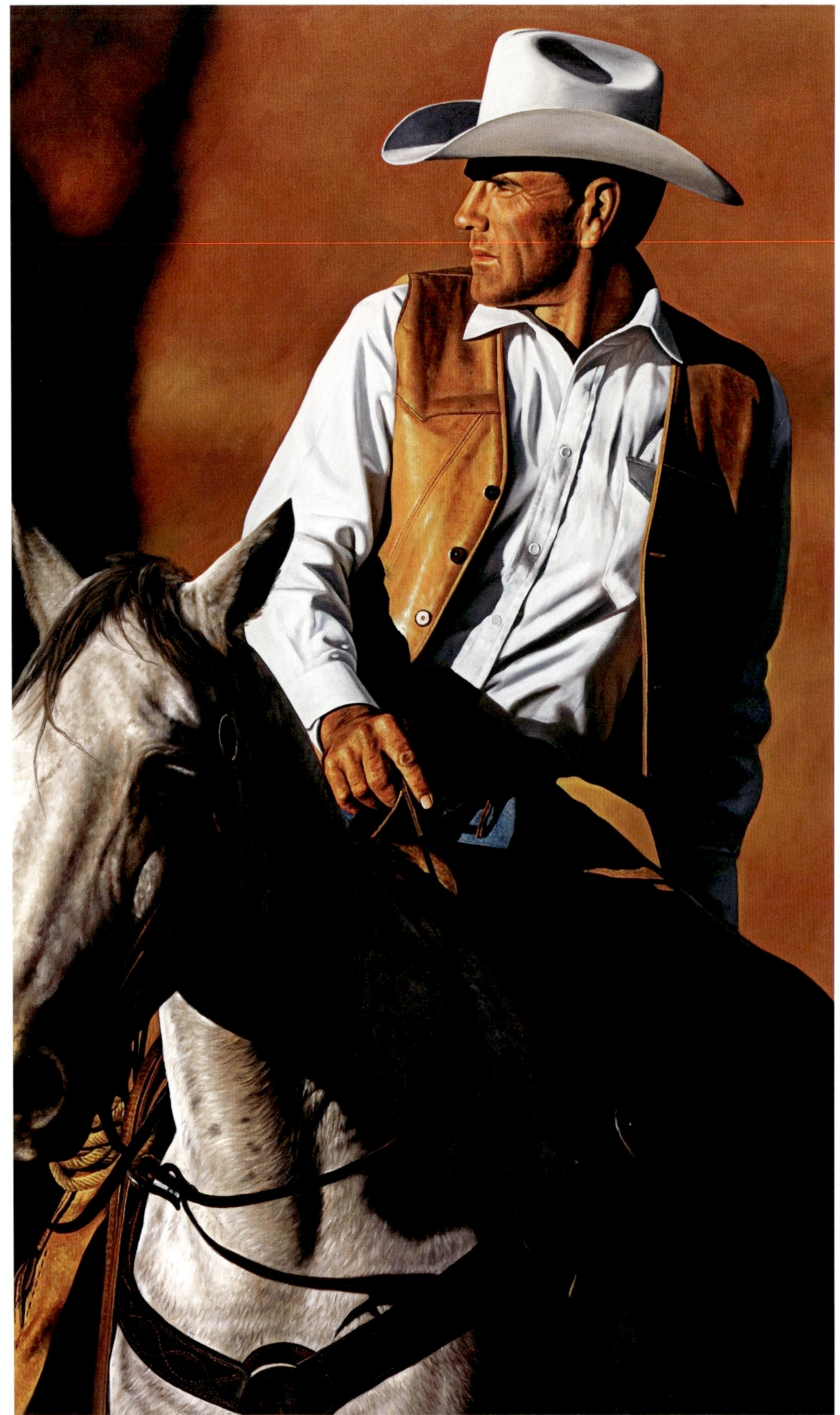

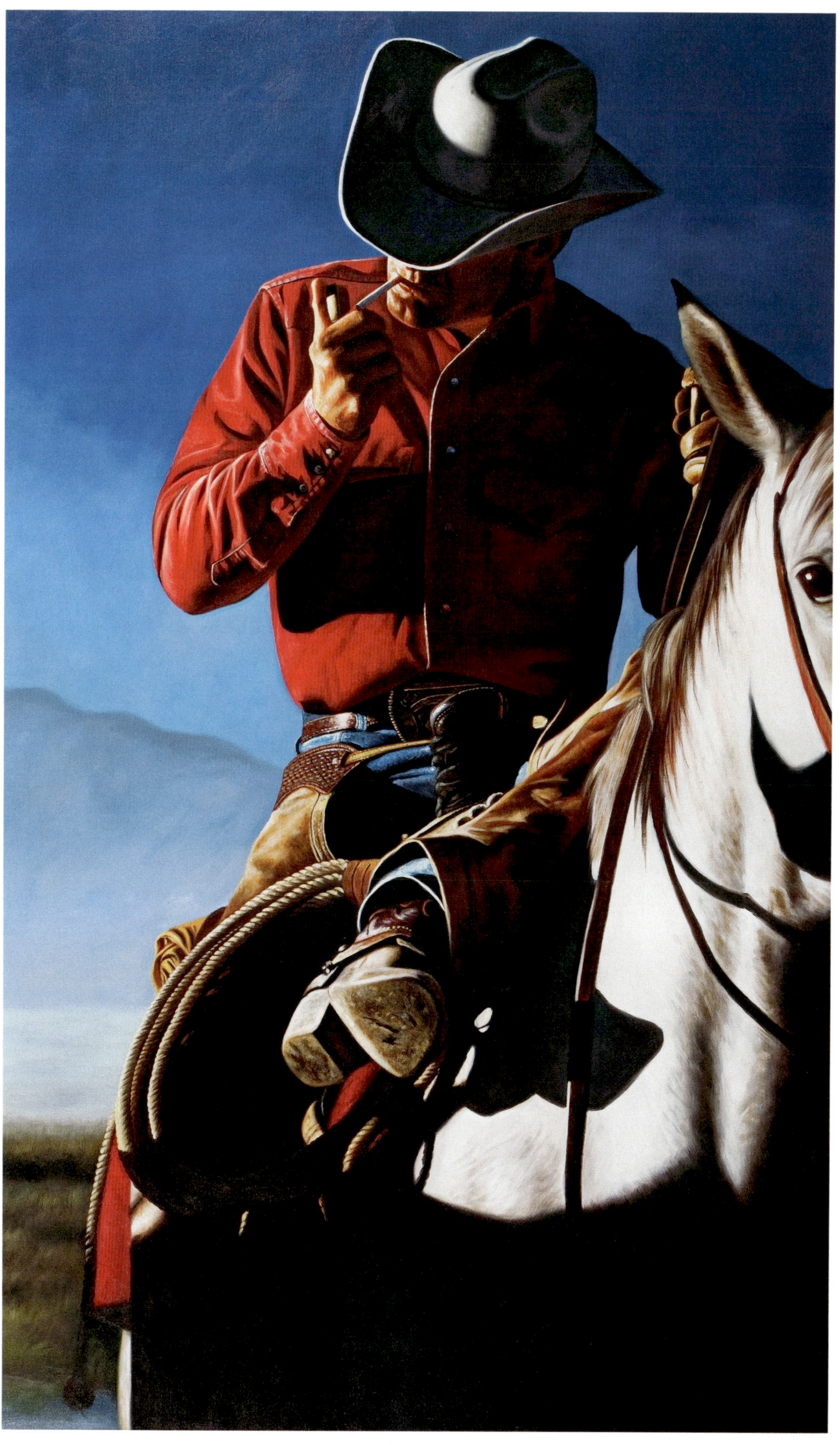

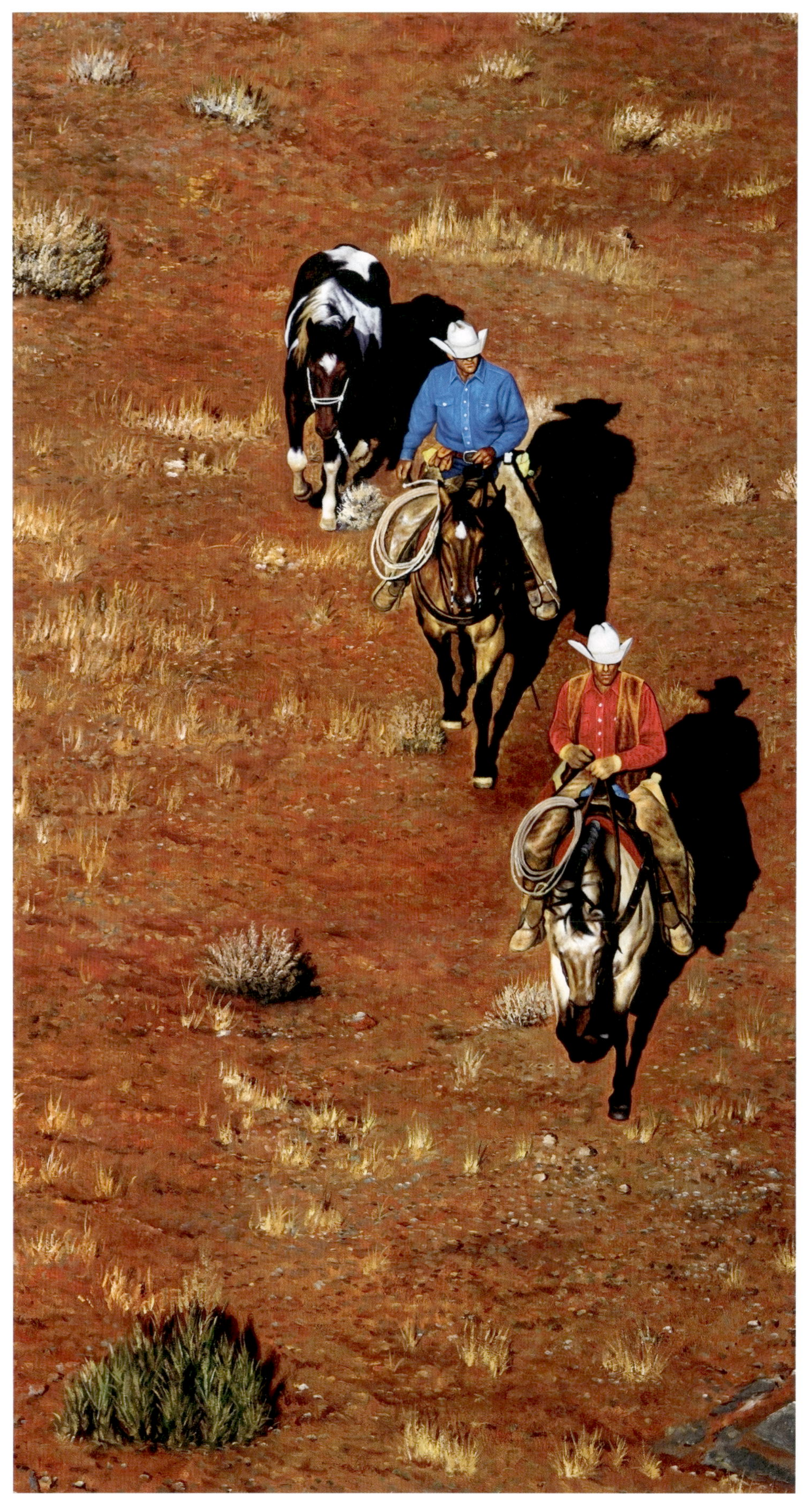

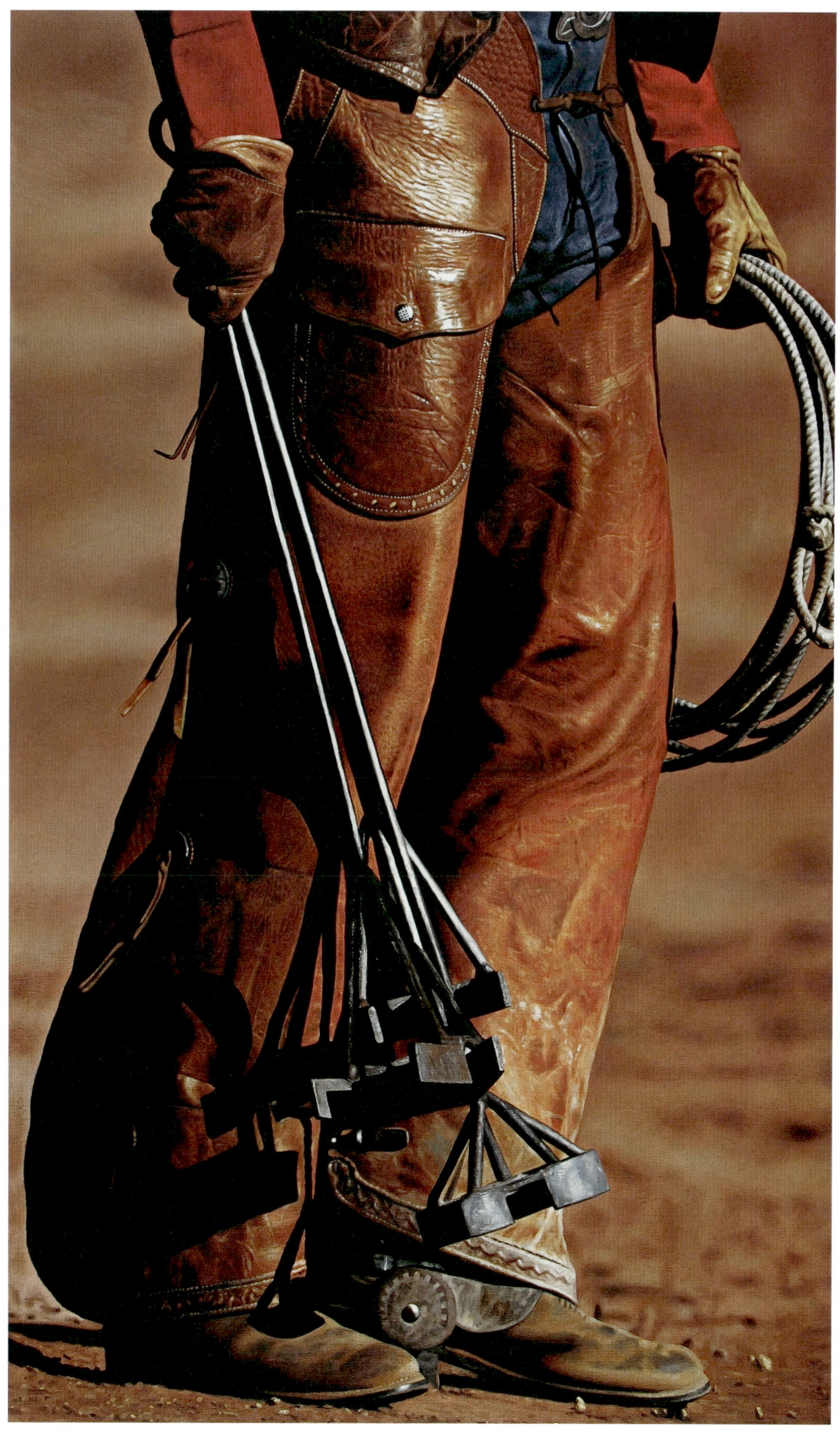

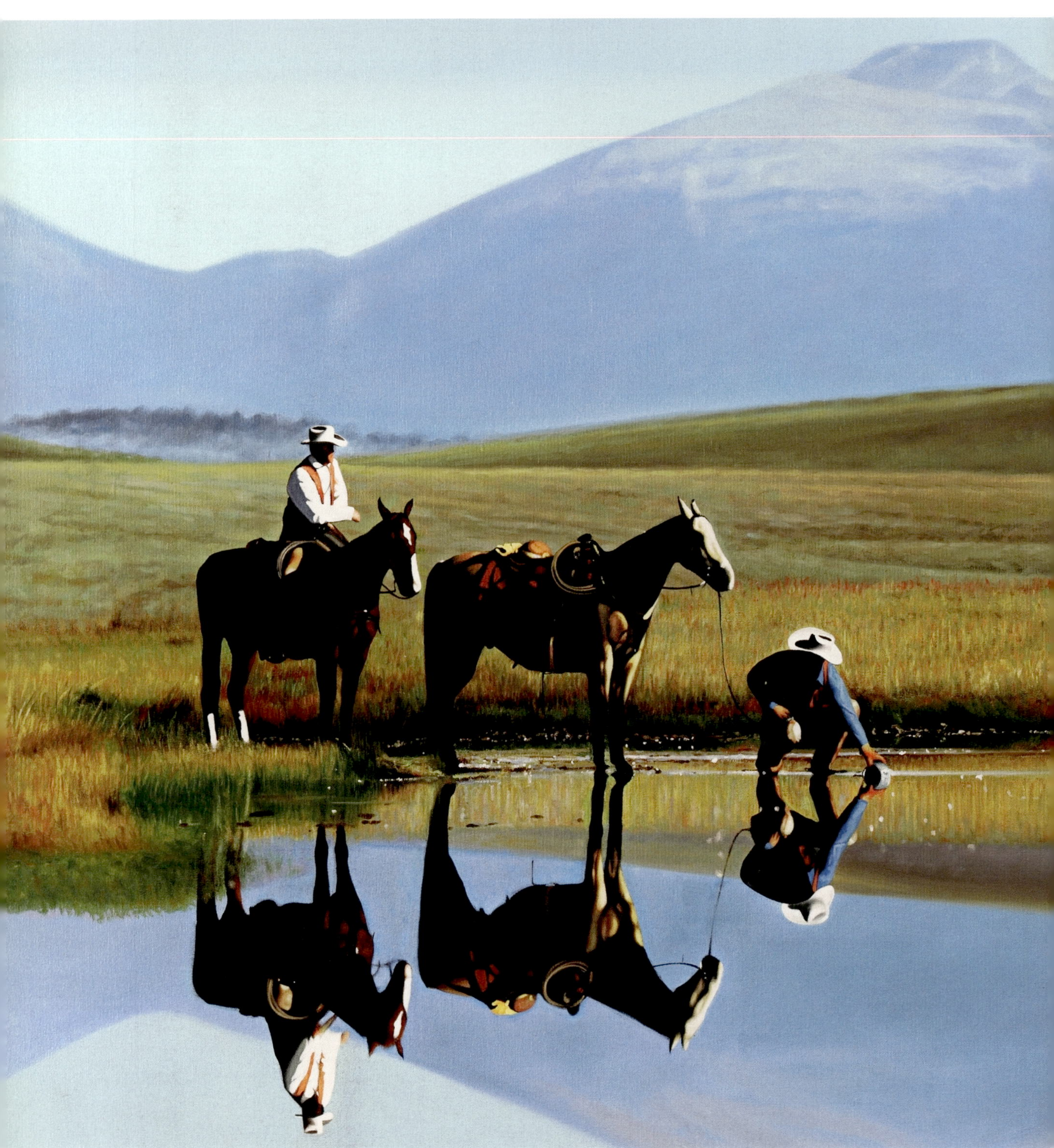

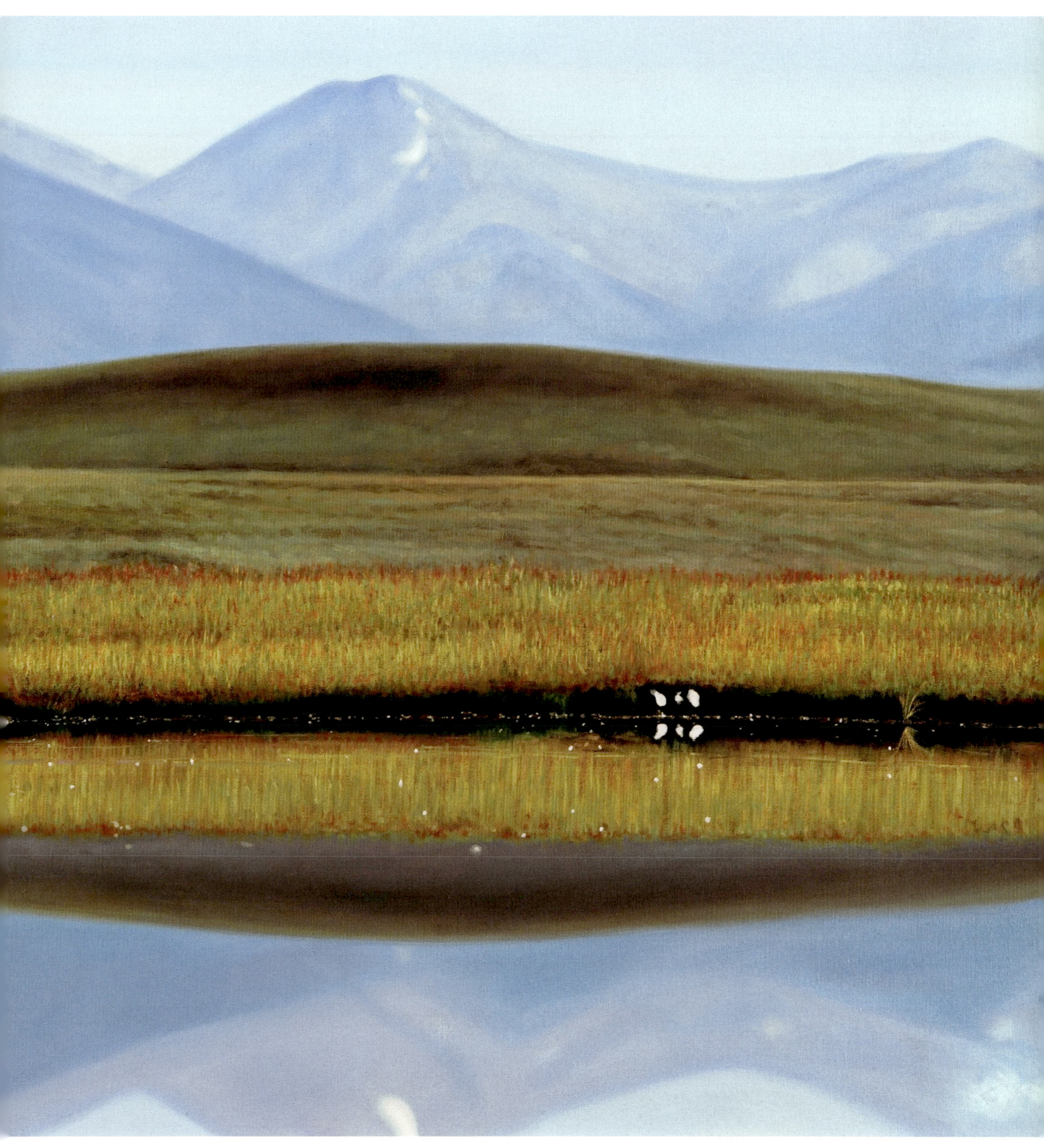

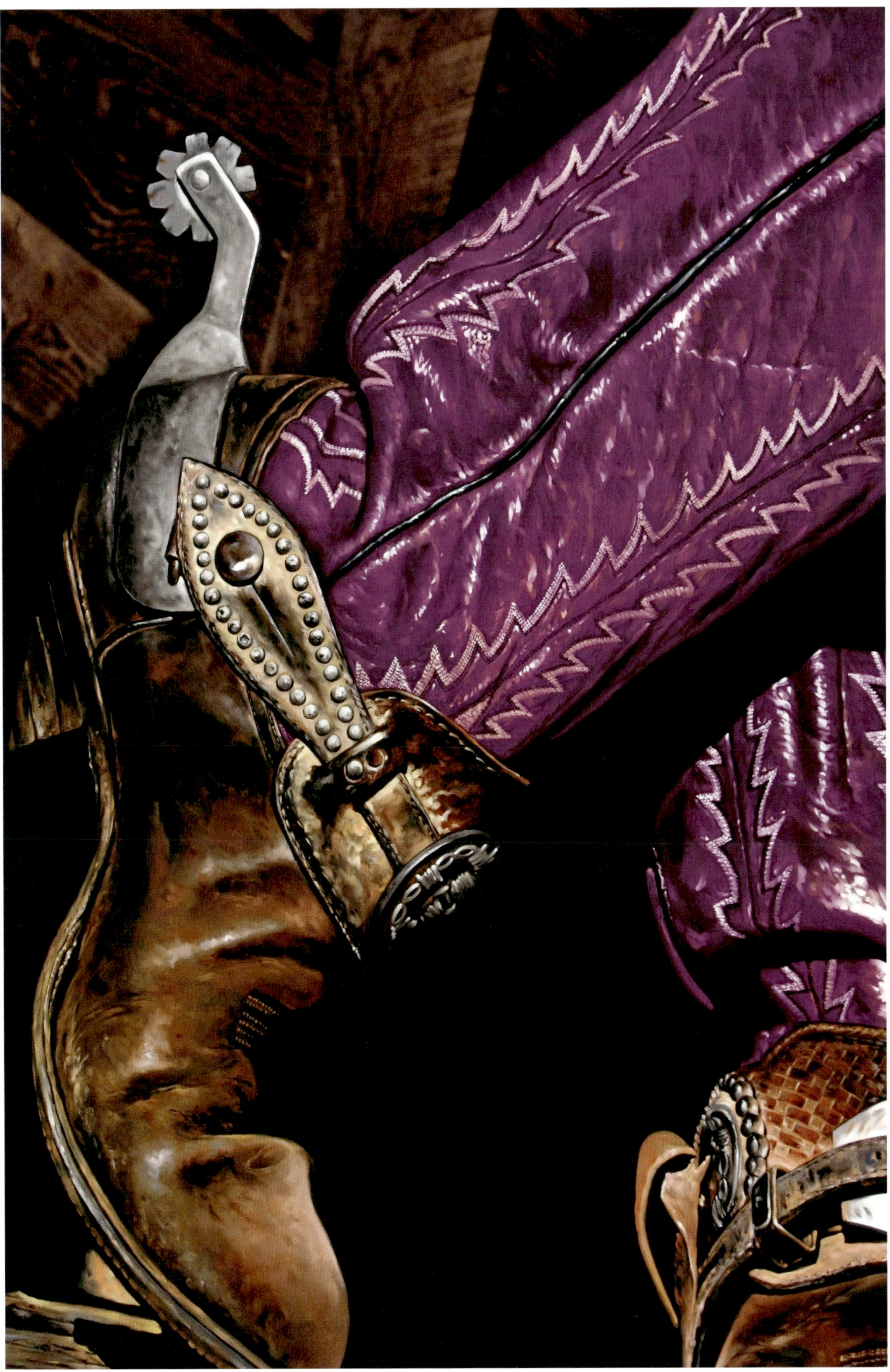

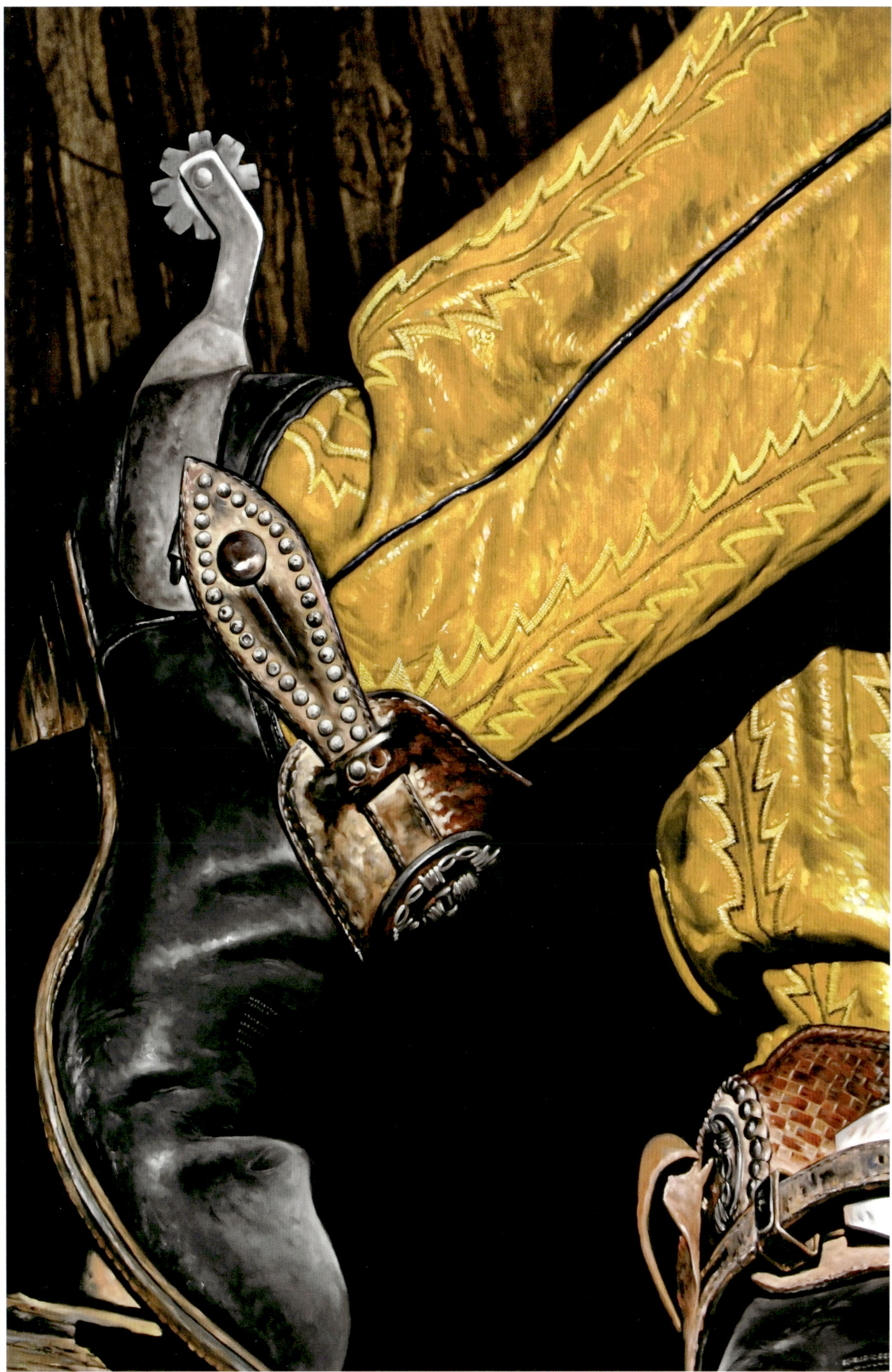

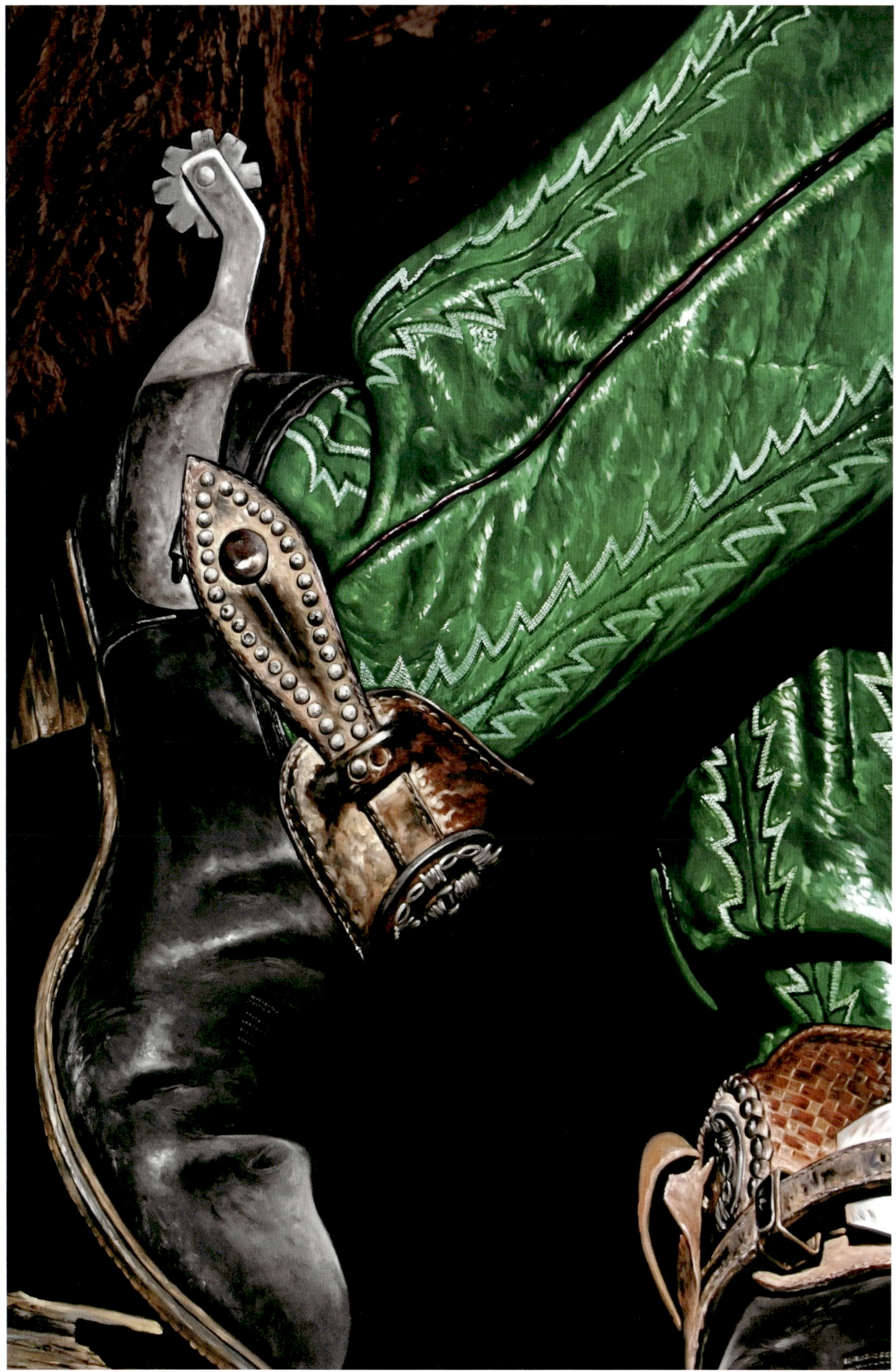

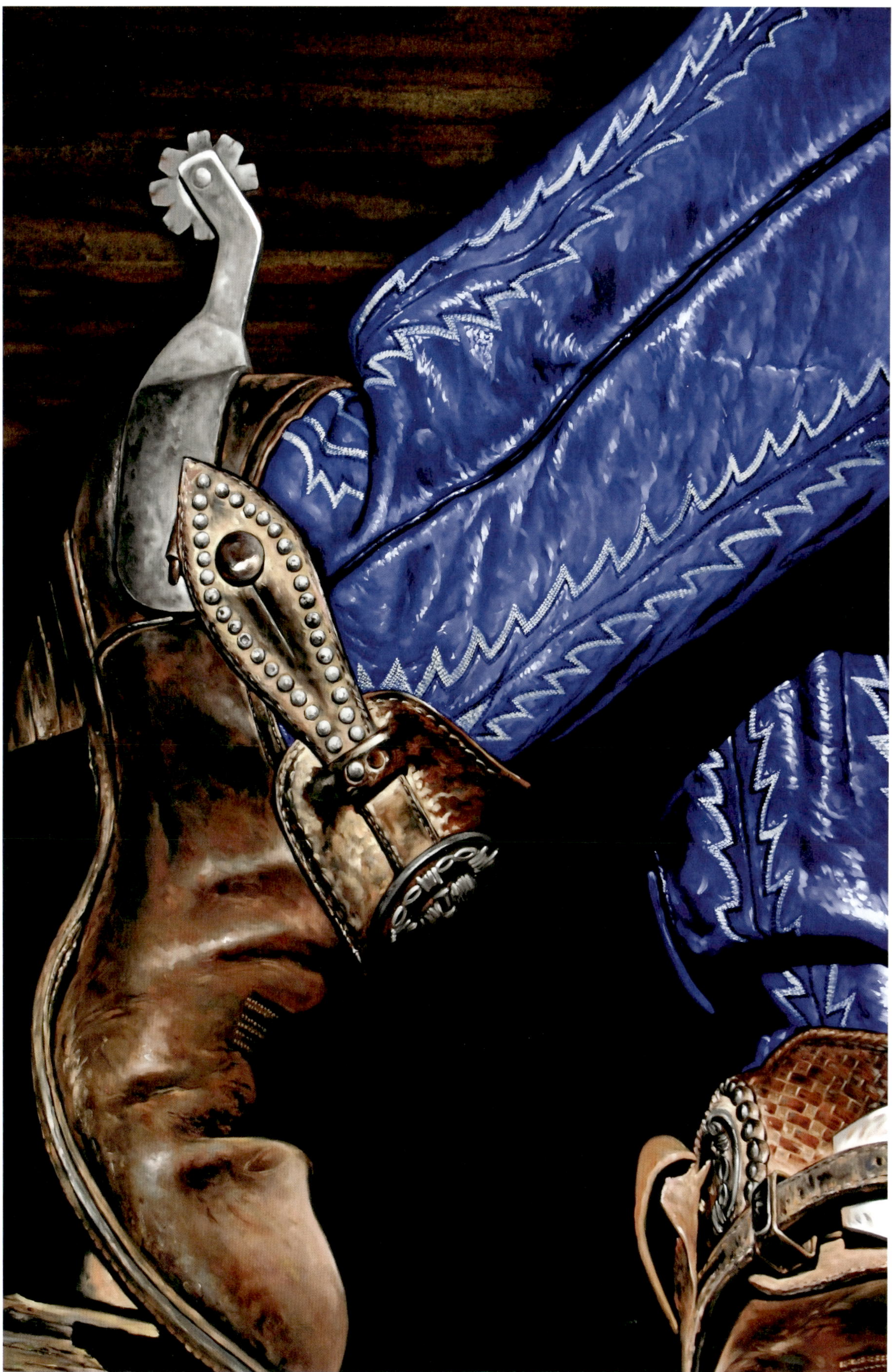

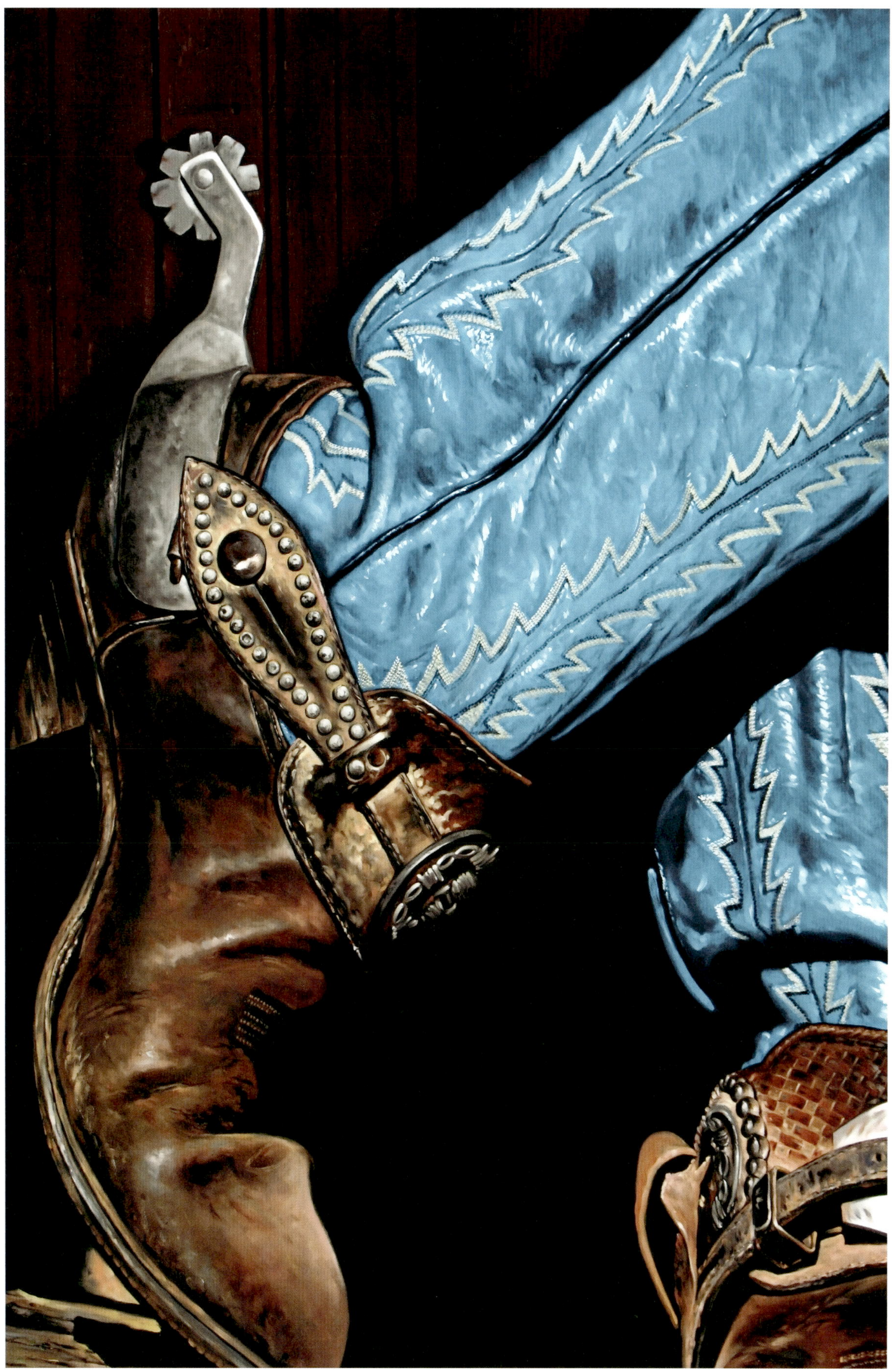

Arles
from: *Fashion*
1999 / 2012
Digital print
80 x 120 cm
p. 198–199

Arles
from: *Fashion*
1999 / 2012
Digital print
100 x 80 cm
p. 200

Arles
from: *Fashion*
1999 / 2012
Digital print
100 x 80 cm
p. 201

Nomads
from: *Fashion (Mongolia)*
2000 / 2012
Digital C-print
75 x 120 cm
p. 202–203

Nomads
from: *Fashion (Mongolia)*
2000
p. 204

Nomads
from: *Fashion (Mongolia)*
2000
p. 205

Spring
from: *Mongolia*
1998
p. 206

Spring
from: *Mongolia*
1998
p. 207

Spring
from: *Mongolia*
1998 / 2012
Digital C-print
120 x 120 cm
p. 208

Spring
from: *Mongolia*
1998 / 2012
Digital print
120 x 120 cm
p. 211

Hotel
from: *Fashion (Mongolia)*
1998 / 2012
Digital C-print
75 x 60 cm
p. 212

Untitled
from: *Fashion (Mongolia)*
1998
p. 213

Untitled
from: *Fashion (Mongolia)*
1998
p. 214

Untitled
from: *Fashion (Mongolia)*
1998
p. 215

Blue
from: *Fashion (Mongolia)*
1998
p. 216–217

Bike Week, Daytona, Florida
from: *Daytona*
1995 / 2012
Digital print
60 x 40 cm
p. 218–219

Bike Week, Daytona, Florida
from: *Daytona*
1995
p. 220–221

Bike Week, Daytona, Florida
from: *Daytona*
1995 / 2012
Digital print
60 x 40 cm
p. 222–223

Bike Week, Daytona, Florida
from: *Daytona*
1995 / 2012
Digital print
40 x 60 cm
p. 224–225

Bike Week, Daytona, Florida
from: *Daytona*
1995 / 2012
Digital print
40 x 60 cm
p. 226–227

Bike Week, Daytona, Florida
from: *Daytona*
1995 / 2012
Digital print
40 x 60 cm
p. 228–229

Miss Nevada
from: *Las Vegas*
1999 / 2012
Digital C-print
75 x 60 cm
p. 231

Cowboy
from: *Las Vegas*
1999 / 2012
Digital C-print
75 x 60 cm
p. 233

Wedding
from: *Las Vegas*
1999
p. 235

Glass Pool
from: *Las Vegas*
1999 / 2012
Digital C-print
100 x 80 cm
p. 237

Everest base camp, Nepal
from: *Fashion (Everest)*
1999 / 2012
Digital pigment print
100 x 330 cm
p. 238–239

Everest base camp, Nepal
from: *Fashion (Everest)*
1999
p. 240–241

Everest base camp, Nepal
from: *Fashion (Everest)*
1999
p. 242

Tanjung Puting, Kalimantan (Borneo), Indonesia
from: *Fashion*
1998 / 2012
Digital C-print
100 x 80 cm
p. 245

Tanjung Puting, Kalimantan (Borneo), Indonesia
from: *Fashion*
1998
p. 247

Salar de Uyuni, Bolivia
from: *Fashion*
2000 / 2012
Digital C-print
100 x 80 cm
p. 249

Untitled, India
from: *Fashion (White Story)*
1998 / 2012
Digital print
112 x 90 cm
p. 251

Untitled, India
from: *Fashion (White Story)*
1998 / 2012
Digital print
112 x 140 cm
p. 252–253

Way Kambas, Sumatra, Indonesia
from: *Fashion*
1999 / 2012
Digital C-print
150 x 120 cm
p. 255

East Coast, Australia
from: *Fashion*
2001 / 2012
Digital C-print
150 x 120 cm
p. 256

Little Flower
from: *Las Vegas*
1999 / 2012
Digital C-print
75 x 60 cm
p. 257

South Africa
from: *Fashion*
1999 / 2012
Digital C-print
75 x 60 cm
p. 259

India
from: *Fashion*
1999
p. 261

India
from: *Fashion*
1999
p. 263

Bintan Island, Indonesia
from: *Fashion*
2000 / 2012
Digital C-print
150 x 120 cm
p. 265

Bintan Island, Indonesia
from: *Fashion*
2000
p. 267

Barry White
from: *Fashion*
1999 / 2012
Digital C-print
150 x 240 cm
p. 268–269

Misfits, Australia
from: *Fashion*
2001 / 2012
Digital C-print
75 x 120 cm
p. 270–271

Boa Vista, Cape Verde Islands
from: *Fashion*
2001 / 2012
Digital C-print
160 x 240 cm
p. 272–273

Cowboy #36
from: *Cowboys*
1998
p. 448–449

Cowboy #61
from: *Cowboys*
2010
Oil on canvas
120 x 350 cm
p. 454–455

Cowboy #102
from: *Cowboys*
2012
Oil on canvas
120 x 180 cm
p. 456

Cowboy #100
from: *Cowboys*
2012
Oil on canvas
120 x 180 cm
p. 457

Cowboy #13
from: *Cowboys*
2008
Oil on canvas
180 x 120 cm
p. 459

Cowboy #74
from: *Cowboys*
2010
Oil on canvas
200 x 120 cm
p. 461

Cowboy #38
from: *Cowboys*
2009
Oil on canvas
120 x 180 cm
p. 462–463

Cowboy #53
from: *Cowboys*
2008
Oil on canvas
180 x 120 cm
p. 465

Cowboy #22
from: *Cowboys*
2007
Oil on canvas
240 x 120 cm
p. 467

Cowboy #47
from: *Cowboys*
2010
Oil on canvas
220 x 120 cm
p. 469

Cowboy #05
from: *Cowboys*
2007
Oil on canvas
120 x 180 cm
p. 470–471

Cowboy #12
from: *Cowboys*
2007
Oil on canvas
120 x 200 cm
p. 472–473

Cowboy #116
from: *Cowboys*
2012
Oil on canvas
120 x 230 cm
p. 474–475

Cowboy #71
from: *Cowboys*
2010
Oil on canvas
150 x 200 cm
p. 476–477

Cowboy #66
from: *Cowboys*
2010
Oil on canvas
200 x 120 cm
p. 478

Cowboy #21
from: *Cowboys*
2009
Oil on canvas
200 x 120 cm
p. 479

Cowboy #44
from: *Cowboys*
2010
Oil on canvas
220 x 120 cm
p. 481

Cowboy #03
from: *Cowboys*
2007
Oil on canvas
200 x 120 cm
p. 483

Cowboy #15
from: *Cowboys*
2007
Oil on canvas
120 x 240 cm
p. 484–485

Cowboy #122
from: *Cowboys*
2012
Oil on canvas
180 x 120 cm
p. 487

Cowboy #123
from: *Cowboys*
2012
Oil on canvas
180 x 120 cm
p. 489

Cowboy #121
from: *Cowboys*
2012
Oil on canvas
180 x 120 cm
p. 491

Cowboy #120
from: *Cowboys*
2012
Oil on canvas
180 x 120 cm
p. 493

Cowboy #119
from: *Cowboys*
2012
Oil on canvas
180 x 120 cm
p. 495

Biography

Hannes Schmid was born in Zurich in 1946 and grew up in Toggenburg. He completed an apprenticeship as an electrical engineer and lighting engineer, and from 1970 studied photography at the Ruth Prowse School of Art in Cape Town, South Africa.

Projects

2012	*Smiling Gecko*, independent charitable project for children in Cambodia
2009	*Divas+Heroes*
2003–	*Cowboys*, painting
2001–2008	*Models*, charitable project for the Swiss Paraplegic Foundation and for Pro Infirmis
2001–2006	*Bonneville. The Final Run*, film and photography for Formula 1
1998–2011	*For Gods Only*, photography and film
1993–2002	Recreation of the Marlboro Man for Leo Burnett / Phillip Morris
1984–2002	*Fashion*
1984–2001	Implementation of numerous independent projects, e.g. in Florida *(Daytona)*, in Belize *(Mennonites)*, in Bolivia *(Potosí)*, the Maha Kumbh Mela in India *(The Flow of Life)*, in Singapore *(Thaipusam)*
1977–1984	*Rockstars*
1974–1977	Travels through Southeast Asia, China, Tibet, sojourns with tribes in West Papua (Irian Jaya), Indonesia *(Dani & Lani)*
1970–1974	Travels through Africa. Landscape and portrait photography, e.g. on Lake Turkana *(El Molos)*, on Kilimanjaro, on Mount Kenya, in Ethiopia, in Sudan and in Egypt

Awards

2011	*Delphic Art Movie Award.* Special prize "Protection of Intangible Heritage" for the film *For Gods Only*
2004	Patronage of UNESCO Switzerland for *For Gods Only*
1992	*LIFE Magazine,* Best Fashion Picture of the Year
1988	*Elle. France,* Best Fashion Photographer

Collections

Fachstelle Kultur des Kantons Zürich (Culture Agency of the Canton of Zurich)

Fotostiftung Schweiz (Swiss Foundation for Photography), Winterthur

Julius Baer Art Collection, Zurich

Museum Folkwang, Essen

Collection Rainer-Marc Frey, Zurich

Collection Per Gunnar Strømberg Rasmussen, Bergen, Norway

Solo Exhibitions

2012	*Hannes Schmid. Photography and Painting, A Different Fashion*, St. Moritz Art Masters, Switzerland
	Momentous, photo12, Maag Areal Zurich, Zurich, Switzerland
2011	*Cowboy*, Edwynn Houk Gallery, New York, USA
	Human Currents, Rubin Museum of Art, New York, USA
	Myth of the West, Edwynn Houk Gallery, Zurich, Switzerland
	Work in Progress, Bank Julius Baer, Zurich, Switzerland
2010	*For Gods Only*, St. Moritz Art Masters, Switzerland
	Never Look Back, Swiss Foundation of Photography, Winterthur, Switzerland
2008	*Men and Machismo*, Mitchell Algus Gallery, New York, USA
	Divas+Heroes, Petit Palais, Montreux Palace, Montreux, Switzerland
	Divas+Heroes, Cultural Centre Zermatt, Zermatt, Switzerland

Group Exhibitions

2012-13	*A Star is Born*, Museum der bildenden Künste Leipzig, Leipzig, Germany
2012	*Shine on You Crazy Diamond*, Ex-Ernst & Young, Zurich, Switzerland
	Scenarios About Europe, Galerie für Zeitgenössische Kunst Leipzig, Leipzig, Germany
2011	*Family Life*, Elaine Levy Project, Brussels, Belgium
	Echoes, Centre Culturel Suisse, Paris, France
2010	*A Star is Born*, Museum Folkwang, Essen, Germany
2009-12	*Who Shot Rock & Roll. A Photographic History*, Brooklyn Museum, New York; Worcester Art Museum, Worcester; Memphis Brooks Museum of Art, Memphis; Akron Art Museum, Akron; Columbia Museum of Art, Columbia; Tucson Museum of Art, Tucson; Annenberg Space for Photography, Los Angeles, USA
2009	*Rockstars*, Galerie Nicola von Senger, Zurich, Switzerland
2008/09	*Born of the Moment and Method*, Walter Randel Gallery, New York, USA
2008	*Looking Back: The White Columns Annual*, White Columns Gallery, New York, USA
2002	*Tribe Art Commission (Moment of a Moment)* touring exhibition, London, Milan, Jakarta, Shanghai

Authors' Biographies

Elisabeth Bronfen is professor of English and American Studies at the University of Zurich. She has contributed numerous essays on visual culture to exhibition catalogues and anthologies. Most recently she has published *Tiefer als der Tag gedacht, Eine Kulturgeschichte der Nacht* (2008), *Crossmappings, Essays zur Visuellen Kultur* (2011), and *Specters of War. Hollywood's Engagement with Military Conflict* (2012).

Gail Buckland is the Distinguished Visiting Professor of the History of Photography at The Cooper Union, New York. She has taught at Columbia College, Chicago; Pratt Institute, Brooklyn; and Sarah Lawrence College, Bronxville, New York where she held the Nobel Chair in Art and Cultural History. Buckland is the author or collaborator on fourteen books. She is the former curator of the Royal Photographic Society of Great Britain and has organized numerous exhibitions in the United States and Europe.

Rainer Egloff gained his doctorate in history at the University of Zurich after training as a bookseller and working as an amateur rock musician. He has published extensively on the social sciences, multidisciplinarity, and popular culture. After many years of transdisciplinary research at the Collegium Helveticum, Zurich, he started working for Swiss Re in 2012, doing research on the early recognition of risk.

Matthias Frehner has been director of the Kunstmuseum Bern since 2002. Previously he worked as the curator of the Oscar Reinhart Collection "Am Römerholz" in Winterthur, as secretary of the Gottfried Keller Foundation and as art editor at the *Neue Zürcher Zeitung*. He studied art history, German literature, and archaeology, writing his doctorate on "Die Geschichte der Schweizer Eisenplastik" (The History of Swiss Iron Sculpture). He has written widely on various themes and artists, including Anker, Segantini, Vallotton, Oppenheim, Hodler, Amiet, Burne-Jones, Derain, as well as looted art and the Kunstmuseum's collection.

Kornelia Imesch Oechslin is professor of Modern and Contemporary Art and Architecture at the University of Lausanne, with a focus on the global art system, art & branding, art & gender, film & art, and Swiss art. She is the co-editor and author of several publications on art and the art business from modern to contemporary art.

Christiane Kuhlmann is the curator of the exhibition *Hannes Schmid. Real Stories*. She studied art history and history, writing her doctorate on dance photography of the 1920s. In 2010 she curated the exhibition *A Star is Born. Photography and Rock since Elvis* at the Museum Folkwang, Essen, where she included works by Hannes Schmid. She has worked for the Museo Picasso in Malaga, the Museum of Contemporary Art in Seville, and the Rijksmuseum Amsterdam. Kuhlmann has published widely, teaches photography at the FH Dortmund, and is chairman of the board of the Kunsthaus Essen.

Ildegarda E. Scheidegger is an art historian working as a specialist at Sotheby's Zurich. She holds a PhD in East Asian arts and is engaged as an art consultant and curator, in art event management, the coaching of artists, as well as an author and editor. In addition she authors texts for public relations and reviews, and gives lectures. Her recent publications include *Mayo Bucher: Moonwalker* (2011) and *Annelies Strba: My Life Dreams* (2012).

Acknowledgments

With this book a window opens on my creative endeavors that could only be accomplished with the backing of my family, friends, and acquaintances. I would like to extend my heartfelt thanks to all those who gave me their trust, patience, and financial support.

Above all I thank my wife Hillary and my two children, Anna and Maximilian, from whom I required a lot of understanding and patience; Simon Huang, my father-in-law, who with the art of his calligraphy has combined the Gods with the earthly; Susanne Zoller, my business partner, who has been an important part of my endeavors for all these years; Jürg Wey, who with all his knowledge and skill consistently brings me forward in new ways, and who has significantly participated in shaping my work; Cherin and Boris Collardi, whose friendship and assistance in recent years have been crucial for my path; Ursina Donnerstag and Gregor Klomp, who supported me in my tasks; Guido Persterer, to whom as gallery owner and friend I have much to be thankful for; Christiane Kuhlmann, who has taken on a lot of effort and work, gone through my archive, and brought my work together, and thus laid the foundation for the exhibit in the Kunstmuseum Bern and for the book; Ildegarda Scheidegger, who has accompanied me for many years, whose work I highly esteem, and under whose responsibility the book and the collaboration with all the authors have become possible; Elisa Bütler, who grew into the whole thing with me and who has always demonstrated competence and shown indefatigable commitment; Stefan Laeng, who with his counsel and help was at my side at all times; Gilio Pasqua, who helped us on all levels with his technical know-how.

Matthias Frehner enabled me to make my work accessible to a broad public. Markus Schürpf with his research on my creative endeavors provided the basis for the book and exhibition. My friend Jens Winter has encouraged me for years. Olivier Vermeulen, with whom I am likewise linked with a wonderful friendship, has been my support for years at Canon Switzerland. Hubert Lüscher also supports me in the realization of my installation projects. And lastly, I also express my gratitude to all of you, my readers and viewers.

Hannes Schmid

Impressum

Publication

Published on the occasion of the exhibition
Hannes Schmid. Real Stories
Kunstmuseum Bern, 13.03.2013–21.07.2013

Edited by
Kunstmuseum Bern, Matthias Frehner
Ildegarda E. Scheidegger

Editor
Ildegarda E. Scheidegger
Astrid Näff

Picture Editing
Christiane Kuhlmann
Jürg Wey

Copyediting
Astrid Näff
Louise Stein

Translations
Astrid Näff
Catherine Schelbert
Ishbel Flett
Fiona Elliot

Design
Jürg Wey, Schmid+Zoller Communications, Zürich

Printing and Binding
Ast & Fischer AG, Wabern

© JRP|Ringier Kunstverlag
Authors and Publisher
© Texts to the conceptual work
Christiane Kuhlmann
Image Copyright
Hannes Schmid

Distributed by
JRP|Ringier
Limmatstrasse 270
CH-8005 Zurich
T +41 (0) 43 311 27 50
F +41 (0) 43 311 27 51
E info@jrp-ringier.com
www.jrp-ringier.com

ISBN 978-3-03764-310-5

JRP|Ringier publications are available internationally at selected bookstores and from the following distribution partners:

Switzerland
AVA Verlagsauslieferung AG
Centralweg 16
CH-8910 Affoltern a.A.
verlagsservice@ava.ch
www.ava.ch

Germany and Austria
Vice Versa Distribution GmbH
Immanuelkirchstrasse 12
D-10405 Berlin
info@vice-versa-distribution.com
www.vice-versa-distribution.com

France
Les presses du réel
35 rue Colson
F-21000 Dijon
info@lespressesdureel.com
www.lespressesdureel.com

UK and other European countries
Cornerhouse Publications
70 Oxford Street
UK-Manchester M1 5NH
publications@cornerhouse.org
www.cornerhouse.org/books

USA, Canada, Asia, and Australia
ARTBOOK|D.A.P.
I55 Sixth Avenue, 2nd Floor
USA-New York, NY 10013
dap@dapinc.com
www.artbook.com

For a list of our partner bookshops or for any general questions, please contact JRP|Ringier directly at info@jrp-ringier. com, or visit our homepage www.jrp-ringier.com for further information about our program.

Exhibition

Curator
Christiane Kuhlmann

Museum of Fine Arts Bern
Matthias Frehner, Director

Assistant to the Director
Christine Büchler-Räz

Finances and Personnel
Andrea Zimmermann

Corporate Communications
Ruth Gilgen Hamisultane
Brigit Bucher
Aya Christen
Rosmarie Joss
Christian Schnellmann
Marie Louise Suter

Shop
Magali Cirasa

Art Education Program
Anina Büschlen
Magdalena Schindler
Beat Schüpbach

Registrar
Ethel Mathier
Franziska Vassella

Conservators
Nathalie Bäschlin
Dorothea Spitza

Exhibition Management
René Wochner

Production Images and Installations
Jürg Wey

Exhibition Technicians
Thomas Bieri, Jan Bukacek, Mike Carol, Andres Meschter, Martin Schnidrig, Simon Stalder, Roman Studer, Volker Thies, Peter Töni, Wilfried von Gunten

Studio Hannes Schmid
Schmid+Zoller Communications, Zürich
Elisa Bütler, Scientific Employee
Stefan Laeng, Sponsorship
Giglio Pasqua, Assistant Picture Editing
Susanne Zoller, Controller